REF 796.42 B479
Benyo, Richard.
Running encyclopedia

OVER
NIGHT

Running
Encyclopedia

Richard Benyo
Joe Henderson

Human Kinetics

Hyde Library
Memphis University School

Library of Congress Cataloging-in-Publication Data

Benyo, Richard.
   Running encyclopedia / Richard Benyo, Joe Henderson.
     p. cm.
   Includes bibliographical references (p.).
   ISBN: 0-7360-3734-9
   1. Running races--History. 2. Runners (Sports)--History. I. Henderson, Joe, 1943- II. Title.

GV1061 .B445 2002
796.42--dc21   2001039460

ISBN: 0-7360-3734-9

Copyright © 2002 by Richard Benyo and Joe Henderson

All rights reserved. Except for use in a review, the reproduction or utilization of this work in any form or by any electronic, mechanical, or other means, now known or hereafter invented, including xerography, photocopying, and recording, and in any information storage and retrieval system, is forbidden without the written permission of the publisher.

"Kardong vs. Buniak" on page 99 is used by permission of its author, Don Kardong. Where indicated in specific entries, some biographical and statistical information is, by permission, from the 2000 Boston Marathon media guide.

Acquisitions Editor: Martin Barnard; **Developmental Editor:** Julie Rhoda; **Assistant Editor:** Carla Zych; **Copyeditor:** Bob Replinger; **Proofreader:** Julie A. Marx; **Graphic Designer:** Robert Reuther; **Graphic Artist:** Kimberly McFarland; **Cover Designer:** Jack W. Davis; **Cover Photographer:** Tom Roberts; **Printer:** United Graphics.

Human Kinetics books are available at special discounts for bulk purchase. Special editions or book excerpts can also be created to specification. For details, contact the Special Sales Manager at Human Kinetics.

Printed in the United States of America   10 9 8 7 6 5 4 3 2 1

Human Kinetics
Web site: www.humankinetics.com

United States: Human Kinetics
P.O. Box 5076, Champaign, IL 61825-5076
800-747-4457
e-mail: humank@hkusa.com

Canada: Human Kinetics
475 Devonshire Road Unit 100, Windsor, ON N8Y 2L5
800-465-7301 (in Canada only)
e-mail: orders@hkcanada.com

Europe: Human Kinetics
Units C2/C3 Wira Business Park
West Park Ring Road, Leeds LS16 6EB, United Kingdom
+44 (0) 113 278 1708
e-mail: hk@hkeurope.com

Australia: Human Kinetics
57A Price Avenue, Lower Mitcham, South Australia 5062
08 8277 1555
e-mail: liahka@senet.com.au

New Zealand: Human Kinetics
P.O. Box 105-231, Auckland Central
09-523-3462
e-mail: hkp@ihug.co.nz

For Drew, dear friend in the long run through life.

—*Richard Benyo*

For my mother, Virginia King Henderson, who landed me
my first writing job and lent me her typewriter to complete it.

—*Joe Henderson*

MEMPHIS UNIVERSITY SCHOOL
FOUNDED 1893

Presented by
Janice Martin
In honor of their son
Jay Martin
On his birthday
December 14, 2003

Contents

Foreword

This book is one of the most complete histories ever compiled on road racing. And a deep and rich history it is, stretching from the 19th century to the 21st. In the *Running Encyclopedia* you'll learn about the amazing runners and landmark events, along with the technological and organizational milestones. Rich Benyo and Joe Henderson want you to take this material personally by remembering the people who inspired you, the event you ran, the techniques you tried, the products you used, the publications you read. While reading the book's manuscript, I wasn't just reviewing the sport's history; I was also reviewing much of my own history as a runner.

When I first started running road races back in 1969, it never occurred to me that those were the "good old days" of road racing. Nor did I have the vaguest idea that my newfound pursuit would lead to a fuller and richer life, a host of good friends, an exciting and fulfilling career, a world of memories, and best of all, a chance meeting with the love of my life.

It all started pretty innocently, as it does for most of us, with a few minutes of running several days a week after years of inactivity. In 1967, I left my job at Time-Life International to become the founding publisher of *New York Magazine*, a weekly that would become the pioneer in a new genre of publishing. We began with the money-raising efforts, opened the office, organized the staff, and did all the rest of the launch activity. Then in April 1968 came the magazine itself. (It occurs to me as I write that sentence that April 1968 was the same month that my friend and *Runner's World* executive editor, Amby Burfoot, won the Boston Marathon.)

For two years there were few breaks from the grind. The countless lunches, dinners, late nights, and constant pressure began to pack some serious weight onto my once-lean frame. I knew that the time had come to do something. I had been a mediocre runner in high school and college, so I decided to revisit my old sport.

Stopwatch in hand, I'd head out the door before work and run as fast as I could for about a half-mile. Over time, I slowed down and added distance. Before long, I entered my first road race near Yankee Stadium. I think the distance was six miles, but I'm not sure.

Now, after more than 30 years of road racing, many of those early races seem to blur into one another. Others, however, stand out in my mind as if they were yesterday—especially my first marathon, Boston 1969. That's right, it was my first marathon; there were no qualifying times in those days, and a $2 entry fee was the price of admission. There wasn't much training information available, so I just ran a lot of miles for a few months. My unwanted weight just fell away, and I had to have my suits altered.

At the starting area in Hopkinton, my old friend, Dr. George Sheehan (not yet the philosopher-king of running), introduced me to a few friends as his protégé. It seemed like a good group of guys. And that's all there were—guys! I ran in a flimsy pair of Tiger Marathon shoes with midsoles so thin that if you stepped on a dime, you could tell if it were heads or tails.

After finishing that Boston in 3:26, I immediately retired from the sport, as so many first-time marathoners do. But before long, the urge returned, and I began running again because I truly enjoyed it. As I became more immersed in the sport, I started training smarter and following the exploits of the top runners of the day: Amby Burfoot; Ron Hill; and the late Buddy Edelen, who would go to sleep in his running clothes so that he wasted no time getting out the door for his morning run.

For Edelen, that morning run was the first of two daily training sessions that bracketed his teaching job. Back then every top runner had a full-time job. There were no professionals in the sport for one good reason: There was no money. No appearance fees, no prize money, no shoe contracts, no agents—nada. The only difference between the guys who won Boston and the rest of us was that they were a lot faster.

After Frank Shorter's Olympic marathon victory in 1972, I remember hearing that he had refused an invitation to run Boston the following April. The race organizers were willing to pay his bus fare from his home in Florida, but they would not agree to airfare! Perhaps the traditionalists of the Boston Athletic Association had not comprehended that Frank was the catalyst for a running movement that was beginning to take hold.

Frank was the right man at the right time. His marathon victory was the brightest moment of the Munich Games (see page 253), which will always be remembered for the tragic massacre of Israeli athletes. Frank was an intelligent, articulate, independent man who captured our imagination. Among my collector items, I still have the Olympic issue of *Life* magazine with Frank on the cover.

In 1976, all of my running friends and I watched Frank run to the silver medal in Montreal. We felt for Frank, who abhorred the rainy weather of the day and was beaten by an East German, Waldemar Cierpinski. Years later, Cierpinski's name came up in the investigations of the systematic doping of East German athletes.

That same year, my dear friend, Fred Lebow, began organizing a five-borough New York City Marathon, the brainstorm of an iconoclastic city worker named George Spitz. I offered to be a sponsor and my new magazine, *New Times*, put up $5,000 and agreed to publish a program for the race. I trained through the summer with two of my friends: Jacques d'Ambroise, the ballet dancer, and Leonard Harris, a writer and television critic. Neither had ever run a marathon, but this endurance event was now catching on as a challenge for ordinary folks.

During New York City Marathon week, Frank Shorter stayed at my house, as we had become good friends. He came in second behind Bill Rodgers. That

Courtesy of George Hirsch/*Runner's World*

Hirsch (middle) on a run in 1978 with Bill Rodgers (left) and Frank Shorter (right).

first year the course made a U-turn around a telephone pole in the Bronx. Bill, who had built up a sizable lead, took the turn and passed Frank coming toward him. Even though there were still six miles to go, Frank congratulated Bill on his run.

Years later we can look back and see that this was one of the milestones in the history of road racing. The torch had been passed from one great champion to the next. The race, with 2,800 runners, was proclaimed a success, and soon other big cities around the world used it as a prototype to model their own marathons. Fred Lebow went on to become the legendary promoter that the sport needed. He had charisma, flair for the media, and street smarts to pull it all together.

A decade after my first Boston Marathon, I achieved my marathon personal record (PR) in the 1979 Boston. It was a cool, rainy day, good for running. Bill Rodgers won the race that day—one of his four Boston victories—setting his own PR. During the first mile of the race, I found myself running next to Joan Benoit. We introduced ourselves: I, a 44-year-old magazine publisher, and she, a 21-year-old college senior.

As the miles passed, we learned that Joan was in second place behind race favorite Patti Lyons. Coming into Wellesley, I said, "Joan, you should know that two years ago, I was with Miki Gorman at this point, and Miki won the race. We're running faster now than I was then." She looked up at me and replied, "George, you made my day."

Courtesy of George Hirsch/*Runner's World*

Joan Benoit (W11) runs beside Hirsch (T142) at Boston 1979, her first major marathon win.

As we moved into the Newton Hills, Joan left me behind. When I got into Boston, I learned from a spectator that Joan had passed Patti and was heading for the victory. Little did I know that this was the first major win for the woman who would go on to be America's most celebrated female road runner.

The next year, President Jimmy Carter boycotted the Olympic Games in Moscow because of the war in Afghanistan. It was a controversial decision that took away Bill Rodgers' best chance at an Olympic medal. As Rodgers had succeeded Shorter, now Alberto Salazar (a track star from the University of Oregon) came along and replaced Rodgers with his three consecutive New York City Marathon wins. Americans seemed to dominate distance running year in and year out.

Although the 1984 Los Angeles Olympics were boycotted by the Soviet Union and a number of the eastern bloc countries, we were all excited about the first women's Olympic Marathon. We knew Joan Benoit had a good chance, but we were concerned about the knee injury that had forced her into surgery just 17 days before the U.S. Olympic Marathon Trials. Tough as always, Joan surged to an early lead and handily defeated her two Norwegian rivals, Grete Waitz and Ingrid Kristiansen.

The running boom that had begun in the 1970s continued to gain new adherents in the 1980s. Jim Fixx and George Sheehan became the leading spokespersons for this movement that captured millions of people. Their books were bestsellers, and our magazine, *Runner's World*, became the sport's bible, reaching hundreds of thousands of readers every month.

Still, I never expected that running would come to affect my personal life so directly. In 1988, I attended the Men's Olympic Marathon Trials, which were held in conjunction with the New Jersey Waterfront Marathon. The day before the race, at the marathon expo, I met a lovely woman who told me she was there to run her first marathon.

I was so taken with her that I tried to find her the next day in the starting area, but the size of the crowd made that impossible. Refusing to give up, I simply started jogging at the very back of the pack and slowly picked up the pace while looking for my new friend. At five miles, I caught up with her and we ran the rest of the distance together, sharing life stories as we went along.

After the marathon, we went our separate ways for a while, but as fate had it, we eventually got back together. Today, my wife, Shay, and I still enjoy putting in some miles on the roads or trails of upstate New York, Idaho, Italy, or wherever we happen to be.

By the late 1980s and early 1990s, as Moroccan leadership in road running went into decline and the entire running movement began to wane, Kenyan and Ethiopian runners came to the fore while many of the "boom" runners moved on to other things. Fred Lebow died of brain cancer in 1994 before the New York City Marathon, and the race that he created would become a moving tribute to him. My son, David, took up running to lose some weight and we ran New York together that year. It was an emotional day as we saw hundreds of T-shirts bearing Fred's name and picture. Running the marathon with my son gave us a special memory that we will always cherish.

In the past few years, the ranks of runners have again swelled, but this second boom is quite different from the first. Now there are as many women as men. Most people run to be fit, lose weight, ease stress, and find companionship. Races, particularly marathons, are bigger than ever, yet the average finishing times are much slower. The new voices of the sport are Jeff Galloway (who teaches his disciples to mix walk breaks with their running during the marathon) and John "the Penguin" Bingham (whose credo of "Waddle on, friends" strikes a warm chord with those in the back of the pack).

At the same time, there is growing hope for Americans to rejoin the ranks of the elite. Khalid Khannouchi, the world record-holder in the marathon, became a U.S. citizen in 2000. The Moroccan-born Khannouchi wants to win Olympic and World medals for his new country and to inspire our younger athletes, many of whom were not yet born when Shorter, Rodgers, and Salazar ruled the roads.

Whether Khannouchi succeeds in his dreams or not, I'm sure the roads will remain full of everyday runners looking for health, fitness, friendship, and personal challenges. And many of these runners will add a touch of spice to their lives and goals by racing on those same roads, as many of us have been doing since we discovered the lure of the road race. This wonderfully detailed book tells us that the history of the sport and our role in it are inseparable.

George A. Hirsch
Publisher, *Runner's World* magazine

Acknowledgments

Many contributors showed as much excitement over this project as the authors did. This started with Martin Barnard and Julie Rhoda, our editors at Human Kinetics and both avid runners.

Information from outside sources was supplied eagerly and quickly, and often in great quantity. Special praise in that regard goes to Marty Post of *Runner's World*, Ryan Lamppa of the Road Running Information Center, and Ken Nakamura, an authority on running matters in Asia and beyond.

The following good people also shared with us their valuable time and invaluable expertise: Marc Bloom, Paul Christman, Bob and Lenore Dolphin, Rich Englehart, Jack Fleming, Ed Fox, Jill Geer, Nobby Hashizume, Janet Heinonen, Madeline Hernandez, Garry Hill, Scott Hubbard, Jeff Johnson, Don Kardong, Ed Kozloff, Dan Lilot, Mike Lundgren, Mark Milde, Jim Oaks, Paul Reese, Kirk Rosenbach, Victor Sailer, Jan Seeley, Mark Shearman, Thomas Steffens, Kathrine Switzer, Cathy Troisi, Andy Yelanak, and Ken Young.

In addition, dozens—maybe hundreds—of the people within the A-to-Z listings supplied information about themselves. We thank them all for helping us corral so much of road-racing history into one volume.

Introduction

Running is at once the most simple and the most varied of sports—and is surely the oldest form of efficient human locomotion. Marion Jones sprinting 100 meters with the grace of a greyhound or gray-haired Paul Reese running across the United States with the gracelessness of a mule are of the same heritage. Running is hardwired in all of us. An infant taking its first steps does not "learn to walk." The infant's first steps are at a run as it launches itself full-tilt into the world.

Unfortunately, in a "civilized" world, childhood is filled with admonitions from concerned parents to "walk, don't run!" Yet children do what comes naturally. They fill their lives with running, with racing each other, with running from one heated activity to the next. The tendency to run through an activity is the deep-seated nature of a child, yet as a society we have tended to take pains to short-circuit it as though running were somehow unseemly or undesirable. The goal of civilization has always been to squeeze the fun out of life.

But in spite of this tendency, there has always been a cadre of dissidents—adults who run for fun, for competition, for increased stamina, and for self-satisfaction. It was this downtrodden elite who fostered and kept running alive and semiwell through the transition period of the 19th and 20th centuries when mechanization attempted to eradicate human locomotion from life in the industrialized world. In some cultures less hamstrung by civilization as we define it, such as Ethiopia and Kenya, running has never been threatened as a legitimate form of transportation, so it should come as no surprise that runners from these countries lead the world in long-distance racing.

College runners and blue-collar club runners perpetuated running in the United States by participating in road races such as the Boston Marathon and San Francisco's Cross-City Race (now Bay to Breakers 12K). During the latter third of the 20th century, citizen participation in running, especially in mass road races, has catapulted the sport into the enviable position as the only major sport where the average practitioner can line up in the same starting field as the gods of the sport and compete against them. Road racing is the most democratic of sports. The fact that it is so simple and therefore so universal also has thrust it to a rarefied place on the international scene. Virtually every country in the world competes in running contests.

The 5K road race and the marathon have emerged as the largest participant sports competitions in the world. Intermediate distances in the seven-mile range have spawned races (the Bay to Breakers 12K and the Bloomsday 12K in Spokane, Washington) that regularly boast more than 50,000 entrants.

Imagine a stadium of baseball fans participating in the game instead of watching it.

As with any popular mass-participation movement, the sport of road racing did not emerge full-blown. It evolved through fits and starts, brilliance and blunders, potential and realization. It evolved because of dedicated people, because of the timely infusion of good ideas, and in some instances by sheer good luck.

A truly comprehensive history of the sport of road racing has never been written. This is our attempt to remedy that lapse. To do justice to the key players and concepts, we have chosen to ignore the chronological narrative format in favor of the encyclopedic approach. This format allows us to pinpoint specific people, places, movements, concepts, and performances and highlight each of them with an individual listing.

We have chosen road racing as the focus of this encyclopedia focus simply because it is universally practiced by the largest number of participants. We have demarcated it at the low end with the incredibly popular 5K and at the high end with the fabled marathon, which is currently enjoying its own spectacular growth. The marathon, in fact, forms the backbone of this book, because it is such a historic (it is, after all, more than 2,500 years old), prestigious, and glamorous event. It highlighted the first modern Olympics in 1896, and Boston has kept it alive since 1897.

We have limited the scope of this book to the organized sport of road racing, as opposed to the activity or exercise of running, because to deal with the subject of running in general would make the book unwieldy and diffuse the focus and audience. In that regard we need to define up front what the book does *not* cover more than what it does. This book does not attempt to cover track, road miles, cross country, ultras, mountain or adventure running, biathlons and triathlons. (By merely running through that list of running's variations, it is easy to see just how diverse a sport and avocation running has become over the years.)

Even confined to covering only road racing from 5K to the marathon, we've topped 1,000 listings. In an attempt to be as inclusive as we could be within those confines, many runners and performances will be found in statistical sidebars accompanying various famous races and important records instead of receiving an individual listing. We have included top performances from major road races, record progressions, age-group records where significant, and separate men's and women's listings.

Because we are preparing this book primarily for an English-speaking (largely American) market, there is a prejudice inherent in the weight of our listings toward that audience. We have acknowledged, however, important international events and performances, especially at venues that have helped shape the sport, such as Fukuoka, Košice, London, Rotterdam, and cities hosting Olympic Marathons.

To highlight outstanding racers and events, numerous profile sidebars are used throughout. These appeared originally in Joe's newsletter, *Running Commentary* (www.joehenderson.com), and are identified by date of publication and updated when required.

We have also secured 100 photographs that capture the history of the sport. In some instances we opted for well-known and often-published photos. But we also searched out photographs that have rarely been seen, especially from the early days of road racing.

As far as what qualifications and prejudices the authors bring to this project, we both worked as editors of *Runner's World* magazine—Joe from 1970 to 1977, Rich from 1977 to 1984. This is Joe's 23rd book and Rich's 17th. Joe is currently West Coast editor of *Runner's World* magazine; Rich is editor of *Marathon & Beyond* magazine. Neither of us began his running career in road racing, but both gravitated to it after a few years, Joe after starting in high school track and Rich after beginning in college cross country. We've both long since forgotten how many races they've run in our lives, but the numbers are deep into the hundreds.

This is our first official collaboration since Joe edited Rich's 1978 book *Return to Running* (Anderson World), although we both feel our occasional joint appearances at races constitute a sort of collaboration. Currently, Joe lives in Eugene, Oregon, while Rich lives in Forestville, California. (Additional information about both can be found in About the Authors at the back of this book.)

We have attempted to bring to this project our love of and fascination with the sport of road racing by fashioning stories instead of merely constructing alphabetized listings. Our hope is that the book can be read and enjoyed either by letting it fall open to any listing or by looking up a specific subject or, for the more ambitious, reading it through from A to Z. (Specifics on how to get the most from the encyclopedia appear in the User's Guide that follows this introduction.) We hope you enjoy the book as much as we've enjoyed scouring through our files and our memories to bring together between two covers the incredible, the outrageous, the seemingly mundane, the startling, the astounding, and the unforgettable people and places that have made road racing perhaps the most practiced adult sport in the world.

Richard Benyo and Joe Henderson

User's Guide

We have constructed *Running Encyclopedia* much like a standard encyclopedia, but with some variations due to the unique nature of road racing and because we wanted to make the book functional as an easy-access resource. Toward that end we have included a goodly number of winners of major competitions, records at various distances, and sidebars from Joe's newsletter, *Running Commentary*, to enlarge the range of the book. We'll be more specific on these aspects in a moment.

The foundation of the book is the alphabetized list of people, places, events, and things related to road racing. These entries have the following features:

- In instances where a female runner has married and taken her husband's name, the listing is under the name the woman raced under in her prime. For example, Lisa Larsen Weidenbach Rainsberger is listed under "Weidenbach" instead of under her maiden name of "Larsen" or her current married name of "Rainsberger."

- We have shied away from formal first names. Hence, Bill Rodgers is not listed as "William" because he's best known by the nickname.

- In the instance of product names, we have listed the current name ("Asics" instead of the long-running "Tiger" running shoes from Japan) or two names, cross-referenced, if the product is known by more than one term ("ERG" and "Electrolyte Replacement with Glucose").

- In the case of races, we have listed them by their popular name and not by a name made complex by the inclusion of a sponsor, which in many instances spanned merely a portion of the race's history. For instance, we list the "Chicago Marathon" instead of the "LaSalle Bank Chicago Marathon."

- We have made great efforts to find birthdates of the runners listed—and, where appropriate, death dates. This has been difficult for people born in the 19th century; in some instances we were able to find only a year of birth. We have listed what birth and death date information we were able to uncover during our research.

- As to the size of listings, there is both method and madness to it. Some listings, such as Frank Shorter's, are extremely important to the history of road racing. His listing, however, is not exhaustive because Frank has been well known for decades and extensive material on him is available to the public. In some instances we did rather extensive listings (Rob de Castella, for instance) to reflect a runner whose importance to the sport is sizable but whose story may not be so available to readers. Because we present brief listings for particular runners does not mean that they are unimportant, only that we felt that relative to certain seminal figures, their contributions were not quite as pronounced.

- In instances where a runner or other person crops up in a sidebar or in historical results of a race but does not have a separate listing, he or she appears in the supplemental index at the back of the book.

- Where it was readily available, we have included Web site addresses for races, organizations, companies, and a few individuals. They are current as of October 1, 2001.

- It must also be noted that this is a dynamic sport, with facts changing constantly. Statistical data in this book is current as of October 1, 2001. (Berlin Marathon, Chicago Marathon, Košice Peace Marathon, world record, and world record progressions data is current as of October 7, 2001.)

- Times throughout the book are listed to the full second, in keeping with current statistical practice. Marks for longer distances that are set in 10ths of a second are rounded up.

We have been as careful as we could to secure reliable information, but mistakes in a manuscript this size are inevitable. We invite readers to send corrections so that we can assemble them for inclusion in the next edition.

Our hope for the book is that it becomes an omnibus history of road racing while also being an easy-to-use source of hard information and a good read of a sport that, to us, is its own reward.

AAU. *See* Amateur Athletic Union.

Abe, Tomoe (b. August 13, 1971). The stringent Japanese training system works best at producing fast young women marathoners who contend for Olympic and World Championship medals. Abe, barely 22, won a bronze at the 1993 Worlds, then took the prestigious Osaka Ladies' Marathon the next spring. Her obvious ultradistance prowess came to the fore in 2000 at the Lake Saroma (Japan) 100K race where she ran a 6:33:11. This shattered the old world record, held by Ann Trason, by nearly half an hour. *See also* Osaka Ladies Marathon; Trason, Ann; World Championships medalists.

Abera, Gezahegne (also spelled Gezahegn or Gezahenge) (b. April 17, 1978). The Kenya-Ethiopia battle for world marathon domination was never more closely fought than at Boston 2000. Ethiopian Abera pushed Kenyan winner Elijah Lagat to the end as both ran the same time (2:09:47). But Abera got in the final word for the year at the Sydney Olympic Games Marathon where he won in 2:10:11, beating Kenyan Eric Wainaina by 20 seconds. Less than a year after winning his Olympic title, Abera won the 2001 World Champioships Marathon by the narrowest of margins. The Ethiopian outkicked Simon Biwott of Kenya, 2:12:42 to 2:12:43. Abera became the first man to achieve the Olympic-Worlds double in the marathon, although Rosa Mota had this earlier for women.

Abera's biggest previous win was Fukuoka 1999 (2:07:54), where he battled France's Mohamed Quaadi over the final two kilometers. It was the first time in the history of Fukuoka that two runners went under 2:08. Abera is a relative newcomer to the marathon, but he is learning fast. In 1998 he placed 3rd at the Addis Ababa Marathon in 2:17:28 at altitude. In his first race in the United States, he placed 4th at the 1999 Los Angeles Marathon with a 2:13:59. Later in 1999 he placed 11th at the World Championships in Seville. Abera trains in his home country of Ethiopia under Dr. Yilma Berta, who also trains Fatuma Roba. *See also* Ethiopian runners; Fukuoka Marathon; Olympic medalists; rankings, *Track & Field News;* World Championships medalists.

Abshire, Brian (b. November 14, 1963). An Olympic steeplechaser in 1988, Abshire has run the fastest American road 5K. His 13:20 came in 1993 with a big assist from gravity on a downhill course in Fontana, California. *See also* record progressions, American; records, American.

accelerations. This racing tactic, also called "surges," is employed most successfully by East Africans. Accelerations involve varying pace suddenly and dramatically to make a move past or away from competitors within a race. *See also* surges.

acclimatization. The runner's body has amazing powers to acclimate, given proper and prolonged exposure to environmental extremes. This is especially true in adapting to hot weather and high altitude. A cool-weather runner can train the body to work well under these conditions, but this athlete remains at a disadvantage to someone with lifelong exposure to heat or oxygen-thin air. *See also* altitude training.

Achilles tendon. The thin band of fibrous tissue connecting the calf and heel is named for the weak link of a Greek hero, and it's the bane of many distance runners. Achilles tendinitis (the painful inflammation of the tendon) and tears are among the most common running injuries. *See also* injuries.

Active.com (www.active.com). *See* online registration.

active rest (or active recovery). *See* cross-training.

Adcocks, Bill (b. November 11, 1941). The Brit was the second man, after Australian Derek Clayton, to run under the five-minute-per-mile pace for a marathon when he ran 2:10:48 while winning Fukuoka in 1968. That earned him the top world ranking for the year from *Track & Field News*, despite his fifth-place finish at the altitude-scrambled Olympics in Mexico City. *See also* Fukuoka Marathon; rankings, *Track & Field News*.

adidas (www.adidas.com). This major German sport-shoe manufacturer was the Microsoft of track shoes from the early 1950s through the early 1970s but was slower than other companies to spot and capitalize on

© Mark Shearman, Athletics-Images.

Bill Adcocks (#57) battles fellow Brit Ron Hill at the 1966 Polytechnic Marathon; two years later Adcocks would be the second man to run a marathon at a sub-5:00 pace.

the boom in road racing. Consequently adidas was only able to gain a tentative toehold in this market, which was dominated by Asics and Nike. As the 1990s closed out, adidas had made another push through extensive marketing and advertising, and it became the official shoe sponsor at Boston in a resurrected attempt to crack the American market. Their late 1990s magazine ad campaign ("Runners. Yeah, we're different.") was one of the most original and controversial in running history. *See also* shoe companies.

Adirondack Marathon (www.adirondackmarathon.org). *See* scenic races.

adventure racing. We believe that *any* race can be an adventure. But in today's parlance the term has come to mean off-road events of great length, which therefore fall outside the scope of this book. The best known of these adventure ventures are the Marathon des Sables (Marathon of Sands in North Africa) and the Eco-Challenge (a multisport, made-for-television wilderness trek at a new location each year).

aerobic capacity. This book is not intended to be a physiology text, but because the term *aerobic* is batted about it demands a brief definition. *Aerobic* literally means "with oxygen" (as opposed to anaerobic, "without oxygen"). Simply put, you run aerobically until your breathing becomes labored. Aerobic capacity is one of the key factors in running success. Aerobic training—longer, gentler running (during which breathing is not labored)—focuses on increasing that capacity.

aerobics. Kenneth Cooper plucked an obscure word from physiology and turned it into a phenomenon. His first *Aerobics* book, published in 1968 (Bantam Books), brought millions of recruits into running and led to a series of books with the *A* word in their titles. As the 1980s rolled in, the term was kidnapped by (primarily) female indoor exercise gurus to describe their form of continuous floor exercises. *See also* anaerobic threshold; books; Cooper, Dr. Kenneth.

African Games. The most crowded cradle of distance runners now conducts continental championships every four years. The marathons are run as part of a full track and field meet, held the year before each Olympics. Trouble is, these marathons often are run in either extreme heat or high altitude. And the best Africans are off competing somewhere else where the stakes are higher.

African runners. Abebe Bikila touched off one of the two most significant trends of the past 50 years (the other was the rise of women's running) with his barefoot marathon victory at the 1960 Olympics—then executed a repeat, with shoes this time, four years later. The Ethiopian's accomplishments signaled the rise of East Africans as world distance running lords. Kenyans and Tanzanians followed, and the power spread across the continent to South Africa and Morocco. *See also* African Games; Bikila, Abebe; Ethiopian runners; Kenyan runners.

African Games Winners

The continent has produced many of the world's fastest marathoners, yet hot weather and altitude have combined to keep the winning times at this meet relatively slow. Note that men's record-holder (*) is Belayneh Dinsamo, who set the world mark the next year.

WOMEN

Year	Place	Athlete	Time
1995	Harare	Jowaine Parrott (South Africa)	2:55:09
1999	Johannesburg	Hiywot Bizaw (Ethiopia)	2:45:35*

MEN

Year	Place	Athlete	Time
1973	Lagos	Mamo Wolde (Ethiopia)	2:27:32
1978	Algiers	Richard Mabuza (Swaziland)	2:21:53
1987	Nairobi	Belayneh Dinsamo (Ethiopia)	2:14:47*
1991	Cairo	Tena Negere (Ethiopia)	2:31:17
1995	Harare	Nicholas Nyengere (Zimbabwe)	2:20:08
1999	Johannesburg	Joshua Peterson (South Africa)	2:19:05

Agee, William (b. December 25, 1905). A 1928 U.S. Olympian, Agee won the national marathon title three years later. He's a member of the RRCA Hall of Fame. *See also* Hall of Fame, RRCA; national marathon champions, U.S.; Olympians, U.S.

age grading. Masters runners devised this system of equalizing times by age and gender. It is sometimes used as a way of cutting through the myriad of age groups and awarding one set of prize money to older runners. The tables are administered by the World Masters Association (WMA), formerly the World Association of Veteran Athletes (WAVA), and are periodically adjusted to reflect the results of increasingly large databases of masters performers. These tables are based not only on what current age-group records are but also on what they *should be* to come into statistical alignment with other marks. *See also* masters racing; World Masters Association.

age-group records. *See* records, American age-group; records, world age-group.

agents. No sooner had running turned openly pro than runners began hiring professionals to do their hard bargaining. (Previously only coaches, spouses, or the athletes themselves were allowed to bargain.) Agents became as important as coaches in deciding where runners would race, and financial incentives became as important as promises of flat courses and fast times. Some runners' agents are part of large operations such as the IMG (International Management Group), but most are relatively small, independent operations. *See also* professional racing.

aided courses. If road records were to mean anything, restrictions on assistance from slope and wind needed to be established. The Athletics Congress (now USA Track & Field) supplied these guidelines in the 1980s. Record-quality courses of any distance must not go downhill by more than one meter per kilometer, and the start and finish can be no farther apart than 30 percent of the total distance (which theoretically negates possible wind assistance). U.S. courses not meeting these standards are labeled "aided," and marks set on them can be called only American bests—not records. The most famous aided course is that of the Boston Marathon. *See also* record progressions, American; record progressions, world; records, American; records, American age-group; records, world; records, world age-group.

Finland's Olavi Suomalainen wins the 1972 Boston Marathon in 2:15:39. Prior to the mid-1950s Boston's course was deemed shorter than the standard 26.22 miles; even now its standard-distance course is considered aided.

AIMS. *See* Association of International Marathons and Road Races.

air sole. There was a time when a running-shoe sole was simply one strip of rubber glued onto another. Then in the late 1970s Nike took the radical step of slipping air pouches into the mix to provide greater impact protection for distance runners (buoying Nike sales through the 1980s, especially when the technology was moved into basketball shoes—specifically the Air Jordan). This move inspired innovations from other companies, ranging from gels to plugs to dual-density midsoles. *See also* Nike.

Alamosa, Colorado. The high-mountain town (more than 7,000 feet above sea level) has a proud history and a vigorous present. It set a precedent for single-race Olympic Marathon Trials when the first qualifying race was run there in 1968. Buddy Edelen, the former world record-holder, had moved to town in an ill-fated attempt to make the team. Alamosa is the home of Deena Drossin, American 5K record-holder, who like many of the town's runners was attracted by the coaching of Joe Vigil. *See also* Drossin, Deena; Edelen, Leonard "Buddy"; Olympic Trials Marathon, U.S.

altitude training. Runners began looking up, toward the mountains, when the 1968 Olympic Games were awarded to Mexico City, approximately 7,500 feet (2,300 meters) above sea level. The fascination with training at altitude—generally considered anything over 5,000 feet (1,600 meters)—grew even stronger when Kenyan and Ethiopian runners from high elevations dominated those Games. Training at altitude can benefit any runner because it conditions the body to work more efficiently in the low-oxygen environment. With altitude training the body produces more of the naturally occurring hormone erythropoietin (EPO), which boosts the oxygen-carrying capacity of the blood. This allows more oxygen to reach the working muscles without the heart having to pump harder. Thus, a runner is able to produce more energy aerobically and to maintain a faster pace. It's no surprise that runner's have flocked to Boulder and Alamosa in Colorado and that Fila and Team USA have established training camps in the California mountains. *See also* acclimatization; Alamosa, Colorado; Boulder, Colorado; erythropoietin; Fila; Team USA.

Amateur Athletic Union (AAU). The governing body of amateur U.S. sports through the 1970s could also be known as Antiquated Attitudes Updated as it struggled through the fight over women's right to compete in distance events, the explosion in road racing, professionalism, and many other issues. The AAU finally surrendered its hold on the sport to The Athletics Congress (TAC) in 1978. *See also* Athletics Congress, The; organizations; USA Track & Field.

American records. *See* record progressions, American; records, American; records, American age-group.

American Running Association (www.americanrunning.org). Founded by Dr.

Richard Bohannon as the National Jogging Association, it evolved into the American Running and Fitness Association before taking its current name. The group offers a variety of services to members, including the publication *Running & FitNews*, a newsletter offering specific running tips and general health advice.

anaerobic threshold (also called lactate threshold). We used to think of it as running at redline pace, as fast as we could go without breaking down. Then the scientists came up with a definition, defining the *threshold* as the fastest pace one can run aerobically, that is, without going into oxygen debt. The significance of this point is that, beyond it, lactic acid produced by fatigue accumulates rapidly in the muscles and blood.

Runners can increase their anaerobic threshold by training at that pace once or twice per week. Two of the best methods of anaerobic threshold training are running repeated intervals of 800 to 2000 meters without allowing the body to recover fully between efforts, and doing tempo runs. The heart-rate monitor provides a way for runners to estimate their anaerobic or lactate threshold in order to regulate and monitor their pace; they can stay just under the pace at which oxygen debt occurs. *See also* heart-rate monitor, interval training; tempo runs.

Analytical Distance Runner, The. *See* Young, Ken.

Andersen, Gabriele (b. March 20, 1945). Her staggering, heat-addled finish at the first-ever women's Olympic Marathon in 1984 was almost as memorable as Joan Benoit's victory. In fairness to Andersen, a long-time U.S. resident who represented her native Switzerland at the Games, she wasn't an inept runner, just a dehydrated and overheated one. The Los Angeles race did her no lasting harm. A few months later she turned 40 and went on to enjoy a productive masters career.

Anderson, Bob (b. December 28, 1947). The eccentric, prickly Kansan pioneered many of today's taken-for-granted institutions, including *Runner's World* (originally *Distance Running News*, begun in 1966), race expos, Corporate Cup, fun runs, 24-hour relays, dual covers on magazines (one for newsstand sales, another for more serious subscribers), and promotional self-covers on subscription covers of magazines. Emulating the running style of fellow Kansan Jim Ryun, Anderson was a decent but not exceptional runner in college. Bob's *Distance Running News* evolved from a request for training information from prominent marathoners, which he assembled and sent out to marathoner wannabes when he decided to move up to that distance. Bob dropped out of college to pursue his magazine dreams and eventually moved to California at the urging of just-hired editor Joe Henderson. The magazine's name was changed to *The Runner's World*, then just plain *Runner's World*.

As the magazine grew, Bob began to publish monthly booklets. The booklets evolved into a book division, which was quite successful in the late 1970s and early 1980s. He also acquired a number of other specialty magazines, such as *Soccer World, Nordic World* (cross-country skiing), and *Down River* (kayaking). As *Runner's World* grew to a circulation of nearly a half million, Bob started other magazines, among them *Fit*, which began to drain profits from *Runner's World*. By 1983 he had begun a mail-order swimsuit company, which increasingly riveted his attention.

A divorce propelled the sale of *Runner's World* to Rodale Press in 1985. Ironically, with *RW* cut loose, Bob has gone back to his original love of running and is a force in the 50-plus age categories in the San Francisco Bay Area, regularly running 10Ks in the mid-30s. See also *Distance Running News*; publications; *Runner's World*.

Anderson, Bob (b. March 20, 1945). The "Other Bob," unrelated to the *Runner's World* founder except by confusion over their shared name, wrote the long-time best-selling book (three million and counting) *Stretching* (Author, 1975). He operates a Colorado-based fitness publications and products business (www.stretching.com). *See also* books.

Anderson, Jon (b. October 12, 1949). While serving conscientious-objector duty by washing dishes in a hospital, the 1972 Olympian in the 10,000 meters won Boston in 2:16:03 on a hot day. He was only the third American man since World War II to win there, but seven more U.S. victories would follow in the next 10 years as Bill Rodgers (twice) and Alberto Salazar set course records. Only later would we realize that the early 1970s to the mid-1980s would stand as the golden era of U.S. marathoning. *See also* Boston Marathon.

Anderson, Owen (b. July 7, 1947). The former college professor filled an important niche when he launched *Running Research News*. Its mission for many years has been to translate the sometimes arcane language of scientific papers published in often obscure journals into terms that runners can understand. Anderson did the same for many years as a *Runner's World* columnist before retiring to work exclusively on his own publication. *See also* publications; *Running Research News*.

Anderson, Ruth (b. July 27, 1929). This now-retired Lawrence Livermore Labs scientist and pioneer women's marathoner (and ultrarunner) began competing in her 40s and continues into her 70s, setting age-group records and helping batter down barriers against participation by women, especially by masters women. She's a member of the RRCA Hall of Fame. *See also* Hall of Fame, RRCA.

annual plans. *See* periodization.

anti-inflammatories. These legal, over-the-counter drugs come in many forms and are mainstays of runners coping with the normal aches and pains of their activity. Overused, however, these so-called NSAIDS (nonsteroidal anti-inflammatory drugs) can mask a serious injury—allowing it to become more serious—or cause gastrointestinal complications.

Anton, Abel (b. October 24, 1962). The Spaniard's times aren't the greatest, but when the starting gun fires, he runs to win, and win he did—1997 and 1999 World Championships Marathon, 1996 Berlin, and 1998 London. *Track & Field News* ranked him number one in the world for 1997. *See also* Berlin Marathon; London Marathon; rankings, *Track & Field News;* World Championships medalists.

apparel. *See* clothing.

Appell, Olga (b. August 2, 1963). After winning the 1991 Pan-American Games Marathon for Mexico, she gained U.S. citizenship and represented her new country internationally. Appell holds the American 10K best for an aided course, 30:55 set at Salt Lake City in 1995. In the same year she won the Los Angeles Marathon. *See also* Bloomsday 12K; Los Angeles Marathon; Pan-American Games; records, American.

Applegate, Liz (b. June 6, 1956). She teaches nutrition at the University of California, Davis but is better known in running for her writing on dietary topics for *Runner's World.* Like all writers for the magazine, she is an avid runner. Her books include *Power Foods* (1991) and *Eat Smart, Play Hard* (2001) both from *RW*'s parent company, Rodale. See also *Runner's World.*

AquaJogger (www.aquajogger.com). One of the most effective cross-training practices is "running" in water—that is, mimicking normal running workouts in the pool when running on land isn't possible or wise because, for example, an injury might be further hampered by impact. The AquaJogger is a product that makes this alternative, low-impact exercise possible. Original design work and testing on this belt was done by Dick Brown, a well-known coach and coauthor of *Fitness Running* (Human Kinetics, 1994) who is no longer connected with the product. *See also* water running; Wet Vest.

arch supports. *See* orthotics; podiatry.

Arimori, Yuko (b. December 17, 1966). Several nations have dominated the marathon internationally during various points in history: the Ethiopians in the 1960s, the Americans in the 1970s, and so forth. There have been several periods of Japanese domination—most recently by Japanese women. In most international competitions, they are a deciding factor; on their home soil they are dominant. Had there been team scoring in the 1992 and 1996 Olympic Marathons, the Japanese women would have won both years.

The standard-bearer during that period was Yuko Arimori, who placed second at Barcelona (2:32:49) and third at Atlanta (2:28:39), each time finishing one place behind Valentina Yegorova. A graduate of the Nippon College of Physical Education, Arimori entered the marathon scene in 1990 with

Yuko Arimori placed second at the 1992 Barcelona Games Marathon and third at the 1996 Atlanta Games Marathon but was dogged by chronic injuries and an adoring public that made life at home in Japan a daily trial.

a debut 2:32:51 at the Osaka Ladies' Marathon, which was good for sixth place. She ran the race again the following year and took second place with a time of 2:28:01. She was picked by the Japanese selection committee to go to Barcelona.

Her silver medal made her a national celebrity at home. With it came the pressures associated with being in the public forum, a pressure that can stress a successful athlete more than running on the roads in races. She also suffered a heel injury, overcompensated, and injured her other heel. She had surgery in late 1994 but was no sooner repaired than she fell and injured her right leg.

Arimori was able to train back to a high level and won the Sapporo Marathon (in 2:29:17), which told the team selectors that she might indeed be in good enough shape to go to Atlanta. She was unable to top Fatuma Roba's sterling performance, but her bronze medal combined with her earlier silver makes her one of the foremost female marathon competitors of all time. She has since retired from international competition. *See also* Olympic medalists; Roba, Fatuma.

Arkansas Marathon. Dating back to 1969, the small race in Malvern, Arkansas, ranks among America's longest lasting. Entry forms are available each spring for the fall race at www.arkansasrunner.com. *See also* oldest races.

Around the Bay 30K (www.aroundthebayroadrace.com). Three years before the opening act of the Boston Marathon, a race of about 19 miles was run in Hamilton, Ontario, Canada. It continues today, standing as one of North America's most venerable events. *See* "Bay Watch" on page 11. *See also* oldest races.

ARRA. *See* Association of Road Racing Athletes.

Asari, Junko (b. September 22, 1969). She enjoyed greater longevity than many of the Japanese marathon prodigies. After winning the 1993 World title, along with the Osaka Ladies' Marathon, she was ranked number one in

Bay Watch

From Joe Henderson's *Running Commentary,* May 1998.

From my hotel room the view was both impressive and intimidating. Not often had I seen an entire course laid out before me, especially one this long.

I looked toward the east at a triangular-shaped bay. At the far end was a narrow opening into Lake Ontario. Steel mills lined the flat southern shore of this bay. To the east, beachside parks and housing. Along the hilly north side, fine homes.

One of the oldest races in North America runs here in the city of Hamilton, Ontario—an hour's drive southwest of Toronto and an hour above Niagara Falls. The Around the Bay 30K was already three years old when the Boston Marathon came into this world.

Billy Carroll fathered the race known locally as "The Bay." He owned a cigar store as his legitimate front for a more lucrative business operating out of the back room. In 1894 he stirred up betting action on The Bay race that he devised. The runners were the "horses." Winning runners back then received a box of cigars for their work. Amid the stogies they found payoffs as large as $15,000.

The early Hamiltonians grew so fast that Jack Caffery, Billy Sherring, and Fred Hughson placed 1-2-3 at Boston in 1900. Sherring went on to win the 1906 Olympic Marathon in Athens.

The betting is long gone, but the race goes on. Sure, it went through some hard years—when it either wasn't run or barely went ahead (accounts vary)—but it's still around to celebrate its 104th birthday.

This is a historic event, and I'm a sucker for history. I wanted to become a tiny part of it. I could feel that history just by looking out the Sheraton window. The bay hadn't changed since 1894, so neither had the course around it—except to shrink from 19-plus miles to a standard 30K.

Down on the street for the start I thought briefly about all the runners who had passed this way before. But quickly my concerns jerked back to the here and now.

Few of the 2,500 entrants this year could honestly say they came here for the history. They were attracted more by the distance and the timing. Thirty kilometers is a distance seldom available for racing but easy to understand. It fills the black hole of the sport, that great void between half- and full marathons. Times make sense at this distance. Three 40-minute 10Ks equal 2:00, three 50s add up to 2:30.

A 30K is nearly three-fourths of a marathon, and the race's late-March date makes The Bay ideal training for a spring marathon. Every other runner I talked to in Hamilton seemed to be working up to Boston, Ottawa, London (the one in Ontario), Pittsburgh, or Cleveland.

Our concerns weren't historic but current. How to dress for a 70-degree day (the week after a foot of snow fell here) . . . how much to save for the hilly last 10K . . . how hard to run with a marathon coming up.

This, of course, was just as it had been for the original runners who competed here 104 years ago. They weren't thinking about their spots in history, only about their races that day.

the world. Little was heard from her again until 1995, when she won the Tokyo Ladies' Marathon. Three quiet years later, she won again at Tokyo. *See also* Osaka Ladies' Marathon; rankings, *Track & Field News;* Tokyo Marathons; World Championships medalists.

Kenya's Delillah Asiago was the queen of the roads in America in 1995, sweeping Bloomsday, Bay to Breakers, and Bolder Boulder. *Runner's World* ranked her tops that year.

© Mark Shearman, Athletics-Images.

Ashenfelter, Horace (b. January 23, 1923). His successes came mostly on the track, the greatest being a steeplechase gold medal at the 1952 Olympic Games. No American had won the event before, and none has since. We recognize him in this road-oriented book because the RRCA named him to its Hall of Fame. *See also* Hall of Fame, RRCA; Hall of Fame, USATF.

Asiago, Delillah (b. February 24, 1972). Kenya's women can move too, though they got a later start at proving it than the men. Asiago holds the current world 12K record. She stood atop the *Runner's World* road rankings in 1995 after sweeping the Bloomsday 12K, Bay to Breakers 12K (where she set her world mark of 38:23), and Bolder Boulder 10K that May. *See also* Bay to Breakers 12K; Bloomsday 12K; Bolder Boulder 10K; rankings, *Runner's World*; records, world.

Asian Games. Japan's long-standing passion with the marathon and its ability to produce marathon talent shows on the accompanying winners' list. But the Japanese women have found a strong new rival in China, and the men in Korea. A full menu of track and field events are run every four years, midway between Olympics.

Asics (www.asicstiger.com). This is the modern name of the Japanese Tiger running shoe company, a brand made popular by future Nike creators Phil Knight and Jeff Johnson when they began operating as Blue Ribbon Sports in the 1960s. Tiger's great innovation was the nylon upper, which quickly became standard in the industry. Asics countered Nike's introduction of the air sole with a gel sole. *See also* Nike; shoe companies.

Association of International Marathons and Road Races (AIMS) (www.aims-association.org). A group of concerned marathon directors banded together to promote, market, and standardize marathons throughout the known universe.

Asian Games Marathon Winners

Perhaps the greatest women's marathon to date was run in this meet—future Olympic gold medalist Naoko Takahashi's solo 2:21:47 in steamy Bangkok. Note that Korean men won the last three races and four of the past five. * = event record.

WOMEN

Year	Place	Athlete	Time
1986	Seoul	Eriko Asai (Japan)	2:41:03
1990	Beijing	Zhao Youfeng (China)	2:35:19
1994	Hiroshima	Zhong Huandi (China)	2:29:32
1998	Bangkok	Naoko Takahashi (Japan)	2:21:47*

MEN

Year	Place	Athlete	Time
1951	New Delhi	Chota Singh (India)	2:42:59
1954	(no marathon)		
1958	Tokyo	Lee Chang Hoon (Korea)	2:32:55
1962	Jakarta	Masayuka Nagata (Japan)	2:34:55
1966	Bangkok	Kenji Kimihara (Japan)	2:33:23
1970	Bangkok	Kenji Kimihara (Japan)	2:21:03
1974	(no marathon)		
1978	Bangkok	Mineteru Sakamoto (Japan)	2:15:30
1982	New Delhi	Kim Yang Kon (Korea)	2:22:21
1986	Seoul	Takeyuki Nakayama (Japan)	2:08:21*
1990	Beijing	Kim Won Tak (Korea)	2:12:56
1994	Hiroshima	Hwang Young Cho (Korea)	2:11:13
1998	Bangkok	Lee Bong Ju (Korea)	2:12:32

Today the association includes other road races besides marathons. The association publishes a twice-yearly magazine called *Distance Running. See also* organizations.

Association of Road Racing Athletes (ARRA). Road racing was toying uneasily with the pay-or-don't-pay question when athletes took matters into their own hands in 1980. This group, cofounded by Don Kardong, was largely responsible for opening up the sport to prize money. *See also* Kardong, Don; organizations; Professional Road Running Organization; professional racing.

Athens, Greece. No city has deeper historic roots in running. It might or might not have been Pheidippides' ultimate finish line, but it was the site of the 1896 and 1906 Olympic Games and it will host the 2004 Games if the city can complete the construction of venues in time. The Greeks also put on the 1997 World Championships. An annual marathon from the Plains of Marathon to the city of Athens is contested each year (www.athensmarathon.com). *See also* historic sites; Olympic Marathon, 1896; World Championships medalists.

Athens (Ohio) Marathon. The Ohio marathon, run in April, isn't as old as its namesake's, but the U.S. version goes back to 1968. A nice touch at the race: winners receive olive wreaths from Greece. *See also* oldest races.

Athletics Congress, The (TAC). Under pressure from the U.S. government, the Amateur Athletic Union was forced (by an act of Congress that allowed organizations to govern only one sport; the AAU had overseen many) to release its longtime hold on track and distance running in 1978. But the "new" governing body for the sport in the United States continued to operate out of the same offices as before, and Ollan Cassell was still in charge. He would not leave that post for almost 20 years, by which time the organization was known as USA Track & Field. *See also* Amateur Athletic Union; Cassell, Ollan; organizations; USA Track & Field.

Athletics West. For a decade from the late 1970s to mid-1980s, Nike sponsored a club designed to give athletes their best chance to excel. Athletic West's greatest successes were Joan Benoit, 1984 Olympic champion, and Alberto Salazar, New York City and Boston winner. The club also supported Tony Sandoval, 1980 Olympic Trials winner, and Mary Decker, who set road records along with her track exploits. *See also* Benoit, Joan Samuelson; Nike; Salazar, Alberto; Sandoval, Tony; Slaney, Mary Decker Tabb.

Atkins, Herm (b. August 30, 1948). In an era when black runners from Africa increasingly filled the front ranks of marathons, few African-Americans competed well (or competed at all) on the roads. Atkins's marathon "record" for black Americans, 2:11:52, has stood since 1979. *See also* Sanders, Odis.

Atlanta Marathon (www.atlantatrackclub.org). Long before Atlanta entertained an Olympics, it had a marathon, founded in 1963. The race runs on Thanksgiving morning and follows many of the same streets as the 1996 Olympic route. *See also* oldest races.

Atlantic City Marathon (www.racegate.com). Long before the coastal city legalized gambling, it held a marathon. Ed League established this race in 1959, and it has been held, usually in October, ever since. *See also* oldest races.

Audain, Anne. See next page.

Avenue of the Giants Marathon (www.humboldt1.com/~avenue). One of the loveliest courses anywhere, the route passes through the giant redwoods of far northern California. A similar route is used each fall for the Humboldt Redwoods Marathon and Half. *See also* Humboldt Redwoods Marathon; scenic races.

Audain, Anne (b. November 1, 1955). The New Zealander was adopted at birth. She was born with severely deformed feet, which weren't corrected surgically until her early teens. Before she emerged as a running phenomenon, she was a teaching phenomenon in her native New Zealand, where she was known as someone who took great strides toward raising both the self-esteem and the goal-setting ability of her charges.

Never a woman to back down from a challenge, in 1981 she and several other athletes were temporarily barred from international competition because they made a show of accepting prize money for their racing. She was a sparkplug in turning road racing into a sport in which an athlete could make a decent living. As the first professional distance runner, she was also the first woman signed to a Nike contract.

She held the world record in the track 5,000 meters, qualified six times for the Olympic Games, won gold and silver medals in the Commonwealth Games, and claimed more road-racing victories than any other woman during the 1980s. She also set the world road 10K record twice, and was the first woman to go under 32:00. Her greatest string of wins came at the Spokane Bloomsday 12K race, where she won seven times between 1980 and

1990. In 1983 she founded the Idaho Women's Fitness Celebration in hopes of inspiring healthy attitudes in women and girls of all ages and abilities. She published her autobiography, *Uncommon Heart*, and maintains an active Web site at www.anneaudain.com. *See also* Bloomsday 12K; Bolder Boulder 10K; Idaho Women's Fitness Celebration; Peachtree 10K; record progressions, world.

© Mark Shearman. Athletics-Images.

Born with severely deformed feet that were surgically corrected many years later, New Zealand's Anne Audain (#560) went on to be the winningest female road racer of the modern era.

Avery, Guy (b. February 21, 1964). A former NCAA Division I runner at Siena College and then a successful coach, Avery founded the highly technical newsletter *Peak Running Performance*, subtitled *Leading-Edge Training and Racing Strategies for Runners*. He later sold it to Road Runner Sports, which publishes the newsletter from San Diego. Avery still offers training advice (www.marathonedge.com). *See also* Road Runner Sports.

Avia (www.avia.com). Avia had the gumption to base its operations on Nike's home turf, the Portland area—which now serves as U.S. headquarters for adidas as well.

Avon Racing Circuits (www.avonrunning.com). Kathrine Switzer's brainchild spread the marathon gospel from 1978 to 1984, when the Avon Marathon stood as the unofficial world championships for women. Switzer revived the concept in the late 1990s, this time with world and national championships at the 10K distance. *See also* "Avon Calling" on next page; Switzer, Kathrine.

Avon Winners

With full backing from her employer, Kathrine Switzer established a quasi-world championships marathon for women. This race opened the way for an official Worlds in 1983 and an Olympic race for women in 1984. Note that three-time Avon winner Lorraine Moller won a medal in the Olympic Marathon. * = event record.

AVON MARATHON

Year	Place	Athlete	Time
1978	Atlanta	Marty Cooksey (U.S.)	2:46:16
1979	Waldniel	Joyce Smith (Britain)	2:36:27
1980	London	Lorraine Moller (New Zealand)	2:35:11
1981	Ottawa	Nancy Conz (U.S.)	2:36:45
1982	San Francisco	Lorraine Moller (New Zealand)	2:36:13
1983	Los Angeles	Julie Brown (U.S.)	2:26:26*
1984	Paris	Lorraine Moller (New Zealand)	2:32:44

AVON GLOBAL 10K

Year	Place	Athlete	Time
1999	New York City	Tegla Loroupe (Kenya)	31:48
2000	Milan	Sonia O'Sullivan (Ireland)	30:59*

Avon Calling

From Joe Henderson's *Running Commentary,* September 1998.

Karen Binder called to ask if I would speak at the Avon women's race she was directing in Portland, Oregon. I agreed but with an unspoken question: why?

The mostly female audience at the talk might also have wondered: why a male speaker? When I spoke I answered without being asked. I said it was because my memory was longer than that of almost everyone there that day. I remembered when women didn't—and weren't even allowed to—run the 10K distance of the weekend's race or anything longer.

Then I recalled running the 1967 Boston Marathon with Kathrine Switzer. We've become friends since, and Kathrine was then in the room. But at the time I'd never heard of her (nor she of me), and I didn't know until afterward that she had run.

That Boston was my first marathon, and it would change my life. Kathrine's wearing of an official number, her run-in with Jock Semple, and the resulting media flurry would change the entire running world.

The incident activated Kathrine's political and promotional instincts. She worked toward acceptance of women at Boston, which came in 1972, and approval of a national championship marathon for women, in 1974. Later she organized the first Avon running circuit, a main reason why the women's marathon won a place in the 1983 World Championships and then the 1984 Olympic Games.

Kathrine revived the Avon circuit this year. I said in Portland, "She's the reason you're all here today, both because of what she does now and did a long time ago."

The first Avon series showed the world how well women could run if given the chance. The second series celebrates how far women have come.

I added at the talk, "Another reason for my being here is that I'm a father. My two daughters now have full opportunity to run, and both have taken it. My mother and sisters never had the chance at the same age."

I've supported women runners since the 1960s without really thinking of it as a women's-rights issue. It was a growth-of-running issue. Running couldn't grow to full potential as long as the national and international rules arbitrarily and unfairly excluded half the population.

Kathrine Switzer wasn't the first woman to run a marathon in the United States, but she was among the first half dozen. She remembers knowing the name of every female marathoner in the world. They seldom topped 1 percent of any field when she ran.

Today, women are marching toward majority status. Twice this year in North America they've accounted for more than half the field at marathons—with 53 percent at the Okanagan International in British Columbia and 55 percent (or some 10,000 women) at Rock 'n' Roll.

The good health of running today is largely the women's doing. The healthiest trend is the feminizing of the sport, and Kathrine Switzer and Avon can take credit for nursing this growth.

Ayres, Ed (b. October 11, 1941). Before helping to found *Running Times*, he placed third in the inaugural New York City Marathon (run in Central Park). Ayres guided *RT* through its startup and several ownership changes before leaving to work for the Worldwatch Institute. *See also* publications; *Running Times*.

B

BAA (Boston Athletic Association). *See* Boston Marathon.

Baby Jogger (www.babyjogger.com). Bicycle technology wedded necessity to create a product that would allow parents to run with their young children. The parents in turn made pests of themselves at larger races by insisting on pushing the carriages through heavy runner traffic. Many races were forced to ban the BJs. Still, they make wonderful training accessories. And an adult version allows Dick Hoyt to compete at Boston (and other races) with his grown-up invalid son Rick.

Bacheler, Jack (b. December 30, 1943). To say he was the third man (placing ninth at Munich in 1972, where Frank Shorter was first and Kenny Moore was fourth) on the greatest Olympic team of modern times doesn't do him justice. Bacheler, a 1968 Olympian in the 5,000 who stood almost six feet seven inches, inspired Frank Shorter's move to Gainesville and heavily influenced his decision to become a marathoner. Bacheler was an accidental marathoner at Munich. He intended to make the 10,000-meter team but was disqualified in that race. Jeff Galloway, who made the 10K team, helped pace Bacheler to his marathon berth. Incredibly, Jack was suffering from a bad head cold the day of the Olympic Marathon. Jack later coached national championship women's teams at North Carolina State University, where he was and is a professor of entomology. *See also* Olympians, U.S.; Olympic Trials Marathon, U.S.; Shea, Julie and Shea, Mary.

Courtesy RunningPast.com

The unmarathon Boston. In 1918, in the midst of World War I (known at the time as the Great War), the Boston Marathon was supplanted by a military relay race, of which this official's ribbon is a relic.

Bakoulis, Gordon Bloch (b. February 14, 1961). It's a female Gordon, and a multitalented one. She ran no high school or college track and entered her first race at 24. By age 30 she'd run a 2:33 marathon and qualified for the World Championships (1991). The former editor of *Running Times* has written books on running and cross-training. She also edited *The Running Times Guide to Breakthrough Running* (Human Kinetics, 2000). *See also* books; *Running Times;* World Championships, U.S.

Stefano Baldini of Italy managed to break through the African stranglehold on distance running in 1996 when he won the World Half-Marathon Championships.

© Mark Shearman. Athletics-Images.

Baldini, Stefano (b. May 25, 1971). Even during times when African runners dominate the long distances, someone occasionally beats them. That someone at the 1996 World Half-Marathon was Baldini of Italy. Baldini also won the 1998 European Championships Marathon, beating the more highly regarded Spaniards and Portuguese. In 2001 he collected a bronze medal in the World Championships Marathon, running 2:13:18. *See also* European Championships; World Championships medalists.

Band-Aids. The traditional nipple saver, particularly for men, who tape themselves to protect against rubbing by their sweaty shirts in this ultrasensitive area. Band-Aids have recently been usurped by Nipgards. *See also* Nipgards.

banned substances. *See* drug testing.

Bannister, Roger (b. March 23, 1929). Normally we wouldn't include a runner who seldom raced beyond one mile. But Bannister's contribution transcended his event. By breaking through the four-minute-mile barrier in 1954, he made runners aware of new possibilities at all distances. For instance, the marathon world record dropped by five minutes between 1954 and 1964. *See also* barrier breakers.

Bare Buns Fun Run (www.ontherun.com/barebuns). A 5K race in Washington State strips runners to the basics and leaves them nowhere to pin their race numbers—but also offers a clothed division for the merely curious. Male runners are left to wonder if they'll be awarded a prize for shortest in their age group. A good account of the race is available in Tim Martin's humorous book *There's Nothing Funny About Running* (Marathon Publishers, 2000). *See also* oddest races.

Barie, Zak (b. May 15, 1954). The Tanzanian was among the first wave of Africans to arrive on the American roads. He held the world 10K record and was the first to break 28:00 on the roads (27:43 in 1984). Zak was *Runner's World*'s top-ranked runner that year. *See also* rankings, *Runner's World*; record progressions, world.

barrier breakers. Round-number barriers abound in this sport. The biggest looming barrier is now the 2:05 marathon for men. Until recently, a 2:20 marathon for women was the long sought after barrier. Naoki Takahashi broke it at Berlin on September 30, 2001 with her 2:19:46. One week later, Catherine Ndereba bettered this time at Chicago with a 2:18:47. Other past barrier crashers under unaided conditions for women include the following: 15-minute 5K, Lydia Cheromei (14:58 in 1997); 2:30 marathon, and Grete Waitz (2:27:33 in 1979); for men: 1:00 road half-marathon, Moses Tanui (59:47 in 1993); and 2:10 marathon, Derek Clayton (2:09:37 in 1967). *See also* Cheromei, Lydia; Clayton, Derek; record progressions, American; record progressions, world; Tanui, Moses; Waitz, Grete.

Barrios, Arturo. See next page.

Barron, Gayle (b. April 6, 1945). An early winner of Atlanta's Peachtree 10K (five victories in the first six years) and the Boston Marathon (1978), Barron has remained active in the sport. She wrote one of the first books for women runners, *The Beauty of Running* (Harcourt Brace Jovanovich, 1980), and now coaches the Atlanta-based Team Spirit marathon-training program. *See also* Boston Marathon; Peachtree 10K.

bars, sports. No, these are not the type that serve drinks and unending telecasts of sports events. They are the bars that a runner eats before, after, and even during training and racing. Canadian marathoner Brian Maxwell's PowerBar, introduced in the mid-1980s, led a rush into a product category that now includes dozens of brands. The bars are today so ubiquitous that some Nevada casinos sell them to gamblers. *See also* Maxwell, Brian; PowerBar.

Bassler, Dr. Tom (birthdate unavailable). The pathologist-runner-iconoclast from California made the famous (and now widely discredited by highly publicized cases to the contrary, notably Jim Fixx's) statement in the early 1970s, "No one who finishes a marathon will ever die of a heart attack."

© Jeff Johnson

Gayle Barron, who dominated the Peachtree Road Race (in Atlanta) and the early runnings of the Atlanta Marathon, won Boston in 1978 with a 2:44:52.

Barrios, Arturo (b. December 12, 1962). Today Arturo Barrios coaches the army distance running team in Boulder, Colorado, and coaches through the Internet. He set world records in the track 10,000 meters (27:08.23 in 1989), road 10K (27:41 in 1986), and track 20,000 meters (56:55.6 in 1991) as well as the hour run (13.11 miles or 21.101 kilometers in 1991), during which he became the first human being to run a track half-marathon in less than an hour (59:59.6).

Born into poverty in Mexico City, he worked his way to a degree in mechanical engineering from Texas A&M University and later became a U.S. citizen after his prime racing years had passed. His running talent became apparent early. At 17, while still in high school, he ran a 4:04 mile, 14:26 for 5,000 meters, and 30:20 for 10,000 meters.

In 1980 Barrios ran for Mexico in the Central American Junior Championships, where he was spotted by a scout from Rice University, who offered him a scholarship. The only problem was that Arturo didn't speak English. So he moved to Texas and enrolled in Wharton Junior College where he studied English, math, and physics. His running in junior college did not improve drastically, but his command of English and his grades did. The promised scholarship to Rice never came through, so he accepted one from Texas A&M. Again, Arturo gave preference to his studies over his training, maintaining the long-term view. In 1985 he placed second to Ed Eyestone in the NCAA 10,000-meter championships.

Once he secured his diploma, Arturo returned to Mexico City, lived on virtually nothing, and took up running seriously.

Mike Sandrock photo

Itinerant marathoners Rich Benyo and Arturo Barrios stage a sit-down strike protesting excessive yard work required by Mike Sandrock outside Boulder, Colorado, in exchange for getting a room for the night.

He trained at high altitudes and won local 10Ks, where he made enough prize money to buy tires for the car his brother had given him to get back and forth to training sessions. In March 1986 he scraped together enough money to buy a one-way ticket to a 10K in Phoenix, Arizona; he hoped the $800 he could win for eighth place would cover a return ticket. The field included Ed Eyestone, Bill Rodgers, Steve Jones, John Treacy, Ibrahim Hussein, and Peter Koech. Arturo ran conservatively in the first half and then opened it up over the last two miles, winning in 27:41, a 10K road world record.

Suddenly an invited runner, he went on a tear, winning 13 of his next 14 races. His loss came at his first Boston Marathon, where he took fifth place in 2:14:09. It was also in 1986 that he made his move to Boulder, the mecca of world-class road racers. He won four Bolder Boulder 10K races, usually with a devastating surge around the four-mile mark, an uphill portion of the course. He also won four times at Bay to Breakers.

During 1987 and 1988 Barrios won 18 major road races, but he was directing his attention to the track. He finished fifth, running for Mexico, in the Seoul Olympics 10,000 meters, but he knew he had more talent to plumb. He ran only two road races in 1989, then concentrated aggressively on the track, racing against the best in Europe. After a few near misses at the world record, the big day came at the Olympic Stadium in Berlin, site of the 1936 Olympics. On August 18, after having several rabbits lead him through the early miles, Arturo ran alone to a new world record of 27:08.23, a record that would stand for four years.

Arturo placed a disappointing fifth at the 1992 Barcelona Olympics, still competing for his native Mexico, and decided to give the marathon his attention. He ran New York in 1993 and took third. At Boston in 1994 he placed fifth in 2:08:23. That fall he was third at New York. He then went to Los Angeles in March 1995 and finished fifth, again after leading much of the race. During the race he pulled a hip muscle, but through judicious recuperation and light training, he was back to normal that summer.

Gradually Arturo's ability to take the field out and keep the pace fast enough to drop most of his competitors faded, but his popularity never did. His name graces an annual 10K race in Southern California that is held to raise money for needy young scholars. He collects used running shoes and cleans them up so that he can take them to his native Mexico and give them to enthusiastic young runners. Although most of the famed runners in Boulder tend to be passed over by younger runners who fail to access the vast storehouses of knowledge possessed by the old guard, Arturo has remained popular with runners of all ages. He takes pains to make himself available to them, even if they often fail to heed his most important bit of advice: "Don't necessarily train harder; train smarter." *See also* Bay to Breakers 12K; Bolder Boulder 10K; national 10K champions, U.S.; Peachtree 10K; rankings, *Runner's World*; record progressions, world.

Bay to Breakers 12K (www.baytobreakers.com). America's largest and wackiest event is also one of the oldest. Begun in 1912 as the Cross-City Race across San Francisco, it remained small until the sport first boomed in the 1970s. By then one of the city's newspapers had taken over as title sponsor. In peak years the organizers boasted a field of 100,000. An exact count was, and is, hard to come by because many of the runners and walkers never bother to enter. The race has the distinction of being one of the first footraces to encourage running in costume. It also was the breeding ground of the now-famous and far-flung concept of centipede running, originated by the UC Davis Aggies Running Club, in which compatible runners tie themselves together in some sort of costume and run in tandem. *See also* biggest races.

Beames, Adrienne (b. July 7, 1941). Before any woman had broken three hours in the marathon, this Australian reportedly ran 2:46:30 in 1971. Mysterious circumstances surrounding this event, and the fact that Beames ran no notable marathons before or after this race, cast doubt on its authenticity. Some authorities place her in the lineage of records; others don't. *See also* records progressions, world.

Beardsley, Dick (b. March 21, 1956). This accident-prone Minnesotan was half of classic "Duel in the Sun" (with Alberto Salazar) at the 1982 Boston Marathon. He still holds the fourth-best U.S. marathon time of 2:08:52 and was cowinner of the first London Marathon in 1981. Beardsley later endured a series of horrific farm and traffic accidents that nearly claimed his life but he rebounded to run marathons again. *See also* "Where's Dick?" on page 26; Hall of Fame, RRCA; London Marathon; Salazar, Alberto; Squires, Billy.

Bay to Breakers Winners

This San Francisco megarace grabs headlines for its size and zaniness. Don't forget, though, that it still is a race, an old and proud one that since the 1980s has brought together some of the world's best runners. The course varied from 7 $1/2$ to 8 miles before settling at its current 12K. Note that Kenny Moore won six times in a row from 1968 through 1973. Winners are from the United States unless otherwise noted. * = event record.

WOMEN

Year	Athlete	Time	Year	Athlete	Time
1971	Frances Conley	50:45	1987	Rosa Mota (Portugal)	39:16
1972	Cheryl Bridges	44:47	1988	Lisa Martin (Australia)	39:16
1973	Cheryl Bridges	45:20	1989	Ingrid Kristiansen (Norway)	39:14
1974	Mary Etta Boitano	43:22	1990	Jill Hunter (Britain)	39:19
1975	Mary Etta Boitano	46:04	1991	Susan Sirma (Kenya)	38:27
1976	Mary Etta Boitano	49:20	1992	Lisa Ondieki (Australia)	38:35
1977	Judy Leydig	47:28	1993	Lynn Jennings	39:14
1978	Skip Swannack	47:02	1994	Tegla Loroupe (Kenya)	39:10
1979	Laurie Binder	43:07	1995	Delillah Asiago (Kenya)	38:23*
1980	Laurie Binder	42:28	1996	Elana Meyer (S. Africa)	38:56
1981	Janice Oehm	41:47	1997	Jane Omoro (Kenya)	39:57
1982	Laurie Binder	42:28	1998	Jane Omoro (Kenya)	38:57
1983	Laurie Binder	41:24	1999	Catherine Ndereba (Kenya)	38:37
1984	Nancy Ditz	42:37	2000	Colleen de Reuck (S. Africa)	38:42
1985	Joan Samuelson	39:54	2001	Jane Ngotho (Kenya)	40:35
1986	Grete Waitz (Norway)	38:47			

MEN

Year	Athlete	Time	Year	Athlete	Time
1912	Robert Vluth	44:10	1957	Jesse Van Zant	44:02
1913	Robert Vluth	40:59	1958	Wilford King	41:17
1914	Oliver Millard	40:47	1959	Wilford King	41:30
1915	Oliver Millard	41:39	1960	Don Kelley	42:00
1916	George Wyckoff	42:33	1961	Jack Marden	41:30
1917	Oliver Millard	41:30	1962	Jim Shettler	41:25
1918	Edgar Stout	42:41	1963	Herman Gurule	40:16
1919	Harry Ludwig	42:45	1964	Jeff Fishback	38:32
1920	William Churchill	40:57	1965	Bill Morgan	38:02
1921	Charles Hunter	40:28	1966	Eric Brenner	41:11
1922	William Churchill	42:56	1967	Tom Laris	38:42
1923	William Churchill	41:56	1968	Kenny Moore	38:15
1924	William Churchill	41:52	1969	Kenny Moore	38:40
1925	Vincenzo Goso	42:50	1970	Kenny Moore	36:29
1926	Frank Eames	42:13	1971	Kenny Moore	36:57
1927	Frank Eames	42:56	1972	Kenny Moore	36:39
1928	Pietro Giordanengo	43:05	1973	Kenny Moore	37:15
1929	Pietro Giordanengo	43:05	1974	Gary Tuttle	37:07
1930	Manuel John	43:10	1975	Ric Rojas	37:18
1931	Jack Keegan	44:28	1976	Chris Wardlaw (Australia)	
1932	Ray Cocking	43:19	1977	Paul Geis	37:03
1933	Jack Keegan	43:31	1978	Gerard Barrett (Australia)	35:17
1934	John Nehi	42:12	1979	Bob Hodge	36:50
1935	Leo Karlhofer	43:51	1980	Craig Virgin	35:11
1936	Joe McCluskey	40:37	1981	Craig Virgin	35:07
1937	Norman Bright	39:52	1982	Rod Dixon (New Zealand)	35:07
1938	Ed Preston	41:15	1983	Rod Dixon (New Zealand)	35:01
1939	Ed Preston	41:14	1984	Ibrahim Hussein (Kenya)	35:11
1940	Ed Preston	42:12	1985	Ibrahim Hussein (Kenya)	34:53
1941	Frank Lawrence	42:39	1986	Ed Eyestone	34:33
1942	James Haran	43:53	1987	Arturo Barrios (Mexico)	34:45
1943	Joseph Wehrly	45:01	1988	Arturo Barrios (Mexico)	34:57
1944	Fred Kline	43:15	1989	Arturo Barrios (Mexico)	34:40
1945	Fred Kline	43:25	1990	Arturo Barrios (Mexico)	34:31
1946	Fred Kline	44:28	1991	Thomas Osano (Kenya)	33:55
1947	Merle Knox	43:52	1992	Thomas Osano (Kenya)	33:57
1948	Fred Kline	44:27	1993	Ismail Kirui (Kenya)	33:42
1949	Merle Knox	42:58	1994	Ismail Kirui (Kenya)	34:03
1950	Elwyn Stribling	42:57	1995	Ismail Kirui (Kenya)	33:58
1951	John Holden	46:09	1996	Thomas Osano (Kenya)	34:35
1952	Jim Shettler	45:34	1997	Joseph Kimani (Kenya)	33:51*
1953	Jesse Van Zant	42:05	1998	Simon Rono (Kenya)	33:58
1954	Jesse Van Zant	42:15	1999	Lazarus Nyakeraka (Kenya)	34:11
1955	Jesse Van Zant	43:42	2000	Reuben Cheruiyot (Kenya)	34:54
1956	Walt Berger	44:56	2001	James Koskei (Kenya)	34:19

 Hyde Library Memphis University School

Where's Dick?

From Joe Henderson's *Running Commentary*, April 1999.

A race director's duties extend beyond directing the runners to include rounding up guests. Rich Benyo spent the Friday before his Napa Valley Marathon at the airport, collecting the speakers for the weekend.

Members of our party strayed as we awaited arrival of the final guest. "Organizing a group of runners is like trying to herd cats," said Rich in resignation and exasperation.

This was quite a collection of talent. It included Lorraine Moller, New Zealand's Olympic Marathon medalist from 1992 who now lives in Colorado; Gayle Barron, women's winner at the 1978 Boston Marathon; John Keston, an Oregon-based Briton who holds the world record for marathoners 70 and older; and George Sheehan III, son of Dr. George and inheritor of his speaking skills.

Our missing person was Dick Beardsley. He wasn't lost, just delayed by his airline. Dick, now 43, is a longtime favorite of mine. In the early 1980s no one in the world ran marathons much better than he did. He linked up with Alberto Salazar in the best road-race finish I've ever seen. They finished two seconds apart at the 1982 Boston Marathon, running times that still rank third and fourth in U.S. history.

Since then Dick has endured a horrific series of accidents. The worst, suffered on his dairy farm, nearly cost him a leg—and his life. That happened 10 years ago. Three traffic mishaps followed, resulting in chronic pain and eventual addiction to pain medication. Dick bottomed out in late 1996 with his arrest for forging prescriptions. He received no jail time but was ordered to undergo treatment and to perform hundreds of hours of community service.

I saw him at Napa last year. He said then, "The arrest was the best thing that could have happened to me. It made me face my problem instead of hiding or denying it." He was then celebrating "one year of sobriety." Of his speaking to student groups, he said, "I would have liked to do that anyway."

Now he could tell us how the second year off drugs had gone, that is, if we ever saw him. Through a series of glitches, the theme of the weekend became, "Where's Dick?" He missed the first evening reception and the dinner that followed, along with all other group meals but one. Dick, a professional radio announcer, spoke brilliantly at the clinics, then seemed to vanish again.

In one of his talks someone asked the inevitable, "Are you running tomorrow?" He told of running only four or five miles a day, then added, "I'd like to go to halfway in the marathon, then see how I feel." The rumor took wing that he planned to finish. But he wasn't immediately available to confirm or deny.

On race morning I saw Dick only briefly, as he pulled off his extra clothes. He had on his race face. Later at the finish line our group asked each other, "Where's Dick?" None of us had seen him on the course.

Finally he walked into the hotel lobby, again wearing his usual relaxed smile. "At halfway I felt like I could have gone on all day," he said. "Two miles later I was looking for a ride on the sag wagon."

That fifteen-mile run was his longest run since the farm accident a decade ago. It celebrated two drug-free years and completion of more than 400 hours of community service. His friends might not be able to find him as often and for as long as they would like. But Dick Beardsley knows right where he is now, and just how far he has bounced back after hitting bottom.

[In 2000 Dick returned to the Napa Valley Marathon and ran all the way, finishing in 3:23. That was his first full marathon in more than eight years. At Grandma's Marathon in 2001, he achieved his goal of coming within an hour of his still-standing course record of 2:09:37. Twenty years later, he ran 2:55:39.]

Although never a road racer, Dave Bedford, one-time 10,000-meter world record-holder, now directs thousands of road racers in his capacity as race director of the London Marathon. Bedford was renowned in his track days for his fierce, drooping mustache and his black socks, an intimidating combination.

© Mark Shearman. Athletics–Images.

Beckford, Darlene (b. December 9, 1961). In the early years of road record-keeping, American Beckford became the first in the world to break 16 minutes in a road 5K by running 15:53 in 1985. *See also* record progressions, American; record progressions, world.

Bedford, Dave (b. December 30, 1949). The former world record-holder in the 10,000 cut a dark figure on the track with his droopy mustache and black socks. He never directed his own efforts toward the roads but now directs the efforts of tens of thousands in the London Marathon. *See also* London Marathon.

Belisle, Polin (b. July 2, 1966). He wormed his way into the Olympic Marathon, not once but twice, for two different countries (Belize and Honduras), under suspicious circumstances. On both occasions, 1988 and 1992, his qualifying times apparently were falsified. Justice was served, though, when he was last to finish at Seoul and first to drop out at Barcelona. *See also* cheaters.

Bemis-Forslund Pie Race. The race—founded in 1891—in Northfield, Massachusetts claims to be the oldest race in North America, but it probably doesn't qualify because it isn't a standard, open road race. Bemis-Forslund is an intramural event on the campus of a prep school, limited to the school community. *See also* oldest races.

Benham, Ed (b. July 12, 1907; d. April 21, 2001). The former jockey did some of his, and the world's, best running after his 80th birthday. He ran the world's best 80-plus marathon of 3:43 and holds American marks for that age group in the 10K and half-marathon. *See also* Hall of Fame, RRCA; records, American age-group; records, world age-group.

Benoit Samuelson, Joan (b. May 16, 1957). Joan Benoit won the first-ever Olympic marathon for women at the 1984 Los Angeles Olympic Games. Employing a run-how-you-feel tactic, Joan ran much as Frank Shorter had at the Munich Games. Finding the early pace too slow for her liking, Joan took the lead while the rest of the field stayed back, feeling she would come back to them—especially considering that Joan had undergone knee surgery just before the U.S. Olympic Marathon Trials. But she never faltered. According to Dave Martin and Roger Gynn's book *The Olympic Marathon* (Human Kinetics, 2000), Benoit's time of 2:24:52 was faster than 13 of 20 of the previous Olympic men's marathon winning times.

Joan Benoit, America's foremost female marathoner, wins the 1983 Boston in a then-world best of 2:22:43.

A native of Maine and graduate of Bowdoin College, Joan was enthusiastic as a high school and college athlete but not outstanding. She ran her first marathon as a lark, entering the 1979 Hamilton (Bermuda) race as a long workout the day after she won the 10K. Joan "jogged" to a second-place finish in 2:50:54. Three months later she entered the Boston Marathon and won it in 2:35:15. She ran the race in a Bowdoin College shirt, wearing a baseball cap backward long before the style became popular among teens. She was voted "Best USA Female Distance Runner" by *Runner's World* magazine that year, and she traveled from Maine to California to receive her award while wearing a sensible Maine sweater and displaying a heartfelt tear in her eye in awe of the honor.

Warm and gregarious with her friends, Joan has a highly developed sense of humor that borders on the outrageous (she's been known to sneak up on running friends and bite them in the butt, earning her the nickname "Barracuda"). But Joan Benoit Samuelson is also a fierce trainer and competitor; this two-edged trait has accounted for a litany of injuries over the years that would have sidelined a lesser human being. It was because of injuries

that she missed the U.S. Olympic Trials in 1988 and 1992, yet she returned to compete in the Trials of 1996 (13th place in 2:36:54) and 2000 (9th in 2:39:59 on a hot day at age 42).

In 1997 a panel of experts reporting to *Marathon & Beyond* magazine voted her the seventh most prominent figure to have an effect on marathoning in the past 25 years. In a subsequent *M&B* poll (in 1999) featuring the best marathoners of all time, she ranked number one ahead of Grete Waitz and Ingrid Kristiansen. The panel of experts put it succinctly: "1984 Olympic gold medal, beat Grete [Waitz] and Rosa [Mota] in 2:24:52 Olympic record; first in Chicago (2:21:21) beating Ingrid [Kristiansen], missing the world record by only 15 seconds; two Boston wins (1979 and 1983), the latter in 2:22:43 world's best at the time." Women's running pioneer Kathrine Switzer wrote, "Joanie was not just a runner but a racer; was totally focused and determined." World masters marathon record-holder Priscilla Welch said she voted for Benoit Samuelson "for a gold in the 1984 Olympics, and for her continued involvement in the sport both actively and through the media. [She's a] fierce competitor and knowledgeable spokesperson for the sport."

Through the 2000 U.S. Women's Marathon Trials, Joan had completed 25 marathons, winning 9 of them. Not to be outdone by her competitive accomplishments, she became a race director and put together the highly competitive and extremely popular Beach to Beacon 10K race in her home state of Maine. She is married and has two children and reputedly still cans some mean jams and jellies from local fruit she herself picks. *See also* Bay to Breakers 12K; Chicago Marathon; Olympians, U.S.; Olympic medalists; Olympic Trials Marathon, U.S.; rankings, *Runner's World*; rankings, *Track & Field News*; record progressions, American; record progressions, world; records, American; records, world.

Following Joan

From Joe Henderson's *Running Commentary,* September 1998.

As the first woman to win an Olympic Marathon, Joan Benoit (now Samuelson) showed her class right after that race by crediting women's running pioneers for making this all possible. Joan has always been the classiest of runners.

A small number of fans and a large group of fellow athletes gathered in Eugene to see why she remains so widely admired so long after her best races were run. She came here 22 years after first running in Eugene's Olympic Trials 1,500 as a teenager. The last time she raced on the Hayward Field track was to finish an American-record marathon 16 years ago.

Now 41, she returned for the World Masters Games in August. This meet isn't to be confused with the World Veterans Championships, a bigger and better-established meet held in Eugene in 1989.

Nike sponsored the Masters Games. Nike also sponsors Joan, and she is a master, so she agreed to give a clinic here. She told her audience, "I can still do the same workouts I once did, but I sure can't recover as quickly." Her mileage has settled at 50 to 60 a week, or little more than half what it was in her record-breaking, medal-winning years.

"Quality over quantity" is her practice as well as her advice to other masters. "The best thing you can do for yourself is give yourself a rest."

Joan could have rested the day after her speech. She could have figured that her job was finished here and headed home to Maine without competing. Or she could have gone through the motions in the 5,000. No one was here to test her, even with the meet open to runners as much as 11 years younger.

She did run but downplayed any talk about setting records. "I always run the way I feel, sometimes by the seat of my pants," she said at her clinic. "I don't really know what I'm in for."

The 90-degree heat and stiff breeze on the backstretch weren't right for record setting. Yet Joan went to the lead and locked right into national-record pace of 16:51. This pace looked very fast, as hers always does because she's so short and her leg turnover is so quick. It's hard to imagine that she once kept up this pace for a marathon. No other American female marathoner has gone that far this fast since 1985.

The U.S. masters 5K record slipped away from her in Eugene as she ran 17:03. Then even after her race had ended she showed her class. She waved off reporters and held off her victory lap. She waited to greet the second and third runners, who finished two to three minutes later.

They couldn't have found anyone better to follow, even from this distance. What Joan Benoit Samuelson has done helps all women runners do what they do.

[Upping her training mileage for the 2000 Olympic Marathon Trials, Samuelson finished ninth in 2:39:59—the highest place and fastest time ever by a master in this event.]

Benyo, Richard (b. April 20, 1946) *See* About the Authors at the back of this book.

Berlin Marathon (www.berlin-marathon.com). A consistently flat, fast, and accurate marathon course where in 1998 Ronaldo da Costa ended the 10-year stall in the men's record with 2:06:05. The following year Tegla Loroupe lowered the 13-year-old women's record to 2:20:43. Loroupe's world record was broken in 2001 when Naoko Takahashi became the first woman to run under 2:20 with her 2:19:46. The marathon is typically held in late September or early October.

Berlin Marathon Winners

Two sub-2:07 men's races in consecutive years (1998 and 1999) and two sub-2:24 women's races in three years (1997 and 1999) stamped Berlin as one of the fastest marathons anywhere. * = event record.

WOMEN

Year	Athlete	Time
1974	Jutta Von Hasse (Germany)	3:22:01
1975	Christin Bochroder (Germany)	3:59:15
1976	Jutta Von Hasse (Germany)	3:05:19
1977	Angelika Brandt (Germany)	3:10:27
1978	Ursula Blaschke (Germany)	2:57:09
1979	Jutta Von Hasse (Germany)	3:07:07
1980	Gerlinde Puttmann (Germany)	2:47:18
1981	Angelika Stephan (Germany)	2:47:24
1982	Jean Lochead (Britain)	2:47:04
1983	Karen Goldhawk (Britain)	2:40:32
1984	Agnes Sipka (Hungary)	2:39:32
1985	Magda Ilands (Belgium)	2:34:10
1986	Charlotte Teske (Germany)	2:32:10
1987	Kerstin Pressler (Germany)	2:31:22
1988	Renata Kokowska (Poland)	2:29:16
1989	Paivi Tikkanen (Finland)	2:28:45
1990	Uta Pippig (Germany)	2:28:37
1991	Renata Kokowska (Poland)	2:27:36
1992	Uta Pippig (Germany)	2:30:22
1993	Renata Kokowska (Poland)	2:26:20
1994	Katrin Dorre (Germany)	2:25:15
1995	Uta Pippig (Germany)	2:25:37
1996	Colleen de Reuck (South Africa)	2:26:35
1997	Catherina McKiernan (Ireland)	2:23:44
1998	Marleen Renders (Belgium)	2:25:22
1999	Tegla Loroupe (Kenya)	2:20:43
2000	Kazumi Matsuo (Japan)	2:26:15
2001	Naoko Takahasi (Japan)	2:19:46*

MEN		
Year	**Athlete**	**Time**
1974	Gunter Hallas (Germany)	2:44:53
1975	Ralf Bochroder (Germany)	2:47:08
1976	Ingo Sensburg (Germany)	2:23:08
1977	Norman Wilson (Britain)	2:16:21
1978	Michael Spottel (Germany)	2:20:03
1979	Ingo Sensburg (Germany)	2:21:09
1980	Ingo Sensburg (Germany)	2:16:48
1981	Ian Ray (Britain)	2:15:42
1982	Domingo Tibaduiza (Colombia)	2:14:46
1983	Karel Lismont (Belgium)	2:13:37
1984	John Skovbjerg (Denmark)	2:13:35
1985	James Ashworth (Britain)	2:11:43
1986	Boguslaw Psujek (Poland)	2:11:03
1987	Suleiman Nyambui (Tanzania)	2:11:11
1988	Suleiman Nyambui (Tanzania)	2:11:45
1989	Alfredo Shahanga (Tanzania)	2:10:11
1990	Steve Moneghetti (Australia)	2:08:16
1991	Steve Brace (Britain)	2:10:57
1992	David Tsebe (South Africa)	2:08:07
1993	Xolile Yawa (South Africa)	2:10:57
1994	Antonio Pinto (Portugal)	2:08:31
1995	Sammy Lelei (Kenya)	2:07:02
1996	Abel Anton (Spain)	2:09:15
1997	Elijah Lagat (Kenya)	2:07:41
1998	Ronaldo da Costa (Brazil)	2:06:05*
1999	Josephat Kiprono (Kenya)	2:06:44
2000	Simon Biwott (Kenya)	2:07:41
2001	Joseph Ngolepus (Kenya)	2:08:47

Berman, Sara Mae (b. 1936). An early Boston Marathon crusader, she "won" that race in the last three years (1969 to 1971) before women were recognized officially. Berman once held the American record, which she set when she became the first woman from this country to break 3:30. *See also* Boston Marathon; record progressions, American.

Best Efforts. *See* Moore, Kenny.

Beurskens, Carla (b. February 15, 1952). Few runners apart from Grete Waitz at New York City have owned a race as much as Beurskens did the Honolulu Marathon from the mid-1980s to mid-1990s. The Dutchwoman won that race 8 times in 10 years, the last three as a master. *See also* Honolulu Marathon; Rotterdam Marathon.

Beverly, Jonathan (b. April 10, 1964). He was serving as editor at *Running Times* as the new century began. See also *Running Times*.

bib. It labels the runner for identification and scoring purposes. Longtime runners still use the earlier term *number*.

biggest races. Such is the growth of the sport that it now takes a race of more than 20,000 to qualify as truly "mega." Entry figures are often inflated, and the truest measure of size is the number of official finishers. Using that standard, the world's largest events are in roughly this order: (1) Bay to Breakers 12K, San Francisco, U.S.; (2) Peachtree 10K, Atlanta, U.S.; (3) Carrefour International 9K, Buenos Aires, Argentina; (4) Bloomsday 12K, Spokane, U.S.; (5) Stramilano 12K, Milan, Italy; (6) Volta a Peu a Valencia 8K, Valencia, Spain; (7) Round the Bay 8.4K, Auckland, New Zealand; (8) City to Surf 14K, Sydney, Australia; (9) Cursa el Corte Ingles 12K, Barcelona, Spain; (10) Bolder Boulder 10K, Boulder, U.S. Largest of the marathons are New York, London, and Chicago. The largest all-women's race is the Grete Waitz 5K (Oslo, Norway). *See also* "Numbers Runners" below.

Numbers Runners

From Joe Henderson's *Running Commentary,* July 2000.

For the best reading of how many people run in America, look to the Road Running Information Center of USATF. Other estimates are based on polling data. RRIC uses actual head counts of racers. Those aren't the numbers who register but those who care enough to finish.

You have to love the trend that the annual tally reveals. Growth, growth, growth every year—more than doubling the total in the past 15 years. Last year, reports the RRIC, "there were an estimated 7.1 million finishers from a total of more than 12,000 U.S. running events." This is up from 6.8 million runners in 1998. This does not mean that more than seven million Americans ran races last year. They were counted every time they raced, and many of the runners weren't U.S. citizens.

The race for biggest racing distance is no contest. The 5K totaled 2.5 million performances, with the Races for the Cure contributing 688,000 to that total. Next largest in size is the 10K at one million, and the 8K (and five mile) at 560,000.

Then comes the marathon. It grew to 435,000 finishers, up 4 percent from the record high (of 419,000) of the previous year despite a trend toward capping entries at this distance. The fifth most popular distance is the half-marathon at 425,000. In prestige, if not in size, the "half" still has a long way to go to overtake its namesake.

[Comparisons of figures for the largest races in the country in 1999, as compiled by the RRIC, with figures from] 10 years earlier reveal the trends in running. Three races topped 30,000 in 1989. Seven of them did by 1999.

Bay to Breakers and Bloomsday, which ranked one and two as the 1980s ended, lost 12,000 and 5,000 finishers respectively in the next decade. Peachtree jumped from sixth to second, mainly because the limit on entrants doubled. Bolder Boulder increased in size by 16,000 in those years and the New York City Marathon by 7,000.

Dropping out of the top 10 during the 1990s were the Crescent City 10K, Great Aloha Run, Bix, Capitol 10K, and Los Angeles Marathon. Women supplied many of the replacements. The two highly ranked Races for the Cure and the Revlon Run for Women are mostly or entirely female.

Biggest U.S. Races

Here are the largest 40 for 2000, the last year for which the Road Running Information Center had compiled complete statistics before this encyclopedia went into production. The RRIC counts finishers from single races (not totals for multievent programs) and doesn't attempt to separate runners from walkers. e = estimated count.

Race (city)	Finishers
Bay to Breakers 12K (San Francisco, CA)	52,474
Peachtree 10K (Atlanta, GA)	50,000e
Race for the Cure 5K (Washington, DC)	47,428
Bloomsday 12K (Spokane, WA)	45,537
Bolder Boulder 10K (Boulder, CO)	40,462
Revlon Run for Women 5K (Los Angeles, CA)	35,974
Chicago Marathon (Chicago, IL)	31,877
Revlon Run for Women 5K (New York, NY)	30,000e
New York City Marathon (New York, NY)	29,375
Race for the Cure Women's 5K (Portland, OR)	25,355
Race for the Cure Coed 5-K (Denver, CO)	25,100e
Race for the Cure 5K (New York, NY)	25,000e
Race for the Cure 5K (Detroit, MI)	24,600e
Race for the Cure 5K (Peoria, IL)	24,000e
Race for the Cure 5K (Philadelphia, PA)	24,000e
Honolulu Marathon (Honolulu, HI)	22,652
Race for the Cure 5K (Pittsburgh, PA)	21,256
Race for the Cure 5K (Dallas, TX)	21,000e
Indy 500 Festival Mini-Marathon (Indianapolis, IN)	18,289
Corporate Challenge 3.5M (Atlanta, GA)	19,000e
Corporate Challenge 3.5M #2 (New York, NY)	18,550
Crescent City Classic 10K (New Orleans, LA)	18,000e
Los Angeles Marathon (Los Angeles, CA)	17,192
Marine Corps Marathon (Washington, DC)	17,048
Club Med Corporate 5K (Miami, FL)	16,400e
Race for the Cure 5K (Cleveland, OH)	16,000e
Race for the Cure 5K (Little Rock, AR)	16,000e
Rock 'n' Roll Marathon (San Diego, CA)	15,918
Boston Marathon (Boston, MA)	15,668
Idaho Women's Fitness Celebration 5K (Boise, ID)	15,200e
Race for the Cure Women's 5K (Denver, CO)	15,200e
Corporate Challenge 3.5M (Chicago, IL)	14,850e
Cooper River Bridge Run 10K (Charleston, SC)	14,144
Corporate Challenge 5K #3 (New York, NY)	13,850e
Great Aloha 8.15M (Honolulu, HI)	13,500e
Corporate Challenge 3.5M #1 (New York, NY)	13,300e
Corporate Challenge 3.5M (Buffalo, NY)	12,600e
Wharf to Wharf 6M (Santa Cruz, CA)	12,500e
Capitol 10K (Austin, TX)	12,000e
Bix 7M (Davenport, IA)	11,883

Big Sur Marathon (www.bsim.org). Races don't come much more dramatically scenic than this one, where runners have the Pacific Ocean to their left nearly all the way. With the scenery, though, come hills—nearly all the way. This race is consistently voted the best marathon in the world by the biannual book *The Ultimate Guide to Marathons* (Marathon Publishers). *See also* scenic races.

Bikila, Abebe. See pages 36-37.

Biktagirova, Madina (b. September 20, 1964). The woman from the former Soviet Union has the dubious honor of being the first Olympic marathoner disqualified for a failed drug test. She tested positive for the mild stimulant norephedrine at the 1992 Games after finishing fourth and returned to racing after a brief suspension. This isn't to say, of course, that she is the only Olympian ever to have used illicit substances. Others who did succeeded in beating the system in place at the time. Biktagirova remains the Los Angeles Marathon record-holder with 2:26:23, set earlier the same year as her Olympic dishonor. *See also* drug testing; Los Angeles Marathon.

Binder, Laurie (b. August 10, 1947). She is one of the rare runners to bridge the gap between successful open and masters careers. Binder won the national marathon title in 1982, then set an American masters record (still standing at 2:35:08) nine years later. She also holds the masters half-marathon mark. At shorter distances, Binder was a three-time Bay to Breakers winner. *See also* "Meet the Penguin" on next page; Bay to Breakers 12K; national marathon champions, U.S.; records, American age-group.

Bingham, John (b. December 13, 1948). Perhaps more commonly known as the Penguin, Bingham tapped into the run-for-fun mood that prevailed at the turn of the last century and instantly developed a huge following. The professional musician and music professor, an untested writer, landed a column in *Runner's World* and followed with a best-selling book, *The Courage to Start* (Simon & Schuster, 1999). *See also* Penguin Brigade.

biomechanics. This is the term for how we run—not how far or how fast, but how we actually move. The science of human movement contributes in many ways to running performance—by correcting flaws in form, by improving the quality and safety of shoes, and by finding solutions to injuries. The profession of podiatry relies heavily on biomechanical principles. *See also* podiatry.

Birch Bay Marathon. Blaine, Washington, hard by the Canadian border, boasts one of the oldest U.S. marathons. It launched in 1969 and is currently run each December. *See also* oldest races

Bix 7M (www.bix7.com). If big races can crop up in small cities such as Bix's hometown of Davenport, Iowa, then they can take root anywhere. This seven-mile race began as part of a tribute to jazz musician Bix Beiderbecke and has grown to more than 14,000 finishers. *See also* biggest races.

Meet the Penguin

From Joe Henderson's *Running Commentary,* September 1998.

The *Runner's World* writing staff is not a big, happy family. We aren't unhappy either, but we aren't a family at all. Some of us hardly know each other.

The miracles of the computer age let most of us writers live anywhere, and we're everywhere: Hal Higdon in Indiana, Don Kardong in Washington, Liz Applegate in California, Marc Bloom in New Jersey.

The closest we come to a staff meeting is leading the *RW* pacing groups at one or two marathons a year. I've visited the home office in Pennsylvania only twice, and never in the past 10 years. I meet the other writers one or two at a time at races, if at all.

I'd never run across our newest columnist until this summer. I knew John Bingham only as the Penguin, the persona he has adopted in his column.

In two years of appearances in the magazine he has gathered a huge following. He's now making his second cross-country tour to meet and entertain his fans. Last summer he traveled for two months by motorcycle. This year he's driving a car and staying out longer, 12 weeks in all. One stop—between San Francisco and Salt Lake City—was Jeff Galloway's camp at Lake Tahoe. I happened to be there, too.

I knew nothing more about him than his name and nickname, and how he spends his summers. I'd seen only one picture of him, a group shot that revealed little. I expected from the Penguin a brash young pup in his 30s, somewhat outsized in height and bulk. Up walked an almost-50-year-old with a graying mustache and round glasses that give him a look of surprise. He introduced himself by his given name, not the acquired nickname.

John Bingham is unimposing physically, at five feet eight inches and 140 pounds. He once was 100 pounds heavier, this during his career as a professional musician and then a PhD student.

His running started at age 43. He now has dropped to part-time teaching of music at Middle Tennessee State University and risen to a starring role in the second running boom. Besides his *Runner's World* column, speaking tour, and heavily visited Web site, he has a book in the works with Simon & Schuster.

When John steps in front of an audience, the quiet-spoken college prof disappears, and he becomes the Penguin. He doesn't lecture or converse on stage. He performs.

Running writing, and by extension speaking, can use more humor. The Penguin supplies it, especially when he performs live. His is one of the most hilarious acts I've ever seen on the running circuit. This is standup comedy worthy of the Improv. His listeners don't giggle or titter politely; they double over with laughter that brings happy tears to their eyes.

The Penguin is no buffoon, though. Behind his humor lies an invitation to everyone, of any size and speed, to fit as comfortably into this sport as he did at his start. He says that much more unites the fast and the slow, the skinny and the heavy, than separates us. We can be one big, happy family when we get to know each other.

[In 1999, John Bingham published *The Courage to Start* (Simon & Schuster). It quickly became one of the best-selling books in the sport.]

Bikila, Abebe (b. August 7, 1932; d. October 22, 1973). Most students of the sport acknowledge Abebe Bikila as the greatest marathon runner who ever lived and, ironically, the most tragic figure in the sport. Bikila was a natural running animal—fluid, low to the ground, with a minimal bob of the head. He was efficiency personified.

Ethiopia, Bikila's homeland in eastern Africa, was cloaked in secrecy when he began racing. The country had been invaded in 1936 by Italy, part of the muscle flexing of the European Axis powers, and the country was ravaged by war. The land was remote to begin with, and Emperor Haile Selassie, distrustful of the world, built on that remoteness. Ethiopia had sent a team of athletes to the 1956 Olympic Games in Melbourne, but their performance had been disappointing.

Onni Niskanen, a Finn, moved to Ethiopia to become the director of athletics. He discovered among the country's military a cadre of fine athletes used to competing in distance events at Addis Ababa, the capital, which sat at an altitude of 8,000 feet. Niskanen trained his runners systematically, and they responded. He set up a marathon course at Addis and ran several trial marathons. In the first one, young Abebe Bikila, a member of the Imperial Palace Guards, ran 2:39:50. In the next trial, he astonished everyone except Niskanen when he ran 2:21:23, more than three minutes faster than the winning time at the previous Olympic Games at Melbourne. A small team was immediately cobbled together and sent to Rome.

Bikila's shoes were falling apart, and he could not find any in Rome to fit, so he ran barefooted, which was widely reported by the press. As an unknown, Bikila did not suffer under the stone of great expectations. Halfway through the race, he and Moroccan Rhadi Ben Abdesselem broke away and commenced a two-man duel.

Arguably the greatest marathoner in the history of the world, Ethiopia's Abebe Bikila became the first to win two Olympic Marathons (1960 in Rome, 1964 in Tokyo).

© Mark Shearman. Athletics-Images.

But as the race wore on, Abdesselem was no match for Bikila, who steadily pulled away, victorious in the capital city of the nation that had attempted to subjugate his own years before. Bikila's 2:15:17 not only won the Olympic gold medal but also tied the Soviet Sergey Popov's world record.

After returning home to rest, Bikila returned to the world stage and went on a marathoning tear. On May 7, 1961, he won on the original Marathon to Athens course in 2:23:45, on July 25 he won in Osaka in 2:29:27, and on October 12 he won in Košice in Czechoslovakia in 2:20:12. In 1963 Bikila and teammate Mamo Wolde traveled to the famed Boston Marathon, a race no Olympic champion had ever won. Under cold conditions, the Ethiopians took the field out on world-record pace, but by the Newton Hills, the cold had caused both of them to cramp. Humiliated, Bikila vanished again into Ethiopia—until 1964.

An Olympic Trial Marathon race at Addis saw Abebe run 2:16:19 with teammate Wolde less than a second behind him. But six weeks before the Tokyo Olympics, Abebe underwent an appendectomy. Essentially, Bikila was out, but he believed otherwise. He continued to train and on October 21 lined up at the starting line in Tokyo. He went out with the leaders and by 20K he was alone in the lead. He won in 2:12:12, another world record and more than four minutes ahead of second-place finisher Basil Heatley. When Bikila finished, he turned onto the infield, lay down, and began doing a series of stretching exercises. Some observers felt that he was rubbing in his overwhelming victory. In fact, he had learned over the years that if he did not immediately stretch following a long run, his muscles stiffened up.

Bikila became the first marathoner to repeat as a gold-medal winner in the Olympics, and both performances were world records. He would attempt to win again in 1968, but he was hobbled with a stress fracture. Teammate Mamo Wolde would win instead. To put Abebe Bikila's career in perspective, of the 13 marathon races in which he competed and in which he completed the course, he won every one except Boston in 1963, where he placed fifth.

On March 22, 1969, Abebe was driving after dark in his Volkswagen Beetle when he swerved to avoid an oncoming vehicle. The car rolled into a ditch, and he suffered the dislocation of the sixth and seventh vertebrae, making him a quadriplegic. In spite of medical attention in a hospital in England, he never regained the use of his legs, although he did regain some use of his arms and competed for a time as an archer. He was a guest at the 1972 Munich Olympics. When Frank Shorter received his gold medal for winning the marathon, he went directly to Bikila to shake his hand. A year later, at the age of 41, Abebe Bikila, the running animal, the image of the perfect marathoner, suffered a stroke and died of a brain hemorrhage, leaving a wife and four children. In 1996, his daughter, Tsige, wrote a biography of her father, *Triumph and Tragedy*, which was published in Addis Ababa. *See also* African runners; Ethiopian runners; Košice Peace Marathon Olympic medalists; rankings, *Track & Field News*; Wolde, Mamo.

Bjorklund, Garry (b. April 22 1951). In the 1976 U.S. Olympic Track and Field Trials, Bjorklund lost a shoe but still managed to make the 10,000-meter team. In 1980 he lost his chance to run an Olympic Marathon to the Carter boycott of the Moscow Games. "BJ" skipped the meaningless Trials Marathon and set a PR of 2:10:20 at Grandma's that summer; his time was just one second slower than the winning time at the Trials.

BJ was raised on a 40-acre farm in Twig, 40 miles outside Duluth, Minnesota. He wasn't much of an athlete in school (the school had an enrollment of 10 boys and 3 girls), being overweight. By seventh grade he had sprung up in height and slimmed down in weight, but his first encounter with competitive running turned him off. The sports in northern Minnesota are hunting and fishing. Once he settled on track, though, he improved rapidly. As a high school freshman he ran a 4:19 mile; by his senior year he was down to 4:05.

Garry Bjorklund, known as BJ, was one of America's top distance runners of the late 1970s and early 1980s. He dogged Bill Rodgers's footsteps at the New York City Marathon and staged a classic duel with Dick Beardsley at the 1981 Grandma's Marathon in Duluth, Minnesota.

Once into college his development continued but at longer distances. He seemed a shoo-in for the 1972 Olympic team but developed a foot injury. He made the 1976 team but finished a disappointing 13th. Once out of college, BJ focussed his concentration to road racing, where he quickly made a name for himself as being one of the only road racers brave enough or talented enough to go out with Bill Rodgers, who at that point dominated the roads. His strong running on the roads through the late 1970s and early 1980s won him a place in the RRCA Hall of Fame. *See also* Hall of Fame, RRCA.

Blake, Arthur (b. January 26, 1872; d. October 23, 1944). The first-ever U.S. Olympic marathoner (and the only one entered in the revival of the Games in 1896) failed to finish at Athens. Although he was in third place at the halfway point, he dropped soon after, a victim of the unaccustomed distance and the hills. He had placed second in the 1,500 meters earlier in the week. *See also* Olympians, U.S.

blisters. Still the occasional bugaboo of some runners, blisters are not nearly the constant and almost universal problem they once were. Improved shoe materials and design, better socks, and stick-on or spray-on products for the feet have combined to reduce blistering to a minor concern.

blood doping. The controversial performance aid stores an athlete's own blood for reinfusion before the race to elevate red blood cell count and hence oxygen transport to muscles, aiding performance in all middle- and long-distance races. A more sophisticated modern version uses the banned substance EPO (erythropoietin) to accomplish the same result. *See also* drug testing; erythropoietin.

blood lactate. *See* anaerobic threshold.

Bloom, Marc (b. February 14, 1947). He edited *The Runner* for nearly the entire life of the magazine and now writes about the sport for *Runner's World* and the *New York Times,* among other publications. He began his editing career doing *The Harrier,* a magazine dedicated to cross country running. He has written many books on the sport, among them *The Marathon: What It Takes to Go the Distance* (Holt, Rinehart ad Winston; 1981) and *Run With the Champions* (Rodale, 2001). See also *Runner, The; Runner's World.*

Bloomsday 12K (www.bloomsday.org). Spokane, Washington, a city of 200,000, attracts a field of nearly 50,000. U.S. Olympian Don Kardong founded the

Bloomsday Winners

The Spokane race was born as a professional event, thanks to Frank Shorter's appearance (and victory) in Bloomsday's first running. New Zealander Anne Audain was a seven-time winner. The distance was about eight miles through 1982, then was reduced to and certified at 12K. * = event record.

WOMEN

Year	Athlete	Time
1977	Joan Ullyot (U.S.)	53:26
1978	Marty Cooksey (U.S.)	43:24
1979	Cathie Twomey (U.S.)	43:56
1980	Gail Volk (U.S.)	46:27
1981	Anne Audain (New Zealand)	41:54
1982	Anne Audain (New Zealand)	40:02
1983	Anne Audain (New Zealand)	39:29
1984	Regina Joyce (Ireland)	40:28
1985	Anne Audain (New Zealand)	39:20
1986	Anne Audain (New Zealand)	38:48
1987	Lesley Welch (U.S.)	39:22
1988	Anne Audain (New Zealand)	39:35
1989	Lynn Williams (Canada)	39:30
1990	Anne Audain (New Zealand)	39:40
1991	Lisa Weidenbach (U.S.)	40:03
1992	Lisa Ondieki (Australia)	39:02
1993	Anne-Marie Letko (U.S.)	39:19
1994	Olga Appell (U.S.)	38:57
1995	Delilllah Asiago (Kenya)	38:31*
1996	Colleen de Reuck (South Africa)	38:48
1997	Kim Jones (U.S.)	40:34
1998	Jane Omoro (Kenya)	40:14
1999	Jane Omoro (Kenya)	39:37
2000	Jane Omoro (Kenya)	40:08
2001	Elana Meyer (South Africa)	39:23 *(continued)*

Bloomsday Winners, *continued*

MEN

Year	Athlete	Time
1977	Frank Shorter (U.S.)	38:26
1978	Bill Rodgers (U.S.)	37:08
1979	Ric Rojas (U.S.)	37:07
1980	Mark Anderson (U.S.)	36:22
1981	Duncan Macdonald (U.S.)	35:34
1982	Henry Rono (Kenya)	35:49
1983	Jon Sinclair (U.S.)	34:55
1984	Ibrahim Hussein (Kenya)	34:33
1985	Paul Davies-Hale (Britain)	34:27
1986	Jon Sinclair (U.S.)	34:25
1987	Steve Binns (Britain)	34:38
1988	Peter Koech (Kenya)	34:22
1989	John Halvorsen (Norway)	34:21
1990	German Silva (Mexico)	34:42
1991	Steve Moneghetti (Australia)	34:52
1992	Yobes Ondieki (Kenya)	33:55
1993	Arturo Barrios (Mexico)	33:55
1994	Josphat Machuka (Kenya)	34:10
1995	Josphat Machuka (Kenya)	33:52*
1996	Lazarus Nyakeraka (Kenya)	34:07
1997	Lazarus Nyakeraka (Kenya)	34:19
1998	Hezron Otwori (Kenya)	34:23
1999	Joshua Chelanga (Kenya)	34:18
2000	Reuben Cheruiyot (Kenya)	34:10
2001	Dominic Kirui (Kenya)	34:29

race in 1977, and it has been rated consistently among the country's best-organized and biggest events. *See also* "If Spokane can..." on next page; biggest races.

Blue Ribbon Sports. *See* Asics; Nike.

body composition. One look at the front-runners in any road race will reveal most of what you need to know about the role of body build in running performance. The winners might be tall or short, but they're almost uniformly lean—sometimes almost skeletally so. Body-fat percentage, if measured, registers in single digits for men and slightly higher for women. So great are the rewards for low body fat that runners sometimes take extreme, even unhealthy, measures to reduce it. Genetically large runners have taken a more positive approach by lobbying for size divisions at races. *See also* Clydesdale division.

If Spokane Can . . .

From Joe Henderson's *Running Commentary,* May 1998.

One spin-off of my trip to Japan last fall was an invitation to write a monthly "Letter from the USA" for *Runners* magazine. It's as simple as an editor asking me questions about running in this country. One of the first was about the Bloomsday phenomenon, which brought this answer:

The Japanese know American distance running mainly by our marathons. Our oldest one, in Boston, is world famous—as is our largest, in New York City. And, of course, Japan supplies the majority of runners for the Honolulu Marathon.

But to me the most amazing American megarace is not a marathon but the less-traveled distance of 12 kilometers. This race isn't run in one of our better-known cities but in Spokane, Washington. Spokane doesn't look anything like Seattle, the sprawling and wet coastal city 500 kilometers to the west. Spokane sits in the sunny and lightly populated high plains of Washington.

The Spokane area's population is only 200,000. Yet this small city hosts one of the largest U.S. races, the Lilac Bloomsday 12K. The event brings out nearly 50,000 runners each spring.

Bloomsday has in some years been *the* biggest U.S. race—at least as the Road Running Information Center judges size, by number of finishers. By this standard Bloomsday has on occasion stood even higher than San Francisco's Bay to Breakers (another 12K—because that happens to be the distance across the city). We know for sure that the Bloomsday had the greatest number of runners, by far, for a city its size. Greater Spokane has less than 5 percent of the population of the San Francisco Bay Area.

How did it happen in Spokane? First, realize that this region has a long tradition of running excellence. Gerry Lindgren, who made the Tokyo Olympic team at age 18, grew up here. Kenyan Henry Rono broke his first world records while attending nearby Washington State University. Spokane is the adopted home of Kim Jones, long one of America's top female marathoners, and Don Kardong, fourth-place finisher in the 1976 Olympic Marathon.

Kardong returned from the Montreal Olympics with the thought of spreading running interest in his community, and he founded Bloomsday the next year. Now occupied as president of the Road Runners Club of America and as a writer for *Runner's World,* he no longer directs the race but remains its elite-athlete coordinator and its guiding spirit.

Bloomsday serves both the class (the emerging professional road runners) and the mass (the growing numbers of fun runners). The race prides itself equally on being one of the first in this country to award prize money to its leaders as well as the one with the largest number of official finishers.

Although Bloomsday attracts runners from throughout the world and across the nation, the majority—60 percent last year—still come from the Spokane area. Six thousand children run the shorter Junior Bloomsday races each year.

In all, about 1 in every 10 residents joins in the running. That amazing figure shows what can happen when an event captures the imagination of a city. At this rate Bay to Breakers would need a half-million local runners, and the New York City Marathon a million, to keep pace.

© Mark Shearman. Athletics-Images.

Irina Bogacheva, from Kyrgyzstan in the former Soviet Union, won Honolulu in 1998 and 1999—at the ages of 37 and 38—and made it look easy.

body temperature. Runners learn to tolerate the extremes of weather, but sometimes temperature goes above or below tolerance levels, harming performance and eventually health itself. Overheating is known as *hyperthermia*; excessive chilling as *hypothermia*.

Bogacheva, Irina (b. April 30, 1961). The woman from Kyrgyzstan has raced best at ages 37 and 38—winning the 1998 and 1999 Honolulu Marathons and Los Angeles in 1999. *See also* Honolulu Marathon; Los Angeles Marathon.

Boileau, Art (b. October 9, 1957). He grew up in Oregon, where he was a college teammate of Alberto Salazar. But Boileau was Canadian by birth and became one of that country's all-time great marathoners with a 2:11:15 PR (set at Boston when he was runner-up to Rob de Castella in 1986). Boileau twice won the Los Angeles Marathon, in 1987 and 1989. *See also* Los Angeles Marathon.

Boitano, Mary Etta (b. March 4, 1963). By age 10, the San Franciscan was already a marathon veteran with a 3:01 time to her credit. At 11 in 1974, she won the first of her three straight Bay to Breakers titles. By her midteens, she had abandoned serious racing. *See also* Bay to Breakers 12K; kids' running.

Bolder Boulder 10K (www.bolderboulder.com). The popular and innovative Colorado race, held each Memorial Day since 1979, draws nearly 40,000 finishers but seems smaller. Its wave-start concept divides runners into more manageable groups of equal abilities and starts each group at one- to two-minute intervals, a practice that other megaraces should imitate. *See also* biggest races; Boulder, Colorado.

Bolder Boulder Winners

Boulder's big 10K has produced incredible records, considering its 6,000 feet of elevation and resulting thin air. Josphat Machuka broke 28 minutes, and fellow Kenyan Delillah Asiago approached 32 minutes. * = event record.

WOMEN

Year	Athlete	Time
1979	Sandy Simmons (U.S.)	39:56
1980	Ruth Hamilton (U.S.)	37:15
1981	Ellen Hart (U.S.)	34:55
1982	Anne Audain (New Zealand)	32:38
1983	Ellen Hart (U.S.)	34:46
1984	Rosa Mota (Portugal)	34:03
1985	Rosa Mota (Portugal)	33:59
1986	Rosa Mota (Portugal)	33:54
1987	Nancy Tinari (Canada)	33:59
1988	Rosa Mota (Portugal)	34:41
1989	Ingrid Kristiansen (Norway)	33:59
1990	Rosa Mota (Portugal)	33:14
1991	Delillah Asiago (Kenya)	33:52
1992	Jill Hunter (Britain)	33:57
1993	Uta Pippig (Germany)	33:39
1994	Nadia Prasad (France)	33:28
1995	Delillah Asiago (Kenya)	32:13*
1996	Elana Meyer (South Africa)	33:22
1997	Libbie Hickman (U.S.)	33:25
1998	Jane Omoro (Kenya)	33:26
1999	Lidia Simon (Romania)	32:30
2000	Derartu Tulu (Ethiopia)	33:09
2001	Deena Drossin (U.S.)	33:25

MEN

Year	Athlete	Time	
1979	Ric Rojas (U.S.)	29:44	
1980	Marc Hunter (U.S.)	29:57	
1981	Frank Shorter (U.S.)	29:29	
1982	Rodolfo Gomez (Mexico)	28:51	
1983	Mark Scrutton (Britain)	28:51	
1984	Herb Lindsay (U.S.)	29:09	
1985	Paul Davies-Hale (Britain)	29:06	
1986	Arturo Barrios (Mexico)	28:46	
1987	Arturo Barrios (Mexico)	29:06	
1988	Rolando Vera (Ecuador)	29:53	
1989	Arturo Barrios (Mexico)	28:59	
1990	Martin Pitayo (Mexico)	28:48	*(continued)*

Bolder Boulder Winners, *continued*

Year	Athlete	Time
1991	Thomas Osano (Kenya)	29:01
1992	Thomas Osano (Kenya)	28:40
1993	Arturo Barrios (Mexico)	29:04
1994	Armando Quintanilla (Mexico)	29:31
1995	Josphat Machuka (Kenya)	27:52*
1996	Simon Rono (Kenya)	28:28
1997	Hezron Otwori (Kenya)	28:55
1998	Simon Rono (Kenya)	28:50
1999	Berhanu Adanne (Ethiopia)	29:00
2000	Joseph Kimani (Kenya)	28:55
2001	James Koskei (Kenya)	29:00

Bone Fone. In the early 1980s, marketers thought runners would buy anything—and they were often correct. The Bone Fone was a weird application of a portable radio. It draped over the shoulders and sent audio from radio stations through the body's bones. Sony Walkman later won that round of the sounds-on-the-run war.

bonk. Old-timers still call it "hitting the wall." The modern term, borrowed from bicycle racing, is "bonking." The most common culprits are unwise pacing and inadequate training. Physiologically, the usual cause is a depletion of energy supplies in the working muscles. *See also* wall, the.

Bonner, Beth (b. June 9, 1942, d. 1998). She is generally acknowledged as the first female to break 3:00 in the marathon and is certainly the first American woman to do so. Her big time of 2:55:22 came in 1971 as the first New York City Marathon women's winner. She had set another world and American record earlier in 1971 with 3:01:42 at Philadelphia. Bonner was killed in a bicycling accident at age 46. *See also* New York City Marathon; record progressions, American; record progressions, world.

books. The all-time best sellers are Jim Fixx's *Complete Book of Running* (Random House, 1977), *Galloway's Book on Running* by Jeff Galloway (Shelter, 1984), Bob Glover and Jack Shepherd's *The Runner's Handbook* (2nd ed., Penguin, 1996), and George Sheehan's *Running & Being* (2nd ed., Second Wind, 1998) as well as the more general fitness volumes *Aerobics* by Kenneth Cooper (Bantam Books, 1968) and *Stretching* by Bob Anderson (Author, 1975). Sales, however, don't always equate with critical acclaim.

The authors of Running Encyclopedia recommend the following, some of which you'll have to search for at used book stores. Rich recommends *The Long Run Solution* by Joe Henderson (World Publications, 1976), *Running*

With the Legends by Mike Sandrock (Human Kinetics, 1996), *Once a Runner* (a novel) by John Parker (Cedarwinds, 1994), *The Complete Runner* (Avon Books, 1974), and *The Boston Marathon* by Tom Derderian (Human Kinetics, 1994). Joe recommends Arthur Lydiard's *Run to the Top* (Jenkins, 1963) and Tom Osler's *Serious Runner's Handbook* (World Publications, 1978). Both recommend Hal Higdon's *On the Run From Dogs and People* (Regnery, 1971).

Bordin, Gelindo (b. April 2, 1959). The only male Olympic gold-medal winner (1988 in 2:10:32) to also win the Boston Marathon (1990 in 2:08:19), the well-respected Italian serves as race director of the Prague International Marathon. Gelindo is respected because he worked his way up through the ranks, his performances were consistent, and he did everything with class. His accomplishments are even more phenomenal when we realize that in 1981 a car struck him while he was training in Italy, and it was presumed he would die of the injuries.

During a three-year period (1988–1990), Gelindo was arguably the best marathoner in the world. But even before the Olympic gold and Boston, he won the 1986 European title and in 1987 won the World Championships bronze. In 1990 he again won the European title. *See also* Boston Marathon; European Championships; Olympic medalists; rankings, *Track & Field News*; World Championships medalists.

Boston Marathon. *See* next page.

Boston Marathon, The. *See* books; Derderian, Tom.

Boulder, Colorado. It's the running capital of the United States, at least in terms of top runners living there. Frank Shorter settled in Boulder between his Olympic years, and other runners have followed ever since. A United Nations of runners has migrated there for high-altitude training and for the laid-back attitude. Longtime residents include Arturo Barrios from Mexico, Priscilla Welch from Britain, and Mark Plaatjes from South Africa. *See also* Bolder Boulder 10K.

Bowerman, Bill (b. 1911; d. December 24, 1999). The legendary University of Oregon track coach is also famous for using his wife's waffle iron to create the revolutionary soles for Nike's Waffle Trainer running shoes in the 1970s (the fumes from the process may have eventually caused health problems). After visiting Arthur Lydiard in New Zealand, Bowerman imported the "jogging" craze to the United States in the 1960s when he wrote one of the first books on the subject, titled simply *Jogging* (Grosset & Dunlap, 1967). A staple of his training program for top athletes—ranging from Bill Dellinger to Kenny Moore to Steve Prefontaine—was the hard-easy approach, which spaced each tough workout or race with one or more days of recovery. *See also* "Bowerman's Gifts" on page 50; coaches; Dellinger, Bill; Hall of Fame, RRCA; Hall of Fame, USATF; Moore, Kenny; Nike; Prefontaine, Steve.

Boston Marathon (www.bostonmarathon.org). The cradle of American marathoning, the race began in 1897 after a group of Boston Athletic Association members returned from the first modern Olympics imbued with the spirit of the marathon event. The race began modestly enough, featuring several dozen runners the first few years. The entrants were primarily blue-collar workers who belonged to competing athletic clubs in the Boston and New York areas, with an increasing contingent of foreign runners thrown in. College runners at first looked down on the race but eventually began slumming by entering.

In the early years the course went through a variety of distances, because it wasn't until the 1908 London Olympic Games that the standard distance of 26 miles, 385 yards was run, and it took years for it to be adopted universally; it wasn't adopted in Boston until 1927. The number of race entrants stayed under 1,000 until 1968, but soon afterward the numbers had exploded to the point that the BAA instituted qualifying times.

The potent BAA eventually fell on hard times as the face of sport in America changed from the local athletic club format. The Boston Marathon offices and the BAA eventually ended up in a pile of cardboard boxes in the massage room of trainer Jock Semple in the Boston Garden. The Running Revolution of the late 1970s was a shot in the arm to the Boston Marathon, but it also presented a challenge from the growth of other urban marathons that offered prize money. Boston was in danger of committing suicide by refusing, in the mid-1980s, to go with the trend. Not to be daunted for long, a new slate of dynamic directors and an infusion of capital and a long-term commitment from John Hancock Insurance Company returned Boston to the front-rank status it deserves. Tom Derderian's *The Boston Marathon* (Human Kinetics, 1994) is an overwhelmingly thorough history of the great race, run on Patriots' Day, the third Monday in April. *See also* Cloney, Will; fastest races; Morse, Guy; oldest races; Semple, John "Jock."

From the collection of Dr. Edward H. Kozloff–Motor City Striders

Ellison "Tarzan" Brown, whose father was a Narragansett Indian, ran how he felt, and in 1936 he felt like leading Boston from start to finish.

Boston Marathon Winners

The world's longest-running marathon has crowned more than 100 male champions and 30 women winners. Many of the men's times listed through the mid-1950s were run on courses shorter than the standard 26.22 miles. Women's winners were unofficial from 1966 to 1971. * = race record.

WOMEN

Year	Athlete	Time
1966	Roberta Gibb (U.S.)	3:21:40
1967	Roberta Gibb (U.S.)	3:27:17
1968	Roberta Gibb (U.S.)	3:30:00
1969	Sara Mae Berman (U.S.)	3:22:46
1970	Sara Mae Berman (U.S.)	3:05:07
1971	Sara Mae Berman (U.S.)	3:08:30
1972	Nina Kuscsik (U.S.)	3:08:58
1973	Jacqueline Hansen (U.S.)	3:05:59
1974	Miki Gorman (U.S.)	2:47:11
1975	Liane Winter (West Germany)	2:42:24
1976	Kim Merritt (U.S.)	2:47:10
1977	Miki Gorman (U.S.)	2:48:33
1978	Gayle Barron (U.S.)	2:44:52
1979	Joan Benoit (U.S.)	2:35:15
1980	Jacqueline Gareau (Canada)	2:34:28
1981	Allison Roe (New Zealand)	2:26:46
1982	Charlotte Teske (West Germany)	2:29:33
1983	Joan Benoit (U.S.)	2:22:43
1984	Lorraine Moller (New Zealand)	2:29:28
1985	Lisa Weidenbach (U.S.)	2:34:06
1986	Ingrid Kristiansen (Norway)	2:24:55
1987	Rosa Mota (Portugal)	2:25:21
1988	Rosa Mota (Portugal)	2:24:30
1989	Ingrid Kristiansen (Norway)	2:24:33
1990	Rosa Mota (Portugal)	2:25:24
1991	Wanda Panfil (Poland)	2:24:18
1992	Olga Markova (Russia)	2:23:43
1993	Olga Markova (Russia)	2:25:27
1994	Uta Pippig (Germany)	2:21:45*
1995	Uta Pippig (Germany)	2:25:11
1996	Uta Pippig (Germany)	2:27:12
1997	Fatuma Roba (Ethiopia)	2:26:24
1998	Fatuma Roba (Ethiopia)	2:23:21
1999	Fatuma Roba (Ethiopia)	2:23:25
2000	Catherine Ndereba (Kenya)	2:26:11
2001	Catherine Ndereba (Kenya)	2:23:53

(continued)

Boston Marathon Winners, *continued*

MEN

Year	Athlete	Time
1897	John J. McDermott (U.S.)	2:55:10
1898	Ronald J. McDonald (Canada)	2:42:00
1899	Lawrence Brignolia (U.S.)	2:54:38
1900	John J. Caffery (Canada)	2:39:45
1901	John J. Caffery (Canada)	2:29:23
1902	Samuel Mellor (U.S.)	2:43:12
1903	John C. Lordon (U.S.)	2:41:30
1904	Michael Spring (U.S.)	2:39:05
1905	Fred Lorz (U.S.)	2:38:26
1906	Timothy Ford (U.S.)	2:45:45
1907	Thomas Longboat (Canada)	2:24:24
1908	Thomas Morrisey (U.S.)	2:25:44
1909	Henri Renaud (U.S.)	2:53:37
1910	Fred L. Cameron (Canada)	2:26:53
1911	Clarence DeMar (U.S.)	2:21:40
1912	Michael Ryan (U.S.)	2:21:19
1913	Fritz Carlton (U.S.)	2:25:15
1914	James Duffy (Canada)	2:25:02
1915	Edward Fabre (Canada)	2:31:42
1916	Arthur Roth (U.S.)	2:27:17
1917	William Kennedy (U.S.)	2:28:38
1918	(not held)	
1919	Carl Linder (U.S.)	2:29:14
1920	Peter Trivoulides (U.S.)	2:29:31
1921	Frank Zuna (U.S.)	2:18:58
1922	Clarence DeMar (U.S.)	2:18:10
1923	Clarence DeMar (U.S.)	2:23:48
1924	Clarence DeMar (U.S.)	2:29:40
1925	Charles Mellor (U.S.)	2:32:01
1926	John Miles (Canada)	2:25:41
1927	Clarence DeMar (U.S.)	2:40:23
1928	Clarence DeMar (U.S.)	2:37:08
1929	John Miles (Canada)	2:33:09
1930	Clarence DeMar (U.S.)	2:34:49
1931	James Henigan (U.S.)	2:46:46
1932	Paul de Bruyn (U.S.)	2:33:37
1933	Leslie Pawson (U.S.)	2:31:02
1934	Dave Komonen (Canada)	2:32:54
1935	John A. Kelley (U.S.)	2:32:08
1936	Tarzan Brown (U.S.)	2:33:41
1937	Walter Young (Canada)	2:33:20
1938	Leslie Pawson (U.S.)	2:35:35
1939	Tarzan Brown (U.S.)	2:28:52
1940	Gerard Cote (Canada)	2:28:29
1941	Leslie Pawson (U.S.)	2:30:38
1942	Joe Smith (U.S.)	2:26:52
1943	Gerard Cote (Canada)	2:28:26
1944	Gerard Cote (Canada)	2:31:51
1945	John A. Kelley (U.S.)	2:30:41
1946	Stylianos Kyriakides (Greece)	2:29:27

Year	Athlete	Time
1947	Yun Bok Suh (Korea)	2:25:39
1948	Gerard Cote (Canada)	2:31:02
1949	Karl Leandersson (Sweden)	2:31:51
1950	Han Kee Yong (Korea)	2:32:39
1951	Shigeki Tanaka (Japan)	2:27:45
1952	Doroteo Flores (Guatemela)	2:31:53
1953	Keizo Yamada (Japan)	2:18:51
1954	Veikko Karvonen (Finland)	2:20:39
1955	Hideo Hamamura (Japan)	2:18:22
1956	Antti Viskari (Finland)	2:14:14
1957	John J. Kelley (U.S.)	2:20:05
1958	Franjo Mihalic (Yugoslavia)	2:25:54
1959	Eino Oksanen (Finland)	2:22:42
1960	Paavo Kotila (Finland)	2:20:54
1961	Eino Oksanen (Finland)	2:23:29
1962	Eino Oksanen (Finland)	2:23:48
1963	Aurele Vandendriessche (Belgium)	2:18:58
1964	Aurele Vandendriessche (Belgium)	2:19:59
1965	Morio Shigematsu (Japan)	2:16:33
1966	Kenji Kimihara (Japan)	2:17:11
1967	Dave McKenzie (New Zealand)	2:15:45
1968	Ambrose Burfoot (U.S.)	2:22:17
1969	Yoshiaki Unetani (Japan)	2:13:49
1970	Ron Hill (Britain)	2:10:30
1971	Alvaro Mejia (Colombia)	2:18:45
1972	Olavi Suomelainen (Finland)	2:15:30
1973	Jon Anderson (U.S.)	2:16:03
1974	Neil Cusack (Ireland)	2:13:39
1975	Bill Rodgers (U.S.)	2:09:55
1976	Jack Fultz (U.S.)	2:20:19
1977	Jerome Drayton (Canada)	2:14:46
1978	Bill Rodgers (U.S.)	2:10:13
1979	Bill Rodgers (U.S.)	2:09:27
1980	Bill Rodgers (U.S.)	2:12:11
1981	Toshihiko Seko (Japan)	2:09:26
1982	Alberto Salazar (U.S.)	2:08:52
1983	Greg Meyer (U.S.)	2:09:00
1984	Geoff Smith (Britain)	2:10:34
1985	Geoff Smith (Britain)	2:14:05
1986	Rob de Castella (Australia)	2:07:51
1987	Toshihiko Seko (Japan)	2:11:50
1988	Ibrahim Hussein (Kenya)	2:08:43
1989	Abebe Mekonnen (Ethiopia)	2:09:06
1990	Gelindo Bordin (Italy)	2:08:19
1991	Ibrahim Hussein (Kenya)	2:11:06
1992	Ibrahim Hussein (Kenya)	2:08:14
1993	Cosmas Ndeti (Kenya)	2:09:33
1994	Cosmas Ndeti (Kenya)	2:07:15*
1995	Cosmas Ndeti (Kenya)	2:09:22
1996	Moses Tanui (Kenya)	2:09:16
1997	Lameck Aguta (Kenya)	2:10:34
1998	Moses Tanui (Kenya)	2:07:34
1999	Joseph Chebet (Kenya)	2:09:52
2000	Elijah Lagat (Kenya)	2:09:47
2001	Lee Bong Ju (South Korea)	2:09:43

Bowerman's Gifts

From Joe Henderson's *Running Commentary,* February 2000.

The best first reaction to Bill Bowerman's death at age 88 came from the runner who knew him best. Olympian-turned-writer Kenny Moore said, "What a career he had. He created the milers, which created the [University of Oregon] program, which created the crowds, which created the audience for his belief that you can be fit no matter how old you are, which created the beginning of the running boom, which created the need for shoes and created the opportunity to form the company that made all those shoes, for which he was properly rewarded."

Moore will someday publish a biography about his teacher (Bowerman never liked to be called "coach") and friend. It will take a book, and an author of Moore's talent, to do his life justice.

The best that can be said at column length is that it's fitting Bowerman should leave us on Christmas Eve 1999. He was the Santa Claus of the century for our sport—delivering gifts as a teacher, author, and inventor.

As an athlete Bowerman didn't run distances but played football and sprinted; he then served in World War II and returned a decorated hero. His service at the University of Oregon earned the school four NCAA titles. What should have been the pinnacle of his coaching career became one of his greatest frustrations. He led the U.S. team at the deeply troubled Munich Olympics.

His proudest legacy is as a distance coach, the greatest this country has ever known. Dozens of his milers broke four minutes. His student and successor as Oregon coach, Bill Dellinger, won an Olympic 5,000 medal.

In a sport given to excess, Bowerman preached moderation. He adopted a hard-easy approach to training, with the hard work coming only every second or third day. He rarely allowed his distance runners to double in a meet. He de-emphasized cross country and indoor racing that spread an athlete's efforts over too much of the year. The irony here is that his best-known athlete was one of his last, Steve Prefontaine. Pre was anything but moderate in approach.

In the early 1960s Bowerman traveled to New Zealand for a lesson that would turn around his physical life and that of his country. He took a "jog" with older New Zealanders, and they exposed his unfitness. He went home, kept running, and cowrote (with Eugene doctor Waldo Harris) the first great book of the running boom, a million seller titled *Jogging.*

Meanwhile Bowerman's tinkering with shoes led him to join with an ex-athlete of his named Phil Knight to start a company that imported Tiger shoes from Japan. They later split from the Japanese to produce their own brand, known as Nike.

Bowerman remained that company's spiritual father. On hearing of his death, Knight said, "Bill was for so many of us a hero, leader, and most of all a teacher. My sadness at his passing is beyond words."

Nike made Bowerman extremely wealthy. He shared that wealth in many ways, most of them unpublicized. For every athletic building he funded on his Oregon campus and every high school track he helped create, he contributed more to university academic programs and community arts activities.

Bill Bowerman will keep on giving. His financial gifts will make his city and state better places to live and learn. His gifts to the sport are priceless, even if the runners who receive them never know their source.

Brantly, Keith (b. May 23, 1962). His long career was highlighted by appearances at the 1996 Olympic and 1999 World Championships Marathons. Domestic honors included winning the 1995 and 1998 national marathon championships and four national 10K titles. He held world and American 5K records. *See also* national marathon champions, U.S.; national 10K champions, U.S.; Olympians, U.S.; Olympic Trials Marathon, U.S.; record progressions, American; record progressions, world; World Championships, U.S.

Brasher, Chris (b. August 21, 1928). As an athlete the British steeplechaser won the 1956 Olympic gold medal. Two years earlier he'd helped pace Roger Bannister to the first sub-four-minute mile. Later, Brasher saw the future of marathoning at New York City and transported the concept to England by founding the London Marathon. *See also* London Marathon.

Breathe Right (www.breatheright.com). In the 1990s runners (and many professional athletes) began appearing at races with strips of tapelike bandages across their noses. This practice had a purpose—Breathe Right convinced them that they could breathe easier by opening up their nostrils with this product, though most of the air a runner takes in comes through the mouth.

Bridges, Cheryl (b. December 25, 1947). She is generally regarded as the first woman to dip into the 2:40s in the marathon, with her 2:49:40 in 1971. This record came less than three months after Beth Bonner's initial smashing of the three-hour barrier. Cheryl's daughter, Shalane Flanagan, has been proving herself as one of the country's top young runners. *See also* Bay to Breakers 12K; Hall of Fame, RRCA; record progressions, American; record progressions, world.

Bright, Bob (birthdate unavailable). The feisty Bright directed the Chicago Marathon in its first heyday, the mid-1980s. He enjoyed spirited battles for talent and recognition against the equally feisty Fred Lebow of New York City. For a time the duel depleted both races. *See also* Chicago Marathon.

Broloppet Half-Marathon (www.broloppet.com). The race in Copenhagen laid claim to being the world's largest first-time event—by far—as well as one of the largest races ever, regardless of age, when in the year 2000 about 80,000 runners crossed the start line to celebrate the opening of a tunnel and bridge spanning approximately 16 kilometers to link Copenhagen, Denmark to Malmo, Sweden. The race is run each May. *See also* biggest races.

Brooks (brookssports.com). When Jerry Turner ran the company in the late 1970s, it was a major force in the industry. Brooks gained controversial number-one rankings from *Runner's World* in the days when readers and manufacturers took those annual *Runner's World* October-issue standings quite seriously. Turner is long out of the company, but the reconstituted Brooks remains a significant player in the shoe marketplace. *See also* shoe companies.

Brown, Barry (b. July 26, 1944, d. 1992). He was the fastest U.S. master marathoner for more than 15 years (a wind-aided 2:15:15 at Twin Cities in 1984). He ultimately committed suicide in the wake of business deals gone sour. *See also* Hall of Fame, RRCA; records, American age-group.

Julie Brown of the United States was one of the most versatile runners of her generation, running world-class races at 800 and 1,500 and at World Cross Country, and running a 2:26 marathon in 1983. She made the U.S. team for the first women's Olympic marathon and also made the first World Championships marathon team.

© Mark Shearman, Athletics-Images.

Brown, Doris. *See* Heritage, Doris Severtson Brown.

Brown, Ellison "Tarzan" (b. September 22, 1914; d. August 23, 1975). Tarzan, an American Indian, would either win Boston or stop along the course to take a swim in a convenient lake. He won that race in 1936 and 1939, and he set American marathon records in 1939 and 1940. His one Olympic experience (1936) ended in a DNF. Brown was easily one of Boston's most colorful characters, among a huge roster of such eccentrics. *See also* Boston Marathon; Hall of Fame, RRCA; Olympians, U.S.; record progressions, American.

Brown, Julie (b. February 4, 1955). Her versatility was unrivaled, even by such legends as Lynn Jennings and Francie Larrieu Smith. Brown competed in world-class 800s and 1,500s, won a World Cross Country title, and ran one of the world's best marathons for her era, a 2:26:26 in 1983. She made the first World Championships and Olympic Marathon teams. *See also* Avon Racing Circuits; Hall of Fame, RRCA; national marathon champions, U.S.; Olympians, U.S.; Olympic Trials Marathon, U.S.; record progressions, American; World Championships, U.S.

Browne, Dan (b. June 24, 1975). The West Point graduate won the national 5K and 10K titles in 1998 and the half-marathon in 2001. *See also* national 5K champions, U.S.; national half-marathon champions, U.S.; national 10K champions, U.S.

Buerkle, Dick (b. September 3, 1947). Rare is the runner who competes nationally in even two decades. Buerkle has done it over a span of *four*. He set an indoor world record in the mile with 3:54.93 in 1978 and made the first of his two Olympic 5,000-meter teams in his 20s. At age 52 he set an American age-group record in the road 5K with 15:38. *See also* records, American age-group.

Buniak, Peter. *See* Drayton, Jerome.

Burfoot, Amby (b. August 19, 1946). His high school coach, John J. Kelley, was the only American to win the Boston Marathon in the 1950s. "The Ambulator" (so named for his low-to-the-ground running style) was the only American to win Boston in the 1960s (with 2:22:17 in 1968). He later became the well-respected editor of *Runner's World* magazine and has served in that position longer than any of his predecessors. He has written a number of excellent books, including *The Principles of Running* (Rodale, 1999) and *The Runner's Guide to the Meaning of Life* (Rodale, 2000). He also edited *Runner's World's Complete Book of Running* (Rodale, 1997). See also "Beyond Winning" on next page; Boston Marathon; Hall of Fame, RRCA; publications; *Runner's World*.

© Jeff Johnson

Amby Burfoot, now editor of *Runner's World* magazine, is led away from the Boston Marathon victory stand by Jock Semple (wearing hat) in 1968, when Amby became the only American in the decade of the 1960s to win the famed race.

Beyond Winning

From Joe Henderson's *Running Commentary,* June 1998.

As a 21-year-old in 1968, Amby Burfoot won the Boston Marathon to worldwide acclaim. He would forever wear the words "former Boston winner" before his name.

He now goes back to run Boston every five years to refresh his aging memories. This was one of those years, the 30th anniversary, and Amby didn't think well of his prospects.

His goal was modest. It wasn't to win in his age group, the 50–54s. "I just want to come within an hour of my '68 time" of 2:22, he told me in early March when he ran the Napa Valley Marathon in a little under four hours. He was hurting before that race, and he hurt more afterward.

Less than two weeks before Boston, Amby said, "I'm a mess. My old Achilles problem has flared up again, and now I've pulled a butt muscle." Amby had written an article on R/W (the run/walk system) this spring for *RW* (that's *Runner's World,* where he is editor). "I might have to use the *walk*-walk to finish at Boston," he said.

I sent him a note of encouragement. It reminded him that all pains magnify before a big race, then magically ease on race day. As long as we both have run, we sometimes forget this truth. "Miracles can happen," I told Amby. "The race atmosphere has amazing curative powers."

Amby's Boston time didn't make news this year. It didn't even appear in the online version of *Runner's World.* I found his result in Boston's database. He ran 3:35, missing his goal of his 1968 time plus one hour but beating his injuries by doing as well as he did. My e-mail to him read: "Miracles *do* happen."

His reply told of winning in another way. He hadn't said anything earlier about his second goal.

Although his walk-break story in the magazine was well received, and though he'd mentioned using the "walk-walk" system, and though I'd told him how more and longer breaks had helped me, he wanted none of that at Boston. He intended to *run* the marathon.

"I resolved not to walk a step this time, and didn't," he said. "A little hard but not the worst I've run, and I'm well pleased." Winning can be as simple, and as difficult, as fighting off the forces that conspire to keep us from starting or finishing.

[Amby continues to lead *Runner's World* pace groups at marathons. He always chooses a four-hour pace and always comes within seconds of the target time. "I'm trying to set a world record for running the most 4:00:00s," he says. His next Boston Marathon anniversary run is scheduled for 2003.]

Bush, George W. (b. July 6, 1946). The man elected president of the United States in 2000—after a marathon-length legal fight in the wake of the election—was a pretty fair marathoner during his days in Texas. He ran 3:44 at the Houston Marathon in 1993.

C

Cabrera, Delfo (b. November 12, 1919). National and continental power in everything, from world military domination to marathon running, flows and ebbs. Argentina enjoyed a brief fling at world glory in the marathon before and after World War II with victories in the Olympic Games of 1932 and 1948. The second of those victories was delivered by Cabrera. Countryman Reinaldo Gorno was runner-up in 1952, but no Argentinean—or Latin American—has won a medal in the event since. Cabrera also won the first Pan-American Games Marathon in 1951. *See also* Olympic medalists; Pan-American Games; rankings, *Track & Field News*; Zabala, Juan Carlos.

Caffery, John (b. 1879; d. 1919). Canadians excelled early in Boston Marathon history, and none more so than 1900 and 1901 winner Caffery, a five-foot-eight-and-a-half-inch, 127-pound runner from Hamilton, Ontario. For the 1900 race, as Tom Derderian recounts in his book *The Boston Marathon* (Human Kinetics, 1994), a team of five Canadians came to Boston from Ontario. "Jack" Caffery, 21, ran for the St. Patrick's Athletic Club in Hamilton and wore the traditional shamrock on his shirt. The race was hot that year for the 29 starters. And there was great confusion at the finish area, where BAA officials were also processing results of a track meet they had been holding at the same time.

When Caffery crossed the finish line, he went to the BAA building only to find that none of the officials were manning the finish area and therefore the clock had not been stopped. The officials wanted to know if Caffery had broken the finish-line tape. He had no idea where it was. He went back outside to the finish area, then returned to the clubhouse, looking for the officials so they could stop the clock. Astonishingly, Caffery was so far ahead that the second finisher had not yet appeared. After searching for the officials throughout the three-story building, Caffery finally found them and they stopped the clock.

Nearly two minutes later teammate Bill Sherring finished, and almost eight minutes after that teammate Fred Hughson arrived, giving the Hamiltonians a 1-2-3 sweep. The following year Caffery returned and repeated his victory, again setting a course record, this time of 2:29:23. His teammate, Bill Davis, a Mohawk Indian, took second place. *See also* Boston Marathon; Sherring, William.

Campbell, John (b. February 6, 1949). John Campbell's life has been defined by hard work. As a youngster in the Ravenbourne section of Dunedin, New

Zealand, he delivered milk from the age of 10. For much of his life he has been a fisherman, a tough job in any country, in any century. And for most of his life he has been a runner—an avocation that serves to leaven his life but to which he brings the same intensity and dedication as he has to every job he has held. Campbell's most notable accomplishments have come as a masters runner. He broke fellow-Kiwi Jack Foster's masters marathon record with a 2:11:04 at Boston in 1990, at age 41. (That record lasted 11 years, with Mohamed Ezzher of France finally breaking it with 2:10:33 in 2001.) Campbell had done a 2:14:19 at Boston as a 40-year-old. In the same period, he also ran 2:16:15 and 2:14:34 at New York City.

On the verge of turning 40, Campbell represented New Zealand in the Seoul Olympic Games with a 12th place finish in the marathon (2:14:08). In 1990 he ran 1:02:28 for the half-marathon in Philadelphia, crushing the then-world mark by an astonishing three minutes. He has retreated somewhat from competitive running lately in the wake of a series of running-related injuries. *See also* Ezzher, Mohamed; Foster, Jack.

camps, running. Adult runners can gather at these camps and act like kids again. Busiest of the camp directors is Roy Benson, with gatherings throughout the country. Jeff Galloway has long-established camps at Lake Tahoe and elsewhere. Both of those camp directors live in Atlanta. On occasion, going into the summer running-camp season, the national and regional running magazines carry directories. Camps vary widely in their constituencies, settings, and teachings. The great majority fall outside the scope of this book, serving high school and college track and cross country runners. Road camps tend to attract adults, who are drawn by the chance to run together and learn various running tricks from well-known teachers. *See also* Galloway, Jeff.

Capitol 10K. This state capitol is in Austin, Texas, where the race draws a five-figure field each March. *See also* biggest races.

carbohydrate loading (also known as carbo loading). The process of super-loading the body with carbohydrates (fuel) entails eating large amounts of carbohydrate-laden foods in anticipation of a race or long run. One method involves a depletion phase of two to three days (five to six days before the event) when carbohydrate intake is kept artificially low, followed by a loading phase of two to three days when runners replenish the depleted glycogen stores by eating high-carbohydrate foods such as pasta, rice, and potatoes. Research by physiologists such as Dave Costill of Ball State University in the 1970s, however, found that straight carbo loading (without the depletion phase) is as successful in superloading the athlete's body with fuel as is the more deleterious depletion-phase routine.

Carlip, Freddi (b. December 22, 1944). Freddi, a.k.a. Miss Road Manners (for her work to bring order from the chaos of legions of first-time racers descending on road races and not knowing what to do once they get there), is the president of the Road Runners Club of America (RRCA), only the third woman to hold that post (after Henley Gabeau and Jane Dolley). Previously she served as vice president, eastern director, and the Pennsylvania state representative, for which she was awarded outstanding state rep of 1990. She served on the task force that redesigned *FootNotes*, the association's quarterly publication, and she was managing editor of the RRCA's 40th anniversary book, *Boom! Forty Years of Running and Writing With the RRCA* (1998).

Freddi lives in Lewisburg, Pennsylvania, has been running since the first running boom of the 1970s, and is an avid racer. She is the editor and publisher of *Runner's Gazette*, a monthly Mid-Atlantic running publication that is the oldest running newspaper in the United States. She served as the first female president of the Buffalo Valley Striders, based in Lewisburg. In her "spare" time she coaches forensics at Lewisburg Area High School, serves on the steering committee of the Community Alliance for Respect and Equality (CARE), and writes poetry when her muse whispers in her ear. Her eclectic knowledge of music has earned her the title of "Music Maven"; her tastes run to doo-wop, which is no surprise because she is from Philadelphia and used to dance on American Bandstand. *See also* Road Runners Club of America; *Runner's Gazette.*

Carlsbad 5K (www.eliteracing.com). Located about 30 miles north of San Diego on the Pacific Ocean, Carlsbad was the setting for the current men's world record, the American women's and men's marks, and several age-group bests. The race is run in early spring on a flat, unaided course, usually in ideal weather. The city also hosts the winter San Diego Marathon. *See also* fastest races; records, American; records, world.

Carrefour International 9K. South America's largest race sends about 50,000 through the streets of Buenos Aires, Argentina, each November. *See also* biggest races.

Carter, Jimmy (b. October 1, 1924). Other recent U.S. presidents have run for exercise and relaxation, but none besides Carter has entered a race while in office. His ended badly as he collapsed of heat exhaustion and did not finish the five-miler.

Cascade Run Off 15K. Long after its demise in the early 1990s, this Portland, Oregon, race boasts marks on the all-time list for this distance. Cascade also claims an important place in professional running history, as in 1981 it openly offered prize money in defiance of existing world and U.S. "amateur" rules. *See also* Association of Road Racing Athletes; professional racing.

Casio. In the mid-1970s it became unfashionable to run with a stopwatch clutched in your fist. A new term—*chronograph*—came into the language when the emerging electronic firms began to market the wrist chronographs. Among the vanguard was Microsel, whose problem-prone chronographs were both unreliable and costly (well over $100). By the end of the decade, however,

Casio had come to the rescue of runners with a relatively inexpensive ($19.95) and reliable chronograph, the F-200. Eventually the technology would become so pedestrian that at least one running magazine has offered a free chronograph with a new subscription. *See also* Microsel; watches, digital.

One of the most dominating American female road racers in the 1970s, Patti Lyons (Catalano) of Quincy, Massachusetts, seemed always a step or two behind Grete Waitz and Joan Benoit.

© Jeff Johnson

Cassell, Ollan (b. October 5, 1937). When the Olympic gold medalist (4 × 400 relay in 1964) took the job in his early 30s as executive director of the country's governing body of running, it was called the Amateur Athletic Union (AAU) and operated under the hidebound policies of that group. He survived the coming of women to the sport, the move to the Athletics Congress (TAC), the professionalization of running, and the coming of USA Track & Field (USATF). When finally voted out of office in 1998, he was in his 60s. *See also* organizations.

Catalano, Patti Lyons (now Dillon) (b. April 6, 1953). No American woman, and few in the world, shone brighter on the roads in the early 1980s. She was the first American woman to break 2:31, 2:30, 2:29, and 2:28; she also set world and American half-marathon records, established an aided world and American 10K best, won four straight Honolulu Marathons (1978 through 1981), and was the top-ranked road runner of 1980 and 1981. Yet Patti Lyons did not come to running by the usual route. She began running in her Quincy, Massachusetts, area to lose weight and had little if any knowledge of the sport. Uncertain about what she was doing, she usually ran after dark in the local cemetery— while wearing clogs! Her talent soon became apparent, and she fell under the coaching of Joe Catalano; they would later marry. Some observers felt Joe ran Patti too hard and too often. She gradually became increasingly prone to injuries and eventually withdrew from the sport for a more quiet existence. *See also* Honolulu Marathon; Peachtree 10K; rankings, *Runner's World*; record progressions, American; record progressions, world.

Catalina Island Marathon (www. pacificsportsllc.com). The hilly race, run in March, travels roads and paths around this rustic island 26 miles across the sea from Los Angeles. *See also* scenic races.

Catuna, Anuta (b. October 1, 1968). The Romanian has done plenty of winning— World Cup Marathon 1995, World Championships silver medal 1995, and New York City 1996. In her 1998 Boston debut, she placed 3rd with a 2:27:34; she returned in 1999 and placed 10th in 2:33:49.

As the 2000 Boston press info states: "Catuna is best known for her stunning 1996 win at the New York City Marathon over world leaders Tegla Loroupe and Joyce Chepchumba. Catuna's finish was crowned with a Romanian national record of 2:28:18. Other New York finishes include fourth in 1994 (2:31:26), fourth in 1997 (2:31:24), and sixth in 1999 (2:32:05). Catuna won gold at the 1995 World Cup Marathon in Athens and set a course record for that year of 2:31:10. At the 1995 World Championships in Sweden, she took home silver in the marathon. Catuna earned bronze at the 1994 and 1995 World Half-Marathon Championships. She won the La Rochelle Marathon in 1993, and in 1994 placed second at the Marrakech Marathon (2:29:39), fifth at the Paris Marathon, and fifth at the European Marathon Championships."

But another fact, having nothing to do with her running but rather with her parents' sense of humor, distinguishes her. The name Anuta Catuna is a palindrome—spelled the same way forward and backward. *See also* New York City Marathon; World Championships medalists; World Cup Marathon.

© Mark Shearman. Athletics-Images.

Romania's Anuta Catuna has been a consistent performer over the years, winning the World Cup Marathon in 1995, World Championship silver in 1995, and New York Marathon in 1996.

Cavanagh, Peter (birthdate unavailable). The British-born shoe and foot researcher of the 1970s ran the Biomechanics Lab at Penn State University. He also orchestrated the *Runner's World* shoe surveys in the late 1970s and early 1980s. He wrote *The Running Shoe Book* (Anderson World, 1980).

Cedarwinds Publishing (www.midpointtrade.com/cedarwinds_publishing _co.htm). Running author John Parker's publishing and bookselling company specializes in running, carrying both original books and bringing back into print hard-to-find classics. Cedarwinds began in the late 1970s with publication of Parker's classic, *Once a Runner. See also* books; Parker, John.

Ceron, Dionicio (b. October 9, 1965). Internationally, he's the most successful of the many fine Mexican road racers—silver medalist in the 1995 World Championship Marathon, winner of the London Marathon three times (1994, 1995, and 1996), winner of Fukuoka and Rotterdam in 1993, and ranked number one in the world in 1993. *See also* Fukuoka Marathon; London Marathon; Peachtree 10K; rankings, *Track & Field News*; Rotterdam Marathon; World Championships medalists.

certified courses. This program, imported to the United States (from England) by Ted Corbitt and the RRCA in the early 1960s, gives meaning to records on the roads by assuring that distances are as advertised. The certification program is now administered by the Road Running Technical Committee (RRTC) of USATF. Race directors can learn the exacting procedures for certification by contacting the RRTC. *See also* Corbitt, Ted; Road Running Technical Committee; USA Track & Field.

chafing. Running quickly becomes a miserable feeling when it rubs you the wrong way. Fortunately, improvements in clothing, shoes, and skin-protection products have reduced painful rubbing. *See also* blisters; Second Skin; Vaseline.

ChampionChip. Another giant step into the brave new world brought fully computerized scoring through a chip worn in the shoelaces of racers. Computers can then monitor racers as they cross through checkpoints and the finish line. Side benefits include the tracking of races (especially marathons) as they unfold by recording splits and the screening of cheaters who don't cross all checkpoints. Expect this technology to extend itself to most races at all road distances by becoming more cost effective through imprinting a "chip" in a barcode format on bib numbers. *See also* "Chipping In" on next page.

charity running. Using races as a fund-raising vehicle changed the face, the pace, and the cost, of road racing—especially the marathon. Most races now have a cause attached, as do many training groups. Contributions work two main ways—as a portion of total race proceeds donated to charity or as pledges solicited by individual runners. Largest of these ongoing efforts is Team in

Chipping In

From Joe Henderson's *Running Commentary,* June 1999.

Following the Boston Marathon from 3,000 miles away has never been easier. The "national TV coverage" doesn't stretch as far as Eugene, where the network that broadcasts the race is absent from our cable system. But this is hardly missed in the online age.

This year my main source of Boston news was *Runner's World Daily.* Uncredited writers typed furiously from the pressroom in Boston, supplying play-by-play on the race.

These reports told only about one race, though—the one at the front. Mike Lundgren, a Kansas City friend, had asked me on Sunday, "Who do you think will win? What do you think the times will be?"

I had to confess not even knowing for sure who was running. Times? Those depended on the luck of the draw and the weather gods. I hoped the draw wouldn't be too lucky, as in wind-blown 1994, and lead to tainted "world records." What I didn't tell Mike was that the race up front that interests running fans so much concerns me the least.

I need to take my races personally to arouse interest. Nowadays I know almost no one at the front. I can't keep the Kenyan names straight because I'm not willing to work hard enough at it. But I do know a growing number of names from the pack. Tracking them at Boston has never been faster.

This news gathering used to take days, even weeks. I'd wait for close friends living far away to make their way home from Boston, then wait for their reports to arrive by phone or mail. That changed last year when Boston went to instant results reporting. The ChampionChip, an inch-square piece of plastic, ties into a runner's shoelaces. It uploads data whenever that person steps on a recording carpet laid across the road. Boston lays these strips at five-kilometer intervals. Splits fly to a computer for posting on the Net. This allows tracing your favorite runners as the race progresses. Go to the Boston home page (www.baa.org), then punch a button labeled "103rd Race Results."

That was the theory, anyway. In fact, the message, "Server busy, try again later," blocked me more often than not. Too many other faraway Boston followers had the same plan. (Visits numbered in the millions.) I did get in early and often enough, though, to learn (before *RW*'s live coverage told me) that Lynn Jennings had run 2:38, that Bill Rodgers and John Campbell seemed to have dropped out, and that Don Kardong finished in 3:25 while talking on his cell phone.

But mostly I checked on names known only to family and friends. I tracked Neil as he finished in the mid-threes, Tim as he realized his prerace fear of not breaking four, and Karin as she finished in the mid-fours.

Watching the Boston Marathon by computer from 3,000 miles away was the next best thing to being there. Even better in some ways, because I never could have checked so often on so many people while standing beside the course. What I missed, though, and what no database could ever replace, was seeing the faces of these folks as they passed—that and celebrating with them later.

Training, which has raised massive amounts of money for leukemia research. Other up-and-comers are Joints in Motion (JIM), which benefits arthritis sufferers, and Team Diabetes. *See also* Team in Training.

Charleston Distance Run. Dr. Don Cohen founded this 15-mile race (along with another brainchild of his, a track and field hall of fame) in the early 1970s. It continues today, each Labor Day weekend, in the face heavy competition from fall marathons. *See also* "Doing the Charleston" below.

Chase Corporate Challenge. *See* corporate racing.

Doing the Charleston

From Joe Henderson's *Running Commentary*, September 2000.

Danny Wells has put a lot of himself into the Charleston (West Virginia) Distance Run. He had finished it every year before dropping out this time with an injury. He also has directed the race for 12 years, and he writes about it as a reporter for the sponsoring newspaper, *The Gazette*.

This is a proud old race, well run since 1973. Now, through no fault of its own, it's in decline. Numbers have dropped steadily in recent years, to one-third of peak size. The latest field was the smallest, at about 650 finishers, since the first year.

This trend concerns and saddens Danny Wells. When he called to interview me for a news story, he spoke more as a runner and race director than as a reporter. "What can we do?" he asked. "We think we're doing things right here, but the race doesn't hold the same attraction as it once did. We added a 5K a few years ago, and it could soon be bigger than the main event."

The problem, I told him, is the big event's distance. The race bills itself as "America's 15-Miler." It might call itself the country's *only* remaining 15—at least the only one with a national reputation. It's one of the few holdouts against the trend of runners flocking to races half-marathon and shorter and to the marathon itself, but leaving the great gap between unfilled.

"Our committee has talked about what to do," said Wells. "One idea is to go along with the trend and change our distance to half-marathon, but we have a history here that we'd like to preserve."

I urged Charleston to hang onto what it has. The runners might return in greater numbers if they see what this distance has to offer. A column of mine for *Runner's World* talked about gap filling. It praised these distances as steps toward a marathon. If I had been training for an October or November marathon, running Charleston would have figured into my plans. There's no better training for a race than by running a race of the right distance, I told Wells, and this one would have been just right. You have people to run with, to hand you drinks, to read you splits, and to cheer you on. It beats slogging out the miles alone.

Charleston still has its loyalists—Danny Wells most prominently, plus blind San Franciscan Harry Cordellos who has run here the past 25 years in a row, and five-time winner Gideon Mutisya of Kenya. I hope they'll have more company in years ahead.

cheaters. They are the bane of road racing, a sport generally considered simple and pure. Cheaters come in many stripes—those who don't run the full distance, those who use a false time to get into races, those who lie about their ages, those who take drugs. Cheating is as old as the first Olympics (when Spiridon Belokas took a ride through the middle portion of the marathon) and as recent as last weekend's big race. Cheating appears to be increasingly common in age-group competitions, not in lying about age (which is easily verified on official ID cards) but among runners who don't go the full distance. Chip technology and on-course video surveillance systems have helped reduce the course-cutting problem. *See also* ChampionChip; drug testing; Ruiz, Rosie.

Chebet, Joseph (b. August 23, 1970). He was easily Kenyan of the year for 1999—winner of the Boston and New York City Marathons and world-ranked number one for the year. The Boston Marathon's 2000 press information included this on Chebet: "Although a few of his peers posted faster times in other races, Chebet was the only runner to tackle and win two of the world's most difficult courses. Chebet beat Ecuador's Silvio Guerra to the line at Boston 1999 with a 2:09:52 finish and then brought home the New York crown the same year with a 2:09:14. Consistently at the top, Chebet's career seven marathons include four wins and three second-place finishes. In his first two tries he proved the victor, recording a 2:10:57 at the 1996 Amsterdam Marathon and a 2:08:23 at the 1997 Turin Marathon. Turning stateside, Chebet began a string of tough second-place finishes. He followed in the footsteps of fellow Kenyan John Kagwe at both the 1997 and the 1998 New York City Marathon (2:09:27, 2:08:48), and in his 1998 debut at Boston (2:07:37) he fell shy of Moses Tanui's win by three seconds. Chebet rates his 1999 Boston win as his career highlight. He has been training to repeat that success in Europe, running twice a day and over a hundred miles a week. He is coached by Dr. Gabriele Rosa of Italy." *See also* Boston Marathon; New York City Marathon.

Chepchumba, Joyce (b. November 6, 1970). Kenyan women started later than the men but are catching up quickly in quality and depth. Chepchumba won Chicago (1998 in 2:23:57 and 1999 in 2:25:59) and London (1997 in 2:26:51 and 1999 in 2:23:22) twice each within a three-year period. She remained busy in late 2000, following her bronze-medal effort in the Sydney Olympic Marathon with the Tokyo Ladies Marathon title just eight weeks later (in 2:24:02). *See also* Chicago Marathon; London Marathon; Olympic medalists; Tokyo Marathons.

Chepkemei, Susan (b. June 25, 1975). This previously little-known Kenyan improved her half-marathon time by four minutes to set a world aided best of 1:05:44 at Lisbon, Portugal, in April 2001. She also won the 2001 Rotterdam Marathon in 2:25:45. *See also* records, world; Rotterdam Marathon.

While other Kenyan women have dominated the longer distances, Lydia Cheromei has dominated the shorter distances. In 1997 she was the first to break 15:00 on an unaided 5K road course.

Cheromei, Lydia (b. May 11, 1977). Long or short, Kenya's women have the record book covered. While Tegla Loroupe holds the marathon record, Cheromei was first to break 15 minutes on an unaided course with 14:58 in 1997. This was a record until 2001 when Paula Radcliffe ran an unaided 14:57. *See also* record progressions, world.

Cherry Blossom 10M (www.cherryblossom.org). Washington, D.C., is the scene of many records at this distance, including the current women's world mark (51:16 by Colleen de Reuck) and the men's U.S. record (46:13 by Greg Meyer). Although in some years the famed cherry blossoms have already been stripped from the trees by rain, the course is scenic and the competition hot for this early spring race. *See also* fastest races; records, American; records, world.

Cheruiyot, Reuben Chesang (b. 1973). The Kenyan prospered in May 2000 when he won Bloomsday and Bay to Breakers, two weeks apart. *See also* Bay to Breakers 12K; Bloomsday 12K.

Cheruiyot, Rose (b. July 21, 1976). Her 15:05 at Carlsbad in 1995 is the fastest unaided women's 5K ever run on U.S. roads. At the time the Kenyan set a world record, since broken by Lydia Cheromei in 1997. *See also* Cheromei, Lydia; record progressions, world.

Chiba, Masako (b. July 18, 1976). The Japanese woman holds the world half-marathon best of 1:06:47 for an aided course. *See also* record progressions, world; records, world.

Chicago Marathon (www.chicagomarathon.com). The Chicago Marathon has had as many ups and downs as the Boston Marathon, but in a much shorter period. The little marathon was taken under the wing of Flair Marketing in the late 1970s and named the Mayor Daley Marathon. The race stirred up the local running community by making big changes rapidly; at the 1978 race, local running clubs staged protests over the starting time (originally noon, then 10:30 A.M.), the increased price of entry ($10), and the T-shirt design, which heavily featured marketing logos.

Chicago Marathon Winners

Chicago has long been one of America's fastest courses—site of the American women's record since 1985, world-record men's races in 1985 and 1999, and the U.S. men's record in 2000. * = race record.

WOMEN

Year	Athlete	Time
1977	Dorothy Doolittle (U.S.)	2:50:57
1978	Lynae Larson (U.S.)	2:59:25
1979	Laura Michalek (U.S.)	3:15:45
1980	Sue Petersen (U.S.)	2:45:03
1981	Tina Gandy (U.S.)	2:49:39
1982	Nancy Conz (U.S.)	2:53:23
1983	Rosa Mota (Portugal)	2:31:12
1984	Rosa Mota (Portugal)	2:26:01
1985	Joan Samuelson (U.S.)	2:21:21
1986	Ingrid Kristiansen (Norway)	2:27:08
1987	(not run)	
1988	Lisa Weidenbach (U.S.)	2:29:17
1989	Lisa Weidenbach (U.S.)	2:28:15
1990	Aurora Cunha (Portugal)	2:30:11
1991	Midde Hamrin-Senorski (Sweden)	2:36:21
1992	Linda Somers (U.S.)	2:37:43
1993	Ritva Lemettinen (Finland)	2:33:18
1994	Kristy Johnston (U.S.)	2:31:34
1995	Ritva Lemettinen (Finland)	2:28:39
1996	Marian Sutton (Britain)	2:30:41
1997	Marian Sutton (Britain)	2:29:03
1998	Joyce Chepchumba (Kenya)	2:23:57
1999	Joyce Chepchumba (Kenya)	2:25:59
2000	Catherine Ndereba (Kenya)	2:21:32
2001	Catherine Ndereba (Kenya)	2:18:47*

MEN

Year	Athlete	Time
1977	Dan Cloeter (U.S.)	2:17:52
1978	Mark Stanforth (U.S.)	2:19:20
1979	Dan Cloeter (U.S.)	2:23:20
1980	Frank Richardson (U.S.)	2:14:05
1981	Phil Coppess (U.S.)	2:16:13
1982	Greg Meyer (U.S.)	2:10:59
1983	Joseph Nzau (Kenya)	2:09:44
1984	Steve Jones (Britain)	2:08:05
1985	Steve Jones (Britain)	2:07:13 *(continued)*

Chicago Marathon Winners, *continued*

Year	Athlete	Time
1986	Toshihiko Seko (Japan)	2:08:27
1987	(not run)	
1988	Alejandro Cruz (Mexico)	2:08:57
1989	Paul Davies-Hale (Britain)	2:11:25
1990	Martin Pitayo (Mexico)	2:09:41
1991	Joseildo Rocha (Brazil)	2:14:33
1992	Jose DeSouza (Brazil)	2:16:14
1993	Luiz Dos Santos (Brazil)	2:13:15
1994	Luiz Dos Santos (Brazil)	2:11:16
1995	Eamonn Martin (Britain)	2:11:18
1996	Paul Evans (Britain)	2:08:52
1997	Khalid Khannouchi (Morocco)	2:07:10
1998	Ondoro Osoro (Kenya)	2:06:54
1999	Khalid Khannouchi (Morocco)	2:05:42*
2000	Khalid Khannouchi (U.S.)	2:07:01
2001	Ben Kimondiu (Kenya)	2:08:52

In the early 1980s the marathon found its legs under race director Bob Bright, who decided to take on New York City for recognition as the predominant fall marathon (Chicago's in October, New York's in November). The battle between the two for top racers and headlines diminished both events and nearly exhausted the Chicago effort. The race went into a decline and was in fact canceled in 1987. But Chicago doesn't stay on the mat for long.

Under the direction of Carey Pinkowski since the late 1980s, the race has come roaring back to become one of the premier races in the world. It's big, it's professionally run, and everyone in the world wants to run it. The course is flat and fast and looped so that it counts as an unaided course. It is so fast that in 1999 Khalid Khannouchi ran the world's first sub-2:06 there, and in 2001 Catherine Ndereba became the second woman to run under 2:20 and the first woman to run under 2:19 there. She ran a 2:18:47 to break the 2:19:46 world record Naoko Takahashi had set just one week earlier at Berlin. *See also* biggest races; Bright, Bob; fastest races; Pinkowski, Carey.

children's running. *See* kids' running.

Chinmoy, Sri (b. August 27, 1931). The Indian-born guru commanded his followers to run long and prosper, and they did. They often took his admonition to ridiculous lengths, organizing events that in some instances went on for literally weeks and covered more than a thousand miles. Sri Chinmoy arrived in the United States in 1964 and has lectured at most of the world's major universities. He's published hundreds of books of poetry and philosophy. He's also completed and exhibited thousands of inspirational paintings and drawings.

A champion athlete in his youth and a lifelong runner, he is also well known in the weightlifting world for his remarkable achievements in the one-arm lift and the leg raise, elevating tremendous amounts of weight. Many of Sri Chinmoy's efforts are geared toward achieving world peace, and numerous garden sites around the world are designated as "Sri Chinmoy Peace-Blossoms" where the faithful can gather to promote love, peace, and unity. *See also* Sri Chinmoy Marathon Team.

chondromalacia. The bane of many a runner, this malady is so common an injury that it became known as runner's knee. It involves a painful wearing away of cartilage under the kneecap. *See also* injuries.

Chriss, Alvin (birthdate unavailable). As an official and lawyer for the Athletics Congress, Chriss helped ease the sport into its professional era. He kept elite runners eligible as amateurs within the rules of the early 1980s by instituting a trust-fund program as an interim step toward open payments. *See also* organizations; professional racing.

Sri Chinmoy has inspired thousands to take up a lifestyle that involves a dedication to aerobic fitness. His groups have since the 1970s organized numerous marathons and ultramarathons around the country.

Christman, Paul (b. October 27, 1942). He's the founder-publisher-editor-writer of *Running Stats*, the longest running of the results publications. Christman, who lives in Boulder, Colorado, also wrote a well-regarded novel, *Purple Runner* (Highgate Lane Press, 1983). *See also* publications; *Running Stats*.

Chronomix. Finish-line timing accuracy and speed improved greatly with the introduction of this product, a handheld digital clock with an attendant printer to record accurately each runner crossing the finish line. It's one of a handful of technical improvements in running that literally changed the sport.

Churchill, William (b. 1886). The 1924 U.S. Olympic marathoner (who placed 23rd at Paris in 3:19:18) won four times at the San Francisco race later to be known as Bay to Breakers. *See also* Bay to Breakers 12K; Olympians, U.S.

chute. It's the promised land for runners, the spot where they slow to a stop after finishing races. But for race officials this funneling system that sorts finishers into order is the storm center where results are accurately recorded—or not.

Cierpinski, Waldemar (b. August 3, 1950). Cierpinski, the second runner in history (after Abebe Bikila) to win a second gold medal in the Olympic Marathon (Montreal 1976 and Moscow 1980) can be considered a victim of the East German state-sponsored sports mills. In the wake of the fall of the Berlin Wall in 1992, information from Stasi files has implicated Cierpinski as the recipient (willingly or not is uncertain at this writing) of performance-enhancing drugs, which were almost certainly instrumental in his Olympic victories. Little has been heard from Cierpinski himself, but much righteous indignation has been expressed by international (and especially American) athletes and sports enthusiasts.

A probably useless movement has been instigated to have Cierpinski return his ill-gotten medals, which as far as 1976 is concerned would elevate Frank Shorter (United States) to the position of the only runner since Bikila to repeat gold in the Olympic Marathon. It would also move Karel Lismont of Belgium to second place, a position he held (again, behind Shorter) in the 1972 Games, and would move Don Kardong of the United States into bronze (third). Little is likely to come of the effort to strip Cierpinski of his medals and move everyone else up in the standings because of the length of time that passed between the transgressions and the revelations.

In the case of Cierpinski, the East German system, for all its vaulted greatness, failed him on several occasions. Reputedly infallible in tracking athletes, evaluating them, selecting them for specific sports, and nurturing them from an early age toward world domination, the system selected Cierpinski at age 12 and sent him to the Aufbau Nienburg, a factory sports club. At the age of 16 he was entered in the annual Spartakaid, in the 1,500-meter steeplechase and the 7.5K road race. For seven years the East German system tried to train Cierpinski as a steeplechaser, but it didn't meld. "Apart from all other reasons," Cierpinski said, "the tempo over the 3,000-meter distance was simply too fast for me. Training for it certainly promoted the development of my basic speed, but the marathon distance was more my cup of tea."

He came upon the marathon almost by accident. "In 1974 I was vacationing in Czechoslovakia and feeling in good humor," he recalled, "so I decided to try a marathon in Košice. I came in third with a 2:20:20." The following year he ran it in 2:17:30 and came in seventh. His first serious marathon came in 1976 (a 2:13:57

Now known as a likely dupe in East German drug experiments, Waldemar Cierpinski won the Olympic Marathon gold in Montreal (1976) and again in Moscow (1980).

© Mark Shearman, Athletics–Images.

at Karl-Marx-Stadt), and six weeks later he won the East German Olympic Marathon Trials. Even though Hans-Joachim Truppel took second in 2:13:44 and Bernd Arnhold third in 2:14:53, the East Germans sent only Cierpinski.

At Montreal he lined up a virtual unknown, set off only by his all-white uniform. The East Germans had jumped through hoops to secure permission for him to wear all white instead of the approved East German uniform because their scientists felt that the white would better reflect the sun and give him an advantage in cooling. The special suit was moot because it rained at Montreal, where Cierpinski put on a surge at 30K to test Shorter, found him weakening, and pulled away. "It was very emotional for me," Cierpinski said. "Earlier, everything had been in Frank's favor, and then it became man to man." By 35K Cierpinski had a 13-second lead; he ultimately won by 51 seconds.

The Americans (and a host of other nations) boycotted the Moscow Olympics in 1980. Some 40 countries competed. Cierpinski won again (with a 2:11:03), this time by 17 seconds over Gerard Nijboer of the Netherlands. In his nine-year career, Cierpinski competed in 26 marathons, winning 11 of them. All of them, of course, are tainted by the persuasive evidence of illegal performance-enhancing drug use. *See also* Olympic medalists; rankings, *Track & Field News;* World Championships medalists.

circuit training. *See* weight training.

City to Surf 14K. Long before hosting the Olympic Games, Sydney had one of the largest road races in the Southern Hemisphere. City to Surf draws fields approaching 40,000 in the mild Australian winter. *See also* biggest races.

Clark, Christine (b. October 11, 1962). A startling winner of the 2000 U.S. Olympic Trials, the treadmill-trained Alaskan, a 37-year-old medical doctor, PRed by seven minutes on a hot day to become the only U.S. female qualifier for the Sydney Games. In Sydney she shaved another two minutes from her fastest time by running 2:31:38 and placing 19th. *See also* "Another Amazing Alaskan" on next page; national marathon champions, U.S.; Olympians, U.S.; Olympic Trials Marathon, U.S.

Clark, James (birthdate unavailable). In 1909 he took the world and American marathon records under 2:50 for the first time by running 2:46:53. *See also* record progressions, American; record progressions, world.

Clarke, Anne (b. September 21, 1909; d. March 3, 2000). This late starter set a basketful of records before dying at age 90. Several 5K and half-marathon records for ages 75–79, 80–84, and 85–89 have outlived her. *See also* records, American age-group.

Clayton, Derek. *See* pages 70-71.

Clifton, Christine (b. August 2, 1972). She debuted in the marathon with 2:32:45 at Chicago 2000. This qualified her for the U.S. Championships team, but she was unable to compete. Christine is the ex-wife of Mark Junkerman, who set the American junior 10K record in 1985 with 29:15.

Another Amazing Alaskan

From Joe Henderson's *Running Commentary,* March 2000.

Roy Reisinger, an Alaskan in exile in Arizona, was out of Internet reach the weekend of the Women's Olympic Marathon Trials. He asked me to pass results to him as soon as the race ended. "Just the top four would be fine," said Roy, "plus how Chris Clark from Anchorage did." He naturally assumed she wouldn't be one of the four, since she was seeded 22nd in this field and had finished more than 50 places below that in the last Trials.

It's fun to shock someone, as I did by telling Roy that only one U.S. runner would go to Sydney—a 37-year-old mother of two boys and medical doctor from Alaska. "That's so neat!" exclaimed Roy. "If anyone should have been knocked out by the heat and humidity, it should have been Clark." This is not only because of where she's from but because "she works full-time as a pathologist, and running has been very much just a part-time thing for her."

Coming from Alaska might not be the handicap it seems. Many years ago I traveled there as Roy's guest at his running camp and came away amazed at the toughness of the Alaskan runners. Only the rugged settle there, and the conditions further toughen those who stay.

Notice that the last two Americans to make amazing breakthroughs in the marathon have Alaskan roots. David Morris, who broke 2:10 last fall, grew up in Anchorage and went to college in Montana (itself not exactly a Sun Belt state). Christine Clark reversed Morris's path. Raised and schooled in Montana, she settled in Anchorage.

These Alaskans aren't just tough. They're also smart. Morris recognized that to run his best he had to leave the country. He migrated to Japan.

My first thought as Clark pulled away from the field in the heat of Columbia was that she must have left Alaska to train. Later I learned that she did, in a way. She ran more than half her miles, and nearly all her fast miles, out of winter cold. Treadmill training in Anchorage gave her a safe, reliable surface and warm "weather," and let her make the most of her minimal 70-mile weeks.

"If a gal from Alaska can do [this well] in this heat, anyone can do it," said Clark at the postrace news conference. Fact is, no one else could do better on this day, and very few in this field could PR by any amount, let alone seven minutes.

Clark and others voiced disappointment that she didn't run just 31 seconds faster, providing Olympic tickets for two other women. But it wasn't her job to run their races for them.

I wrote last fall about how David Morris gives hope to American men that they can shed the "national inferiority complex" in the marathon. He dropped from 2:15 marathoner to 2:09 in one race.

Another Alaskan, Christine Clark, went from 2:40 to 2:33 on a day when this shouldn't have happened. She gives hope to everyone who's older than the average Trials runner, has much going on in his or her life besides running, and believes in miracles.

[Clark improved her PR by two more minutes at the Sydney Games, placing 19th.]

Clayton, Derek (b. November 17, 1942). For more than a dozen years from the late 1960s through the early 1980s, Australia's Derek Clayton held the world's best time in the marathon more on psychology than physiology. A larger-than-typical distance runner, Clayton trained hard and raced hard, giving no quarter and expecting none. He was (relatively) big, he was strong, and he was single-minded. "Every race I ran," he said years later, "was a race I'd trained hard to win. And if another runner attempted to beat me, I saw it as that runner attempting to take something that was mine." Clayton's larger-than-life persona helped to erect a barrier through which other road racers could not break. Derek set the world's fastest time in the marathon on December 3, 1967, at Fukuoka, at that time considered to be the unofficial men's marathon championship of the world. The course was a very legitimately measured out-and-back route on which Clayton scorched to a 2:09:37, breaking the record by an astounding 2:23. Seiichiro Sasaki was a minute and a half behind him in second place.

Considering Clayton's Fukuoka time, his strength, and his courage to run hard from the gun, it is surprising that controversy continues to surround his race at Antwerp on May 30, 1969, when he broke his own record with a startling 2:08:34. Because of major construction projects in Antwerp in the wake of his victory, it is impossible to go back and remeasure the course in an effort to silence once and for all the claim by critics that the course was short. Other competitors that day performed as expected based on their proven talents and levels of fitness, further supporting Derek's claim that the course was accurate.

Derek was not a favorite with the crowd or with fellow runners, and that may account in part for the persistent sniping at his record. During the days following the 2:08:34 performance, Clayton recounted in graphic detail the agonies he went through, from passing blood-impregnated stools to discharging black bile. His oft-told tale of how his body suffered in the wake of his effort served as a psychological warning sign to runners who might attempt to top his feat and thereby steal his glory. As a result, his record stood un-

til October 1981, when it apparently was broken in New York City by Alberto Salazar, a runner Clayton himself predicted would be the one to do it. (Unfortunately, the New York course would be found to be a mite short and Salazar's world record would be disallowed.) But with Salazar's breach of the Clayton mark, the psychological wall was also breached, and two months later Australian Rob de Castella also broke Clayton's mark by 16 seconds—this time at Fukuoka with a time of 2:08:18. In a matter of two months, Derek lost the world record and the Australian record. He was philosophical about the loss: "He had what it took to break my record," he said of Salazar. "He proved that, with the right training, it can be done. . . . Now I don't have to hear this bloody 'short course' crap anymore."

Clayton's legacy is both real and constructed. A big man for a marathoner (six feet two and more than 160 pounds), Clayton never ran well in the heat; big runners have trouble dissipating heat. And Derek did train like a madman. There were persistent rumors of his doing back-to-back 200-plus-mile weeks. He did nothing to dispel those rumors, although years later when he worked as assistant to the president of *Runner's World*, he admitted that he had not done 200-mile weeks, although he'd come close. "Why should I tell them I didn't run 200 milesn a week?" he asked. "Let them go out there and run themselves into the bloody ground trying to match what they think I'm doing."

Today Clayton lives with his family in Beaumaris in Australia, where he works as a glass merchant and importer in North Melbourne. Our favorite quote from a road racer famous for great quotes sums up Derek Clayton the competitor: "In the marathon, I always like to have someone next to me at 15 miles—so I can grind him into the ground." *See also* Fukuoka Marathon; record progressions, world.

Cloney, Will (b. October 29, 1911). He was the last of the old-style Boston Marathon directors, who defended the amateur ideal in the face of changing running realities. Cloney yielded in the 1980s as the race declined and required more professional management. *See also* Boston Marathon.

clothing. The miracle fibers—polypro, Gore-Tex, Coolmax, Supplex, Lycra, and others—tamed the weather and made possible more comfortable running year-round by dissipating sweat or holding in heat, as necessary.

Clydesdale division. Age divisions? Gender divisions? Why not weight divisions? The Clydesdales, heavyweights of the sport, fought for and in some races won this designation and recognition. Originally this division recognized only men above 200 pounds, but many weight categories now exist for both males and females.

coaches. Long-distance runners are generally an independent lot. But behind most of the best runners has stood a strong coach: Pat Clohessy for Rob de Castella, Bill Dellinger for Alberto Salazar, Billy Squires for Dick Beardsley, Bob Sevene for Joan Benoit Samuelson, Bill Bowerman for Kenny Moore. Others, such as Arthur Lydiard, have coached in a broader sense through their writings. *See also* Bowerman, Bill; Dellinger, Bill; Lydiard, Arthur; Sevene, Bob; Squires, Billy.

© Mark Shearman. Athletics–Images.

Some of the greatest road races in the world took place during the preprofessional era at Commonwealth Games Marathons. In this 1990 Commonwealth shootout in Auckland, Steve Moneghetti (#56) tries to keep a leg up on Steve Jones (#1114), Douglas Wakiihuri (#571), and Rob DeCastella (#27).

Columbus Marathon (www. Columbusmarathon.com). Competition is stiff in October and November with Chicago, New York City, and Marine Corps falling within the same time frame. But Columbus has found its niche by promising a midsized marathon with fast times and professional payoffs.

Commonwealth Games. In the preprofessional era (before the 1980s), this was one of the world's great races, with winners including Ron Hill and Rob de Castella (twice). The Games are open to competitors from countries currently in the British Commonwealth and are contested on even-numbered years that are not Olympic years.

Commonwealth Games Marathon Winners

The gathering of the former British Empire occurs every four years, halfway between Olympics. Note that Australians Lisa Martin Ondieki and Rob de Castella are two-time winners. * = event record.

WOMEN

Year	Place	Athlete	Time
1986	Edinburgh	Lisa Martin (Australia)	2:26:07
1990	Auckland	Lisa Martin (Australia)	2:25:28*
1994	Victoria	Carole Rouillard (Canada)	2:30:41
1998	Kuala Lumpur	Heather Turland (Australia)	2:41:24

MEN

Year	Place	Athlete	Time
1930	Hamilton	Duncan Wright (Scotland)	2:43:43
1934	London	Harold Webster (Canada)	2:40:36
1938	Sydney	Johannes Coleman (South Africa)	2:30:50
1950	Auckland	Jack Holden (England)	2:32:57
1954	Vancouver	Joseph McGhee (Scotland)	2:39:36
1958	Cardiff	David Power (Australia)	2:22:46
1962	Perth	Brian Kilby (England)	2:21:17
1966	Kingston	Jim Alder (Scotland)	2:22:08
1970	Edinburgh	Ron Hill (England)	2:09:28
1974	Christchurch	Ian Thompson (England)	2:09:12*
1978	Edmonton	Gidamis Shahanga (Tanzania)	2:15:40
1982	Brisbane	Rob de Castella (Australia)	2:09:18
1986	Edinburgh	Rob de Castella (Australia)	2:10:15
1990	Auckland	Douglas Wakiihuri (Kenya)	2:10:27
1994	Victoria	Steve Moneghetti (Australia)	2:11:49
1998	Kuala Lumpur	Thabiso Moqhabi (Lesotho)	2:19:15

Complete Book of Running, The. Jim Fixx used his $25,000 advance to take a year off from his magazine editing job and indulge himself in writing about running—never expecting to produce a publishing sensation. The book (Random House, 1977) would become the all-time leader among running books, standing atop the *New York Times* best-seller list for all topics for 60 weeks in a row during 1977–1978 and selling close to one million hardbound copies. *See also* books; Fixx, Jim.

Complete Book of Running for Women, The. Claire Kowalchik, a former editor at *Runner's World*, compiled this book (Pocket Books, 1999), which has sold well among the burgeoning population of female runners.

Complete Runner, The. *See* books.

Concannon, Joe (b. April 22, 1939; d. February 16, 2000). The long-time *Boston Globe* running writer was more than a newsman. He also coauthored a book, *Marathoning* (Simon & Schuster, 1980), with Bill Rodgers and founded the Litchfield Hills seven-mile road race in his Connecticut hometown. *See also* Boston Marathon.

Conditioning of Distance Runners. This slim treatise, written by Tom Osler and published by Ross Browning's *Long Distance Log* in 1967, became one of the first great advice books for runners. *See also* books; Osler, Tom.

Connectors (www.connectingconnectors.com). The women's running group, inspired by Oprah Winfrey's marathoning escapades and promoted by Tawni Gomes, now numbers more than 30,000 members who meet on the Internet for mutual motivation and the sharing of tips and experiences. *See also* "Connector in Chief" on next page; Gomes, Tawni; Winfrey, Oprah.

Conover, Mark (b. May 28, 1960). He was a surprising winner at the 1988 Olympic Trials, but an injury kept him from finishing at the Seoul Games. Later he fought off Hodgkin's disease and came back to qualify for the Trials again in 1996. Since then he has coached at Cal Poly in San Luis Obispo, California. *See also* Olympians, U.S.; Olympic Trials Marathon, U.S.

Converse (www.converse.com). Better known for its basketball sneakers, the company enjoyed a brief run of popularity in our sport during the 1980s when Arthur Lydiard was with the corporation. He designed some of the best running shoes ever, but they enjoyed only modest popularity and soon faded from the marketplace. *See also* Lydiard, Arthur; shoe companies.

Conz, Nancy (b. May 1, 1957). One of America's first great female marathoners, she peaked too soon for Olympic opportunity. Conz won the 1981 Avon, 1981 national championships, and 1982 Chicago titles. *See also* Avon Racing Circuits; Chicago Marathon; national marathon champions, U.S.

Connector in Chief

From Joe Henderson's *Running Commentary,* October 1999.

You can't just decide to start a movement. It has to come to you because you had a good idea at the right time and have the personality and business savvy to attract and then direct an organized following. Three movers converged at the same spot this summer. Each has gained legions of followers.

Jeff Galloway leads the most popular brand of marathon-training program. His devotees sometimes call themselves Gallowalkers for the breaks they take. Jeff invited John Bingham to his camp at Squaw Valley, California. John leads the Penguin Brigade. The camp also put Tawni Gomes on the program. If you don't know the name already, you will. A year ago Gomes (rhymes with homes) ran her first marathon with a group that had met on the Internet. Inspired by the weight loss and running efforts of Oprah, they called themselves Connectors.

Tawni and the others finished the race. A *Runner's World* writer was on hand to tell about it, and the magazine featured the Connectors last February. Reaction to a postmarathon appearance on Oprah's show and then the *RW* cover story changed Tawni's life, which already had undergone a private but dramatic transformation.

In her mid-30s she was successful in her business life but was not dealing well with the business of living. She openly admits now to having been overweight, bulimic, domestically abused, and suicidal not long ago. Running saved her, she says. It did more than that. Going public with her story brought hundreds and then thousands of others, mainly women, forward to share similar stories with each other.

When Tawni came to the Galloway camp this summer, she had quit her sales job. But she was still selling, now marketing hopes instead of products. "We now have more than 10,000 Connectors!" she exclaimed. (Tawni uses exclamation points even when she speaks.) The number is approaching 15,000 worldwide, and she connects with them almost daily with a mass e-mailing.

Her laptop came along to the Squaw Valley camp, where Connectors nearly filled the weekend session. "This is the only way I can keep up with my mail. I get about a hundred personal notes a day, and it was close to a thousand after the *Runner's World* article came out."

Tawni quit her job this summer to write a book about her experiences since starting to run less than two years ago. She has done consulting work for *RW*. The publishers recognize the potential size of her movement. There are a lot more overweight people, looking to become fit, than there are serious long-time runners looking to go farther and faster. Tawni Gomes has struck a mother lode even wider and deeper than the one John "Penguin" Bingham has struck. She said at camp, "John hopes to sell a million of his books because it will mean he has reached that many people with his message. I'd like to do the same."

She's thinking big, and why not? The market for her message is bottomless in a world where fatness is much more common than fitness.

[In 2000 Tawni Gomes published her book, *No More Excuses!* (Paper Chase, 2000). Her Connectors group had more than tripled in size.]

Coogan, Gwyn (b. August 21, 1965). She won the 1998 national marathon and 1999 national half-marathon titles and placed fourth in the 1996 U.S. Olympic Marathon Trials after making the 1992 team in the 10,000 meters. *See also* Coogan, Mark; national half-marathon champions, U.S.

Coogan, Mark (b. May 1, 1966). Gwyn's husband, Mark, competed in the 1996 Olympic Marathon, was runner-up in the 1995 Pan-American Games Marathon, and won the 1996 national 5K title. He would have returned to the Olympics in 2000 after placing third in the Trials but lacked a qualifying time. *See also* national 5K champions, U.S.; Olympians, U.S.; Olympic Trials Marathon U.S.; Pan-American Games.

Cooksey, Marty (b. July 18, 1954). She's another of the women born on the wrong side of the cusp of full recognition. Her resume includes Avon Marathon (the inaugural race) and national marathon titles in 1978, a win at the second Bloomsday in 1978, the first national 5K championship in 1986, and aided world and American bests in the half-marathon. *See also* Avon Racing Circuits; Bloomsday 12K; national 5K champions, U.S.; national marathon champions, U.S.; record progressions, American; record progressions, world.

cool down. This track athletes' practice of winding down after a race or interval run is not widely practiced among many road runners, except in the loosest sense of walking around to cool off, and maybe doing a little stretching.

Coolmax. *See* clothing.

Cooper, Dr. Kenneth (b. 1931). In December 2000 in Dallas, the city turned out to celebrate the 30th anniversary of Kenneth Cooper's Aerobics Institute, an oasis within the city where Kenneth and his scientists test, evaluate, and train folks to attain general fitness and, by so doing, to enhance their lives. The former college miler and air force doctor started a generation of Americans running for health with his 1968 book *Aerobics* (Bantam Books), in which he assigned points for various workouts leading to a weekly fitness score. Many of his followers, accustomed to leading ambitious lives, took their fitness to the roads, swelling the number of road racers in the United States.

Dr. Cooper was one of his own guinea pigs, running the Boston Marathon in the mid-1960s. In the mid-1970s his Cooper Institute (www.cooperins.org) conducted one of the first major research projects on distance runners when he assembled several dozen top U.S. racers for extensive tests in everything from $\dot{V}O_2$max to blood chemistries, then compared them to good runners, untrained lean men, and average young men. He continued to publish books based on his findings, one of the most popular being *The Aerobics Way* (M. Evans, 1977). In the wake of Jim Fixx's death while running in 1984, Dr. Cooper published *Running Without Fear,* an examination of how and why Fixx had died, with an admonition to the rest of the nation not to let Fixx's death deter them from finding fitness through running. Among the findings from his 30 years of research is that the optimal amount of running needed for fitness is 3K to 5K of running three to five days a week. *See also* aerobics.

Cooper River Bridge Run (www.bridgerun.com). This 10K in Charleston, South Carolina, packs more than 12,000 runners onto the bridge each spring. *See also* biggest races.

Coppess, Phil (b. September 2, 1954). The Iowan is the only American to hold a current world record with his long-standing best in the seldom-run 30K distance. He ran that time en route to a victory in the 1985 Twin Cities Marathon. Coppess also won the 1981 Chicago Marathon. *See also* Chicago Marathon; records, American; records, world.

Corbitt, Ted (b. January 31, 1919). The likable African-American physical therapist and distance runner was the father of American ultrarunning and cofounder of the RRCA, including its invaluable course-certification program. He was a 1952 Olympic marathoner and 1954 national marathon champion but became better known later for his ultra efforts. He worked most of his life as a massage therapist, specializing in sports. In April 2000, after years of injuries and ill health, he showed up (at age 81) at a Sri Chinmoy six-day race in New York and completed 240 miles. *See also* certified courses; Hall of Fame, National Distance Running; Hall of Fame, RRCA; national marathon champions, U.S.; Olympians, U.S.

Cordellos, Harry (b. 1937). The blind San Franciscan once ran a 2:57 marathon at Boston in the 1970s. He also took up a number of other sports, including diving and water skiing. He told his story in his autobiography, *Breaking Through* (Anderson World, 1981).

corporate racing. Bringing company employees together to run on teams as a way to encourage both teamwork and health was pioneered by *Runner's World* Corporate Cup in the 1970s. Company running now enjoys its greatest participation in the Chase Corporate Challenge 3.5M race series. See also "Fast Companies" on next page.

Costes, Nick (b. August 2, 1926). He appeared to break 2:20 twice at Boston, but that course turned up short both times. A 1956 Olympian and 1955 national marathon champion, Costes later became a college coach at Troy State in Alabama. He authored the book *Interval Training* (World Publications, 1972). *See also* Hall of Fame, RRCA; national marathon champions, U.S.; Olympians, U.S.

Costill, Dr. David (b. February 7, 1936). The former Ball State University professor and head of that institution's Human Performance Lab, Dave was a pioneer at using distance runners for experiments in human physiology. Dave describes himself as an athlete who turned to science. Captain of the swim

Fast Companies

From Joe Henderson's *Running Commentary,* October 1999.

The short novel and the movie with the same title, *The Loneliness of the Long-Distance Runner,* are fine works of literature and film. But they're poorly named.

Running is not inherently a lonely activity, and runners are loners only if they want to be. The sport has an active social side that becomes more active all the time. Runners team up for relay races such as Oregon's wildly popular Hood to Coast. They train for marathons in Galloway groups and fund-raising programs. And they run in workplace-based races.

I write a column for a Japanese magazine called *Runners.* In that country the major corporations employ top athletes in exchange for their running services. The editors asked me if U.S. companies do anything like this.

Not in any widespread or systematic way, they don't. The shoe companies do support elite runners, but these athletes only represent the firms and don't work there day by day. They seldom share more than a uniform bearing the company logo and rarely get together for training or even share a coach.

We don't have a corporate program like those in Japan that nurtures the big names of the sport. But we have the opposite—a growing trend toward companies spawning teams of workers who happen to run. Talent isn't a requirement, and no one is employed based on his or her running resume. This is a hobby practiced outside work hours but with full support from coworkers, often including the top executives.

The traditional running-club system plays a relatively minor role in the U.S. sport. Our population is too scattered for runners to gather for regular training as club teams. Americans come together mainly for school and, later, for work. High school and college teams have long been the bedrock of the sport in this country, and now a major growth area is company teams. This is a natural development because work is where adult runners spend the biggest chunk of their time. The people they get to know best outside the family are those who share their job site.

So naturally they team up for training before or after work, or during their lunch hour. Rarely do they have an official coach, but the more experienced runners advise the recent arrivals and recruit new members. Running together leads to racing together, both outside and within the corporate community. Relays of widely varying lengths enjoy unprecedented popularity in this country. The recent Hood to Coast Relay included dozens of company teams in its total of more than 1,000.

Company-only racing got its start about 20 years ago when *Runner's World* magazine sponsored the Corporate Cup, which was largely a track meet. A New York City-based financial institution took this concept to the streets, where it exploded in size.

The Chase Corporate Challenge is now a nationwide series of events. At the odd distance of $3\frac{1}{2}$ miles, it doesn't frighten newcomers but still serves as a good speed test for experienced runners. Several of these events ranked among the largest of any type in the United States last year [in 1998]. A corporate race in New York City and another in Atlanta drew more than 20,000, and six events fielded more than 10,000. The numbers will be even higher in the company-racing season just ending [in 1998].

This movement is as healthy for companies as it is for individuals. Coworkers join each other outside work to build fitness and team spirit, which in turn serve them well on the job.

team at Ohio State University, he later coached swim teams in the schools where he taught. In 1964, while teaching at State University of New York at Cortland, he became the coach of the cross country team because no one else wanted the job.

As a biology teacher, Dave was curious about the physiological significance of athletic performance. While working on his doctorate, he began conducting "little testing projects" with his swimmers and later with his cross country runners. In 1966 he moved to Ball State. Since then he has been a visiting professor in Europe on many occasions, made scientific presentations on virtually every continent on earth, and has published hundreds of scientific articles. He also wrote the then-definitive book on running from the scientist's viewpoint, *A Scientific Approach to Distance Running* (Track & Field News, 1979). An avid runner for many years and a veteran of the Boston Marathon, he eventually returned to his first love, swimming, after encountering a number of running-related injuries.

Cote, Gerard (b. July 28, 1913). The personable French-Canadian won four Boston Marathons in an eight-year period before, during, and after World War II. His victories came in 1940 (2:28:28), 1943 (2:28:25), 1944 (2:31:50), and 1948 (2:31:02). *See also* Boston Marathon.

From the collection of Dr. Edward H. Kozloff—Motor City Striders

Gerard Cote came to Boston from Canada in 1940 to win over John A. Kelley by 3 1/2 minutes; he celebrated by smoking a big cigar and drinking Scotch and port wine while the press interviewed him.

Cotton, Terry (b. August 7, 1954). He set an American half-marathon best, breaking an hour, on a much-aided course at Fontana, California. *See also* records, American.

Courage to Start, The. John Bingham's hot-selling book, published in 1999 by Simon and Shuster, is the bible of the Penguin Brigade. *See also* Bingham, John; Penguin Brigade.

Cox, Bucky (b. July 11, 1972). In what would likely be considered child abuse these days, Bucky Cox was trained to run marathons as a five-year-old by Ray Foster of the University of Kansas, a researcher at the university's Bureau of Child Research in the late 1970s. Bucky's first marathon was Lawrence, Kansas, over the Fourth of July weekend in 1978 when the temperature hit 94 degrees. He finished 63rd out of 67 with a time of 5:25:09 as 32 runners dropped out, primarily from heat exhaustion.

Foster explained his training technique in a "Looking at People" report from Mary Erickson in *Runner's World* in September 1978: "We select a level of demand that is essentially insignificantly higher than the current level, and we base our decisions on data. Bucky is reinforced with a token system of nickels for good running—running freely, easily, at a decent pace. He is also rewarded for the absence of bitching and for being polite while running—for example, thanking people who stop their cars to let us pass." What does Bucky think about while running? "Running," Bucky responded, "makes me lose my mind."

Crater Lake Marathon. This race is run in August through Oregon's only national park. *See also* scenic races.

Crescent City Classic 10K (www.ccc10K.com). When the weather cooperates, as it did in 1984, the flat New Orleans course used for the early spring race is one of the fastest anywhere. Mark Nenow set the current American aided best of 27:22 in 1984. *See also* biggest races; fastest races.

Crim 10-Mile. Flint, a hard-luck industrial city in Michigan, is an unlikely spot for one of the country's best races, held each August. Cathy O'Brien set a still-standing American (at the time, also world) record of 51:47 on this demanding course in 1989. *See also* Kenyan runners; O'Brien, Cathy.

cross country racing. It's outside the realm of this book, but successful crossovers to and from road racing are common. The list of World Cross Country champions is dotted with top roadies: Julie Brown, Grete Waitz, Ingrid Kristiansen, John Treacy, Craig Virgin (see next page), and Carlos Lopes.

cross-training. Runners have the triathletes to thank for giving us permission to try complementary activities. The other two-thirds of triathlons—swimming and bicycling—remain the most popular alternatives, as active recovery during periods of injury or simply to round out physical development. But cross-country skiing, water running, and rowing are gaining converts. And good old walking is the simplest and most practical option. The term *cross-training* can also encompass strength and flexibility exercises in their many forms. *See also* weight training; stretching exercises; triathlon and duathlon; walk breaks; water running.

Cruz, Alejandro (b. February 10, 1968). The Mexican won at Chicago in 1988 (in 2:08:57) and was the top-ranked all-distance road racer four years later. *See also* Chicago Marathon; rankings, *Runner's World.*

Cummings, Paul (b. September 5, 1953; d. September 17, 2001). One of the Stormin' Mormons (along with Ed Eyestone and Henry Marsh), his Olympic experience came in the track 10,000. But Cummings was more active as a road racer, holding world and American half-marathon records and the U.S. 20K mark. He won the first national half-marathon championship in 1987. *See also* national half-marathon champions, U.S.; record progressions, American; record progressions, world.

© Mark Shearman

One of the most versatile American runners, Craig Virgin twice won the World Cross Country title, made three Olympic 10,000-meter teams, and placed second at Boston with a 2:10:26.

Cunha, Aurora (b. May 31, 1959). The Portuguese woman got around; she was the winner of the 1988 Tokyo, 1990 Chicago, and 1992 Rotterdam marathons. *See also* Chicago Marathon; Rotterdam Marathon; Tokyo Marathons.

Curp, Mark (b. January 5, 1959). His best racing came in the great gap between the 10K and the marathon. Curp was first in the world to break 1:01 in the half-marathon and is the current American record-holder at this distance. *Runner's World* named him as the world's top road racer in 1987 and 1988, and the RRCA made him a hall of famer in 2000. *See also* Hall of Fame, RRCA; national half-marathon champions, U.S.; rankings, *Runner's World*; record progressions, American; record progressions, world; records, American.

da Costa, Ronaldo (b. June 7, 1970). In 1998 the Brazilian broke the decade-old world's best marathon time with a startling 2:06:05 (a 45-second improvement) at the Berlin Marathon. He was so in control that day that when he crossed the finish line he did a cartwheel and then danced the samba for the crowds. A hero in his homeland to the point that he can no longer train there because everyone he runs past wants to shake his hand or slap him on the shoulder, he has taken up training at more neutral places throughout the world, including San Diego and Lanzarote, a remote island.

Ronaldo da Costa's story is one of a hard-working runner making it from poverty to affluence. The son of a farm laborer, he is 1 of 12 children. He had to leave school early to help support his family. With his $200,000 for breaking the world record, da Costa built his family a new house. Unfortunately, he continues to

© Mark Shearman, Athletics–Images.

Brazil's Ronaldo da Costa set a new world's best marathon mark of 2:06:05 in 1998 and was so filled with energy that he did a cartwheel at the finish line. His record lasted a year.

struggle to regain the level of fitness that shattered the world record. His record was broken by Khalid Khannouchi at Chicago in 1999. *See also* Berlin Marathon; record progressions, world.

Dadi, Tesfaye (b. March 19, 1969). He shares the world junior marathon record with fellow Ethiopian Nagesh Dube. Both ran 2:12:49 in separate races in the late 1980s. *See also* Dube, Nagesh; records, world age-group.

Daniels, Dr. Jack (b. April 26, 1933). The man with the memorable name has held a day job as a cross country and track coach at Cortland State College in New York since 1986, but his coaching extends far beyond the campus. He guided Jerry Lawson and Ken Martin to sub-2:10 marathons and Lisa Martin Ondieki to a sub-2:24, and has taken a sabbatical to do research and provide guidance to post-collegiate runners on the Farm Team in Palo Alto, California. Daniels also coaches through his research and writings, notably *Daniels' Running Formula* (Human Kinetics 1998). Dr. Daniels brings to coaching a knowledge of physiological principles that few other coaches possess, and he has practical experience as an athlete and coach that few other scientists have gained. He was himself an Olympic medalist, earning a silver in the 1956 modern pentathlon and a bronze in the 1960 team competition. *See also* Lawson, Jerry; Martin, Ken; Martin Ondieki, Lisa.

Davies, Clive (b. August 7, 1915; d. April 25, 2001). A Welshman transplanted to the United States, he ran a marathon in 2:42:44 at age 64, which was then the fastest in the world for this age group. It remains the American over-60 mark more than 20 years later, as does his 65–69 record of 2:42:49. *See also* Hall of Fame, RRCA; records, American age-group.

Davies-Hale, Paul (b. June 21, 1962). The Brit won the Bolder Boulder 10K in 1985 and won the Chicago Marathon in 1989 with 2:11:25. *See also* Chicago Marathon; Bolder Boulder 10K.

Davis, Marc (b. December 17, 1969). This 1996 U.S. Olympic steeplechaser is America's 5K road record-holder (13:24 at Carlsbad in 1996) as well as the national champion at that distance in 1997. He's known also for his many tattoos, some of which commemorate his running feats. *See also* national 5K champions, U.S.; record progressions, American; records, American.

Daws, Ron (b. September 25, 1938; d. 1992). He never liked the title given to his first book (an autobiography), *The Self-Made Olympian* (World Publications, 1977), but it was apt. Few runners have stretched their limited talent further than Daws, who made the U.S. Olympic Marathon team in 1968 after being no more than a journeyman runner through high school and college. His tremendous insights into racing allowed him to coach then-wife Lorraine Moller in her early years as a marathoner. They later divorced, and Daws died of a heart attack on the eve of Moller's greatest triumph, a bronze medal at the Barcelona Olympics. *See* Hall of Fame, RRCA; national marathon champions, U.S.; Olympians, U.S.; Olympic Marathon Trials, U.S.

Deacon, Bruce (b. December 5, 1966). Canada's lone entry in the men's 2000

Olympic Marathon had the misfortune of being knocked down in the opening rush. He still finished but in a much slower time than he'd hoped. Deacon, who ran his first marathon at age 13, had his best international effort at the 1995 World Championships, where he placed 11th. His marathon PR is 2:13:35.

Dead Runners Society (storm.cadcam.iupui.edu/drs). These Deads aren't Jerry Garcia fanatics but runners who get together by way of their computers—and at annual conventions—to chat about their favorite sport. Chris Conn is credited with founding the group in 1991. Its name derived from the movie *Dead Poets Society*. From an original membership of about 50, the virtual running community has grown to about 1,700 as this book goes to press.

de Bruyn, Paul (b. October 7, 1907). The German immigrant to the United States won the 1932 Boston Marathon after having already been selected to the 1932 German Olympic team. He had worked as a sailor for North German Lloyd Steamships and then lived in New York City where he shoveled coal in the basement of the Wellington Hotel. A true German, he loved beer but, living in the United States, was caught in the middle of Prohibition. He was built big for a marathoner, some 163 pounds, but he was strong. He would also qualify for the German Olympic team in 1936 while waiting to become an American citizen. Once he did so, de Bruyn volunteered for the U.S. Navy in World War II; in 1945 he received battle injuries that ended his running career. He was later elected to the RRCA Hall of Fame. *See also* Boston Marathon; Hall of Fame, RRCA.

From the collection of Dr. Edward H. Kozloff—Motor City Striders

Paul de Bruyn, a German living in America, won the 1932 Boston. Immediately after winning, he asked for a beer, but America was in the midst of Prohibition.

de Castella, Rob (b. February 27, 1957). There was nothing elegant about the way Rob de Castella ran. He didn't float over the road like Bill Rodgers or skim over the surface like Frank Shorter. He appeared to attack the ground brutally, yet he did so in an efficient, ground-devouring manner. And he was intelligent about his running and racing, a student of the art and science of running. During the time he spent training in Boulder, Colorado, in the 1980s he trained hard but conservatively, never burning a workout so hard that he went to a race toasted or overtrained. Like Emil Zatopek and fellow Australian Derek Clayton before him, "Deek's" secret (if it can be called a secret) was simple—straightforward hard work and a passion for racing.

Deek came from a relatively large family—four brothers and two sisters. His father, Rolet, an executive with the Nestlé Corporation, was an amateur runner. As a youngster, Deek would accompany him to races. In school, Deek joined the cross country team and scored a point or two, but he was usually the number-four or number-five man on the squad. He was not a natural athlete but he made up for it with enthusiasm.

In one of those coincidences that seem almost divinely arranged, in the fall of 1971 he ran into Pat Clohessy, who was coaching cross country at Deek's new school. Clohessy had been a formidable runner himself in his college years. Under Clohessy's guidance, Deek blossomed. By his senior year in 1974, he broke world-renowned Herb Elliott's Australian junior two-mile record by running 8:46. But Clohessy saw Deek as a long-distance runner. Clohessy continued to train Deek after high school, but the athlete had to learn the hard way to "train smarter, not harder," which meant modifying his lifestyle (i.e., cutting out the late-night partying) to allow hard workouts to take

Rob "Deek" DeCastella was not an elegant runner, but he was intelligent and hard working; by applying science and art to road racing, he became one of the best of all time.

hold on a resting body.

He added some stability to his life by marrying Gayelene Clews, a talented runner herself, in 1980. During this period Deek made the commitment to racing longer distances, where Pat Clohessy felt his real talents lay. In his first marathon, the Victoria Championship of 1979, he won with a 2:14:44, then followed that with a 2:13:23 win in the Australian national championship marathon. The 1980 Australian Olympics Marathon Trials were on the horizon, so Deek took a year off from his schooling, and he and Gayelene moved to the mountains where he began

© Mark Shearman. Athletics-Images.

training 145 to 150 miles per week—and in the process ran himself into the ground. He backed off and was able to recover enough to take second place (2:12:24) in the Trials. In spite of the U.S. boycott of the Moscow Olympics, Australia sent a team, and Deek finished 10th in 2:14:31.

He returned to Australia to start a job as a bio-lab technician and to train for Fukuoka, where he ran 2:10:44 but finished eighth. He went home with a determination to back away from racing and to train for the 1981 Fukuoka. A month before that race, Alberto Salazar set a new world best at New York City of 2:08:13. Deek won Fukuoka with a 2:08:18, the fastest time ever on a loop or out-and-back course and 1:18 faster than countryman Derek Clayton's course record. Salazar's New York time was later adjusted when the course was found to be short, and Deek suddenly had the world's best marathon time.

It is difficult to recall anyone who so quickly stormed and conquered the marathon world as did Rob de Castella in 1980 and 1981; he consistently improved with each race he ran, as much by thinking through the process as by running through it. Next came the 1982 Commonwealth Games in Brisbane, a meeting of former British colonies, where Deek was the overwhelming favorite. The field was dominated by two Tanzanians, Gidamis Shahanga and Juma Ikangaa, who took off immediately and vanished from sight while the rest of the field ran more conservatively. When Deek hit 18 miles and realized that the two were not coming back to him, he went out after them, catching a struggling Shahanga at 23 miles but encountering a feisty Ikangaa at 24. The two battled back and forth until Deek prevailed in 2:09:18.

Deek, a combination of brain and brawn, seemed to be unstoppable, able to win at will. The next stop on his tour of

the marathon world was a *mano-a-mano* meeting with undefeated Alberto Salazar at Rotterdam in 1983. His competition didn't come from Salazar, however, but from Portuguese Carlos Lopes. Only a last-minute sprint saved Deek's win (2:08:37) by a mere two seconds; he ran the final mile in 4:32. He went into the first-ever World Track and Field Championships Marathon in Helsinki later that year as the favorite and proved his strength with a 2:10:03 win.

Then it was on to the 1984 Los Angeles Olympic Games, where he was the clear favorite. But Olympic Marathons are often strange affairs. He finished fifth in 2:11:12. In retrospect, he felt he might have taken too much time off racing to focus on training specifically for the Olympics, and he became caught up in the hype surrounding the Games. He put together a string of sub-2:10s, including a third at Chicago in 1985 in 2:08:48. At Boston in 1986 he set a new course record of 2:07:51. That August he repeated as Commonwealth Games winner. Three weeks later he finished third at New York.

At the 1988 Seoul Games he could finish only 8th after missing eight weeks of training because of a bad back. His training was also sour before the 1990 Commonwealth Games, where he finished 13th; he'd been nursing a leg injury.

He accepted a job as director of the Australian Institute of Sport, where he put in 60-hour weeks and trained to race, but it was too much. At Barcelona for his fourth Olympic marathon, he ran badly. Afterward he gradually phased out of racing, having already proved to everyone's satisfaction that he was one of the best runners the sport had ever produced. *See also* Boston Marathon; Commonwealth Games; Fukuoka Marathon; rankings, *Track & Field News;* record progressions, world; Rotterdam Marathon; World Championships medalists.

Decker Slaney, Mary. *See* Slaney, Mary Decker Tabb.

de Coubertin, Pierre (b. 1863). The Frenchman created the modern Olympic Games—only to have the Greeks attempt to make him persona non grata once they got going. *See also* Olympic Marathon, 1896.

DeHaven, Rod (b. September 21, 1965). Winner of the 2000 U.S. Olympic Trials Marathon, he ran a brilliant tactical race in humid heat to become the lone U.S. male qualifier for the Games. Unfortunately, he caught an intestinal flu being passed around during the Games and struggled to finish. Taking some of the sting out of that disappointment was his sixth-place finish with a PR of 2:12:41 at the 2001 Boston Marathon. No American man had placed higher since 1987. DeHaven also competed in the 1999 Worlds and is a three-time winner (1994, 1998, and 2000) of the national half-marathon title. *See also* national half-marathon champions, U.S.; national marathon champions, U.S.; Olympians, U.S.; Olympic Trials Marathon, U.S.; World Championships, U.S.

dehydration. *See* drinks, running.

delayed-onsert muscle soreness. *DOMS* refers to the odd sensation of feeling worse the *second* day after a hard race or workout than the first day. Stiffness and soreness usually peak 24 to 48 hours after a serious bout of activity, then gradually begin to loosen their hold.

D'elia, Toshiko (b. January 2, 1930). The longtime long-distance runner from the New York City area really blossomed when she turned 70. She set age-group records in the 5K (24:36) and 10K (48:53), both in 2000. *See also* records, American age-group.

Dellinger, Bill (b. March 23, 1934). The Olympic 5,000-meter bronze medalist (1964) became the longtime University of Oregon coach, serving from the late 1960s to the late 1990s. He worked with a raft of star distance runners, most notably Alberto Salazar. The year 2000 brought him both wonderful and terrible developments, as the USATF voted him into its hall of fame and he suffered a stroke. *See also* coaches; Hall of Fame, National Distance Running; Hall of Fame, USATF.

DeMar Clarence. *See* page 81.

Dengis, Pat (b. 1900; d. 1939). He was inducted into the RRCA Hall of Fame for winning three U.S. marathon titles—1935, 1938, and 1939. Dengis, from Baltimore, also finished second in the 1935 and 1938 Boston Marathons. *See also* Hall of Fame, RRCA; national marathon champions, U.S.

DeNinno, Lynn (b. November 7, 1961). She twice won the women's national 10K title, in 1990 and 1991. *See also* national 10K champions, U.S.

DeMar, Clarence (b. June 7, 1888; d. June 11, 1958). It would be difficult to locate a more truly legendary road racer than DeMar, due both to his extreme individualism and the statistical games revolving around "What if?" scenarios about his life. Born near Cincinnati, DeMar at age seven used to dogtrot rather than walk to school and soon developed a reputation as a kid who never walked anywhere. In this way he was not unlike Kenyan children of a century later. When his father died, young Clarence helped bring in some money for his mother and five younger siblings by selling pins, needles, thread, and soap, sometimes trotting between 10 and 20 miles in a day's work.

At 10, his mother moved the family to Warwick, Massachusetts, where a relative had a house in which they could live rent free. At one point, Clarence injured his ankle while skating. It became infected, and he nearly lost his foot. Even with a free house, however, the DeMar family couldn't make it and broke up. Clarence was sent to the Farm School on Thompson's Island in Boston Harbor. After graduating at age 16, DeMar continued his education at the Maple Lawn Academy. His love of education would continue throughout his life. He read constantly and dreamed of becoming a sports hero, but his efforts in each sport ended in failure and frustration. He entered the University of Vermont and continued to trot everywhere, going so far as to convince the physical education instructor that he was getting enough exercise without wasting a class to get more.

He read in newspapers about races of great distances in foreign countries. "One morning the thought came to me," he reported in his autobiography, *Marathon* (Cedarwinds, 1937), "that I could run a marathon, and perhaps go abroad and represent my country." Clarence went out for the cross country team, but his efficient, ground-eating style didn't set well with the

Clarence DeMar won his seventh Boston in 1930 at age 41, astonishing the medical experts who had said he had a bad heart; he outlived most of the "experts."

From the collection of Dr. Edward H. Kozloff–Motor City Striders

team captain, who wanted him to run up on his toes. It would not be the last time Clarence's ideas came into conflict with ideas held by others. In his first interclass meet (four miles) he beat the team captain.

Clarence cut short his college career, however, when at age 21 he was legally able to help support his mother. He moved in with her at her home in Melrose and remained for 20 years, working as a printer in Boston. He ran to and from work, carrying a clean shirt under his arm. Although he'd never run more than 10 miles in his life, over Christmas of 1909 he ran from Reading to Boston (20 miles) and then back out to Melrose (7 miles). He did the run in three hours "without much exertion." On February 22, 1910, in rain and sleet, he won a 10-mile handicap race from Boston to Chestnut Hill and back.

DeMar had his eyes set on the marathon distance and on April 19 entered his first Boston Marathon, where he took second place, less than a minute behind the winner. Over the summer DeMar raced frequently on the roads, then went into training over the winter for Boston, running 100 miles a week. At Boston, he took the lead at 19 miles and won in 2:21:40, breaking the course record by three minutes. He won the next eight races he entered and in the fall won the Brockton Marathon, making him 10 for 10 for the year.

In hopes of going to the 1912 Olympics, Clarence sat out that year's Boston Marathon and ran a 10-mile qualifier. But through a series of managerial and coaching disasters, the marathoners were worn down by the time they reached Stockholm and fared badly in competition. DeMar had been examined by a doctor who told him he had an irregular heart. That warning, along with an increasing workload and DeMar's growing feeling that running was a vainglorious thing to do, left him little time to train and race. He received his AA degree from Harvard and served as scoutmaster for Troop 5 in Melrose, where, instead of racing on weekends, he took the scouts camping. This lasted for five years, during which many experts believe DeMar missed the prime of his racing career.

In 1917 Clarence returned to running. He took third at Boston that spring and won the Brockton Fair Marathon in the fall in course-record time. Then the war came, and although army doctors confirmed he had a "runner's heart" (an enlarged heart), he was drafted for service. He effectively lost two additional years of prime racing to the military.

He spent the Boston Marathon day of 1920 canoeing with his scouts. For Boston 1921, DeMar was making repairs to the Boy Scout cottage. But in 1922 he decided to train for Boston and won in 2:18:10, knocking 47 seconds off the course record of the time (the course that year was measured at 24 miles and 1,242 yards). He came back in 1923 and won Boston again, in spite of having a shoe come loose when a cyclist struck by a car careened into him. He won again in 1924, when the course was set at the now-standard 26 miles, 385 yards. DeMar made the 1924 Olympic team and placed third. He finished second in the 1925 Boston and third in 1926, then went on a tear, winning his next five marathons: Baltimore (May 1926), Sesquicentennial at Philadelphia (June 1926), Port Chester (October 1926), Baltimore again (March 1927), and Boston (April 1927). He won Boston again in 1928 and 1930, in the latter year at age 41. He also won the national marathon title every year from 1926 through 1929.

In all, Clarence DeMar won Boston an amazing 7 times. Some argue that had he trained and raced through the prime of his running career, when he instead backed away from his running, he would have easily won Boston more than 10 times. It is not difficult to hear DeMar dispelling that theory with the comment, "You don't win what you don't run."

DeMar's last race in 1957, at age 68, was a 15K that he ran despite intestinal cancer and a colostomy. The longevity of his career brought to light for many scientists that performing at a high level was possible as one aged. His best time at Boston once the race distance was standardized was 2:29:40 at age 36; he slowed to 3:58:37 at age 66. *See also* Boston Marathon; Hall of Fame, National Distance Running; Hall of Fame, RRCA; national marathon champions, U.S.; Olympians, U.S.; Olympic medalists.

DeMar-velous

From Joe Henderson's *Running Commentary,* November 1991.

A recently republished book tells about its author winning the Boston Marathon repeatedly. It tells of training with high mileage and about overtraining. It tells of racing after age 40 and of adjusting for aging.

It isn't Bill Rodgers's new book, although in *Masters Running and Racing* (Rodale, 1991) Rodgers does pay homage to this other author. Rodgers wrote, "One of my favorite running books is Clarence DeMar's autobiography, *Marathon."*

In terms of doing the most and doing it longest, DeMar ranks as the best marathoner in U.S. history. He was the last American to run in three Olympic races and the last between 1924 and 1972 to win a medal. DeMar won seven Boston Marathons between 1911 and 1930, a record that will never be broken. His last win at age 41 still makes him the oldest Boston winner ever. He was the first great master, though that word didn't enter running language for almost 40 years after he'd turned 40.

DeMar wrote *Marathon* in 1937. The book's material has aged so well that John Parker of Cedarwinds Publishing (Box 13618, Tallahassee, FL 32317) has reissued it. I just reread it and was reminded again of how little is new in this sport.

The physical rules haven't changed since DeMar trained for his first Boston Marathon win 80 years ago. He got good by running lots of miles and got hurt from running too many, too fast. "I covered nearly a hundred miles per week in practice for a couple of months with several 20-mile jaunts," he said. "The first of many physical difficulties I have met before races annoyed me at this time. My right knee became stiff, [but] I didn't go to see a doctor because I had a sneaking notion that he would tell me not to run until the knee got well."

DeMar called the 1912 Olympic Marathon his most disappointing race. Considered a favorite, he finished 12th and blamed this poor showing on overtraining. The coach made U.S. marathoners run 20 miles a day when they should have been tapering. "We didn't race," DeMar recalled, "but neither did we loaf. Alone, I'd have run much slower part of the time. Eventually, a week or so before the race, with the nervous strain of trying to make good every day instead of once a fortnight, I went stale."

He found, as today's runners are rediscovering, that a long training run every two weeks or so worked best for him. He could go long if the pace was right.

DeMar was an early ultramarathoner who sometimes entered a 44-mile race as training for Boston. At this distance, he wrote, "one can slow down 25 percent from a marathon. Instead of 10 miles per hour, $7^1/_2$ is satisfactory. I found that I could run this slower pace indefinitely without the nervous strain of the marathon."

DeMar later became one of the first lifers in the sport. He promised after winning at Boston in 1930, "I'll keep running as long as my legs will carry me." He kept running Bostons until 1954 and continued racing until shortly before his death four years later at age 70.

As Clarence DeMar came to terms with aging, he wrote, "No longer does my success depend on the amount of practice I do. Frequently, a rest and just a little practice cause me to make a better showing. No longer does slow practice always produce the best race. Sometimes speedwork causes me to do better.

"So the older I get, the less dogmatic and sure I become as to the best way for anyone to get into physical condition. Not only are there individual differences, but the same individual has to change his method of training over a period of years—even as old people change their glasses."

Colleen de Reuck holds world records at 10 miles and 20K and was ranked number one in 1993 and 1997.

Densimo, Belaine. *See* Dinsamo, Belayneh.

DeOliveira, Carmen (b. August 17, 1965). The Brazilian is the South American marathon women's record-holder at 2:27:41.

Derderian, Tom (b. March 8, 1949). The former top New England runner (2:19 marathon PR) wrote the definitive running history book, *The Boston Marathon* (Human Kinetics, 1996). He competed in the 1972 and 1976 U.S. Olympic Trials in the marathon. He has worked as a magazine editor, a college coach, and in research and development for major shoe companies Nike and Reebok; he holds three U.S. patents for running shoes and apparel. *See also* Boston Marathon.

de Reuck, Colleen (b. April 13, 1964). She splits her training time between her native South Africa (for which she competed in the Olympic Marathon in 1992 and 2000) and her adopted hometown of Boulder, Colorado. De Reuck holds the current 10-mile (51:16 in 1998) and 20K (1:05:11 in 1998; Esther Wanjiru's faster time is pending) world records and earned the top road ranking in 1993 and 1997. She became a U.S. citizen in late 2000. *See also* Bay to Breakers 12K; Berlin Marathon; Bloomsday 12K; Honolulu Marathon; rankings, *Runner's World*; records, world.

DeRios, Maria Trujillo. *See* Trujillo, Maria.

Deseret News 10K (www.deseretnews.com/run). The Salt Lake City course is one of the fastest, with the downhill slope more than canceling out the penalty of altitude. Olga Appell ran 30:55 here, an aided American best for women. Race day also includes a marathon on a much more challenging course than the 10K. These events are always run on Pioneer Day in July. *See also* fastest races.

Detroit International Marathon (www.freep.com/marathon). This event has operated under several different names and on various courses, but with a legacy dating back to 1963 it is one of the country's longest-running marathons, contested each August. *See also* Kurtis, Doug; oldest races.

diary, running. *See* logbooks.

Dickerson, Marianne (b. November 14, 1960). Her one great performance came on a big stage. As a 22-year-old she was silver medalist (behind Grete Waitz) at the first World Championships Marathon in 1983, setting her permanent PR of 2:31:09. No American woman has won a medal since in that event. *See also* World Championships, U.S.

did not finish. Results listings usually use the initials DNF for the dreaded "did not finish."

diet. *See* bars, sports; carbohydrate loading; drinks, running; foods, runners'.

Dillon, Patti. *See* Catalano, Patti Lyons.

Dinsamo, Belayneh (also spelled Densimo, Belaine) (b. June 18, 1966). Although the Ethiopian never again approached his world-record time of 2:06:50 at Rotterdam in 1988, he wasn't a one-race wonder. He also won the 1987 African Games, Rotterdam 1989 and 1996, and the 1990 Fukuoka. *See also* African Games; Fukuoka Marathon; rankings, *Track & Field News*; record progressions, world; Rotterdam Marathon.

Belayneh Dinsamo set the world's best marathon time of 2:06:50 at Rotterdam in 1988, a record that would last a decade.

Dipsea Trail Run (www.dipsea.org). It's mainly a trail race, but this one attracts the road-racing crowd. The Dipsea, 7.1 miles, which runs each June through Marin County, California, was the inspiration for the movie *On the Edge* that starred Bruce Dern.

directors, race. Behind every good race stands a strong race director. Some are paid for their work (such as Guy Morse at Boston), but most are volunteers (such as Les Smith at Portland). The mark of a truly enduring race is how it survives a change in directors. Good examples of positive changes are Allan Steinfeld taking over from the late Fred Lebow at New York City and Carey Pinkowski rebuilding a floundering Chicago Marathon. *See also* officials, volunteer; *Road Race Management*.

Discovery USA (www.fila.com). Italian Dr. Gabriele Rosa brought to the United States, in 2000, this Fila-funded program that had worked successfully in Kenya. It identifies running prospects through a series of physiological tests, then brings the best of them together for periodic training camps. *See also* Fila; Rosa, Dr. Gabriele.

Distance Running News. *See* Anderson, Bob; *Runner's World*.

distances, metric and English. American runners speak a strange hybrid language on distances. Most races are run in kilometers, yet splits are given at mile points and runners train by miles per week. In typical revolutionary fashion, Americans have rejected repeated attempts by various factions to shove the metric system down their throats. On the other hand, much of the world still understands the meaning of the word *miler*.

Ditz, Nancy (b. June 25, 1954). In the late 1980s Ditz could lay claim to being the top American female marathoner. She placed 7th (first U.S. finisher) at the 1987 Worlds and 17th (again the top American) at the 1988 Olympics. Winner of the 1985 national marathon title, she won at Los Angeles in 1986 and 1987. *See also* Los Angeles Marathon; national marathon champions, U.S.; Olympians, U.S.; Olympic Trials marathon, U.S.; World Championships, U.S.

Distance Conversions

Metric-distance races	Mile-system equivalents
1,500 meters (1.5K)	.93 mile
3,000 meters (3K)	1.86 miles
5,000 meters (5K)	3.11 miles
8,000 meters (8K)	4.97 miles
10,000 meters (10K)	6.21 miles
12 kilometers	7.46 miles
15 kilometers	9.32 miles
20 kilometers	12.43 miles
half-marathon (21.1K)	13.11 miles
25 kilometers	15.54 miles
30 kilometers	18.64 miles
marathon (42.2K)	26.22 miles
Mile-distance races	**Metric-system equivalents**
1 mile	1,609 meters (1.61K)
2 miles	3,218 meters (3.22K)
5 miles	8,045 meters (8.01K)
10 miles	16.09 kilometers
20 miles	32.18 kilometers

Dixon, Rod (b. July 13, 1950). Better known as a track runner, the New Zealander had extraordinary range. He won an Olympic medal at 1,500 meters in 1972 and won the 1983 New York City Marathon in 2:08:59 after a stirring duel with England's Geoff Smith. *See also* Bay to Breakers 12K; New York City Marathon.

DNF. *See* did not finish.

Doctor Scholl's (www.drscholls.com). The manufacturer of foot-protective devices for runners sponsored a series of high-quality 10Ks in the mid-1980s.

Dorre-Heinig, Katrin (b. October 6, 1961). An incredibly consistent competitor, Dorre-Heinig had major international marathon victories in three decades, both before and after the reunification of Germany (she was from the East). Dorre-Heinig has run more sub-2:30s than any other woman

East German Katrin Dorre has run more sub-2:30s than any other woman in the world. She's won consistently in three different decades: Osaka four times, Tokyo three times, and London twice.

in the world. She was bronze medalist at the 1988 Olympics and 1991 Worlds, World Cup winner in 1985, four-time winner of Osaka, and three-time winner at Tokyo and London. *See also* Berlin Marathon; London Marathon; Olympic Games; Osaka Ladies Marathon; Tokyo Marathons; World Championships medalists; World Cup Marathon.

Dos Santos, Luiz (b. April 6, 1964). Before Ronaldo da Costa's rise to glory, the top Brazilian was Dos Santos—bronze medalist in the 1995 Worlds (2:12:49), 1993 and 1994 Chicago winner (2:13:15 and 2:11:16), and 1995 champ at Fukuoka (2:09:30). *See also* Chicago Marathon; Fukuoka Marathon; World Championships medalists.

Douglas, Scott (b. June 29, 1964). The talented youngish writer-editor (in a field dominated by geezers) was once editor of *Running Times* and has coauthored books with Bill Rodgers (*Complete Idiot's Guide to Running and Jogging*, 1998) and Pete Pfitzinger (*Road Racing for Serious Runners*; Human Kinetics, 1999 and *Advanced Marathoning*; Human Kinetics, 2001). As a fund-raiser for the Road Runners Club of America, Douglas ran the full length of the C&O Canal Towpath, 184 miles, in late 2000. *See also* Pfitzinger, Pete; Rodgers, Bill.

Drayton, Jerome See next page.

drinks, running. Gatorade (from Quaker Oats now, though it began life as a drink for University of Florida football players) started the trend toward mixed drinks on a national level, and they've flowed freely ever since. Gatorade was developed to provide sugar to working muscles as well as to replace the electrolytes and salts lost in sweat, and that's just what the early formulas tasted like. It has improved. Other pioneers include ERG ("Gookinaid") and Exceed (from Ross Labs, the same folks who make Head and Shoulders). The theory behind these drinks is that because runners sweat out more than water, they need a drink that mixes other nutrients with water.

Drossin, Deena (b. February 14, 1973). She set an American 5K record of 15:08 in one of her infrequent road appearances in 2000 at Carlsbad. Drossin's ambitions in track and cross country are more serious. She won the 2000 Olympic Trials 10,000, made the team in the 5,000, and twice has placed in the top dozen (2000 and 2001) at the World Cross Country Championships. She also won the 2001 Bolder Boulder 10K. *See also* Bolder Boulder 10K; record progressions, American; records, American.

drug testing. Unavoidable in the world of high-stakes racing, it catches relatively few road racers. Is this because distance runners rarely cheat or because the tests can be beaten? Probably some of both. Traditionally the testing has been conducted by governing bodies of the sport. In 2001, however, several major marathons banded together to institute their own tests for the banned blood-boosting substance synthetic EPO. *See also* cheaters; erythropoietin.

duathlon. *See* triathlon and duathlon.

Dube, Nagesh (b. May 20, 1968). He has shared the current world junior marathon record of 2:12:49 with fellow Ethiopian D-man, Tesfaye Dadi, for more than a decade. *See also* Dadi, Tesfaye; records, world age-group.

duct tape. The Nobel Prize committee ought to come down to earth on some of their scientific awards and give the prize to inventions that help people on a daily basis. One of those inventions is duct tape (sometimes referred to as "200-mph tape" by auto racers whose pit crews literally tape a damaged car together with the stuff so it can get back into a race), an innovative toe protector and blister proofer for runners.

Drayton, Jerome (b. January 10, 1945). With his trademark sunglasses and sinister mustache, Jerome became Canada's greatest marathoner (as voted by members of the Track-Canada News Group in 1999). His current Canadian national record has stood since he posted it in 1975. After winning Boston in 1977, the acerbic Jerome ruffled Beantown feathers by suggesting that they supply water to runners along the course; the following year it was taken care of.

Although he is forthcoming to direct questions, Jerome remains one of the great enigmas of marathoning because he is so seldom available to field questions. He has worked since 1975 as a fitness, recreation, and sports administrator for the Ministry of Citizenship, Culture and Recreation of the Ontario government. He lives in Toronto, where he has resided since 1956 when he immigrated to Canada.

He was born Peter Buniak in Germany in 1945 to Ukrainian and Russian parents and lived in Munich (as did Frank Shorter and Kathrine Switzer) until age 11, the year his mother, who had left for North America the year before, was able to send for him. "Originally, she had wanted to move to the United States," Jerome reported, "but changed her mind when informed of the USA's policy of compulsory enlistment for military service for its young men. Having survived the Second World War and particularly, as a teenage mother, she had no intention of living with the risk of seeing me go off to war."

He began competitive running quite by accident at age 18 at the annual Mimico High School track and field meet, as he reports in an extensive personal data form

Canada's Jerome Drayton (a.k.a. Peter Buniak) set off a backlash by complaining after this 1977 win at Boston that no water was available along the course. After the citizens of Boston cooled down, water stations were set up along the course for the first time in 1978. Drayton remains the Canadian marathon record-holder.

© Jeff Johnson

completed as an alumni of the Toronto Olympic Club. "We didn't really have a track—just a grass field with a chalk line around it and one corner almost at a 50-degree angle. I entered the half-mile, one-mile, and two-mile events. My reason for entering was that I'd been asked by a friend to do it, in order to divert the amorous attentions of his dream girl from the reigning high school distance champion.

Without any knowledge of training methods and very little preparation, I won all three races. However, my friend failed to get the girl. So did I!"

His wins moved him on to the regional high school meet, where he didn't win any races but caught the attention of the Toronto Olympic Club (TOC) scout. A coach had another runner take Jerome out on an eight-mile run, and he hated it. He quit TOC but rejoined in 1965 after a box lacrosse teammate suffered a debilitating cross-check. Andy Boychuk, then Canadian marathon record-holder, 1967 Pan-American Games Marathon champ, and fellow TOC member, challenged Jerome to try a marathon by saying, "You're not a man until you've run a marathon."

He entered his first marathon on June 2, 1968, in Detroit, where the weather was hot and where he would need a 2:24 to qualify for the Canadian Olympic team. He went out way too fast, committed all the novice sins, and finished in 2:23:57; Andy Boychuk was 22 seconds behind him. Boychuk later ran a faster marathon and was named to the team instead of Jerome, so Jerome went out and ran on the same course Boychuk had, turning in a Canadian record of 2:17:51. The altitude of Mexico City was a problem for Jerome, however, and he dropped at 15 miles, while Boychuk took 10th place in 2:28:40.

But Jerome liked the Olympic experience and felt that in the marathon he'd found his event. On October 8, 1969, he returned to Detroit's Motor City Marathon, and this time the weather was perfect. He ran a 2:12:00, a North American record. He was invited to the prestigious Fukuoka Marathon in Japan, at that time considered the men's international championship, and won the race in 2:11:13, again a North American record, and the third fastest marathon of all time. He was voted

by *Track & Field News* as the number-one marathoner in the world. He returned to Fukuoka in 1975 and won with a 2:10:09, at that time the sixth fastest time in history, but he was frustrated, knowing that he could have broken 2:10 had it not been for his agreeing to wear untested racing flats the Japanese Tiger running-shoe company had pushed on him. The time was still his personal best and remains the Canadian record.

At the Olympics in 1976 (see accompanying poem at the end of the profile), he took sixth place with a 2:13:30 while suffering a heavy cold. He decided to retire from the sport, but his withdrawal was short lived. He returned to Fukuoka later that year to win the race again, this time with a 2:12:35. He continued to race at a high level. He won a hot Boston (in which archrival Bill Rodgers dropped out) in 1977 with 2:14:46 and that fall took second in New York City (2:13:52) behind Rodgers (2:11:28). He also took second in the Commonwealth Games in Edmonton in August 1978 with a 2:16:13. He worked on curing a chronic leg problem in 1979 with an eye toward the Moscow Olympics in 1980, but the boycott effectively ended his career.

In 1997 an accident on a stationary bike caused a knee injury that reduced his running. He swims and lifts weights four to six days a week. To honor his accomplishments, a special banquet was held in conjunction with the 1997 Royal Victoria Marathon in British Columbia. American marathoner Don Kardong, who finished two places in front of Jerome at the 1976 Olympics, prepared and delivered the following poem. "Karel" is pronounced "Carol"; "twoney" refers to the Canadian two-dollar coin. *See also* Boston Marathon; Fukuoka Marathon; rankings, *Track & Field News.*

Kardong vs. Buniak

The stadium was quiet, with the marathoners set,
Listening for the gun to send them off.
Then bang! we sprang and I know I'll never forget
The cheers and cries and shouts of "Mazeltov!"

It was pretty heady company, this world-class elite
Surrounding me and circling the track.
They were, I'm sure, the finest group that I would ever meet.
They were studs, and I was just a hack.

There was Frankie S., the golden boy, the Munich wunderkind,
And Boston Bill, the second Yankee thriller.
And Yank number three, why that was me, but a medal? God forbid!
Guys like me were essentially there as filler.

But I thought if I ran wisely, if I held my cards real tight,
I might bluff my way to a second or a third.
I would cruise and then surge, pass some stragglers and I then might
Get a bronze—was that so hideously absurd?

So I toured les rues du Montreal, throwing bottles to the fans,
And I kept my distance from the front-end pack.
Then feeling fine at mile nine, I picked it up, unleashed my plans,
And made my move from way, way back.

I passed a few, then I passed some more, then a whole bunch after that,
'Til someone cried, "You're thirty seconds from the bronze."
I was near, but it's also clear I was empty, weak and flat,
Like a lurching, sputtering race car at Le Mans.

Still, I set my sights as well as I might, and I started reeling them in.
I passed Viren and Lismont and then Jerome Drayton,
I had moved up to the bronze spot from a place clear back at tin.
Now down the road that ole finish line was waitin'.

But my legs were tight and try as I might I was struggling to keep up the pacin',
I was thirsty and hot and my vision had already blurred.
And with a mile left to go I heard footsteps back there chasin'.
Chasin' me, that is, and trying to steal my third.

It was Drayton, so I thought, when I turned to get a look,
A Canadian, a twoney and a looniac.
I would have to race the local boy, it was just my rotten luck
To have to challenge the hero, Peter Buniak.

It would be a classic battle to the finish, me and him,
A North American duel for third place.
And the stadium was filled that day, was stacked up to the brim,
With Yankees and Canadians cheering the race.

So we sprinted hard down Sherbrooke, and we raced a long downhill,
And my rival broke away as we passed through the gate.
I was hobbling though, by then, as he moved up for the kill,
I struggled to catch him but I finished three seconds late.

Well, I thought, as I crouched panting past the line and catching my breath,
At least the Canadian fans will be pleased with his medal.
That man was tough, he was rough, he sealed my death.
And now for a lousy fourth I'll have to settle.

And it was really much, much later, when the fans had left for slumber,
And I was sitting with a hops and barley fix,
That I found that Karel Lismont was the guy who did that number
On me. And Jerome Drayton? He was six.

So now I'm in a quandary, since this dinner is honoring Drayton,
I've put myself over somewhat of a barrel.
It should obviously be Jerome that I stand congratulatin',
Instead, I have to look for a man named . . . Karel.

© Jeff Johnson

Benji Durden, now a coach living in Boulder, Colorado, was one of the top American marathoners in the early 1980s. He was one-third of the trio of Americans to go under 2:10 at the 1983 Boston Marathon. Greg Meyer won (in 2:09:00) and Ron Tabb took second.

Dunn, Jerry (b. January 29, 1946). At the risk of encouraging such things, we report that Dunn holds the record for most marathons in one year. He ran 200 in 2000 but often arrived in a city early and took multiple trips over the marathon course—counting them all in his total. He chronicles this on his Web site (www.marathonman.org).

Durden, Benji (b. August 28, 1951). He picked the wrong years to peak. Durden was a member of the U.S. Olympic team to nowhere in 1980. He then ran a sub-2:10 marathon at Boston 1983 in a year when two other Americans finished in front of him. Later he became a widely respected coach of road racers in the runner-rich Boulder area. *See also* Hall of Fame, RRCA; Olympians, U.S.; Olympic Trials Marathon, U.S.; World Championships, U.S.

Dyrgall, Vic (b. October 8, 1917). The 1952 Olympian (13th and top American at Helsinki) won national marathon titles in 1949 and 1952. *See also* Hall of Fame, RRCA; national marathon champions, U.S.; Olympians, U.S.

E

East Bay. *See* mail-order companies.

economy, running. The economy of motion in running refers to the amount of energy working muscles require to run at a given pace. Becoming a more "efficient" runner is all about minimizing the amount of energy used in running that impedes forward motion—things such as overstriding or moving the arms excessively from side-to-side.

Edelen, Leonard "Buddy" (b. September 22, 1937; d. 1997). Leonard "Buddy" Edelen was in a class apart from other American runners from 1962 through 1965. At his best he could beat anyone in the world in the marathon. Discounting Alberto Salazar's disputed world mark in New York in 1981, Edelen was the last American man to hold world's best, with 2:14:28 in 1963. A year earlier he became the first U.S. runner to break 2:20. His national record lasted six years (though Amby Burfoot came within a second of it in 1968). Edelen finished sixth at the 1964 Tokyo Olympics while suffering from sciatica, picked up shortly after he won the Trials—by 20 minutes! *See also* "Buddy's Record" on next page; Hall of Fame, RRCA; Košice Peace marathon; national marathon champions, U.S.; Olympians, U.S.; rankings, *Track & Field News*; record progressions, American; record progressions, world.

Edmonton, Alberta, Canada. The capital city of Alberta was the site of the 1978 Common-

© Mark Shearman. Athletics–Images.

Dissatisfied with training in the United States, Buddy Edelen went to England to teach school and to train with the best; it worked. He set a world's best of 2:14:28 in 1963.

wealth Games Marathon and the 2001 World Championships—the first running of the Worlds in the Western Hemisphere. The traditional Edmonton Festival Marathon course was radically altered to better show off the city for the Worlds.

Buddy's Record

From Joe Henderson's *Running Commentary,* January 1992.

Leonard "Buddy" Edelen is a figure from history. But few of us ran when he did, and little was known about him even then. Now we can read his full story. Lawyer-writer Frank Murphy has published Edelen's biography, titled *A Cold Clear Day.*

Edelen didn't get a chance to claim fame and wealth on the American roads. Little was happening there in 1960. After failing badly in the Olympic Trials 10,000, Edelen fled to Europe. He took a low-paying job teaching school and never earned more than $500 for a race. Fred Wilt sent him training advice from Indiana. Buddy became a marathoner in 1962. He went the distance four times in the last half of that year and in the final race set an American record of 2:18:57.

No one in the world had yet broken 2:15, and Edelen didn't look like he would be the first when he lined up for England's Polytechnic Marathon on June 15, 1963. He'd won his big race of the spring, breaking Abebe Bikila's course record at Athens four weeks earlier.

"Buddy had no particular plan for this marathon," writes Frank Murphy of the Poly. "He had trained well, and that gave reason for hope, even surprise. If it came, that would be good. But if it did not, it would be no worry."

The mix was perfect: a well-trained, relaxed runner in a great field on a fast course. The Poly was then one of the world's top four marathons (along with Boston, Fukuoka, and Košice). The 1963 field included future sub-2:10 man Ron Hill.

Today, the English course would be as debatable as New York's was when Salazar ran so fast there. Murphy describes the point-to-point route from Windsor Castle to Chiswick as "flat to gently downhill, with no significant [up]hills to worry a runner." In 1963, a tailwind gave some help at the Poly. But temperatures in the 70s canceled much of that benefit.

Edelen ran the fastest time in history, 2:14:28. Then he had to weather months of rumors that the course was short. A remeasurement finally put the shortage at 32 yards, and he'd added nearly twice that amount by taking a wrong turn.

He rolled on toward the Olympics with a 2:15:10 at Košice that fall and a 20-minute victory at the 1964 U.S. Trial. He then resumed hard work within a week of the Trial. In that first workout, Edelen felt, in Murphy's words, "the first sign of the injury every athlete fears. It was the injury from which he would not recover."

Sciatica hobbled him at the Tokyo Olympics, where he placed sixth. His greatest marathon may have been his last, when in 1965 he came within six seconds of his best time despite complaining to his diary that "the sciatica was sheer hell the last six miles."

Buddy Edelen went on to teach at Adams State College and now lives in Tulsa. At 54, he won't trust his legs to race but they still let him run.

[Edelen died in 1997 of cancer at age 59.]

efficiency, running. *See* economy, running.

ekiden. The Japanese word for a marathon road relay, the *ekiden* is usually run as roughly three 5Ks, two 10Ks, and the odd 7.2K. World Championships were contested in this event through 1998. The ekiden (Anglicized pronunciation "ECK-uh-din") traces its roots to an ancient Japanese mail-delivery system, a sort of human Pony Express in which runners handed messages one to the next. In Japan the runners still wear a sash that simulates a mail pouch. *See also* relays; World Marathon Relay.

Electrolyte Replacement with Glucose (ERG). In the 1970s San Diego Marathoner Bill Gookin formulated this alternative to Gatorade, said to meet better the specific needs of runners. It was inevitably nicknamed "Gookinaid." *See also* drinks, running.

Elite Racing (www.eliteracing.com). The San Diego-based company conducts races—among them the Carlsbad 5K, Rock 'n' Roll Marathon, and Country Music Marathon—and produces a television series featuring top races, also called *Elite Racing*, on ESPN. *See also* Carlsbad 5K; Reavis, Toni; Rock 'n' Roll Marathon; television.

El Mouaziz, Abdelkader (also spelled Abdelkhader) (b. January 1, 1969). Just six weeks after placing seventh in the 2000 Olympic Marathon, this Moroccan won the New York City Marathon. He was the 1999 London winner in 2:07:57 and set a PR of 2:07:11 at London in 2001. El Mouaziz became the top marathoner in his country by default when Khalid Khannouchi changed his citizenship to the United States. *See also* London Marathon, New York City Marathon.

El Ouafi, Boughera (b. October 18, 1898). The North African colonial won the 1928 Olympic

When Khalid Khannouchi gave up his Moroccan citizenship to become a U.S. citizen, Abdelkader El Mouaziz became Morocco's top marathoner; he won London in 1999 and New York in 2000.

© Mark Shearman. Athletics-Images.

From the collection of Dr. Edward H. Kozloff–Motor City Striders.

Boughera El Ouafi, an Arab born in Algeria, ran in the 1928 Amsterdam Olympic Marathon wearing the uniform of France. He won the gold medal, after having placed seventh at the Paris Olympics four years before. This picture is on a tobacco card from the late 1920s.

gold for France in the marathon in 2:32:57, giving an early hint about the wave of Africans to arrive decades later. The next native of that continent to win at the Games was Alain Mimoun, who also ran for France, in 1956. *See also* Mimoun, Alain; Olympic Marathon 1900 to 2000.

Emmons, Julia (b. July 29, 1941). She has long been a solid presence on the active running scene in Atlanta as executive director of the Atlanta Track Club, which hosts the Peachtree 10K and Atlanta Marathon. Emmons also directed the marathons at the 1996 Olympic Games, and she has served in various capacities with USA Track & Field. *See also* Atlanta Marathon; Peachtree 10K; Professional Road Running Association.

Endurance. *See* Gebrselassie, Haile; movies.

entry limits. One penalty of the expansion of the sport in all racing distances, and particularly the marathon, has been that not everyone can run everywhere. Some races (Boston, Olympic Marathon Trials) are limited by time standards. Others (the New York City Marathon is the best example) draw the line at how many runners can enter. *See also* "Full Marathons" on next page; qualifying times.

Full Marathons

From Joe Henderson's *Running Commentary,* June 1999.

America no longer produces any of the world's best marathoners, but we bring out the *most*. Some critics in this country would connect these two facts. They would say that our country now places too much emphasis on participating in marathons and not enough on excelling in them.

Americans certainly turn out in great numbers. More than 400,000 people, a record high, entered our marathons last year. A handful of these events are big enough to earn the title *megaraces*. The New York City Marathon regularly tops 30,000 entrants. Honolulu has risen above that figure on occasion. Three other marathons in this country—Los Angeles, Rock 'n' Roll, Chicago—stand at or near 20,000 [1999 figures].

Many of them could be bigger yet, and others could grow just as large, if they allowed unlimited entries. More than 50,000 would run New York if the streets and bridges could accommodate that many. Instead, this race cuts off entries when they reach a specified number that changes from year to year. It fills within days—months before race day.

The Boston Marathon is the only annual race in this country to restrict entries through qualifying times. Even while requiring performances as fast as 3:10, the race draws more than 12,000 runners. Boston showed its immense popularity by easing requirements in 1996; the field exploded to almost 40,000.

Restricting race fields is the most talked-about trend of the moment in this country. "Full marathon" has taken on a new meaning. It no longer distinguishes the 42-kilometer event from the half-marathon; it designates events that have filled to capacity and are accepting no more runners.

This happens in events as large as the New York City Marathon and as small as Napa Valley (which topped out at 1,800 runners this year). Perhaps the hottest ticket is for St. George in Utah. *Runner's World* once designated its course as fastest in the United States, and marathoners have lined up to enter ever since.

People who apply too late for the full races are now voicing some frustration. Many of the complaints come from self-proclaimed "serious runners," who blame less-serious participants for shutting them out. The purists claim that marathons are running contests—not the walk-when-you-feel-like it, take-as-long-as-you-wish events they now appear to be in this country.

The purists' wrath is directed especially at the fastest-growing group of marathoners, those who participate as organized groups to raise money for charity. The biggest and best-known is Team in Training, which collects funds for leukemia research.

The *Washington Post* carried a story this spring that quoted runners who couldn't get into the 16,000-person Marine Corps Marathon. They complained that 25 percent of spots were reserved for the charities, which in turn kept that many "real runners" from entering this October event that filled up in March.

This conflict strains the traditionally friendly relations between marathoners of all abilities and sours the welcoming atmosphere of our races. It's unfortunate and unnecessary in a country where dozens of other marathons would be thrilled to take in runners displaced by the few races that put up the "sold out" sign.

EPO. *See* erythropoietin. *See also* drug testing.

Equinox Marathon (www.equinoxmarathon. org). Alaskans run on cross-country ski trails each September while waiting for the snow to fly. They've done this since 1963, making Equinox, run on a mix of roads and trails, one of the oldest marathons. *See also* oldest races.

ERG. *See* Electrolyte Replacement with Glucose.

erythropoietin (EPO). This naturally occurring hormone in the blood (in low levels) is responsible for stimulating red blood cell production and thus increasing the capacity of the blood to transport oxygen to working muscles. Synthetically produced EPO is the drug of choice among some elite distance runners (and many elite endurance cyclists), producing effects similar to altitude training. Although the drug is hard to detect at present, reliable blood tests are being developed. *See also* drug testing.

Espinosa, Andres (b. February 4, 1963). The Mexican held the North American marathon record at 2:07:19 until new U.S. citizen Khalid Khannouchi broke it in 2000. Espinosa was the 1993 New York City winner. *See also* New York City Marathon.

Ethiopian runners. A hotbed of distance-running talent for even longer than its East African neighbor, Kenya, Ethiopia (formerly Abyssinia) first burst onto the distance-running landscape in 1960 with Abebe Bikila's Olympic Marathon gold at Rome. Then came his repeat performance at Tokyo in 1964 and a gold by teammate Mamo Wolde in Mexico City in 1968.

Subjugated by Italy before World War II, Ethiopia shuttered its borders following the war, so little news escaped. Haile Selassie ruled as emperor of Ethiopia from 1930 from the capital Addis Ababa, surrounding himself with a palace guard and a standing army to maintain his dominion. Foreign coaches were brought into the country in the wake of a poor tentative showing at the 1956 Olympics at Melbourne. From that coaching a distance-running force was created, built on Addis Ababa's high altitude, the fact that most Ethiopians traveled by foot, and the government's authority to impose armylike discipline on runners.

Even during the 1960s, when Ethiopian marathoners were dominant on the world stage, their appearances outside the country were carefully orchestrated. After a period in the late 1970s and early 1980s when East African countries were no longer dominating the sport of long-distance running, they staged a telling comeback in the 1990s—a comeback that has only continued to grow. Ethiopian women took their place among the world leaders in the 1990s, most dramatically in the person of Fatuma Roba, the Atlanta Olympic Marathon champion and three-time Boston winner. *See also* Abera, Gezahegne; Bikila, Abebe; Gebrselassie, Haile; Roba, Fatuma; Wolde, Mamo; World Marathon Relay.

ethylene vinyl acetate (EVA). This lighter, more shock-absorbent material was invented in 1974 by David Schwaber for use in Brooks running shoes to replace the typical rubber midsoles. It became an industry standard for many years until Nike introduced their "air" and Asics their gel midsoles.

Eugene, Oregon. The self-proclaimed "running capital of the United States" was the site of two Olympic Trials that selected the country's best marathon teams ever. Frank Shorter went on to win a gold in 1972, and in 1976 Shorter won silver while Kenny Moore and Don Kardong tied for fourth. *See also* Olympians, U.S.; Olympic Trials Marathon, U.S.

European Championships. Another once-great marathon race that has suffered at the hands of professional big-city marathons in recent years, the European Championships remains one of the biggest prizes a runner from Europe can win. And they don't have to compete against anyone from Africa!

EVA. *See* ethylene vinyl acetate.

even pacing. *See* negative splits; pacing.

Exceed. Produced by Ross Labs, Exceed is worthy sports-drink competition for Gatorade. When Exceed began to show its muscle, Quaker Oats, owner of Gatorade, stepped up to the plate with massive advertising and marketing and beat it back. *See also* drinks, running.

Once one of the most competitive marathon races in the world, the European Championships (pictured here in Budapest in 1998) have fallen on hard times as many of the most competitive athletes turn instead to big-city, big-money races.

European Championships Marathon Winners

Sergey Popov set a world record in the 1958 continental race. Two women from Portugal, Rosa Mota and Manuela Machado, have won all five races to date. * = event record.

WOMEN

Year	Place	Athlete	Time
1982	Athens	Rosa Mota (Portugal)	2:36:04
1986	Stuttgart	Rosa Mota (Portugal)	2:28:38
1990	Split	Rosa Mota (Portugal)	2:31:27
1994	Helsinki	Manuela Machado (Portugal)	2:29:54
1998	Budapest	Manuela Machado (Portugal)	2:27:10*

MEN

Year	Place	Athlete	Time
1934	Turin	Armas Toivonen (Finland)	2:52:29
1938	Paris	Vaino Muinonen (Finland)	2:37:29
1942	(not run)		
1946	Oslo	Mikko Heitanen (Finland)	2:24:55
1950	Brussels	Jack Holden (Britain)	2:32:14
1954	Berne	Veikko Karvonen (Finland)	2:24:52
1958	Stockholm	Sergey Popov (USSR)	2:15:17
1962	Belgrade	Brian Kilby (Britain)	2:23:19
1966	Budapest	Jim Hogan (Britain)	2:20:05
1970	Athens	Ron Hill (Britain)	2:16:48
1974	Rome	Ian Thompson (Britain)	2:13:19
1978	Prague	Leonid Moiseyev (USSR)	2:11:58
1982	Athens	Gerard Nijboer (Holland)	2:15:16
1986	Stuttgart	Gelindo Bordin (Italy)	2:10:54
1990	Split	Gelindo Bordin (Italy)	2:14:02
1994	Helsinki	Martin Fiz (Spain)	2:10:31*
1998	Budapest	Stefano Baldini (Italy)	2:12:01

expos. The great shopping mall and meet-and-greet gathering places at road races, expositions, or expos, are typically held one or two days before the running itself. Before expos appeared at road races, *Runner's World* held "open houses," essentially one-company expos open to visiting runners.

Eyestone, Ed (b. June 15, 1961). A rangy runner with wide-ranging talents, he was a three-time NCAA champion on the track and a 1988 and 1992 Olympic marathoner who also competed in the 1995 Worlds. At home he won national 10K, half-marathon, and marathon titles and set an American 25K record (1:14:38 in 1991) that still stands. Eyestone now coaches distance runners at his alma mater, Brigham Young University. *See also* "Ahead for

Ed" on next page; Bay to Breakers 12K; Hall of Fame, RRCA; national half-marathon champions, U.S.; national marathon champions, U.S.; national 10K champions, U.S.; Olympians, U.S.; Olympic Trials Marathon, U.S.; Peachtree 10K; records, American; World Championships, U.S.

© Mark Shearman, Athletics—Images.

Ed Eyestone was one of America's most flexible runners. He ran for the U.S. Olympic marathon team in 1988 and 1992 and now coaches at his alma mater, Brigham Young.

Ahead for Ed

From Joe Henderson's *Running Commentary,* June 2000.

Possibly the toughest job in college sports (and high school, for that matter) is coaching distance runners. The job offers little glory and low pay, especially if the coach is a track assistant.

The bigger test, though, is the competitive year. Other sports have a season. Running has seasons that bump into each other—cross country leading to indoor track to outdoor track to racing that extends well into the summer for some runners. The coach never gets much of an off-season.

Ed Eyestone knows all of this. He sampled it while coaching for three years at Weber State. Then his dream job opened up. Brigham Young University, his old school, offered to make him its cross country coach and track assistant. He couldn't say yes fast enough. The burden of multiple-season coaching doesn't bother him. He's familiar with the routine from his own running career (three-time NCAA champion at BYU and later a two-time Olympian).

Eyestone is from the first generation of runners who spent all of their postcollege years in a professional sport. Some have trouble, as their talents wane, with finding a job for the rest of their working lives. Ed prepared for this shift. Trained in exercise science (and writing a monthly column for *Runner's World* on the subject), he isn't just an old jock who goes into coaching by default.

He reminds me most of Steve Plasencia. He too has an academic background in the science of exercise. A few years ago Steve began coaching distance runners at his alma mater, the University of Minnesota. Plasencia's running didn't end there. He enjoyed several more years of top-level masters running before vowing this spring to ease off at age 43.

Ed Eyestone turns 40 in June 2001. He has masters plans of his own, running races as they fit into BYU's busy year.

Ezzher, Mohamed (b. April 26, 1950). The Moroccan-born Frenchman broke the long-standing world masters marathon record with 2:10:33 at Paris in April 2001. He was the first runner 40 years of age or older to crack 2:11. *See* records, world age-group.

F

Falmouth. The annual seven-mile race on Cape Cod, Massachusetts, has long drawn many of the world's best runners. The cofounder was Tommy Leonard, famed bartender at Boston's now-defunct Eliot Lounge, a runners' hangout, especially over Boston Marathon weekend.

Fanelli, Gary (b. October 24, 1950). The clown prince of road racing is best known for running in his many disguises, including Elwood Blues and Chester Polyester. But he also had 2:14:16 marathon speed at one time. He represented American Samoa in the Olympics and holds that country's marathon record at 2:25:35, set at the Seoul Games. At a Boston Marathon expo in the early 1980s, while Gary did his Elwood Blues shtick before an amused crowd, the marathon's gatekeeper Jock Semple stage-whispered, "Look a' that foolishness. He's up thar ruinin' my race 'n eeeevvverythin' it stands fer. Why, I oughta . . . ."

fartlek. This form of interval training, developed by the Scandinavians, is more free flowing than track intervals in that the intervals of a fartlek can be run between telephone poles or road signs or two-story houses. The idea is to include in a regular run surges of faster running, ranging anywhere from half a minute (or less) to three minutes long (or more). Translated from Swedish, the term means "speed play." We had to include it here because the word is so much fun to say and write and because we're sure that to the regular walking-around world it sounds gross.

fastest races. A race can be fast simply because the fastest people run there and they would be speedy on almost any course. *Runner's World* once judged the St. George Marathon to be the fastest race in the United States at that distance (and the race sold out quicker than ever before the next year). This race is aided—by a significant net loss in elevation and potentially by a tailwind—as are many of the races that appear to be fastest: Boston (in its weather-friendly years), the Deseret News 10K, Pittsburgh 10K, and especially the Alta 8K in Utah and Fontana 5K and Half-Marathon in California. Fast unaided courses depend heavily on favorable weather, so it's difficult to say which unaided courses will rank consistently at the top. *See also* aided courses; records, American; records, world.

Fifty-Plus Fitness Association (www.50plus.org). Longevity expert Walter Bortz, MD, is the guiding force behind this organization, which promotes active aging. The group also gives the Emil Zatopek Award at its annual convention and road race.

Fifty Staters (50+D.C.). A loose organization run by founder Dean Rademaker, 50+D.C. is made up of runners who've completed a marathon in all U.S. states and D.C. As the year 2001 began, the group boasted 130 members, some of whom had made multiple trips through all the states. Many have gone on to race in all the Canadian provinces, and some on all continents.

Fila (www.fila.com). A relatively new player in the high-stakes running-shoe game, the Italian company supports many of the top Kenyans. Dr. Gabriele Rosa also scouts out and coaches many of Fila's athletes. He started the Discovery USA program in 2000 to mimic Discovery Kenya, which has operated successfully since 1991. *See* Discovery USA; Rosa, Dr. Gabriele; shoe companies.

Filutze, Barbara (b. June 21, 1946). In her late 40s she was peerless among American women her age. The Pennsylvanian still holds national age 45–49 records for 5K (17:14), 10K (35:57 plus 34:40 aided), and the marathon (2:45:11). *See also* records, American age-group.

financial awards. *See* professional racing.

5K. Formerly looked down on as merely a fun run, it is now the most popular road-race distance. Much of its growth comes from the wildly popular Race for the Cure and Corporate Challenge (at a slightly longer 3.5 miles) series. Five kilometers is the perfect place for a novice to begin and for a vet to do speedwork. *See also* distances, metric and English.

Fixx, Jim (b. 1932; d. 1984). An overweight smoker, the magazine editor took up running, became addicted to it, and wrote *The Complete Book of Running* (Random House, 1977), the sport's all-time hardbound best-seller. Critics of running took ill-disguised delight in his death, which occurred while he was running at age 52. But by making the lifestyle changes he did, he outlived his father by a decade. And yes, that is Jim's leg on the cover of the book. *See also* "Fixx-ation" on next page; books; *Complete Book of Running, The.*

Fiz, Martin (b. March 3, 1963). In the 1990s Spanish men showed a special knack for peaking at championship races. They won three straight World Marathon Championships, starting with Fiz's victory in 1995. He also won the European title in 1994 and Rotterdam in 1995 with 2:08:57—the year he led the world rankings. *See also* European Championships; rankings, *Track & Field News*; Rotterdam Marathon; World Championships medalists.

Fleet Feet (www.fleetfeet.com). The running boom of the 1970s (Running Boom I) spawned many chains of running shops in the United States. The major survivor is Fleet Feet, founded by marathoner-ultrarunner-triathlete

Fixx-ation

From Joe Henderson's *Running Commentary,* December 1998.

This is getting old—14 years old, to be exact. Whenever any runner dies, for whatever reason, some reporter will march out the name of Jim Fixx and suggest that running is to blame. It happened again, predictably, this fall when Florence Griffith Joyner died. That was quite a reach, to compare a 54-year-old marathoner with a 38-year-old ex-sprinter. FloJo was no quick Fixx.

Two reporters from the *Chicago Tribune* really outdid themselves. They linked three deaths from unrelated ailments. The only connection was that the three victims all were, or had been, runners of some sort.

The *Tribune*'s story ran under the headline "Marathon Death Stirs Questions." It began by reporting that a 43-year-old woman, Kelly Barrett, had died after collapsing 24 miles into the marathon. She went into cardiac arrest in a medical tent and never recovered. Fair enough. That was news. But then the reporters continued into speculation that bordered on an indictment of all distance running.

"Barrett's death raises questions that have attended the deaths of famous athletes ranging from marathoner Jim Fixx in 1984 to Olympic sprinter Florence Griffith Joyner in September," wrote Jeremy Manier and Julie Deardorff. "Many physicians wonder if the grueling trial of a 26-mile marathon is worth the risk."

The writers quoted a cardiologist. He said that moderate exercise is good for our health, but marathons aren't moderate or healthy. Then the story quoted a source who wasn't an expert or unemotional. Kelly Barrett's unnamed brother said he couldn't see why anyone runs marathons "just because some bozo in ancient Greece did it. I don't think people are designed to run that far. And for what—to say you did it? It seems so senseless."

This report went on to say that 300 runners asked for medical help at the Chicago Marathon. Casual readers might think that number high if they don't notice that the figure is 1.5 percent of the day's runners and it included all conditions from blisters on up. Deaths in U.S. road races each year number about one in a million runners, from all causes.

Back to the three deaths noted in the story. To link them is to compare apples, tomatoes, and potatoes. Jim Fixx didn't die while running a marathon but during a routine training run. He was found to have badly clogged coronary arteries, the most common cause for a fatal attack in a runner.

Florence Griffith Joyner was never a distance runner (her longest race was a 5K), and she retired from sprinting nearly 10 years before her death. Its cause (discovered after the *Chicago Tribune* story appeared) wasn't a heart condition but complications of epilepsy, and she died in bed.

Kelly Barrett's death, the only one of the three with any connection to a marathon, resulted from a rhythm disturbance in her heartbeat—a different condition from Fixx's.

These cases don't relate to each other in any way except their outcome. They don't label distance running as dangerous.

Sally Edwards. Fleet Feet still thrives with Tom Raynor in charge, with three dozen stores nationwide.

Tom Fleming (#5), two-time winner of the New York City Marathon, has consistently been an advocate of high-mileage training. Here he trails Geoff Smith at the 1984 Boston Marathon.

Fleming, Tom (b. July 23, 1951). A two-time winner of the New York City Marathon (1973 and 1975) when it was still run within Central Park, hard-training (high mileage combined with plenty of racing and speedwork) Jersey Tom found a coveted title at Boston barely eluding him. He took 2nd there in 1973 and 1974, 3rd in 1975, 6th in 1977, 10th in 1978, and 4th in 1979. A 4:12 miler, he had a marathon PR of 2:12. He is today an outstanding coach, working with runners such as Joe LeMay. *See also* LeMay, Joe; New York City Marathon.

flexibility. *See* stretching exercises.

Flores, Doroteo (b. February 11, 1922). Top runners from Central America are extremely rare today, but in 1952 Flores, from Guatemala, won at Boston in 2:31:53. He followed up with a gold medal in the 1955 Pan-American Games Marathon. *See also* Boston Marathon; Pan-American Games.

fluid intake. *See* drinks, running.

Fontana, California. This city is the scene of a superaided half-marathon and lesser-aided 5K races. The courses descend at far more than the one-meter-per-kilometer limit for records. Current American men's "bests" (another designation for aided times) at both distances were set here. *See* fastest races; records, American.

foods, runners'. Runners are a marketer's dream. They're always looking for an edge they can take by mouth. Supplements are wildly popular in running. As for actual nourishment, runners take it from a variety of energy bars and gels. Early entries here were PowerBar, GU, and PowerGel. The marketers are doubly thrilled because after runners make it cool to consume these items, the public gets into the act and begins devouring them. Consider the ubiquity of PowerBars and their imitators. *See also* bars, sports.

Footnotes (www.rrca.org). As official publication of the Road Runners Club of America, it stands second in circulation only to *Runner's World* among U.S. magazines. *See also* Road Runners Club of America.

Forshaw, Joseph (b. May 13, 1880; d. November 26, 1964). A rare three-time Olympian, his first appearance was in the semiofficial Games of 1906. Forshaw won the bronze medal in 1908 behind Johnny Hayes for the only two-medal performances ever by U.S. marathoners at a fully recognized Games. *See also* Olympians, U.S.; Olympic medalists.

Foster, Jack (b. May 23, 1932). The New Zealander rewrote the entire concept of aging when, in 1974 at the Commonwealth Games Marathon at Christchurch, he took the silver medal behind Ian Thompson by running 2:11:19. Foster was 41 years old. In the process, he beat world record-holder Derek Clayton of Australia and world-beater Ron Hill of England. Foster trained hard, running off-road across the hills of New Zealand. His secret was that he never ran himself into the ground—and he ran with a glee fueled

Jack Foster of New Zealand put a spike in the heart of the idea that age robs you of speed; at the 1974 Commonwealth Games, at age 41, he took second place with a 2:11:19.

© Mark Shearman. Athletics-Images.

by his love of the sport. His Commonwealth medal was hardly a fluke. He'd already competed in the 1972 Olympics, and in 1975 he traveled to Honolulu and won the race outright, knocking six minutes off the course record with 2:17:24, improving on Jeff Galloway's winning time of the previous year.

Although Foster retired from serious running in his 50s because of chronic leg problems and some breathing problems, he didn't stagnate. Instead, he jumped into competitive cycling, his fitness translating nicely across disciplines. Foster is credited, rightly so, with spearheading a renaissance of masters running. His world record for a masters marathon was first broken in 1990 by fellow New Zealander John Campbell, who uncorked a 2:11:04 at Boston, also at age 41. Sticklers felt that Foster's mark of 2:11:19 was still the world record, however (because Boston is an aided course) until Mohamed Ezzher broke the record at Paris in 2001 with a time of 2:10:33. *See also* Honolulu Marathon; records, world age-group.

four-hour marathon. In Running Boom I, the big goal was to break three hours, or to run slightly faster than seven minutes per mile. The big goal of the average marathoner in Running Boom II is to break four hours, or a little faster than nine minutes per mile. Dave Kuehls even wrote a briskly selling book titled *Four Months to a Four-Hour Marathon* (Perigree, 1998). *See also* Kuehls, Dave; Running Boom II; three-hour marathon.

Fowler, Robert (b. 1882; date of death unknown). His record in two Olympics is two DNFs. Two other U.S. Olympians, Mike Ryan and Michael Spring, share that honor. Fowler, however, set world and American marathon records of 2:52:46 in 1909. *See also* Olympians, U.S; record progressions, American; record progressions, world.

Fox, Terry (b. July 28, 1958; d. 1980). People who run the annual May marathon in Vancouver, Canada, have a psychological advantage over other marathoners. The race begins on the street in front of B.C. Place, one of the few remnants of that city's Expo 1986. To reach the start, most runners must walk across the plaza at B.C. Place Stadium. On the plaza, facing West Georgia Street, is an arch built in tribute to Terry Fox, a young man from British Columbia who, after losing a leg to cancer in 1977, set out in the spring of 1980 to run across Canada from east to west to raise money for cancer research.

He referred to his journey as "The Marathon of Hope." As the cancer spread and he was forced off the course in Thunder Bay, Ontario, he said, "I want to live. And if I can get out there again and finish the run, I will." He never did. The cancer killed him, but it didn't even dent his dream. He raised some $20 million during his 3,339-mile trek.

The Terry Fox Arch is a favorite meeting place of runners about to compete in the Vancouver International Marathon, and it serves as an inspiration to put your best into going the distance. In 1983 a film of Terry Fox's life, *The*

Terry Fox Story, was released. Leslie Schrivener wrote a biography, *Terry Fox: His Story*, which was published in 1981 by Canada's McClelland and Stewart Ltd.

fractures, stress. *See* injuries.

Frank, Norm (b. June 20, 1931). America's most prolific marathoner has run the distance more than 700 times and is still going. Although he long ago broke the seemingly unbeatable record of 524 by Sy Mah, both totals pale beside that of German Horst Preisler, who in 2000 logged his 1,000th race of marathon or longer distance. *See also* Mah, Sy; Preisler, Horst.

Frank, William (b. December 12,1879; date of death unknown). The 1906 U.S. Olympian won a bronze medal at Athens in 3:00:47. *See also* Olympians, U.S.; Olympic medalists.

Freihofer's Run for Women (www.freihofersrun.com). Albany, New York, is the perennial site of the national 5K and the scene of several records. Freihofer's Bakery is a loyal sponsor, and George Regan is the longtime director of the race, usually held in late May or early June. *See also* national 5K champions, U.S.; records, American.

Fujita, Atsushi (b. November 6, 1976). The placement of his listing is fitting. It comes right before Fukuoka, the scene of his biggest day. In 2000 Fujita not only won that race in course-record time but also beat the reigning Olympic gold medalist and defending Fukuoka champion, Gezahenge Abera, and set Japanese and Asian records of 2:06:51. *See also* Fukuoka Marathon.

Fukuoka Marathon. Long before there was a World Cup Marathon or a World Championship Marathon, there was—and still is—the Fukuoka Marathon, an invitation-only, men-only race that has been run in Japan since 1947. Because the course is an out-and-back and therefore unaided, it is a preferred venue for serious marathoners who want to post a legitimate time while running against the best in the world.

In many years the caliber of the Fukuoka Marathon has far outshone the Olympic Marathon field. It has also been the site of two world records (Derek Clayton's 2:09:37 in 1967 and Rob de Castella's 2:08:18 in 1981). It has also helped make legends of Frank Shorter (who won four years in a row, 1971 to 1974), Jerome Drayton (three wins: 1969, 1975, and 1976), and Toshihiko Seko (who won three years in a row, 1978, 1979, 1980, then again in 1983). Traditionally run in early December, the weather is typically excellent for good performances.

Fultz, Jack (b. August, 27, 1948). He won the hottest Boston Marathon ever, the infamous 1976 "Run for the Hoses" when the starting-line temperature shimmered at 97 degrees F. Fultz ran 2:20:19 that year but PRed with 2:11:18 while placing fourth in 1978. He now coaches runners who are part of a spe-

Fukuoka Marathon Winners

This race became the model for Japanese races that followed. It has remained single-sex even after the arrival of women in the sport, and it became invitational after the arrival of the masses. For more than a quarter century starting in the mid-1950s, it was the world's preeminent annual race for men. * = event record.

Year	Athlete	Time
1947	Toshikazu Wada (Japan)	2:45:45
1948	Saburo Yamada (Japan)	2:37:25
1949	Sinzo Koga (Japan)	2:40:26
1950	Shunji Koyanagi (Japan)	2:30:47
1951	Hiroyoshi Haigo (Japan)	2:30:13
1952	Katsuo Nishida (Japan)	2:27:59
1953	Hideo Hamamura (Japan)	2:27:26
1954	Reinaldo Gorno (Argentina)	2:24:55
1955	Veikko Karvonen (Finland)	2:23:16
1956	Keizo Yamada (Japan)	2:25:15
1957	Kurao Hiroshima (Japan)	2:21:40
1958	Nobuyoshi Sadanaga (Japan)	2:24:01
1959	Kurao Hiroshima (Japan)	2:29:34
1960	Barry Magee (New Zealand)	2:19:04
1961	Pavel Kantorek (Czechoslovakia)	2:22:05
1962	Toru Terasawa (Japan)	2:16:19
1963	Jeff Julian (New Zealand)	2:18:01
1964	Toru Terasawa (Japan)	2:14:49
1965	Hidekuni Hiroshima (Japan)	2:18:36
1966	Mike Ryan (New Zealand)	2:14:05
1967	Derek Clayton (Australia)	2:09:37
1968	Bill Adcocks (Britain)	2:10:48
1969	Jerome Drayton (Canada)	2:11:13
1970	Akio Usami (Japan)	2:10:38
1971	Frank Shorter (U.S.)	2:12:51
1972	Frank Shorter (U.S.)	2:10:30
1973	Frank Shorter (U.S.)	2:11:45
1974	Frank Shorter (U.S.)	2:11:32
1975	Jerome Drayton (Canada)	2:10:09
1976	Jerome Drayton (Canada)	2:12:35
1977	Bill Rodgers (U.S.)	2:10:56
1978	Toshihiko Seko (Japan)	2:10:21
1979	Toshihiko Seko (Japan)	2:10:35
1980	Toshihiko Seko (Japan)	2:09:45
1981	Rob de Castella (Australia)	2:08:18
1982	Paul Ballinger (New Zealand)	2:10:15
1983	Toshihiko Seko (Japan)	2:08:52
1984	Takeyuki Nakayama (Japan)	2:10:00
1985	Masanari Shintaku (Japan)	2:09:51

Year	Athlete	Time
1986	Juma Ikangaa (Tanzania)	2:10:06
1987	Takeyuki Nakayama (Japan)	2:08:18
1988	Toshihiro Shibutani (Japan)	2:11:04
1989	Manuel Matias (Portugal)	2:12:54
1990	Belayneh Dinsamo (Ethiopia)	2:11:35
1991	Shuichi Morita (Japan)	2:10:58
1992	Tena Negere (Ethiopia)	2:09:04
1993	Dionicio Ceron (Mexico)	2:08:51
1994	Boay Akonay (Tanzania)	2:09:45
1995	Luiz Dos Santos (Brazil)	2:09:30
1996	Lee Bong Ju (Korea)	2:10:48
1997	Josia Thugwane (South Africa)	2:07:28
1998	Jackson Kibiga (Kenya)	2:08:48
1999	Gezahegne Abera (Ethiopia)	2:07:54
2000	Atsushi Fujita (Japan)	2:06:51*

cial fund-racing effort for cancer research at the Boston Marathon. *See also* Boston Marathon.

fun runs. *Runner's World* instigated this nationwide (later worldwide) program of races at several distances in an informal setting, launched in 1973. A list of fun-run sites was carried for many years in the back of the magazine until the sheer volume became too unwieldy. The concept set the style for mass-migration events that followed in later decades. See also *Runner's World.*

Gabeau, Henley (b. February 14, 1944). Preface all her credentials with Road Runners Club of America. She was its first female president (from 1989 to 1990), its first paid executive director (1990 to 2001), and a member of its hall of fame (inducted in 1985). Henley was the right woman in the right place at the right time as women's running came of age in the 1980s.

She was also extremely active in U.S. team leadership roles: manager of the 1982 women's IAAF World 10K Championships team, coach and manager of the junior men's cross country team for the IAAF World Championships in Warsaw in 1987, manager of the 1989 women's ekiden team competing in Japan, 1991 manager of the women's team competing in the IAAF World 15K Championships in the Netherlands, manager of the track and field women's team at the IAAF World Indoor Championships in Toronto in 1993, manager of the women's 1995 team at the Pan-American Games in Argentina, and track and field athletics chief records officer at the 1996 Olympic Games.

On the running side, Henley took fourth place in the 1976 Marine Corps Marathon and won the 1977 and 1979 North Carolina Track Club Marathon. She has a 10K PR of 39:25 and a marathon PR of 3:08. *See also* Hall of Fame, RRCA; Road Runners Club of America.

Gailly, Etienne (b. November 26, 1922). The gutsy Belgian led the marathon in Olympic Stadium at the 1948 London Games, but his pacing was erratic He was passed twice—by Delfo Cabrera and Tom Richards—before he staggered, exhausted, across the finish line to salvage the bronze medal. *See also* Olympic medalists.

Galloway, Jeff. *See* page 114.

Galloway's Book on Running. First self-published in the mid-1980s, then picked up by Shelter Publishing, Jeff's book probably ranks second in sales only to Jim Fixx's similarly named *The Complete Book of Running*—and may rank first by the end of the current decade. *See also* books; Galloway, Jeff.

Garcia, Salvador (b. November 1, 1963). The grim-faced Mexican peaked in a five-month period of 1991–1992, winning New York City in the fall of 1991 and Rotterdam the next spring. *See also* New York City Marathon; Rotterdam Marathon.

Galloway, Jeff (b. July 12, 1945). Although he is frequently identified with the marathon, Jeff was never an Olympic marathoner. He competed in the 10,000 meters in the 1972 Olympics—something of a fluke because he and friend Jack Bacheler made the team in the "wrong" events (see sidebar below). Jeff rose to prominence in the late 1970s with a national chain of franchised running stores called Phidippides, which spawned summer running camps (especially at Squaw Valley near Lake Tahoe).

After an oversaturation of running books in the wake of the running boom of the late 1970s to early 1980s, a trough developed when most of the books went out of print. In 1984 Jeff jumped into that trough by self-publishing *Galloway's Book on Running*, which he sold and promoted at his camps, at talks he gave, and through what was left of his chain of running stores.

Between the book and Jeff's tireless personal appearances, his fame grew tremendously. He began putting together marathon-training groups and in the 1990s expanded their appeal by preaching the use of walking breaks during marathons to make the event accessible to more people. To further accommodate the growing lust for information on marathon running, he published *Marathon!* (1996).

Jeff's wife, Barbara, runs marathons, and the couple has two sons who've inherited their parents' good running genes. The Galloways live in Atlanta, where Jeff was the sparkplug behind the founding of the now-famous July 4 Peachtree 10K Road Race in Atlanta. *See also* "Galloway Gallantry" below; books; camps, running; Hall of Fame, RRCA; Honolulu Marathon; Peachtree 10K; Phidippides; walk breaks.

Galloway Gallantry

From Joe Henderson's *Running Commentary,* September 2000.

Nominations are due this month for the RRCA's Browning Ross Award. It honors those like Ross, one of the organization's founders, for lifetime achievements in and service to the sport.

My first impulse was to cast a vote for Jeff Galloway, but I went with someone older, 81-year-old Ted Corbitt. Jeff, at 55, still has much of his life to live and his good work to continue. I think of him now, though, because of a note received from reader Ron Marianetti. At a Galloway camp this summer, Ron heard that Jeff had given up his spot on the 1972 Olympic Marathon team and wanted details.

When you hear that Jeff was an Olympian, it's easy to assume that it was as a marathoner. He has built much of his reputation around giving marathon advice. But he made the 10,000 team at the 1972 Trials, while his Florida Track Club teammate Jack Bacheler finished fourth but was disqualified for a bumping incident.

The marathon was run after the 10 that year. It would have been Jeff's better event, and the 10 would have been Jack's. As it was, Jeff paced his buddy through the marathon, then stepped aside at the end to let him place third. (Frank Shorter and Kenny Moore tied for first.) Jeff and Jack would have preferred to switch events, but officials wouldn't hear of it.

Bacheler went on to finish ninth at the Olympics. Galloway, who didn't make the 10,000 final, surely could have been a contender at his better distance. But I've never once heard him voice any regrets over his choice to help a friend. This story helps explain why Jeff became the revered figure he is in the sport.

Gareau, Jacqueline (b. March 10, 1953). While Rosie Ruiz was trying to figure out what a split was in a post-1980-Boston interview, the real winner of that race forever lost her moment in the spotlight; the award ceremony on a later date was little consolation. Gareau was for real, though, unlike faker Ruiz. Jacqueline was Canada's first (and still only) female winner at Boston and her country's first to break 2:30 (with 2:29:27 in 1983). She also represented Canada in the first Olympic Marathon for women but didn't finish. *See also* Boston Marathon.

Gatorade (www.gatorade.com). This product is the largest-selling sports drink in the Americas. *See* drinks, running.

Gebrselassie, Haile (b. April 18, 1973). Just recently a road racer, the two-time Olympic 10,000-meter champion has an excellent chance to break the marathon record should he choose to run his first serious race at that distance. His only known attempt was a low-key 2:38 as a teenager, an event featured in the documentary film on his life, *Endurance*. He won the 2001 Half-Marathon World Championships by one second over fellow Ethiopian

Haile Unlikely

From Joe Henderson's *Running Commentary*, August 2000.

Fred Lebow didn't make many wrong guesses about what would happen in the sport. But he missed by more than a mile when he forecast a sub-two-hour men's marathon by the year 2000.

Talk of this otherworldly time resurfaced with news that Haile Gebrselassie's marathon debut is coming in 2001. A *Washington Post* report says he "confides to friends that he will be satisfied with his efforts only if he can perform the almost superhuman feat of breaking the two-hour barrier."

It won't happen. Not next year, anyway, not for Geb and maybe not for anyone else in our lifetime.

Think about what running a two-hour marathon would mean. It would average about 4:35 per mile, or 28:25 for each 10K, and the best anyone has done so far is 4:48 and 29:45. Think of the percentages. Breaking the current record by 4.53 percent would equate to slashing 10 seconds from the mile mark. Think of half-marathon times. Few runners have ever broken one hour while stopping at that point, and the fastest of them (Paul Tergat at 59:17) is less than a minute under an hour. Think of marathon history. Almost six more minutes would have to come off the record. Marathoners took 32 years to trim the last six minutes, and 11 years to go from sub-2:07 to sub-2:06.

The barriers of 2:05, 2:04, 2:03, 2:02, and 2:01 still stand in the way of sub-2:00, and they grow taller each time. Gebrselassie might clear one or two of them, but even he isn't a big enough runner to leap them all. Let's celebrate incremental improvements instead of setting marathoners up to fail.

[Gebrselassie announced after winning his second straight Olympic 10,000—by less than a tenth of a second from Paul Tergat—that his road-racing plans were on indefinite hold because of chronic Achilles problems that required surgery after the 2000 Games. Tergat debuted in the marathon at London in 2001, placing second in 2:08:15.]

Tesfaye Jifar in 1:00:03. See also "Haile Unlikely" on page 123; Ethiopian runners; movies; World Half-Marathon Championships.

Geigengack, Bob (b. January 9, 1907; May 25, 1987). He coached both George Sheehan and Frank Shorter, 40 years apart, long before their road-running days. *See also* Hall of Fame, USATF.

Geiger, Betty Springs (b. June 12, 1961). She won the 1984 (32:51) and 1986 (32:13) national 10K and was cochamp (with Francie Larrieu Smith, 32:14) in 1985. She married her coach, Rollie Geiger, who still coaches track and field at North Carolina State University. *See also* national 10K champions, U.S.; Peachtree 10K; record progressions, American.

Roberta Gibb frequently ran the Boston Marathon in the 1960s, years before women were formally admitted. She hid in the bushes at the start and emerged when the starting gun was fired. This photo is from 1968.

© Jeff Johnson

gel. Asics provided this heel- and sole-cushioning innovation in the 1980s as an answer to Nike's introduction of air soles. Gel shoes remain prominent, as do air models, 20 years later. *See also* Asics; shoe companies.

gels. This basic food group of long-distance runners was first developed as GU out of Berkeley, California. Essentially, it's an energy goop, high in carbohydrate, that an endurance athlete can carry easily in a pocket and squeeze out of a Mylar-like packet directly into the mouth while on the run. *See also* foods, runners'; GU; PowerBar.

Gibb Welch, Roberta (b. 1942). Before Kathrine Switzer ran Boston with a number, free spirit Bobbi Gibb ran it numberless, just for the joy of it. She "won" three years straight—1966 (3:21:40), 1967 (3:27:17), and 1968 (3:30:00)—when the gentlemen in charge still considered women beneath recognition. *See also* Boston Marathon; Hall of Fame, RRCA.

Githuka, Peter (b. February 14, 1969). The Kenyan holds the current world 8K record with his 22:03 set at Kingsport, Tennessee, in 1996. *See also* records, world.

Giusto, Matt (b. November 25, 1966). This U.S. track Olympian also won a pair of national road titles, the 5K in 1994 (13:53) and the 10K in 1996 (27:59). *See also* national 5K champions, U.S.; national 10K champions, U.S.

Glasser, Dr. William (b. 1925). In 1976 he published the book *Positive Addiction*, which gave high praise to the psychological benefits of distance running. "I believe there are a number of addictions that are as good as [negative] addictions are harmful," he writes in the first chapter. "I call them positive addictions because they strengthen us and make our lives more satisfying. They exist in sharp contrast to the common or negative addictions like alcohol or heroin, which always weaken and often destroy us." His other best-seller was *Control Theory: A New Explanation of How We Control Our Lives* (1984). Sadly, his concept that we are in control of our own lives failed to take as the nation become more victim-oriented through the 1980s and 1990s.

Glover, Bob (birthdate unavailable). With coauthor Jack Shepherd, Bob has written one of the longest running and most authoritative series of running training books on the market, *The Runner's Handbook* (originally published by Penguin in 1978). Bob knows of what he speaks. A runner since the 1960s, he put together what he called the Hue Olympics in Vietnam in 1969, in a burned-out stadium that had been headquarters for the North Vietnamese Army. He was for a long time the fitness director of the New York City West Side YMCA. He eventually moved his talents to the New York Road Runners Club as the director of its educational programs. He founded and coached the elite women's running team, Atalanta.

It was Jack Shepherd who contributed the writing expertise to put Bob's training ideas on paper. Jack was a senior editor at *Look* magazine in the 1960s and has written for many of the major magazines in the United States. One of Jack's books, *The Forest Killers* (1975), was nominated for a National Book Award. He began Bob's running program and was so impressed that he insisted it be put between the covers of a book. The rest, as they say, is history. One of Bob's subsequent books, *The Competitive Runner's Handbook* (revised in 1999), was cowritten with his wife, Shelly-Lynn Florence Glover. *See also* books; New York Road Runners Club.

glycogen. This is the fuel of choice for the endurance-running body. Carbohydrate loading tends to increase the supply of glycogen, and lack of glycogen is the main reason for hitting the wall. *See also* carbohydrate loading; wall, the.

Gomes, Tawni (b. December 13, 1965). She lost 100 pounds after being inspired by Oprah Winfrey's marathon training, then founded a mass movement (the Connectors) based on Oprah's book, *Make the Connection* (1996). Gomes quit her job to devote her time to keeping a connection with her disciples, and she wrote a book of her own, *No More Excuses!* (2000). *See also* Connectors.

Gomez, Rodolfo (b. October 30, 1951). Best known for his stirring—and losing—"duel in the dust" with Alberto Salazar as they turned into the final

Rodolfo Gomez is best remembered for his late-race duel with Alberto Salazar at New York in 1982. Now a coach in his native Mexico, Gomez won Tokyo in 1981 and Rotterdam in 1982.

Central Park segment of the 1982 New York City Marathon, the Mexican did some impressive winning of his own—including the 1981 Tokyo Marathon and 1982 Rotterdam. Gomez is now a well-known and much-respected coach in Mexico. *See also* Bolder Boulder 10K; Rotterdam Marathon; Tokyo Marathons.

Gompers, Paul (b. February 4, 1964). A child prodigy of marathoning, he set an American junior record of 2:15:28 in 1983 that still stands. He matured into an Olympic Trials fourth placer in 1988 at age 24. *See also* records, American age-group.

Gookinaid. *See* Electrolyte Replacement with Glucose (ERG).

Gordon, Dave (b. August 30, 1959). Five years after breaking onto the international scene by winning the Honolulu Marathon, Gordon ran in the 1987 World Championships but didn't finish. *See also* Honolulu Marathon; World Championships, U.S.

Gore, Al (b. March 31, 1948). He was the highest-ranking U.S. government official (second-term vice president at the time) to finish a marathon when he slipped in under five hours at the 1997 Marine Corps Marathon while running with his two daughters.

Gore-Tex (www.goretex.com). Al Gore may have claimed to invent the Internet, but he didn't invent Gore-Tex, which predates the Internet. This was—and still is—a revolutionary fabric woven tight enough to keep out raindrops but loose enough to allow perspiration to percolate through. Gore-Tex is a real boon for running in inclement weather. Early proponents of the fabric were Early Winters and Moss Brown. *See also* clothing.

Gorman, Miki (b. August 9, 1935). Born in China of Japanese parents, Michiko Suwa emigrated to Pennsylvania in 1964, where she developed secretarial skills and worked as a nanny for an army colonel. When she married Michael Gorman, a businessman, she gave up her career and shut herself off from the outside world because of her naturally shy nature and her broken English.

Wanting to improve her body after they moved to Los Angeles in the late 1960s, she was eventually lured to the L.A. Athletic Club. But exercise classes bored her, so she tried running. There were not a great number of female runners, so she ran with the male members of the club—indoors. She received encouragement from most of her male teammates, which escalated once her obvious talents became apparent. She fell under the influence of the fabled coach Laszlo Tabori. He had her enter a marathon to use the first 10 miles as a training run. Urged on by the crowd, who informed her she was in the lead, she completed the entire marathon in 3:30, although she was walking at the end.

On December 2, 1973, she entered the Western Hemisphere Marathon in Culver City, California, and ran 2:46:36, an American record. The following spring she went to Boston and won by six minutes with a 2:47:11. She was 38 years old, long past what at that time was considered retirement age for runners.

After turning 40, Miki twice won New York City (1976 and 1977) when the race was brought out of Central Park and run

Miki Gorman become one of the world's most accomplished female road racers in the 1970s after she took up running as a way of improving her body image.

through the five boroughs. She also won Boston in 1977 with a 2:48:33. She stood all of five feet one, weighed 83 pounds, and was listed in the program as "housewife." She almost single-handedly redefined what mature women were capable of running. *See also* Boston Marathon; Hall of Fame, RRCA; New York City Marathon; record progressions, American; Tabori, Laszlo.

Gorno, Reinaldo (b. June 18, 1918). He didn't quite reach the gold-medal peak of fellow Argentineans Juan Carlos Zabala and Delfo Cabrera, but he did chase Emil Zatopek with a silver at the 1952 Olympics (2:25:35). Gorno also won at Fukuoka in 1954 (2:24:55). *See also* Fukuoka Marathon; Olympic medalists.

governing bodies. Start by knowing that the International Olympic Committee (IOC) has little direct power over road running (except the Olympic Marathon). Most of those policies, for the Games and globally, are made by the International Association of Athletics Federations (IAAF)—which governs all track and field. The IAAF is made up of hundreds of national governing bodies. In the United States, the franchise belongs to USA Track & Field (previously known as The Athletics Congress, or TAC, and before that as the Amateur Athletic Union, or AAU). Under the blanket of USATF fall many groups that guide the activities of runners—long-distance running committees for men and women; the Road Running Information Center (RRIC), which keeps records; and the Road Running Technical Committee (RRTC), which certifies courses.

Running USA, a newer independent body of various types of racing entities (individual races, shoe companies, suppliers, etc.), serves as a promotional group for high-level running as a whole. Road Runners Club of America (RRCA) is a consortium of hundreds of local member clubs. *See also* Amateur Athletic Union; Athletics Congress, The; International Association of Athletics Federations; International Olympic Committee; organizations; Road Runners Club of America; Running USA; USA Track & Field; U.S. Olympic Committee.

Grandfather Mountain Marathon (http://users.boone.net/lamarreca/gmmbear.htm). As the name suggests, this is a toughie as well as an oldie—dating from 1968. The race usually is run in July and has an elevation gain of 1,719 feet. *See also* oldest races.

Grandma's Marathon (www.grandmasmarathon.com). This race offers one of the few chances to run a fast marathon in the summertime. Grandma's runs along the shore of Lake Superior, finishing in Duluth, Minnesota. Under the direction of Scott Keenan since its inception in 1977, it is considered one of the most popular and well-run marathons in the United States.

Great Aloha Run. While the Honolulu Marathon draws a majority-Japanese field, the city's other big race of 8 1/4 miles caters mainly to homegrown runners. Great Aloha, run in February, boasts more than 14,000 finishers. *See also* biggest races.

Great Race 10K (www.rungreatrace.com). A slightly downhill course in Pittsburgh attracts runners in search of fast—if aided—times. This race is run in September. *See also* fastest races.

Green, Harry (also known as Henry) (b. July 15, 1886; date of death unknown). The Brit set the world marathon record in 1913, becoming the first to break 2:40 (with a 2:38:17). *See also* record progressions, world.

Green, Jim (b. November 27, 1932). He had the good luck and misfortune to peak at the same time as John J. Kelley and often followed Kel across the finish line. They placed 1-2, with Green second, in the 1959 Pan-American Games Marathon. *See also* Kelley, John J.

Green, Norm (b. June 27, 1932). The Baptist pastor was one of the few human beings who have lived a half century to break 2:30 in the marathon. His best time after 50 was 2:25:51. He holds American 50–54, 55–59, and 60–64 records for the half-marathon and 50–54 and 55–59 records for the marathon. *See also* Hall of Fame, RRCA; records, American age-group.

Greenspan, Bud (b. September 9, 1926). The filmmaker, with trademark glasses apparently glued to his forehead, has documented many Olympic Marathons and has done more than anyone to preserve film of the Olympic Games. In one of its first marketing moves, Dreamworks SKG Television packaged an eight-volume set of Greenspan's films of the Olympic Games track and field competition throughout the years, along with a 224-page coffee-table book highlighting the 100 greatest moments in Olympic history and reproductions of the Olympic Games posters from 1896 through 1996. The package was marketed as a centennial celebration under the title *The Olympiad: Greatest Moments. See also* movies.

Gregory, Louis (b. July 10, 1905). The RRCA Hall of Famer was an excellent marathoner in pre-World War II years, winning the 1940 national title in 2:35:10. *See also* Hall of Fame, RRCA; national marathon champions, U.S.

Greig, Dale (b. May 15, 1937). She set a women's world marathon record in 1964 as the first to break 3:30. The Brit ran 3:27:45 on the British Isle of Wight. *See also* record progressions, world.

Grimes, Dan (b. January 30, 1959). He's a rare individual who has seen the sport from both sides—as a competitor in the World Championships Marathon (1987) and as an official who presided over the USATF men's long-distance committee at the turn of the new century. *See also* USA Track & Field; World Championships, U.S.

Groos, Margaret (b. September 21, 1959). She's best remembered as the 1988 Olympic Marathon Trials winner, but she found perhaps more success in the 10K. She held world and American 10K records as the first to break 33:00 (with 32:47 in 1979) and was winner of the 1989 national 10K. *See also* national marathon champions, U.S.; national 10K champions, U.S.; Olympians, U.S.; Olympic Trials Marathon, U.S.; record progressions, American; record progressions, world.

Groundhog Run (www.childrenstlc.org). It's not an event for the claustrophobic, because the February 5K and 10K are run completely underground at the Hunt Midwest Underground Caves in Missouri. *See also* oddest races.

GU (www.gusports.com). The original sports gel, GU was invented in Berkeley, California, the same city that spawned PowerBars. *See also* foods, runners', gels.

Gynn, Roger (b. September 19, 1935). The British running historian worked with Dr. David Martin to capture the statistical history of marathoning, including their master book, *The Olympic Marathon* (Human Kinetics, 2000). Gynn and Martin also collaborated on *The Marathon Footrace* (1979), published by Charles C Thomas. *See also* Martin, David.

half-marathon. This is a poorly named race. It is half a marathon (13.1 miles) only in length, not in training or pace. Men have run this distance in less than an hour, and women under 1:07. Of course, no one has come close to doubling those times in a marathon. The half is the only individual road race with an annual World Championship race, dating from 1992 when Liz McColgan (Britain) and Benson Masya (Kenya) were the individual winners. *See also* national half-marathon champions, U.S.; World Half-Marathon Championships.

Hall of Fame, National Distance Running (www.distancerunning.com). Unlike the much older and far larger Road Runners Club of America Hall of Fame, the National Distance Running Hall of Fame has a building housing memorabilia of its members. This shrine, which inducted its first members in 1998, is located in Utica, New York. See also "Left-Out Standouts" on page 134.

Hall of Fame, Road Runners Club of America (www.rrca.org). The Road Runners Club of America has enshrined members in its hall since 1971, making this

National Distance Running Hall of Fame Inductees

This is the newest of the halls of fame that honor runners. The first four classes of inductees are the following:

Year	Inductees	
1998	Ted Corbitt	Bill Rodgers
	Joan Samuelson	Frank Shorter
	Kathrine Switzer	
1999	John A. Kelley	Nina Kuscsik
	Francie Larrieu Smith	
2000	Clarence DeMar	Steve Prefontaine
	Alberto Salazar	Grete Waitz
2001	Bill Dellinger	Lynn Jennings
	Fred Lebow	Craig Virgin

Road Runners Club of America Hall of Fame Inductees

Listed alphabetically within year of induction are the members of this hall. Some inductees are honored for efforts other than road racing.

Year	Inductees		
1971	Bob Campbell	Clarence DeMar	Leonard "Buddy" Edelen
	John J. Kelley	Browning Ross	
1972	Ted Corbitt	Fred Faller	Louis Gregory
	John A. Kelley	Joseph Kleinerman	
1973	Tarzan Brown	Victor Dyrgall	James "Hinky" Henigan
	Peter McArdle	Paul Jerry Nason	
1974	Pat Dengis	Leslie Pawson	Mel Porter
	Charles Robbins	Fred Wilt	
1975	Horace Ashenfelter	Don Lash	Joseph McCluskey
1976	Robert Johnson	George Sheehan	Curtis Stone
1977	Eino Pentti	Greg Rice	Frank Shorter
1978	John Hayes	Bill Rodgers	Aldo Scandurra
1979	Joe Henderson	Ray Sears	Gar Williams
1980	Ruth Anderson	Nina Kuscsik	Thomas Osler
	William Steiner		
1981	Hal Higdon	Steve Prefontaine	Ken Young
1982	William Agee	Roberta Gibb Welch	William "Billy" Mills
1983	Ed Benham	Paul de Bruyn	Gabe Mirkin
1984	Clive Davies	Jacqueline Hansen	Joan Samuelson
	Bob Schul	Kathrine Switzer	Craig Virgin
1985	Henley Gabeau	Gordon McKenzie	Alex Ratelle
	John "Jock" Semple	Louis White	
1986	Doris S. Brown Heritage	Nick Costes	Ron Daws
1987	Bill Bowerman	Hugh Jascourt	Don Kardong
	Francie Larrieu Smith		
1988	Garry Bjorklund	Cheryl Bridges Flanagan	Thomas Hicks
	Kenny Moore		
1989	Dick Beardsley	Herb Lorenz	Sy Mah
	Harold Tinsley		
1990	Pat Porter	Alberto Salazar	Max Truex
1991	Barry Brown	Lynn Jennings	Fred Lebow
1992	Jeff Darman	Jeff Galloway	Ted Haydon
1993	Jack Bacheler	Norm Green	Mary Slaney
1994	Julie Brown	Amby Burfoot	Marion Irvine
1995	Ann Trason	George Young	
1996	Ed Eyestone	Jerry Kokesh	Pete Pfitzinger
1997	Kim Jones	Jon Sinclair	
1998	Benji Durden	Doug Kurtis	
1999	Gerry Lindgren	Tony Sandoval	
2000	Mark Curp	John Tuttle	
2001	Miki Gorman	Greg Meyer	

USA Track & Field Hall of Fame Inductees

Here are USATF Hall of Fame members with connections to road racing, listed by their year of induction. Many are also in the RRCA and NDR Halls of Fame.

Year	Inductees
1975	Horace Ashenfelter, Ted Haydon
1976	Billy Mills, Steve Prefontaine, Joie Ray
1977	Greg Rice
1978	Bob Giegengack
1980	John A. Kelley
1981	Bill Bowerman, Fred Wilt, George Young
1988	Cordner Nelson
1989	Frank Shorter
1990	Doris Severtson Brown Heritage
1991	Bert Nelson, Bob Schul
1994	Fred Lebow
1995	Marty Liquori
1996	Joe McCluskey
1998	Francie Larrieu Smith
1999	Bill Rodgers
2000	Bill Dellinger

by far the largest of the halls, though there is no physical hall (it's a paper organization). New inductions are made each year at the RRCA convention. *See also* "Left-Out Standouts" on next page.

Hall of Fame, USA Track & Field (www.usatf.org). The USA Track & Field Hall is what the name implies, a shrine for track and field greats. But a few people from road racing have sneaked in as well. The hall is now located in Indianapolis but will move to New York City in 2002. *See also* "Left-Out Standouts" on next page.

Ron Daws finishes the 1969 Boston Marathon. Daws experimented with extremely light running shoes and with training methods that would maximize his limited running talent. He was successful to the point that he made the 1968 Olympic Marathon team and was inducted into the RRCA Hall of Fame in 1986.

© Jeff Johnson

Left-Out Standouts

From Joe Henderson's *Running Commentary*, April 2000.

Classes of 2000 await induction into two halls of fame. Joining the older one at the Road Runners Club of America will be former half-marathon world record-holder Mark Curp and Olympic marathoner John Tuttle. The National Distance Running Hall of Fame in Utica, New York, will add seven-time Boston winner Clarence DeMar; well-remembered Steve Prefontaine; America's only two-time sub-2:09 marathoner, Alberto Salazar; and Grete the Great Waitz (the only non-American member to date).

While collecting material for the *Running Encyclopedia*, I noticed many glaring absentees from these halls. I share the blame because as an RRCA voter I've never nominated any of them. Here, alphabetically, are the 10 missing persons who most need to be remembered in the next round of voting:

- Marianne Dickerson. The only American female medalist in a World Championships Marathon, she earned a silver (behind Waitz) in the first one.

- Patti (Catalano) Dillon. Set three American marathon records and was the first to break 2:30.

- Jim Fixx. Wrote the sport's all-time best-selling book, one that contributed mightily to Running Boom I.

- Miki Gorman. Two-time winner at both Boston and New York City, she achieved three of those victories as a master.

- Bob Kempainen. Fastest American marathoner ever [See Khannaouchi update at end of this sidebar] at 2:08:47 and twice an Olympian.

- Greg Meyer. Last U.S. man to win at Boston (in 1983) and still the fourth-fastest American at 2:09:00.

- Cathy O'Brien. The only American woman to date to run in two Olympic Marathons, 1988 and 1992, and the U.S. junior and high school record-holder.

- Mark Plaatjes. Won the 1993 World Championships Marathon shortly after winning his U.S. citizenship.

- Lisa (Weidenbach) Rainsberger. Remembered most for her three near misses in the Olympic Trials, she was a Boston and Chicago winner.

- Steve Spence. The only American man ever to win a World Championships Marathon medal, a bronze in 1991.

Add Khalid Khannouchi to this list of nominees as soon as he runs his first race as an American.

[Khannouchi set an American record of 2:07:01 in his first marathon as a citizen, at Chicago 2000.]

Halvorsen, John (b. August 17, 1966). Women from Norway have excelled as the men from that country seldom have. An exception is Halvorsen, who won the Bloomsday 12K in 1989 and was that year's top-ranked world road racer. *See also* Bloomsday 12K; rankings, *Runner's World*.

Hansen, Jacqueline (b. November 20, 1948). As a pioneering female runner, she was the first woman to go under 2:45 (1974) and the first to go under 2:40 (1975), as well as the second official Boston winner (1973). "She's not like me; she doesn't preach sermons," her husband, Tom Sturak, told writer Truman Clark in 1978. Sturak, a renowned runner in his own right and a confirmed pot stirrer, has certainly egged on wife Jacqueline over the years. In the same interview, Jacqueline referred to Tom as "a liberated man," who back then was a strong advocate of women's running. "I'm motivated by competition," Sturak said back in 1978. "Jacqueline is not; she's goal oriented. Jacqueline wants to do things no other woman has done."

Coached by the famed Laszlo Tabori and egged on by Sturak, Jacqueline blossomed into one of the most celebrated road racers of the 1970s and one of the principal sparkplugs behind getting the women's marathon onto the international race schedule. She joined Nike in working behind the scenes to get a women's marathon into the Olympic Games and worked in conjunction with other runners' groups (male, female, and mixed) to guarantee that it would happen. The fact that the first women's Olympic Marathon was run in her hometown of Los Angeles made it doubly satisfying for her. The only way it could have been more satisfying would have been bringing it off eight years earlier when she was at her competitive peak. *See also* Boston Marathon; Hall of Fame, RRCA; Honolulu Marathon; International Runners Committee; record progressions, American; record progressions, world; Tabori, Laszlo.

hard-easy training. This principle is Bill Bowerman's greatest training legacy. The Oregon coach, an inveterate experimenter, found that none of his runners could train hard more than a few days in a row. On the other hand, most of them thrived when an easy day or even multiple easy days separated the hard sessions. One of his most loyal disciples was Kenny Moore, who was no stranger to hard work but would run as little as 30 minutes on his easy days. Moore ran in two Olympic Marathons. *See also* Bowerman, Bill; Moore, Kenny.

Harper, Cheryl (b. April 15, 1962). She took advantage of the rules and set the current American 8K (aided) best of 24:41 (1997) on a steeply downhill course in Utah. *See also* records, American.

Hartshorn, Gordon (b. December 5, 1938; d. August 18, 1998). The Texan ran 74 marathons in as many weeks, a "world record" at the time—all the while fighting a losing battle with prostate cancer. *See also* "Finish Lines" on next page.

Finish Lines

From Joe Henderson's *Running Commentary,* February 1999.

Gordon Hartshorn first became a name to me a few years ago when he wrote to say that he planned to run a marathon every weekend from 1996 through 2000, for a total of about 200 races. He approached me for publicity, at least, and for help finding sponsorship if I could give it.

I offered him little more than encouragement, but he didn't hold that against me. Gordon subscribed to my newsletter even before we met. He renewed for another two years when there was little reason to think he would stick around long enough to read all the issues.

I'll back up here and say that the Texan's path first crossed mine in 1996, at the Canadian Rockies Marathon in Canmore, Alberta. That weekend he bought a copy of my George Sheehan biography, *Did I Win?* Much of that book deals with George's final race against prostate cancer. He lost it but won by his definitions: "Winning is doing the best you can with what you are given" and "Winning is never having to say I quit."

Gordon looked healthy and ran tirelessly that weekend. He confided, though, "I have prostate cancer too but am not letting it rule my life. I'm taking no special treatments but just letting it take its natural course."

Its course cut short his streak at 74 weeks in July 1997. His last and hardest race had entered its final lap. I didn't hear how it ended until reading about the inevitable outcome in *Marathon & Beyond* magazine.

Gordon had written for the magazine. In doing so he'd become friends with editor Rich Benyo. Rich wrote, "Many of you first met Gordon, who died of prostate cancer, in our November/December 1997 issue. His 'My Most Unforgettable Marathon' piece recaptured the events of Gordon's 1996 Midnight Sun Marathon, run in Nanisivik, above the Arctic Circle."

A year later that marathon would be his 74th and last. His death came in August 1998, shortly before his 60th birthday.

When I wrote to ask Rich for a fact about Gordon, he wrote, "It was a bit otherworldly to exchange e-mails with Gordon during the last several months. He valiantly went through the end of his life in a very heroic and inspiring way. Although it sounds silly, I should have removed his file from the rest of the 'active' files. But I can't yet come to do it, because his file still seems pretty damned vibrant."

I know what Rich means. After hearing of Gordon's death, I had a couple of eerie after-life encounters with him. His name still appears on my active list of subscribers. I'm reluctant to remove it. While looking up details about him, I went to the Internet. Up popped his Web site, opening with two pictures of him running. I hope the site stays alive and draws visitors to pay respects to a runner worth remembering.

Hash House Harriers (www.harrier.org). Without a doubt, this is the world's most absurd running club. We can't do better in describing it than to let the official "About Hashing" document stand by itself: The Hash House Harriers is a social club of runners that has been described as "a drinking club with a running problem." Ex-pat British businessmen, accountants, lawyers, civil servants, and so on started the Hash in 1938 in Kuala Lumpur, Malaysia. It is a club based on the old English game of hares and hounds in which one or two members would be given a head start of several minutes and would drop shredded paper as the "scent." The hounds would then follow, after the pre-scribed time, and attempt to catch the hares. The hares would lay the trail in a straight or obvious line but then would stop laying trail and run off in another direction and begin laying the trail after 100 meters or so. When the hounds discovered that they were no longer on trail, they would fan out in all directions in search of the "scent" and would call to the others when one of them again discovered the trail.

The founder of the Hash, A.S. "G" Gispert, discovered the Springgit Harriers, one of the paper-chase clubs, in Malacca in 1937. He introduced Ronald "Torch" Bennett to the concept, and the stage was set. When "G" returned to Kuala Lumpur in 1938, he became a member of the Federated Malay States Volunteer Reserves, which trained on Mondays. "G" and many of the other ex-pat Brits were housed in barracks in the Royal Selangor Club where he and "Torch" would often discuss starting a harrier club in K.L. (Kuala Lumpur). Finally, in about December of 1938, "G" convinced about a dozen others to follow his inaugural paper trail.

Gispert then suggested the name "Hash House Harriers" in mock allusion to the mess at the Selangor Club, where many of them dined. The runs were held Monday evenings after reserve training and were followed by refreshment in the form of Tiger beer. A.S. "G" Gispert was killed in battle defending Singapore from the Japanese on February 11, 1942. The Hash has grown from those humble beginnings to include thousands of chapters and tens of thousands of hashers worldwide.

Hatch, Sidney (b. December 6, 1885; date of death unknown). The two-time U.S. Olympian in the marathon placed 8th in 1904 and 14th in 1908. *See also* Olympians, U.S.

Haydon, Ted (b. 1911; d. 1985). The University of Chicago Track Club coach and longtime friend of road running promoted races in his area in the late 1950s and 1960s when no one else was interested. He was an assistant coach of the 1972 Olympic team, where U.S. marathoners finished 1-4-9. Haydon belongs to both the USATF and RRCA Halls of Fame. *See also* Hall of Fame, RRCA; Hall of Fame, USATF.

Hayes, Johnny (b. April 10, 1886; d. August 23, 1965). He became an Olympic marathon winner in the 1908 race when Dorando Pietri was disqualified after receiving assistance inside the stadium. Hayes became the first world and American record-holder (at 2:55:19) in this first race at what would later become the standard distance of 26 miles, 385 yards. He also was the first to

The great rematch of the 1908 Olympic marathon race between Johnny Hayes and Dorando Pietri occurred in January 1910.

break 3:00. *See also* Hall of Fame, RRCA; Olympians, U.S.; Olympic medalists; record progressions, American; record progressions, world.

headsets. The ubiquitous, portable, music and talk radio sets entertain and inform runners who aren't satisfied listening to companions, to the sounds around them, or to their own thoughts. Some races discourage runners from wearing headsets as a safety concern. *See also* Walkman.

Heart of America Marathon (ctc.coin.org/hoa). Labor Day weekend in Columbia, Missouri, has included this marathon since 1960. *See also* oldest races.

heart-rate monitor. This high-tech training tool gained popularity in the 1990s as pulse replaced pace as the prime measurement of effort for many runners. One of many helpful books on the subject is John Parker's *Heart Monitor Training for the Compleat Idiot* (Cedarwinds, 1999). *See also* aerobic threshold; Polar.

heat. It's the distance runner's number-one environmental enemy. We can warm up on all but the coldest days, but avoiding overheating becomes increasingly difficult as the temperature rises above the comfort zone. Heat cramps, heat exhaustion, and even heat stroke can result—particularly when high humidity combines with high temperature. The body has great powers to adapt to hot conditions, however, given adequate exposure to it in training and proper hydration. Race directors also look out for the runners' interests by scheduling most events at cooler hours of the day and in seasons of the year likely to have kinder temperatures. *See also* body temperature; clothing; drinks, running.

Heatley, Basil (b. December 25, 1933). The Brit went into the 1964 Olympic Games as world record-holder in the marathon (2:13:55 in 1964). He lost both the race and the record to Abebe Bikila but still ran a strong second in Tokyo. *See also* Olympic medalists; record progressions, world.

Heffner, Kyle (b. September 12, 1954). Along with U.S. "teammates" Tony Sandoval and Benji Durden, the 25-year-old Heffner did not go to the 1980 Olympics through no fault of his own. He qualified third at Buffalo with a PR of 2:10:55, but President Carter called a boycott of the Moscow Games. *See also* Olympians, U.S.; Olympic Trials Marathon, U.S.

Heinonen, Janet (b. January 10, 1951) and **Heinonen, Tom** (b. July 1, 1945). Running definitely runs in the Heinonen family. Tom won the 1969 national marathon title, competed internationally in cross country, and has coached national-championship women's teams and individuals at the University of Oregon. His wife, Janet, a runner since the 1960s, coauthored *All About Road Racing* (Tafnews, 1979) with Tom and wrote *Running for Women* (*Sports Illustrated*, 1979) herself. She publishes a monthly newsletter, *Keeping Track* (www.runnersworld.com/keepingtrack), and writes a monthly column for *Runner's World* Online (www.runnersworld.com). Their son Erik was one of the country's top high school cross country runners in 2000.

Held, Dan (b. October 15, 1965). He made the successful leap from international marathons to ultras of the same level. Held competed in the 1997 World Championships Marathon (and had a 2:13:50 PR at that distance), then three years later placed fourth in the World 100K. *See also* World Championships, U.S.

Helgerson, Jay (birthdate unavailable). The first runner known to us to have completed a marathon a week for a full year, he pulled off the feat in the late 1970s. To facilitate his record, a northern California running club put together a marathon just for him on a weekend devoid of marathon-length races.

Hellebuyck, Eddy (b. January 22, 1961). He ran for Belgium in the 1996 Olympic Marathon, then gained his U.S. citizenship in time to represent this country in the 1999 World Championships. Hellebuyck, a 2:11 marathoner who has run 2:16 as a master, is a longtime resident of Albuquerque, New Mexico, where he and his wife, Shawn, serve as agents for top runners. In 2001 Eddy tied the American masters 10K record with 29:37 and broke the half marathon mark with 1:05:18. He competed in the 2001 World Championships Marathon as a 40-year-old, placing 38th in 2:28:01. *See also* World Championships, U.S.

Helsinki, Finland. It was the first city to host both an Olympic Games (1952) and a World Championships (the debut meet in 1983). Rome, Athens, and Tokyo have since been the scene of both meets. The 1952 Helsinki Olympics was the setting of perhaps the greatest feat in distance running when Czechoslovakian runner Emil Zatopek won gold in the 5,000 meters, 10,000 meters, and his first-ever marathon. *See also* Olympic Marathon, 1900 to 2000; World Championships medalists; Zatopek, Emil.

Henderson, Joe (b. June 3, 1943). *See* About the Authors at the back of this book.

Henigan, Jimmy (b. April 25, 1892; d. February 27, 1950). The 1931 Boston winner (2:46:46) competed in the Olympic Marathons on either side of that win, 1928 and 1932, placing 39th and not finishing. *See also* Boston Marathon; Hall of Fame, RRCA; Olympians, U.S.

Jimmy Henigan, pictured here back at the cardboard box factory the day after running Boston in 1931.

Courtesy of Dr. Edward H. Kozloff–Motor City Striders

Heritage, Doris Severtson Brown (b. September 17, 1942). Women's running today is taken for granted, yet relative to long-distance running in general it is only recently that women have enjoyed equal status with men. Back in the Dark Ages of the 1950s, one of the most seminal women ever to lace on a pair of running shoes was Doris Severtson of Gig Harbor, Washington. Her career as a runner started when the Tacoma Parks Department in Washington State put on a junior Olympics in 1958. Doris took second place in the 50-yard dash and first in the 75-yard dash, the longest event contested for girls. She also won the long jump, and that feat caught the attention of folks from the Tacoma MicMac Team, which recruited her. When the club's 440-yard runner was away at the AAU Nationals in 1959, the coaches tapped Doris, who proceeded to run 59.4—a national record.

When the 800 meters was put on the Olympic program for 1960,

Doris moved up in distance and set a national record of 2:19. Trying out for the U.S. Olympic team, she lowered that time to 2:13.4, but she was beaten at the Trials by Pat Daniels, who went to the Games. She also competed in the 1967 and 1971 Pan-American Games in the 800 meters, taking second place both times. She competed in the 1,500 meters at the 1972 Olympics but tripped on the curb and broke her foot.

Her true calling was in longer distances. She won the first five World Cross Country meets, beginning in 1967. She ran her first marathon in Vancouver, Canada, on May 29, 1976, and ran a 2:47:35, at that time the world's record for a female debut marathon. Her pioneering efforts on behalf of women's running, accoplished primarily by breaking barriers herself, are beautifully chronicled in the Frank Murphy book, *The Silence of Great Distance* (WindSprint Press, 2000). Doris is the longtime track and cross country coach at Seattle Pacific University. *See also* Hall of Fame, RRCA; Hall of Fame, USATF.

Hickman, Libbie Johnson (b. February 17, 1965). Born in Billings, Montana, but residing in Colorado, Libbie earned her stripes as a track runner. But in her 30s she branched out to do some road racing and found it to her liking. She quickly became a 2:28 marathoner. She won national titles in the half-marathon in 1998 (1:13:29) and in 2000 (1:11:01) and national 10K titles in 1998, 1999, and 2000. She made the 10,000 final at the Sydney Olympics, where she placed 16th.

Libbie began her running career at age eight when her father timed her against her brothers. She went to high school in Egypt where her father worked for an oil company. She ran in college at Colorado State but recalled, "I was not as serious about my running then. I concentrated on the 1,500 meters. As a senior I realized that I only had one year left to run. I moved up to the 3,000 meters and got serious."

She graduated with a BS in science/physiology, with a chemistry minor. When she isn't competing, she and her husband, Walter, renovate rental properties. She loves gardening and would love to have the time to do it full time. She is just now realizing her full potential on the roads. *See also* Bolder Boulder 10K; national half-marathon champions, U.S.; national 10K champions, U.S.

Hicks, Thomas (b. January 7, 1875; d. December 2, 1963). The American won this country's first gold medal in the first Olympic Marathon held in the United States—St. Louis in 1904. Hicks was declared the winner after Fred Lorz was disqualified for taking a ride. Hicks himself took strychnine and alcohol during the race, a practice not illegal at the time. *See also* Hall of Fame, RRCA; Olympians, U.S.; Olympic medalists.

Higdon, Hal (b. June 17, 1931). Although he has been associated with long-distance running as both a journalist and competitor for decades, Hal has, over the years, dipped his foot into many a pond. He began his journalistic career as a cartoonist for a service-group magazine while continuing his running career, which now extends six decades. In the 1970s and 1980s he wrote extensively about auto racing, in both feature articles and books, and he wrote a landmark book on the infamous Leopold and Loeb trial, *The Crime of the Century* (University of Illinois Press, 1999).

The primary focus of his writing has been running, however, where he has been a contributor to *Runner's World* since its second issue (when it was called *Distance Running News*) in 1966. He has also written numerous books on the subject of running, from the lighthearted *On the Run From Dogs and People* (Regnery, 1971) to the highly practical *Marathon: The Ultimate Training Guide* (Rodale, 1999).

He placed fifth (first American, with a PR of 2:21:55) in the 1964 Boston Marathon and has since been a fierce age-group competitor. He was also instrumental in the founding of the Road Runners Club of America. In his spare time he continues to refine his artistic talents, displaying his artwork at various venues. He spends quite a bit of his time training groups of runners to complete the Chicago Marathon, and he has an active Web site (www.halhigdon.com), where some of his artwork can be enjoyed. *See also* books; Hall of Fame, RRCA; *On the Run From Dogs and People; Runner's World.*

Ron Hill of Great Britain, one of the world's top marathoners in the 1960s, heads toward a 2:10:30 victory in the 1970 Boston Marathon.

© Jeff Johnson

Higgins, Norm (b. November 18, 1936). A New York City Marathon winner (1971) and national champion (1966), Higgins ran 2:15:52 in 1971, when few Americans were yet breaking 2:20. He later coached Olympic track runner and road record-setter Jan Merrill. *See also* Merrill, Jan; national marathon champions, U.S.; New York City Marathon.

Hill, Ron (b. September 25, 1938). Now known for an unbroken streak of running days dating from 1964, the British runner was once one of the world's finest marathoners. He was the second runner (after Derek Clayton) to break 2:10. He won Commonwealth, European, and Boston titles in 1970 and held the top world ranking that year. *See also* Boston Marathon; Commonwealth Games; European Championships; rankings, *Track & Field News;* streakers.

hills. Shakespeare never ran a road race, as far as we know. Yet he wrote a lament for runners with his line that hills "draw out the miles and make them wearisome." Hills worry some runners so much that race directors advertise their courses as "flat and fast" or "slightly rolling." Other runners, however, seek out hilly racecourses for the challenge. They train on hills, either as they occur naturally on training routes or, as a form of interval training, hill repeats.

Hiroshima, Kurao (b. December 5, 1928). The name Hiroshima had already left an indelible mark on the world when the runner by this name won twice at Fukuoka, in 1957 and 1959. *See also* Fukuoka Marathon.

Hirsch, George (b. June 21, 1934). George is the publisher of *Runner's World* magazine, a position he probably never imagined he'd hold back in 1977 when he published a prototype of *The Runner* magazine, which was to compete with *Runner's World* for a decade. George has long had magazine ink in his blood. He graduated from Princeton in 1956 with a major in American and modern European history. That dovetailed nicely with his being a naval officer stationed on an old LST in Naples from 1957 to 1960. Upon his return he went to Harvard Business School. Then in 1962 he began work at Time-Life International.

In 1967 Hirsch joined Clay Felker, and they spent a year raising money to launch *New York Magazine*, which created a completely new genre of magazine. George worked with writers such as Tom Wolfe, Jimmy Breslin, Gloria Steinem, and Adam Smith. In 1973 he founded *New Times Magazine*, a youthful answer to stodgy *Time* and *Newsweek*. Although a critical success, the magazine ended publication in January 1979.

By that time George had moved his attention to *The Runner*, a publication that provided an outlet for his passion for long-distance running and proved a worthy opponent to *Runner's World*. Following an unsuccessful run for Congress in New York's Silk Stocking District in 1986, George sold *The Runner* to Rodale, which had purchased *Runner's World* from Bob Anderson. George came aboard as *RW* publisher, and the continued success of the magazine is a matter of record. The circulation is more than a half million, and the magazine has spawned eight international editions as well as *Runner's World* Online (www.runnersworld.com).

George ran his first marathon in Boston in 1969 and has run more than 25 marathons; his fastest was a 2:38 at Boston 1979. His most memorable marathon was New York City in 1994, which he ran with one of his four sons. He ran a 2:59 at the California International Marathon on the verge of turning 60, and won the 60-year age-group in Chicago the following year. He has also worked as an expert commentator at numerous marathons, including New York, Boston, and several Olympics. He lives with his wife, Shay, in his beloved New York City. See also the foreword; *Runner's World*; *Runner, The*.

historic sites. Runners can visit Olympic, World Championships, and other famous courses, and often run races on all or parts of them. Examples in the United States are the Atlanta, Los Angeles, and St. Louis Marathons, all of which touch past Olympic routes. *See also* Olympic Marathon, 1900 to 2000.

hitting the wall. *See* wall, the.

Hodge, Bob (b. August, 3, 1955). He was a 2:10:59 American marathoner at a time (1979) when that level of running wasn't uncommon. Hodge also won Bay to Breakers (1979) and national 10K (1982) titles. *See also* Bay to Breakers 12K; national 10K champions, U.S.

Holden, Jack (b. March 13, 1907). The British marathoner is the oldest winner of a major championship with his 1950 European (2:32:14) and Commonwealth Marathon (2:32:57) titles at age 43. *See also* Commonwealth Games; European Championships; rankings, *Track & Field News*.

Honikman, Basil (b. January 26, 1937). The longtime head of the Road Running Information Center became executive director of Running USA in 2000. *See also* Road Running Information Center; Running USA.

Honolulu Marathon (www.honolulumarathon.org). It's the largest international race held in the United States, with two-thirds of the more than 20,000 runners flying in from Japan each December. *See also* "Times Up" on page 147; biggest races; Scaff, Dr. Jack.

The Honolulu Marathon has long been one of the most international of American marathons, drawing roughly two-thirds of its 20,000-plus field from Japan. The December race runs past Diamondhead and is a mecca for slow runners. The race stays open until the last runner finishes.

Honolulu Marathon Winners

No one has dominated a major marathon as Carla Beurskens has Honolulu. The Dutchwoman won here 8 of 10 times in the years from 1985 through 1994. This race prides itself as a discoverer of talent—none greater than then little-known Josia Thugwane, who previewed his Olympic victory by winning at Honolulu in 1995.
* = race record.

WOMEN

Year	Athlete	Time
1973	June Chun (U.S.)	3:25:31
1974	Cindy Dalrymple (U.S.)	3:01:59
1975	Jacqueline Hansen (U.S.)	2:49:24
1976	Kim Merritt (U.S.)	2:44:44
1977	Cindy Dalrymple (U.S.)	2:48:08
1978	Patti Lyons (U.S.)	2:43:10
1979	Patti Lyons (U.S.)	2:40:07
1980	Patti Catalano (U.S.)	2:35:26
1981	Patti Catalano (U.S.)	2:33:24
1982	Eileen Claugus (U.S.)	2:41:11
1983	Annick Loir-Lebreton (France)	2:41:25
1984	Patti Gray (U.S.)	2:42:50
1985	Carla Beurskens (Netherlands)	2:35:51
1986	Carla Beurskens (Netherlands)	2:31:01
1987	Carla Beurskens (Netherlands)	2:35:11
1988	Cyndie Welte (U.S.)	2:41:52
1989	Carla Beurskens (Netherlands)	2:31:50
1990	Carla Beurskens (Netherlands)	2:33:34
1991	Ritva Lemettinen (Finland)	2:40:11
1992	Carla Beurskens (Netherlands)	2:32:13
1993	Carla Beurskens (Netherlands)	2:32:20
1994	Carla Beurskens (Netherlands)	2:37:06
1995	Colleen de Reuck (South Africa)	2:37:29
1996	Ramila Burangulova (Russia)	2:34:28
1997	Svetlana Vasilieva (Russia)	2:33:14
1998	Irina Bogacheva (Kyrgyzstan)	2:33:27
1999	Irina Bogacheva (Kyrgyzstan)	2:32:36
2000	Lyubov Morgunova (Russia)	2:28:31*

MEN

Year	Athlete	Time
1973	Duncan Macdonald (U.S.)	2:27:34
1974	Jeff Galloway (U.S.)	2:23:02
1975	Jack Foster (New Zealand)	2:17:24
1976	Duncan Macdonald (U.S.)	2:20:37
1977	Jeff Wells (U.S.)	2:18:38
1978	Don Kardong (U.S.)	2:17:05
1979	Dean Matthews (U.S.)	2:16:13
1980	Duncan Macdonald (U.S.)	2:16:55
1981	Jon Anderson (U.S.)	2:16:54
1982	David Gordon (U.S.)	2:15:30

(continued)

Honolulu Marathon Winners, *continued*

Year	Athlete	Time
1983	Kevin Ryan (New Zealand)	2:20:19
1984	Jorge Gonzales (Puerto Rico)	2:16:25
1985	Ibrahim Hussein (Kenya)	2:12:08
1986	Ibrahim Hussein (Kenya)	2:11:43*
1987	Ibrahim Hussein (Kenya)	2:18:26
1988	Gianni Poli (Italy)	2:12:47
1989	Simon Robert Naali (Tanzania)	2:11:47
1990	Simon Robert Naali (Tanzania)	2:17:29
1991	Benson Masya (Kenya)	2:18:24
1992	Benson Masya (Kenya)	2:14:19
1993	Lee Bong Ju (South Korea)	2:13:16
1994	Benson Masya (Kenya)	2:15:04
1995	Josia Thugwane (South Africa)	2:16:08
1996	Erick Kimaiyo (Kenya)	2:13:23
1997	Erick Kimaiyo (Kenya)	2:12:17
1998	Mbarak Hussein (Kenya)	2:14:53
1999	Jimmy Muindi (Kenya)	2:16:45
2000	Jimmy Muindi (Kenya)	2:15:16

Hood to Coast Relay (www.ndirect.com/htc/). The largest race of its type in the United States has more than 12,000 runners, in teams of 12, traveling more than 190 miles from the shoulder of Mt. Hood to the Pacific coast in Oregon. Runners average three five-mile legs, while teammates accompany them in vans. *See also* relays.

Houston Marathon (www.compaqhoustonmarathon.com). One of the country's finest and fastest races, it hosted the 1992 Women's Olympic Trials. A short-coming is that the south Texas weather in January can vary widely—from raining and near freezing one year to in the 80s the next.

How They Train. Published in 1959 by *Track and Field News*, it was one of the first great books of advice on, well, how specific runners train. Dozens of runners contributed reports on their training for editing by Olympian Fred Wilt, who later coached Buddy Edelen to his marathon world record. *See also* Wilt, Fred.

Huber, Vicki (b. May 29, 1967). The two-time U.S. track Olympian held the national 5K record (15:14 in 1992) that another Olympian, Deena Drossin, broke in 2000. Both times were run at Carlsbad. *See also* record progressions, American.

Hudson, Brad (b. September 30, 1966). He qualified twice for the World Championships Marathon but didn't finish either time, in 1991 and 1993. *See also* World Championships, U.S.

Times Up

From Joe Henderson's *Running Commentary,* November 1998.

Time approaches again for the annual Japanese mass migration to the Honolulu Marathon in December. I'm not sure if this is still true, but a few years back when I last ran there Honolulu was Japan's largest marathon with more than 20,000 runners from that country.

Americans love this race because they get the feel of a foreign marathon without leaving the United States. Japanese love it because they get to travel abroad, yet the majority of marathoners still speak their language.

On this side of the Pacific we wonder why Honolulu is so popular with the Japanese. One answer is obvious: Few vacation spots on earth are more attractive than Hawaii. Another answer is more to the point: No race is friendlier than Honolulu to the slow marathoner. It imposes no firm cutoff time for finishing, so runners can essentially take all day if need be. As a result Honolulu's median time is above five and a half hours. That means that half the field takes longer than that to finish.

Such leniency is almost unheard of in Japan, where the traffic pressures on crowded city streets and country roads won't allow closures for more than five hours. Nearly all marathons in the United States are more generous than that.

Modern realities of the sport have forced races to ease their time limits. When I first ran marathons in the 1960s, the watches stopped and the streets reopened (if they were ever closed at all) after four hours. No one protested because back then hardly anyone ran slower than 4:00. Today more than half the field in most races is still on the course at the four-hour mark. The sport has changed dramatically, and race policies and practices have changed with it.

Marathoning here has grown from the back of the pack. That is, its current vitality is fueled by slower runners, by those who mix running and walking, and by pure walkers. (One of the little secrets behind the growth of "running" in this country is the major contribution of people who walk at least some of the distance.)

No marathon can afford to eliminate the people who take more than twice as long as the leaders to finish. So the successful races here have adapted in several ways to the changing demographics. The most obvious adaptation is an easing of time limits. I know of no marathon in this country that stops timing sooner than five hours. The typical cutoff time is six to seven hours, which allows finishing at a quick walking pace.

Marathons that must operate under time constraints, imposed by public agencies, still try to accommodate the slower finishers. As time elapses, the streets and roads open again to traffic. But the races aren't heartless. They don't usually pull the remaining marathoners from the course. They're simply asked to move to the sidewalks and to be careful at unprotected intersections—as they would in training. Officials still greet them with times, medals, T-shirts, and refreshments as their long day's work ends.

Human Kinetics (www.humankinetics.com). The Champaign, Illinois-based publisher is the most prominent source of running books in the 1990s and beyond; HK was the original publisher of *Marathon & Beyond* magazine. *See also* books.

Humboldt Redwoods Marathon (www.northcoast.com/~hrm). Run in October, it follows essentially the same spectacular course as the spring Avenue of the Giants race but does so in reverse. Humboldt also includes a half-marathon. *See also* Avenue of the Giants Marathon; scenic races.

humidity. *See* heat.

Hunt, Thom (b. March 17, 1958). A high school prodigy (4:03 miler), Hunt went on to set the American half-marathon record twice and the national 10K mark. He now helps organize the Rock 'n' Roll Marathon in San Diego. *See also* record progressions, American; Rock 'n' Roll Marathon.

Hunter, Jill (b. October 14, 1966). The current world 25K record-holder from England (1:24:26 in 1991) was the top-ranked road racer in 1991. *See also* Bay to Breakers 12K; Bolder Boulder 10K; rankings, *Runner's World*; records, world.

Hussein, Ibrahim. *See* page 139.

Hwang Young Cho (b. March 22, 1970). The 22-year-old South Korean won the 1992 Olympic Marathon (2:13:23) but was bedeviled by injuries after that. He retired after winning the 1994 Asian title (2:11:23). *See also* Asian Games; Olympic Marathon, 1900 to 2000; rankings, *Track & Field News*.

hydration. *See* drinks, running; heat.

hyperthermia. *See* heat.

hypothermia. *See* body temperature.

Hussein, Ibrahim (b. June 3, 1958). Ibrahim was one of the first Kenyans to excel at the marathon and remains one of the most respected and well liked of all marathoners. His demeanor has always been open, approachable, and friendly. He speaks English and his native Nandi fluently, and does well with Arabic and Swahili. He is a 1984 graduate of the University of New Mexico, where he majored in economics.

One of the nicest marathoners when not racing, Ibrahim developed a reputation as one of the fiercest competitors on the block—strong, determined, and equipped with 47-second 400-meter speed. He needed it at the 1988 Boston Marathon, when in one of the most exciting finishes in the long history of the race he outkicked Juma Ikangaa at the finish line to win by one second with a 2:08:43.

Hussein grew up idolizing 1968 Olympic

gold medalist Kip Keino. The middle of five children, Ibrahim grew up Muslim, yet he was educated at St. Patrick's Catholic boarding school 60 miles from his home because it was the best school in Kenya, both academically and athletically. Inexperienced in the steeplechase, Ibrahim tried it and won himself a scholarship to the University of New Mexico. In the early 1980s he tried his hand at road racing and easily won major races such as Bloomsday and Bay to Breakers, incorpo-

rating his devastating kick. After learning some lessons about how marathoning isn't as easy as it looks, he went on a tear. He won Honolulu three years in a row (1985–1987) and won New York in 1987. His debut at Boston only whetted his appetite for more. He placed fourth in 1989, first in 1991 (2:11:06), and first again in 1992 (2:08:14). *See also* Bay to Breakers 12K; Bloomsday 12K; Boston Marathon; Honolulu Marathon; New York City Marathon; Peachtree 10K.

© Mark Shearman

Ibrahim Hussein (#0581) was one of the first Kenyans to announce to the world that the floodgates were opening; his 1988 Boston finish against Ikangaa (#0936) was one of the best ever.

IAAF. *See* International Association of Athletics Federations.

Idaho Women's Fitness Celebration (www.bkbltd.com). New Zealander Anne Audain founded this race in her adopted hometown of Boise, and she remains its spokeswoman. Run in early fall, the Celebration 5K is primarily a women's event, ranking among the country's largest. *See also* Audain, Anne; biggest races.

Igloi, Mihaly (b. 1909; d. 1998). He brought advanced training methods to the United States in the late 1950s when he defected with several of his elite athletes from Hungary. Igloi coached Jim Beatty to world records and laid the foundation for Bob Schul's Olympic gold medal in the 5,000. Laszlo Tabori carries on the legacy of Igloi's interval-based methods as a coach in southern California. *See also* "Igloi's Boys" on next page; Tabori, Laszlo.

Ikangaa, Juma. *See* page 154.

Ikenberry, Judy (b. September 3, 1942). She won the first U.S. women's marathon championship after the AAU finally gave full approval to the event in 1974. Judy now works with husband Dennis Ikenberry in a race-scoring business called Race Central. *See also* "Living History" on page 153; national marathon champions, U.S.

Richard Benyo photo

Judy Ikenberry, one of the pioneers of women's road racing, now runs a company specializing in scoring road races.

Igloi's Boys

From Joe Henderson's *Running Commentary,* February 1998.

If you think U.S. distance running is depressed now by world standards, you should have seen it in the 1950s. Horace Ashenfelter was the golden exception, winning the Melbourne Olympic steeplechase.

Otherwise the Americans ran the long races as expected, which was poorly. None of the 1,500-meter runners reached the final, the highest 5,000 or 10,000 finish was 18th, and no marathoner placed better than 20th. In 1956 America's first sub-four-minute mile was still two years away. U.S. records in the 5K and 10K were minor league by world standards. Eastern Europeans—Czechs, Soviets, Hungarians—were the "Africans" of their time. Mihaly Igloi-coached runners in Hungary were setting many of the records.

Igloi, who died this January at age 89, was an unlikely candidate to lead the United States out of the distance-running wilderness. He was never completely understood or widely imitated here, and so his contribution was never fully appreciated.

He might never have come here if political battling hadn't driven him out of Hungary shortly after the Melbourne Olympics. He came to America looking for personal freedom, not athletic opportunity. There was little of the latter here, where Igloi's limited English barred him from traditional coaching jobs in high schools and colleges.

The coach first set up a training camp in the San Francisco Bay Area, attracting a small band of athletes. They later moved with him to Los Angeles.

Igloi showed how quickly an inspired coach and a few runners could reverse a country's fortunes. This had happened by the early 1960s. The Igloi group included Max Truex, Jim Beatty, and Bob Schul. Truex, a dropout in the 10,000 in the 1956 Olympics, placed sixth at Rome while hugely improving the American record. In 1962 Beatty ran the world's first sub-four-minute mile indoors. And of course in 1964 Schul became America's first—and still only—Olympic 5,000 winner.

Igloi used an interval-based training system, using complex mixtures of distances and paces that only he (and perhaps his protégé Laszlo Tabori) understood. Nearly all the training was on the track, with the coach always watching. This approach obviously worked well for the few runners lucky enough to join him—and to tolerate the intensity and uncertainty of his program. Igloi's boys set 49 world records.

But the mysterious method was almost inseparable from the man, who said little about it publicly and wrote even less. He had to be there to make it work, and it didn't transfer well to other coaches or to athletes training on their own.

Timing also worked against Igloi. His coaching contemporary was Arthur Lydiard, whose runners won twice at the 1960 Olympics and whose ways were the opposite of Igloi's. The New Zealander called for lots of running away from the track—and out of the coach's sight. This system appealed more to runners than camping at the track for hours each day.

Lydiard, who never met a microphone or reporter he didn't like, had a gift for promotion that Igloi never tried to develop. Lydiard explained himself often and well, and his methods caught on worldwide.

Igloi's didn't. So he and his system, and his success, are little remembered now—except by the people who ran for him. One is Orville Atkins, a marathoner. Orville was an Igloi boy in the mid-1960s, and he later wrote, "Coach Igloi gave me his time and patience only because I asked for it. I respect him and thank him. I was lucky to work and learn under a man who was strong willed, stubborn and a genius to boot."

Living History

From Joe Henderson's *Running Commentary,* December 1999.

Running seminars work the same way as study in school. Learning isn't confined to the lecture halls but continues in the hallways, at meals, and on the streets outside.

I attended a race directors' conference in Portland this fall, sitting on a couple of panels. As usually happens at events like this, I learned more than I taught—and heard the weekend's best story outside the classroom. It had both a shocking start and a happy end.

Judy Ikenberry sat beside me for one of the panel discussions. My thought while glancing over at her was this: she looks too young and lively to be a monument to women's running history. As Judy Shapiro, she began running in the late 1950s and ran as far as the officials at the time would let her. That was little more than a mile. Later she married her coach, Dennis Ikenberry, and graduated in distances as the slowly relaxing rules allowed. In 1974 she won the first U.S. women's marathon title, setting a PR of 2:54 while beating better-known runners such as first official Boston champion Nina Kuscsik.

Later still, the Ikenberrys set up a race-scoring business called Race Central, based in southern California. That was Judy's reason for being on the Portland panel, because her company scores the Portland Marathon along with dozens of others each year.

After the talk we walked back to our separate hotels together. Judy said then what she hadn't mentioned in her talk. "We're thinking of cutting back on our business. Dennis is 65 and starting to talk about retirement. I'm only 57, but I haven't been well the past year and need to slow down."

She looked as energetic as I'd seen her in any of our annual visits. I asked what had gone wrong. She gave a grim story the lightest possible telling. "I'm happy just to be here," she said. "I died in June." There's a line guaranteed to capture attention. Judy explained that she'd felt symptoms while riding her bicycle and knew what might be happening. "I have a terrible family history of heart disease and high cholesterol," she said.

During examination for her condition, Judy's heart stopped and was electrically jolted back to life. She required immediate bypass surgery, from which she recovered in time for her daughter's wedding. "She would never have forgiven me if I hadn't been there," said Judy. Tracing a line from lower stomach to upper chest, she said, "I now have a nice little scar to remind me to take better care of myself." She added, "I know I need to stay far away from gambling casinos. I've already used up all of my good luck."

At lunch that Saturday in Portland, Judy had taken charge of having get-well cards signed for race director Les Smith's wife. Nadine had fallen the night before and broken an arm. No one at the conference knew better than Judy Ikenberry how good getting better could feel.

iliotibial band syndrome. It's not a musical group but a knee injury so common that it's known by its initials—ITB. This band runs from the outer thigh to behind the knee. *See also* injuries.

Ikangaa, Juma (b. July 19, 1957). When we think of the African domination of the marathon, we typically associate the Ethiopians (Abebe Bikila, Mamo Wolde) with the 1960s and the Kenyans (too many to list) with the late 1980s through the turn of the century. Yet one of the most dominating figures during the 1980s was a Tanzanian, Juma Ikangaa. A diminutive athlete (five feet three inches and 117 pounds) with the heart of a lion, he ran six sub-2:09s. During his career, the soft-spoken, gentle lion won New York City (2:08:01, 1989, course record), Fukuoka (1986), Tokyo (1984 to 1986), Melbourne, and Beijing. He was a fierce competitor, often compared to Steve Jones—a runner who took the field out fast and kept the pedal to the metal.

Ikangaa was the youngest of six children. He did what many older people in the United States say they used to do; he took himself to school and back each day, running 10 miles in each direction. After high school, he entered the military and in Cairo won the Army Games 5,000- and 10,000-meter races. Ikangaa burst upon the world marathon scene at the 1982 Commonwealth Games at Brisbane, Australia, where, after running his first marathon only the month before, he took the field out at a pace that surprised favorite Rob de Castella—so much that de Castella let Juma and teammate Gidamis Shahanga go, until he realized they weren't coming back. De Castella caught up, and at 24 miles he and Juma waged one of the epic battles in marathon history, with de Castella ultimately winning—barely.

"I train to run the marathon as fast as I can," Juma said. Like other front-runners, he always chose marathons with stellar fields. After a disappointing 6th at the 1984 Los Angeles Olympics, Juma pretty much took 1985 off, then returned in 1986 with a 3rd (2:08:39) at Beijing, a 2:08:10 win at Tokyo, and a win at Fukuoka in 2:10:06. In 1987 he ran his first Boston, where he placed 11th and then went on a buying spree in Beantown with his appearance money, purchasing clothes to give to children back in Tanzania. That fall he returned to Beijing, and this time he won.

In February 1988 he went back to Tokyo and took 2nd with a 2:08:42. He came back to Boston looking for not just a win to wipe out his 11th-place finish from the year before but to set a world record. He took the field through 10 miles in 47:57, gradually dropping the world-class field except for Kenyan Ibrahim Hussein. An African had never won at Boston, although many had tried, including Ethiopians Bikila and Wolde. With a mile to go, Hussein was on Ikangaa's shoulder. They both sprinted, but Hussein sprinted a mite faster and won by one second (2:08:43). Some consider it the best Boston race of all time.

Disappointed, Juma returned to Africa where it is rumored he ran 220-mile weeks, an astonishing volume if it is true. He spoke of winning the 1988 Olympic Marathon and then winning Boston the following spring. But after leading for a time at Seoul, Juma eventually fell back and finished seventh. At Boston in 1989 he took the field out even faster than the year before (a 1:02:23 half-marathon split), but in the final miles was outdueled by Ethiopian Abebe Mekonnen. Juma lost with a 2:09:56. Still looking for a win in an American marathon, he went to New York City that fall and ran against Olympic champion Gelindo Bordin of Italy, Steve Jones (defending New York champ), and world record-holder Belayneh Dinsamo (2:06:50) of Ethiopia. He burned everyone down with 4:34-per-mile surges. He won in 2:08:01, setting a course record that still stands.

In 1990 he returned to Boston, intent on winning the famed race; in fact, he came to Boston stating he was going to break the world record. He went out at a world-beating pace (half-marathon in 1:02:01), but Gelindo Bordin passed him in the final miles to become the first Olympic Marathon gold medalist ever to win Boston. For Juma, it was three second places at Boston.

Gradually, the fierce training Juma did in order to dominate races began to take its toll, wearing him down. In all, he ran in roughly 40 marathons at a world-class pace, taking the fields out at breakneck speeds. Along with Steve Jones, Juma Ikangaa took the marathon to a new level, pushing the pace from the first step to the last stride. In the process, Juma's sense of humor, graciousness, and genuine regard for people made him one of the most popular road runners of his era. *See also* Boston Marathon; Fukuoka Marathon; New York City Marathon; rankings, *Track & Field News*; Tokyo Marathons.

© Mark Shearman. Athletics–Images.

Tanzanian Juma Ikangaa was one of the smaller African road racers but he had the heart of a lion. He typically took the field out at a suicide pace and tried to burn his competitors.

Indy 500 Festival Mini-Marathon (www.500festival.com). The nation's largest half-marathon—with 18,500 finishers in 1999—runs part of its course as one lap of the famous Indianapolis Motor Speedway. The race starts and finishes in downtown Indianapolis, several weeks before the auto race of late May. The event is the centerpiece of the Masters Indy Life Circuit and serves as the USATF masters half-marathon championships. *See also* biggest races.

injuries. In any year a majority of the running population will be injured. But we must define *injury*. Most running injuries are minor in that they don't disrupt daily life. Most are self-inflicted, and most eventually heal if the cause is rooted out and corrected. The leading injuries among runners are chondromalacia ("runner's knee") and iliotibial band (ITB) syndrome of the knee, Achilles tendinitis of the lower leg, stress fractures of the lower leg and foot, plantar fasciitis of the foot, and injuries brought on by stretching while the muscles are still cold.

International Association of Athletics Federations (IAAF) (www.iaaf.org). Formerly the International Amateur Athletic Federation, the IAAF now deals largely with professional and semipro athletes in all track and field events. The organization, based in Monte Carlo, Monaco, regulates track and field as a whole on the world stage, with its biggest event being the every-other-year World Championships, which include marathons for men and women. *See also* organizations.

International Olympic Committee (IOC) (www.olympic.org). The group of aristocrats is in charge of selecting Olympic sites and conducting the Olympic Games. Many of the actual decisions on the track and field segment of the Games, however, are left to the IAAF. *See also* Olympic Marathon, 1900 to 2000; organizations.

International Runners Committee (IRC). The now defunct group, supported by Nike, lobbied in the late 1970s and early 1980s for a women's Olympic Marathon. Its leader was Jacqueline Hansen, former world record-holder at that distance. The IRC disbanded shortly after the women's marathon joined the Olympic schedule for the 1984 Games. *See also* Hansen, Jacqueline; organizations.

Internet. *See* online registration. *See also Web sites for individual events, organizations, and companies.*

interval training. Traditional intervals—short bursts of speed, separated by recovery breaks—aren't a favorite of many runners. But interval work is a necessity for improving speed. Leading proponents of intervals have been runner Emil Zatopek and coach Mihaly Igloi. A broader application of the interval principle (breaking up a big piece of work into smaller chunks) is the practice of taking walk breaks during long runs. *See also* Igloi, Mihaly; walk breaks; Zatopek, Emil.

Inubushi, Takayuki (b. August 11, 1972). The former Asian marathon record-holder from Japan ran 2:06:57 at Berlin in 1999. His mark fell in 2000 to Atsushi Fujita. *See also* Fujita, Atsushi.

IOC. *See* International Olympic Committee.

Irvine, Sister Marion (b. October 19, 1929). A Catholic nun and educator, she is the oldest American runner to qualify for a U.S. Olympic Trials. She ran the 1984 Trials Marathon at age 54 after qualifying with 2:51:01. She holds the American 60–64 record for the 5K. *See also* "Second to Nun" below; Hall of Fame, RRCA; records, American age-group.

Isphording, Julie (b. December 5, 1961). So naive was she as a 22-year-old running in the first U.S. Olympic Trials Marathon for women that she didn't know until crossing the finish line that she'd finished third and made the team. An injury kept Isphording from finishing at the Los Angeles Games, but she returned to that city in 1990 to win the L.A. Marathon. Julie now hosts a radio program on running in Cincinnati. *See also* Los Angeles Marathon; Olympians, U.S.; Olympic Trials Marathon, U.S.

Second to Nun

From Joe Henderson's *Running Commentary,* August 2000.

A woman wrote to tell me of her lofty goal and to ask a question. She's several years from reaching it and wondered if she'd be first to do so.

"My name is Michelle Hamel," she said. "Presently I can run a 3:10 marathon, and I have a long-term goal of going to the Olympic Trials in 2004. At that time I will be 50 years young." She asked, "Has there been a 50-year-old woman to go to the Trials yet? If not, I would like to be the first."

She wouldn't be second to none, I had to tell her. But she could be second to a nun. The only 50-plus runner to make the Olympic Trials so far was Sister Marion Irvine, who qualified in 1984 by running 2:51:01. She was 54 then and had only been running since her late 40s. (Sister Marion no longer is the fastest over-50 American. That record belongs to Shirley Matson. Her time of 2:50:26, run in 1991, wasn't quite fast enough for the Trials the next year.)

The exchange of notes with Michelle Hamel gives me an excuse to talk more about Sister Marion. I see her each summer at Jeff Galloway's running camp, which reconvened last month at Lake Tahoe. She is always the life of this party. She tells un-nun-like jokes and wields a mean paddle on the raft trip, while waging a water war on nearby boaters from our group.

Marion is 70 and has long since downsized her running to a recreational level. Someone at camp mentioned that she's now semiretired from her life's work in education. "Our order doesn't recognize the word 'retired,'" she corrected. "The preferred term is 'working part-time.'" Her emphasis has shifted to political and human-rights issues, such as campaigning against the death penalty.

She now has time that wasn't available in her racing days. She's spending some of it watching others run. "I'll be in Sacramento for all of the Trials," she said as she left the Galloway camp in July. "The big news, though, is that I'm going to Sydney for the Games. I have to sleep on someone's floor to get there, but I'm going and never thought this would be possible."

IT band. *See* iliotibial band syndrome.

Ivanova, Zoya (b. March 14, 1952). A much-decorated runner in the last days of the Soviet Union, she was silver medalist in the 1987 World Championships (2:32:38) and the World Cup winner (2:30:39) that same year. Ivanova also won at Tokyo in 1982 (2:34:26) and Los Angeles in 1989 (2:34:42). *See also* Los Angeles Marathon; Tokyo Marathons; World Championships medalists; World Cup Marathon.

Jackson Day Race (www.runnotc.org). The New Orleans 9K, run each January, stretches back to the early years of the last century. *See also* oldest races.

Janicki, Don (b. April 23, 1960). He ran his first marathon as a teenager and won his first national championship—in the half-marathon—in his 30s. Janicki competed in two World Championship Marathons, 10 years apart (21st and leading American in 1987; did not finish in 1997). *See also* national half-marathon champions, U.S.; World Championships, U.S.

Jasper to Banff Relay. The Canadian 177-mile relay race ran north to south along the eastern side of the Rockies and was a model for the Hood to Coast Relay. The big difference between Jasper to Banff and most modern relays is that each of the 12 members of the J-B team ran only one long leg of 10 to 12 or more miles, far longer than those of other relays. Also everyone started together in Jasper (rather than in waves), an experience made possible because the race was limited to only 120 teams. Following the 2000 running, the organizers canceled the race because they were burned out after nearly 20 years and faced additional restrictions, such as running only in daylight. The Edmonton, Alberta, running community talked about jumping in to save it, but the timing was extremely bad as Edmonton was gearing up to host the 2001 World Championships. The J-B race will likely be revived at some point. *See also* Hood to Coast Relay; relays.

Jennings, Lynn (b. July 1, 1960). She's one of the most versatile runners, female or male, in U.S. history. Best known for cross country (three World titles) and track (Olympic and World Indoor medals), she also is American road record-holder at 8K (25:02 in 1991), 10K (31:06 in 1990), and 12K (39:14 in 1993). She is a six-time winner of the national 5K, a four-time winner of the national 10K, and a member of the RRCA and National Distance Running Halls of Fame. Jennings ran her first marathon, in 2:46, as a teenager and her second, in 2:38, more than 20 years later. Both were at Boston. *See also* "Looking Up to Jennings" on next page; Bay to Breakers 12K; Hall of Fame, National Distance Running; Hall of Fame, RRCA; national 5K champions, U.S.; national 10K champions, U.S.; Peachtree 10K; record progressions, American; records, American.

Jimmy Stewart Relay. *See* relays.

Looking Up to Jennings

From Joe Henderson's *Running Commentary,* December 1991.

Lynn Jennings makes my short list of most-admired athletes. She's a runner for all seasons: world champion in cross country, Olympian in outdoor track, American record-holder indoors, and owner of world and U.S. road marks.

Jennings's versatility and year-round consistency are unmatched. But a runner needs more than talent to become a favorite. Lynn has more. She gives you a firm hand-shake, looks you in the eyes, calls you by name, and says what she thinks. She also takes commitments seriously.

Jennings committed herself last year to run the National Women's 8K Champion-ship in Alhambra, California, but couldn't go because of an ankle sprain. She prom-ised then to be there in 1991 and she was. Before racing, she gave a clinic for the area's high school runners. She admitted her failures: running herself into knee sur-gery in high school and retiring three times while still young.

In her mid-20s, Jennings decided, "I was born to be a runner. When I told that to my parents, they supported my decision but weren't thrilled. I could see Dad thinking he had just spent $40,000 on my Princeton education so I could run around in sneakers the rest of my life."

Lynn also wasn't shy about telling her strengths. "I'm one of the wiser runners out there on the circuit," she said. "I never ignore what my body tells me, and I never get overuse injuries." Yet she confessed to pushing nearer the edge this year than ever before. The Alhambra 8K would be her third road race in less than three weeks, a far busier schedule than Jennings prefers.

But she made no excuses about feeling tired or this being her down season. She wasn't coy about her intentions. Lynn said, "I want to break 25:02. That's the existing world record. I've been thinking about that for a couple of months. I'm not thinking I *might* be able to do it. I'm thinking I *will* do it."

Alhambra's $100,000 incentive to break the record was more than a publicity gim-mick. Races often get ink and airplay with such bonus offers while taking little risk of paying off. Not Alhambra. Organizers there had to buy an insurance policy costing about one-fifth that amount. And Jennings stood a good chance of earning the bonus because she already held the 8K mark.

But records can't be scheduled, even by the most determined runners and gener-ous sponsors. They can't order perfect conditions. The weather this last Saturday in October turned un-Californian. After five years of drought, heavy rains suddenly blew through Alhambra. The rain could have improved Jennings's chances if it had simply cooled the temperature and cleared out the smog. But the storm also brought wind, a headwind for the hard part of the out-and-back course.

Lynn might have given up her record attempt before it started. Instead, she raced to the halfway mark 19 seconds faster than record pace before turning into the wind. It slowed her to 25:23. Not a record but an admirable try.

[Jennings did her finest running after this story appeared. She won a bronze medal in the 10,000 meters at the 1992 Olympic Games, a bronze and silver in the 3,000 meters at the 1993 and 1995 World Indoor Championships, and her third World Cross Country title, and she competed in her third Olympics.]

jog. A synonym for slow running, almost universally despised among "real" runners, *jog* used to refer to casual running in the 1960s. The word is coming back into vogue as runners slow their pace, using the term as a self-effacing synonym for a very easy run.

Jogbra (www.championjogbra.com). A great supporter of women's running is the Jogbra. The first Jogbra Sports Bra was constructed in the early 1980s from two jockstraps sewn together by two women athletes who couldn't find a supportive bra for running. That first design is now part of the permanent collection at the Smithsonian and the Metropolitan Museum of Art's Costume Collection. *See also* clothing.

Jogging. Bill Bowerman's groundbreaking (or ground-pounding) book was written with W.E. Harris, MD, and published in 1967 (Grosset & Dunlap). It was inspired by Bowerman's being taken on a "jog" by New Zealand coach Arthur Lydiard, and it preceded Dr. Kenneth Cooper's *Aerobics* by a year. As Cooper would do later, Bowerman promoted running for its health and fitness benefits. *See also* books; Bowerman, Bill; Lydiard, Arthur.

Johnson, Jeff (b. September 29, 1941). With Phil Knight, Jeff founded Blue Ribbon Sports as a vehicle through which they could sell Japanese Tiger (now Asics) running shoes to American runners. Jeff, like a handful of running entrepreneurs throughout the country, drove to road races with the trunk of his car stuffed with Tiger running shoes so he could sell them to the local runners. No running stores existed at the time; about as close as you could get to buying running shoes was to mail order New Balance shoes or, as of 1966, to order Tiger shoes from Phil and Jeff through a center-spread mail-order ad in the new running magazine, *Distance Running News* (forerunner of *Runner's World*). Prices (for the TG-22 Road Runner) started at $7.95. In the magazine's second year Jeff Johnson put together the first-ever running-shoe comparison report.

When Knight and Johnson began to have troubles with Tiger, they joined Oregon coach Bill Bowerman to come up with their own American-made running shoe, Nike. The name, legend has it, came to Jeff in a dream. After working with Nike for many years to develop the brand and produce increasingly better shoes, Jeff retired early.

One of his greatest contributions to the sport lies not in the development of better running shoes but in the historical record of running he created as a photographer starting in the 1960s. Many of those images appear in this book to represent road racing during that era. Jeff spent much of the 1990s developing the Farm Team, a San Francisco Bay Area running team that he coached for many years. ("Farm" refers to its location in the Stanford University area, long known to Bay Area residents as the Farm.) He spent half of each year in California and the other half in New Hampshire while developing the team, which recently reached the point where Jeff was able to turn the administrative responsibilities over to others, Stanford coach Vin Lananna among them. *See also* air sole; Asics; Blue Ribbon Sports; Bowerman, Bill; Knight, Phil; Nike; shoe companies.

Johnson, Libbie. *See* Hickman, Libbie Johnson.

Johnston, Kristy (b. June 3, 1965). The sub-2:30 U.S. marathoner should have been an Olympian in 2000 but missed out because of a confusing qualifying system and a hot day at the Trials (where she finished second). She also missed the 1993 Worlds because of injury, after being the leading qualifier. Johnston won the 1994 Chicago Marathon. *See also* Chicago Marathon; Olympic Trials Marathon, U.S.

Joints in Motion (JIM). This running-based charitable effort raises funds to combat arthritis. *See also* charity running.

Jones, Kim Rosenquist (b. May 2, 1958). She enjoyed one of the longest and most productive marathon careers of any American but was always one place away from the winner's laurels in big-time marathons. Of her seven best marathon times, six are for second place and one is for third—2:26:40 at Boston 1991 (second), 2:27:50 at Berlin 1991 (second), 2:27:54 at New York City 1989 (second), 2:29:34 at Boston 1989 (third), 2:30:00 at Boston 1993 (second), 2:30:50 at New York City 1990 (second), and 2:31:24 at Chicago 1995 (second).

Two of her biggest victories came at Twin Cities, in 1986 and 1989. She is the third fastest American of all time at 2:26:40, a three-time member of U.S. World Championships teams (with an eighth place in 1993), national marathon winner in 1986, and 1997 10K champion. She also holds the world and American 30K records of 1:47:41, set en route to a 1986 marathon.

Kim won the 1991 Philadelphia Distance Run Half-Marathon in 1:12:53. She was ranked America's best marathoner in 1993. Her best 10-mile time is 53:33, and her best 10K is 32:23. She also won the 1997 Bloomsday in her then hometown of Spokane. Since turning 40 in 1998, she has had some sterling masters performances. *See also* Bloomsday 12K; Hall of Fame, RRCA; national marathon champions, U.S.; national 10K champions, U.S.; records, American; records, world; World Championships, U.S.

Jones, Steve. *See* page 153.

Jong Song Ok (b. August 18, 1974). The little-known North Korean woman pulled a big upset by winning the 1999 World Championships Marathon—then abruptly retired before the Sydney Olympics at age 25. *See also* World Championships medalists.

junior division. It's defined internationally as runners who haven't yet turned 20 in the current calendar year. *See also* records, American age-group; records, world age-group.

junk miles. This disparaging label applies to slow miles and extra miles run largely or solely for the sake of putting bigger numbers in the logbook or avoiding a day with zero mileage.

Jones, Steve (b. August 4, 1955). Born in Tredegar, Wales, son of a steelworker, Steve Jones grew up tough and rugged, qualities he transferred to his running. During his youth Steve was two ticks to the hoodlum side of the law. He began smoking cigarettes at age 12 and continued for seven years. He hung out with punks, was pursued by the Ebbw Vale police for minor troublemaking, and he occasionally held down three jobs at once—paperboy, milk delivery boy, and butcher boy.

At 15 he signed up for the Air Training Corps of the Royal Air Force. At about the same time he was conned into entering a local 5K cross country race; he finished 5th, which qualified him for the regional, where he placed 6th, which sent him to the nationals, where he placed 23rd. He was hooked but not quite hooked enough to give up smoking cigarettes for another four years. Additionally, he never trained—only raced.

At 18 he joined the Royal Air Force, becoming a jet-fighter mechanic. And he took up running seriously, training like a madman, twice a day, sometimes three times daily, always hard. Like Emil Zatopek, Jones claimed to have little talent other than a talent for working hard. Still something of an unknown in his own country, when the World Cross Country Championships came to Wales in 1977, he was not picked for the team, which angered him. In an attempt to show officials

One of the toughest competitors in marathon running, Steve Jones, a jet fighter mechanic in the RAF, ran fast and hard from the start of a race. In the process he set world bests in the half-marathon and marathon. During one spree, he ran three sub-2:08:30 marathons in a one-year period.

how wrong they were in passing him over, he eventually became Wales cross country champion an amazing nine times! He concentrated on cross country and track (first the steeplechase, then the 5,000 and 10,000).

Agent Bob Wood had been trying to lure Steve to the marathon, and in the fall of 1983 Jones went to Chicago. Unfortunately, he pulled a tendon in his foot the night before the race and although he felt comfortable aerobically, his foot caused him to favor one leg, which ultimately hobbled him. He was still with the lead pack when he limped off the course at 16 miles.

Jones placed a disappointing eighth in the 10,000 meters at the 1984 Los Angeles Olympics. He came over early for Chicago that year, using some road races as warm-ups for the marathon. He lost to Carlos Lopes, gold medalist in the marathon at Los Angeles, by six seconds in a 15K race in Texas, then won a half-marathon in Ohio in just over 62 minutes after stopping to help right a wheelchair competitor who had fallen over. He came to Chicago hoping to break the Welsh national marathon record of 2:12. With sponsorship from Beatrice Foods, director Bob Bright brought in a sterling field to compete against the glitter of New York City's fall marathon. The field went out fast and instead of slowing down, they just kept going harder. Although he had gone beyond 20 miles only once in training, Steve felt strong until the final miles, when his legs became sore. But still he pushed, crossing the finish line in 2:08:05, a world record. In a little over two hours, Steve Jones went from unknown to road-racing king.

In March of 1985 he proceeded to break the world record in the half-marathon with a 1:01:14 at Birmingham, England. It was a perfect tune-up for the London Marathon in April where, in spite of stopping to relieve himself in the wake of stomach cramps, he ran 2:08:16. Five weeks before the 1985 Chicago Marathon, Steve went to Utah to train at altitude and to run several tune-up road races. At Chicago, he went out fast from the gun, passing the rabbit at two miles (reached in 9:28). Since Jones set his world record at Chicago in 1984, Carlos Lopes had lowered it to 2:07:12 in April in Rotterdam. That day at Chicago, Steve missed Lopes's mark by one second—and along with it a $50,000 bonus. But in the process he accomplished the seemingly impossible—three sub-2:08:30s within a one-year period.

At the 1986 European Championships Marathon at Stuttgart, Jones hit the wall hard at 20 miles while enjoying a commanding lead. Rather than drop out, he stayed in and struggled through to 20th place in 2:22:12. He took it easy in 1987, then ran 8th (2:14:07) at Boston in April 1988. The British officials felt he was a has-been and didn't bother to pick him for the team going to Seoul. Then, two days before the New York City Marathon, Reebok, his sponsor, refused to re-sign him. He entered New York as an independent and proceeded to run the second-fastest time on the course (2:08:20), winning by more than three minutes.

In October 1992 at age 39 he ran a disappointing 2:29 at New York. His fortunes changed when he became a masters runner, though; he has run consistently well in masters road racing and continues to do so while working for Reebok, who was happy to re-sign him after his New York City win back in 1988. He lives and trains in Boulder, Colorado. *See also* Chicago Marathon; London Marathon; New York City Marathon; rankings, *Track & Field News;* record progression, world.

J.Y. Cameron Five-Mile. The Buffalo, New York, race is one of the country's oldest, founded a year before the Boston Marathon (1896). *See also* oldest races.

K

Kagwe, John (b. January 9, 1969). The Boston Marathon billed the Kenyan this way as he came into the 2000 race: "A top finisher in some of the world's toughest marathons, Kagwe takes on Boston a fourth time this year. Kagwe is best known for his 1997 and 1998 New York City Marathon wins. In 1997, he broke the tape in 2:08:12 (second fastest time run on the course), despite stopping to tie his shoe twice. He defended his New York title in 1998 (2:08:45) after outsprinting Joseph Chebet in the final stretch by three seconds. Kagwe is past champion of the 1995 Pittsburgh Marathon (2:10:24) and champion of the 1997 Prague International Marathon (2:09:07). At Boston, he's aiming to get away from the fifth position, having earned the spot last year in 2:13:58 and the year before in 2:08:51.

"In Kagwe's 1994 marathon debut, he finished Boston 16th in 2:11:52. Additional marathons include 1999 New York (5th, 2:09:39), 1995 New York (5th, 2:11:42), and 1996 New York (4th, 2:10:59). In 1997, Kagwe ran his personal best half-marathon, placing 2nd at the Philadelphia Distance Run in 61:18. Kagwe trains in Kenya and the Philadelphia area. During this past winter, he placed 1st in the Kenya Prisons Provincial Cross Country Championships (8K) in 26:55, and in March finished 2nd at the Newark Distance Classic 20K in 60:46." In the 2000 Boston race, he placed 6th in 2:12:26. *See also* New York City Marathon.

Kantorek, Pavel (b. February 8, 1930). The Czech won the Košice Marathon three times (1958 with 2:29:38, 1962 with 2:28:30, 1964 with 2:25:56) and Fukuoka in 1961 (2:22:05). *See also* Fukuoka Marathon; Košice Peace Marathon.

Kardong, Don (b. December 22, 1948). If road racing has a Renaissance man, it is Don Kardong. (His nearest rival is probably Hal Higdon.) The fact that Don missed the bronze medal in the 1976 Olympic Marathon by a mere three seconds is only one part of his story. A graduate of Stanford University (psychology major, 1971) and the University of Washington (BA in English, 1974), Don was as much a threat at the longer distances on the track (see the second Steve Prefontaine movie, *Without Limits*) as he was on the roads.

In the wake of his fourth-place finish at Montreal in a PR of 2:11:16, he did what many other outstanding American runners did in the 1970s: he opened a running store. (He had worked as an elementary school teacher while training for the Olympic Games.) The store was in his adopted hometown, Spokane, Washington, where he's lived since getting married. To encourage more people to run, so they'd wear out their running shoes and come to him to buy more, he created the Lilac Bloomsday 12K Run—one of the country's largest races and one of the few megaraces in the country not held in a major city. He also won the 1976 Peachtree Road Race in Atlanta and the 1978 Honolulu Marathon.

Long a contract writer for *Runner's World* magazine, Don has collected his writings in two books, *Thirty Phone Booths to Boston: Tales of a Wayward Runner* (Macmillan, 1985) and *Hills, Hawgs and Ho Chi Minh* (Keokee, 1996). He has also written *Bloomsday: A City in Motion* (Cowles, 1989). He has dedicated a great deal of his life to helping the sport of road racing grow, the pinnacle of which was his four-year term (1996–2000) as president of the Road Runners Club of America. He has also experimented with ultrarunning, his first such effort a winning one in the tough Le Grizz 50-miler. He was also a founding member and past president (1981–1995) of the Association of Road Racing Athletes, an organization representing the interests of world-class long-distance runners.

Don is a humorist and much sought after as a speaker. He also does some coaching of runners over the Internet. He is married, has two daughters, and lives in Spokane. Don is widely acknowledged as one of the all-time good guys of road racing. *See also* Bloomsday 12K; Hall of Fame, RRCA; Honolulu Marathon; Olympians, U.S.; Olympic Trials Marathon, U.S.; Peachtree 10K; Road Runners Club of America; USA Track & Field.

Karvonen, Veikko (b. January 5, 1926). The Finns dominated distance running in the 1920s and 1930s, and again briefly in the 1970s. Karvonen was an in-betweener, with his marathon career peaking in the 1950s. He was bronze medalist in the 1956 Olympics, winner of the 1954 European title, winner of the 1955 Fukuoka, and had a top world ranking in 1951, 1954, and 1955. *See also* European Championships; Fukuoka Marathon; Olympic Marathon, 1900 to 2000; rankings, *Track & Field News.*

Kelley, John A. (b. September 6, 1907). On April 20, 1981, at the 85th running of the famed Boston Marathon, John A. Kelley of East Dennis, Massachusetts, ran in his 50th Boston Marathon. Kelley, 73, took twice as long as race winner Toshihiko Seko to finish the course, but despite foul weather, nearly every one of the more than a million spectators stayed until "Old John" Kelley (to differentiate him from "Young John" Kelley, see next entry, no relation) finished the course.

Bandy-legged, Irish to the hilt, high-spirited, and an amateur painter, Kelley won Boston twice, a decade apart (1935 and 1945), and took second place seven times. Ultimately, "Old John" would compete in 61 Boston Marathons and would complete 58 of them. In 1993 he stepped down from running the fabled race to serve as perpetual honorary grand marshal of the race.

John A. Kelley, twice winner of the Boston Marathon (1935 and 1945), ran Boston more than any other human being. He eventually became the honorary grand marshal of the event.

John Kelley was born the eldest of 10 children. In 1921 his father took him to see his first Boston Marathon race, and he was fascinated. He ran track and cross country in high school. Unfortunately, he graduated into the Great Depression; with no job at hand, he took up road racing, doing numerous 5- and 10-mile races. He ran his first marathon on St. Patrick's Day 1928 in Rhode Island on an out-and-back course where he went out too fast and spent the second half able to see the finish line ahead but seemingly unable to get any closer. He finished in 3:17. The next month he ran his first Boston, where he dropped out at Cleveland Circle, one of only three times that he did not finish the famed race.

His second attempt at Boston came in 1932, when he again dropped out—this time at Wellesley near the halfway mark. He was running with the leaders, however, when he dropped. In 1933 he took 37th place and the following year he took 2nd.

In 1935 Kelley won the race in 2:32:08. The following year, "Tarzan" Brown won, guaranteeing himself a place on the 1936 Olympic team. A marathon was held in Washington, D.C., to pick the remaining two Olympic marathoners. Kelley took second place and was off to Berlin, where he did not do well, but did finish, unlike his two teammates.

In March of 1937 Kelley ran a 20-mile race in Medford, which he considers probably the best race of his long career. He beat Walter Young, an amateur boxer from Canada, by three minutes. Kelley's advisers told him to back off to rest for Boston, which he did. In that race, he

From the collection of Dr. Edward H. Kozloff—Motor City Striders

and Young battled it out for 23 miles, exchanging the lead 16 times, until Young used his superior strength to pull away, winning by six minutes.

Kelley's win at Boston in 1945, a decade after his first win, takes second place to his performance at the famed Yonkers Marathon (which he ran 29 times), where he won in 1935 and again in 1950—an amazing 15-year spread between wins, the latter win coming at age 42. The Yonkers Marathon for many years served as the U.S. national marathon championship; "Old John" won it in 1948 and 1950. He made the Olympic Marathon team for the third time in 1948 at age 40. (The second time was in 1940, but the Games were canceled because of World War II.)

As to his performance at his 50th Boston in 1981, Kelley ran it in 4:01:25 and blames his failure to break four hours on all the publicity surrounding his 50th Boston. "I could have done a much better time, you know, on my 50th," he lamented afterward, "if I hadn't given in to all the people who wanted some of my time before the race. I'm still learning lessons about my running . . . ." In 1992 a biography of "Old John" Kelley, *Young at Heart*, was published; it was written by Frederick Lewis and Dick Johnson. *See also* Boston Marathon; Hall of Fame, National Distance Running; Hall of Fame, RRCA; Hall of Fame, USATF; Olympians, U.S.; national marathon champions, U.S.

Kelley, John J. (b. December 24, 1930). It is impossible to relate the story of John J. Kelley (sometimes referred to as "The Younger" to differentiate him from the similarly named but unrelated John A. Kelley) without introducing John "Jock" Semple, the fiery Scot who was for many years the keeper of the flame at the Boston Marathon. In 1948, Jock first laid eyes on Young John Kelley. It was an Olympic year, and one of the U.S. Olympians, Vic Dyrgall, was brought in for the July 4 15K race at Fall River, Massachusetts, so the crowd could get a look at an Olympian while he raced as a last tune-up for the Games. Dyrgall went out fast, as expected, but two high school runners latched onto him and stayed with him; the smaller of the two was wearing taped-together track shoes with the spikes removed. In the 100-degree

Courtesy of Dr. Edward H. Kozloff-Motor City Striders

John J. Kelley virtually owned the Yonkers Marathon. He won eight times: 1956 through 1963. This victory was in 1960.

heat and on a rough road, the tape unwound, the shoes disintegrated, and the kid was running in bare feet, which began to bleed on the rough surface. At four miles the kid dropped out and Jock, in a car following the leaders, stopped to pick him up. John J. Kelley had found his Boston Athletic Association (BAA) angel.

It was only Johnny Kelley's second road race. Ten days later he ran a handicap race at Haverhill and won both the time and place trophies while Jock Semple watched. Jock claimed for years that he was not only Johnny's coach but also Johnny's father figure; Johnny's father had died early in his life. Johnny went to Boston University in 1950 on a running scholarship, which meant he had to work 15 hours a week at the dorm cafeteria to make ends meet. And he had to spend additional time walking the line between the dictates of his college track coach, Doug Raymond, and his road-racing coach, Jock Semple. Raymond demanded repeat laps; Jock sampled all sorts of training and even wanted to introduce a new concept called *fartlek*. When Emil Zatopek exploded onto the scene, Johnny modified his training to imitate the great Czech.

Johnny decided to train for the 1953 Boston Marathon and didn't dare tell Doug Raymond until two weeks before. Johnny, the first American to finish, took fifth place. The next year he was again the first American but placed seventh. In the meantime, a vacuum had formed at the Boston Marathon, into which crusty old Jock had been sucked as torch carrier and guardian. At this point Young Johnny's career was interrupted by a year and a half in the army. When he returned, Boston had grown. Boston 1956 was a barnburner, a battle to the finish that produced astonishingly fast times. Antti Viskari set an apparent world record of 2:14:14. Kelley was in second place, a mere 20 seconds back. Unfortunately, a subsequent remeasuring of the course found it 1,100 yards short.

Johnny went to the Melbourne Olympics but under hot conditions finished 25th. He thought about giving up running. But he was back at Boston on April 20, 1957. He and his wife, Jessie, stayed the night before with grizzled veteran and namesake Johnny "The Elder" Kelley. Jock Semple thought the arrangement was perfect. Old Johnny even joked with people that Young Johnny was his son. Young Johnny won Boston that day (in 2:20:05, a course record) and fulfilled Jock Semple's dream of bringing a victory home for the BAA. Johnny was the only American to win Boston in the 1950s.

Kelley's association with Boston, however, overshadows his much more incredible feat. Each year, a month after Boston, the AAU Marathon Championships were held on the tough Yonkers, New York, course. Johnny Kelley won the Yonkers race an astounding eight years in a row, from 1956 through 1963! During that same time period, he also won the Pan-American Games Marathon in 1959 and set American marathon records in 1956 and 1957, becoming the first American to dip under 2:25.

He enjoyed a distinguished career as an English teacher in Groton, Connecticut, where one of his high school students was Amby Burfoot, who would also run cross country under Johnny's guidance and go on to win the 1968 Boston Marathon—the only American to win Boston in the decade of the 1960s. These days, Young Johnny and his wife operate a running store in Groton, while Johnny pens stories of his unforgettable years of running with the leaders. *See also* Boston Marathon; fartlek; Hall of Fame, RRCA; national marathon champions, U.S.; Olympians, U.S.; Pan-American Games; record progressions, American; Semple, John "Jock"; Zatopek, Emil.

Kellner, Gyula (b. April 11, 1871; d. July 28, 1940). The Hungarian ultrarunner was one of only four non-Greeks in the first Olympic Marathon and the only foreigner to complete the race. He was awarded third place after protesting Spiridon Belokas's accepting a ride. *See also* Olympic medalists.

Kempainen, Bob (b. June 18, 1966). Now a medical doctor practicing in Seattle, Bob took breaks from his medical school studies to become the fastest U.S. marathoner ever with an aided 2:08:47 at Boston in 1994. He's still the fastest U.S.-born marathoner, though naturalized citizen Khalid Khannouchi has since lowered the American record to 2:07:01.

Bob was not an exceptional runner in high school, but coach Vin Lananna recruited him to Dartmouth, where he began to bloom. He ran a 30:14 10,000 as a freshman; by his senior year (1988) he had pared that time down to 28:43 and placed third in the NCAA Championships. Following college Bob concentrated on the 10,000 on the track, but no great breakthroughs came, although he did take second in the USATF nationals. He and coach Lananna decided it was time to move up in distance.

In 1991 Bob ran the Twin Cities Marathon and took 2nd place in 2:12:12. The following year he placed 3rd at the U.S. Olympic Trials in the event and went to Barcelona, where he finished 17th in 2:15:53. In 1993 he ran New York City, placing 2nd in 2:11:03. From 1994 to 1996 Bob ranked as the top U.S. marathoner. He ran his 2:08:47 at Boston in 1994, and although he only placed 7th and the tailwind and downhill slope aided the performance, he was seen as the renaissance of American marathoning.

His toughness and work ethic in the face of medical studies were topped at the 1996 U.S. Olympic Trials Marathon where, because of severe stomach cramps he endured projectile vomit, front and center on the television coverage. His distress seemed only to stir him to greater efforts. He won the trials in 2:12:45 and became a legend of running through adversity. Some considered his stomach problems an embarrassment, but most long-distance runners identified with his perseverance. Postings such as this appeared on Internet sites: "This guy has to be one of the toughest runners alive, because he was throwing up while running, and he actually pulled away from his competition as he did so!"

Bob wanted to vindicate what he viewed as his poor 1992 Olympic performance, but he went into the 1996 Games suffering from tendinitis in the iliotibial bands in both legs. He decided to run anyway and had the worst marathon of his career, a 2:18:38 for 31st place. "This is the first marathon I really died in," he said afterward. He then wound down his running career and concentrated on completing his medical studies. *See also* Olympians, U.S.; Olympic Trials Marathon, U.S.; record progressions, American; records, American.

Kenyan runners. Kenya burst onto the world running map at the 1968 Mexico City Olympics in the person of Kip Keino, who beat favored American Jim

Ryun in the 1,500 meters and set an Olympic record in the process. Keino also took second in the 5,000 meters, and teammate Naftali Temu won the 10,000. (Ethiopia, Kenya's East African rival, made its own strong showing. Mamo Wolde took second in the 10,000 and then won the marathon, an event the Ethiopians dominated in the 1960s.) Keino became a national hero and did much to give running a cachet in Kenya that it had not enjoyed before.

The range of the Kenyan runners took a radical spike in the 1980s when Ibrahim Hussein, educated in the United States, and Douglas Wakiihuri, who went to Japan to train under the legendary coach Kiyoshi Nakamura, moved up to the marathon and began to dominate any race they entered. Kenyan running experienced another radical spike in the 1990s when Italian clothing (and later running-shoe) giant Fila established Discovery running programs in Kenya under coach Dr. Gabriele Rosa. Suddenly Kenyans came out of Africa in droves and began to dominate road races at 5K and 10K and then migrated into the marathon.

Until the 1980s no African had ever won the Boston Marathon. In 1988 three dozen Africans came to Boston as the race made the big shift to a professional level and drew one of its best-ever international fields. It included Olympic marathon medalists Gelindo Bordin and John Treacy, New York City winner Orlando Pizzolato and fellow Italian Gianni Poli, Steve Jones, previous Boston winner Geoff Smith, John Campbell from New Zealand, and a handful of Japanese. The race featured five runners under 2:10 and a classic first-place battle between Kenya's Ibrahim Hussein and Tanzania's Juma Ikangaa. The winner's column at the Boston Marathon would never be the same again. Except for Gelindo Bordin's 1990 breaking of the Boston curse against Olympic men's gold medalists, every Boston from then on was won by an African—usually a Kenyan.

A little behind on the time curve, but not to be denied as a dominating force, were African women, led by Kenyan Tegla Loroupe. At the 2000 Olympic Games, Eric Wainaina took silver in the marathon, and Joyce Chepchumba took bronze. The Kenyans seem to have an unending supply of eager, dedicated long-distance runners ready to compete anywhere in the world at a high level. *See also* "Embrace Every Race" on next page; Fila; Rosa, Gabriele.

Keston, John (b. December 5, 1924). A perfect argument that it is never too late to start a running program, John Keston did not begin running until he was 55—as a method of controlling mild hypertension. But once he got up a head of steam, it would take a series of untimely accidents to slow him from his age-group marathon world-record rampage. A member of the Royal Air Force in Italy during World War II, John took up the career of an itinerant actor with the Shakespearian Company in Britain. He was eventually lured to teach at a small college in the American Midwest, where he taught theater arts while continuing to pursue his acting and singing.

Once into running, he quickly found he had a talent for it and began gravitating to the marathon, where his PR is 2:52:32. His world-record hunt involved

Embrace Every Race

From Joe Henderson's *Running Commentary,* October 1998.

Beverly, a volunteer at the Crim Races, drew the early shift. She was making her first airport runs at six o'clock on a Sunday morning, and I was the first weekend guest to be escorted away from Flint, Michigan.

We talked about the recent divisive and depressing two-month strike against General Motors that had Flint as its epicenter. We didn't talk about the city's image, which took a beating in the movie *Roger and Me.* That portrayal is still a sore point with the city's loyalists. As we pulled into the airport, Beverly said, "When you talk to people about Flint, tell them we're nice here." And they are.

I've traveled here for 11 of the Crim's past 13 runnings and never met with anything but niceness. This even extends to the residents who have nothing to do with the running event. One year I ran through one of the poorer neighborhoods. From a porch I heard the shout, "Run, white boy, run!" The shouter was African-American, as were all his neighbors.

I've gotten lots of mileage from this story in years since. But in fairness to Flint I note here that the comment was jovial, not menacing. It didn't lead to an adrenaline-charged upping of pace or quick retreat to a paler part of town.

Flint has always welcomed this runner, even where he's in the minority. And the Crim Race has long embraced runners of all nationalities and shadings. I walked into the hospitality room at the Radisson on race eve. The faces there were mostly dark, and the dominant language was Swahili. I felt again like someone from a minority group but not unwelcome.

Kenyans accounted for the top eight men and top three women at Crim. Last year's leading male was Moroccan, and a Mexican has won here in recent years. Asians will eventually arrive. This points out an oddity of U.S. road racing. Although the elite is multiracial, the overall field is quite white.

Talk of racism rumbled through the sport this spring when certain events allegedly tried to limit the number of Kenyans. But the bigger problem went unaddressed in that discussion. That is how to diversify the rest of the pack.

Some racial and ethnic minorities in this country fight an everyday battle against messages telling them they can't keep pace because they look, talk, and act differently from the dominant culture. Everyone needs to find ways to win. Running in races is one of those ways. Go the distance at whatever pace you can handle, and you can feel like just as big a winner as the person who finishes first.

"Everyone can win" has become a cliche in running. But it's still a rare concept in sports and even rarer in life at large. This running mantra has yet to reach all cultures. So far, the racing that made superstars of black Africans—as well as Arabs, Asians, and Latin Americans—hasn't transferred widely enough to Americans of similar descent and lesser ability.

U.S. road running resembles a party to which only one ethnic group was invited. This was never the intent but is still the result. Both sexes now run together, as well as all ages and every degree of ability (and disability). There is a continuing need for all Americans to embrace every race. We runners, like the people of Flint, all need to put out the word that we're nice folks who welcome everyone to our parties.

pursuing a sub-3:00 marathon at increasingly advanced ages. He became the oldest person in history to break 3:00 when he did so at nearly 70 years of age at the Clackamas River Canyon Marathon in 1994. (This honor has since been claimed by Canadian Ed Whitlock.) Another attempt came in 1996 at the Twin Cities Marathon where he ran 3:00:58 at age 71!

Keston thought his pursuit of world age-group records had come crashing down when he had a serious bicycling accident that necessitated him having pins put into his hip. As he was recovering, he slipped on ice while building a new house and broke his ankle. His time away from running was not wasted, however; he used it to pursue a career as an actor. He won the primary role in the computer game Riven, the successor to the wildly popular Myst. By 2000 he'd recovered enough to become the oldest American man to break 3:30 for the marathon, finishing the Portland Marathon in 3:23:01. He also set a national age 76 record, bettering the old mark of 3:34:42 set by Ed Benham in 1983. *See also* records, American age-group; records, world age-group; Whitlock, Ed.

Khannouchi, Khalid (b. December 22, 1971). In an era when the typical native-born American takes his country and everything else for granted, immigrants continue to set the tone of appreciating America as the land of opportunity. Khalid Khannouchi could well be the poster boy for immigrants who earned the American dream the hard way. Born in Morocco (homeland of many an outstanding runner), Khalid emigrated to America in the early 1990s and took menial jobs such as dishwasher in a restaurant to subsist while he honed his running.

He eventually married his coach-agent, Sandra, while battling persistently to become a better runner and to work his way through American bureaucracy. Khalid gradually became stronger and faster. In his marathon debut in Chicago in 1997 he set a debut world record of 2:07:10. When he came back to Chicago in 1999, he was caught in a morass of bureaucratic ineptitude. His citizenship application was trapped in limbo because the official who had been handling it had been indicted on taking bribes, thereby freezing every file he had touched. With an ability to focus on the matters of the moment, Khalid ran the perfect negative-split marathon, hanging back in the first half and making his move once he was into the final 10K, building speed like a freight train, not taking the lead until the final mile, and crossing the finish line in a new world record of 2:05:42!

He had hoped to become an American citizen in time to try out for the 2000 Olympic marathon team (which would have put the U.S. men's team in an entirely different posture than the one in which it ended up) but his citizenship didn't come through until it was too late to qualify. When Morocco offered to put him on their Olympic team, Khalid refused, citing the lack of support he'd received there as a young runner and his intention of running for the United States. Instead of going to the Trials, he ran London, where he placed third in 2:08:36 but was injured in the wake of the race.

He worked on recuperating over the summer and was not in 100 percent shape when he returned to Chicago in the fall of

2000 as defending champion and an American citizen. Again he didn't dictate the pace but laid back in the pack, hoping for a tactical race rather than an all-out speed fest. The field was extremely deep, sporting seven sub-2:07 marathoners. "Before the race I was scared," Khalid said. "I didn't want to make any mistakes and embarrass myself in front of the crowd. It was important to me as an American to win the race." He won with a 2:07:01, then wrapped himself in the American flag. "This one is for America," he said.

His win virtually rewrote the American record books. His performance eclipsed both David Morris's unaided-course record of 2:09:32 and Bob Kempainen's aided best 2:08:47. Perhaps Khalid's presence inspired other Americans, as the United States had 8 men in the top 20 and 4 women in the top 10 that year in Chicago. His first appearance in a U.S. uniform was discouraging as he dropped out of the 2001 World Championships Marathon in the 16th mile with blistered feet. *See also* Chicago Marathon; Peachtree 10K; rankings, *Runner's World*; record progressions, American; record progressions, world; records, American; records, world; World Championships, U.S.

© Mark Shearman, Athletics-Images

Khalid Khannouchi left his native Morocco to become a U.S. runner. He ran a debut record 2:07:10 at Chicago 1997, then set the world record of 2:05:42 in 1999.

kids' running. Acknowledging the need to build a future runner base in an aging sport, many races now offer shorter events for the youngsters. The Junior Bloomsday, for instance, draws thousands of youngsters on a weekend when they won't get lost in the shuffle of the big event. *See also* "When Can We Start?" on next page; Boitano, Mary Etta; Cox, Bucky.

Kilauea Volcano Marathon (www.bishopmuseum.org/vac/home.html). In the annals of odd races, this ranks right up there. It runs each summer through the moonscape of a crater on the Big Island of Hawaii. *See also* oddest races; scenic races.

Kilby, Brian (b. February 26, 1938). To the British of another era, the Commonwealth Games (previously the Empire Games) and the European Championships were almost as important as the Olympics. Kilby swept both marathon titles in the summer of 1962. *See also* Commonwealth Games; European Championships; rankings, *Track & Field News*.

kilometer distances. *See* distances, metric and English.

Kimaiyo, Eric (b. 1969). The Honolulu Marathon has long served as a proving ground for Kenyan runners. Kimaiyo proved himself with wins there in 1996 (2:13:23) and 1997 (2:12:17). *See also* Honolulu Marathon.

Kimaiyo, Hellen (b. September 8, 1968). This Kenyan strung together three victories in a row at Peachtree—1996 through 1998. *See also* Peachtree 10K.

Kimani, Joseph (b. September 1, 1972). Other Kenyans have won more races, but none has set more records. Kimani formerly held the world 10K record (27:20 in 1996) and currently holds the 12K mark (33:31 in 1997), as well as the fastest 10K on an aided course (27:04 in 1996). He ran all of these times in U.S. races. *See* Bay to Breakers 12K; Bolder Boulder 10K; Peachtree 10K; records, world.

Kimihara, Kenji (b. March 20, 1941). The Japanese marathoner bracketed his silver-medal performance in the 1968 Olympics with victories at the 1966 Boston (2:17:11) and the 1966 (2:33:23) and 1970 (2:21:03) Asian Games. *See* Asian Games; Boston Marathon; Olympic medalists.

Kipketer, Sammy (b. September 29, 1981). At an age when U.S. runners are leaving home for college, this 18-year-old Kenyan traveled halfway around the world to set the world 5K record. He ran 13:00 at the renowned Carlsbad race in 2000. Kipketer returned to Carlsbad the next year, as a graybeard of 19, to tie his record of 13-flat. A week later he broke the world 10K record with 27:18. *See also* record progressions, world; records, world.

Kiplagat, Lornah (b. May 1, 1974). Chicago 2000 featured one of the fastest two-woman finishes ever. Kiplagat came out second best to fellow Kenyan Catherine Ndereba but ran 2:22:36. Earlier Lornah had won the 1997 and 1998 Los Angeles Marathons. She was also the winner of the 2000 and 2001 Peachtree 10Ks. *See also* Los Angeles Marathon; Peachtree 10K.

When Can We Start?

From Joe Henderson's *Running Commentary,* February 2000.

I was in no hurry to start running marathons, taking nine years and hundreds of shorter races to work up the nerve to try my first one. When it finally came, at Boston, it made me feel young again. I was nearly 24 then—which, at a time when few runners lasted past their teens, seemed old for a runner.

Boston told me I wasn't so old—or odd—after all, because most of the runners there were my senior. Some were graybeards of 30 or more. We've come around to that again, where the marathon is mainly an older-folks home.

So where does this leave runners in their early 20s or younger? Out, or at least feeling out of place? They might feel that way when looking at the faces of today's marathoners.

A high school runner, Mark Bahnuk, asked me to comment on this subject recently for a class paper he was writing. He didn't say if a marathon was in his near future but wanted to know if anyone his age should go this far. My feelings on the subject aren't strong one way or another.

I've known many who finished with no ill effects. Bruce Deacon jumps to mind. Canada's current top marathoner ran his first at 13. I've known others—usually those who were pushed into this by their parents or coaches, or went in unprepared—who washed out prematurely. I could name, but won't, a girl and a boy whose fathers were coaching them to become Olympians as teenagers. Neither ever ran in the Trials.

Mark Bahnuk's questions, and my answers, follow:

"What is the earliest age when someone should begin marathon training?"

This limit is usually set for the runner by the marathons themselves. Most impose age restrictions. If qualified by age, then a young runner who *chooses* (this is the key word; the goal can't be chosen for him or her by an overzealous coach or parent) and has done some long-distance training already can go into marathon training.

"Do you feel it is fair that in most marathons it is necessary to be 18 or older?"

This is as much a practical concern as a physical one. Marathons worry about liability issues from letting minors run. And they have the public-relations concern of appearing to promote "child abuse."

"Do you feel that the stress levels reached during the marathon have a greater effect on someone that is younger than the average marathoner?"

I take a rather unusual view on this question. It's my observation that mature runners are more likely to be hurt by the marathon than young ones. Youthful bodies can absorb more abuse and bounce back from it quicker because they have more resiliency.

"Do you feel that training for a younger marathoner should be different than for a normal marathoner?

The principles are the same—long runs are most important, followed closely in value by recovery days. One complication that few adults have to deal with is their commitment to high school cross country and track teams. Fitting marathon training and recovery into these schedules can be quite a challenge.

Kiprono, Josephat (b. December 12, 1973). The Kenyan is among the few marathoners who've broken 2:07 *twice*. His PR of 2:06:44 came while winning at Berlin in 1999. He tied the Rotterdam course record of 2:06:50 while winning in 2001. *See also* Berlin Marathon; Rotterdam Marathon.

Kirtland, Julia (b. March 15, 1965). Her big breakthrough year was 1997, when she won the national marathon title (2:37:46) and ran that distance at the World Championships (36th in 2:49:43). *See also* national marathon champions, U.S.; World Championships, U.S.

Kirui, Ismail (b. February 20, 1975). The young Kenyan won the Bay to Breakers 12K three straight years (1993 through 1995). *See also* Bay to Breakers 12K.

Klecker, Janis (b. July 18, 1960). She excelled at everything from 5Ks (national champion) to ultramarathons but is best known as a 1992 Olympian and Trials winner. A dentist, she is married to Barney Klecker, himself an outstanding runner, especially within the ultra world where he once held the world record for 50 miles. *See also* national 5K champions, U.S.; national marathon champions, U.S.; Olympians, U.S.; Olympic Trials Marathon, U.S.

Kleinerman, Joe (birthdate unavailable). As a runner, he earned a spot in the RRCA Hall of Fame. As an official, he continued working in the New York Road Runners office into his 80s. *See also* Hall of Fame, RRCA; New York Road Runners Club.

Klochko, Lyubov (b. September, 26, 1959). The Ukrainian woman won the Los Angeles Marathon in 1993 and 1996, and Tokyo in 1989. *See also* Los Angeles Marathon; Tokyo Marathons.

knee injuries. *See* injuries.

Knight, Phil (b. 1938). The former University of Oregon trackman started by selling Japanese running shoes in the mid-1960s; he now sells Nike shoes to the Japanese—and to everyone else. A revealing insider's look into the rise of Phil Knight and Nike was penned in the book *Swoosh: The Unauthorized Story of Nike and the Men Who Played There* (Harper Collins, 1991). *See also* air sole; Blue Ribbon Sports; Bowerman, Bill; Johnson, Jeff; Nike; shoe companies; Tiger.

Koech, Peter (b. February 18, 1958). The Kenyan holds the current world 10-mile best for an aided course—44:45 at a 1997 race in the Netherlands. *See also* Bloomsday12K; records, world.

Kokowska, Renata (b. December 4, 1958). The Polish woman is a three-time winner of the Berlin Marathon—2:29:16 in 1988, 2:27:36 in 1991, and 2:26:20 in 1993. *See also* Berlin Marathon.

Hannes Kolehmainen of Finland was Olympic champion in 1920 at Antwerp.

From the collection of Dr. Edward H. Kozloff–Motor City Striders

Kolehmainen, Hannes (b. December 9, 1889; d. November 11, 1966). The Finn won the 1920 Olympic Marathon, the Games' first in which there was no controversy. He set a world record of 2:32:36 on the Antwerp course that measured more than half a kilometer longer than the 42.2K distance needed. *See also* Olympic medalists; record progressions, world.

Kosgei, Japhet (b. 1968). The Kenyan backed up his 1999 Rotterdam win by beating the field at Tokyo 2000. *See also* Rotterdam Marathon; Tokyo Marathons.

Košice Peace Marathon (www. mmm.sk/). The Czechoslovakian city hosted one of the first international marathons, starting in 1924 and surviving through many periods of turmoil both inside and outside that country. When the split-up of the country came, the Czech Republic retained Prague, and Košice became part of Slovakia. The race now is run in October.

Kostrubala, Thaddeus (b. 1930). Born in Chicago, Kostrubala received his MD from the University of Virginia. He taught in medical schools and related departments in Northwestern University, Tufts University, California State University, and the University of California, and for many years was associated with the San Diego Marathon Clinic. He was a pioneer in using running as a central therapeutic technique in his medical practice. He put his ideas into the popular 1976 book *The Joy of Running* (Lippincott).

Košice Peace Marathon Winners

The Czech race has endured World War II, the Iron Curtain, the Soviet invasion, the split of Czechoslovakia into two countries (the Czech Republic and Slovakia), and the coming of bigger-money races worldwide. Here are the men's winners since the beginning and the women's since they joined the race in 1980. (* = event record)

WOMEN

Year	Athlete	Time
1980	Sarka Balcarova (Czechoslovakia)	2:50:15
1981	Christa Vahlensieck (West Germany)	2:37:46
1982	Gillian Burley (Britain)	2:43:26
1983	Raisa Sadreydinova (USSR)	2:34:41
1984	Christa Vahlensieck (West Germany)	2:37:19
1985	Lucia Byelayeva (USSR)	2:38:19
1986	Christa Vahlensieck (West Germany)	2:41:08
1987	Christa Vahlensieck (West Germany)	2:38:40
1988	Christa Vahlensieck (West Germany)	2:39:03
1989	Alena Peterkova (Czechoslovakia)	2:31:28*
1990	Carol McLatchie (U.S.)	2:46:00
1991	Maria Starovska (Czechoslovakia)	2:46:00
1992	Dana Hajna (Czechoslovakia)	2:43:27
1993	Yelena Plastinina (Ukraine)	2:42:11
1994	Ludmila Melicherova (Slovakia)	2:40:27
1995	Guliya Tazetdinova (Russia)	2:43:03
1996	Guliya Tazetdinova (Russia)	2:44:28
1997	Violetta Kryza (Poland)	2:38:56
1998	Violetta Kryza (Poland)	2:46:23
1999	Katarina Jedinakova (Slovakia)	2:55:39
2000	Ivana Martincova (Czechoslovakia)	2:46:17
2001	Galina Zhulyeva (Ukraine)	2:36:55

MEN

Year	Athlete	Time
1924	Karol Halla (Czechoslovakia)	3:01:35
1925	Pal Kiraly (Hungary)	2:41:55
1926	Paul Hempel (Germany)	2:57:02
1927	Jozsef Galambos (Hungary)	2:48:26
1928	Jozsef Galambos (Hungary)	2:55:45
1929	Paul Hempel (Germany)	2:51:31
1930	Istvan Zelenka (Hungary)	2:50:59
1931	Juan Zabala (Argentina)	2:33:19
1932	Jozsef Galambos (Hungary)	2:43:15
1933	Jozsef Galambos (Hungary)	2:37:54
1934	Josef Sulc (Czechoslovakia)	2:41:27
1935	Arturs Motmillers (Latvia)	2:44:58
1936	Gyorgy Balaban (Austria)	2:41:08
1937	Desire Leriche (France)	2:43:42
1938–44	(not run)	*(continued)*

Košice Peace Marathon Winners, *continued*

1945	Antonin Spiroch (Czechoslovakia)	2:47:22
1946	Mikko Hietanen (Finland)	2:35:03
1947	Charles Heirendt (Luxembourg)	2:36:06
1948	Gosta Leandersson (Sweden)	2:34:47
1949	Martti Urpalainen (Finland)	2:33:46
1950	Gosta Leandersson (Sweden)	2:31:21
1951	Jaroslav Strupp (Czechoslovakia)	2:41:08
1952	Erkki Puolakka (Finland)	2:29:10
1953	Walter Bednar (Czechoslovakia)	2:53:33
1954	Erkki Puolakka (Finland)	2:27:21
1955	Evert Nyberg (Sweden)	2:25:40
1956	Thomas Nilsson (Sweden)	2:22:06
1957	Ivan Filin (USSR)	2:23:58
1958	Pavel Kantorek (Czechoslovakia)	2:29:38
1959	Sergey Popov (USSR)	2:17:46
1960	Sam Hardicker (Britain)	2:26:47
1961	Abebe Bikila (Ethiopia)	2:20:12
1962	Pavel Kantorek (Czechoslovakia)	2:28:30
1963	Buddy Edelen (U.S.)	2:15:10
1964	Pavel Kantorek (Czechoslovakia)	2:25:56
1965	Aurele Vandendriessche (Belgium)	2:23:47
1966	Gyula Toth (Hungary)	2:19:12
1967	Nedo Farcic (Yugoslavia)	2:20:54
1968	Vaclav Chudomel (Czechoslovakia)	2:26:29
1969	Demissie Wolde (Ethiopia)	2:15:37
1970	Mikhail Gorelov (USSR)	2:16:27
1971	Gyula Toth (Hungary)	2:21:44
1972	John Farrington (Australia)	2:17:35
1973	Vladimir Moseyev (USSR)	2:19:02
1974	Keith Angus (Britain)	2:20:09
1975	Chang Sop Choe (North Korea)	2:15:48
1976	Takeshi Soh (Japan)	2:18:43
1977	Chun Son Goe (North Korea)	2:15:20
1978	Chun Son Goe (North Korea)	2:13:35*
1979	Jouni Kortelainen (Finland)	2:15:12
1980	Aleksey Lyagushev (USSR)	2:15:25
1981	Hans-Joachim Truppel (East Germany)	2:16:58
1982	Gyorgy Sinko (Hungary)	2:18:48
1983	Frantisek Visnicky (Czechoslovakia)	2:16:52
1984	Li Dong Meng (North Korea)	2:18:59
1985	Valentin Starikov (USSR)	2:17:13
1986	Frantisek Visnicky (Czechoslovakia)	2:18:43
1987	Erwin Nederlof (East Germany)	2:14:49
1988	Michael Heilmann (East Germany)	2:17:52
1989	Karel David (Czechoslovakia)	2:18:39
1990	Nikolay Kolesnikov (USSR)	2:20:28
1991	Vlastimil Bukovjan (Czechoslovakia)	2:18:21
1992	Wieslaw Palczynski (Poland)	2:16:24
1993	Wieslaw Palczynski (Poland)	2:14:11
1994	Petr Pipa (Slovakia)	2:15:03
1995	Marnix Goegebeur (Belgium)	2:13:57
1996	Marnix Goegebeur (Belgium)	2:17:41
1997	Thar Chaldi (Morocco)	2:16:22
1998	Andzej Krzyacin (Poland)	2:14:29
1999	Robert Stefko (Slovakia)	2:14:10
2000	Ernest Kipyego (Kenya)	2:14:35
2001	David Kariuki (Kenya)	2:13:27

Kristiansen, Ingrid (b. March 21, 1956). When combining the words *marathon* and *Norway*, the natural response is Grete Waitz—the Norwegian schoolteacher who burst upon the road-racing scene at the New York City Marathon in 1978 by breaking the world record on her first marathon attempt. But her younger countrywoman, Ingrid Kristiansen, has a slew of accomplishments in running that place her in the same stratosphere. She held world records in 5,000 meters, 10,000 meters, and marathon simultaneously (something no other runner, male or female, had ever done); she had the world's best times in the road 10K, 10 miles, 15K, half-marathon,

Norway gave the world two marathon world record-setters in Grete Waitz and (pictured here in Oslo) Ingrid Kristiansen. Ingrid's record 2:21:06 at London 1985 lasted 13 years.

and marathon; she ran 15 sub-2:35 marathons; and she won world championships on the roads, on the track, and in cross country.

But she didn t begin her athletic career as a runner; she started as an elite cross-country skier. In 1971 she was the Norwegian cross-country skiing champion—at age 15! Eventually, she divided her year between cross-country skiing in the winter and being Norway's number-two distance runner behind Grete Waitz (who also regularly cross-country skied). Her initial crossover into marathoning came in 1977 when she ran a 2:45:15.

She made the shift to primarily running in 1980 when she won the Stockholm Marathon in 2:34:25 and was named to the Norwegian Olympic team, which then proceeded to join the U.S. boycott of the Moscow Games. The marathon had not yet been introduced as an Olympic event for women, so for 1980 she would have had to compete on the track. In the fall Ingrid went to the New York City Marathon, where Grete Waitz won for the third straight year and Ingrid placed third. The next year she took second at New York behind New Zealand's Allison Roe. Earlier in the year Ingrid set the world record for 5,000 meters by running 15:28.4 in Oslo.

During that period, she also worked full-time as a medical engineer; she didn't give up her day job until 1983. That same year she gave birth to her son Gaute; five

© Mark Shearman. Athletics–Images.

months later she won the Houston Marathon in 2:27:51, just two minutes off Grete Waitz's world record. She ran the London Marathon in April of 1984 and won with a 2:24:26, then began keying in on the first women's Olympic Marathon in Los Angeles. She disappointed herself with a fourth-place finish and soon after realized that she had a mental block in feeling that she could not beat Grete Waitz, who had placed second in L.A. Her new world record of 14:58.89 in the 5,000 meters at the Bislett Games later that year assured her that she could run faster than Grete. She did manage to place higher than Grete in the Norwegian Cross Country Championships.

She was concentrating again on London in the spring of 1985, where she planned to go after Joan Benoit's 2:22:43 world's best mark (a mark Joan had set after Grete Waitz had lowered the world mark four times straight between 1978 and 1983). Ingrid ran London in 2:21:06! In July she broke the world record in the 10,000 meters, becoming the first woman to go under 31 minutes. She went to Chicago in the fall and went head to head with Joan Benoit Samuelson but lost to Joan's 2:21:21 effort.

The following spring Ingrid easily won the Orange Bowl 10K in Miami, then went to Boston in April and won in 2:24:55. She returned to Bislett Stadium in July and again lowered her 10,000-meter world mark, to 30:13.74. The next month she regained her 5,000-meter world record.

At London in April 1987 she attempted to be the first woman to go under 2:20 for the marathon but slowed in the second half and ran 2:22:48; four minutes behind her, Priscilla Welch set the world women's masters record. In Rome that summer Ingrid easily won the 10,000 meters in the World Championships. And on the roads she was unstoppable. She ran a 10-mile world record (50:31) in Amsterdam, then a 15K world record

(47:15) at the IAAF Championships.

The following year she returned to London for an attempt to be the first to break 2:20. She went through the halfway mark at 1:10 but faltered in the late miles to finish in 2:25:41, making it her fourth London win. She went into the Olympics as the odds-on favorite to win the gold in the 10,000 meters. She went out as though the race were hers, but after seven laps she dropped off to the inside of the track, the victim of a broken bone in the arch of her right foot.

In 1989 she started the year by winning the New Bedford Half-Marathon in a new world record of 1:08:32. In early April she set a course record at the Freedom Trail 10K in Boston. Again at Boston she went for the sub-2:20, but the temperatures went up in the second half of the race and she had to settle for a win with a 2:24:33. In the fall she went to New York, again to attempt a sub-2:20, but the heat again stifled her effort, and she won in 2:25:30.

Ingrid backed off in 1990 to give birth to a second child and went through a difficult pregnancy. She came back in 1991 at age 35 to run a half-marathon in Holland in 1:09:05. But she missed the 1992 Olympics because of a series of injuries and gradually withdrew from racing, concentrating more on her family life, which had always been more important to her anyway. In spite of her not being as well known as Grete Waitz and Joan Benoit, some observers of the sport consider Kristiansen the greatest female distance runner ever. Today she lives with her family outside Oslo, in a modest home surprisingly devoid of trophies and reminders of her glorious years on the roads. She offers advice to runners through her Web site: www.ingrid-kristiansen.com. *See also* Bay to Breakers 12K; Bolder Boulder 10K; Boston Marathon; London Marathon; New York City Marathon; record progressions, world.

Kuehls, Dave (b. November 21, 1960). The *Runner's World* writer wrote two fast-selling books as the 1990s ended: *4 Months to a 4-Hour Marathon* (Perigree, 1998) and *Run Away From Fat* (Perigree, 1999).

Kurtis, Doug (b. March 12, 1952). Doug is probably best known for his marathon consistency and durability. Over a 14-year span, he ran 73 sub-2:20 marathons, an average of five sub-2:20s a year. In 1989 alone, Doug ran 12 sub-2:20 marathons, another world record (broken first by El Hadi Moumou of Morocco with 13 in 1994, who was supplanted by Italian Giorgio Calcaterra with 16 in 2000). In 1989 all Americans combined ran only 62 sub-2:20s.

Another unparalleled record is his total number of marathon victories, which is 39! Next down on the list is Bill Rodgers with 21. These victories included winning his hometown of Detroit six straight years, Seattle five straight years, and others such as Fox Cities, Las Vegas, Austin, and Arizona. He is the only masters runner ever to win Grandma's Marathon outright. His best masters performance was the 1994 Boston Marathon, where he won the masters division with 2:15:47.

Doug ran 184 marathons; he raced on every continent but Antarctica and in more than 40 U.S. states. He is a five-time U.S. Olympic Marathon Trials qualifier; he first qualified in 1980 and later become the oldest qualifier in 1992 and 1996. His awards include RRCA Masters Runner of the Year in 1992, 1993, and 1994, and he was twice voted Michigan Runner of the Year. He is currently the race director of the Detroit International Marathon. *See also* Detroit International Marathon; Hall of Fame, RRCA.

Kuscsik, Nina (b. January 2, 1939). One of the initial handful of American women running pioneers (along with Roberta Gibb, Doris Brown Heritage, Jacqueline Hansen, and Kathrine Switzer), Nina started running after reading Bill Bowerman's book *Jogging* and Dr. Ken Cooper's *Aerobics* and assuming, "hey, I can do that too." Once she began running, she couldn't get enough; she became a pioneer not only in marathoning but also in ultrarunning. (Back in the 1970s, she held the world women's record at 50 miles—6:35:53.)

Her first marathon was Boston 1969, before women were officially admitted. As soon as they were admitted to Boston (1972), she won it—in 3:08:58. She also won New York City that year, when it was still run in Central Park, as well as the following year.

Nina came to running in a roundabout way. She started her sports career by playing basketball as a teen but dropped that at 15 when she suffered from a chronically dislocated shoulder. She moved to roller skating and at age 20 won the National One-Mile Speed Skating Championship in 1959—and again in 1960. She then moved to ice skating and won the 1961 International Silver Skates All-Around Title. She also joined a bike club, won the New York State Championship for women, and in a 23-mile handicap race defeated all comers, men and women. For a time, Nina gave up sports and her work as a nurse, preferring to stay home with her kids. Eventually, she began exercising again and took her first run by accident. She was riding her bike, got a flat, had no spare, and had to run home.

Her most enduring legacy is her activism on behalf of women's running. In 1977 the AAU adopted a resolution that Nina wrote, calling for the addition of a women's marathon to the Olympic Games. Gordon Bakoulis, former editor of *Running Times* and a U.S. Olympic Marathon Trials competitor, interviewed Nina in 2000 and asked her what she would most like to be remembered for. "I guess for my love of running," Nina answered, "and that my pioneering work created opportunities for other women."

It is ironic that someone who did so much to advance women's running was, like her pioneering friends, just behind the curve they helped create. She ran her PR (2:50:22) in 1977. By the time the women's marathon had been placed in the Olympic Games, she was no longer capable of running the sub-2:51:16 needed to run in the Trials. In the wake of several knee surgeries, she still runs for relaxation, fitness, and enjoyment, often in Central Park, but no longer competes. She continues to work at Mount Sinai Hospital. *See* Boston Marathon; Hall of Fame, National Distance Running; Hall of Fame, RRCA; New York City Marathon.

lactate threshold. *See* anaerobic threshold.

Lagat, Elijah (b. June 19, 1966). America doesn't have a monopoly on over-weight people. Fat even happens in Kenya. Throughout the world doctors diagnose youngsters as overweight and recommend getting more exercise. This happened to Elijah, prompting him to take up running.

On his first trip to Boston in 2000 he won (2:09:47) in one of the closest and most exciting finishes ever. His rival was soon-to-be Olympic champion Gezahegne Abera of Ethiopia. The Boston Marathon press department released this information on Elijah Lagat before the 2000 race: "The experienced Kenyan brings one of the fastest personal best times to the race. He was the winner of the 1997 Berlin Marathon (2:07:41) and the champion of the 1998 Prague Marathon (2:08:52). Other notable finishes include 7th at the 1996 Rotterdam Marathon in 2:11:54, 2nd at the 1997 Turin Marathon in 2:09:19, 10th at the 1998 Chicago Marathon in 2:10:33, 5th at the 1999 Paris Marathon in 2:08:50, and 6th at the 1999 New York City Marathon in 2:09:59. Lagat extends his talents to the half-marathon as well, recording the fourth-fastest time in 1999 with his first-place finish at Route du Vin Half-Marathon in Grevenmacher, Luxenbourg." *See also* Abera, Gezahegne; Berlin Marathon; Boston Marathon; Kenyan runners.

Lake Tahoe Marathon (www.laketahoemarathon.com). This high-altitude race on the California-Nevada border is run in October. *See also* scenic races.

Lamppa, Ryan (b. June 25, 1959). He serves as record-keeper and chief writer-editor for the Road Running Information Center in Santa Barbara, California. As such he contributed heavily to the statistical side of this book. *See also* Road Running Information Center; Running USA.

Langlace, Chantal (b. January 6, 1955). France's only world record-setter in the marathon did it twice, with 2:46:24 (1974) and 2:35:15 (1977). *See also* record progressions, world.

largest races. *See* biggest races.

Larrieu Smith, Francie (b. November 23, 1952). Francie picked up where Doris Severtson Brown Heritage left off as a pioneering U.S. female distance runner, but her career lasted even longer. Francie qualified for the Olympic

Games five times; the first time was in 1972 when she ran the 1,500 meters at age 19. Her final Olympic appearance was at the 1992 Olympic Games in Barcelona, where, having been selected to do so by her teammates, she carried the U.S. flag during opening ceremonies and then placed 12th in the marathon at age 39. In between came one of the most illustrious running careers in American history.

In a career spanning four decades, she set 35 American records in distances from 1,000 to 10,000 meters. She made 28 national teams and won 21 national titles. She ran the 1,500 in her first two Olympic appearances (and would have run that distance in Moscow if not for the boycott), missed the 1984 Games, then came back to take fifth in the 10,000 meters in the 1988 Games. She also ran in the 1987 and 1991 World Championships in the 10,000. In 1991 she picked up a silver medal in the World Cup Marathon.

Her older brother, Ron, was an Olympic 10,000-meter runner in the 1964 Olympics. Francie lives with her husband, Jimmy, in Georgetown, Texas, and is a college running coach. *See also* Hall of Fame, National Distance Running; Hall of Fame, RRCA; Hall of Fame, USATF; Heritage, Doris Severtson Brown; national 10K champions, U.S.; Olympians, U.S.; Olympic Trials Marathon, U.S.; Peachtree 10K.

Larsen, Lisa. *See* Weidenbach, Lisa Larsen.

Lasseter, Carol. *See* Rice, Carol Lasseter.

Las Vegas International Marathon and Half-Marathon (www.lvmarathon.com). A winter date (early February) and a generally downhill course produce some of the fastest U.S.—aided—race times, especially in the half-marathon. The marathon dates from 1967. *See also* fastest races; oldest races.

Lauck, Anne Marie Letko (b. March 7, 1969). Born in Rochester, New York, and raised in New Jersey, she attended Wake Forest and Rutgers. Coached by the legendary Dick Brown, she is a two-time Olympian. After placing 10th in the marathon at the 1996 Atlanta Games, she finished 3rd at the U.S. Olympic Trials Marathon in 2000, but because of a lack of an "A" standard qualifying time, she was not eligible to go to Sydney. She quickly regrouped and went into training for the Track and Field Trials, where she placed 4th in the 10,000 meters (32:02) and 5th in the 5,000 (15:34). When two women who had qualified in front of her pulled out to run other distances, she went to Sydney in the 5K.

Anne Marie competed in the 10,000 meters at both the 1993 and 1999 World Championships. She placed third at the 1994 New York City Marathon and took fifth in the 10,000 meters at the 1992 World Cup. She won the New York Mini Marathon (10K) in 1994 with a 31:52. Rarely did Americans win either the Bloomsday 12K or Peachtree 10K in the 1990s—and she won both. *See also* Bloomsday 12K; national 10K champions, U.S.; Olympians, U.S.; Olympic Trials Marathon, U.S.; Peachtree 10K; rankings, *Runner's World.*

Lawson, Jerry (b. July 2, 1966). This colorful, inconsistent runner was the first American to break 2:10 (with 2:09:35 at Chicago 1997) on a verified, unaided course. He was one of only three Americans, along with Bob Kempainen and David Morris, to break 2:10 on any course in the 1990s. *See also* Daniels, Dr. Jack; Kempainen, Bob; Morris, David; record progressions, American.

Lazaro, Francisco (b. January 8, 1891; d. 1912). The Portuguese runner died the day after collapsing at the too-hot Olympic Marathon at Stockholm in 1912, a probable victim of heat stroke. His death remains the only death in the history of the Olympic Marathon.

Lebow, Fred. *See* page 190.

Lee Bong Ju (b. October 11, 1968). Like many Koreans, this runner found a way to perform well in the biggest races of the 1990s. Lee followed his silver-medal race at the Atlanta Olympics in 1996 with victories at Fukuoka that same year and at the 1998 Asian Games. Then he won Boston in 2001. Earlier he had won the 1993 Honolulu Marathon. *See also* Asian Games; Boston Marathon; Fukuoka Marathon; Honolulu Marathon; Olympic medalists; rankings, *Track & Field News.*

Lelei, Sammy (b. August 14, 1964). He was the hot Kenyan of the early to mid-1990s, winning the Peachtree 10K in 1992 and the 1995 Berlin Marathon in 2:07:02. *See also* Berlin Marathon; Peachtree 10K.

LeMay, Joe (b. December 5, 1966). Talk about near misses! LeMay qualified for the 1996 U.S. Olympic 10,000 by place but lacked the time needed to run in the Atlanta Games. Four years later he had the second-fastest qualifying time, 2:13:55, but didn't place well enough in the Trials to reach Sydney. A talented writer, he is a columnist for *Marathon & Beyond.* He is coached by Tom Fleming. *See also* Fleming, Tom.

Lemettinen, Ritva (b. September 9, 1960). Finnish women sometimes had the same winning touch as the men of Finland's storied past. Lemettinen won the Chicago Marathon in 1993 (2:33:18) and 1995 (2:28:39) and Honolulu in 1991 (2:40:11). *See also* Chicago Marathon; Honolulu Marathon.

Leonard, Tommy (b. August 15, 1933). For decades he was the "host" at the Eliot Lounge, the most famous of watering holes for Boston runners. Tommy also cofounded the extremely successful Falmouth Road Race, a seven-miler on Cape Cod. More recently he has been seen hosting a Boston race weekend gathering at the Back Bay Brewery across the street from the Boston finish line. *See also* Falmouth.

Lepper, Merry (birthdate unavailable). The first American woman to hold a world marathon mark and the first to run under 3:40, she ran 3:37:07 in the 1963 Western Hemisphere race. *See also* record progressions, world.

Lebow, Fred (originally named Lebowitz) (b. 1932, d. 1994). An immigrant from Transylvania, Fred eluded the Nazis in the 1940s and escaped to America. He arrived with very little—a limited education in religious studies—but a will to work hard to make it in America. He became a garment-district executive and took up running in 1969. It wasn't long before this became his passion. In the same year he began to run, he joined the RRCA, New York Area Club (RRC-NYA).

The next year Mayor John Lindsay closed Central Park to vehicular traffic on weekends. Vince Chiappetta and Fred Lebow joined to put on a four-lap marathon in the park: The New York City Marathon was born. The next year Beth Bonner ran the first legitimate sub-3:00 marathon for a woman at that race.

In 1973 Fred took over as president of RRC-NYA. Admittedly difficult to work

Legendary New York City Marathon race director Fred Lebow (right) pictured here beside George Hirsch (left) and Bill Rodgers (center) in 1978.

Courtesy of George Hirsch/Runner's World

with, he became a whirlwind, tossing off assorted ideas for increasing the club's involvement in the city and in the growing running community worldwide. At the 1975 marathon the idea was floated by George Spitz to take the race out of the park. In conjunction with the U.S. Bicentennial, the race was expanded to cover all five boroughs, a phenomenal accomplishment for a 1,700-member club. The move would forever alter the landscape for big-city marathons. In 1977 the club changed its name to the New York Road Runners Club and introduced the Corporate Challenge. In 1978 Fred hired Allan Steinfeld to help him organize events, introduced the Empire State Building Run-Up, and invited Grete Waitz to the New York City Marathon, where, in her first marathon, she broke the world record. The club moved to what came to be known as the International Running Center (9 East 89th Street) and initiated the Fifth Avenue Mile.

Fred was diagnosed with brain cancer in 1990. Two years later, for the first time, he ran in his own marathon with his friend Grete Waitz in an emotional attempt to use a positive attitude to overcome the cancer. During race weekend Random House released *The New York Road Runners Club Complete Book of Running*, put together by Fred, author Gloria Averbuch, and "friends"—a loose collection of unlikely contributors whom Fred had touched in some way, from supermodel Kim Alexis to TV anchorman Tom Brokaw, and from shock-jock Don Imus to four-time New York winner Bill Rodgers. Fred's indomitable spirit was unable to defeat the cancer, and he died in 1994. His friend and yin to his yang, Allan Steinfeld, became race director. *See also* Hall of Fame, National Distance Running; Hall of Fame, RRCA; Hall of Fame, USATF; New York City Marathon; Steinfeld, Allan.

Lester, Steve (b. December 29, 1942). No master has ever been better at running downhill rapidly. He holds national aided-course bests for 5K (age 45–49) and 10K (45–49 and 50–54). *See* records, American age-group.

Letko, Anne Marie. *See* Lauck, Anne Marie Letko.

Leydig, Jack (b. January 14, 1944). The success of the running boom in the 1970s was due in part to the noteworthy international accomplishments of American long-distance runners and to a generation's decision that it was going to do everything it could to retard aging. But it was facilitated by a little army of agents in various hotbeds of running around America—runners who couldn't get enough running and who couldn't do enough to make it successful. Every major running center has one of these driven people who pushed running to the next plateau.

Because this book's authors both lived in the San Francisco Bay Area in the 1970s, we are most familiar with Jack Leydig, the local sparkplug of running, who not only kept it going but kept raising the bar in unique ways. Jack grew up on the San Francisco Peninsula but went to school at Southern Illinois University, where he was a 4:16 miler. After graduation in 1968, he returned to San Mateo County and joined the West Valley Track Club (WVTC). It was a fateful day, for over the following decade he would essentially become the benign dictator of peninsula running, spewing forth one wonderful idea after another while everyone else tried merely to keep up.

He had no sooner taken over the WVTC presidency in 1969 than he began putting together more races. One of the most famous was the 5 × 5-mile loop West Valley Marathon, about as flat and fast as ever a marathon could be; it was several times the national championship course. He put together a cross country series at Crystal Springs Reservoir. In 1972 he unveiled the Christmas Relays, an event that set standards for other famous relays to come. The course ran for 50 miles between Santa Cruz and Half Moon Bay along famed Highway 1 (Pacific Coast Highway), changing directions every other year. Featuring seven-person teams and two handicapped starts, the race became so popular that by 1978 the road was jammed with relay traffic and the California Highway Patrol begged him to cancel it, which he did for 1979. Jack reopened the relays on a nearly five-mile loop around San Francisco's Lake Merced, where it is still run annually.

Jack also created the *WVTC Newsletter*, which he turned into a full-fledged 70-page magazine in 1971 that he renamed *NorCal Running Review*. In the mid-1970s Jack established one of the first point-based racing circuits in running. When he returned to San Mateo way back in 1968, he began arriving at races in his VW microbus, stocked with running shoes and equipment for sale to equipment-starved runners. He still has the 1968 VW—with more than a half-million miles on its odometer.

Jack's personality drew hot runners to the club—Don Kardong, Duncan Macdonald, Bill Clark, Domingo Tibaduiza, and Alvaro Mejia (who was running for WVTC when he won Boston in 1971). Jack was no slouch himself; he ran his PR of 2:25:15 at Boston in 1972 for 22nd place. For the past several decades, Jack has operated Jack's Athletic Supply, supplying T-shirts to local races. Runners like Jack, who were bitten big time by the running bug, made the sport special during the Running Revolution.

Lima, Vanderlei (b. August 11, 1969). Ronaldo da Costa, former marathon record-holder, wasn't the lone Brazilian star of the late 1990s. Lima won the 1999 Pan-American Games Marathon gold medal (2:17:20) and was the Tokyo winner in 1996 (2:08:38). *See also* Pan-American Games; Tokyo Marathons.

Lindgren, Gerry (b. March 9, 1946). Like many runners of his era—Billy Mills and Steve Prefontaine also jump to mind—Lindgren would have been a ter-

---

Fame Reclaimed

From Joe Henderson's *Running Commentary*, January 1999.

Gerry Lindgren was a hero of my youth. I was young then, and he was even younger.

At 18 he wasn't just the best ever for his age. This kid from Spokane with pixyish size and a squeaky voice looked and sounded like a high school freshman. Yet he was one of the world's best distance runners, period. Americans liked his prospects of winning a 10,000 medal, maybe even gold, at the 1964 Olympics. And why not? Gerry had beaten the mighty Soviets that summer, and he'd won the Trials.

He didn't win at Tokyo, didn't come close on Billy Mills's golden day. We'll never know how Gerry might have done if he hadn't been running his race on a sprained ankle. We do know that he tied Mills for the world six-mile record the next year, at age 19. At Washington State, Gerry set an NCAA record for titles won.

Injuries began catching up with him in his early 20s, and he never made another Olympic team. Then adult life caught up with him. Details are vague, and rumors are best left buried. It's enough to say that he disappeared from home, family, and business in the 1980s.

When spotted running in Honolulu, he denied being—or knowing—this person called Lindgren. He used the name Gail Young. Supported by new friends in Hawaiian running, he eventually reclaimed his own name and along with it some of the fame that is rightfully his. He again runs races as Gerry Lindgren and now works as a freelance coach in the islands.

Much as I'd admired him early, then rooted for his comeback later, I had never met Gerry. I'd seen him run only twice. Now I was in Honolulu for a talk at NikeTown. Keala Peters of Nike arranged a dinner the night before.

"This started as an intimate gathering, but it keeps growing," she said. "We now have 15 coming." She ran through the guest list. I knew about half of the people personally, and most of the others by name. They were a mix of top runners, coaches, writers, and officials. One name in particular grabbed my interest: Gerry Lindgren. It happened that I sat next to him at dinner.

At 52 he retains some of the look that he had at 18. The years in hiding didn't speed up his aging. His hair is its original color, and his lines are few. His voice is still boyish, and his sense of humor impish. This is the guy who once told Honolulu writer Mike Tymn (who sat on my other side) that he still had "a four-minute mind, but nine-minute legs." Well, not quite. He'd run his latest 10K in 36 minutes.

Gerry ordered a vegetarian meal. He's strict in his eating, to the point of avoiding milk and egg products. When the log-sized burrito arrived, he asked the waiter, "Did someone put a live chicken in here?"

As he worked through the burrito, I asked how he thought he might have done in the long-ago Olympics if not for the ankle sprain. "Some people built me up as a possible medalist. But I was just a kid who didn't really know what he was doing."

The 35 years since then have taught him a lot.

rific road racer if opportunities had been available to him in the 1960s and early 1970s. As it was, he made the Olympic 10,000-meter team at age 18 and set a world six-mile record in 1965. The onetime wonder boy now runs and coaches in Honolulu. *See also* "Fame Reclaimed" on page 192; Hall of Fame, RRCA.

Lindgren, Mavis (b. April 2, 1907; d. 2001). She began running in her 60s and continued marathoning into her 90s. Mavis holds the over-90 world and American marathon records at 8:53:08. *See also* records, American age-group; records, world age-group.

Lindsay, Herb (b. November 12, 1954). The unusually well-muscled Michigan runner was a dominant road racer of the early 1980s. He held world and American half-marathon records, and was the first to break 1:02. His resume also includes victories at the Bolder Boulder 10K and the national 10K. *See also* barrier breakers; Bolder Boulder 10K; national 10K champions, U.S.; rankings, *Runner's World*; record progressions, American; record progressions, world.

Liquori, Marty (b. June 4, 1949). The former child-star miler—the last American, until Alan Webb in 2001, to break the four-minute mile in high school and an Olympian as a college freshman—grew up to be a road-race broadcaster and producer of *ESPN's Running and Racing* (www.runningandracing.com). Liquori was an early spokesman for Team in Training, which raises funds to combat leukemia, a disease he himself has. *See also* Hall of Fame, USATF; Team in Training; television.

Lisbon, Portugal. The city is scene of the world's fastest (aided) half-marathon. Kenyan Paul Tergat ran a world best of 59:06 there. *See also* fastest races.

Lismont, Karel (b. March 8, 1949). The consistently good Belgian runner was second to Frank Shorter in the 1972 Olympic Marathon and third to Shorter's second in

© Mark Shearman. Athletics–Images.

Belgium's Karel Lismont is one of the best least-known road racers in the world; he took silver to Shorter's gold at Munich and bronze to Shorter's silver at Montreal.

1976. Lismont continued running in the Games through 1984 while compiling one of the longest world-class marathoning careers ever. *See also* Berlin Marathon; Olympic medalists.

logbooks. The most important book that runners read is the one they write themselves. This is their record of training and racing distances and times, experiences, and observations. Many specially designed logs are available, but a blank notebook serves as an equally good place to start this personal writing.

London 1908. This Olympic Marathon gave the race its now-standard distance. It went up from the previous 40K (25 miles), more or less, to accommodate the Royal family's viewing. London also hosted the 1948 Games, using a different course than the 1908 route. *See also* Olympic Marathon, 1900 to 2000.

London Marathon (www.london-marathon.co.uk). Olympic gold-medal steeplechaser (1956) Chris Brasher of England (also one of the rabbits for Roger Bannister's first sub-4:00 mile) visited the New York City Marathon in October 1979 and wondered to himself if London could possibly pull off something similar. Instead of keeping his wondering to himself, he wrote an article for the *London Observer* titled "The World's Most Human Race," which ended

One of the largest and most successful marathons in the world, the scenic London Marathon was modeled after the New York City Marathon.

London Marathon Winners

Not many races can say that they debuted with a tie for first. Dick Beardsley and Inge Simonsen shared the first London title. In 1985 Ingrid Kristiansen set a world record that would last 13 years. * = event record.

WOMEN

Year	Athlete	Time
1981	Joyce Smith (Britain)	2:29:57
1982	Joyce Smith (Britain)	2:29:43
1983	Grete Waitz (Norway)	2:25:29
1984	Ingrid Kristiansen (Norway)	2:24:26
1985	Ingrid Kristiansen (Norway)	2:21:06*
1986	Grete Waitz (Norway)	2:24:54
1987	Ingrid Kristiansen (Norway)	2:22:48
1988	Ingrid Kristiansen (Norway)	2:25:41
1989	Veronique Marot (Britain)	2:25:56
1990	Wanda Panfil (Poland)	2:26:31
1991	Rosa Mota (Portugal)	2:26:14
1992	Katrin Dorre (Germany)	2:29:39
1993	Katrin Dorre (Germany)	2:27:09
1994	Katrin Dorre (Germany)	2:32:34
1995	Malgorzata Sobanska (Poland)	2:27:43
1996	Liz McColgan (Britain)	2:27:54
1997	Joyce Chepchumba (Kenya)	2:26:51
1998	Catherina McKiernan (Ireland)	2:26:26
1999	Joyce Chepchumba (Kenya)	2:23:22
2000	Tegla Loroupe (Kenya)	2:24:33
2001	Derartu Tulu (Ethiopia)	2:23:56

MEN

Year	Athlete	Time
1981	Dick Beardsley (U.S.) and Inge Simonsen (Norway)	2:11:48
1982	Hugh Jones (Britain)	2:09:24
1983	Mike Gratton (Britain)	2:09:43
1984	Charlie Spedding (Britain)	2:09:57
1985	Steve Jones (Britain)	2:08:16
1986	Toshihiko Seko (Japan)	2:10:02
1987	Hiromi Taniguchi (Japan)	2:09:50
1988	Henrik Jorgensen (Denmark)	2:10:20
1989	Douglas Wakiihuri (Kenya)	2:09:03
1990	Allister Hutton (Britain)	2:10:10
1991	Yakov Tolstikov (USSR)	2:09:17
1992	Antonio Pinto (Portugal)	2:10:02
1993	Eamonn Martin (Britain)	2:10:50
1994	Dionicio Ceron (Mexico)	2:08:53
1995	Dionicio Ceron (Mexico)	2:08:30
1996	Dionicio Ceron (Mexico)	2:10:00
1997	Antonio Pinto (Portugal)	2:07:55
1998	Abel Anton (Spain)	2:07:57
1999	Abdelkader El Mouaziz (Morocco)	2:07:57
2000	Antonio Pinto (Portugal)	2:06:36*
2001	Abdelkader El Mouaziz (Morocco)	2:07:11

with this fateful line: "I wonder whether London could stage such a festival? We have the course, a magnificent course . . . but do we have the heart and the hospitality to welcome the world?" Other folks in London, stirred by Brasher's words, wondered the same thing. After all, it was at the 1908 Olympics that the now-standard distance of 26 miles, 385 yards was established.

Londoners came together to found the London Marathon Charitable Trust Ltd., which promised that the residents of London would never be asked to ante up tax money to bail out the marathon. On March 29, 1981, the first London Marathon was run. Sponsored by Gillette for roughly $75,000 U.S., the first running featured 8,000 runners. Incredibly, the first race ended in a 2:11:48 tie between America's Dick Beardsley and Norway's Inge Simonsen.

The race has grown to be one of the largest, most popular, and best organized in the world. Dave Bedford, former world 10,000-meter record holder, is currently the director. The race has also spawned excellent competition. In 2000 Spain's Antonio Pinto set a European marathon record there with 2:06:36. *See also* Bedford, Dave; Brasher, Chris.

Long Distance Log. The scrappy little results-centered magazine, edited by Browning Ross, predated *Runner's World* by nearly a decade. *LDL* also published one of the first modern books on training, Tom Osler's *Conditioning of Distance Runners* in 1967. Ross shut down his publication in 1975, as bigger and better-funded competitors took over what he had started. *See also* "Logging On" on next page; *Conditioning of Distance Runners;* publications; Ross, Browning.

Long Island Marathon (www.lirrc.org). Only five marathons in the United States have a longer history than this one, which launched in 1958. *See also* oldest races.

Long Run Solution, The. *See* books; About the Authors at the back of this book.

long runs. *Long* is in the eye of the beholder, but in broad terms it means running considerably longer—say, twice as long—as the typical day's run. Arthur Lydiard popularized the practice of weekly long runs in the 1960s. It's no coincidence that the first boom in marathon participation followed. Training long led naturally to racing long. *See also* Lydiard, Arthur.

long slow distance (LSD). Although you can get high from it, it has nothing to do with illegal drugs. This is a form of long, gentle training widely credited to Joe Henderson, who wrote a book on the subject in 1969. Henderson in turn credits the concept to Arthur Newton, Arthur Lydiard, and Ernst Van Aaken. *See also* About the Authors at the back of this book; Lydiard, Arthur; Newton, Arthur; Van Aaken, Dr. Ernst.

Logging On

From Joe Henderson's *Running Commentary,* April 1999.

Pete League needed to downsize his publication collection. This meant parting reluctantly with the magazines once edited by one of his closest friends, the late Browning Ross. Trashing the old *Long Distance Logs* would have been a sacrilege. So Pete offered them to his running friends, myself included.

I've long since stopped saving all magazines that arrive here, because they'd soon leave me no room to live. My practice of finding a good adoptive home for reading material is the same as Pete's. He indulged my request to cram a large envelope full of *Logs* and send them to me for a nostalgic review, before I passed them to the next eager reader. The package arrived 40 years after I first subscribed to the magazine in which my work would make its first appearance in a national publication.

Breaking into the *Log* took no skill. All I needed in the winter of 1961 was an envelope and a stamp for mailing a handwritten note. Browning Ross printed my letter, not because it said anything special but because it helped fill space. That was the beauty of the *Log*. Anyone, writer or runner, could break in there.

The *Log* covered all of us—and I do mean *all,* right back to the last finisher and often even the DNFs. A magazine could do that then without being a thousand pages long.

The early copies were mimeographed on the backs of old test papers. Browning Ross was a teacher at the time. He'd graduated to semistandard magazine format by the time I arrived as a subscriber three years later. But the *Log* never grew beyond a hobby for him and was never accused of being slick.

Its format was small, the size of a paperback book cover instead of standard 8 $\frac{1}{2}$ by 11. The photos were always black and white, and often a hazy gray. Browning was known to run the same cover two months in a row. Publication schedules depended on how much material had accumulated and how busy he was elsewhere. He might mail a month early or a month late, and he never put any statute of limitations on the age of race results.

The *Log* was never a moneymaker. Subscriptions were cheap. Advertising was sparse. The one-man staff sold shoes from the back of his car to support his hobby. At its peak the *Log* attracted about 1,000 readers. Browning knew most of us personally, and we knew each other because our names went to everyone else whenever we ran a road race.

Results usually appeared in the form received. Browning attempted no uniformity of presentation—or organization by date, distance, or region.

We didn't mind. We read for content, not style. We read to see our own names (though we'd committed the times to memory months earlier) and to see how our friends were doing. We read for their letters . . . and for tidbits on training . . . and for articles duplicated from other publications, exactly as printed originally . . . and for Browning's own sly and wise comments.

Browning Ross logged out as a publisher in 1975. No old copies of *Long Distance Log* remain with me permanently, but most of the memories do.

loop. Many runners refer to all their routes as "loops." In fact, a loop course is more precisely defined as one that doesn't repeat itself—it features neither an out-and-back nor a multiple-lap design—but finishes where it starts.

Tegla Loroupe of Kenya broke Ingrid Kristiansen's world marathon record in Rotterdam 1998 with a 2:20:47, then chipped 4 seconds off that time a year later in Berlin.

© Mark Shearman. Athletics-Images.

Lopes, Carlos (b. February 18, 1947). He became the hero to every aging runner at the 1984 Olympics as the oldest man, at 37, ever to win the marathon—setting a Games record of 2:09:21 that stands today. His encore? Merely a world record of 2:07:12, the first sub-2:08 time, the following spring at Rotterdam after he turned 38. In an earlier phase of his career, the Portuguese runner won a World Cross Country title and an Olympic silver medal in the 10,000, both in 1976. He would win the cross country title again nine years later. *See also* Olympic medalists; rankings, *Track & Field News*; record progressions, world; Rotterdam Marathon;.

Lore of Running. *See* Noakes, Dr. Tim.

Loroupe, Tegla (b. May 9, 1973). The women's marathon record crept closer to the 2:20 barrier when Kenya's Loroupe broke the Ingrid Kristiansen record that had stood for 13 years. She ran a controversial (male-paced) 2:20:47 at Rotterdam in 1998, then improved to 2:20:43 a year later in Berlin. Other major wins included New York City 1994 and 1995, Rotterdam 1997 and 1999, and London 2000. She also won the World Half-Marathon Championships three straight years from 1997 to 1999. *See also* "Tegla Lo-record" on next page; "Avon Racing Circuits; Bay to Breakers 12K; Berlin Marathon; London Marathon; New York City Marathon; rankings, *Track & Field News*; record progressions, world; Rotterdam Marathon; World Half-Marathon Championships.

Lorz, Fred (b. 1880; d. 1992). He tried to accept gold at the 1904 St. Louis Olympics after catching a car ride at mile three. Unlike later cheaters, he had real talent, as shown the next spring when he won Boston. *See also* Boston Marathon; cheaters; Olympians, U.S.

Tegla Lo-record

From Joe Henderson's *Running Commentary,* June 1998.

Various stories of mine have been viewed as unkind to Kenyans. I seemed to say that their dominance of distance running has become too great. Some commentators have even called this concern racist.

So you might wonder what I think of Kenyan Tegla Loroupe's record in the marathon. She ran 2:20:47 this spring to take down the mark that had shrugged off all threats for 13 years. My answer might surprise you. I'm happy—or at least relieved—that Loroupe is the new record-holder, and almost as pleased that she set it at Rotterdam and not at, say, Boston.

One problem with Kenyans is that so many are so good. They come and go so quickly that we don't get much chance to memorize their names, let alone learn of their personalities. Loroupe came and stayed. We got to know her and to like her. If asked to name two runners from Kenya, you probably would make her one of them. Like "Grete" or "Ingrid," just the first name "Tegla" will do.

My fear was that some unknown runner, most likely from China, would break this record in some little-known race. Then all sorts of suspicions would have infected the mark.

Loroupe's marathon credentials were well known. She wasn't a new arrival from the short races (such as Catherina McKiernan of Ireland, another possible record-breaker, who debuted in 2:23 last year). Tegla had won at New York City as long ago as 1994. She had come closer than any other active contender, with 2:22:07 at Rotterdam last year, to Ingrid Kristiansen's record of 2:21:06.

I overlook Uta Pippig here. She came within 40 seconds of the Kristiansen time at Boston in 1994 but has been injured much of the past two years, which brings up two more items about Loroupe.

- She too was hurt last fall. A back injury was misdiagnosed as career threatening, and she was confined briefly to a cast. As often happens with forced rests, she came back better than ever.

- Boston is my favorite race, but it isn't a course for setting legitimate records. It's point-to-point, downhill, and subject to aiding winds—such as those that blew Pippig in 1994. If Loroupe had run her time at Boston, it would have been widely and wrongly labeled a record.

She ran instead at flat, out-and-back Rotterdam. There still are no official world records for marathons, but when standards are finally adopted this type of unaided course will surely qualify.

Loroupe's mark carries only one taint. Two Kenyan men accompanied her, setting the pace and breaking the wind. This sort of assistance is probably inevitable, and often incidental rather than planned, as long as women and men run their marathons side by side.

Five years ago the women's records at distances 1,500 and up were all the property of Europeans. Now the last of those is gone, and Tegla Loroupe becomes the first black African woman to hold a record in an Olympic event. She's so right for it that I'd now like to see her be first under 2:20.

[Loroupe dropped the record by another four seconds, to 2:20:43, at Berlin in 1999. Her record was bettered at Berlin in 2001 by Naoko Takahashi, who ran the first sub-2:20 women's marathon–2:19:46, and then at Chicago by Catherine Ndereba who ran a 2:18:47 one week later.]

Los Angeles Marathon Winners

Tapping into the excitement of the 1984 Olympics, the annual marathon began little more than a year later. Winners included John Treacy, silver medalist at the L.A. Games, and Julie Isphording, member of the first U.S. women's team. * = event record.

WOMEN

Year	Athlete	Time
1986	Nancy Ditz (U.S.)	2:36:27
1987	Nancy Ditz (U.S.)	2:35:24
1988	Blanca Jaime (Mexico)	2:36:11
1989	Zoya Ivanova (USSR)	2:34:42
1990	Julie Isphording (U.S.)	2:32:25
1991	Cathy O'Brien (U.S.)	2:29:38
1992	Madina Biktagirova (Russia)	2:26:23*
1993	Lyubov Klochko (Ukraine)	2:39:49
1994	Olga Appell (U.S.)	2:28:12
1995	Nadia Prasad (France)	2:29:48
1996	Lyubov Klochko (Ukraine)	2:30:30
1997	Lornah Kiplagat (Kenya)	2:33:50
1998	Lornah Kiplagat (Kenya)	2:34:03
1999	Irina Bogacheva (Russia)	2:30:31
2000	Jane Salumae (Estonia)	2:33:33
2001	Elena Paranonova (Russia)	2:36:58

MEN

Year	Athlete	Time
1986	Ric Sayre (U.S.)	2:12:59
1987	Art Boileau (Canada)	2:13:08
1988	Martin Mondragon (Mexico)	2:10:19
1989	Art Boileau (Canada)	2:13:01
1990	Pedro Ortiz (Colombia)	2:11:54
1991	Mark Plaatjes (South Africa)	2:10:29
1992	John Treacy (Ireland)	2:12:29
1993	Joseildo Rocha (Brazil)	2:14:29
1994	Paul Pilkington (U.S.)	2:12:13
1995	Rolando Vera (Ecuador)	2:11:39
1996	Jose Luis Molina (Mexico)	2:13:23
1997	El Maati Chaham (Morocco)	2:14:16
1998	Zebedayo Bayo (Tanzania)	2:11:21
1999	Simon Bor (Kenya)	2:09:25*
2000	Benson Mbithi (Kenya)	2:11:55
2001	Stephen Ndungu (Kenya)	2:13:13

Los Angeles Marathon (www.lamarathon.com). Along with New York City, Chicago, and Honolulu, Los Angeles is one of several U.S. marathons with a history of 20,000-plus fields. L.A. also has the rare honor of having hosted two Olympic Games. The marathon, run in March, touches parts of the Olympic courses used in 1932 and 1984. *See also* biggest races.

Louis, Spiridon. *See* page 202.

LSD. *See* long slow distance.

Lycra. *See* clothing.

Lydiard, Arthur (b. July 6, 1917). It would be difficult to imagine a single individual in the second half of the 20th century who has had more of an influence on running than New Zealand's Arthur Lydiard. A shoemaker by trade, Arthur formulated revolutionary ideas about training to run, many of which he tried out on himself in the 1950s. Other New Zealand coaches ridiculed the ideas of the outgoing and gregarious Lydiard, who went against using hard track workouts as the basis of good training. Instead, he preached plenty of long-distance training to build a base before building other stories, such as strength and speed, on the fitness house. Even when he scoured his neighborhood in Auckland for some likely runners to train under his methods, then took them to the 1960 Rome Olympics where two of them won golds on the track and the third took bronze in the marathon, he didn't receive full respect at home.

So he packed his bags and took them to Finland, a country where Paavo Nurmi's teachings—hard track workouts and lots of them—had sustained the Finns until the 1960s. Lydiard made a believer of the Finns. Pekka Vasala, who trained under Lydiard and won the gold medal in the 1,500 meters for Finland at the 1972 Munich Games, put it this way: "He instituted long training runs throughout the winter, hill springing exercises, and more. After Finland's triumph at the 1972 Munich Olympics [where Lasse Viren also won the 10,000 and 5,000], Lydiard's success was without doubt. I owe much of my success to his unique training approach."

By 1972 Lydiard's methods had become established in certain circles in the United States, having been sneaked into the country in Bill Bowerman's 1967 book, *Jogging* (Grosset & Dunlap). It is safe to say that Arthur Lydiard's teachings form the basis of every successful marathon-training book published in the United States during the past three decades. Yet, paradoxically, Lydiard is once again in eclipse; his theories of high-mileage weeks to build a base have been denounced by scientific types who preach lower total mileage (70 to 80 miles per week), often with disastrous results. Lydiard's base of high-mileage is still practiced in Africa, where runners train two to three times a day and amass very high weekly mileage, much of it at a relaxed, controlled pace. *See also* books; Bowerman, Bill; coaches; *Run to the Top*.

Louis, Spiridon (also spelled Loues) (b. January 12, 1873; d. March 26, 1940). Spiridon Louis was the hero of the first modern Olympic Games held in Athens in 1896. Although the athletes in the revival of the ancient Olympic Games were overwhelmingly Greek (230 of 311 total athletes from 13 countries), Greece fared badly in the competition. A special marathon event was created (complete with a special winner's cup) and was scheduled for the closing day of the Games. The race was set to run the classic course from the town of Marathon to the city of Athens made famous in the legend of Pheidippides. There were 18 entries and 17 starters: one each from Australia, the United States, France, and Hungary, and the rest Greeks. This race was not the first marathon, however; Greece had held two qualifying marathons (February 27 and March 12, 1896) to pick their team.

During the March race, which was run under atrocious conditions, a water carrier named Spiridon Louis took sixth place and barely qualified for the Olympic race. But Louis's job transporting water to Athens was perfect training for the marathon. He loaded jugs of water onto a wagon pulled by a horse, then jogged next to it to and from the city. He had also served as a soldier. His commander, Papadiamantopolous, was the starter for the Olympic Marathon and rode his horse ahead to the stadium to alert the waiting crowds of the progress of the race.

Although the race began at two o'clock in the afternoon, the weather was cool and favorable for long-distance running. In the early going, the foreign runners took the lead, but their fast early pace eventually caught up with them and they began to falter. Louis ran steadily, and at 35K he caught the Australian, Edwin Flack, who held the lead. They stayed near each other for several kilometers. At 37K Louis's girlfriend was waiting to give him orange slices, and the course was downhill. He picked up the pace, and the rest of the field failed to respond. As Louis approached the stadium, Papadiamantopolous rode ahead and informed King Georgios of Louis's lead; word spread around the stadium, and the crowd went wild. The weather had turned warmer as the runners neared Athens, and Louis was covered with perspiration and road dust. Crown Prince Konstantinos and Prince Georgios ran out to meet Louis and ran the final stretch into the stadium with him. He finished in 2:58:50, 13 seconds in front of Kharilaos Vasilakos.

Louis was showered with all sorts of gifts—including, it is reported, the hand of the daughter of the industrialist George Averoff, a shipping tycoon who had helped fund the Olympics. However, she was a prize Louis did not accept. King Georgios offered Louis anything he wanted; he requested a better cart and a younger horse to haul his water. He never competed again. He married his girlfriend Eleni the next spring, and they produced three sons. Louis, a fan of Adolf Hitler, was brought to the 1936 Olympics in Berlin to celebrate 40 years of Olympic competition. He died four years later and is buried in his hometown of Amaroussion. *See also* Olympic Marathon, 1896.

Lyons, Patti. *See* Catalano, Patti Lyons.

Macdonald, Duncan (b. January 15, 1949). Macdonald competed alongside his Stanford teammate Don Kardong at the 1976 Olympic Games. Duncan ran the 5,000 there, but he was equally at home on the roads and at longer distances. He was a three-time Honolulu Marathon titlist (2:27:34 in 1973, 2:20:37 in 1976, and 2:16:55 in 1980) and the winner of Kardong's Bloomsday 12K race in 1981. *See also* Bloomsday 12K, Honolulu Marathon; Kardong, Don.

Machado, Manuela (b. August 9, 1963). Rosa Mota's Portuguese successor had a good run of success in the mid-1990s, winning the World Championships Marathon in 1995 (2:25:39) and collecting silvers in 1993 and 1997. She also won two European Marathon Championship titles in a row, 1994 (2:29:54) and 1998 (2:27:10). *See also* European Championships; World Championships medalists.

Machala, June (b. January 1, 1931). She holds American records for the 5K, 10K, and half-marathon in the 65–69 age group (22:07, 45:04, and aided 1:39:21), and for the 10K and half-marathon in the 70–74 age group (48:30 and aided 1:42:13). *See also* records, American age-group.

Machuka, Josphat (b. December 12, 1973). In little more than a year's time, this Kenyan won three lucrative U.S. races—the Bloomsday 12K in 1994 and 1995 and the Bolder Boulder 10K in 1995. *See also* Bloomsday 12K; Bolder Boulder 10K.

Mackinac Island Run (www.gaultracemanagement.com). The island in Upper Michigan is off-limits to auto traffic. This makes it a runner's paradise, especially on the Saturday in September when the Mackinac Island eight-mile race circles the island and runners' only concern is dodging the road apples. *See also* scenic races.

Magee, Barry (b. February 6, 1934). He was the least known of New Zealand's medal trio at the 1960 Rome Olympics. Together with winners Murray Halberg and Peter Snell, Magee—third in the marathon (2:17:19)—touched off the Lydiard Revolution in distance training. Magee also won the 1960 Fukuoka (in 2:19:04) about three months after Rome. *See also* Fukuoka Marathon; Olympic medalists.

Mah, Sy (b. 1926; d. 1988). He amassed more marathon finishes (524) than anyone until Norm Frank, in 1994, and then others surpassed his total. However, Mah's "record" came during years when marathoning opportunities were less plentiful than they are now. He also contributed as a coach, teacher, and motivator of marathoners in his native Canada and at the University of Toledo. *See also* "Mah's Ways" on next page; Frank, Norm; Hall of Fame, RRCA; Preisler, Horst.

mail-order companies. Catalog companies sprang up to offer runners shoes and equipment at attractive prices. These include East Bay (www.eastbay.com), Road Runner Sports (www.roadrunnersports.com), and the National Running Center (www.nationalrunningcenter.com). Traditional running stores, which offer service and individualized fittings along with sales, aren't pleased when their customers order by mail.

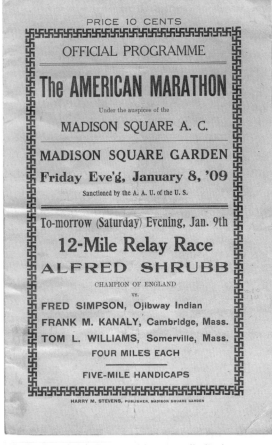

PRICE 10 CENTS

OFFICIAL PROGRAMME

The AMERICAN MARATHON

Under the auspices of the

MADISON SQUARE A. C.

MADISON SQUARE GARDEN

Friday Eve'g, January 8, '09

Sanctioned by the A. A. U. of the U. S.

To-morrow (Saturday) Evening, Jan. 9th

12-Mile Relay Race

ALFRED SHRUBB

CHAMPION OF ENGLAND

vs.

FRED SIMPSON, Ojibway Indian

FRANK M. KANALY, Cambridge, Mass.

TOM L. WILLIAMS, Somerville, Mass.

FOUR MILES EACH

FIVE-MILE HANDICAPS

HARRY M. STEVENS, PUBLISHER, MADISON SQUARE GARDEN

Courtesy RunningPast.com

When organized opportunities were limited, runners would run anywhere at anytime. In this instance, a January 8, 1909, program advertises "The American Marathon," which was actually a 12-mile indoor race between Alfred Shrubb of England and a relay team of American runners who would run four miles each.

Mamabolo, Titus (b. January 7, 1941). The world 50-plus marathon record-holder from South Africa broke 2:20 (with a 2:19:29 in 1991) in his second half century. *See also* records, world age-group.

Manley, Mike (b. February 14, 1942). In younger years he made an Olympic team (1972) as a steeplechaser. Later he became the first American master to break 2:20 in the marathon (as well as 2:19 and 2:18, all in the same 1983 race in which he ran 2:17:02). He now coaches many top runners in Eugene, Oregon. *See also* coaches.

marathon. It almost seems too obvious to mention. But how can we call this a complete book without a listing for the central event of road racing? The marathon, of course, takes its name from the Greek coastal town by the same name. This was the scene of the historic and Olympic events that launched the race. The marathon arrived at its current distance—42.2 kilometers or 26.2 miles—not in Greece but in England, at the 1908 Olympics. *See also* Olympic Marathon, 1896; Olympic Marathon, 1900 to 2000.

Mah's Ways

From Joe Henderson's *Running Commentary,* December 1991.

Willie Williamson gives guided tours through Sy Mah's past. He first takes his visitors running along the Brookside loop near the University of Toledo campus where Mah taught. "I never come here without thinking about Sy," said Williamson on one recent tour. He had started running in Mah's class at the university and later helped teach it.

Willie is now keeper of the Mah legend. Swiss daughters didn't want that task when their dad died of cancer three years ago. One of them told Williamson, "Take whatever you want from his papers, and we'll dispose of the rest." These included records from the 524 marathons that Sy had run.

"He was a packrat who never threw anything away," said Williamson. "It would have taken someone a year to go through everything he saved. I did what I could, but 90 percent of it is gone forever." What's left fits into two albums, a videotaped interview with Mah from the mid-1980s, and Willie's memory bank. I looked at the albums, watched the tape, and pumped Sy's friend for facts before going onstage at a sports medicine conference dedicated to Sy.

"Sy Mah spent his last 20 years breaking the rules," I said at the program on ultraendurance sports. "He was an exercise scientist who didn't follow the rules of exercise science." Mah ran more marathons than anyone else. But he didn't train for them, taper for them, or recover from them in the approved ways.

One school of marathon training insists on increasing the average daily mileage to at least eight or nine. Another school requires stretching the long training run to about marathon length. Mah did neither. He did no marathon training beyond what the marathons themselves gave him. Nor did he heed widely reported findings on how long it takes to rest up for a marathon or to get over one. He would never insert the recommended number of easy weeks before or after.

Sy averaged one marathon every other week for almost 20 years, often doubled on a weekend, sometimes tripled on a three-day weekend, and once ran five marathons in nine days. Yet he wasn't so much breaking rules as *making* those that worked for him.

The standard rules fit the typical marathoner: one who does little else but run, who runs nearly every day and often hard, and who runs marathons—along with all other races—as fast as possible. Sy Mah wasn't typical.

His first rule was to *run* marathons, not race them. He usually ran at least a minute per mile slower than his best possible pace, and he often stopped to walk with runners who were having trouble. Mah's second rule was to mix sports instead of being a running specialist. He combined triathlons, canoe events, and ski races with the runs. Sy's third rule was to train little during the week and to save his big efforts for the weekends.

"He didn't care much for any kind of training," said Williamson. "That's one reason why he ran so many marathons, so he wouldn't need to do much else. I doubt if he ran more than 20 miles a week between races, and his runs were very rarely longer than five or six miles."

Mah lived for his marathon weekends. On the videotape that his friend saved, Sy says, "My weekends were very full and tremendously exciting."

Marathon & Beyond (www.marathonandbeyond.com). The publication is the bastard offspring, birthed in January 1997, of *The Marathoner*, which perished in 1979 after a brief run. Rich Benyo delivered and nurtured both publications as editor. *M&B* was published for its first two years by Human Kinetics, then taken over by Benyo and publisher Jan Seeley. *See also* About the Authors at back of this book; *Marathoner, The*; publications.

marathon, first U.S. If you guessed Boston, try again; that's the oldest surviving American marathon but not the first. New York City Olympic fans came back home in 1896 and were so inspired by the road event they'd witnessed in Athens that they put on their own marathon from Stamford, Connecticut, to the Knickerbocker Athletic Club on Columbus Circle in downtown Manhattan. There were 30 entrants but only 10 finishers, which wasn't bad considering that the weather was miserable, with mud and slush. John McDermott won in 3:25:55; he would also win the first Boston Marathon the following spring. *See also* McDermott, John.

Marathoner, The. As a way of spreading marathon news throughout the year rather than hoarding it until the increasingly huge annual February issue, *Runner's World* published this magazine in 1978 as an oversized, perfect-bound quarterly at the then outrageous price of $2.50 per copy. Created by Rich Benyo, the magazine lasted only five issues because of its being tied on a *Runner's World* profit-and-loss sheet to *On the Run*, a biweekly tabloid that failed miserably. *See also* About the Authors at back of this book; *Marathon & Beyond*; publications; *Runner's World*.

Marathon, Plains of. This was the site of an epic battle from which Pheidippides supposedly ran to Athens with news of victory, birthing the marathon legend that led to inclusion of the event in the 1896 revival of the Olympic Games. The Olympic race started at the historic site on the Greek coast, as does the current annual Athens Marathon. *See also* Athens, Greece; Olympic Marathon, 1896.

Marchiano, Sue (b. November 5, 1954). The 1989 World Cup Marathon winner (in 2:30:48) is the only American, male or female, to claim an international title since Joan Benoit Samuelson won at the 1984 Olympics. Marchiano led the U.S. team to a silver medal in the World Cup race. *See also* World Cup Marathon.

Mardi Gras Marathon (www.mardigrasmarathon.com). This Mardi Gras tradition in New Orleans goes back to 1965, though the race is usually held in January, before the annual festivities. For several years the race was run across the Lake Pontchartrain Bridge, resulting in extremely fast times when the wind was right. *See also* oldest races.

Marek, Steve "Superman" (birthdate unavailable). The Superman-costumed runner and race organizer befriended and defended Rosie Ruiz after her 1980 Boston Marathon debacle. Previously Marek had trouble with the New York

RRC's Fred Lebow, who had banned Marek from races for lining up in the front and impeding faster runners and for falsifying his New York Marathon entry by claiming to be a sub-3:00 marathoner. *See also* Ruiz, Rosie.

Marine Corps Marathon (www.marinemarathon.com). The alternative to New York City, Marine Corps is also run in the fall, offering no prize money but drawing a five-figure field. It is known in recent years for the rapid and early filling of its field as well as for being the race where celebs (Oprah, Al Gore) go for their marathon debuts. The racecourse passes many of Washington, D.C.'s best-known sights. *See also* biggest races.

Markova, Olga (b. August 6, 1968). In the chaotic first years after the breakup of the Soviet Union, some runners thrived. Free of former restrictions on travel, Russian Markova spent much of her time running in—and winning—U.S. races, including Boston in 1992 (2:23:43) and 1993 (2:25:27). *See also* Boston Marathon; rankings, *Runner's World*.

Martin, Dr. Dave (b. October, 1, 1939). If Dave Martin had done nothing more than write (with partner Roger Gynn) the several books he did on marathoning, his contribution to road racing would be impressive. But Dave has done so much more for the science of the sport that it's difficult to keep track of it all. A professor and researcher at Georgia State University (Atlanta) in the Department of Cardiopulmonary Care Sciences, he has researched and written extensively on athletic physiology, served on numerous committees directly related to American track and field efforts, and conducted research on elite U.S. distance runners to improve their training and racing results.

His first major book (with Gynn) was *The Marathon Footrace* (Charles C Thomas, 1979), a definitive 469-page study on the sport. He later wrote *Training Distance Runners* (Human Kinetics, 1991 and 1997) with Peter Coe, father of two-time Olympic 1,500-meter gold medalist Sebastian Coe. And in 2000 (again with Gynn) he published a 512-page opus, *The Olympic Marathon* (Human Kinetics).

Dave is a fellow in the American College of Sports Medicine, as well as a contributing member of the Association of Track and Field Statisticians, the International Marathon Medical Directors Association, the Association of International Marathons, and the International Society of Olympic Historians. In 1978 the U.S. Olympic Academy selected him to be one of its three representatives to the International Olympic Academy. He has over the years amassed a data bank of more than 44,000 marathon performances from around the world. He has run 29 marathons. *See also* Gynn, Roger.

Martin, Eamonn (b. October 23, 1961). The Brit won major marathons on both sides of the Atlantic in the mid-1990s—London in 1993 and Chicago in 1995. *See also* Chicago Marathon; London Marathon.

Martin, Jennifer (b. October 23, 1961) The Pan-American Games allows two runners per event per country, not three like the Olympics. In the 1995 Pan-

Lisa Martin (now Ondieki) was one of the dominating forces in road racing during the 1980s. Here she competes in cross country at Oregon in 1981.

© Jeff Johnson

Am Marathon, the American women went 1-2, with Martin (in 2:44:10) trailing America's only winner, Maria Trujillo. *See also* Pan-American Games; Trujillo, Maria.

Martin, Ken (b. October 8, 1958). A former steeplechaser at the University of Oregon, Martin broke a six-year drought in sub-2:10 U.S. marathons in 1989 by running a 2:09:38 at New York City. (The last to do it had been his ex-teammate from Oregon, Alberto Salazar.) Martin also won the 1984 and 1985 national marathon championships. *See also* Martin, Lisa; national marathon champions, U.S.

Martin, Lisa (now Ondieki) (b. May 12, 1960). Like her ex-husband Ken Martin, she began her college career at the University of Oregon—she as a hurdler. Each move up in distance suited the Australian better. She was the marathon silver medalist at the Seoul Olympics in 1988, won the first Commonwealth Games women's marathon title in 1986 (and repeated in 1990), and won New York City in 1992. Her PR of 2:23:51 is still one of the fastest times ever run in a women's race, in this case the Osaka Ladies' Marathon. *See also* Bay to Breakers 12K; Bloomsday 12K; Commonwealth Games; New York City Marathon; Olympic medalists; Osaka Ladies' Marathon.

Masback, Craig (b. March 31, 1955). The former world-class miler has breathed new life into the USATF since taking over as executive director of the struggling governing body of the American sport in the late 1990s. Masback was a middle-distance runner himself, a world-class miler, and he understands the needs of runners better than his predecessors did. He ran during the professional sport's coming of age and later worked as a television commentator, so he appreciates the realities of big-money sports. *See also*; USA Track & Field.

masters racing. A one-time fringe movement for over-40 runners now accounts for nearly half of any U.S. road-racing field. National and world championships for masters are run at a variety of road distances, and many races award prize money to masters. *See also* records, American age-group; records, world age-group.

Masya, Benson (b. May 14, 1970). The reformed boxer from Kenya won the first World Half-Marathon race ever contested in 1992 with 1:00:24. Two years later he was the world's top-ranked road racer, primarily for victories at the 1994 Peachtree 10K (28:01) and the 1992 Honolulu Marathon (2:14:19). *See also* Honolulu Marathon; Peachtree 10K; rankings, *Runner's World*; World Half-Marathon Championships.

Matson, Shirley (b. November 7, 1940). With 2:50:26 she broke the seemingly unbeatable American over-50 marathon record held by Sister Marion Irvine. Matson also holds multiple national 50-plus marks in the 5K (17:28 in the 50–54 age group) and 10K (35:57 in the 50–54 age group), as well as the national 55–59 half-marathon record. In 2001 she broke another of Sister Marion Irvine's records, taking the over-60 10K American mark with 40:28. *See also* Irvine, Sister Marion; records, American age-group.

Maui Marathon (www.mauimarathon.com). The Hawaiian race is run each March, about three months after Honolulu. *See also* scenic races.

Mavis, Stan (b. February 26, 1955). Americans did much of the early record setting on the roads simply because the big races were in the United States and the standards for records were in place. Mavis set a world and American half-marathon mark of 1:02:16 in 1980. *See also* record progressions, American; record progressions, world.

maximum oxygen uptake ($\dot{V}O_2$max). The ability to consume oxygen in large amounts and use it with great efficiency is a primary factor affecting distance running potential.$\dot{V}O_2$max, as it's nicknamed, can be improved greatly with training. It is usually measured during a treadmill run in a physiology lab.

Maxwell, Brian (b. March 14, 1953). A Canadian Olympic marathoner and near winner at Boston (third in 1977), Brian could run a 2:14 marathon but wasn't able to go to Moscow in 1980 to prove his mettle. A coach at the University of California at Berkeley, he struck it rich with his creation and marketing of a portable sports bar called PowerBar. *See also* PowerBar.

May, Carey (b. July 19, 1959). The U.S.-educated (at Brigham Young University) Irishwoman won the Osaka Ladies' Marathon in 1983 (2:29:23) and 1985 (2:28:07). She later married Canadian marathoner Dave Edge. *See also* Osaka Ladies' Marathon.

May, Marian (b. 1954). She's believed to be the first woman to win a mixed marathon when, in 1975, she ran 3:02:51 in Alaska as a 21-year-old.

McArdle, Peter (b. March 22, 1929; d. June 24, 1985). The bald-pated Irish immigrant looked like a man among boys when he ran the 1964 Olympic Marathon for the United States. He placed 23rd in Tokyo but was the Pan-American Games bronze medalist a year earlier. McArdle died while running at age 56. *See also* Hall of Fame, RRCA; Olympians, U.S.

McArthur, Kennedy (b. February 10, 1882). South Africa, a nation rich in distance runners, has had only two Olympic gold medalists in the marathon. McArthur was the first, in 1912. Josia Thugwane ended the subsequent 84-year drought at the Atlanta Games. *See also* Olympic medalists.

McCluskey, Joe (b. June 2, 1911). The RRCA Hall of Famer won a bronze medal as a steeplechaser in the 1932 Olympics. His road credentials included a 1936 win at Bay to Breakers. *See also* Bay to Breakers 12K; Hall of Fame, RRCA.

McColgan, Liz (b. May 24, 1964). After winning the bronze medal at 10,000 in the Seoul Olympics in1988, the Scot increasingly turned her attention to the roads. Her honors include a New York City Marathon victory in 1991, the World Half-Marathon title in the event's first year, 1992, and wins at the Tokyo and London Marathons. She holds the current world 10K road record of 30:39 and held two earlier marks at that distance as well as two former 5K records. *See also* London Marathon; New York City Marathon; record progressions, world; records, world; Tokyo Marathons; World Half-Marathon Championships.

McDermott, John (birthdate unavailable). He placed first in two historic first races—the maiden marathon run in the United States, from Stamford to New York City in 1896, and the inaugural Boston the following spring. *See also* Boston Marathon; marathon, first U.S.

McDonagh, Jim (b. February 14, 1924). Born in Ireland, McDonagh was a great master runner before the term was coined. He made the U.S. Pan-American Games Marathon team in 1967 at age 43.

McDonald, Ronald (b. 1875, d. September 3, 1947). No, he's not the clown who works pushing hamburgers to kids. This McDonald was a 1900 Olympian who placed seventh at Paris two years after his Boston victory. *See also* Boston Marathon; Olympians, U.S.

McGillivray, Dave (b. August 22, 1954). He has played an ever-increasing role in recent years as technical director of the Boston Marathon—to the point that in June 2000 he was appointed race director when long-running director Guy Morse was elevated to executive director. Dave's greatest triumph was starting 39,000 runners smoothly at the 1996 race. He runs the marathon course each year after most of the runners have finished.

Dave is comfortable with organizational challenges. In 1978 he put together a 3,200-mile run from Medford, Oregon, to his hometown of Medford, Massachusetts—a trip he'd been planning for some four years. Along the way he raised funds for Boston's Jimmy Fund, which benefits a number of causes. A 2:29 marathoner, he knocked off 40 miles a day for 80 days. *See also* Boston Marathon; Morse, Guy.

McGlone, Fred (birthdate unknown). National marathon championships continued during World War II. McGlone won twice, in 1942 and 1943. *See also* national marathon champions, U.S.

McKenzie, Gordon (b. June 26, 1927). After his disappointment in the 1960 Olympic Marathon (where he placed 48th), McKenzie came back to win a silver medal at the 1963 Pan-American Games. His English wife, Chris, was a pioneering female runner in the New York City area. *See also* Hall of Fame, RRCA; Olympians, U.S.

Dave McGillivray promoted races in the 1980s, and in 2000 he was promoted to second in command at the Boston Marathon. He is shown here finishing the 1985 edition of that famed race.

McKiernan, Catherina (b. November 30, 1969). Experience? Who needs experience? McKiernan ran 2:23:44 while winning her first marathon (Berlin in 1997), recording the world's fastest debut. In her second marathon the following spring, the Irishwoman won London in 2:26:26 and gained top world ranking in the event for 1998. *See also* Berlin Marathon; London Marathon; rankings, *Track & Field News*.

McLatchie, Carol (b. October 28, 1951). She now chairs the women's long-distance committee of USATF and as a runner was a Košice Marathon champion (in 1990) and World Cup Marathon team member. *See also* Košice Peace Marathon; rankings, *Runner's World*; USA Track & Field.

McMahon, William (b. March 3, 1910). His year was 1936, into which he crowded a U.S. marathon title and a run at the Berlin Olympics, where he didn't finish. *See also* national marathon champions, U.S.; Olympians, U.S.

measurement, course. *See* certified courses; distances, metric and English.

medalists, Olympic. *See* Olympic medalists.

medalists, World Championships. *See* World Championships medalists.

Medoff, Marshall (b. December 30, 1937). The lawyer-promoter nearly killed off the Boston Marathon in the early 1980s, usurping it from Will Cloney in an attempt to turn it into his own money machine, as the race made its first halting steps from the old to the new way of doing business. The John Hancock Company rescued the marathon with a major infusion of sponsorship dollars in 1986. *See also* Boston Marathon.

megamarathoners. This subspecies of marathoner emphasizes quantity of races. The 50 + D.C. group recognizes as "mega" those runners who have completed the marathon distance at least 100 times. *See also* Fifty Staters.

Mekonnen, Abebe (b. January 9, 1964). The Ethiopian circled the globe winning races: Rotterdam (1986 in 2:09:08), Tokyo (1988 in 2:08:33, 1991 in 2:10:26, and 1993 in 2:12:00), and Boston (1989 in 2:09:06). *See also* Boston Marathon; Rotterdam Marathon; Tokyo Marathon.

Mellor, Charles (b. December 27, 1893, d. February 11, 1962). His Olympic career complete (he'd placed 12th in the 1920 Games and 25th in the 1924), Mellor excelled in 1925. That year he won at Boston in 2:32:01 and took the

From the collection of Dr. Edward H. Kozloff—Motor City Striders

Chicago's Chuck Mellor won Boston in 1925, a year when Clarence DeMar, coming off an Olympic bronze medal, hoped to win, but came up 38 seconds short.

first U.S. marathon championship ever awarded in 2:33:01. *See also* Boston Marathon; national marathon champions, U.S.; Olympians, U.S.

Melpomene. This Greek woman reputedly ran the 1896 Olympic marathon course in Athens, although there is no real evidence. David Martin and Roger Gynn say in *The Olympic Marathon* that this may have been the same woman as Stamata Revithi, who was refused entry but ran the course in 5½ hours on race day. *See also* Revithi, Stamata.

Melpomene Institute (www.melpomene.org). Based in Minnesota's Twin Cities, this organization researches and promotes women's running and, more generally, women's wellness.

Merrill, Jan (b. June 18, 1956). A track Olympian (1,500 at Montreal), she set world and American 10K records twice, at 32:30 and 32:04. She was coached by Norm Higgins, a national marathon champion. *See also* Higgins, Norm; record progressions, American; record progressions, world.

Merritt, Kim (b. May 22, 1955). She reached her running peak young. She was just 20 years old when she won at New York City in 1975 and at Boston the next spring at the hot "Run for the Hoses," and she was 22 when she set an American record of 2:37:57 in 1977. *See also* Boston Marathon; Honolulu Marathon; national marathon champions, U.S.; New York City Marathon; record progressions, American.

metric distances. *See* distances, metric and English.

Meyer, Elana (b. October 10, 1966). She's no slouch at other distances, but in the half-marathon she has few if any equals. The South African won the world half-marathon title in 1994, and she has set the world record four times—the last being the current record of 1:06:44, set in 1999. (Susan Chepkemei ran faster on an aided course in 2001.) *See also* Bay to Breakers 12K; Bloomsday 12K; Bolder Boulder 10K; Peachtree 10K; record progressions, world; records, world; World Half-Marathon Championships.

© Mark Shearman. Athletics-Images.

South African Elana Meyer owns the half-marathon distance. She won the World Half title in 1994 and set the world record three different times, including the current record of 1:06:44.

Meyer, Greg (b. September 18, 1955). The last American man to win Boston (1983) is often overshadowed by his friend Bill Rodgers in spite of Meyer's better PR (2:09:00). Greg also won at Chicago in 1982, holds the current American 10-mile record of 46:13, and has held world and national marks at 10K. *See also* Boston Marathon; Chicago Marathon; Hall of Fame, RRCA; record progressions, American; record progressions, world; records, American.

Michelsen, Albert "Whitey" (b. August 5, 1893). The 1928 and 1932 Olympian placed ninth and seventh, respectively. In 1925 he set a world and American marathon record of 2:29:02, as the first to break 2:30. *See also* Olympians, U.S.; record progressions, American; record progressions, world.

Microsel. The first of the mass-marketed digital chronographs were advertised in running magazines in 1977 and 1978; they sold for more than $100 and were in the shop for repairs every two weeks. Microsel was quickly knocked out of the market by a much less expensive ($19.95)—and infinitely more reliable—Casio model. *See also* Casio.

Midnight Run. The New Year's Eve race, founded in the mid-1960s, was adopted by *Runner's World* in the early 1970s in Los Altos Hills, California, near the magazine's home base of Mountain View. The event was later mimicked by *The Runner* magazine in its hometown of New York City and continued there as an *RW* production after the two magazines joined. The distance has varied between the original 10K and 5K. While it was in Los Altos at the 8K distance, Alberto Salazar and Grete Waitz set world records on its course.

midsoles. *See* ethylene vinyl acetate.

Mihalic, Franjo (b. March 9, 1920). The Yugoslav enjoyed three straight banner years—silver medalist in the 1956 Olympics, top world ranking in 1957, and Boston winner in 1958 (2:25:54). *See also* Boston Marathon; Olympic medalists; rankings, *Track & Field News*.

Milan, Italy. *See* Stramilano.

mile distances. *See* distances, metric and English.

Miles, Johnny (b. October 30, 1905). The well-named Canadian won the 1926 and 1929 Boston Marathons. *See also* Boston Marathon.

Mills, Billy (b. June 30, 1938). For a time before the 1964 Olympics, Mills thought his prospects looked better in the marathon than in the 10,000 meters. We all now know better, as his victory in the 10,000 was one of the biggest upsets in Olympic history. He carried through with his marathon obligation, placing 14th in that anticlimactic race at Tokyo. A decent film, *Running Brave*, was made of his life story. *See also* Hall of Fame, National Distance Running;

Hall of Fame, RRCA; Hall of Fame, USATF; movies; Olympians, U.S.

Mimoun, Alain (January 1, 1921). Consistently a follower of his dear friend Emil Zatopek on the track, Mimoun finally won the Olympic Marathon in 1956 when defending champion Emil (who placed sixth) was coming off surgery; Alain waited at the finish line for Emil to finish. Alain had taken second to Emil in both the 5,000 and 10,000 in the 1952 Games and had placed second to Emil in the 10,000 at the 1948 Games. The African-born Frenchman previewed the coming age when runners from that continent would dominate distance racing. *See also* Olympic medalists; rankings, *Track & Field News*.

minimarathon. This inexact term can describe any distance from a 5K upward.

Mini Marathon, New York City (www.nyrrc.org). *Mini,* in this case, means a 10K women's race, long held in Central Park with a variety of sponsors.

Mintz, Ida (b. October 15, 1905). The American holds the world women's marathon record of 5:10:04 in the lightly populated over-80 age group. *See also* records, American age-group; records, world age-group.

© Mark Shearman. Athletics–Images.

Billy Mills (#722) was entered in both the marathon and the 10,000 meters in the 1964 Olympics; he forged a dramatic victory in the 10,000, which later served as the anchor for the film *Running Brave*.

Miranda, Oscar (birthdate unavailable). The Cuban-American was caught cheating at Boston after claiming to win a masters title. His attempted scam preceded that of fellow Cuban-American Rosie Ruiz. *See also* cheaters.

Mirkin, Dr. Gabe (birthdate unavailable). He reached the RRCA Hall of Fame both for his writing efforts in recent years including *The Sports Medicine Book* (Little, Brown; 1978) and for his promotional work in the sport as far back as the 1960s, when Dr. Mirkin was an avid racer himself. *See also* Hall of Fame, RRCA.

Mizuno (www.mizunousa.com). The Japanese company has made running shoes for almost a century but hasn't rivaled Asics for sales in the U.S. market.

Moiseyev, Leonid (b. October 21, 1952). The Soviet marathoner won the European title (in 2:11:58) and led the world rankings in 1978. *See* European Championships; rankings, *Track & Field News.*

Moller, Lorraine (b. June 1, 1955). Lorraine is one of the longest-running, best-performing female marathoners in the world. She has the distinction of being the only woman to have run in and finished the first four women's Olympic Marathons: 1984 (5th in 2:28:31), 1988 (34th in 2:37:52), 1992 (3rd in 2:33:59), and 1996 (46th in 2:42:21). Born in Butaruru, New Zealand, Lorraine is one of the pillars of the women's running movement who helped make the women's Olympic Marathon a reality. Much of her marathoning career both paralleled and supported Kathrine Switzer's leadership at Avon Products to establish and grow an international marathon series for women that would serve as living, breathing, panting proof that sufficient interest existed in several dozen countries to justify the women's marathon in the Olympic Games. She won three of the annual Avon Marathon championships.

Although Lorraine began as a track runner, like many of the female road-racing pioneers, and was quite successful at it (she took the bronze in the 1,500 meters at the 1983 Commonwealth Games, for instance), she gravitated to longer distances as the road races escalated and it

New Zealand's Lorraine Moller competed in the first four women's Olympic Marathons, taking a bronze in Barcelona in 1992. Here she wins the 1984 Boston Marathon.

© Jeff Johnson

became obvious that her talent lay in distances not run on tracks. She won her very first marathon (Grandma's, June 23, 1979). Less than two months later she won the Avon International Women's Marathon in London (2:35:11). She was both impressive and consistent, winning the first eight marathons she entered. She won the Avon International Women's Marathon (San Francisco) again in 1982 and in 1984 (Paris). Earlier that year she had also won Boston (2:29:28). She won the Osaka Ladies' Marathon three times (1986, 1987, and 1989).

As she was in the ascension in her marathon career, she met 1968 U.S. Olympic marathoner Ron Daws in Minnesota and married him in 1981. For a time he served as her coach, but the relationship was tempestuous. By sad coincidence, she received news of Daws's death while she was in Barcelona two days before she was to compete in the 1992 Olympic Marathon, where she would win the bronze. The two had become estranged several years before.

In her career, Lorraine won 15 of 28 marathons. She was also instrumental in forcing the issue of above-the-table payment of prize money to road racers when, in 1981 at the Cascade Run Off 15K in Portland, Oregon, she joined fellow New Zealanders Allison Roe and Anne Audain, Domingo Tibaduiza of Colombia, and a group of U.S. runners in accepting cash. The New Zealand federation banned Lorraine and Anne from international competition; Allison Roe returned to New Zealand and was eventually reinstated. Six weeks after the incident, the matter came to a head at the Crim 10-Miler in Flint, Michigan; other runners refused to run in the race if Lorraine was allowed to compete for fear of being "contaminated." The race's biggest draw, Bill Rodgers, walked to the starting line and effectively defused the situation. Boulder, Colorado, journalist and running author Michael Sandrock put it this way in his book *Running With the Legends*: "Moller and Audain were responsible in large part for altering the framework of women's running, not just in New Zealand, but around the world as two of the first women to make their living from running road races."

Lorraine set the masters world on fire immediately upon turning 40. She holds world age-group records at 5K (16:03) and four miles (21:05). Hers has easily been one of the longest-running careers in women's running history—some 23 years as a world-class athlete. In 2000 she became a mother for the first time at age 45. *See also* Avon Racing Circuits; Boston Marathon; Daws, Ron; Olympic medalists; Osaka Ladies' Marathon; rankings, *Runner's World*.

Moneghetti, Steve (b. September 26, 1962). He had a career somewhat like fellow Australian Ron Clarke a generation earlier—with fast times and high finishes but none of the Olympic medals that he wanted so dearly. The closest Moneghetti came was fifth at Seoul. However, he won the 1994 Commonwealth title and was the bronze medalist at the 1997 Worlds. *See also* Berlin Marathon; Bloomsday 12K; Commonwealth Games; rankings, *Track & Field News*; Tokyo Marathons; World Championships medalists.

monitor, heart-rate. *See* heart-rate monitor; Polar.

Monti, David (b. January 25, 1960). Running publishing moved into a new era when the New Yorker began issuing *Race Results Weekly* by e-mail in the mid-1990s. *See* publications.

Moore, Kenny (b. December 1, 1943). Eclipsed by his excellent contract writing for *Sports Illustrated* on the subject of running, the appearance of his bare butt in the film *Personal Best,* and his stints (with Robert Towne) in writing film scripts (including *Without Limits*) is the fact that Kenny Moore was one of the most dominant American road racers of the late 1960s and early 1970s. Kenny was a graduate student in fine arts at the University of Oregon at Eugene, America's running mecca. In 1968 he ran literally anywhere they'd draw a starting line. During that period he came to own the historic San Francisco Bay to Breakers road race.

On May 5, 1968, he traveled to Modesto, California, to run against Australia's Ron Clarke and America's Gerry Lindgren in the 5,000 meters, then to San Francisco for the 10 A.M. start the next day at the Bay to Breakers race. Even though he took several wrong turns in the Golden Gate Park portion of the course, he won by 46 seconds. He made the trek to Bay to Breakers an annual ritual as he won every race from 1968 to 1973, frequently breaking the course record in the process. He so dominated the race during that period that author Len Wallach in his history of the race titled *The Human Race* (The Hearst Corporation, 1978) devoted two entire chapters to Kenny: "1968 and 1969: Ken Moore's First Two Victories," and "1970, 1971, 1972 and 1973: The Moore Years Continue." The movie-star handsome Moore even managed to get time off from service in the U.S. military in the early 1970s to keep his streak going.

At the Mexico City Olympics in 1968, where Mamo Wolde made it three in a row for Ethiopia, Kenny placed 14th (top American) in 2:29:50 after leading in the early going. Had there been a team title, Moore's effort along with that of George Young (16th) and Ron Daws (22nd) would have clinched it for the United States. In the 1972 Games, Moore narrowly missed a medal as the United States had its greatest modern team finish ever: Frank Shorter first, Kenny Moore fourth (2:15:40), and Jack Bacheler ninth.

Kenny Moore's influence on running continued during the 1970s and 1980s in his regular writing on the subject for *Sports Illustrated,* where he kept running in front of the sports-following public with his well-crafted, insightful features. Some of his best writing was eventually collected between hard covers in *Best Efforts* (Doubleday, 1982). He currently lives in Hawaii. *See also* Bay to Breakers 12K; Hall of Fame, RRCA; movies; national marathon champions, U.S.; Olympians, U.S.; Olympic Trials Marathon, U.S.; record progressions, American.

Morishita, Koichi (b. September 5, 1967). The Japanese runner's victory in the 1992 Tokyo Marathon previewed his silver-medal performance at the Olympics that year. *See also* Olympic medalists; Tokyo Marathons.

Moroccan runners. One of the few countries to challenge Kenya's dominance on the roads, Morocco fielded the only team ever to beat the Kenyan men at the World Marathon Relay (in 1994). Morocco is also the birthplace of the current marathon world record-holder, Khalid Khannouchi, and homeland of

London and New York City Marathon winner Abdelkader El Mouaziz. *See also* El Mouaziz, Abdelkader; Khannouchi, Khalid; World Marathon Relay.

Morris, David (b. May 17, 1970). Sub-2:10 marathons are few and far between for Americans, and even fewer are run on unaided courses. Fastest on a course with no possibility of help from terrain or wind was Morris, who ran a surprising 2:09:32 at Chicago in 1999 after training in Japan; it was a PR by five minutes. In 2000, Khalid Khannouchi, who had become an American citizen between the 1999 and 2000 Chicago Marathons, usurped Morris as American record-holder with a 2:07:01, while Dave ran 2:12:00 in the same race. *See also* "David Who" on next page; national half-marathon championions, U.S.; record progressions, American; records, American; World Championships, U.S.

Morrisey, Thomas (b. September 2, 1888; d. October 1, 1968). Olympic success has never guaranteed success at Boston, and vice versa. Morrisey won Boston in 1908, then DNFed at the London Games. *See also* Boston Marathon; Olympians, U.S.

Morse, Guy (b. June 1, 1951). In July 2000 Guy was promoted to executive director of the Boston Athletic Association and is now responsible for the direction of the organization, including the Boston Marathon and year-round BAA events. The year 2000 was Guy's 16th year with the BAA. He was originally

Photo courtesy BAA

For years Guy Morse (left) has been the guiding light behind the Boston Athletic Association and the famed Boston Marathon.

David Who?

From Joe Henderson's *Running Commentary,* December 1999.

I've pretty much sat out the what's-wrong-with-America's-marathoners debate. Plenty of voices already shout theories and accusations without me adding mine. But mainly I don't want to dwell on negatives or appear to criticize individual Americans who are running as well as they can.

Still, there's no denying that U.S. marathon performances have slipped badly—not only versus the rest of the world but against the country's own past standards. This isn't opinion. It's statistical fact.

The fastest men's time was run in 1981, and the women's record has stood since 1985. Through late October, America's top man ranked 197th in the world for the year and the best woman, 177th—both the lowest ever. No American man or woman had yet met the Olympic qualifying standards of 2:14 and 2:33.

One race changed all of that. Within $2^1/_2$ hours at Chicago, two runners reversed an almost unbroken decade of decline in U.S. marathoning.

One we knew well. Libbie Hickman lopped nearly five minutes from her PR with 2:28:34. (Kristy Johnston also went under the Olympic entry time.) This was a time waiting to happen. Hickman's world-class track marks signal that she'll go much faster.

The surprise of Chicago, the reason American road runners can take heart, was David Morris. You're excused here if you would have asked before October 24, "David who?" He brought a best time of 2:15:25 into this race. He'd run that last year and had seldom been seen on this country's roads since then.

That's because the Alaska-born, Montana-educated Morris took a job with Honda in Japan and ran for its corporate team. The nice twist here is that Moroccan Khalid Khannouchi had to come to this country to find himself as a runner. Morris had to leave the United States and the air of negativity about what marathoners here can't do anymore.

A 1:02:00 half-marathon hinted at what Morris might do in a marathon. Yet halves aren't good predictors of longer-range success. (Note that Todd Williams once ran just over an hour but hasn't yet broken 2:11 in the marathon.)

Morris's Japanese coach told him he was ready for 2:08. David chose a more conservative sub-2:10 goal. Significantly, though, he also chose not to settle into the sub-2:14 pace group arranged for would-be American Olympic qualifiers. (None of them made it.) Instead he would run with the big guys—staying with them well enough to place fourth in 2:09:32.

That's an American record for a loop course, the fastest run on any type of course in five years. But before getting too excited about this time, realize that one man can't turn around American marathoning all by himself. Many others tried and failed to meet the Olympic standard at Chicago.

Morris's own time still falls short of what Bill Rodgers ran 20 years ago. Four other Americans also have gone faster. We do David Morris no favors by calling him the savior of U.S. men's marathoning. But we can cheer his progress, wish him more of it, and hope that he encourages others to shed the national inferiority complex. Morris, 29, surely will lead other Americans to think, "If he can improve that much, why can't I?"

[His record fell to Khalid Khannouchi in 2000, but Morris remains the fastest U.S.-born runner on a record-quality course.]

brought on to stabilize the Boston Marathon and to bring it into the modern world of professionally run marathons after the race floundered throughout the early 1980s. In 1985 Guy worked with the BAA Board of Governors to put together a long-term, major commitment from John Hancock Financial Services, which was then unprecedented in the world of sponsorship.

Beginning with the 1986 race, the Boston Marathon once again attracted the top runners in the sport by annually awarding the world's largest prize purse. At the same time, the local communities have been generously reimbursed for their support and cooperation. Guy also spearheaded the formation of the Boston Marathon Organizing Committee, which brought together some 60 staff members, consultants, and volunteers to handle medical, transportation, water distribution, security, scoring and timing, communications, and all other vital services. The "100th" (actually 99th, as no race was run in 1918) running of the marathon in 1996 brought an estimated $140 million to the greater Boston area.

Not satisfied, Guy built a community outreach program that has allowed the BAA to offer services to a variety of local audiences, including the annual Boston Marathon Jimmy Fund Walk (established in 1989) and a youth running program that was unveiled in 1997. A native of Marlboro, Massachusetts, Guy is a graduate of Northeastern University. He resides, with his wife and four children, in the Cape Cod community of Centerville. *See also* Boston Marathon; McGillivray, Dave.

Mota, Rosa (b. June 29, 1958). Portugal, where Rosa Mota was born, was not culturally supportive of the concept of women being independent and pursuing careers in sports. Rosa, though, was encouraged by her family, especially her father. Raised in Porto, a coastal town famed for aged port, she was an active child whose lifestyle lent itself to her doing well in running. She excelled early in local competitions, as did her sister Paula. Remembering the environment in which they ran, Paula told writer Mike Sandrock, "Women at that time were not going out. They stayed at home. When we ran through the streets, they would say, 'Go home! Go home and help your mother wash the dishes.' Things like that."

High schools did not have sports programs, so Rosa joined a series of sports clubs, ultimately landing with a small, local club. She ran well from 1975 through 1980, mostly at shorter distances, because at that time those distances were the only ones available for women. But in 1980 she met Dr. Jose Pedrosa, who would become her coach and would mold her into one of the most consistently well-trained and least overtrained female distance runners in the world. That preparation accounts in large part for a world-class career studded with key victories at tough international events over a decade. Although she was eclipsed in most minds by Grete Waitz, Joan Benoit, and Ingrid Kristiansen for most of her career, Rosa's accomplishments equaled and in some respects surpassed those of her peers.

When Dr. Pedrosa and Rosa met, she was at a low ebb in her running, becoming increasingly tired in the legs. Her inclination at that time was to quit the sport

© Mark Shearman. Athletics-Images.

Rosa Mota (here working out in Lisbon in 1986) was long overshadowed by Waitz, Benoit, and Kristiansen, yet some of her accomplishments equal or surpass theirs. Working against a Portuguese society that saw women in more traditional roles, she trained eagerly and it paid off. She capped her career with gold at Seoul.

entirely, but Jose Pedrosa (nicknamed "Ze") diagnosed her problem as being not in her legs but in her lungs. Although the condition was not well understood at the time, Ze found that she suffered from exercise-induced asthma. Once convinced her problem was medical and not mental, Rosa came back quickly. On the last day of 1981, she raced at the famed São Silvestre New Year's Eve Race in São Paulo, Brazil, and handily won; she would win it a total of six times.

In the spring of the following year, the Portuguese federation picked her to be on their team going to the European Championships in Athens. She wanted to try the marathon (it would be her first), but the federation wanted her in the 3,000 meters. They compromised; if she ran the 3,000, they would also allow her to try the marathon. The race organizers had decided to use the original Marathon course (of 490 B.C.) from the Plain of Marathon to Athens, the same course that had been used in the first Olympic marathon in 1896. The course is hilly and usually hot, calling for strategic running rather than all-out racing. Ze advised Rosa to begin conservatively and let the other women burn themselves out. She began at the back of the pack and gradually moved up, winning the race easily.

It was an enormous boost for her native Portugal. Suddenly those who had criticized her for running instead of washing dishes were her strongest supporters. Encouraged by her victory, she increased her mileage and decided to see what kind of a marathoner she could be if she concentrated on it. She quickly reeled off a string of marathons, becoming faster in each one. In April 1983 she ran Rotterdam in 2:32:27; she took fourth in the first-ever World Championships with a 2:31:50; then she traveled to the United States to compete in shorter road races, where she did very well. She was taken aback when she was given money for her performances. That fall she ran in, and won, the Chicago Marathon in 2:31:12, setting a course record.

At the first women's Olympic Marathon, Los Angeles in 1984, Rosa was considered to be racing out of her class and not a factor. She surprised everyone, including herself, by taking third behind Joan Benoit and Grete Waitz with a time of 2:26:57, knocking more than four minutes off her PR. That fall she returned to Chicago and broke her own course record by five minutes with 2:26:01.

In 1985 the Chicago race was set as a barnburner with new world record-holder Ingrid Kristiansen going up against Joan Benoit, from whom she'd taken the record, and Rosa thrown in for spice. The three of them ran hard; Joan won, Ingrid took second, and Rosa placed third with 2:23:29, making this the seventh marathon in a row in which she had improved her previous time. In 1986 she managed to defend her European Championships gold at Stuttgart.

Then in April 1987 she went to Boston and won in 2:25:21. That summer she won the World Championships in Rome by an astonishing seven minutes with a 2:25:17.

Her gold medal at the Seoul Olympics was almost preordained. With four kilometers to go, she passed Jose Pedrosa as he stood on the sidelines and told her to "Go!" She went—and won in 2:25:40; it was the first time a Portuguese woman had ever won a track and field medal in the Olympics. She suffered sciatic pain early in 1989 but still managed to take second at the Los Angeles Marathon. In 1990 she seemed to be back in good health. She won the Osaka Ladies' Marathon and that summer won the gold at the European Championships for the third straight time.

Then Rosa began to experience medical and injury problems. She had an ovarian cyst removed in May 1991. She suffered from stomach problems that caused her to drop out of the World Cup Marathon in London. Then she dropped out of the World Championships Marathon in Tokyo. She began to aim for the 1992 Olympic Marathon in Barcelona, but less than two weeks before the race she suffered hip problems and did not race.

Rosa continued to live in her native Porto and in 1995 was elected to the Portuguese Parliament. By any standards, her career was stellar. She ran competitively for nearly two decades, during which she won gold at the European, World, and Olympic Marathons, a feat no other woman has matched. *See also* Bay to Breakers 12K; Bolder Boulder 10K; Boston Marathon; Chicago Marathon; European Championships; London Marathon; Olympic medalists; Osaka Ladies' Marathon; rankings, *Track & Field News;* Rotterdam Marathon; Tokyo Marathons; World Championships medalists; World Cup Marathon.

Moving Pictures

From Joe Henderson's *Running Commentary,* May 2000.

I blame the oversight on being a word guy. I've never had anything to do with the illustrations and layout of my work, only with the words, so my thoughts on the visual are few.

Rich Benyo is more versatile. My partner on the encyclopedia project noticed that the preliminary entry list I'd compiled, reaching thousands of entries, never once mentioned running movies.

The list of those that fit within our limits—including racing scenes from road events, 5K to marathon—is short. Outside these boundaries lie those with running titles (*The Running Man,* an Arnold Schwarzenegger thriller, and *Marathon Man,* a look at sadistic dentistry) that are about this sport in name only. Out too are the recent *Without Limits* and *Prefontaine,* because Pre was never a road racer. *Personal Best* is a track film with marathoner Kenny Moore playing another brand of athlete. The 1960s classic *Loneliness of the Long Distance Runner* is only marginally about running, and not long distance running at that.

In the maybe category falls *On the Edge,* whose Dipsea-like race runs partly on the roads and whose cast includes serious runner-actor Bruce Dern and several actual road racers. *Running Brave* has no footage of Billy Mills's anticlimactic Olympic Marathon, which he ran after winning the 10,000.

The fictional movies with road racing at their heart are mostly forgettable. Joanne Woodward in *See How She Runs,* Michael Douglas in *Running,* and Ryan O'Neal in *The Games* come across as actors trying and failing to look like runners. They lack The Look.

The videos I like best are the real ones. I much prefer the Steve Prefontaine documentary, *Fire on the Track,* to either of the dramatic productions. *Endurance* is a true story, with Haile Gebrselassie playing himself. In an unintentionally comical scene he pretends to be a novice marathoner and almost trips over his feet at six-minute-mile pace.

Best of the lot are the various Olympic films, because real runners run real races. Setting a high early standard was director Leni Reifenstahl with her *Olympia,* an almost-four-hour look at the 1936 Games. Bud Greenspan directed the 1984 Olympic summary, *Sixteen Days of Glory.* The Munich Games report, *Visions of Eight* (the combined effort of eight directors), carries memorable footage of Frank Shorter's marathon victory.

Nothing I've ever watched on screen is as memorable as the marathon in *Tokyo Olympiad* by Kon Ichikawa. The late-race, slow-motion close-ups of an apparently tireless Abebe Bikila give a look into the face of the future in this sport.

Mount Evans Race. This 14-mile event in Colorado traveled the highest paved highway in the United States, starting at about 10,000 feet and topping out above 14,000. The race enjoyed popularity in the 1970s but was discontinued in the early 1980s when its sponsor dropped out.

Mount Washington Race. One of the steepest road races, this event ascends the highest mountain in the northeastern United States, climbing more than

4,000 feet in less than seven miles.

movies. The sport has been the subject of many movies—some fictional and some factual, some memorable and some forgettable. The "Moving Pictures" sidebar above introduces many of them.

Moving Comfort (www.movingcomfort.com). This was the first company (founded by Ellen Wessel and Elizabeth Goeke in 1977) to make clothing designed specifically for women.

Winners of the 2000 Honolulu marathon, Jimmy Muindi (Kenya) and Lyubov Morgunova celebrate on Waikiki Beach.

© Mark Shearman. Athletics—Images.

Muhrcke, Gary (b. August 10, 1940). The firefighter won the first New York City Marathon in 1970. Years later he raised eyebrows in the city by winning the Empire State Building Run-Up while on disability leave from the fire department. *See also* New York City Marathon.

Muindi, Jimmy (b. August 14, 1973). The Kenyan won two Honolulu Marathons, 1999 in 2:16:45 and 2000 in 2:15:16. *See also* Honolulu Marathon.

Murphy, Frank (b. December 25, 1952). The Kansas City attorney wrote two excellent books about runners. His first was the biography of Buddy Edelen, *A Cold Clear Day* (Wind Sprint Press, 1992). Later, Murphy penned *The Silence of Great Distance* (Wind Sprint Press, 2000), tracing the history of women's running. *See also* books; Edelen, Leonard "Buddy."

Murphy, John and **Murphy, Suzanne** (birthdates unavailable). Cheaters in road races usually act alone. At the 1997 Boston this husband-wife team, having given their ages as 64 for him and 59 for her, tried and failed to get away with turning in times they couldn't have legitimately run. *See also* cheaters.

Musyoki, Michael (b. May 28, 1956). He graduated from the University of Texas at El Paso and went on to become one of the first great Kenyans on the U.S. roads. He set the world half-marathon record twice (1:01:36 in 1982 and 1:00:43 in 1986) and was the top-ranked road racer of 1982. *See also* Peachtree 10K; rankings, *Runner's World*; record progressions, world.

N

NAIA. *See* National Association of Intercollegiate Athletics.

Nakayama, Takeyuki (b. December 20, 1959). Twice he finished in the next place out of the medals in Olympic Marathons—at Seoul and Barcelona. But the Japanese runner hardly ended his career empty-handed. His winnings included the 1986 Asian Games (2:08:21), Fukuoka in 1984 (2:10:00) and 1987 (2:08:18), and Tokyo in 1990 (2:10:57). *See also* Asian Games; Fukuoka Marathon; rankings, *Track & Field News;* Tokyo Marathons.

Napa Valley Marathon (www.napa-marathon.com). First run in 1979 from Calistoga, California, in the northern end of the famed wine-growing valley to Napa in the south, the course holds the distinction of never having been altered a foot over its two-plus-decade existence. Site of the RRCA National Marathon Championships since 1998, the March race is considered one of the most beautiful marathons in the United States. *See also* scenic races.

nasal strips. *See* Breathe Right.

Nason, Jerry (b. April 14, 1909; d. June 19, 1986). His long-term reporting on the Boston Marathon from the 1930s through the 1980s for the *Boston Globe* earned him a spot in the RRCA Hall of Fame. *See also* Hall of Fame, RRCA.

National Association of Intercollegiate Athletics (NAIA). The better-known National Collegiate Athletic Association (NCAA) hasn't yet caught up with the NAIA. The confederation of smaller colleges has conducted a marathon for decades along with its track and field championships. Occasionally the junior colleges have conducted marathons at their national meet.

National Distance Running Hall of Fame. *See* Hall of Fame, National Distance Running.

national 5K champions, U.S. The men have run this championship distance sporadically since 1979. The women started later but have selected a winner more years, including Lynn Jennings six times. The national 5K site is generally selected through a bidding process, but some races, such as Freihofer's Run for Women, hold onto a championship event because of superior sponsorship and organization. *See also* Freihofer's Run for Women.

U.S. National 5K Winners

This championship race is run regularly for women but only sporadically for men. Note Lynn Jennings's six victories. * = event record. + = short course short.

WOMEN

Year	Athlete	Time
1986	Marty Cooksey	15:54
1987-1988	(not run)	
1989	Judi St. Hilaire	15:27
1990	Lynn Jennings	15:31
1991	Janis Klecker	16:22
1992	Shelly Steely	15:30
1993	Lynn Jennings	15:35
1994	Lynn Jennings	15:37
1995	Lynn Jennings	15:25*
1996	Lynn Jennings	15:21+
1997	Elva Dryer	15:29
1998	Lynn Jennings	15:46
1999	Cheri Kenah	15:31
2000	Libbie Hickman	15:35
2001	Collette Liss	15:47

MEN

Year	Athlete	Time
1979	Odis Sanders	14:44
1980	Odis Sanders	15:04
1981	Odis Sanders	14:37
1982-1989	(not run)	
1990	Terry Brahm	13:56
1991-1993	(not run)	
1994	Matt Giusto	13:53
1995	Tim Hacker	13:55
1996	Mark Coogan	13:57
1997	Marc Davis	13:43*
1998	Dan Browne	13:05+
1999-2001	(not run)	

national half-marathon champions, U.S. Parkersburg, West Virginia, is the semipermanent home of this championship event. It serves as one of the qualifiers for the World Half-Marathon Championships. *See also* World Half-Marathon Championships.

national marathon champions, U.S. The oldest of the road championships has been run for men since the 1920s and for women since they gained full

U.S. National Half-Marathon Winners

Men have contested this distance for national titles most years since the late 1980s, but the women have run it only occasionally. Note that Olympic marathoners Anne Marie Lauck, Ed Eyestone, Rod DeHaven, and Steve Spence all are half-marathon winners. * = event record.

WOMEN

Year	Athlete	Time
1989	Diane Brewer	1:13:00
1990-1992	(not run)	
1993	Elaine Van Blunk	1:12:06
1994	(not run)	
1995	(not run)	
1996	Anne Marie Lauck	1:12:10
1997	(not run)	
1998	Libbie Hickman	1:13:29
1999	Gwyn Coogan	1:12:36
2000	Libbie Hickman	1:11:01*
2001	Milena Glusac	1:12:13

MEN

Year	Athlete	Time
1987	Paul Cummings	1:02:32*
1988	Mark Stickley	1:02:42
1989	(not run)	
1990	Mark Curp	1:03:37
1991	Jon Sinclair	1:03:44
1992	Don Janicki	1:03:44
1993	Ed Eyestone	1:03:19
1994	Rod DeHaven	1:03:38
1995	Steve Spence	1:04:42
1996	Alfredo Vigueras	1:04:42
1997	David Morris	1:05:53
1998	Rod DeHaven	1:03:42
1999	Todd Williams	1:04:24
2000	Rod DeHaven	1:03:06
2001	Dan Browne	1:03:55

recognition in the 1970s. In Olympic years the Trials winner also becomes national champion.

National Masters News (www.nationalmastersnews.com). You don't need to be over 40 to read this fine monthly magazine, founded by Al Sheahen in 1980. Its coverage of the sport is geared toward runners age 30 and above. *See also* masters racing; publications.

U.S. National Marathon Winners

The national marathon is the longest-running U.S. road championships. Note that Joan Samuelson, Bill Rodgers, and Frank Shorter never won a title. * = race record.

WOMEN

Year	Athlete	Time
1974	Judy Ikenberry	2:55:18
1975	Kim Merritt	2:46:15
1976	Julie Brown	2:45:33
1977	Leal Reinhart	2:46:34
1978	Marty Cooksey	2:41:49
1979	Susan Petersen	2:46:17
1980	Susan Munday	2:43:17
1981	Nancy Conz	2:36:46
1982	Laurie Binder	2:39:46
1983	Julie Brown	2:26:26*
1984	Katy Schilly	2:32:40
1985	Nancy Ditz	2:31:36
1986	Kim Rosenquist	2:32:31
1987	Janis Klecker	2:36:12
1988	Margaret Groos	2:29:50
1989	Nan Doak-Davis	2:33:11
1990	Jane Welzel	2:33:25
1991	Maria Trujillo	2:35:39
1992	Janis Klecker	2:30:12
1993	Linda Somers	2:34:11
1994	Linda Somers	2:33:42
1995	Debbie K. Morris	2:34:42
1996	Jenny Spangler	2:29:54
1997	Julia Kirtland	2:37:46
1998	Gwyn Coogan	2:33:37
1999	Kim Pawelek	2:37:56
2000	Christine Clark	2:33:31

MEN

Year	Athlete	Time
1925	Charles Mellor	2:33:01
1926	Clarence DeMar	2:45:06
1927	Clarence DeMar	2:40:23
1928	Clarence DeMar	2:37:08
1929	Clarence DeMar	2:43:47
1930	Karl Koski	2:25:22
1931	William Agee	2:32:38
1932	Clyde Martak	2:58:18
1933	Melvin Porter	2:53:46
1934	Melvin Porter	2:48:04
1935	Patrick Dengis	2:53:53
1936	William McMahon	2:38:15
1937	Melvin Porter	2:44:22

Year	Athlete	Time	
1938	Patrick Dengis	2:39:39	
1939	Patrick Dengis	2:33:46	
1940	Lou Gregory	2:35:10	
1941	Bernard Smith	2:36:07	
1942	Frederick McGlone	2:37:54	
1943	Frederick McGlone	2:39:09	
1944	Charles Robbins	2:40:49	
1945	Charles Robbins	2:37:14	
1946	John A. Kelley	2:50:29	
1947	Ted Vogel	2:40:11	
1948	John A. Kelley	2:48:33	
1949	Victor Dyrgall	2:38:50	
1950	John A. Kelly	2:45:56	
1951	Jesse Van Zant	2:37:12	
1952	Victor Dyrgall	2:38:39	
1953	John Lafferty	2:50:31	
1954	Ted Corbitt	2:46:14	
1955	Nick Costes	2:31:13	
1956	John J. Kelley	2:24:53	
1957	John J. Kelley	2:24:56	
1958	John J. Kelley	2:21:01	
1959	John J. Kelley	2:21:55	
1960	John J. Kelley	2:20:14	
1961	John J. Kelley	2:26:54	
1962	John J. Kelley	2:27:40	
1963	John J. Kelley	2:25:18	
1964	Buddy Edelen	2:24:26	
1965	Gar Williams	2:33:51	
1966	Norm Higgins	2:22:51	
1967	Ron Daws	2:40:07	
1968	George Young	2:30:48	
1969	Tom Heinonen	2:24:43	
1970	Robert Fitts	2:24:11	
1971	Kenny Moore	2:16:49	
1972	Edmund Norris	2:24:43	
1973	Doug Schmenk	2:15:48	
1974	Ronald Wayne	2:18:53	
1975	Gary Tuttle	2:17:27	
1976	Gary Tuttle	2:15:15	
1977	Ed Schelegle	2:18:11	
1978	Carl Hatfield	2:17:21	
1979	Tom Antczak	2:15:28	
1980	Frank Richardson	2:13:54	
1981	Robert Johnson	2:29:14	
1982	Joel Menges	2:32:29	
1983	Pete Pfitzinger	2:14:45	
1984	Ken Martin	2:11:24	
1985	Ken Martin	2:12:57	
1986	Bill Donakowski	2:10:41*	
1987	Ric Sayre	2:13:54	
1988	Mark Conover	2:12:26	
1989	Bill Reifsnyder	2:12:09	
1990	Steve Spence	2:12:17	*(continued)*

U.S. National Marathon Winners, *continued*

Year	Athlete	Time
1991	Bill Reifsnyder	2:12:39
1992	Steve Spence	2:12:43
1993	Ed Eyestone	2:14:34
1994	Paul Pilkington	2:12:13
1995	Keith Brantly	2:14:27
1996	Bob Kempainen	2:12:45
1997	Dave Scudamore	2:13:48
1998	Keith Brantly	2:12:31
1999	Alfredo Vigueras	2:14:20
2000	Rod DeHaven	2:15:30

national records. *See* record progressions, American; records, American; records, American age-group.

National Running Center. *See* mail-order companies.

national 10K champions, U.S. The first titles at this distance went to two of the biggest names in American running history, Mary Decker and Bill Rodgers.

U.S. National 10K Winners

Two legends, Mary Decker Slaney and Bill Rodgers, won the first road titles at this distance. Note that Keith Brantly's three titles spanned 10 years. * = event record.

WOMEN

Year	Athlete	Time
1978	Mary Decker	34:39
1979	Karin Von Berg	34:26
1980	Dana Slater	33:26
1981	Laura Craven	35:43
1982	Kathy Boyle	36:36
1983	Judi St. Hilaire	33:43
1984	Betty Springs	32:51
1985	Francie Larrieu Smith and Betty Springs	32:14
1986	Betty Springs	32:13
1987	Lynn Jennings	32:19
1988	Lynn Jennings	32:39
1989	Margaret Groos	33:11
1990	Lynn DeNinno	34:37
1991	Lynn DeNinno	35:11

Year	Athlete	Time
1992	Lynn Jennings	32:42
1993	Jody Hawkins	33:22
1994	Lynn Jennings	31:48*
1995	Colette Murphy	32:30
1996	Anne Marie Lauck	33:16
1997	Kim Jones	32:49
1998	Libbie Hickman	31:57
1999	Libbie Hickman	32:49
2000	Libbie Hickman	32:47

MEN

Year	Athlete	Time
1978	Bill Rodgers	28:37
1979	Herb Lindsay	28:35
1980-1981	(not run)	
1982	Bob Hodge	29:30
1983	Steve McCormack	29:58
1984	Mark Finucane	29:55
1985	Keith Brantly	28:39
1986	Dirk Lakeman	27:49*
1987	Keith Brantly	28:47
1988	Ed Eyestone	30:01
1989	Keith Brantly	28:55
1990	Harry Green	28:56
1991	Gordon Sanders	30:02
1992	John Trautmann	28:46
1993	Ed Eyestone	28:39
1994	Arturo Barrios	28:43
1995	Keith Brantly	29:12
1996	Matt Giusto	27:59
1997	Todd Williams	28:50
1998	Dan Browne	29:08
1999	Phillimon Hanneck	28:51
2000	Scott Strand	29:01

Ndereba, Catherine (b. July 21, 1972). Boston 2000 press info tells her story this way: "World leader on the roads, Ndereba remains untouchable from the 5K to 10 miles. Named Road Racer of the Year by *Running Times* in 1999, 1998, and 1996, and ranked number one by *Runner's World* for the same three years as well as for 2000, 'Catherine the Great' has slowed her pace only once—to give birth to daughter Jane in 1997. In 1999, she ran away with the world's fastest times for 5K (Riverfest Run, 15:09), 12K (Bay to Breakers, 38:37), 15K (Utica Boilermaker, 48:52, course record), and 10 miles (Broad Street Run, 53:07, course record).

"Additional highlights include setting a course record of 32:05 at the Beach to Beacon 10K in Cape Elizabeth, Maine. The following weekend she ran to a third win at the Falmouth Road Race, where she owns the course record (35:37, 1996). Proving she's a contender at greater distances, Ndereba ran a personal best 69:23 for the individual bronze and team gold at the '99 Palermo IAAF World Half-Marathon Championships, and improved her time to 69:02 at this year's Half-Marathon of Two Lakes in Como, Italy. Debuting at the marathon distance at Boston last year ('99), Ndereba was the only woman to keep pace with winner Fatuma Roba up to the Newton Hills. Catherine returns to Boston (in 2000) to better her 2:28:27 sixth place, and to improve her personal best 2:27:34, which she recorded with a second-place finish at the 1999 New York City Marathon."

She went on to win the Boston Marathon in 2000 after a hard-fought duel with Fatuma Roba (2:26:11 versus Roba's 2:26:27 third place). Then in Chicago that fall Ndereba won in 2:21:32, the fourth-fastest time in the history of women's marathoning. She became the second woman (after Ingrid Kristiansen, who did it in 1986) to win Boston and Chicago in the same year. Ndereba extended her string of victories by repeating as Boston winner in 2001, with 2:23:53. She became the second woman ever to run under 2:20 when, at the 2001 Chicago Marathon, she set the new world record of 2:18:47, beating Naoko Takahashi's first sub-2:20 marathon time of 2:19:46 set just a week earlier at Berlin. *See also* Bay to Breakers 12K; Boston Marathon; Chicago Marathon; rankings, *Runner's World*; record progressions, world; records, world.

Ndeti, Cosmas. *See* page next page.

negative splits. The term, which refers to running the second half of a race or training run faster than the first half, is a misnomer; we never hear the term *positive splits* applied to running the second half slower. Negative splitting is one of racing's most positive experiences because it often results in PRs.

Negere, Tena (b. October 5, 1972). The Ethiopian man won the 1991 African Marathon (2:31:17) and 1992 Fukuoka (2:09:04). *See also* African Games; Fukuoka Marathon.

Nelson, Bert (b. November 17, 1921; d. 1994) and **Nelson, Cordner** (b. August 6, 1918). The brothers cofounded *Track & Field News* in 1948, and their company published books on distance running when no one else did. They were fans of the sport from their earliest years and track athletes in their youth. Both Nelsons were inducted into the USA Track & Field Hall of Fame. *See also* Hall of Fame, USATF; publications; *Track & Field News*.

Nenow, Mark (b. November 16, 1957). Only one American has run 10,000 meters faster—be it on the track (where his national record stood from 1986 to 2001 when it was broken by Meb Keflezighi) or the road (where he had a world aided best of 27:22 in 1984 that still stands as a U.S. record). He was the first American to break 28 minutes on the road, and his 27:48 (unaided course) remains a national mark. *See* also "Leaving a Mark" on page 236; Hall of Fame, USATF; record progressions, American; record progressions, world; records, American.

Ndeti, Cosmas (b. November 24, 1971). Ndeti won the Boston Marathon three years in a row—1993 (2:09:33), 1994 (2:07:15), and 1995 (2:09:22). But he may be more remembered for 1996 when, in interviews leading into the race, he predicted—nay, prophesied—that he would win his fourth straight Boston, that he had been assured by God that he would. He led a prayer meeting in Hopkinton before the race, but his fourth in a row was not to be.

The Kamba tribesman from Kenya made quite an impression on the Boston field in 1993 as, after running conservatively with his friend Benson Masya, he moved up through the stellar field like a firebrand. With Christian messages written on his running shoes, he felt confident he would make a good showing. But even he hadn't expected to do as well as he did that April afternoon. He was in his own groove, passing runners at will. In the final miles he was running a full 15 seconds per mile faster than anyone else. As his competition began to slow, he accelerated, turning in a 1:04:10 second half, which is impressive because the second half of the course is where they keep all the uphills. The top 10 for the day read like a United Nations—Kenya, Korea, Namibia, Japan, Kenya, United States, Kenya, Italy, United States, Venezuela—as Ndeti won in 2:09:33.

The following year, 1994, the press wrote off Cosmas, as much for his overconfidence as for his proselytizing. He carried his one-year-old son around with him. (Gideon Boston Ndeti had been born two days before his 1993 Boston win.) When Cosmas was interviewed, he invariably brought God into the discussion. Between the beaming about his son and his extreme confidence that God would find a way for him to repeat as number one, Cosmas was turning off the press in a big way. Besides, he wasn't coming into Boston with any good recent performances.

American Keith Brantly went out hard, but the pack played it cautiously. Cosmas, in spite of having been advised by Alberto Salazar not to use the 1993 tactic of laying back, stayed in the rear of the big lead pack just watching what developed. At 14 miles the pack caught Brantly, but Cosmas continued to hang back, watching and waiting. Once into the final 10K the race broke open. Although Mexico's Andres Epinosa still looked strong, Cosmas felt confident he could catch him, and he did, creating a four-second lead that he held to the end—in the process setting a course record of 2:07:15. His once-a-day training based on the way he felt had paid off; the three-sessions-a-day for the other Kenyans must have been too much for them.

Cosmas went back to Kenya a huge hero, and he reveled in it. He bragged that he would win again. In fact, he bragged that he could win many more times. And at the 1995 Boston start he once again stayed at the back of the lead pack, watching, waiting, looking for weaknesses in the other runners. Moses Tanui, who lived and trained in the same town as Cosmas, didn't particularly like Ndeti's braggadocio or his seemingly lackadaisical attitude toward practice races. Tanui challenged Ndeti until Cosmas dropped him at 23 miles. For the third year in a row, Cosmas won Boston, this time in 2:09:22.

In 1996 Cosmas Ndeti was confident he would win—perhaps overconfident. But Moses Tanui wanted it more. Along Beacon Street, Tanui pulled away and won with a 2:09:16 to Cosmas's third-place 2:09:51. *See also* Boston Marathon; Kenyan runners.

Leaving a Mark

From Joe Henderson's *Running Commentary,* February 1991.

Mark Nenow, fastest American since the mid-1980s in the track 10,000 and road 10K, is talking about retiring at age 33. Chronic hamstring problems lead him to doubt if he'll race seriously again. I'll be sorry to see him go. We all could use him as a model for simplifying our running.

I met Nenow at a running seminar in Houston shortly after he'd set his world road best. He spoke without notes and answered questions with lots of "I don't knows." But his nonanswers had much to say.

Nenow didn't know his weight and resting pulse. He didn't want his blood tested or his muscles biopsied. He didn't use a computer to determine his training schedule. He didn't remember his times from recent races. He didn't keep such records in a diary.

He said he entered competition with only the most general plan: "Stick my nose in it and run with the leaders as long as I can. That way, I either make a breakthrough or die like a dog."

Nenow was a refreshing throwback to a low-tech era. He certainly worked hard, running the high mileage at a fast pace needed to compete at his level. But the way Nenow approached that work separated him from his contemporaries. He concerned himself only with the generalities of training steadily and racing hard, and let the specifics take care of themselves.

Such looseness required great faith that the instincts guiding him were the proper ones. Nenow trusted himself to do the right things without help from a team of coaches and scientists, and without the backing of elaborate plans and logbooks.

His way didn't always work. He never peaked at the right time to make an Olympic team. Yet he recovered quickly from disappointment. Failures were less devastating when expectations weren't excessive, and successes were all the more satisfying when they weren't planned.

Nenow said that all of his big improvements came as surprises. Because he didn't set time goals, he set no artificial limits on himself. He once passed the midpoint of a 10,000-meter race faster than his 5,000 personal record. More number-conscious runners might have thought, "Uh-oh, I can't keep going at this pace. Better slow down." Nenow kept going, willing to risk "dying like a dog." He didn't die but improved his 10,000 time by nearly a minute.

In recent years Mark enlisted a coach and began training more traditionally. He listened to advisers who said that the marathon would be his best event, tried two, ran into injuries, and never quite reached his old standards again.

At his best, he may have been short on knowledge of running theory and statistics, but he was long on wisdom. Anyone with a little know-how can complicate something simple, but only the wise can simplify something complicated. Mark Nenow's lesson to us all was not to let the planning and analyzing get in the way of the doing and enjoying.

[Nenow's track 10,000 record lasted through mid-2001, and his national best for the road 10K still stood as the book went to press.]

Neppel Darrah, Peg (b. August 16, 1953, d. October 16, 1981). Her career—and life—were all too brief, but she ran brilliantly in the years before she died of cancer at age 28. Neppel set world and American 10K records and won the Peachtree 10K in 1977. *See also* Peachtree 10K; record progressions, American; record progressions, world.

New Balance (www.newbalance.com). The New England company made the first widely distributed shoes for road racers—a red-and-white leather model, circa 1960, with ripple soles. The company has long taken pride in offering width sizing in its shoes, a rarity in this industry. New Balance offered $1 million for the first person to break the U.S. national marathon best during two years of the late 1990s, but no one collected. *See also* shoe companies.

Newton, Arthur (b. January 31, 1883, d. July 19, 1950). A case can be made for Newton as the first great American marathoner. In the 1900 Paris Games he finished fifth at age 17 to runners who knew short-cuts through the city. He came back as the bronze medalist at the 1904 St. Louis Games. This Arthur Newton is not to be confused with a same-named South African ultrarunner a generation younger. *See also* Olympians, U.S.; Olympic medalists.

New York City Marathon (www.nycmarathon.org). Many people in the world find it difficult to swallow New Yorkers' apparent arrogance. They take their special place in the world as if it is understood that they deserve it—as though they were French or something. But it is that sense of entitlement that gives them the confidence to try the impossible—and often to pull it off. No better example is needed than the New York City Marathon. New Yorkers took a leadership role, announcing to the rest of the world that there are heights to which the marathon had not yet been taken but, "hey, stand back while we show you how."

When the NYC Marathon was brought out of Central Park and run through the city's five boroughs to help celebrate the country's bicentennial in 1976, many people were skeptical. Even some of the movers and shakers within the New York Road Runners Club were skeptical that it could be accomplished. But through a combination of audacity and caution (running the course where it would least affect Sunday traffic, which meant running it along the river and even going up some steps), George Spitz's crazy idea that it could be

Kim Merritt, winner of the 1975 New York City Marathon, is shown here closing in on the finish line of the extremely hot 1976 Boston Marathon, the race that became known as the Run for the Hoses.

pulled off, Manhattan Borough president Percy Sutton's willingness to support such an effort, and Fred Lebow's ramrodding it through his club, the event came together. Big-city marathoning would never be the same.

The template of megamarathons everywhere, the NYC Marathon continues to show the way. Inspired by the constantly expanding vision of Fred Lebow and wrenched to success by the organizational expertise of Allan Steinfeld, the race continues to thrive. *See also* biggest races; Lebow, Fred; New York Road Runners Club; Steinfeld, Allan.

New York City Marathon Winners

The race was first run entirely within Central Park, then graduated to the streets of the five boroughs in 1976. Note that no woman finished the first year, 1970. The 2001 New York City Marathon also serves as the U.S. Marathon National Championships. * = race record.

WOMEN

Year	Athlete	Time
1971	Beth Bonner (U.S.)	2:55:22
1972	Nina Kuscsik (U.S.)	3:08:41
1973	Nina Kuscsik (U.S.)	2:57:07
1974	Kathrine Switzer (U.S.)	3:07:29
1975	Kim Merritt (U.S.)	2:46:14
1976	Miki Gorman (U.S.)	2:39:11
1977	Miki Gorman (U.S.)	2:43:10
1978	Grete Waitz (Norway)	2:32:20
1979	Grete Waitz (Norway)	2:27:33
1980	Grete Waitz (Norway)	2:25:42
1981	Allison Roe (New Zealand)	2:25:29
1982	Grete Waitz (Norway)	2:27:14
1983	Grete Waitz (Norway)	2:27:00
1984	Grete Waitz (Norway)	2:29:30
1985	Grete Waitz (Norway)	2:28:34
1986	Grete Waitz (Norway)	2:28:06
1987	Priscilla Welch (Britain)	2:30:17
1988	Grete Waitz (Norway)	2:28:07
1989	Ingrid Kristiansen (Norway)	2:25:30
1990	Wanda Panfil (Poland)	2:30:45
1991	Liz McColgan (Britain)	2:27:32
1992	Lisa Ondieki (Australia)	2:24:40*
1993	Uta Pippig (Germany)	2:26:24
1994	Tegla Loroupe (Kenya)	2:27:37
1995	Tegla Loroupe (Kenya)	2:28:06
1996	Anuta Catuna (Romania)	2:28:18
1997	F. Rocha-Moser (Switzerland)	2:28:43
1998	Franca Fiacconi (Italy)	2:25:17
1999	Adriana Fernandez (Mexico)	2:25:06
2000	Lyudmila Petrova (Russia)	2:25:45

MEN

Year	Athlete	Time
1970	Gary Muhrcke (U.S.)	2:31:38
1971	Norman Higgins (U.S.)	2:22:54
1972	Sheldon Karlin (U.S.)	2:27:52
1973	Tom Fleming (U.S.)	2:19:25
1974	Norbert Sander (U.S.)	2:26:30
1975	Tom Fleming (U.S.)	2:19:27
1976	Bill Rodgers (U.S.)	2:10:10
1977	Bill Rodgers (U.S.)	2:11:28
1978	Bill Rodgers (U.S.)	2:12:12
1979	Bill Rodgers (U.S.)	2:11:42
1980	Alberto Salazar (U.S.)	2:09:41
1981	Alberto Salazar (U.S.)	2:08:13
1982	Alberto Salazar (U.S.)	2:09:29
1983	Rod Dixon (New Zealand)	2:08:59
1984	Orlando Pizzolato (Italy)	2:14:53
1985	Orlando Pizzolato (Italy)	2:11:43
1986	Gianni Poli (Italy)	2:11:06
1987	Ibrahim Hussein (Kenya)	2:11:01
1988	Steve Jones (Britain)	2:08:20
1989	Juma Ikangaa (Tanzania)	2:08:01*
1990	Douglas Wakiihuri (Kenya)	2:12:39
1991	Salvador Garcia (Mexico)	2:09:28
1992	Willie Mtolo (South Africa)	2:09:29
1993	Andres Espinosa (Mexico)	2:10:04
1994	German Silva (Mexico)	2:11:21
1995	German Silva (Mexico)	2:11:00
1996	Giacomo Leone (Italy)	2:09:54
1997	John Kagwe (Kenya)	2:08:12
1998	John Kagwe (Kenya)	2:08:45
1999	Joseph Chebet (Kenya)	2:09:14
2000	Abdelkader El Mouaziz (Morocco)	2:10:09

New York Road Runners Club (www.nyrrc.org). Begun in 1958 in the dawning days of the RRCA with a membership of 47 serious runners and Ted Corbitt as president, the NYRRC (originally known as the Road Runners Club–New York Association), the club has become the world's largest running organization. It now boasts some 34,000 members, its own clubhouse, its own bimonthly magazine *(New York Runner)*, one of the world's most famous marathons, and one of the most crowded schedules of races (more than 70 each year) of any organization in the world. The club also hosts regular social events, running classes with famed author Bob Glover, yoga classes, deep-water running classes, health walking, active-isolated stretching classes, group runs, a Central Park Safety Program, youth and senior programs, a senior fitness program, a junior road runners club series, City Sports for Kids, the New York Road Runners Foundation, and the Achilles Track Club for disabled runners (which is currently 5,000 strong). There's something for everyone. *See also* Corbitt, Ted; Glover, Bob; Lebow, Fred; New York City Marathon; Steinfeld, Allan.

Nijboer, Gerard (b. August 18, 1955). The Dutch runner is in the same position as Frank Shorter. Both might have been Olympic gold medalists (Shorter in 1976 and Nijboer in 1980) if drug-taking charges against Waldemar Cierpinski could have been proven at the time. Nijboer finished second at the depleted Moscow Games in 1980 (in 2:11:20), then won the European title two years later (in 2:15:16). *See also* European Championships; Olympic medalists.

Nike (www.nike.com). Reportedly named by Jeff Johnson when it came to him in a dream, Phil Knight's company evolved from Blue Ribbon sports, which sold imported Tiger shoes from Japan in the 1960s. The company began to produce its own brand in the 1970s after Bill Bowerman invented the

© Jeff Johnson

Phil Knight, an advocate of the long-distance running teachings of Oregon's Bill Bowerman, eventually teamed up with the coach to found Nike.

waffle sole. Nike grew into the largest and most influential shoe company in the world and injected large amounts of money into distance running before heading off into other, more glamorous sports such as basketball and golf. For a critical history of the company, see *Swoosh: The Unauthorized Story of Nike and the Men Who Played There* by J.B. Strasser and Laurie Becklund (Harper Collins, 1991). *See also* air sole; Asics; Bowerman, Bill; Johnson, Jeff; Knight, Phil; shoe companies.

Nipguards (www.nipguards.com). *See* Band-Aids.

Noakes, Dr. Tim (b. 1949). The About the Author section in Noakes's landmark book *Lore of Running* (Oxford University Press, 1985; Human Kinetics, 1991) offers this summary: "Timothy Noakes was a runner 'before running became popular' and has competed in more than 70 marathon and ultramarathon races. His experiences as a runner, a physician and an exercise physiologist motivated him to write *Lore of Running*, the most complete book available on running. Dr. Noakes is the Liberty Life Professor of Exercise and Sports Science and director of the Bioenergetics of Exercise Research Unit of the Medical Research Council of the University of Cape Town. He is an editorial board member for many international sport science journals and the 1991 president of the South African Sports Medicine Association. Noakes is also a Fellow of the American College of Sports Medicine." *See also* books.

Norris, Ed (birthdate unavailable) and **Norris, Fred** (b. September 4, 1921). Fred came to the United States from Britain to start college at age 39. Son Ed was the 1972 national marathon champion (in 2:24:43), and together they were one of the fastest father (2:19)-son (2:24) marathon teams ever. *See also* national marathon champions, U.S.

Nurmi, Paavo (b. January 24, 1897). Although he did little road racing, multi-Olympic medalist and world record-setter Nurmi was a pioneer and innovator of long-distance running, inspiring Emil Zatopek and everyone else who wanted to go long fast.

nutrition. *See* foods, runners'.

Nyakeraka, Lazarus (b. 1976). *Runner's World* ranked the Kenyan first among road racers in 1996. He won Bloomsday that year and the next, and Bay to Breakers in 1999. *See also* Bay to Breakers 12K; Bloomsday 12K; rankings, *Runner's World.*

Nyambui, Suleiman (b. June 13, 1953). The U.S.-educated Tanzanian won the 1987 and 1988 Berlin Marathons. *See also* Berlin Marathon.

Nzau, Joseph (b. April 14, 1952). His Chicago Marathon victory in 1983 earned the Kenyan the top road ranking that year. He had first come to the United States to attend the University of Wyoming. *See also* Chicago Marathon; Peachtree 10K; rankings, *Runner's World.*

Oakley (www.oakley.com). This company pioneered the oh-so-light, oh-so-cool, oh-so-costly sunglasses for runners and other athletes. Now if we can just talk runners into taking them off and letting us see their eyes when posing for photos or accepting awards.

O'Brien, Cathy Schiro (b. July 19, 1967). She's a rarity—a child star who matured into one of the country's finest runners. When she was 16 years old in 1984, she ran in the first-ever U.S. Women's Marathon Trials and set a still-standing U.S. junior record of 2:34:24. She finished ninth after running as high in the field as fourth at the 24-mile mark. Without missing a beat, she traveled to San Diego's Balboa Park and won the annual Kinney National High School Cross Country finals by a 16-second margin.

Cathy Schiro (O'Brien) was the youngest American woman to qualify for the Olympic Marathon Trials. She did so in 1984 at age 16.

When the 1988 Olympic Marathon Trials came around, she was back in the thick of it, placing 3rd, but her 40th place at the Seoul Games disappointed her. Not to be daunted, the next year she set a world 10-mile record of 51:47, which remains the American record. USATF ranked her the number-one female road runner in 1990. In 1991 she won the Los Angeles Marathon with a PR of 2:29:38.

In 1992 Cathy was back at the Olympic Marathon Trials. During the race, as the lead group approached the water station at 15 miles, Janis Klecker fell. Cathy put on the brakes, turned around, and helped her up. Janis went on to win the Trials while Cathy qualified some 14 seconds back. At the Barcelona Olympics, Cathy was the first American finisher with a 10th place overall.

She qualified for the Olympic Marathon Trials again in 1996 but turned her attention instead to the 10,000 meters, in which she placed ninth at the Trials. In 1997 she won the Mount Washington Road Race on her first try. She lives in New England and has a young son born in April 2000. She remains the only American woman to make two Olympic Marathon teams. *See also* Los Angeles Marathon; Olympians, U.S.; Olympic Trials Marathon, U.S.; Peachtree 10K; records, American age-group.

oddest races. Some events aren't content to be just another weekend 5K. They stretch the definition of road races by running on beaches, up—and sometimes down—mountains (Pikes Peak Marathon), up the stairwells of tall buildings (Empire State Building Run-Up in New York City), through caves (Groundhog Run in Missouri), or in volcano craters (Kilauea Volcano Marathon). One of the oddest variations on the theme is the Bare Buns Fun Run in Washington State. *See also* Bare Buns Fun Run; Groundhog Run; Kilauea Volcano Marathon; Pikes Peak Marathon.

officials, volunteer. *See* volunteers.

Ohio River Road Runners Club Marathon (www.orrrc.org). Since its inception in 1967, this modest April event in Dayton has quietly aged into one of the country's longest-running marathons. *See also* oldest races.

Oksanen, Eino (b. May 5, 1931). The strongly built Finn, nicknamed "The Ox," won the Boston Marathon three times in a four-year stretch—1959, 1961, and 1962. He ranked number one in the world in 1959. *See also* Boston Marathon; rankings, *Track & Field News*.

Old Kent Riverbank 25K (www.riverbankrun.com). This race in Grand Rapids, Michigan, is one of the few occupying the black hole of distance racing between half-marathon and marathon. Run in May, the race is the site of the current world American women's record. *See also* Benoit Samuelson, Joan.

Tom Longboat, an Onodaga Indian from Canada, was one of the greatest distance runners of the early 1900s. In 1907 he won the Boston Marathon (one of the oldest marathons) in driving sleet and rain.

From the collection of Dr. Edward H. Kozloff–Motor City Striders

oldest races. Several North American events begun in the 19th century are into the 21st—most prominently the Boston Marathon. Races in Buffalo and New Orleans are just as old, and the Around the Bay 30K in Hamilton, Ontario, dates from 1894. *See also* Around the Bay 30K; Jackson Day Race; J.Y. Cameron File-Mile.

Olympia. *See* movies.

Olympia, Washington. What better place name could the United States Olympic Committee have chosen as the site of the first women's Olympic Marathon Trials in 1984? The city now hosts the annual Capital City Marathon (www.capitalcitymarathon.org).

Oldest U.S. Marathons

Many current marathons in the United States predate the first running boom. Listed here are the long-running survivors inaugurated in 1969 or earlier and still operating as 2000 ended. Many have gone through name and course changes, as well as interruptions in operation. Here we give the beginning year and number of runnings through 2000. Thanks go to Ken Young and his publication *Analytical Distance Runner* (www.mattoleriver.com) for his additions and corrections to our original list.

Race (city)	Year started	Runnings through 2000
Boston (Boston, MA)	1897	103
Yonkers (Yonkers, NY)	1907	76
Western Hemisphere (Culver City, CA)	1948	53
Philadelphia (Philadelphia, PA)	1954	44
Pikes Peak (Manitou Springs, CO)	1956	45
Long Island (East Meadow, NY)	1958	43
Atlantic City (Atlantic City, NJ)	1959	42
Heart of America (Columbia, MO)	1960	41
Washington's Birthday (Greenbelt, MD)	1962	39
Atlanta (Atlanta, GA)	1963	38
Detroit International (Detroit, MI)	1963	38
Equinox (Fairbanks, AK)	1963	37
Race of Champions (Holyoke, MA)	1963	38
Twin Cities (Minneapolis–St. Paul, MN)	1963	38
Mardi Gras (New Orleans, LA)	1965	36
San Diego (Carlsbad, CA)	1965	36
Las Vegas (Las Vegas, NV)	1967	34
Ohio River RRC (Dayton, OH)	1967	33
Palos Verdes (Palos Verdes, CA)	1967	34
Athens (Athens, OH)	1968	33
Grandfather Mountain (Boone, NC)	1968	33
Arkansas (Malvern, AK)	1969	32
Birch Bay (Blaine, WA)	1969	32
Paavo Nurmi (Upson, WI)	1969	32

Olympians, U.S. These are the country's running royalty, the runners who have made the team in the marathon since 1896. First to join this group was Arthur Blake, who failed to finish the inaugural Olympic Marathon. First to finish one was Arthur Newton, who placed fifth in 1900. The first woman couldn't have done better; she is 1984 gold medalist Joan Benoit. *See also* "Our Royalty" on next page.

Our Royalty

From Joe Henderson's *Running Commentary,* May 2000.

The nearest U.S. running has to a royal family is its Olympic marathoners. This lineage reaches back more than 100 years to the first Olympian—Arthur Blake, who dropped out along the road from Marathon to Athens in 1896—and is carried on this year by the lone woman and man headed to Sydney, Christine Clark and Rod DeHaven.

The majority of male Olympians have gone to the big racecourse in the sky. Relatively few are still able to run, let alone race. Our elder statesman is John A. Kelley, still active at almost 93.

Women had to wait so long for their race, though, that all the U.S. Olympic runners are still living. Most of the dozen still run and race—notably Joan Benoit Samuelson, who won the first Games and broke into the top 10 at this year's Trials.

As I sorted out all the royals for listing in the *Running Encyclopedia,* fascinating facts popped up. Many of them surprised me. I'd always thought, for instance, that Munich was the golden Games for American men. Frank Shorter, Kenny Moore, and Jack Bacheler placed 1-4-9. This was the best team showing in modern times but not the best ever.

The high came at the chaotic St. Louis Olympics of 1904. American Fred Lorz "won" but was disqualified for hitching a ride. But his teammates Thomas Hicks and Arthur Newton stepped up to take gold and bronze medals. Other Americans placed 6-7-8 that year, when entries per country were unlimited and the United States sent 18 marathoners.

Other royal family facts include the following:

- Arthur Newton, future medalist, was the first American to finish an Olympic marathon as he placed fifth in 1900. He ran the Paris race at age 17, still the youngest U.S. runner to compete at this level.

- Medals came often in those early Games. Americans won six of them between 1904 and 1912, including Thomas Hicks's in 1904 and Johnny Hayes's four years later.

- Hayes set the first world mark at 26 miles, 385 yards (2:55:19) while winning the first race at this distance. It didn't become standard, though, until the 1924 Games.

- Durable as he was, Clarence DeMar was neither the oldest Olympian (at 40 in 1928) nor the first three-time finisher. James Henigan ran in the 1932 Games at age 41. Joseph Forshaw ran in 1904, 1906, and 1908 and, like DeMar, he was once a bronze medalist.

- DeMar's medal in 1924 was the last for the United States until Frank Shorter's almost a half century later. No one from here broke into the top dozen between 1932 and 1964, so the current drought has a precedent.

- We all know about Billy Mills's 10,000-meter upset at Tokyo in 1964. But did you realize he ended those Games by finishing 14th in the marathon? And did you know that he is the only surviving member of that U.S. marathon team, as both Buddy Edelen and Peter McArdle have passed on?

- Do you recall that Frank Shorter contended for a medal in the 10,000 at Munich in 1972? He placed fifth in that race, a week before winning the marathon.

- Single-race Trials don't have a long history. They only date from 1968. Earlier the selection was usually made from results of two to four races.

- The Trials adopted qualifying times in 1972. Prior to that, anyone could enter.
- Joan Benoit's victory in the first women's Olympic Marathon was the last time any American has claimed a single-digit finish. Cathy O'Brien (1992) and Anne Marie Lauck (1996) both placed 10th.
- O'Brien is the only two-time Olympic woman to date. She made her first team, for Seoul, at age 20—which is years younger than anyone who even competed in this year's Trials.
- The best women's team finish (10-12-21) came at Barcelona. In fact, that's the only time three U.S. women have finished, and it can't happen again until at least 2004.
- The last time an American man reached the top 10 was 1976, when Shorter and Don Kardong placed 2-4—or 1-3, if history ever amends itself.

U.S. Olympic Marathoners

Here are all the runners who have qualified for the Games. Note the early flurry of men's medalists—six between 1904 and 1912, including winners Thomas Hicks and John Hayes. Note also that the 1906 Games were not formally considered Olympics, though sanctioned by the International Olympic Committee. These Games, named the Intercalated Games were held in Athens as a celebration of the 10 year anniversary of the 1896 games.* = Trials winner.

WOMEN

Year	Place	Athlete	Time
1984	Los Angeles	1. Joan Benoit*	2:24:52
		36. Julie Brown	2:47:33
		Julie Isphording	DNF
1988	Seoul	17. Nancy Ditz	2:33:42
		39. Margaret Groos*	2:40:59
		40. Cathy O'Brien	2:41:04
1992	Barcelona	10. Cathy O'Brien	2:39:42
		12. Francie Larrieu Smith	2:41:09
		21. Janis Klecker*	2:47:17
1996	Atlanta	10. Anne Marie Lauck	2:31:30
		31. Linda Somers Smith	2:36:58
		Jenny Spangler*	DNF
2000	Sydney	19. Christine Clark*	2:31:38

MEN

Year	Place	Athlete	Time
1896	Athens	Arthur Blake	DNF
1900	Paris	5. Arthur Newton	4:04:12
		6. Dick Grant	unknown
		7. Ronald MacDonald	unknown

(continued)

U.S. Olympic Marathoners, *continued*

Year	Place	Athlete	Time
1904	St. Louis	1. Thomas Hicks	3:28:53
		3. Arthur Newton	3:47:33
		6. David Kneeland	unknown
		7. Henry Brawley	unknown
		8. Sidney Hatch	unknown
		11. Harry Devlin	unknown
		13. John Furla	unknown
		Edward Carr	DNF
		Joseph Fowler	DNF
		John Foy	DNF
		William Garcia	DNF
		Thomas Kennedy	DNF
		John Lorden	DNF
		Fred Lorz	DNF
		Samuel Mellor	DNF
		Guy Porter	DNF
		Frank Pierce	DNF
		Michael Spring	DNF
1906	Athens	3. William Frank	3:00:47
		12. Joseph Forshaw	unknown
		Robert Fowler	DNF
		Michael Spring	DNF
1908	London	1. John Hayes	2:55:19
		3. Joseph Forshaw	2:57:11
		4. Alton Welton	2:59:45
		9. Lewis Tewanima	3:09:15
		14. Sidney Hatch	3:17:53
		Thomas Morrisey	DNF
		Mike Ryan	DNF
1912	Stockholm	3. Gaston Strobino	2:38:43
		4. Andrew Sockalexis	2:42:08
		7. John J. Gallagher	2:44:20
		8. Joseph Erxleben	2:45:48
		9. Richard Piggott	2:46:41
		10. Joseph Forshaw	2:49:50
		12. Clarence DeMar	2:50:47
		16. Lewis Tewanima	2:52:42
		17. Harry Smith	2:52:34
		18. Thomas Lilley	2:59:36
		John Reynolds	DNF
		Mike Ryan	DNF
1920	Antwerp	7. Joseph Organ	2:41:30
		12. Charles Mellor	2:45:30
		Arthur Roth	DNF
1924	Paris	3. Clarence DeMar	2:48:14
		16. Frank Wendling	3:05:10
		18. Frank Zuna	3:05:53
		23. William Churchill	3:19:18
		25. Charles Mellor	3:24:07
		Ralph Williams	DNF
1928	Amsterdam	5. Joie Ray	2:36:04
		9. Whitey Michelsen	2:38:56
		27. Clarence DeMar	2:50:42
		39. James Henigan	2:56:50
		44. William Agee	2:58:50
		Harvey Frick	DNF

Year	Place	Athlete	Time
1932	Los Angeles	7. Whitey Michelsen	2:39:38
		11. Hans Oldag	2:47:26
		James Henigan	DNF
1936	Berlin	18. John A. Kelley	2:49:33
		Tarzan Brown	DNF
		William McMahon	DNF
1940	Tokyo/Helsinki;	Don Heinicke	
	cancelled, however	John A. Kelley	
	U.S. team selected	Les Pawson	
1944	London; *cancelled*		
1948	London	14. Ted Vogel	2:45:27
		21. John A. Kelley	2:51:56
		24. Olavi Manninen	2:56:49
1952	Helsinki	13. Vic Dyrgall	2:32:53
		36. Thomas Jones	2:42:50
		44. Ted Corbitt	2:51:09
1956	Melbourne	20. Nick Costes	2:42:20
		21. John J. Kelley	2:43:40
		Dean Thackwray	DNF
1960	Rome	19. John J. Kelley	2:24:58
		30. Alex Breckinridge	2:29:38
		48. Gordon McKenzie	2:35:16
1964	Tokyo	6. Buddy Edelen	2:18:13
		14. Billy Mills	2:22:56
		23. Pete McArdle	2:26:25
1968	Mexico City	14. Kenny Moore	2:29:50
		16. George Young*	2:31:15
		22. Ron Daws	2:33:53
1972	Munich	1. Frank Shorter*	2:12:20
		4. Kenny Moore*	2:15:40
		9. Jack Bacheler	2:17:39
1976	Montreal	2. Frank Shorter*	2:10:46
		4. Don Kardong	2:11:16
		40. Bill Rodgers	2:25:15
1980	Moscow;	Benji Durden	
	U.S. boycotted	Kyle Heffner	
		Tony Sandoval*	
1984	Los Angeles	11. Pete Pfitzinger*	2:13:53
		15. Alberto Salazar	2:14:19
		John Tuttle	DNF
1988	Seoul	14. Pete Pfitzinger	2:14:44
		29. Ed Eyestone	2:19:09
		Mark Conover*	DNF
1992	Barcelona	12. Steve Spence*	2:15:21
		13. Ed Eyestone	2:15:23
		17. Bob Kempainen	2:15:53
1996	Atlanta	28. Keith Brantly	2:18:17
		31. Bob Kempainen*	2:18:38
		41. Mark Coogan	2:20:27
2000	Sydney	69. Rod DeHaven*	2:30:46

Olympic Marathon, 1896. The first modern Olympics at Athens in 1896 was a resounding success because of the invention of the marathon—and because of the victory of the home team in that event by a humble shepherd and water carrier named Spiridon Louis. Those Olympic Games did not come into being without a marathon struggle.

Baron Pierre de Coubertin, the Frenchman who thought up the idea of an Olympic revival, was often frustrated by the negative responses of other nations' leaders who should have supported him, and his idea for the Games was almost stolen from him. The baron had dedicated his life, and his health and fortune, to the idea of promoting peace between nations though friendly competition. In the process he pulled up his native France by its athletic bootstraps by encouraging what he called "muscular Christianity." De Coubertin was inspired by the British practice of heavily promoting sports in schools and universities, and by the exuberant affinity of American schoolboys for team sports. The baron's persistence overcame obstacles that would have deterred anyone who had more common sense than blind idealism.

As the 19th century drew toward a close, de Coubertin had convinced Greece (as the cradle of Olympic competition) to host the first modern Olympic Games. He had hoped to use Mount Olympus as the site of the Games, but it proved unsuitable for modern requirements, so Athens was chosen instead. As enthusiasm among the Greeks increased and they developed plans for the Games, they began to shunt de Coubertin into the background, going as far as attempting to dissociate him from the very concept of the modern Olympics. They envisioned the Olympics as a wholly Greek enterprise with no share of the glory going to a Frenchman.

Ultimately, through weeks of negotiations and intercessions from several influential patrons and several nations, the problem was resolved amicably, and the Greeks turned their attention away from making de Coubertin persona non grata and toward trying to raise the capital necessary to construct a suitable stadium and other facilities. Michel Breal, another Frenchman, felt it would be nice to place a novelty event in the Games in honor of the legend of the run from Marathon to Athens. He proposed such a marathon event and offered a silver cup as the first prize. De Coubertin liked the idea and had little trouble selling it to the Greek hosts because the marathon-run concept was drenched in Greek history.

The first Olympic Marathon is traditionally thought of as the first marathon ever run. In actuality it was the third, but Greece also has the distinction of being the home of the first two marathons. As soon as the Greeks heard that a long-distance race would be included in the Olympic Games to commemorate their victory against the Persians on the Plains of Marathon, they became excited beyond belief. Naturally they felt it was a matter of national pride that a Greek should win the event. Thus the Greek Olympic Committee immediately set about searching villages and cities alike for anyone capable of making a good showing.

The first marathon trial was held as part of the Pan-Hellenic Sports Celebration (the Greek national championships) and was open only to members of sporting clubs signed up to compete. The race was on March 10, 1896, over the Olympic course, which ran from the bridge at Marathon to the new stadium in Athens. A dozen club members competed. Charilaos Vasilakos took first in 3:18, Spiridon Belokas second in 3:21, and Dimitrios Deliyannis third in 3:33.

Two weeks later, on March 24, an open race was conducted over the same course.

This time there were 38 entrants. They were apparently a hardier group than the club runners because their times were significantly better. The winner of the open trials, a man listed as Lavrentis, ran the course in 3:11:27. Second place was taken by Ioannis Vrettos in 3:12:30, third by Eleftherios Papasimeon in 3:13:37, fourth by Elias Kafetzis in 3:15:50, and fifth by Spiridon (listed in some accounts as Spyros) Louis (or Loues or Louys), a shepherd and water hauler, in 3:18:27.

On Sunday, April 10, 1896, 16 Olympic competitors—a dozen Greek runners and four foreigners—lined up on the far side of the bridge at Marathon before a crowd of several hundred. Spectators filled the Panathenaic Stadium to watch several track finals while the tension of the marathon built to a frenzy as news of the runners' progress was brought from messengers on horseback. The official Greek historian for the event summed up nicely what was riding on this contest: "If only the Cup of Marathon would be gained by a child of the soil!" was the ardent wish of every Greek person. All kinds of rewards were promised to the victor, should he be a Greek. Some hotelkeepers had pledged to give him free board and lodging—some for a fixed term of years, some for his whole lifetime. Tailors, barbers, and hatters offered their services. Professionalism was already creeping into the Olympics, in the guise of national pride.

Three of the foreigners had placed first, second, and third three days earlier in the 1,500 meters, but none of them had any previous experience at distances approaching the marathon. The foreigners were Edwin Flack (Australia), Arthur Blake (United States), Albin Lermusiaux (France), and Gyula Kellner (Hungary); Kellner was the only one of the four with some marathon-length running experience. For an account of how the race unfolded, see the Louis, Spiridon (the winner) entry.

The Greeks experienced both elation and shame that day. The Hungarian, Kellner, who apparently had finished fourth, protested at the finish line that Spiridon Belokas had taken a carriage ride to get in front of him. The protest was investigated personally by Crown Prince Nicholas, and Belokas, the first marathon cheat, was disqualified. *See also* Belokas, Spiridon; Blake, Arthur; cheaters; de Coubertin, Pierre; Kellner, Gyula; Louis, Spiridon.

Olympic Marathon, 1900 to 2000 (www.olympic.org). The marathon event, seen more as a novelty act than a sport, had something of a sordid history in the Olympic Games in the first half of the 20th century. Many of the courses were badly measured, poorly marked (especially Paris in 1900), shoddily officiated if officiated at all, and often run at a time of day to maximize suffering (1904 St. Louis, for example). A quick look at some of the highlights and lowlights of the Olympic Marathon in the 20th century follows.

1900: The course in Paris in 1900 ran through the city's streets and was so badly marked that local runners were able to take shortcuts, robbing the favored Arthur Newton of a win.

1904: The Games were welded to the St. Louis World's Fair and actually surpassed the Paris Games as the worst organized in history. The marathon was run in 90-degree temperatures with 90 percent humidity, and there was only one water stop along the entire 24-mile course. Fred Lorz (United States) was crowned, then disqualified for cheating by taking an automobile ride. American Thomas Hicks eventually was declared the winner.

1908: At London what would become the official marathon distance was established at 26 miles, 385 yards, after the 385 yards was added to accommodate the royal family's view of proceedings. Italian Dorando Pietri came into the stadium first but was disqualified after repeatedly falling down and being helped up by officials. The second finisher across the line, American Johnny Hayes, was eventually crowned the winner.

1912: At Stockholm the marathon was again run during the hottest part of the day. Half of the starters never finished, many of them collapsed, and one of them, Francisco Lazaro of Portugal, died the next day.

1916: The Games were canceled because of World War I.

1920: In Antwerp the marathon was held for once without major disasters surrounding it. Hannes Kolehmainen of Finland won.

1924: The Games were moved from Amsterdam to Paris to accommodate Baron de Coubertin's retirement. Near disaster was averted when the heat wave that had ravaged the 10,000-meter cross country race the day before gave way to more temperate weather in time for the marathon. Finland's Albin Stenroos won by nearly six minutes.

1928: In Amsterdam the course was relatively flat, but the temperature was 61 degrees with 93 percent humidity. Moroccan Boughera El Ouafi, running for France, won with a 25-second margin.

1932: Los Angeles offered surprisingly favorable weather and a flat, fast course. Argentina's Juan Zabala won in 2:36.

From the collection of Dr. Edward H. Kozloff–Motor City Striders

Argentinian Juan Zabala, shown here training in New York City in 1932, won the Los Angeles Olympics marathon later that year in 2:31:36.

1936: The "Nazi Olympics" in Berlin were marked not only by Jesse Owens's rebuke of Aryan supremacy but by a horrendous misrepresentation in the marathon. Because Japan had attacked and occupied Korea, Korean marathoners Sohn Kee Chung and Nam Sung Yong were forced to compete wearing Japanese uniforms and using Japanese names (Kitei Son and Shoryu Nam, respectively). Sohn and Nam took first and third. In 1988 at the Seoul Olympics, Sohn ran the final leg of the Olympic torch relay and, at age 76, inserted several jumps of joy as he rounded the track.

1940 and 1944: The Games were canceled because of World War II.

1948: The drama of the marathon again took center stage at London. Etienne Gailly, a 21-year-old ex-paratrooper from Belgium, led the race, but Delfo Cabrera of Argentina passed him with the stadium in sight. Gailly put on a furious rush and retook the lead, but his sprint came too early to carry him to victory. When Gailly entered the stadium, the 70,000 spectators were stunned to see him nearly unconscious. As the crowd watched in disbelief, Cabrera passed Gailly to take the gold and Britain's Tom Richards passed him to take the silver. But the crowd's concentration was on Gailly, who finally managed to stagger across the finish line. At the awards ceremony, Gailly was too exhausted to attend, and the rumor circulated that he had died. He recovered fully.

1952: The Helsinki Games were important because they were the first Games in which the Soviets participated. The star of the Games, however, was Emil Zatopek of Czechoslovakia, who won the 5,000 and 10,000 meters, then elected to run the Olympic Marathon as his first race at that distance. He won in Olympic record time (2:23:04), the only time a runner has swept all three distance events at the Games.

1956: At Melbourne, Emil Zatopek was back, but he was coming off a recent hernia operation. The day went to Alain Mimoun of Algeria running under the French colors.

1960, 1964, and 1968: The three Olympic Marathons of the 1960s belonged to Ethiopia. In 1960 at Rome, barefooted Abebe Bikila, considered by some to be the greatest marathoner ever, won the race in a world-record-tying time of 2:15:17. He came back in 1964 at Tokyo to win again, breaking the world record with a 2:12:12 and becoming the first gold-medal marathoner to repeat. In 1968 at Mexico City Bikila ran injured, and dropped at 17K with a stress fracture in his leg. His teammate Mamo Wolde went on to win, completing the sweep of the 1960s for Ethiopia.

1972: At Munich, Frank Shorter of the United States found the early going too slow for his liking and moved away from the field. The others expected him to come back, but he never did. He won in the town in which he was born, in 2:12:20. Teammate Kenny Moore took fourth.

1976: In Montreal, Frank Shorter attempted to match Bikila's doubling of marathon gold but was unseated by East German Waldemar Cierpinski, relegating Shorter to second place. Years later, captured Stasi files indicated that Cierpinski was the recipient of performance-enhancing drugs. The offense was too far in the past by then for the IOC to do anything about rectifying the situation.

1980: The Games were hosted by Moscow, but much of the world boycotted them over the USSR's invasion of Afghanistan. The move was decidedly against the spirit of the Games. With a diminished field, Cierpinski again won gold, the first (and still only) runner to match Bikila's feat. Again, the victory has since been tainted due to the evidence of drug use.

1984: The Los Angeles Games were significant because this was the first time a women's Olympic Marathon was contended. American Joan Benoit, taking a page from Frank Shorter's 1972 win, found the early going too pedestrian, so she moved ahead forcefully and never looked back. Her time of 2:24:52 stood as the women's Olympic record until the 2000 Games. On the men's side, 37-year-old Carlos Lopes of Portugal set an Olympic record of 2:09:21. The first three men were on the track at the same time, which played well because the men's marathon had been choreographed (appropriately) as part of the Closing Ceremonies.

1988: In Seoul, Rosa Mota of Portugal, one of the most dominant women in the sport, won the gold by 13 seconds over Lisa Martin. For the men, Italy's Gelindo Bordin won by 15 seconds over Douglas Wakiihuri of Kenya.

1992: In Barcelona, Russian Valentina Yegorova won the women's side, and Hwang Young Cho of Korea won for the men. In both races the winning margin was less than 30 seconds.

1996: At Atlanta, Fatuma Roba of Ethiopia won the women's marathon by a two-minute margin, in 2:26:05. For the men, South African Josia Thugwane won by just three seconds over Lee Bong Ju of Korea; it was the first time a South African had won since 1912.

2000: Japan's Naoko Takahashi won Japan's first women's gold medal at Sydney, setting an Olympic record of 2:23:14. Ethiopia returned to its winning ways as Gezahegne Abera of Ethiopia picked up the men's gold medal.

Olympic medalists. The highest honor in the sport is a first, second, or third place at the Games. Records, they say, can be taken away, but an Olympic medal is forever.

Olympic Marathon Medalists

Although Olympic marathoning dates back to the first Games—for men, anyway—the distance didn't settle at the now-standard 42.2K, or 26.2 miles until the 1924 Games. The 1908 race was the first run at this length. Note that solid evidence exists for Waldemar Cierpinski's use of banned substances, but no action has been taken to rewrite the results from 1976 and 1980. * = Olympic record.

WOMEN

Year	Place	Distance	Athlete	Time
1984	Los Angeles	standard	1. Joan Benoit (U.S.)	2:24:52
			2. Grete Waitz (Norway)	2:26:18
			3. Rosa Mota (Portugal)	2:26:57
1988	Seoul	standard	1. Rosa Mota (Portugal)	2:25:40
			2. Lisa Martin (Australia)	2:25:53
			3. Katrin Dorre (East Germany)	2:26:21
1992	Barcelona	standard	1. Valentina Yegorova (Russia)	2:32:41
			2. Yuko Arimori (Japan)	2:32:49
			3. Lorraine Moller (New Zealand)	2:33:59

Year	Place	Distance	Athlete	Time
1996	Atlanta	standard	1. Fatuma Roba (Ethiopia)	2:26:05
			2. Valentina Yegorova (Russia)	2:28:05
			3. Yuko Arimori (Japan)	2:28:39
2000	Sydney	standard	1. Naoko Takahashi (Japan)	2:23:14*
			2. Lidia Simon (Romania)	2:23:22
			3. Joyce Chepchumba (Kenya)	2:24:45

MEN

Year	Place	Distance	Athlete	Time
1896	Athens	40K	1. Spiridon Louis (Greece)	2:58:50
			2. Charilaos Vasilakos (Greece)	3:06:03
			3. Gyula Kellner (Hungary)	3:06:35
1900	Paris	40.26K	1. Michel Theato (France)	2:59:45
			2. Emile Champion (France)	3:04:17
			3. Ernst Fast (Sweden)	3:37:14
1904	St. Louis	40K	1. Thomas Hicks (U.S.)	3:28:53
			2. Albert Corey (France)	3:34:52
			3. Arthur Newton (U.S.)	3:47:33
1906	Athens	41.86K	1. William Sherring (Canada)	2:51:24
			2. Johan Svanberg (Sweden)	2:58:21
			3. William Frank (U.S.)	3:00:47
1908	London	42.2K	1. John Hayes (U.S.)	2:55:19
			2. Charles Hefferon (South Africa)	2:56:06
			3. Joseph Forshaw (U.S.)	2:57:11
1912	Stockholm	40.2K	1. Kennedy McArthur (South Africa)	2:36:55
			2. Christian Gitsham (South Africa)	2:37:52
			3. Gaston Strobino (U.S.)	2:39:43
1920	Antwerp	42.75K	1. Hannes Kolehmainen (Finland)	2:32:36
			2. Jüri Lossmann (Estonia)	2:32:49
			3. Valerio Arri (Italy)	2:36:33
1924	Paris	standard	1. Albin Stenroos (Finland)	2:41:23
			2. Romeo Bertini (Italy)	2:47:20
			3. Clarence DeMar (U.S.)	2:48:14
1928	Amsterdam	standard	1. Boughera El Ouafi (France)	2:32:57
			2. Manuel Plaza (Chile)	2:33:23
			3. Martti Marttelin (Finland)	2:35:02
1932	Los Angeles	standard	1. Juan Carlos Zabala (Argentina)	2:31:36
			2. Samuel Ferris (Britain)	2:31:55
			3. Armas Toivonen (Finland)	2:32:12
1936	Berlin	standard	1. Sohn Kee Chung (Japan)	2:29:20
			2. Ernest Harper (Britain)	2:31:24
			3. Nam Sung Yong (Japan)	2:31:42
1948	London	standard	1. Delfo Cabrera (Argentina)	2:34:52
			2. Thomas Richards (Britain)	2:35:08
			3. Etienne Gailly (Belgium)	2:35:34
1952	Helsinki	standard	1. Emil Zatopek (Czechoslovakia)	2:23:04
			2. Reinaldo Gorno (Argentina)	2:25:35
			3. Gustaf Jansson (Sweden)	2:26:07

(continued)

Olympic Marathon Medalists, *continued*

Year	Place	Distance	Athlete	Time
1956	Melbourne	standard	1. Alain Mimoun (France)	2:25:00
			2. Franjo Mihalic (Yugoslavia)	2:26:32
			3. Veikko Karvonen (Finland)	2:27:47
1960	Rome	standard	1. Abebe Bikila (Ethiopia)	2:15:17
			2. Rhadi Ben Abdesselem (Morocco)	2:15:42
			3. Barry Magee (New Zealand)	2:17:19
1964	Tokyo	standard	1. Abebe Bikila (Ethiopia)	2:12:12
			2. Basil Heatley (Britain)	2:16:20
			3. Kokichi Tsuburaya (Japan)	2:16:23
1968	Mexico City	standard	1. Mamo Wolde (Ethiopia)	2:20:27
			2. Kenji Kimihara (Japan)	2:23:31
			3. Mike Ryan (New Zealand)	2:23:45
1972	Munich	standard	1. Frank Shorter (U.S.)	2:12:20
			2. Karel Lismont (Belgium)	2:14:32
			3. Mamo Wolde (Ethiopia)	2:15:09
1976	Montreal	standard	1. Waldemar Cierpinski (E.Germany)	2:09:55
			2. Frank Shorter (U.S.)	2:10:46
			3. Karel Lismont (Belgium)	2:11:13
1980	Moscow	standard	1. Waldemar Cierpinski (E. Germany)	2:11:03
			2. Gerard Nijboer (Holland)	2:11:20
			3. Satymkul Dzhumanazarov (USSR)	2:11:35
1984	Los Angeles	standard	1. Carlos Lopes (Portugal)	2:09:21*
			2. John Treacy (Ireland)	2:09:56
			3. Charlie Spedding (Britain)	2:09:58
1988	Seoul	standard	1. Gelindo Bordin (Italy)	2:10:32
			2. Douglas Wakiihuri (Kenya)	2:10:47
			3. Ahmed Salah (Djibouti)	2:10:59
1992	Barcelona	standard	1. Hwang Young Cho (Korea)	2:13:23
			2. Koichi Morishita (Japan)	2:13:45
			3. Stephan Freigang (Germany)	2:14:00
1996	Atlanta	standard	1. Josia Thugwane (South Africa)	2:12:36
			2. Lee Bong Ju (Korea)	2:12:39
			3. Eric Wainaina (Kenya)	2:12:44
2000	Sydney	standard	1. Gezahegne Abera (Ethiopia)	2:10:11
			2. Eric Wainaina (Kenya)	2:10:31
			3. Tesaye Tola (Ethiopia)	2:11:10

Olympic Trials Marathon, U.S. (www.usatf.org). Few other countries pick their Olympic teams in such a straightforward—some would say brutal—way as the United States: a single race with the leaders going to the Games and the others, regardless of past performances, staying home. This wasn't always the system. For most of Olympic history, American officials chose runners from performances in multiple races. The first single race was run in 1968 at Alamosa, Colorado. Qualifying times for runners to even enter the Trials debuted in 1972. Women adopted this format at their first Trials in 1984. *See also* Olympians, U.S.

U.S. Olympic Trials Marathons

Single-race Marathon Trials became the rule in 1968, when a high-altitude race was required for picking the Mexico City team. Qualifying times have been used since 1972. * = Trials record.

WOMEN

Year	Place	Athlete	Time
1984	Olympia, Washington	1. Joan Benoit	2:31:04
		2. Julie Brown	2:31:41
		3. Julie Isphording	2:32:26
1988	Pittsburgh, Pennsylvania	1. Margaret Groos	2:29:50*
		2. Nancy Ditz	2:30:14
		3. Cathy O'Brien	2:30:18
1992	Houston, Texas	1. Janis Klecker	2:30:12
		2. Cathy O'Brien	2:30:26
		3. Francie Larrieu Smith	2:30:39
1996	Columbia, South Carolina	1. Jenny Spangler	2:29:54
		2. Linda Somers Smith	2:30:06
		3. Anne-Marie Lauck	2:31:18
2000	Columbia, South Carolina	1. Christine Clark	2:33:31
		2. Kristy Johnston	2:35:36
		3. Anne Marie Lauck	2:36:05

MEN

Year	Place	Athlete	Time
1968	Alamosa, Colorado	1. George Young	2:30:48
		2. Kenny Moore	2:31:47
		3. Ron Daws	2:33:09
1972	Eugene, Oregon	1. (tie) Frank Shorter	2:15:58
		1. (tie) Kenny Moore	2:15:58
		3. Jack Bacheler	2:20:30
1976	Eugene, Oregon	1. Frank Shorter	2:11:51
		2. Bill Rodgers	2:11:58
		3. Don Kardong	2:13:54
1980	Buffalo, New York	1. Tony Sandoval	2:10:19*
		2. Benji Durden	2:10:41
		3. Kyle Heffner	2:10:55
1984	Buffalo, New York	1. Pete Pfitzinger	2:11:44
		2. Alberto Salazar	2:11:45
		3. John Tuttle	2:11:50
1988	Jersey City, New Jersey	1. Mark Conover	2:12:26
		2. Ed Eyestone	2:12:49
		3. Pete Pfitzinger	2:13:09
1992	Columbus, Ohio	1. Steve Spence	2:12:43
		2. Ed Eyestone	2:12:51
		3. Bob Kempainen	2:12:54
1996	Charlotte, North Carolina	1. Bob Kempainen	2:12:45
		2. Mark Coogan	2:13:05
		3. Keith Brantly	2:13:22
2000	Pittsburgh, Pennsylvania	1. Rod DeHaven	2:15:30
		2. Peter DeLaCerda	2:16:18
		3. Mark Coogan	2:17:04

Omoro, Jane (b. December 3, 1967). This Kenyan did lots of winning at the shorter road distances around the turn of the century: Bay to Breakers in 1997 and 1998; Bloomsday in 1998, 1999, and 2000; and Bolder Boulder in 1998. *See also* Bay to Breakers 12K, Bloomsday 12K, Bolder Boulder 10K.

Once a Runner. *See* books; Parker, John.

Ondieki, Lisa Martin. *See* Martin, Lisa.

Ondieki, Yobes (b. February 21, 1961). The world's first sub-27-minute 10,000 runner on the track occasionally raced well on the roads too. The Kenyan set a world 5K record of 13:26 in 1989 and won Bloomsday in 1992. Yobes is the ex-husband of Lisa (Martin) Ondieki. *See also* Bloomsday 12K; Martin, Lisa; record progressions, world.

online registration. Runners became wired (that's *wired*, not weird) in the 1990s. One consequence of this was a dramatic swing toward registering for races by way of Web sites—either through sites for individual events or through registration services such as Active.com (formerly known as Racegate.com), which process registration for multiple races.

On the Edge. *See* Dipsea Trail Run; movies.

On the Run From Dogs and People. Running has turned out shelves of books. They're generally long on practical advice and missionary zeal but short on humor. Hal Higdon's *On the Run From Dogs and People* (Regnery, 1971) is a notable exception. *See also* books; Higdon, Hal.

Organ, Joseph (b. August 3, 1892; date of death unknown). The 1920 U.S. Olympian placed seventh at Antwerp and set an American marathon record of 2:41:30 (the first sub-2:45 time for an American). *See also* Olympians, U.S.; record progressions, American.

orthotics. Custom-made shoe inserts, usually prescribed by podiatrists, came into vogue in the 1970s—thanks in large measure to ringing endorsements from Dr. George Sheehan. Orthotics are intended to compensate for the oversights of nature and the abuse heaped on feet, legs, and even the lower back by runners. *See also* podiatry.

Osaka Ladies' Marathon. It's another race in the Japanese style—an international, invitational, single-sex marathon in the Fukuoka mold. The race, launched in 1982, is generally held each March. Leading Osaka's list of multiple winners are Katrin Dorre (four times), Lorraine Moller (three times) and Lidia Simon (three times). This is perhaps the only marathon ever canceled (in 1995) by the devastating after effects of an earthquake.

Osano, Thomas (b. June 4, 1970). The Kenyan won three times at Bay to Breakers (1991, 1992, and 1996) and twice at Bolder Boulder (1991 and

Osaka Ladies' Marathon Winners

Winners of the Japanese women-only race follow. Note Katrin Dorre's four victories over a 13-year span. * = race record.

Year	Athlete	Time
1982	Rita Marchisio (Italy)	2:32:55
1983	Carey May (Ireland)	2:29:23
1984	Katrin Dorre (East Germany)	2:31:41
1985	Carey May (Ireland)	2:28:07
1986	Lorraine Moller (New Zealand)	2:30:24
1987	Lorraine Moller (New Zealand)	2:30:40
1988	Lisa Martin (Australia)	2:23:51
1989	Lorraine Moller (New Zealand)	2:30:21
1990	Rosa Mota (Portugal)	2:27:47
1991	Katrin Dorre (Germany)	2:27:43
1992	Yumi Kokamo (Japan)	2:26:26
1993	Junko Asari (Japan)	2:26:26
1994	Tomoe Abe (Japan)	2:26:09
1995	(canceled because of major earthquake)	
1996	Katrin Dorre (Germany)	2:26:04
1997	Katrin Dorre (Germany)	2:25:57
1998	Lidia Simon (Romania)	2:28:31
1999	Lidia Simon (Romania)	2:23:24
2000	Lidia Simon (Romania)	2:22:54*
2001	Yoko Shibui (Japan)	2:23:11

1992). *See also* Bay to Breakers 12K; Bolder Boulder 10K; Peachtree 10K; rankings, *Runner's World.*

Osler, Tom (b. April 26, 1940). The groundbreaking author wrote his booklet *Conditioning of Distance Runners* in 1966 *(Long Distance Log)* and its highly regarded sequel, *Serious Runner's Handbook* (World Publications) 12 years later. Osler is widely credited with introducing walking breaks to U.S. runners. *See also* Hall of Fame, RRCA; walk breaks.

Osoro, Ondoro (b. December 3, 1967). Besides holding the world record for the most letter *o*s in his name, Osoro has run the fastest debut marathon ever—2:06:54 while winning Chicago in 1998, dethroning Khalid Khannouchi and earning the top world ranking that year. He was selected for the 2000 Kenyan Olympic team, but shortly after that announcement was made he was wounded by a carjacker. *See also* Chicago Marathon; rankings, *Track & Field News.*

O'Sullivan, Sonia (b. November 28, 1969). The Villanova-schooled Irishwoman is best known for her work on the track, where she's among the world's best at 1,500 through 5,000. Her rare forays onto the road have resulted in the current world 8K best (aided) of 24:27, set in 1999, and an Avon world 10K title in 2000. *See also* Avon Racing Circuits; records, world.

Otwori, Hezron (b. December 25, 1976). His victories at Bloomsday and Bolder Boulder in May 1998 netted the Kenyan the top world ranking that year. *See also* Bloomsday 12K; Bolder Boulder 10K; rankings, *Runner's World*.

overuse injuries. The most common cause of running injuries is overdoing the running—too much, too fast, too often. The resulting damage is labeled *overuse*. *See also* injuries.

oxygen debt. The faster you run, the harder you breathe to keep up with the body's oxygen requirements. At a certain point you can't take in enough to satisfy those needs immediately. You must repay the debt after you slow down or stop. Runners can tolerate oxygen debt only for short distances. *See also* anaerobic threshold.

Paavo Nurmi Marathon (www.hurleywi.com). Finn-heavy northern Wisconsin has conducted this August race in Hurley since 1969, honoring Finland's greatest running hero. *See also* oldest races.

pace groups. "Rabbits" running to set the pace for leaders of a race have long been a familiar sight in the sport. A more valuable application of this concept is when an experienced pacer leads a group that is organized to run a specific time, as with the *Runner's World* pacing groups at various marathons and Team in Training pace groups. *See also* Team in Training.

pacing. Running is a rare sport because its participants must perfect the art of doing less than their best. That is, they don't run all out at any moment (except possibly in the homestretch) but instead ration their efforts over the entire distance. They pace themselves, in other words. Most of the best races are run at a pace that is nearly the same from mile to mile. *See also* negative splits; splits.

Paffenbarger, Dr. Ralph (b. October 21, 1922). The Stanford University epidemiologist is world renowned for his research linking regular exercise with longevity. He started running himself at age 45, ran near-three-hour marathons, and was one of the first Western States 100 finishers.

Page, Alan (b. August 7, 1945). In the late 1970s, then Chicago Bear Page, an eight-time all-pro defensive lineman, took up running with his wife, Diane. She had started running in an attempt to cut the withdrawal symptoms when she stopped smoking. Page—all six feet three inches and 222 pounds of him—kept expanding his range, and in 1979 he ran Grandma's Marathon in 3:57:39. When asked which was more challenging, football or the marathon, he said, "The marathon is far more physically demanding. Three hours and 57 minutes is a long time to be in motion." Eventually his off-season marathon-running hobby cost Page his job with the Minnesota Vikings because he lost too much weight to play football. Not to be deterred, the resourceful Page became a judge in the Twin Cities.

Pagliano, John (b. July 10, 1939). He was one of the first podiatrists to recognize what his profession had to offer runners. John brought a wealth of practical experiences as a marathoner and ultrarunner to his practice. He was one of the first sports medicine professionals to create a database of his patients, from which he drew information for numerous studies of runners and their injuries. He was also a pioneer in prescribing orthotics for injured runners. He continues to live and practice in southern California and writes a monthly column for *National Masters News*. See also *National Masters News*; podiatry.

Painter, Trina (b. June 24, 1966). She set the current American 20K record of 1:07:07 in 1995. Good as this mark is, it's overshadowed by the nearly-as-fast time that Joan Samuelson ran for the longer and more commonly contested half-marathon. *See also* records, American.

Palm, Evy (b. January 13, 1942). One of the first great masters runners, the Swede still ranks among the all-time best. No woman her age (47 at the time) or older has run a faster marathon than her 2:31:05 at the 1989 London Marathon.

© Mark Shearman, Athletics-Images.

In the early 1990s Poland's Wanda Panfil was nearly unbeatable. She won the 1991 World Championships and the 1991 Boston following 1990 wins at London and New York.

Palos Verdes Marathon (www.raceplace.com/pvmarathon). The hilly course on suburban L.A.'s Palos Verdes Peninsula has been the scene of this marathon since 1967. "P.V.," as it's known locally, is usually run in May. *See also* oldest races.

Pan-American Games (www.iaaf.org). A once-coveted opportunity to compete internationally has lost its luster in the pro era. The every-four-years meet brings together runners throughout the Americas.

Panfil, Wanda (b. January 26, 1959). As the 1990s began, no one in the world ran better marathons than did this Polish citizen. Topping her list of honors are the 1991 World Championship Marathon, a Boston win the same year, and London and New York titles in 1990. *See also* Boston Marathon; London Marathon; New York City Marathon; rankings, *Track & Field News*; World Championships.

Paris, France. Along with Athens, London, and Los Angeles, Paris is a two-time host of the Olympic Games. A

Pan-American Games Marathon Winners

The hemispheric meet provided Frank Shorter with his first marathon victory. Olga Appell won for Mexico before becoming an American citizen, and Maria Trujillo triumphed for the United States after she represented Mexico in the Olympics. * = event record.

WOMEN

Year	Place	Athlete	Time
1987	Indianapolis	Maricarmen Cardenas (Mexico)	2:52:06
1991	Havana	Olga Appell (Mexico)	2:43:36
1995	Mar del Plata	Maria Trujillo (U.S.)	2:43:56
1999	Winnipeg	Erika Olivera (Chile)	2:37:41*

MEN

Year	Place	Athlete	Time
1951	Buenos Aires	Delfo Cabrera (Argentina)	2:35:01
1955	Mexico City	Doroteo Flores (Guatemala)	2:59:10
1959	Chicago	John J. Kelley (U.S.)	2:27:55
1963	Sao Paulo	Fidel Negrete (Mexico)	2:27:56
1967	Winnipeg	Andy Boychuk (Canada)	2:23:03
1971	Cali	Frank Shorter (U.S.)	2:22:40
1975	Mexico City	Rigoberto Mendoza (Cuba)	2:25:03
1979	San Juan	Radames Gonzalez (Cuba)	2:24:09
1983	Caracas	Jorge Gonzales (Puerto Rico)	2:12:43*
1987	Indianapolis	Ivo Rodrigues (Brazil)	2:20:13
1991	Havana	Alberto Cuba (Cuba)	2:19:27
1995	Mar del Plata	Benjamin Paredes (Mexico)	2:14:44
1999	Winnipeg	Vanderlei Lima (Brazil)	2:17:20

Paris Marathon is now run each spring. *See also* Olympic Marathon, 1900 to 2000.

Parker, John (b. April 16, 1947). A teammate of Jack Bacheler, Frank Shorter, and Jeff Galloway in the heyday of the Florida Track Club, Parker graduated to writing and then to publishing. His 1994 book, *Once a Runner*, still ranks as one of the best running novels ever penned. He publishes books and distributes running titles under the company name Cedarwinds. *See also* books; Cedarwinds Publishing.

Paul, Wesley (b. January 25, 1969). The Missouri boy of Chinese descent was breaking four hours in the marathon at age seven, and three hours a few years later. As often happens with child stars, he vanished from the sport in his early teens. *See also* kids' running.

RUNNING ENCYCLOPEDIA

263

From the collection of Dr. Edward H. Kozloff–Motor City Striders

Rhode Island's Leslie Pawson arrived in Boston in 1938 and staged a classic duel with John A. Kelley; Pawson was stronger and won in 2:35:34.

Pawson, Leslie (b. February 3, 1905). The three-time Boston winner—1933, 1938, and 1941—had the misfortune of peaking at the wrong time to run in an Olympics. He qualified for the 1940 Games, which were canceled because of World War II. *See also* Hall of Fame, RRCA; Olympians, U.S.

PB. *See* personal record (PR).

Peachtree 10K (www.atlantatrackclub. org). A prototype for the megaraces to come, the race is traditionally run on the Fourth of July. The two original winners from 1970, Jeff Galloway and Gayle Barron, grew into giants of the sport. *See also* Barron, Gayle; biggest races; Galloway, Jeff.

Peachtree 10K Winners

Atlanta on July 4 is all but guaranteed to be steamy. Yet this race is the hottest ticket in town, filling to its 50,000 capacity months in advance. Note that future Olympian Jeff Galloway won the first race and that future Boston winner Gayle Barron collected five of the first six Peachtree titles. * = event record.

WOMEN

Year	Athlete	Time
1970	Gayle Barron (U.S.)	49:13
1971	Gayle Barron (U.S.)	45:17
1972	Gillian Valk (U.S.)	47:42
1973	Gayle Barron (U.S.)	40:37
1974	Gayle Barron (U.S.)	38:40
1975	Gayle Barron (U.S.)	38:04
1976	Janice Gage (U.S.)	39:13
1977	Peg Neppel (U.S.)	36:00
1978	Mary Decker (U.S.)	33:52
1979	Heather Carmichael (New Zealand)	33:39
1980	Patti Catalano (U.S.)	32:49
1981	Allison Roe (New Zealand)	32:39
1982	Anne Audain (New Zealand)	32:39
1983	Grete Waitz (Norway)	32:02

1984	Betty Springs (U.S.)	32:55
1985	Grete Waitz (Norway)	32:02
1986	Grete Waitz (Norway)	32:10
1987	Lynn Jennings (U.S.)	32:22
1988	Grete Waitz (Norway)	32:10
1989	Judi St. Hilaire (U.S.)	32:05
1990	Cathy O'Brien (U.S.)	32:04
1991	Dorthe Rasmussen (Denmark)	32:42
1992	Francie Larrieu Smith (U.S.)	31:49
1993	Uta Pippig (Germany)	32:15
1994	Anne Marie Letko (U.S.)	31:57
1995	Joan Nesbit (U.S.)	32:20
1996	Hellen Kimaiyo (Kenya)	30:52*
1997	Hellen Kimaiyo (Kenya)	31:21
1998	Hellen Kimaiyo (Kenya)	31:52
1999	Elana Meyer (South Africa)	31:34
2000	Lornah Kiplagat (Kenya)	30:52*
2001	Lornah Kiplagat (Kenya)	30:58

MEN

Year	Athlete	Time
1970	Jeff Galloway (U.S.)	32:22
1971	Bill Herron (U.S.)	30:58
1972	Scott Eden (U.S.)	31:10
1973	Bill Blewett (U.S.)	31:22
1974	Wayne Roach (U.S.)	30:47
1975	Ed Leddy (Ireland)	29:52
1976	Don Kardong (U.S.)	29:14
1977	Frank Shorter (U.S.)	29:20
1978	Mike Roche (U.S.)	29:00
1979	Craig Virgin (U.S.)	28:31
1980	Craig Virgin (U.S.)	28:40
1981	Craig Virgin (U.S.)	28:04
1982	Jon Sinclair (U.S.)	28:17
1983	Michael Musyoki (Kenya)	28:22
1984	Filbert Bayi (Tanzania)	28:35
1985	Michael Musyoki (Kenya)	27:58
1986	John Doherty (Ireland)	27:56
1987	Joseph Nzau (Kenya)	28:34
1988	J.P. Ndayisenga (Belgium)	28:17
1989	Ibrahim Hussein (Kenya)	28:13
1990	Dionicio Ceron (Mexico)	28:23
1991	Ed Eyestone (U.S.)	28:34
1992	Sammy Lelei (Kenya)	27:57
1993	Thomas Osano (Kenya)	28:05
1994	Benson Masya (Kenya)	28:01
1995	Simon Morolong (South Africa)	28:00
1996	Joseph Kimani (Kenya)	27:04*
1997	Joseph Kimani (Kenya)	27:53
1998	Khalid Khannouchi (Morocco)	27:47
1999	Khalid Khannouchi (Morocco)	27:45
2000	Alene Emere (Ethiopia)	28:04
2001	John Korir (Kenya)	28:19

Peak Running Performance (www.roadrunnersports.com). Guy Avery created this technical publication, which translates scientific findings into practical terms, then sold it to Road Runner Sports. *See also* Avery, Guy.

peaking. This involves aiming training and racing toward producing the best performances when they count the most. The masters of this technique have been coach Arthur Lydiard and multiple Olympic gold medalist Lasse Viren. *See also* Lydiard, Arthur; periodization; Viren, Lasse.

Penguin Brigade. *See* Bingham, John.

perceived exertion. Swedish psychophysiologist Gunnar Borg devised a measuring stick for estimating effort by using the runner's perception of how easy or hard the effort is. The 20-point Borg scale yields results similar to those calculated by heart monitors.

periodization. The tongue-twisting word *periodization* identifies a method of focusing on different types and intensities of training and racing at different times of the year. The system got a big push from Arthur Lydiard in the 1960s when the runners he coached won Olympic medals and set records. Their training plan was structured through a prescribed set of training periods, each with a different emphasis: endurance and base work, followed by hill training, speed building, and finally the peak racing season. *See also* Lydiard, Arthur; peaking.

personal best (PB). *See* personal record.

personal record (PR). In this case, PR doesn't stand for either public relations or Puerto Rico, but for personal record. It's the holy grail of all racers, known as PB (personal best) outside the United States. It gives them the possibility of winning no matter where they finish. The digital watch has been a great boon to checking PRs instantly and accurately. *See also* watches, digital.

Petersen, Sue (b. September 6, 1944). A frequent racer and sometimes big winner in the early years of women's marathoning, the Californian won the 1979 national title in 2:46:17 and Chicago in 1980 (2:45:03). She often ran with her husband, the two of them wearing matching running outfits. *See also* Chicago Marathon; national marathon champions, U.S.

Peters, Jim. *See* next page.

Pfeffer, Kirk (b. July 30, 1956). Injuries kept him from realizing his vast potential as a marathoner, but he held the American half-marathon record twice (1:02:32 in 1979 and 1:02:14 in 1981) and was the first from his country to break 1:03. His normal marathon strategy was to go out at a suicidal pace and hope that he could hold on longer than the competition. He was, for example, on world-record pace at the 1979 New York City Marathon on a day when no one could have kept up the pace in the unseasonable heat. *See also* record progressions, American.

Peters, Jim (b. October 24, 1918). Great Britain's Jim Peters is famous in road-racing circles as the staggering, overheated runner who nearly won the Commonwealth Games Marathon in Vancouver, Canada, in 1954. Always one to go out fast and control the pace, Jim started fast on an exceedingly hot day on a hilly course and entered the stadium with an overheated brain. He wobbled first in one direction, then the other, while the crowd watched, enthralled and appalled at the same time. He staggered and fell, then picked himself up only to fall again. In some 11 minutes inside the stadium, Jim Peters covered all of 180 yards. Officials stood by helplessly, not wanting to repeat what had happened at the 1908 Olympics when the Italian Dorando Pietri had been assisted to the finish and hence disqualified. But when Peters was 200 yards from the finish, the masseur of the British team walked onto the track and carried him off. He was taken to a Vancouver hospital and put into a bed next to marathon teammate Stan Cox who, in the confusion brought on by the heat, had run headlong into a steel telephone pole.

The incident effectively ended the running career of Jim Peters. He retired from running, studied optometry, and opened a shop in London. The career that wound down in the wake of the Vancouver incident was one of the most brilliant of any runner in history. Four times Jim Peters lowered the world marathon mark. He was the first human being to run the marathon in less than 2:25 and 2:20.

Born to a poor family (his father was a railroad worker) in Homerton in east London, his running talent emerged as a byproduct of his soccer. He first shone as a middle-distance runner, but his coach, Johnny Johnson, moved him up to longer distances, where he excelled. He won the English national title in the 6-mile (predecessor of the 10K) in 1946 and took the 10-mile title in 1947. His local prowess didn't translate at that point onto the world stage, however. He went to the 1948 Olympic Games as a 10,000-meter runner, only to be embarrassed by being lapped by Emil Zatopek.

Peters retired at age 29, but his coach lured him back into running, insisting that Peters's true talents lay in the very long distances. Jim ran in relative obscurity, racing seldom, training intensely. "At lunch time, I would go to a track and run six miles, working against the clock until I could run five-minute miles," he recalled. "Then at night I would run 10 miles at a 5:15 pace." He became famous for his rolling gait and his training to hold his breath as a means of increasing his lung size. The 2:25 barrier in the marathon had not yet been broken. Johnson and Peters, however, were training to have Jim break 2:20.

In the spring of 1951 Peters ran several shorter road races; he won the Wigmore 15 in 1:26:55. The following month he won the Essex 20 in 1:47:08. One of the most important marathons of the era was the Polytechnic Marathon (from Windsor Castle to Chiswick). Jim was entered in the 1951 Polytechnic, as was the reigning marathon king in England, Jack Holden, who had beaten Jim in the Finchley 20-mile a few months before. As was his strategy, Jim went out fast, but the older Holden stuck right with him. At 13 miles Holden threw in a surge and by 18 miles had a 200-yard lead. But Jim fought back, passed Holden, and went on to win in 2:29:28, a British record. His closest rival was five minutes back. Five weeks later he entered the tough and hilly AAA championship at Perry Barr in Birmingham, where he ran 2:31:42, again five minutes ahead of the second-place finisher.

The 1952 Polytechnic Marathon was also the AAA championships and the qualifier for the Olympic Games. Jim ran an astounding 2:20:43, lowering the world-best marathon mark by almost five minutes. The course was remeasured and found to be 260 yards too long! Peters's performance at the Helsinki Olympics was unsatisfactory, however. His archrival, Emil Zatopek, defeated Peters after Jim had been transported to the Games in a drafty converted military plane. But Jim was not embarrassed enough to quit the sport.

His 1953 marathon rampage was exquisite. At the Polytechnic in June he finally broke 2:20 with a 2:18:41 on a course found to be 156 yards too long. At the British championships at Cardiff on July 25, in a rainstorm, he ran 2:22:29, a world record for an out-and-back course. At the fourth annual Enschede Marathon in the Netherlands in September, he ran 2:19:22, another world record for an out-and-back course. Three weeks later he was in Finland for the Turku Marathon, where he broke his own world record by six seconds with a 2:18:35; the second-place finisher was seven minutes back. At the 1954 Poly, he lowered his record to 2:17:40.

Then came his near-fatal day at Vancouver in 1954. Jim felt he was capable of 2:15 under perfect conditions, and even in the overwhelming heat he was on pace for a 2:20 finish. But the fates were against him. With the promise of heat at the Melbourne Games in 1956, Jim gave up marathoning. Two decades later, when asked what he'd like to see different about his career, he was as blunt as always: "I'd be a hypocrite if I didn't say it. But I wish there'd been some money in it." *See also* rankings, *Track & Field News*; record progressions, world.

Pfitzinger, Pete (b. August 29, 1957). Having learned from the New Zealanders (his wife, Chris, is one), he knew how to peak at exactly the right time. Pfitzinger was a two-time Olympic marathoner—and both times the leading American finisher, with an 11th in Los Angeles and a 14th in Seoul. He previewed his Olympian future by winning the 1983 national marathon title; he won San Francisco that year and again in 1986. The next year he took third at New York City. In 1984 he was ranked as America's number-one marathoner by *Track & Field News*, received the DeCelle Award as America's best distance runner, and was voted Runner of the Year by the Road Runner's Club of America.

Pete holds an MBA degree in marketing from Cornell University and an MS in exercise science from the University of Massachusetts, Amherst—which he puts to good use as the manager of UniSports Centre for Sport Performance in Auckland, New Zealand. He is the author (with Scott Douglas) of two books, *Road Racing for Serious Runners* (Human Kinetics, 1999) and *Advanced Marathoning* (Human Kinetics, 2001). He also writes a column, "The Pfitzinger Lab Report," for *Running Times* magazine. *See also* Hall of Fame, RRCA; national marathon champions, U.S.; Olympians, U.S.; Olympic Trials Marathon, U.S.

Pheidippides (also spelled Phidippides). This Greek hemerodromos (messenger) was the marathon's patron saint. Legend has him dying at the gates of Athens after running from the Plain of Marathon some 25 miles away to announce victory over the invading Persians. But he was too good a runner for that fate. Earlier in the campaign he had run to Sparta and back (roughly 300 miles) to sue for assistance against the Persians. The legend of his dying at the gates of Athens was concocted several hundred years after the fact. In fact, it was likely some other runner who bore the message of victory to Athens, and likely that he also made the trip successfully. That was, after all, the messenger's job.

Phidippides. Under this alternative spelling, Jeff Galloway wove together in the 1970s and 1980s an impressive franchise system of running stores across the United States. Although the chain was broken up in the 1980s, there are still several independently owned Phidippides stores, and Jeff himself still owns the original in Atlanta. *See also* Galloway, Jeff.

Philadelphia Distance Classic. Record half-marathons set here include the current—and long-standing—U.S. marks of 1:00:55 by Mark Curp and 1:08:34 by Joan Benoit Samuelson. The race is run in September. *See also* record progressions, American; record progressions, world; records, American.

Philadelphia Marathon (www.philadelphiamarathon.com). Long before Philadelphia's prestigious half-marathon began, the city had an annual marathon, now run in November. It reaches all the way back to 1954. *See also* oldest races.

Piercy, Violet (birthdate unavailable). Women have finished marathons for at least three-quarters of a century. The Brit is generally credited as the first record-holder in the women's marathon and the first to break four hours, with 3:40:22 in 1926. *See also* record progressions, world.

Pietri, Dorando (b. October 16, 1885). The gutsy Italian runner came into London Olympic stadium (1908) in the lead, repeatedly collapsed, and was disqualified when he was helped up. This allowed the American Johnny Hayes to step in as gold medalist. *See also* Hayes, Johnny; London 1908.

Pikes Peak Marathon (www.pikespeakmarathon.org). It isn't a road race but a mountain climb, and it isn't a marathon because it is as much as two miles longer. But we cite it here as one of the oldest U.S. races at (approximately) this distance, first run in 1956. The event is actually two races, run on

From the collection of Dr. Edward H. Kozloff–Motor City Striders

One of the great Olympic marathon finishes: Dorando Pietri is helped across the finish line in 1908 at London and is disqualified.

successive days in August. The first is the ascent, which climbs to the peak and takes about as long to complete as a standard marathon. The second race, the up-and-down marathon, is an ultra in time and effort. *See* oddest races; oldest races.

Pilkington, Paul (b. October 12, 1958). He's best remembered as the rabbit who went on to win the 1994 Los Angeles Marathon, the national marathon championship that year. Ironically, he DNFed in his one major international championship race, the 1995 Worlds. *See also* Los Angeles Marathon; national marathon champions, U.S.; rabbits; World Championships, U.S.

Pinkowski, Carey (b. June 30, 1957). A one-time high school star who broke nine minutes for two miles, he later ran at Villanova. His big contribution, though, has come as the director who in the late 1980s restored the struggling Chicago Marathon to its former glory—and then far exceeded it. *See also* Chicago Marathon.

Pinto, Antonio (b. March 22, 1966). Europe's fastest marathoner ran 2:06:36 while winning his third London Marathon in 2000, complementing his wins in 1992 and 1997. The Portuguese runner also won 1994 Berlin. *See* Berlin Marathon; London Marathon.

Pippig, Uta. *See* page next page.

Pitayo, Martin (b. January 10, 1960). The Mexican was a frequent victor in the United States in his prime racing years. His best year was 1990, when he won the Bolder Boulder 10K and the Chicago Marathon. *See also* Bolder Boulder 10K; Chicago Marathon; rankings, *Runner's World*.

pit stops. These don't have the same meaning to runners as they do to auto racers. A runner's pit stops aren't for repairs or refueling but for answering nature's calls.

Pittsburgh, Pennsylvania. The city hosted the 1988 women's and 2000 men's U.S. Olympic Trials Marathons. It's also home to the annual Pittsburgh Marathon and the superfast Great Race 10K. *See also* Great Race 10K; Olympic Trials Marathon, U.S.

Pizzolato, Orlando (b. July 30, 1958). A two-time winner at the New York City Marathon (1984 and 1985), the Italian was so dominant in one of his victories that he had time to stop repeatedly to work out cramps. *See also* New York City Marathon.

Plaatjes, Mark (b. June 2, 1962). Born in South Africa, he ran his best marathon time of 2:08:59 there. But his mixed-race heritage denied him opportunity in that country, and his South African citizenship denied it abroad during the apartheid years. He emigrated to the United States, became a citizen, and won the marathon at the 1993 World Championships. He's still the only U.S. marathon gold medalist in that event. *See also* Los Angeles Marathon; World Championships, U.S.; World Championships medalists.

Pippig, Uta (b. September 7, 1965). It would be difficult to think of a female runner who has so charmed the sports-crazy Boston crowds as Uta Pippig, an escapee from East Germany and three-time winner at Boston (1994, 1995, and 1996). Her unrestrained joy at running in the lead at Boston was at once infectious and charming, and Bostonians took her to their hearts as one of their own. It was particularly devastating to her Boston fans when, in 1998, it was announced that she had been suspended by her German federation for testing positive for performance-enhancing drugs. Athletes who use performance-enhancing drugs appear mannish and unlovely to fans; these descriptions never applied to the lovely Uta.

Uta Pippig and her coach (and later husband) Dieter Hogen escaped from East Germany to West Berlin in January 1990. Uta is one of a handful of female road racers who burst onto the scene in the 1990s after the tremendous surge in women's running in the 1980s. In winning Boston in 1994, she ran 2:21:45, the third fastest marathon ever by a woman at that time. She was 28 years old then, still looking forward to what are considered prime years for a marathoner. Many observers felt she would be the first female to dip below the 2:20 barrier, and she certainly made some heroic attempts.

Uta had been launched as a marathoner at an early age but didn't mature into the role until much later. Not long after she and Dieter escaped from East Germany, she traveled to Boston and took second place in the 1990 race, in 2:28:03. That September the Berlin Marathon would be a very special event. The Berlin Wall had come down earlier in the year (not long after Uta escaped), and for the first time the course of the Berlin Marathon would venture onto East German soil. Uta Pippig, so recently an East German, won the race in 2:28:37. In 1991 she returned to Boston, and although she ran faster than the previous year (2:26:52), she finished third—just in

Uta Pippig of East Germany became the darling of Boston, where she won three years in a row (1994 to 1996), and her enthusiasm won thousands of fans. In 1998 her German federation suspended her on drug charges.

© Mark Shearman, Athletics-Images

front of Joan Samuelson. Uta returned to Boston in 1992 and again took third, this time with a 2:27:12.

In 1993 she focused on the World Championships in Stuttgart. To get some races on her legs, she traveled to America and competed in a series of road races. But when her time came to race the 10,000 meters in Stuttgart, she went in tired and finished ninth. She and Dieter bought a house in Boulder, Colorado, where she began picking up her training volume for New York City. Under hot conditions, she won by 2½ minutes in 2:26:24.

She spent the winter cross-country skiing in Germany and attempted to rest before refiring her hard training program toward Boston 1994. To test herself, Uta ran the Kyoto, Japan, half-marathon in February. Her time of 1:07:59 indicated that she was in good shape with speed to spare. In Boston to prepare for the marathon, she caught a cold, so she ran conservatively in the middle miles, then lowered the boom. She finished in 2:21:45, her PR and the Boston women's record. Her accomplishment brought her instant media fame, and her friendly, outgoing style combined with her attractiveness didn't slow her down. But the media demands cut into her racing and resting. She had studied to be a doctor in East Germany, but little beyond physics transferred to the Western world, so for several years she restudied for a medical degree. She put her studies on hold, however, when she set off in pursuit of the elusive sub-2:20.

Back at Kyoto in February 1995, she ran one second faster in the half-marathon than she had the year before. At Boston again, she faced a headwind that made a run for the record impractical. She went instead for the win and finished in 2:25:11. In September she won the Berlin Marathon for the third time with a 2:25:37. She returned to Boston for the 100th running in 1996 and won for the third time in 2:27:12 in spite of gastrointestinal troubles reputed to be a perforated intestine. Uta represented Germany in the Olympic Marathon in Atlanta where she went out fast, hoping to break the field early, but a leg injury forced her to drop out. She finished fourth at Boston in 1997 with a 2:28:51 in spite of an injured leg, then took time off from racing in hopes of allowing herself time to recover fully.

The German Athletics Association administered an unannounced out-of-competition test on her in late October 1998 while she was in Boulder, Colorado, and suspended her for an abnormally high ratio of testosterone. When her suspension ended in 2000, she began a comeback by entering some minor road races to test her fitness and speed while in the process of pursuing American citizenship. *See also* Berlin Marathon; Boston Marathon; New York City Marathon; rankings, *Track & Field News*; record progressions, world.

plantar fasciitis. One of the most common and persistent of running injuries, plantar fasciitis affects the arch and heel of the foot. It is associated with an inflammation or tear of the plantar fascia along the bottom of the foot. *See also* injuries.

Plasencia, Steve (b. October 28, 1956). As one of America's most durable runners, he competed at high levels for nearly 20 years. Steve is the oldest American to run in the World Championships Marathon, placing 10th in 1995 at age 38. He set 40-plus American records for the 5K (14:25), 10K (29:37), and half-marathon (1:05:27) and now coaches at the University of Minnesota. *See also* records, American age-group; World Championships, U.S.

Plumer, PattiSue (b. April 27, 1962). The track Olympian also dabbled in road racing, where she merely set world and American 5K records with 15:31 in 1986. *See also* record progressions, American; record progressions, world.

podiatry. The foot docs became runners' first line of defense against injuries in the 1970s. Specialists such as Richard Schuster, John Pagliano, Steve Subotnick, and Joe Ellis often prescribed orthotics to compensate for irregularities in biomechanics. *See also* injuries; orthotics; Pagliano, John; Subotnick, Dr. Steve.

Polar (www.polarusa.com). The company is the most prominent producer of heart-rate monitors, which runners have adopted in growing numbers as a way to measure effort and intensity of their training. *See also* heart-rate monitor.

Poli, Gianni (b. November 5, 1957). He gave Italy its third straight victory at the New York City Marathon in 1986 (after Orlando Pizzolato won in 1984 and 1985). Poli ran 2:11:06 in New York, then won Honolulu two years later with 2:12:47. *See also* New York City Marathon; Honolulu Marathon; Pizzolato, Orlando.

polypropylene. The miracle fabric introduced in the early 1980s helped revolutionize distance runners' clothing by providing a lightweight, breathable fabric that wicks moisture from the skin. *See also* clothing.

Polytechnic Marathon. The "Poly," one of the world's greatest races for much of the 20th century, generally followed the route of the 1908 Olympic Marathon. Six world records were set here between 1952 and 1965, three of them by Jim Peters and one by Buddy Edelen. *See also* Edelen, Leonard "Buddy"; Peters, Jim; record progressions, American; record progressions, world.

Popov, Sergey (b. September 21, 1930). The Soviet runner set a world marathon record of 2:15:17 when he won the European title in 1958. He went into the Rome Olympics as the favorite. Then along came Abebe Bikila, who tied Popov's world record while winning the first of two Olympic golds in the event. *See also* European Championships; rankings, *Track & Field News;* record progressions, world.

Porter, Mel (birthdate unavailable). The RRCA Hall of Famer won national marathon titles in 1933 (with 2:53:46), 1934 (2:48:04), and 1937 (2:44:22). *See also* Hall of Fame, RRCA; national marathon champions, U.S.

Porter, Pat (b. May 31, 1959). America's winningest cross country runner in national meets (with eight titles in a row) could also tear up the roads. He was the first U.S. runner to break 14:00 at 5K, with 13:46 in 1986. *See also* record progressions, American.

Portland Marathon (www.portlandmarathon.org). The Oregon race is a model of efficient organization, without a big budget, paid staff, or pro runners. Attorney Les Smith oversees the operation and conducts a how-to seminar for race directors on Friday and Saturday of race weekend. *See also* Smith, Les.

postmarathon syndrome. This form of PMS appears first as muscle soreness lasting several days. A period of weariness that can last for weeks or even months follows. The entire period of this syndrome is also known as the postmarathon blues. *See also* delayed-onset muscle soreness.

PowerBar (www.powerbar.com). Brian Maxwell, a Canadian Olympian and coach at the University of California at Berkeley, founded a company that pioneered sports bars and later spun off related products. Maxwell sold to Nestlé in 2000 for reportedly $100 million. PowerBars supplied a large dose of easily digested carbohydrates in a convenient form for eating before, during, or after runs. *See also* Maxwell, Brian.

PR. *See* personal record.

Prasad, Nadia (b. October 6, 1967). As a French citizen she won the Bolder Boulder 10K in 1994 (33:28 at high altitude) and the Los Angeles Marathon in 1995 (2:29:48). She has since become a U.S. citizen and lives in Boulder. *See also* Bolder Boulder 10K; Los Angeles Marathon.

Prefontaine, Steve (b. January 25, 1951, d. May 30, 1975). As far as we are able to determine, he never ran a road race. But "Pre" almost surely would have gone looking for new challenges—and wealth—on the roads if he'd lived into his 30s and 40s. A guiding spirit of Nike, Pre became the center of an entire industry after his death. He has been the subject of two dramatic movies, a documentary film, and the biography *Pre!* by Tom Jordan (Tafnews, 1977). *See also* Hall of Fame, National Distance Running; Hall of Fame, RRCA.

Preisler, Horst (b. 1935). The world's most prolific marathoner, the German reached 1,000 races of this distance or beyond at the Berlin Marathon in 2000. Up to that point he had averaged 38 marathons and ultras a year. *See also* streakers.

products for runners. Runners are always looking for the winning edge, and marketers are always willing to hold out the promise of better performance by hawking various products. Fortunately, running is a very simple sport, so deliciously outrageous items don't usually make it. All a runner really needs are some comfortable clothes and a good pair of running shoes.

Over the years, though, there have been some unusual products offered. One of our favorites was the Bone Fone, a pair of speakers that draped over a runner's shoulders much like a heavyweight scarf. Before the Sony Walkman walked all over the competition, you could buy the Cronus Strider, a miniradio that attached to your running shorts and featured a single hearing-aid-like phone on a wire. It wasn't stereo like the Bone Fone, but it was much more compact, less expensive, and less obvious.

Before there were heart-rate monitors, there was Genesis. Marketed by Biometrics of Minneapolis, Genesis strapped around your wrist and looked like Dick Tracy's wrist radio. A heart-beat monitor slipped over one of your fingers and connected to the wrist controller by a wire. The shortcoming was that this was still the Dark Ages of electronics (1980), and the digital numbers worked just fine—as long as you didn't move. Once you started running, the Genesis threw fits trying to calibrate fast enough to produce a meaningful reading.

Most of the worthless products did not come in the form of an honest yet misdirected effort to produce a better product, but rather in the form of some sort of oral supplement that was going to knock significant time off your PR. On the upside, many of the advances in products for runners (carbohydrate replacement drinks, energy bars, energy gels, digital watches, Gore-Tex, air soles, reflective gear, etc.) not only helped running but also eventually expanded to a more general market where they were accepted, in part, because they'd first been road tested in marathons. *See also* Bone Fone; Gore-Tex; Walkman.

professional racing. Dashing for cash isn't new. As long as runners have raced each other, some have run for the money. Marathons of the early 1900s awarded prize purses. More recently, invitational races paid runners under the table as far back as the 1970s (and maybe earlier). Payments began to be made openly in the early 1980s, thanks in large part to the efforts of the Association of Road Racing Athletes (ARRA) as well as a relaxing of amateur rules. *See also* Association of Road Racing Athletes.

Professional Road Running Organization (www.prro.org). The latest incarnation of ARRA, this group promotes the interests of the pros. The Peachtree 10K serves as the permanent site of the final race, subtitled the "Race of Champions." *See also* Association of Road Racing Athletes.

progressions of records. *See* record progressions, American; record progressions, world.

pronation. This term, introduced to the running public by Dr. George Sheehan in the early 1970s, brought podiatrists into the mainstream of sports medicine. Pronation is an inward rolling of the foot when the foot strikes the ground while running. Some of this motion is normal, but in excess it sets up the runner for a wide range of injuries. *See also* injuries; podiatry.

PRRO. *See* Professional Road Running Organization.

publications. The monthly *Runner's World* magazine, with a circulation topping a half million, is the major publication in the world for road racers. *FootNotes*, the quarterly magazine of the Road Runners Club of America, has a circulation of roughly 150,000 and is read avidly by RRCA members. Also a player is *Running Times*, which has been published since the 1970s. *Marathon & Beyond*, the new kid on the block (1997), covers marathons. Also prominent is *National Masters News*, a monthly tabloid covering masters road racing and track and field. *Peak Running Performance* and *Running Research News* are journals reporting on cutting-edge training methods and scientific material about running. *Running Stats* and *Race Results Weekly* report the happenings at races. *Running & Fit News* is the official monthly newsletter of the American Running Association and carries medical and training news for runners. The sport is also blessed with a number of regional magazines and club newsletters. See also *FootNotes; National Masters News; Peak Running Performance; Race Results Weekly; Runner's Gazette; Runner's World; Running & Fit News; Running Stats; Running Research News; Running Times*.

pulse rate. *See* heart-rate monitor.

Puma (www.puma.com). The German shoe company was at one time a fierce rival of adidas when the two companies were owned by feuding brothers. In the race for dominance of the road-shoe field, Puma has never been more than an also-ran. *See also* shoe companies.

Q

qualifying times. The sport of road running as a whole has largely resisted imposing entry times on runners. Anyone who enters soon enough can run, and anyone who betters a cutoff time can finish. Two exceptions in the United States are the Boston Marathon, which has limited entries by time for more than 30 years to control the size of field, and the Olympic Trials, which has set standards for almost that long to allow only truly qualified contenders for the team to compete.

quality training. This term, referring to training at a high level of intensity, is a backhanded slap at any running done at lower effort. We don't talk of the opposite of quality training as "quantity training"; we refer to it as "junk mileage" or "LSD". *See also* junk miles; long slow distance.

Quax, Dick (b. January 1, 1948). Like fellow New Zealander Rod Dixon, Quax showed a great range of talent in his running. He was an Olympic silver medalist in the 5,000 meters, a sub-4:00 miler, and later a 2:10 marathoner. In September 1979 at the Nike–Oregon Track Club Marathon in Eugene, Dick ran his first marathon. Observers of the sport assumed that an Olympic track medalist would jog through the marathon to get a feel for it. Instead he ran the fastest first marathon in history—2:11:13.

© Mark Shearman, Athletics–Images.

New Zealand's Dick Quax was a big man and a powerful runner. He took silver at the Olympic 5,000 meters and later knocked off a 2:10 marathon, showing a tremendous range of talent.

"This was just an experiment," he stated after his debut. "I still want to run both the 10,000 and the marathon at Moscow." But Quax had two strikes against him. New Zealand had a very strenuous qualifying standard; before a runner would even be considered for the team, he was required to break 2:13 twice. Then there was the matter of the boycott of the Moscow Games by the United States and most of its allies. Quax later became a successful coach, one of many who worked with Mary Decker Slaney during their years with the Nike-sponsored club Athletics West. *See also* Athletics West; Dixon, Rod; Slaney, Mary Decker Tabb.

R

rabbits. Races hire these two-legged bunnies to ensure a fast pace up front. This practice has led to controversy when men pace women, as in Tegla Loroupe's 1998 world-record race at Rotterdam, and when the rabbit goes on to win the race, as Paul Pilkington did at the 1994 Los Angeles Marathon. *See also* Loroupe, Tegla; pace groups; Pilkington, Paul.

Race for the Cure (www.raceforthecure.com). One of the most successful fund-raising series, it draws tens of thousands of runners and walkers (most of them women) to its races in some cities. Race for the Cure events attract attention to and funds for breast-cancer research. The largest are run in Washington, D.C., and Portland, Oregon. These runs, held in dozens of U.S. cities, were the brainchild of the Susan B. Komen Foundation. In Canada a similar series is called Run for the Cure. *See also* biggest races; charity races.

Race of Champions (www.harriers.org). The second-oldest marathon in Massachusetts (after Boston), the Race of Champions in Holyoke has been a fixture on the New England schedule since 1963. The race is run in May, a few weeks after the Boston Marathon. *See also* oldest races.

Race Results Weekly (www.raceresultsweekly.com). New York City runner David Monti was first to offer a complete and current set of results online. His subscription newsletter is e-mailed most Mondays of the year; this is followed by a midweek update. *See also* Monti, David; publications.

racing distances. *See* distances, metric and English.

racing flats. Now fading from the runners' vocabulary, *flats* is an old term used to distinguish these models from spiked shoes used by track annd cross country runners. Some longtime road runners still refer to their lightweight racing shoes by this name.

Radcliffe, Paula (b. December 17, 1973). After setting the pace, and a PR, in the 2000 Sydney Olympic 10,000 meters, the British woman came back to win the World Half-Marathon. She repeated the win in 2001. Radcliffe set the current world 8K road record of 24:38 in 1999 and ended her summer 2001 track season by jumping into a 5Kroad race—where she set a world record of 14:57 on an unaided course. She's an outspoken advocate of stricter drug

One of the rising stars of road and track, Paula Radcliffe of England won the 2000 World Half-Marathon Championships. At Sydney, she took the field out in the 10,000 meters and hung on for a PR.

testing in distance running. *See also* records, world; World Half-Marathon Championships.

Raines, Albert (birthdate unavailable). A world record is a world record, even when you hold it for less than three weeks. Raines, an American, set the marathon mark of 2:46:05 in May 1909, only to lose it to Henry Barrett of Britain later that month. *See also* record progressions, American; record progressions, world.

Rainsberger, Lisa. *See* Weidenbach, Lisa Larsen.

rankings, *Runner's World* (www.runnersworld.com). *The Runner* magazine started these rankings in the late 1970s; *RW* continued them when the magazines merged. These are the leaders for races (at any road race distance) run in the United States each year, even if the runners come—as they usually do—from outside the country.

rankings, *Track & Field News* (www.trackandfieldnews.com). The venerable magazine has ranked the world's marathoners since *T&FN* launched, more than 50 years ago.

Runner's World Road Rankings

Annual rankings are based largely on road races run in the United States but are open to athletes from all countries who run here. *The Runner* magazine began naming the top man and woman in 1979 (masters men in 1980 and masters women in 1981), and the practice continued when that magazine joined *Runner's World* several years later.

Year	Men	Women
1979	Bill Rodgers (U.S.)	Joan Benoit (U.S.)
1980	Herb Lindsay (U.S.)	Patti Catalano (U.S.)
1981	Herb Lindsay (U.S.)	Patti Catalano (U.S.)
1982	Mike Musyoki (Kenya)	Joan Benoit (U.S.)
1983	Joseph Nzau (Kenya)	Grete Waitz (Norway)
1984	Zakariah Barie (Tanzania)	Grete Waitz (Norway)
1985	Simeon Kigen (Kenya)	Grete Waitz (Norway)
1986	Arturo Barrios (Mexico)	Ingrid Kristiansen (Norway)
1987	Mark Curp (U.S.)	Teresa Ornduff (U.S.)
1988	Mark Curp (U.S.)	Lisa Weidenbach (U.S.)
1989	John Halvorsen (Norway)	Ingrid Kristiansen (Norway)
1990	Martin Pitayo (Mexico)	Maria Trujillo (U.S.)
1991	Steve Kogo (Kenya)	Jill Hunter (Britain)
1992	Alejandro Cruz (Mexico)	Olga Markova (Russia)
1993	Thomas Osano (Kenya)	Colleen de Reuck (South Africa)
1994	Benson Masya (Kenya)	Anne Marie Letko (U.S.)
1995	Phillimon Hanneck (Zimbabwe)	Delillah Asiago (Kenya)
1996	Lazarus Nyakeraka (Kenya)	Catherine Ndereba (Kenya)
1997	Khalid Khannouchi (Morocco)	Colleen de Reuck (South Africa)
1998	Hezron Otwori (Kenya)	Catherine Ndereba (Kenya)
1999	John Korir (Kenya)	Catherine Ndereba (Kenya)
2000	Reuben Cheruiyot (Kenya)	Catherine Ndereba (Kenya)

Year	Masters Men	Masters Women
1980	Roger Robinson (New Zealand)	none selected
1981	Herb Lorenz (U.S.)	Karen Scannell (U.S.)
1982	Dan Conway (U.S.)	Cindy Dalrymple (U.S.)
1983	George Keim (U.S.)	Cindy Dalrymple (U.S.)
1984	Don Coffman (U.S.)	Cindy Dalrymple (U.S.)
1985	Barry Brown (U.S.)	Priscilla Welch (Britain)
1986	Mike Hurd (Britain)	Priscilla Welch (Britain)
1987	Mike Hurd (Britain)	Gabriele Andersen (U.S.)
1988	Bob Schlau (U.S.)	Barbara Filutze (U.S.)
1989	Wilson Waigwa (Kenya)	Laurie Binder (U.S.)
1990	John Campbell (New Zealand)	Priscilla Welch (Britain)
1991	John Campbell (New Zealand)	Laurie Binder (U.S.)
1992	Pierre Levisse (France)	Nancy Grayson (U.S.)
1993	Nick Rose (Britain)	Carol McLatchie (U.S.)
1994	Martin Mondragon (Mexico)	Suzanne Ray (U.S.)
1995	Martin Mondragon (Mexico)	Lorraine Moller (New Zealand)
1996	Antoni Niemczak (Poland)	Jane Welzel (U.S.)
1997	Craig Young (U.S.)	Jane Welzel (U.S.)
1998	Peter Koech (Kenya)	Tatyana Pozdnyakova (Ukraine)
1999	John Tuttle (U.S.)	Tatyana Pozdnyakova (Ukraine)
2000	Simon Karori (Kenya)	Tatyana Pozdnyakova (Ukraine)

Track & Field News World Marathon Rankings

Track & Field News has ranked the world's top 10 athletes in all track and field events since the 1940s for men and since the 1970s for women. These ratings are based more on competitive records than on fast times, though the two factors often go together. Here are the number-one ranked marathoners year by year.

WOMEN

Year	Athlete	Country
1976	Christa Vahlensieck	West Germany
1977	Christa Vahlensieck	West Germany
1978	Grete Waitz	Norway
1979	Grete Waitz	Norway
1980	Grete Waitz	Norway
1981	Allison Roe	New Zealand
1982	Grete Waitz	Norway
1983	Grete Waitz	Norway
1984	Joan Benoit	U.S.
1985	Joan Samuelson	U.S.
1986	Grete Waitz	Norway
1987	Rosa Mota	Portugal
1988	Rosa Mota	Portugal
1989	Ingrid Kristiansen	Norway
1990	Rosa Mota	Portugal
1991	Wanda Panfil	Poland
1992	Valentina Yegorova	Russia
1993	Junko Asari	Japan
1994	Uta Pippig	Germany
1995	Uta Pippig	Germany
1996	Fatuma Roba	Ethiopia
1997	Hiromi Suzuki	Japan
1998	Catherina McKiernan	Ireland
1999	Tegla Loroupe	Kenya
2000	Naoko Takahashi	Japan

MEN

Year	Athlete	Country
1947	Yun Bok Suh	Korea
1948	Delfo Cabrera	Argentina
1949	Martti Urpalainen	Finland
1950	Jack Holden	Britain
1951	Veikko Karvonen	Finland
1952	Emil Zatopek	Czechoslovakia
1953	Jim Peters	Britain
1954	Veikko Karvonen	Finland

Year	Athlete	Country
1955	Veikko Karvonen	Finland
1956	Alain Mimoun	France
1957	Franjo Mihalic	Yugoslavia
1958	Sergey Popov	USSR
1959	Eino Oksanen	Finland
1960	Abebe Bikila	Ethiopia
1961	Abebe Bikila	Ethiopia
1962	Brian Kilby	Britain
1963	Buddy Edelen	U.S.
1964	Abebe Bikila	Ethiopia
1965	Morio Shigematsu	Japan
1966	Mike Ryan	New Zealand
1967	Derek Clayton	Australia
1968	Bill Adcocks	Britain
1969	Jerome Drayton	Canada
1970	Ron Hill	Britain
1971	Frank Shorter	U.S.
1972	Frank Shorter	U.S.
1973	Frank Shorter	U.S.
1974	Ian Thompson	Britain
1975	Bill Rodgers	U.S.
1976	Waldemar Cierpinski	East Germany
1977	Bill Rodgers	U.S.
1978	Leonid Moiseyev	USSR
1979	Bill Rodgers	U.S.
1980	Waldemar Cierpinski	East Germany
1981	Alberto Salazar	U.S.
1982	Alberto Salazar	U.S.
1983	Rob de Castella	Australia
1984	Carlos Lopes	Portugal
1985	Steve Jones	Britain
1986	Juma Ikangaa	Tanzania
1987	Takeyuki Nakayama	Japan
1988	Belayneh Dinsamo	Ethiopia
1989	Juma Ikangaa	Tanzania
1990	Gelindo Bordin	Italy
1991	Hiromi Taniguchi	Japan
1992	Hwang Young Cho	Korea
1993	Dionicio Ceron	Mexico
1994	Steve Moneghetti	Australia
1995	Martin Fiz	Spain
1996	Lee Bong Ju	Korea
1997	Abel Anton	Spain
1998	Ondoro Osoro	Kenya
1999	Joseph Chebet	Kenya
2000	Gezahegne Abera	Ethiopia

Ratelle, Alex (b. September 12, 1924). The Minnesota anesthesiologist served notice in the late 1970s that over-50 runners aren't to be taken lightly. Even though he only started running seriously in his 40s, he began to knock off age-group records. It was in 1965 that a friend persuaded him to go into training with him to run the Boston Marathon, which Alex did in 1966 at a pedestrian (considering his later exploits) 3:53. But at age 52 he ran 2:35:43, at age 53, 2:31:56, and at age 54, 2:32:34.

Alex was four times the American Masters Runner of the Year; he set some 15 U.S. age-group records. In 2000 Alex was inducted into the Minnesota Track and Field Hall of Fame. As anyone who knows running will tell you, Minnesota takes its running heroes (Dick Beardsley, Bob Kempainen, Ron Daws, Janis Klecker, etc.) very seriously.

Minnesota maintains a Web site of its age-group record-holders into the advanced ages, and it is clearly Alex Ratelle territory: 33:23 10K at age 56 in 1981; 52:35 15K at age 56 in 1981; 2:30:41 marathon at age 56 at Grandma's in 1981; 35:30 10K at age 60 in 1985; 2:43:21 marathon at age 60; 2:14:29 20-mile at age 66 in 1990; 2:59:38 marathon at age 65 in 1989. On the Boston Marathon's Web site Alex holds the fifth and eighth best veterans' performances. Obviously he's another living, breathing reminder that it's never too late to start running. *See also* Hall of Fame, RRCA.

From the collection of Dr. Edward H. Kozloff–Motor City Striders

Known as a miler, Joie "Chesty" Ray began his career as a five-miler in 1912 at the age of 18. He stood five feet five inches tall and weighed only 118 pounds at that time, but he bulked up to 127 pounds when he moved down to the mile.

Rawson, Larry (b. January 20, 1942). The former steeplechaser is a familiar and authoritative voice on U.S. road-race and track telecasts. *See also* television.

Ray, Joie (b. April 13, 1894; d. May 13, 1978). He was one of the first top American track athletes to jump up to the marathon, placing fifth at the 1928 Olympics. Ray later gained attention for running a mile for time on each birthday until late in his life. *See also* Hall of Fame, USATF; Olympians, U.S.; Olympic Marathon, 1900 to 2000.

Reavis, Toni (b. January 2, 1948). The busiest of the road-race broadcasters, he appears regularly as the host of ESPN's *Elite Racing* show. *See also* television.

record progressions, American. Records are made to be broken, we're told. And in the accompanying lists we show how often, by how much, and by whom the national marks have been broken through the years.

American Record Progressions

Here is how the records have dropped at the four most commonly run distances—5K, 10K, half-marathon, and marathon. Times in the three shorter distances were run on courses accurate in distance and unaided by wind or terrain. Aided times are listed for the marathon for historical purposes, but records now (since the early 1980s) must be set on unaided courses. In keeping with current practice, marks originally recorded in 10ths of a second are rounded to the next higher full second. Thanks go to Marty Post of *Runner's World* for supplying these lists. Records are current through October 1, 2001.

WOMEN'S 5K

Time	Athlete	Place	Date
16:10	Mary Shea	Raleigh, NC	February 13, 1983
15:53	Darlene Beckford	Tampa, FL	February 9, 1985
15:31	PattiSue Plumer	Carlsbad, CA	June 1, 1986
15:26	Judi St. Hilaire	Albany, NY	June 3, 1989
15:25	Judi St. Hilaire	Ft. Myers, FL	February 16, 1991
15:14	Vicki Huber	Carlsbad, CA	March 29, 1992
15:08	Deena Drossin	Carlsbad, CA	March 26, 2000

Note: Judi St. Hilaire ran 14:57 on an aided course in Fall River, MA, on May 20, 1990. This remains the American best for 5K.

MEN'S 5K

Time	Athlete	Place	Date
14:34	Tony Bateman	Virginia Beach, VA	July 21, 1979
14:03	Keith Brantly	Tampa, FL	February 9, 1985
13:46	Pat Porter	Newcastle, England	March 26, 1986
13:32	Steve Scott	Carlsbad, CA	June 1, 1986
13:31	Steve Scott	Carlsbad, CA	March 27, 1988
13:26	Greg Whitely	Freeport, Bahamas	February 13, 1993
13:24	Marc Davis	Carlsbad, CA	March 31, 1996

Note: Brian Abshire ran 13:20 on an aided course in Fontana, CA, on June 5, 1993. This remains the American best for 5K.

WOMEN'S 10K

Time	Athlete	Place	Date
34:52	Julie Shea	Washington, DC	October 10, 1976
34:15	Peg Neppel	New York, NY	June 10, 1977
33:30	Martha White	New York, NY	June 3, 1978
32:47	Margaret Groos	Boston, MA	October 8, 1979
32:30	Jan Merrill	Purchase, NY	October 4, 1980
32:24	Patti Catalano	Boston, MA	October 13, 1980
32:04	Jan Merrill	Boston, MA	October 12, 1981
31:52	Mary Decker	Eugene, OR	May 1, 1983

(continued)

American Record Progressions, *continued*

Time	Athlete	Place	Date
31:38	Mary Decker	Eugene, OR	May 6, 1984
31:34	Lynn Jennings	Raleigh, NC	November 13, 1988
31:06	Lynn Jennings	Orlando, FL	March 3, 1990

Note: Olga Appell ran 30:55 on an aided course in Salt Lake City, UT, on July 24, 1995. This remains the American best for 10K.

MEN'S 10K

Time	Athlete	Place	Date
28:36	Bill Rodgers	Purchase, NY	September 23, 1978
28:24	Greg Meyer	Boston, MA	June 23, 1979
28:12	Thom Hunt	Phoenix, AZ	February 1, 1981
28:04	Alberto Salazar	Miami, FL	January 9, 1982
28:02	Alberto Salazar	Miami, FL	January 15, 1983
28:01	Alberto Salazar	Phoenix, AZ	March 5, 1983
27:59	Mark Nenow	Mobile, AL	March 10, 1984
27:48	Mark Nenow	Phoenix, AZ	March 2, 1985

Note: Mark Nenow ran 27:22 on an aided course at New Orleans, LA, on April 1, 1984. This remains the American best for 10K.

WOMEN'S HALF-MARATHON

Time	Athlete	Place	Date
1:14:04	Patti Lyons	Manchester, England	September 23, 1979
1:13:26	Joan Benoit	New Orleans, LA	January 18, 1981
1:11:16	Joan Benoit	San Diego, CA	March 7, 1981
1:09:14	Joan Benoit	Philadelphia, PA	September 18, 1983
1:08:34	Joan Benoit	Philadelphia, PA	September 16, 1984

MEN'S HALF-MARATHON

Time	Athlete	Place	Date
1:05:54	Thom Hunt	San Diego, CA	July 4, 1977
1:04:27	Thom Hunt	San Diego, CA	July 4, 1978
1:03:14	Larry Cuzzort	Dayton, OH	October 14, 1979
1:02:32	Kirk Pfeffer	Las Vegas, NV	December 7, 1979
1:02:16	Stan Mavis	New Orleans, LA	January 27, 1980
1:02:14	Kirk Pfeffer	Philadelphia, PA	September 20, 1981
1:01:47	Herb Lindsay	Manchester, England	September 20, 1981
1:01:43	George Malley	Philadelphia, PA	September 19, 1982
1:01:32	Paul Cummings	Dayton, OH	September 25, 1983
1:00:55	Mark Curp	Philadelphia, PA	September 15, 1985

Note: Terry Cotton ran 59:41 on an aided course in Fontana, CA on April 19, 1986. This remains the American half-marathon best.

WOMEN'S MARATHON

Time	Athlete	Place	Date
3:21:19	Sara Berman	Atlantic City, NJ	September 28, 1969
3:02:53	Caroline Walker	Seaside, OR	February 28, 1970
3:01:42	Beth Bonner	Philadelphia, PA	May 9, 1971
2:55:22	Beth Bonner	New York, NY	September 19, 1971
2:49:40	Cheryl Bridges	Culver City, CA	December 5, 1971
2:46:36	Miki Gorman	Culver City, CA	December 2, 1973
2:43:55	Jacqueline Hansen	Culver City, CA	December 1, 1974
2:38:19	Jacqueline Hansen	Eugene, OR	October 12, 1975
2:37:57	Kim Merritt	Eugene, OR	September 11, 1977
2:36:24	Julie Brown	Eugene, OR	September 10, 1978
2:35:15	Joan Benoit	Boston, MA	April 16, 1979
2:31:23	Joan Benoit	Auckland, New Zealand	February 3, 1980
2:30:58	Patti Catalano	Montreal, Canada	September 6, 1980
2:29:34	Patti Catalano	New York, NY	October 26, 1980
2:27:51	Patti Catalano	Boston, MA	April 20, 1981
2:26:11	Joan Benoit	Eugene, OR	September 12, 1982
2:22:43	Joan Benoit	Boston, MA	April 18, 1983
2:21:21	Joan Samuelson	Chicago, IL	October 21, 1985

MEN'S MARATHON

Time	Athlete	Place	Date
2:55:19	John Hayes	London, England	July 24, 1908
2:52:46	Robert Fowler	Yonkers, NY	January 1, 1909
2:46:53	James Clark	New York, NY	February 12, 1909
2:46:05	Albert Raines	New York, NY	May 8, 1909
2:41:30	Joseph Organ	Antwerp, Belgium	August 22, 1920
2:38:28	Frank Zuna	London, England	May 30, 1925
2:29:02	Albert Michelsen	Port Chester, NY	October 12, 1925
2:28:52	Ellison Brown	Boston, MA	April 19, 1939
2:27:29	Ellison Brown	Salisbury, MA	May 30, 1940
2:26:52	Bernard Smith	Boston, MA	April 19, 1942
2:24:53	John J. Kelley	Yonkers, NY	September 30, 1956
2:20:05	John J. Kelley	Boston, MA	April 20, 1957
2:18:55	Buddy Edelen	Fukuoka, Japan	December 2, 1962
2:14:28	Buddy Edelen	Chiswick, England	June 15, 1963
2:13:28	Kenny Moore	Fukuoka, Japan	December 7, 1969
2:11:12	Eamonn O'Reilly	Boston, MA	April 20, 1970
2:10:30	Frank Shorter	Fukuoka, Japan	December 3, 1972
2:09:55	Bill Rodgers	Boston, MA	April 21, 1975
2:09:27	Bill Rodgers	Boston, MA	April 16, 1979
2:08:51	Alberto Salazar	Boston, MA	April 19, 1982
2:08:47	Bob Kempainen	Boston, MA	April 18, 1994
2:07:01	Khalid Khannouchi	Chicago, IL	October 22, 2000

Note: Boston times are now considered to be aided, and thus are American bests rather than records. The progression of records on unaided courses since the 1970s is as follows: (continued)

American Record Progressions, *continued*

Time	Athlete	Place	Date
2:10:30	Frank Shorter	Fukuoka, Japan	December 3, 1972
2:10:20	Tony Sandoval	Eugene, OR	September 9, 1979
2:10:20	Jeff Wells	Eugene, OR	September 9, 1979
2:10:04	Pat Petersen	London, England	April 23, 1989
2:10:04	Jerry Lawson	Chicago, IL	October 20, 1996
2:09:35	Jerry Lawson	Chicago, IL	October 9, 1997
2:09:32	David Morris	Chicago, IL	October 24, 1999
2:07:01	Khalid Khannouchi	Chicago, IL	October 22, 2000

record progressions, world. Here is how the world road records have improved through the years. We include women's and men's times for the most commonly run distances.

World Record Progressions

This is how the records have improved in the four most widely run distances—5K, 10K, half-marathon, and marathon. The times are for unaided courses except in the marathon where some performances helped by terrain and wind are listed for historical purposes. Marks originally recorded in 10ths of a second are rounded up to the next higher full second according to current practice. Thanks go to Marty Post of *Runner's World* for supplying these lists. Records are current through October 7, 2001.

WOMEN'S 5K

Time	Athlete	Place	Date
16:10	Mary Shea (U.S.)	Raleigh, NC	February 13, 1983
15:53	Darlene Beckford (U.S.)	Tampa, FL	February 9, 1985
15:31	PattiSue Plumer (U.S.)	Carlsbad, CA	June 1, 1986
15:30	Liz McColgan (Britain)	Carlsbad, CA	May 27, 1988
15:20	Lynn Williams (Canada)	Carlsbad, CA	April 2, 1989
15:11	Liz McColgan (Britain)	Carlsbad, CA	April 14, 1991
15:10	Elana Meyer (South Africa)	Providence, RI	October 16, 1994
15:05	Rose Cheruiyot (Kenya)	Carlsbad, CA	April 2, 1995
14:58	Lydia Cheromei (Kenya)	Bern, Switzerland	June 8, 1997
14:57	Paula Radcliffe (Britain)	London, England	September 2, 2001

Note: Three runners have run aided 14:57s—Judi St. Hilaire (U.S.) at Fall River, MA, on May 20, 1990; Sue Lee (Canada) at Fontana, CA, on April 6, 1991; and Liz McColgan (Britain) at Chicago on October 27, 1991.

MEN'S 5K

Time	Athlete	Place	Date
14:03	Keith Brantly (U.S.)	Tampa, FL	February 9, 1985
13:35	Steve Harris (Britain)	Newcastle, England	March 26, 1986
13:32	Steve Scott (U.S.)	Carlsbad, CA	June 1, 1986
13:31	Steve Scott (U.S.)	Carlsbad, CA	March 27, 1988
13:26	Yobes Ondieki (Kenya)	Carlsbad, CA	April 2, 1989
13:12	William Mutwol (Kenya)	Carlsbad, CA	March 29, 1992
13:00	Sammy Kipketer (Kenya)	Carlsbad, CA	March 26, 2000
13:00	Sammy Kipketer (Kenya)	Carlsbad, CA	April 1, 2001

WOMEN'S 10K

Time	Athlete	Place	Date
34:52	Julie Shea (U.S.)	Washington, DC	October 10, 1976
34:15	Peg Neppel (U.S.)	New York, NY	June 10, 1977
33:30	Martha White (U.S.)	New York, NY	June 3, 1978
32:47	Margaret Groos (U.S.)	Boston, MA	October 8, 1979
32:41	Grete Waitz (Norway)	Inglewood, CA	November 4, 1979
32:30	Jan Merrill (U.S.)	Purchase, NY	October 4, 1980
32:24	Patti Catalano (U.S.)	Boston, MA	October 13, 1980
32:04	Jan Merrill (U.S.)	Boston, MA	October 12, 1981
31:45	Anne Audain (New Zealand)	Cleveland, OH	May 16, 1982
31:43	Anne Audain (New Zealand)	Boston, MA	October 11, 1982
31:32	Grete Waitz (Norway)	Miami, FL	January 15, 1983
31:31	Ingrid Kristiansen (Norway)	Miami, FL	February 1, 1986
31:07	Liz McColgan (Britain)	Orlando, FL	February 21, 1987
30:59	Liz McColgan (Britain)	Orlando, FL	February 6, 1988
30:39	Liz McColgan (Britain)	Orlando, FL	March 11, 1989

MEN'S 10K

Time	Athlete	Place	Date
28:36	Bill Rodgers (U.S.)	Purchase, NY	September 23, 1978
28:24	Greg Meyer (U.S.)	Boston, MA	June 23, 1979
28:00	M. Motshwarateu (S. Africa)	Purchase, NY	October 4, 1980
27:43	Zak Barie (Tanzania)	Phoenix, AZ	March 3, 1984
27:41	Arturo Barrios (Mexico)	Phoenix, AZ	March 1, 1986
27:40	Addis Abebe (Ethiopia)	Jakarta, Indonesia	January 24, 1993
27:24	William Sigei (Kenya)	New Orleans, LA	April 16, 1994
27:20	Joseph Kimani (Kenya)	Cleveland, OH	May 5, 1996
27:18	Sammy Kipketer (Kenya)	Brunssum, Netherlands	April 8, 2001

Note: Joseph Kimani (Kenya) ran 27:04 on an aided course in Atlanta, GA, on July 4, 1996. This is the world best for 10K.

(continued)

World Record Progressions, *continued*

WOMEN'S HALF-MARATHON

Time	Athlete	Place	Date
1:14:04	Patti Lyons (U.S.)	Manchester, England	September 23, 1979
1:13:26	Joan Benoit (U.S.)	New Orleans, LA	January 18, 1981
1:11:16	Joan Benoit (U.S.)	San Diego, CA	March 7, 1981
1:09:14	Joan Benoit (U.S.)	Philadelphia, PA	September 18, 1983
1:08:34	Joan Benoit (U.S.)	Philadelphia, PA	September 16, 1984
1:08:32	Ingrid Kristiansen (Norway)	New Bedford, MA	March 19, 1989
1:07:59	Elana Meyer (South Africa)	East London, S. Africa	May 18, 1991
1:07:59	Uta Pippig (Germany)	Kyoto, Japan	March 20, 1994
1:07:58	Uta Pippig (Germany)	Kyoto, Japan	March 19, 1995
1:07:36	Elana Meyer (South Africa)	Kyoto, Japan	March 9, 1997
1:07:29	Elana Meyer (South Africa)	Kyoto, Japan	March 8, 1998
1:06:44	Elana Meyer (South Africa)	Tokyo, Japan	January 15, 1999

Note: Susan Chepkemei (Kenya) ran an aided 1:05:44 in Lisbon, Portugal, on April 1, 2001. This is the world half-marathon best.

MEN'S HALF-MARATHON

Time	Athlete	Place	Date
1:02:31	Nick Rose (Britain)	Dayton, OH	October 14, 1979
1:02:16	Stan Mavis (U.S.)	New Orleans, LA	January 27, 1980
1:01:47	Herb Lindsay (U.S.)	Manchester, England	September 20, 1981
1:01:36	Michael Musyoki (Kenya)	Philadelphia, PA	September 19, 1982
1:01:32	Paul Cummings (U.S.)	Dayton, OH	September 25, 1983
1:01:14	Steve Jones (Britain)	Birmingham, England	August 11, 1985
1:00:55	Mark Curp (U.S.)	Philadelphia, PA	September 15, 1985
1:00:43	Michael Musyoki (Kenya)	Newcastle, England	June 8, 1986
1:00:10	Matthews Temane (S. Africa)	East London, S. Africa	July 25, 1987
59:47	Moses Tanui (Kenya)	Milan, Italy	April 3, 1993
59:17	Paul Tergat (Kenya)	Milan, Italy	April 4, 1998

Note: Paul Tergat ran an aided 59:06 in Lisbon, Portugal, on March 26, 2000. This is the world half-marathon best.

WOMEN'S MARATHON

Time	Athlete	Place	Date
3:40:22	Violet Piercy (Britain)	Chiswick, England	October 3, 1926
3:37:07	Merry Lepper (U.S.)	Culver City, CA	December 16, 1963
3:27:45	Dale Greig (Britain)	Isle of Wight	May 23, 1964
3:19:33	Millie Sampson (New Zealand)	Auckland, NZ	July 21, 1964
3:15:23	Maureen Wilton (Canada)	Toronto, Canada	May 6, 1967
3:07:27	Anni Pede-Erdkamp (W. Germany)	Waldniel, W. Germany	September 16, 1967
3:02:53	Caroline Walker (U.S.)	Seaside, OR	February 28, 1970
3:01:42	Beth Bonner (U.S.)	Philadelphia, PA	May 9, 1971
2:46:30	Adrienne Beames (Australia)	Werribee, Australia	August 31, 1971
2:46:24	Chantal Langlace (France)	Neuf Brisach, France	October 27, 1974
2:43:55	Jacqueline Hansen (U.S.)	Culver City, CA	December 1, 1974
2:42:24	Liane Winter (Germany)	Boston, MA	April 21, 1975
2:40:16	Christa Vahlensieck (W. Germany)	Dulmen, W. Germany	May 3, 1975
2:38:19	Jacqueline Hansen (U.S.)	Eugene, OR	October 12, 1975
2:35:16	Chantal Langlace (France)	Oyarzun, Spain	May 1, 1977

Time	Athlete	Place	Date
2:34:48	Christa Vahlensieck (W. Germany)	West Berlin, Germany	September 10, 1977
2:32:30	Grete Waitz (Norway)	New York, NY	October 22, 1978
2:27:33	Grete Waitz (Norway)	New York, NY	October 21, 1979
2:25:42	Grete Waitz (Norway)	New York, NY	October 26, 1980
2:25:29	Grete Waitz (Norway)	London, England	April 17, 1983
2:22:43	Joan Benoit (U.S.)	Boston, MA	April 18, 1983
2:21:06	Ingrid Kristiansen (Norway)	London, England	April 21, 1985
2:20:47	Tegla Loroupe (Kenya)	Rotterdam, Holland	April 19, 1998
2:20:43	Tegla Loroupe (Kenya)	Berlin, Germany	September 26, 1999
2:19:46	Naoka Takahashi (Japan)	Berlin, Germany	September 30, 2001
2:18:47	Catherine Ndereba	Chicago, IL	October 7, 2001

Note: Some sources question the validity of Adrienne Beames's 2:46:30. The alternative progression follows.

Time	Athlete	Place	Date
2:55:22	Beth Bonner (U.S.)	New York, NY	September 19, 1971
2:49:40	Cheryl Bridges (U.S.)	Culver City, CA	December 5, 1971
2:46:36	Miki Gorman (U.S.)	Culver City, CA	December 2, 1973

MEN'S MARATHON

Time	Athlete	Place	Date
2:55:19	John Hayes (U.S.)	London, England	July 24, 1908
2:52.46	Robert Fowler (U.S.)	Yonkers, NY	January 1, 1909
2:46:53	James Clark (U.S.)	New York, NY	February 12, 1909
2:46:05	Albert Raines (U.S.)	New York, NY	May 8, 1909
2:42:31	Henry Barrett (Britain)	London, England	May 26, 1909
2:40:35	Thure Johansson (Sweden)	Stockholm, Sweden	August 31, 1909
2:38:17	Harry Green (Britain)	London, England	May 12, 1913
2:36:07	Alexis Ahlgren (Sweden)	London, England	May 31, 1913
2:32:36	Hannes Kolehmainen (Finland)	Antwerp, Belgium	August 22, 1920
2:29:02	Albert Michelsen (U.S.)	Port Chester, NY	October 12, 1925
2:27:49	Fushige Suzuki (Japan)	Tokyo, Japan	March 31, 1935
2:26:44	Yasuo Ikenaga (Japan)	Tokyo, Japan	April 3, 1935
2:26:42	Sohn Kee Chung (Korea)	Tokyo, Japan	November 3, 1935
2:25:39	Yun Bok Soh (Korea)	Boston, MA	April 19, 1947
2:20:43	Jim Peters (Britain)	Chiswick, England	June 14, 1952
2:18:41	Jim Peters (Britain)	Chiswick, England	June 13, 1953
2:18:35	Jim Peters (Britain)	Turku, Finland	October 4, 1953
2:17:40	Jim Peters (Britain)	Chiswick, England	June 26, 1954
2:15:17	Sergey Popov (USSR)	Stockholm, Sweden	August 24, 1958
2:15:17	Abebe Bikila (Ethiopia)	Rome, Italy	September 10, 1960
2:15:16	Toru Terasawa (Japan)	Beppu, Japan	February 17, 1963
2:14:28	Buddy Edelen (U.S.)	Chiswick, England	June 15, 1963
2:13:55	Basil Heatley (Britain)	Chiswick, England	June 13, 1964
2:12:12	Abebe Bikila (Ethiopia)	Tokyo, Japan	October 21, 1964
2:12:00	Morio Shigematsu (Japan)	Chiswick, England	June 12, 1965
2:09:37	Derek Clayton (Australia)	Fukuoka, Japan	December 3, 1967
2:08:34	Derek Clayton (Australia)	Antwerp, Belgium	May 30, 1969
2:08:18	Rob de Castella (Australia)	Fukuoka, Japan	December 6, 1981
2:08:05	Steve Jones (Britain)	Chicago, IL	October 21, 1984
2:07:12	Carlos Lopes (Portugal)	Rotterdam, Holland	April 20, 1985
2:06:50	Belayneh Dinsamo (Ethiopia)	Rotterdam, Holland	April 17, 1988
2:06:05	Ronaldo da Costa (Brazil)	Berlin, Germany	September 20, 1998
2:05:42	Khalid Khannouchi (Morocco)	Chicago, IL	October 24, 1999

records, American. Standardization of distances and certification of courses made possible the keeping of records. American record-quality courses must be certified by USATF and must not be aided by elevation drop or wind.

American Road Records

These are the marks officially recognized by USA Track & Field. "a" indicates an aided mark that is considered an American best for this distance when the time is faster than the accepted record. Marks are current through October 1, 2001.

WOMEN

Distance	Athlete	Time	Place	Date
5K	Deena Drossin	15:08	Carlsbad, CA	March 26, 2000
	Judi St. Hilaire	14:57a	Fall River, MA	May 20, 1990
8K	Lynn Jennings	25:02	Washington, DC	May 12, 1991
	Cheryl Harper	24:41a	Alta, UT	September 13, 1997
10K	Lynn Jennings	31:06	Orlando, FL	March 3, 1990
	Olga Appell	30:55a	Salt Lake City, UT	July 24, 1995
12K	Lynn Jennings	39:14	San Francisco, CA	May 16, 1993
15K	Lisa Weidenbach	48:28	Portland, OR	June 18, 1989
10M	Cathy O'Brien	51:47	Flint, MI	August 26, 1989
20K	Trina Painter	1:07:07	New Haven, CT	September 4, 1995
Half–Mar.	Joan Benoit	1:08:34	Philadelphia, PA	September 16, 1984
25K	Joan Samuelson	1:24:43	Grand Rapids, MI	May 10, 1986
30K	Kim Rosenquist	1:47:41	St. Paul, MN	October 12, 1986
	Lisa Weidenbach	1:43:27a	Albany, NY	March 24, 1985
Marathon	Joan Samuelson	2:21:21	Chicago, IL	October 21, 1985

MEN

Distance	Athlete	Time	Place	Date
5K	Marc Davis	13:24	Carlsbad, CA	March 31, 1996
	Brian Abshire	13:20a	Fontana, CA	June 5, 1993
8K	Alberto Salazar	22:04	Los Altos, CA	January 4, 1981
	Larry Smithee	21:03a	Alta, UT	September 19, 1998
10K	Mark Nenow	27:48	Phoenix, AZ	March 2, 1985
	Mark Nenow	27:22a	New Orleans, LA	April 1, 1984
12K	Steve Spence	34:26	Spokane, WA	May 7, 1989
15K	Todd Williams	42:22	Jacksonville, FL	March 11, 1995
10M	Greg Meyer	46:13	Washington, DC	March 27, 1983
20K	Paul Cummings	59:13	New Bedford, MA	March 15, 1987
Half–Mar.	Mark Curp	1:00:55	Philadelphia, PA	September 15, 1985
	Terry Cotton	59:41a	Fontana, CA	April 19, 1986
25K	Ed Eyestone	1:14:38	Indianapolis, IN	October 13, 1991
30K	Phil Coppess	1:31:49	St. Paul, MN	October 6, 1985
Marathon	Khalid Khannouchi	2:07:01	Chicago, IL	October 22, 2000

records, American age-group. As the sport has aged, so has the demand for record keeping among the older ages. Younger runners also receive recognition in the junior category, for those under 20. Little special attention is paid to runners in their 20s and 30s because most of the overall fastest times come at these ages.

American Age-Group Records

USA Track & Field keeps many more records than those we have room to list here. Marks are kept for all standard distances in five-year age groups. The listings below are for the four major events—5K, 10K, half-marathon, and marathon. A junior is a runner who is under 20 years of age throughout the calendar year in which the race is run. "a" = aided time; "p" = pending record. Records are current through October 1, 2001.

WOMEN'S 5K

Age group	Athlete	Time	Date
Junior	Jamie Park	16:39	April 14, 1991
40–44	Ruth Wysocki	16:06	May 31, 1997
	Ruth Wysocki	15:44a	September 20, 1997
45–49	Barbara Filutze	17:14	June 5, 1993
50–54	Shirley Matson	17:28	April 14, 1991
55–59	Shirley Matson	18:32	April 13, 1997
60–64	Marion Irvine	19:53	November 11, 1990
65–69	June Machala	22:07	May 31, 1997
70–74	Gerry Davidson	24:38	April 14, 1991
	Toshiko D'elia	24:18p	October 22, 2000
75–79	Anne Clarke	27:17	August 22, 1987
80–84	Anne Clarke	29:23	September 30, 1989
85–89	(no official record)		
90 and up	Tiny Riley	48:35p	June 3, 1995

MEN'S 5K

Age group	Athlete	Time	Date
Junior	(no official record)		
40–44	Steve Plasencia	14:25	December 15, 1996
	John Tuttle	14:19p	September 11, 1999
	Steve Blum	14:15a	June 3, 1995
45–49	Doug Bell	15:07	April 13, 1997
	Nolan Smith	15:00p	June 4, 1995
	Steve Lester	14:34a	September 24, 1988
50–54	Sal Vasquez	15:38	November 23, 1991
	Dick Buerkle	15:38p	September 11, 1999
	Steve Lester	15:11a	September 30, 1995
55–59	Vic Heckler	16:07	September 27, 1997
	Tom Curry	15:35a	May 31, 1997
60–64	Jim O'Neil	17:00	June 1, 1986

(continued)

American Age-Group Records, *continued*

Age group	Athlete	Time	Date
65–69	Warren Utes	18:21	September 30, 1989
70–74	Warren Utes	18:01	September 30, 1990
75–79	Warren Utes	19:24	September 30, 1995
80–84	Dudley Healy	24:52	October 2, 1994
	Warren Utes	22:14p	June 25, 2000
85–89	Gifton Jolley	28:26	December 5, 1992
90–94	Lloyd Walters	40:32	January 26, 1992
	Abe Weintraub	40:32p	August 5, 2000
95 and up	Marion McAnelly	48:55	May 13, 1995

WOMEN'S 10K

Age group	Athlete	Time	Date
Junior	Katie Ishmael	32:33	August 3, 1984
40–44	Ruth Wysocki	33:22	March 22, 1997
45–49	Barbara Filutze	35:57	April 12, 1992
	Barbara Filutze	34:40a	September 29, 1991
50–54	Shirley Matson	35:57	March 2, 1991
55–59	Shirley Matson	38:55p	October 27, 1996
60–64	Shirley Matson	40:28p	September 29, 2001
65–69	June Machala	45:04	October 31, 1998
70–74	June Machala	48:30p	March 24, 2001
75–79	(no official record)		
80–84	Hedy Marque	56:17	April 26, 1998
85–89	(no official record)		
90 and up	(no official record)		

MEN'S 10K

Age group	Athlete	Time	Date
Junior	Mark Junkerman	29:15	March 2, 1985
40–44	Steve Plasencia	29:37	August 1, 1998
	Eddy Hellebuyck	29:37p	March 25, 2001
	Craig Young	29:27a	September 28, 1997
	John Tuttle	29:27a-p	April 17, 1999
45–49	Bill Rodgers	30:50	May 16, 1993
	Steve Lester	30:10a	July 4, 1988
50–54	Ray Hatton	31:48	May 23, 1982
	Steve Lester	31:12a	July 1, 1995
55–59	Jim O'Neill	32:27	September 26, 1993
60–64	Jim O'Neil	34:27	August 4, 1985
65–69	(no official record)		
70–74	Alfred Funk	41:09	September 21, 1984
75–79	Warren Utes	40:12	September 17, 1995
80–84	Ed Benham	45:28	August 8, 1987
85–89	Paul Spangler	58:50	May 3, 1984
90 and up	Paul Spangler	1:14:49	January 20, 1990

WOMEN'S HALF-MARATHON

Age group	Athlete	Time	Date
Junior	(no official record)		
40–44	Laurie Binder	1:13:57	September 15, 1991
	Honor Featherston	1:13:54a	February 4, 1995
45–49	(no official record)		
50–54	Rae Baymiller	1:19:40	September 19, 1993
	Joan Ottaway	1:18:42a	February 11, 1996
55–59	Shirley Matson	1:23:09	October 20, 1996
60–64	Barbara Miller	1:29:49	October 17, 1999
65–69	June Machala	1:39:40	May 1, 1998
	June Machala	1:39:21a	February 1, 1998
70–74	Marcie Trent	1:58:27	May 28, 1988
	Mary Storey	1:50:03a	June 4, 1994
	June Machala	1:42:13 a-p	February 4, 2001
75–79	Anne Clarke	2:26:24	June 14, 1987
	Algene Williams	2:06:34a	April 28, 1991
80–84	(no official record)		
85–89	(no official record)		
90 and up	(no official record)		

MEN'S HALF-MARATHON

Age group	Athlete	Time	Date
Junior	Jay O'Keefe	1:04:42	September 18, 1983
40–44	Steve Plasencia	1:05:27	May 1, 1998
	Eddy Hellebuyck	1:05:18p	January 28, 2001
	Craig Young	1:05:01p	February 7, 1999
	Craig Young	1:03:33a	February 1, 1998
45–49	Bill Rodgers	1:08:05	June 6, 1993
	Gary Romesser	1:07:14a	February 11, 1996
50–54	Norm Green	1:09:30	September 16, 1984
55–59	Norm Green	1:10:23	September 20, 1987
60–64	Norm Green	1:16:55	September 19, 1993
65–69	Michael Bertolini	1:23:50	September 15, 1985
	James Talley	1:20:29a	April 19, 1986
70–74	John Keston	1:27:44	May 2, 1997
	John Keston	1:25:24a	February 9, 1997
75–79	Warren Utes	1:30:19	May 2, 1997
80–84	Ed Benham	1:40:30	December 10, 1988
85–89	(no official record)		
90 and up	(no official record)		

(continued)

American Age-Group Records, *continued*

Age group	Athlete	Time	Date
Junior	Cathy Schiro	2:34:24	May 12, 1984
	Jenny Spangler	2:33:52a	June 11, 1983
40–44	Laurie Binder	2:35:08	October 6, 1991
45–49	Barbara Filutze	2:45:11	October 6, 1991
50–54	Shirley Matson	2:50:26	October 6, 1991
55–59	Margaret Miller	3:07:21	July 11, 1982
	Rae Baymiller	2:52:14p	October 11, 1998
	Sandra Kiddy	3:05:48a	December 8, 1991
60–64	Helen Dick	3:15:30	October 21, 1984
	Barbara Miller	3:14:50p	December 11, 1997
	Barbara Miller	3:11:57a	April 16, 2000
65–69	Whayong Semer	3:36:57	October 2, 1993
70–74	Agnes Reinhard	4:13:03	October 20, 1996
	Marcie Trent	4:11:54a	March 13, 1988
75–79	Anne Clarke	4:49:08	October 20, 1985
	Helen Klein	4:31:05a	December 6, 1998
80–84	Ida Mintz	5:10:04	October 20, 1985
85–89	Ida Mintz	6:53:50	October 28, 1990
90 and up	Mavis Lindgren	8:53:08	September 28, 1997

MEN'S MARATHON

Age group	Athlete	Time	Date
Junior	Paul Gompers	2:15:28	December 10, 1983
40–44	Ken Judson	2:17:02	December 8, 1990
	Barry Brown	2:15:15a	September 30, 1984
45–49	Bob Schlau	2:26:43	January 15, 1995
	Jim Bowers	2:21:32a	June 16, 1984
50–54	Norm Green	2:25:51	December 2, 1984
	Jim O'Neill	2:25:46a	February 4, 1989
55–59	Norm Green	2:33:49	May 1, 1988
	Norm Green	2:27:42a	October 11, 1987
60–64	Clive Davies	2:42:44	October 28, 1979
65–69	Clive Davies	2:42:49	September 13, 1981
70–74	John Keston	3:00:58	October 6, 1996
75–79	Warren Utes	3:18:10	October 15, 1995
80–84	Ed Benham	4:17:51	October 6, 1991
	Ed Benham	3:43:27a	October 11, 1987
85–89	(no official record)		
90 and up	Sam Gadless	8:10:44a	November 2, 1997
	Abe Weintraub	7:25:12p	November 5, 2000

records, world. There were only unofficial "world records" in road racing as this book was completed. Listed on pages 298-300 are the best times run on courses that meet the strict standards employed in the United States, where road records do receive official blessing.

World Road Records

Official world records for road races don't yet exist. But they'll arrive eventually, and when they do they'll at least need to meet the same high standards as U.S. records. These are the times that meet those standards. "a" = aided time; "p" = pending record. Note that Paul Tergat set the 15K, 10-mile, and 20K records en route to a half-marathon. Records are current through October 7, 2001.

WOMEN

Athlete	Time	Place	Date
5K			
Paula Radcliffe (Britain)	14:57	London, England	September 2, 2001
Judi St. Hilaire (U.S.)	14:57a	Fall River, MA	May 20, 1990
Liz McColgan (Britain)	14:57a	Chicago, IL	October 27, 1991
Sue Lee (Canada)	14:57a	Fontana, CA	April 6, 1991
8K			
Paula Radcliffe (Britain)	24:38	Balmoral, UK	April 23, 1999
Sonia O'Sullivan (Ireland)	24:27a	Loughrea, Ireland	October 17, 1999
10K			
Liz McColgan (Britain)	30:39	Orlando, FL	March 11, 1989
12K			
Delillah Asiago (Kenya)	38:23	San Francisco, CA	May 21, 1995
15K			
Elana Meyer (S. Africa)	46:57	Cape Town, S. Africa	November 2, 1991
10M			
Colleen de Reuck (S. Africa)	51:16	Washington, DC	April 5, 1998
Ingrid Kristiansen (Norway)	50:31a	Amsterdam, Netherlands	October 11, 1987
20K			
Colleen de Reuck (S. Africa)	1:05:11	New Haven, CT	September 7, 1998
Wang Xiuting (China)	1:05:11a	Miyazaki, Japan	January 6, 1993
Esther Wanjiru (Kenya)	1:04:01p	Kobe, Japan	December 11, 2000
Half-marathon			
Elana Meyer (South Africa)	1:06:44	Tokyo, Japan	January 15, 1999
Susan Chepkemei (Kenya)	1:05:44a	Lisbon, Portugal	April 1, 2001
25K			
Jill Hunter (Britain)	1:24:26	Indianapolis, IN	October 13, 1991
30K			
Kim Rosenquist (U.S.)	1:47:41	St. Paul, MN	October 12, 1986
Lisa Weidenbach (U.S.)	1:43:27a	Albany, NY	March 24, 1985
Marathon			
Catherine Ndereba (Kenya)	2:18:47	Chicago, IL	October 7, 2001

(continued)

World Road Records, *continued*

MEN

Athlete	Time	Place	Date
5K			
Sammy Kipketer (Kenya)	13:00	Carlsbad, CA	March 26, 2000
Sammy Kipketer (Kenya)	13:00	Carlsbad, CA	April 1, 2001
8K			
Peter Githuka (Kenya)	22:03	Kingsport, TN	July 20, 1996
Larry Smithee (U.S.)	21:03a	Alta, UT	September 19, 1998
10K			
Sammy Kipketer (Kenya)	27:18	Brunssum, Netherlands	April 8, 2001
Joseph Kimani (Kenya)	27:04a	Atlanta, GA	July 4, 1996
12K			
Joseph Kimani (Kenya)	33:31	Evansville, IN	May 10, 1997
15K			
Paul Tergat (Kenya)	42:04	Milan, Italy	April 4, 1998
10M			
Paul Tergat (Kenya)	45:12	Milan, Italy	April 4, 1998
Paul Koech (Kenya)	44:45a	Zaandam, Netherlands	September 21, 1997
20K			
Paul Tergat (Kenya)	56:18	Milan, Italy	April 4, 1998
Half-marathon			
Paul Tergat (Kenya)	59:17	Milan, Italy	April 4, 1998
Paul Tergat (Kenya)	59:05a	Lisbon, Portugal	March 26, 2000
25K			
Rodgers Rop (Kenya)	1:13:44	Berlin, Germany	May 6, 2001
30K			
Phil Coppess (U.S.)	1:31:49	St. Paul, MN	October 6, 1985
Marathon			
Khalid Khannouchi (Morocco)	2:05:42	Chicago, IL	October 24, 1999

records, world age-group. Some of the world age-group marks are incredible, as shown in the accompanying lists. Priscilla Welch's 2:26:51 marathon run in her 40s, for instance, has remained unchallenged for more than years.

recovery time. Racing is challenging and exciting, but it's also taxing. Every full effort requires rest and easy days afterward. This is the concept behind Bill Bowerman's hard-easy routine. Jack Foster, the masters marvel from New Zealand, introduced one of the most widely used formulas for race recovery—one easy day for every mile of the race. *See also* Bowerman, Bill; Foster, Jack.

World Age-Group Marathon Records

These are believed to be the best marathon times for the various 10-year age groups, along with the fastest junior runners. Internationally a runner can compete as a junior if he or she is under 20 years of age throughout the calendar year in which the race is run. "a" = aided time; "p" = pending record. Thanks go to Marty Post of *Runner's World* for supplying these lists. Records are current as of October 1, 2001.

WOMEN

Age group	Athlete	Time	Date
Junior	Sun Yingjie (China)	2:25:45	April 11, 1998
40–49	Priscilla Welch (Britain)	2:26:51	May 10, 1987
50–59	Beverly Lucas (Australia)	2:44:12	July 13, 1997
60–69	Barbara Miller (U.S.)	3:14:50	December 11, 1999
	Barbara Miller (U.S.)	3:11:57a	April 16, 2000
70–79	Pat Trickett (Britain)	3:48:14	April 27, 1997
80–89	Ida Mintz (U.S.)	5:10:04	October 20, 1985
90 and up	Mavis Lindgren (U.S.)	8:53:08	September 28, 1997

MEN

Age group	Athlete	Time	Date
Junior	Negash Dube (Ethiopia)	2:12:49	October 18, 1987
	Tesfaye Dadi (Ethiopia)	2:12:49	October 8, 1988
40–49	Mohamed Ezzher (France)	2:10:33	April 8, 2001
50–59	Titus Mamabolo (South Africa)	2:19:29	July 20, 1991
60–69	Luciano Acquarone (Italy)	2:38:15	July 28, 1991
70–74	Ed Whitlock (Canada)	3:00:24	May 13, 2001
80–89	Ed Benham (U.S.)	4:17:51	October 6, 1991
	Ed Benham (U.S.)	3:43:27a	April 27, 1997
90 and up	Josef Galia (Germany)	7:34:26	1990
	Abe Weintraub (U.S.)	7:25:12p	November 5, 2000

Reebok (www.reebok.com). The British shoemaker enjoyed a great run of success in the 1980s and early 1990s, but its strength in the running marketplace has waned since then.

Reese, Paul (b. April 17, 1917). He's best known for running enormous distances in his older years—across the United States at age 73 and then all the remaining states by age 80—and writing three books about his adventures. But long before doing all that, Paul was one of the country's best age-group road racers. His marathoning peaked at age 55, when he ran 2:39.

registration. *See* online registration.

Reifsnyder, Bill (b. April 12, 1962). The runner from the home of Little League baseball—Williamsport, Pennsylvania—won two national marathon titles, 1989 and 1991. *See also* national marathon champions, U.S.

relays. Road relay racing, a longtime fixture in Britain and Japan, was slower to take root in North America but is now a hot item here. The Jasper to Banff Relay in Alberta, Canada, set a tone that served as a model for the wildly popular Hood to Coast Relay in Oregon and the smaller but gorgeously scenic Calistoga to Santa Cruz Relay in California. Most of these relays, in turn, should credit the Christmas Relays of the 1970s put on by Jack Leydig and the West Valley Track Club in San Mateo, California. The seven-runner, 50-mile relay ran from Half Moon Bay to Santa Cruz one year and in the reverse direction the next year, all of it along the spectacular California Pacific Coast Highway (Highway 1). The event was so popular that the California Highway Patrol canceled it. Marathon-length relays, called ekidens in Japan, gave rise to the World Marathon Relay Championships (which came and went in the 1990s). The most popular race of this length in the United States is the Jimmy Stewart Relay. A growing number of standard marathons also have added relay divisions. *See also* ekiden; Hood to Coast Relay; Jasper to Banff Relay; Leydig, Jack; World Marathon Relay.

repeats. *See* interval training.

rest. It once was a four-letter word to runners, and still is to those who proudly call themselves "streakers" (those who never skip a day's run). But increasingly runners are recognizing that they sometimes gain by *not* running on some days. Rest is especially valuable when recovering from the immediate effects of a race or an injury. Dr. George Sheehan did much to ease the stigma associated with resting when he wrote of improving his performances by running every other day. *See also* Sheehan, Dr. George; streakers.

Revithi, Stamata (b. 1865; date of death unknown). *See* Melpomene.

Revlon Run for Women. This 5K is the largest U.S. event for women outside the Race for the Cure series. It's run in Los Angeles, usually in the spring, and draws nearly 20,000 entrants. *See also* biggest races.

Rice, Carol Lasseter (b. October 26, 1942). The longtime publisher of *Running Times* got into running in 1982 and got hooked big time. She has steered the *RT* ship through a number of owners and an even larger number of editors. *See also* publications; *Running Times*.

Richards, Arne (b. October 18, 1932; d. March 26, 1979). The pioneering road racer and promoter of the sport died too young—at 46—while on a run. He was an early stalwart in the Road Runners Club of America and an adviser to *Distance Running News* (later *Runner's World*) in its Kansas infancy.

Richardson, Frank (b. February 26, 1955). The Iowan won Chicago and the national marathon title in 1980. *See also* Chicago Marathon; national marathon champions, U.S.

ride & tie. A sort of three-member duathlon conceived in the 1970s is raced by a team of three—two runners and one horse. A runner rides the horse along the course, dismounts, ties the horse, and proceeds on foot. When the second runner arrives, he or she remounts the horse, passes the first runner, and ties the horse farther up the course so that the trailing runner can re-mount it. For best results the horses must be specially trained to accept the constant changing of runner-riders. An entire book, titled *Ride & Tie: The Challenge of Running and Riding* (World Publications, 1978) was written on this unique sport.

Rim Rock Run (www.rimrockrun.org). The November race of 37K passes through a mini-Grand Canyon called the Colorado National Monument, near Grand Junction. *See also* "Monumental Event" on next page; scenic races.

road miles. Fred Lebow of the New York Road Runners Club came up with the idea to run a mile race on the streets of his city. He got Fifth Avenue Candy Bar to sponsor the Fifth Avenue Mile, which soon found imitators in many other cities. Often road miles are run downhill on straight courses or are wind aided to produce artificially fast mile times compared with those produced on a track.

Road Race Management (www.rrm.com). This monthly newsletter for event-organizing insiders helps spread info on how it's done and how to do it better. *RRM* is edited and published by *Running Times* cofounder Phil Stewart, who himself directs the popular Cherry Blossom 10-mile race in Washington, D.C. *See also* Cherry Blossom 10M; publications; Stewart, Phil.

Road Runners Club of America (RRCA) (www.rrca.org). This grassroots organization, a national club composed of local clubs, is patterned after its British counterpart. Now more than 40 years old, the RRCA flourished as "official" organizations ignored road racing. RRCA's many contributions include starting a course-certification program, establishing record keeping for road races, helping postcollegiate runners stay involved through the Roads Scholars program, and publishing *FootNotes*. *See also* Carlip, Freddi; Gabeau, Henley; Kardong, Don.

Road Runners Club of America Hall of Fame (www.rrca.org). *See* Hall of Fame, RRCA.

Road Runner Sports. *See* mail-order companies.

Monumental Event

From Joe Henderson's *Running Commentary,* January 2000.

This used to be a time of maximum fear. The plane descended, but it wasn't the prospect of a rough landing that scared me. It was coming into a city for the first time and knowing no one there.

This happens so seldom now, with so many of my trips being encores, that I welcome newness. I also know what to expect, even from temporary strangers. They are runners too. We speak the same language, and I can count on the greeting to be warm.

I'd never traveled within 300 miles of Grand Junction, Colorado. I'd met my hosts, Dave Eisner and Dan Peterson, only by e-mail. We all trusted that we'd recognize each other at the airport. And we did, immediately.

They're so proud of their Rim Rock Run course that they whisked me right there for a tour. The race of 22-plus miles (37K) passes entirely through Colorado National Monument, a mini-Grand Canyon that's not at all small.

I knew only what Don Kardong's story in *Runner's World* had told about the park and race: that it's one of the few federal (read: public, as in our) lands to allow races . . . that the roadside features red-rock walls . . . that the course climbs for most of its first 11 miles, then descends by the same amount . . .that the race is a marathon in time and effort . . . that only about 400 runners get to race here each November.

The drive showed steeper canyons and more spectacular rock formations than I'd imagined. It also showed I'd made the right decision not to enter the race unprepared. A four-mile run along a fairly flat trail was plenty long for me, though the two hosts went super-slowly for the sake of their flatlander guest.

On race day I asked for a ride in the press vehicle. "We don't have one," said director Katie Hill. "But you can drive behind the sheriff's deputy who leads the field." Hill is a quietly tough woman who led the fight to keep this course open to runners when a new park superintendent decreed "no more racing in *my* park." Katie and committee went all the way up to Interior Secretary Bruce Babbitt to preserve the event.

My drive was surprisingly tense. Lead runner Tom Borschel left all competition behind in the third mile, and my rental car became his de facto pacesetter. The deputy hadn't led a race before, and his pace was erratic. He either pulled too far ahead or slowed down so much that Tom almost ran up my tailpipe. But what could I do—honk? Between watching the car in front of me and Tom in my rearview mirror, I couldn't spare much attention for the scenery. A better tour would have to come later.

The first night home from Grand Junction, my wife and I rented *American Flyers.* It's an early Kevin Costner movie about bicycle racing. The acting and story are forgettable, but we watched the video for its memorable scenery.

Its featured bike race travels through the Colorado National Monument, along the same course I'd driven that Saturday. My plan was to infect Barbara with the same excitement I feel about returning. Next time I won't see it as the leader does, but at little more than half his pace and without any car windows blocking the view.

Road Running Information Center (RRIC) (www.usaldr.org). This office, now officially part of USA Track & Field, grew out of the independent National Running Data Center founded by Ken Young in the 1970s. Headed by Basil Honikman, the Santa Barbara-based RRIC keeps national statistics and records for long-distance racing and publishes a weekly Internet report and a newsletter, *On the Roads*. *See also* Honikman, Basil; Lamppa, Ryan.

Road Running Technical Committee (RRTC) (www.usaldr.org). This USATF body sets standards for course measurement and maintains an official list of certified courses in the United States.

Roads Scholars (www.rrca.org). RRCA awards four to six annual "scholarships" to runners needing financial assistance to train and race at a higher level. These athletes are selected according to need and racing potential. *See also* Road Runners Club of America.

Roba, Fatuma (b. December 18, 1973). Olympic Marathon races are frequently peppered with surprise performances. Unknowns or unexpecteds come on in a big way and make a name for themselves while well-known, proven stars fade on the big day. At 22, Fatuma Roba of Ethiopia was not a marathon novice when she arrived in Atlanta for the 1996 Olympic Games. She'd won her first-ever marathon in Ethiopia's capital, Addis Ababa, in July 1993 and had won races earlier in 1996 in Marrakech (in 2:30:50) and in Rome. But she was certainly not considered a favorite at Atlanta.

She came into that Olympic race surprisingly well recovered from her 2:29:05 at Rome in March, and she ran aggressively. Once she asserted herself at the front, her run appeared effortless; she was even enjoying herself enough to smile at and wave at supporters running along the sidewalk carrying an Ethiopian flag. When you can beat Russia's defending champion Valentina Yegorova by exactly two minutes (2:26:05 versus 2:28:05) while setting a personal best, it's difficult not to smile.

Fatuma proceeded to prove that her win was not a fluke by putting a stranglehold on the Boston Marathon for the next three years (1997 in 2:26:24, 1998 in 2:23:21, 1999 in 2:23:25). She returned in 2000 to be part of one of the most dramatic duels (with Catherine Ndereba for most of the race) and closest finishes in the race's history: Kyrgyzstan's Irina Bogacheva nipped Roba for second place at the finish line by thrusting herself across the line like a sprinter as Fatuma faded. Fatuma placed ninth in the Sydney Olympic Marathon, running 2:27:38 in the fastest mass finish in Games history.

Like many an Ethiopian marathoner, Fatuma grew through poverty. Her father was a farmer in the little village of Bokeji. Like many Ethiopian youth, she traveled extensively by foot. This, along with the altitude of much of Ethiopia, combined to produce a champion. Her three wins at Boston equal the accomplishments of Rosa Mota and Uta Pippig on that famed course. *See also* Abera, Gezahegne; Boston Marathon; Ethiopia; Olympic medalists; rankings, *Track & Field News*.

Robbins, Dr. Charlie (b. 1920). A two-time national marathon champion during the war years of 1944 and 1945, "Doc" Robbins later was recognized throughout New England for running his races barefooted, in stocking feet, or in Aquasocks. *See also* Hall of Fame, RRCA; national marathon champions, U.S.

Robinson, Roger (b. May 15, 1939). Roger's running career milestones go way back. In 1966 he represented England in the World Cross Country Championships, and 11 years later he represented his adopted New Zealand in the same international race. He won many provincial championships in Canterbury (1968–1974) and Wellington (1974–1979), but his running exploded when he turned 40. He has won the masters division in numerous marathons— Boston, New York, Vancouver, Canberra, Christchurch, and Winstone. He has also won gold and silver medals in the World Veteran Games. In New Zealand, where running is taken quite seriously, he passed a five-year stretch during which he was unbeaten in more than 100 races. *Runner's World* magazine named him the 1980 Masters Male of the Year.

Roger has also developed an enviable reputation as a skilled and sensitive writer on the subject of running. A professor of English at Victoria University of Wellington in New Zealand, he has published a great deal of academic writing, including (with Nelson Wattie) the massive 1998 *Oxford Companion to New Zealand Literature*. His writing on running has appeared in virtually every major running magazine in the world, and many of his early efforts were collected in the highly acclaimed 1986 book *Heroes and Sparrows: A Celebration of Running* (Southwestern, 1968). Roger is married to running pioneer and promoter Kathrine Switzer. *See also* rankings, *Runner's World*; Switzer, Kathrine.

Rocha, Joseildo (b. February 22, 1965). The Brazilian won the Chicago Marathon in 1991 (2:14:33) and the Los Angeles Marathon in 1993 (2:14:29). *See also* Chicago Marathon, Los Angeles Marathon.

Rock 'n' Roll Marathon (www.rnrmarathon.com). The largest first-time marathon drew almost 20,000 runners to San Diego in 1998 with the promise of hearing rock bands every mile. The inaugural race, however, turned out to be something of a disaster. It was started more than a half hour late, aid stations ran out of water, and many of the bands were taking breaks when the runners passed their locations. The promoters, however, asked for forgiveness and rectified the problems by year two. *See also* biggest races.

Rodgers, Bill (b. December 23, 1947). Four wins at Boston and four wins at New York are the statistics usually quoted when someone is speaking of Bill Rodgers's road-racing career. Although he was born in Connecticut and went to high school there, he was known to the media and to fans of the sport as "Boston Billy" because he later lived, ran, and worked in Boston and because, for a time he treated the Boston Marathon as though it were a race created for his exclusive use. For a person who appears to be continually startled by the world around him, Bill is a serious student of the sport of running. As a competitor, he was accustomed to dominating the pace of a race from the front. Perennially more accessible than any other competitor of his time, Bill's boy-next-door persona housed a fierce, nearly maniacal racing spirit. During the height of his competitive career he was referred to as "King of the Roads," in part because of one period in the late 1970s when he won 22 road races in a row, including everything from the 10K to the marathon.

An outstanding high school cross country runner in Newington High School in Connecticut in the mid-1960s, Bill went on to Wesleyan University, where Jeff Galloway was two grades ahead of him and where Amby Burfoot (1968 Boston winner) was one year ahead and his roommate. After college, Bill drifted away from running, took up smoking and hanging out at bars, and battled for conscientious objector status with the draft board. To earn the C.O., he was required to put in community service, which he did by pushing dead bodies around on gurneys at Peter Bent Brigham Hospital.

A little at a time he drifted back to running, even though he had not entirely given up smoking. He began materializing at local road races, a fellow in raggedy clothes who on occasion ran brilliantly. He drifted into longer and longer road races, tried Boston in 1973, and dropped out after running much too fast for the conditions. Two years later he won the race in 2:09:55, setting an American record by breaking Frank Shorter's mark by 35 seconds. Bill so dominated the race that he took time to walk through aid stations to make sure he could drink water and went so far as to stop on Heartbreak Hill to retie his shoelace.

In 1976 he ran with Frank Shorter at the front of the Olympic Trials Marathon in Eugene, Oregon, before finishing a close 2nd. Although Bill again ran at the front in the Olympic Marathon, he dropped back later in the race because of cramping, placing 40th in 2:25:15. That fall, however, as part of the Bicentennial celebration, the New York City Road Runners

Bill Rodgers sports the high-tech running clothing of 1975 as he wins his first of four Boston Marathons, this one in 2:09:55, a new American record by 35 seconds.

Club brought its marathon out of Central Park and onto the streets of the five boroughs. Bill won the race handily in 2:10:10.

In 1977 he dropped out at Boston but won in Amsterdam on May 12, repeated in New York on October 23, and then won Fukuoka on December 4. He again won Boston in 1978 and repeated in New York in the fall. In 1979 he won Boston for a third time, breaking his own American record with a 2:09:27, and in the fall he won his fourth consecutive New York City Marathon, coming from behind on a very hot day. In 1980 he won Boston for the fourth time but missed his chance at another Olympics; the U.S. decided to boycot the games and he didn't run the Trials to nowhere.

Unlike many road-racing champions who retire from the racing scene after they pass 35 years old, Bill has continued training and competing at a high level, winning numerous masters age-group titles through the years. He continues to operate the Bill Rodgers Running Center in Boston and follows an ambitious racing and guest-appearance schedule. He has written several books, including *Masters Running and Racing* (with Priscilla Welch and Joe Henderson, Rodale, 1991), *Marathoning* (with Joe Concannon, Simon & Schuster, 1980), and *Bill Rodgers' Lifetime Running Plan* (with Scott Douglas, Harper Collins, 1996). He lives in Melrose, Massachusetts. *See also* "Ambassador Bill" on next page; Bloomsday 12K; Boston Marathon; Fukuoka Marathon; New York City Marathon; Hall of Fame, National Distance Running; Hall of Fame, RRCA; national 10K champions, U.S.; Olympians, U.S.; Olympic Trials Marathon, U.S.; rankings, *Runner's World*; rankings, *Track & Field News*; record progressions, American; record progressions, world.

Roe, Allison (b. May 30, 1956). It is obvious that movie-star attractive Allison Roe from New Zealand never met a sport she didn't like. Before she took up running, she was outstanding at high jumping, tennis, swimming, and water skiing. After she eased out of marathon running, she was outstanding as a triathlete. Statuesque and charming, she seemed to come out of nowhere in the early 1980s, make a shocking impression, and then vanish—like the Lone Ranger of running.

Naturally, it wasn't quite that simple. She ran in the 1975 World Cross Country Championships in Morocco as a teenager, and, while pursuing her other sports, eased into the marathon. She ran a relatively modest 2:51 at the Choysa Marathon in Auckland in 1980, then made a huge leap in performance. She traveled to Eugene, Oregon, in September for the Nike–Oregon Track Club Marathon and ran 2:34:29. At the next year's Choysa Marathon she ran 2:36:16.

Then in April 1981 Allison journeyed to Boston, but her presence was overshadowed by the promised duel between Joan Benoit and Patti Catalano. Benoit came into the race strong, but it wasn't to be her day. It was—and it wasn't—to be Patti Catalano's. She set an American record and broke the Boston course record with a 2:27:51, but for the third year in a row she placed second. Roe had performed like a beautifully oiled machine, shattering the women's record for the course by nearly eight minutes by running a 2:26:46!

Roe wasn't finished for the year. In October she went to New York City and stopped Grete Waitz's domination of the course (Grete had won in 1978, 1979, and 1980) by running a course record (and, it was thought, a world record) of 2:25:29. In the same race, Alberto Salazar apparently broke the men's world record with a 2:08:13. Upon remeasurement, however, the course was found to be 150 meters short, so the records were disallowed. Roe's performance, though, wasn't. She had completely dominated marathoning in 1981, but she soon branched off into triathlons. Her impact on road racing was sudden, and it was brilliant, and it was short. *See also* Boston Marathon; New York City Marathon; Peachtree 10K; rankings, *Track & Field News*; record progressions, world.

Ambassador Bill

From Joe Henderson's *Running Commentary,* August 1998.

Bill Rodgers's grand entrance was well orchestrated. Officials at the Fifth Season 8K in Cedar Rapids, Iowa, asked him to pass through the starting crowd from back to front as the announcer shouted his praises. Bill went along with the plan, because he agrees to almost anything. The crowd respectfully parted to let him pass but stayed close enough to shake his hand and pat his back as he jogged forward.

This scene illustrates the phenomenon that is Bill Rodgers. He receives royal treatment at races, yet retains the common touch. This helps explain why he remains so popular, even among runners whose memories don't reach back to his prime racing years of 1975–80. These admirers don't come to see him for what he once did but for who he is now.

His hosts in Cedar Rapids arranged for him to give away hats carrying a "Bill Rodgers Running Center" logo. He signed hundreds of them, and the recipients couldn't have been happier if he had handed them $20 bills. He spoke briefly on two occasions, saying little that bears repeating here. His message didn't matter. He could have spoken in Urdu, and his audiences would have been just as pleased to have him with them.

Bill isn't at his best on stage, but no running celebrity does better one to one. He puts each runner at ease and makes each one feel important. His almost-namesake Will Rogers said he "never met a man he didn't like." Bill Rodgers seems never to meet a runner who doesn't like him.

The Cedar Rapids event was just another stop on his endless road. He has done this a thousand times since the 1970s and couldn't be faulted for just going through the well-rehearsed motions. But he doesn't. He still genuinely enjoys his work, and the runners he visits can tell.

Bill has collected several nicknames over the years. They don't quite fit anymore. "Boston Billy" is too regional for someone whose fame and efforts span the country. "King of the Roads" makes him sound too regal and distant from the rest of us. We might call him an "elder statesman" of the sport. But that makes him sound older than he is. The term that fits best is "ambassador." He spreads through deeds and words the news of what's good and right about running.

Bill is one of the world's most youthful 50-year-olds but is not ageless. The mileage lines around his mouth and eyes have deepened, and his running times have slowed. But his slow is still the envy of runners 10 or more years younger. He ran 26:02 in the Cedar Rapids 8K and beat all masters.

Bill's competitive fires haven't gone cold. He still talks about breaking records for his age group, still talks about staying ahead of the first woman in any race, still talks of competition with his contemporaries (such as almost-50-year-old John Campbell of New Zealand). But he is just as likely to downplay his times to cut the apparent distance between himself and his audiences. He'll let dozens of local runners say they "beat Bill Rodgers," as happened in a Cedar Rapids fun run while he was playing his diplomatic role. No one does it better.

Rojas, Ric (b. February 6, 1952). He was part of the first wave of American talent rolling into Boulder to train. His credentials include wins at Bay to Breakers (1975), the Bloomsday 12K (1979), and the Bolder Boulder 10K

(1979). He now coaches runners in Boulder and competes as a master himself. *See also* Bay to Breakers 12K; Bloomsday 12K; Bolder Boulder 10K.

Rome. Another of the cities that have hosted more than one international championship, Rome was the site of the 1960 Olympics and the 1987 Worlds. *See also* historic sites; Olympic Marathon, 1900 to 2000; World Championships medalists.

Rono, Simon (b. April 9, 1972). Kenyans often enjoy a profitable month or so in the United States. Rono's came in May 1998 when he won Bay to Breakers and Bolder Boulder. *See also* Bay to Breakers 12K; Bolder Boulder 10K.

Rop, Rodgers (b. 1973). The current 25K world record-holder from Kenya ran 1:13:44 at Berlin in 2001. *See* records, world.

Rosa, Dr. Gabriele (birthdate unavailable). The sometimes controversial Italian coach of Fila-linked Kenyans set up a program called Discovery Kenya to scout and develop talent in that country, then attempted to mimic that program by establishing Discovery USA in 2000. With his medical background he's not immune to rumors of aiding his athletes with performance-enhancing drugs. *See also* coaches; Discovery USA; Fila.

Rosenquist Jones, Kim. See Jones, Kim Rosenquist.

Ross, Browning (b. April 26, 1924, d. 1998). The publisher of the seminal *Long Distance Log* was the sparkplug behind the founding of the Road Runners Club of America, which now gives an annual award in his name for lifetime service to the sport. He was a 1948 Olympian in the steeplechase. *See also* Hall of Fame, RRCA; *Long Distance Log*; publications.

Roth, Arthur (b. May 10, 1892; date of death unknown). He won Boston in 1916, the year that World War I canceled the Olympics. Roth reached the Games four years later but DNFed there. *See also* Boston Marathon; Olympians, U.S.

Rotterdam Marathon (www.rotterdammarathon.nl). The consistently fast April marathon was built with world records in mind, and men and women responded. Carlos Lopes, Belayneh Dinsamo, and Tegla Loroupe all set their world marks here. *See also* fastest races.

Round the Bay 8.4K. One of the world's largest races is run in one of the world's smallest countries, New Zealand. Auckland, where the "Bay" race is run each autumn with a field of more than 40,000, was a birthplace of the mass-running movement, thanks to Arthur Lydiard. *See also* biggest races.

Rousseau, Vincent (b. July 26, 1962). This Belgian won the 1993 World Half and 1994 Rotterdam Marathons. A sub-2:08 marathoner, he retired early rather than run Olympics and World Championships at hot-weather sites. *See also* Rotterdam Marathon; World Half-Marathon Championships.

Rotterdam Marathon Winners

The Dutch race established itself early as one of the fastest when Carlos Lopes set a world record in the fifth year. Then Belayneh Dinsamo ran the first sub-2:07 (a world mark that lasted 10 years). Tegla Loroupe set the first of her records on this course. * = event record.

WOMEN

Year	Athlete	Time
1981	Marja Wokke (Holland)	2:43:23
1982	Mathilde Heuinig (West Germany)	2:54:03
1983	Rosa Mota (Portugal)	2:32:27
1984	Carla Beurskens (Holland)	2:34:54
1985	Wilma Rusman (Holland)	2:35:32
1986	Elinor Ljungros (Sweden)	2:41:06
1987	Nelly Aerts (Belgium)	2:41:24
1988	Hong Yanxiao (China)	2:37:46
1989	Elena Murgoci (Romania)	2:32:03
1990	Carla Beurskens (Holland)	2:29:47
1991	Joke Kleyweg (Holland)	2:34:18
1992	Aurora Cunha (Portugal)	2:29:14
1993	Anne van Schuppen (Holland)	2:34:15
1994	Miyoki Asahina (Japan)	2:25:52
1995	Monica Pont (Spain)	2:30:34
1996	Lieve Slegers (Belgium)	2:28:06
1997	Tegla Loroupe (Kenya)	2:22:07
1998	Tegla Loroupe (Kenya)	2:20:47*
1999	Tegla Loroupe (Kenya)	2:22:48
2000	Anna Isabel Alonso (Spain)	2:30:18
2001	Susan Chepkemei (Kenya)	2:25:45

MEN

Year	Athlete	Time
1981	John Graham (Britain)	2:09:28
1982	Rodolfo Gomez (Mexico)	2:11:57
1983	Rob de Castella (Australia)	2:08:37
1984	Gidamis Shahanga (Tanzania)	2:11:12
1985	Carlos Lopes (Portugal)	2:07:12
1986	Abebe Mekonnen (Ethiopia)	2:09:08
1987	Belayneh Dinsamo (Ethiopia)	2:12:58
1988	Belayneh Dinsamo (Ethiopia)	2:06:50*
1989	Belayneh Dinsamo (Ethiopia)	2:08:40
1990	Hiromi Taniguchi (Japan)	2:10:56
1991	Rob de Castella (Australia)	2:09:42
1992	Salvador Garcia (Mexico)	2:09:16
1993	Dionicio Ceron (Mexico)	2:11:06
1994	Vincent Rousseau (Belgium)	2:07:51
1995	Martin Fiz (Spain)	2:08:57
1996	Belayneh Dinsamo (Ethiopia)	2:10:30
1997	Domingos Castro (Portugal)	2:07:51
1998	Fabian Roncero (Spain)	2:07:26
1999	Japhet Kosgei (Kenya)	2:07:09
2000	Kenneth Cheruiyot (Kenya)	2:08:22
2001	Josephat Kiprono (Kenya)	2:06:50*

Now synonymous with *cheat*, Rosie Ruiz pretends to have won the 1980 Boston Marathon, upstaging the real winner, Jacqueline Gareau of Canada.

Royal Victoria Marathon (www. royalvictoriamarathon.com). It features a gorgeous seaside setting in parks on Vancouver Island in British Columbia, where the run falls on the early October Canadian Thanksgiving weekend. *See also* scenic races.

RRCA. *See* Road Runners Club of America.

RRIC. *See* Road Running Information Center.

RRTC. *See* Road Running Technical Committee.

Ruegger, Sylvia (b. February 23, 1961). Canada's longtime marathon record-holder set her mark of 2:28:36 at Houston in 1985. The year before, she'd placed eighth in the inaugural Olympic Marathon.

Ruiz, Rosie (birthdate unknown). She took the "T"—the subway—in Boston in 1980, jumped into the marathon for the final miles, and claimed to be the winner, robbing Jacqueline Gareau of Canada of her glory. All subsequent cheaters would be accused of "pulling a Rosie." *See also* cheaters.

Runner, The. George Hirsch created the magazine in 1978 to compete with *Runner's World.* Eventually, in 1987, he sold the New York City-based publication to *RW's* then-new owner, Rodale Press in Pennsylvania. *See also* Hirsch, George; publications; *Runner's World.*

Runner's Gazette (www.runnersgazette.com). One of the longest-running of the regional publications is based in Pennsylvania. Created by Ed Gildea, the co-founder of the Switchback Scamper 10K, the *Gazette* was shortly thereafter taken over by now-RRCA president Freddi Carlip and moved to Lewisburg, Pennsylvania. The publication can lay claim to being the longest-running newspaper devoted to long-distance running. *See also* Carlip, Freddi; Running Network, The.

Runner's Handbook, The. A steady seller since the mid-1970s, this book by Bob Glover and Jack Shepherd has spawned several sequels, including *The Competitive Runner's Handbook* (Viking, 1983). *See also* books; Glover, Bob.

runner's high. The endorphin-fueled feeling (which occurs when the brain releases endorphins as a result of exercise) is said to kick in after about 20 minutes of running and supposedly keeps us coming back for more.

Runner's World (www.runnersworld.com). The world's largest running magazine was founded in 1966 by Bob Anderson in his Kansas bedroom under the name *Distance Running News*. Anderson wanted to learn about running marathons, and he solicited information from a number of well-known long-distance runners of the time. The information was so thorough that Anderson decided to publish it and share it with other runners. Circulation rose to nearly a half million before Anderson sold to Rodale Press in 1985, and the magazine moved from California (where Anderson had moved in 1970) to Pennsylvania. Although at the height of the late 1970s running boom Bob Anderson would claim that the magazine was responsible for the huge surge in participation in long-distance running, his claim was unfounded because the magazine was not made available to newsstands until the November 1977 issue. Before that, you had to know another runner to know of the magazine's existence. And that (runner talking to runner, i.e., word of mouth) is essentially how the magazine grew in the late 1970s from an insider's monthly to a national phenomenon.

Over the years *RW* was responsible for many innovations to the sport of long-distance running (fun runs, Corporate Cup competition, National Running Week, New Year's Eve Midnight Run, marathon expos) and to magazine publishing (dual covers—a serious cover for subscribers and a "lighter" cover for newsstand sales, a protective cover for subscribers issues on which promotions could be carried, regional editions, etc.). Unfortunately, Anderson's expansion of his empire outside the area of running in the mid-1980s led to the magazine's cash-flow problems and its eventual sale to Rodale. Yet credit must be given where it is due. Bob Anderson's little magazine was ahead of its time, and once it got up to speed it generated the power to influence the sport it covered. *See also* Anderson, Bob; publications.

***Runner's World* Online** (www.runnersworld.com). Since 1996 the magazine has published an electronic Monday-through-Friday newsletter nearly every week of the year. See also *Runner's World.*

***Runner's World* rankings.** See rankings, *Runner's World.*

Running. *See* movies.

Running & Being (www.georgesheehan.com). Published in 1978 (Simon & Schuster), the best selling of George Sheehan's many books made the national sales lists for books of all types at a time when Jim Fixx's book led those lists. *R&B* was republished (Second Wind II) in 1998 in a 20th anniversary edition. *See also* books; Sheehan, Dr. George.

Running and Racing (www.runningandracing.com). Produced by Marty Liquori, the TV series on ESPN emphasizes road racing but also includes some triathlon coverage. *See also* Liquori, Marty; television.

Running Boom I. The boom of the 1970s came from two directions—people wanting to get fit by running and marathoners wanting to run fast times. Their heroes were Frank Shorter and Bill Rodgers. After a miniboom in 1968 following the publication of Dr. Kenneth Cooper's *Aerobics*, Frank Shorter's marathon gold in the 1972 Munich Games ratcheted up the sport. The 1976 Games added more fuel, as did the move of the New York City Marathon out of Central Park and onto the streets of the five boroughs, and the 1977 publication of Jim Fixx's *Complete Book of Running*. Ironically, it was Fixx's death in 1984 that helped put that boom on the skids.

Running Boom II. The boom that has continued since the 1990s brought a bigger and slower group of runners (and run-walkers) than its predecessor and continues to drive participation in road races to an all-time high. These runners' heroes are Jeff Galloway and John "Penguin" Bingham. *See also* "Booming Louder" on next page.

Running Brave. *See* Mills, Billy; movies.

Running Commentary (www.joehenderson.com). *See* About the Authors at the back of this book.

Running magazine. Nike bought up a small magazine and led a short-lived charge into the running publishing fray. *Running* magazine was a critical success but a financial flop in the early 1980s when it became apparent that no self-respecting competing shoe company would advertise in a magazine owned by Nike. Contributing writers included Ken Kesey and Hunter S. Thompson. *See also* Nike; publications.

Running Network, The (www.runningnetwork.com). A national alliance of primarily regional running publications allows smaller-circulation magazines to pool their circulation in order to approach national advertisers. *See also* publications.

Running Research News (www.rrnews.com). Owen Anderson's newsletter makes practical sense of the lab findings. *See also* Anderson, Owen; publications.

Running Room Canada, The (www.runningroom.com). John Stanton's ambitious—and growing—chain of running stores is nearly saturating Canada, and there is every indication that when the market is right he'll expand to the United States. The company is based in Edmonton, site of the 2001 World Championships.

Booming Louder

From Henderson's *Running Commentary,* August 1999.

Runner's World labeled it the "Second Running Boom." This isn't just a ploy to boost the magazine's circulation. This boom is real, it's big, and it's unlike the First Boom.

Back in the 1970s we experienced a sudden 10-fold increase in the number of runners and races. Most of the runners at that time were young men, and most of them took their racing quite seriously. That type of runner never went away, of course. The young and fast men will always be with us, but their portion of the running population is shrinking.

The total population of runners has never shrunk since the First Boom. It didn't end with a "Bust" in the 1980s. The growth simply leveled off. Then the sport began to grow again in the 1990s—but in different ways than before. Running today is

- bigger. At the peak of the First Boom, marathon entrants in the United States never topped 100,000. The current number is more than four times greater.

- shorter *and* longer. The most popular distance of the First Boom was 10 kilometers. In fact, the majority of races were 10Ks. Now the most popular racing distances are 5K (with women's and corporate events contributing heavily to that growth) and marathon.

- slower. In the First Boom the typical midpack time for a 10K was 40 to 45 minutes and for the marathon, 3:00 to 3:30. In the Second Boom we've added 10 minutes to the median 10K time and one hour to the marathon.

- older. Most of the runners from the First Boom still run in the Second, and they naturally have aged by 20-plus years. They're joined by newcomers who discovered the sport in their middle age. The largest age groups at races are now late 30s and early 40s. (The exception to this trend is the women in their 20s. This is the fastest growing segment of women—who overall are the fastest growing group of runners, now numbering 50 percent at many races.)

- friendlier. This isn't to say the runners of the First Boom were antisocial, but they tended to be loners. The Second Boom runner is more likely to join a club, train with a coach in an organized program, run a race with a company team, or enter an event that raises money for charity. Runners today also treat races more as social events and vacations, and less like the serious athletic contests that races once were.

Only the quality and depth of performances by leading Americans are now depressed. By all other standards—total number of runners, variety of runners (in terms of ability, age, size, and sex), events for runners, and resources available to runners—this is the best time ever to be a runner in the United States.

Running Stats (www.runningstats.com). Paul Christman has published his newsletter, featuring primarily results from road races as well as track races over 3,000 meters, almost weekly since the mid-1980s. *See also* Christman, Paul; publications.

Running Times (www.runningtimes.com). One of the country's oldest and largest running magazines dates from 1977, when Ed Ayres was the initial editor. *RT* has endured through many changes of ownership, location, and editors. *See also* Ayres, Ed; Bakoulis, Gordon; Beverly, Jonathan; publications; Rice, Carol Lasseter.

Running USA (www.runningusa.org). This confederation of running events, organizations, and media was founded as the sport headed into the new century to look after the business and promotional interests of running.

Running With the Legends. *See* books; Sandrock, Mike.

Run to the Top. Arthur Lydiard's (with Garth Gilmour) trend-setting book from the early 1960s (Jenkins, 1963) changed the way the world viewed distance-running training, both for elite athletes and exercisers. In the 1990s Lydiard issued the similarly titled *Running to the Top* (Meyer & Meyer Fachverlag und Buchhandel GmbH, 1997) with similar material. *See also* books; Lydiard, Arthur.

RW. See *Runner's World*.

Ryan, Mike (b. January 1, 1889; date of death unknown). He won the 1912 Boston Marathon, but his luck in the Olympics was not as good. He DNFed at the 1908 and 1912 Games. Ryan later became a U.S. Olympic Marathon coach who was much despised by his charges (especially Clarence DeMar) for his overbearing ways. *See also* Boston Marathon; Olympians, U.S.

Ryan, Mike (b. December 26, 1941). A New Zealander unrelated to the other Mike Ryan, he won the Fukuoka Marathon in 1966 and swam against the altitude-trained African tide to win a bronze medal in the 1968 Olympics. *See also* Fukuoka Marathon; Olympic medalists; rankings, *Track & Field News*.

Sachs, M.L. (b. September 7, 1951) and **Sacks, M.H.** (birthdate unavailable). The two researchers with almost the same name were among the first to establish firmly the link between running and good mental health. Together they wrote *Psychology of Running* (Human Kinetics, 1982). Two years later Michael Sachs, now an associate professor in the Department of Physical Education at Temple University, joined with Gary W. Buffone to edit one of the seminal books studying running—*Running As Therapy: An Integrated Approach* (Jason Aronson, 1997). Sachs is a member of the Science Advisory Board of *Marathon & Beyond*. *See also* Glasser, Dr. William; Kostrubala, Thaddeus; *Marathon & Beyond*.

St. George Marathon (www.stgeorgemarathon.com). The point-to-point course features a generous net elevation loss. When *Runner's World* named it the fastest marathon in America, runners flocked to this small city in southern Utah. Times run in this October race are considered aided, but they still qualify for Boston and the Olympic Trials. *See also* fastest races.

St. Hilaire, Judi (b. September 5, 1959). A track Olympian (10,000 in 1992), St. Hilaire holds the American 5K best, shares the world best for an aided course (14:57 in 1990), and is the only U.S. woman to break 15 minutes on any type of course. She held the unaided American 5K record twice, including the first sub-15:30 (15:26 in 1989). In the 1980s she won national 5K and 10K road titles, and she continues to race well as a master. *See also* national 5K champions, U.S.; national 10K champions, U.S.; Peachtree 10K; record progressions, American; record progressions, world; records, American; records, world.

St. Louis. It was the first of only three U.S. cities to host an Olympics. In 1904 the St. Louis Olympic Marathon was run as part of the World's Fair and was the scene of cheating and drug scandals. The race featured the first U.S. Olympic marathon gold medalist, Thomas Hicks. The Third Olympiad Memorial Marathon, run each February, commemorates those Games. *See also* Hicks, Thomas; historic sites; Lorz, Fred; Olympic Marathon, 1900 to 2000.

Salah, Ahmed (also spelled Saleh) (b. December 31, 1956). He put the tiny East African country of Djibouti on the running map. Salah won the World Cup Marathon in 1985 (2:08:09) and 1987 (2:10:55), was silver medalist at

Ahmed Salah (on the left, with Douglas Wakiihuri of Kenya at London in 1989), from the little country of Djibouti, went on a tear in the mid-1980s, winning the 1985 and 1987 World Cup Marathons.

the 1987 and 1991 World Championships, and collected the bronze at the 1988 Olympics. *See also* Olympic medalists; World Championships medalists; World Cup Marathon.

Salazar, Alberto. *See* page next page.

Salmini Films. Ambrose Salmini's company produces movies and TV shows on running. *See also* television.

Samuelson, Joan Benoit. *See* Benoit Samuelson, Joan.

San Blas Half-Marathon (www.sanblas.org). The longtime international half-marathon is run each winter in Coamo, Puerto Rico.

Salazar, Alberto (b. August 7, 1958). The consistently tough-minded, hard-training, and cocky racer typically backed up his seemingly outrageous promises of performance. His place in marathon history was undermined by instances of poor course measurements and mediocre—for him—performances at international events. A protégé of Bill Rodgers and the hotshoes of the Greater Boston Track Club and its enigmatic coach, Bill Squires, Alberto (known then as "the Rookie") went to college in Oregon. There he came under the watchful eye of coach Bill Dellinger, who had his hands full preventing Alberto from training himself into the ground. Dellinger, a shrewd observer of talent, also teased the running world and made Alberto impatient by holding him back from the marathon until Dellinger felt he was ready. That time came after the frustration of making the 1980 Olympic team in the 10,000 meters and then not being able to run in Moscow (because of the U.S. boycott).

Alberto's efficient, low-to-the-ground running style seemed perfect for the marathon. Even world record-holder Derek Clayton thought so and said so. When Salazar entered his first marathon (New York City) in 1980, in the box provided for predicted finish time he wrote "2:10," what would then have been the fastest debut marathon of all time. On October 26, Alberto ran 2:09:41, even faster than he'd predicted, and ended Bill Rodgers's four-year monopoly of the New York City Marathon. (Rodgers finished fifth after a group of leading runners got tangled up at 14 miles and fell into a heap; emerging star Dick Beardsley finished ninth after extricating himself from the tangle.) But Alberto wasn't satisfied. He had quickly but carefully made himself the best road racer in America. At the *Runner's World* Five-Mile Invitational road race in Los Altos, California, on January 4, 1981 he ran 22:04; he'd predicted that he would

break 22. The course didn't quite measure out at five miles, costing him a world record at that distance, but the time stood up as a record at the slightly shorter 8K. It remains the American mark.

For New York City 1981 he predicted that he would run 2:08:01, which would break Australian Derek Clayton's 12-year-old record of 2:08:34. His prediction was again just a mite off. He ran 2:08:13, breaking Clayton's record. In another reversal of fortune, however, the New York course was later found to be short, so his world record wasn't to be. (Ironically, it would be Australian Rob de Castella who would break Clayton's record with a 2:08:18 at Fukuoka in 1981. In his 1981 NYC win Salazar had broken the psychological logjam that had been erected by Clayton's excruciatingly detailed tale of what it took to break 2:09, and now a slew of runners would go not only under 2:09 but under 2:08.)

In spring 1982 Alberto went to Boston for his first try at the historic course near where he'd grown up in Wayland, Massachusetts, after being brought out of Cuba at age two. He came in as the favorite, but not everyone was buying the hype. Billy Squires, who had coached Salazar while he was still in high school, had changed camps. He was now coach of the New Balance Track Club, and one of his charges was Dick Beardsley, who'd run a 2:09:36 at Grandma's Marathon in 1981. Hailing from the cold fastness of Minnesota, Beardsley was the opposite of Alberto. Whereas it was all a reporter could do to search out Salazar before or after a race in hopes of getting a quote, Beardsley was glib, quotable, seemingly lighthearted, and cooperative. Whereas Alberto expected to dictate when and if anyone would talk to him, Dick Beardsley seemed genuinely surprised that someone wanted to talk with him.

If we were to pick the top 10 marathon duels of all time, the 1982 Boston battle

© Mark Shearman. Athletics-Images.

Alberto Salazar was the prince of the American roads in the wake of Shorter and Rodgers. He dominated domestic marathons but failed to win at major international competitions.

between Salazar and Beardsley would be among the top 3. The two literally pounded each other over the length of the course. In the final miles, the lead see-sawed back and forth. Dick led, but when he tried to surge to get away from Alberto and thus avoid having to outkick him at the finish, Dick developed a hamstring cramp. Alberto went around and opened a three-second lead. Dick stepped into a pothole and the change of angle of impact seemed to take care of the hamstring. He increased his pace. But as Dick tried to catch up, the accompanying motorcycle police drifted between the two runners.

Dick weaved his way through the motorcycles and continued to gain. But as he came up to Alberto with 200 meters to go, Alberto went to his arms and sprinted. Dick's response was too little too late. Alberto finished in 2:08:52, a course record in spite of the heat; Dick was two seconds back. (For an outstanding recreation of "The Duel," see Hal Higdon's book *Boston*, Rodale, 1996.) Salazar's Boston time stood for the next 12 years as the fastest by an American until Bob Kempainen bettered it at Boston in 1994.

Although Alberto would again win New York City that fall, Boston 1982 was the zenith for both him and Beardsley. Neither would again rise that high. Alberto would develop mysterious medical problems that may have begun cutting into his performances after 1982. He ran 2:10:10 at Rotterdam 1983 in a staged duel with de Castella and finished 5th. His performance at the Los Angeles Olympics in 1984 was very un-Alberto-like, resulting in a 15th-place finish in 2:14:19. Ten years later, after extensive medical attention, he traveled to South Africa and won the prestigious Comrades Marathon Ultra (53.8 miles) in 5:38:39. Today he works for Nike in Beaverton, Oregon, and lives the life of a happy family man, putting more time into watching his children play sports than he puts into his training. He has coached world-class athletes (including Mary Slaney) and is the author of two books: *Alberto Salazar Treadmill Training and Workout Guide* (Hatherleigh, 2000) and *Alberto Salazar's Guide to Running* (McGraw-Hill, 2001). *See also* Boston Marathon; Hall of Fame, National Distance Running; Hall of Fame, RRCA; New York City Marathon; Olympians, U.S.; Olympic Trials Marathon, U.S.; rankings, *Track & Field News;* record progressions, American; record progressions, world; records, American.

Sanders, Odis (b. June 16, 1959). A rare African-American champion in road racing, Sanders won the first three national 5K championships, in 1979 (14:44), 1980 (15:04), and 1981 (14:37). He now runs as a master, based in Eugene, Oregon. *See also* national 5K champions, U.S.

San Diego Marathon (www.sdmarathon.com). It traces its roots to the old Mission Bay Marathon, founded in 1965. The current version of this January race would more accurately be known as the San Diego *County* Marathon because it is run in Carlsbad. *See also* oldest races.

Sandoval, Tony (b. May 19, 1954). The marathoner of enormous talent never had a chance to display it on the greatest of all stages. Still young and experienced, he finished fourth behind fellow ex-Stanford runner Don Kardong at the 1976 Trials. Sandoval was at his best in 1980, winning the Trials that led nowhere in the boycott year. In 1979 he and Athletics West teammate Jeff Wells both ran 2:10:20 to set an American record for an unaided course. Sandoval's 2:10:19 remains a Trials record. He now works as a medical doctor in his native New Mexico. *See also* Hall of Fame, RRCA; Olympians, U.S.; Olympic Trials Marathon, U.S record progressions, American.

Sandrock, Mike (b. April 15, 1958). He has the best job in the best U.S. city for rubbing shoulders with elite runners. Mike works as a reporter-editor with Boulder's daily newspaper. His book *Running With the Legends* (Human Kinetics, 1996) features many of the city's resident runners. *See also* books.

São Sylvestre. This world-class New Year's Eve race of about 12K runs through the streets of São Paolo, Brazil.

Saucony (www.saucony.com). This U.S. shoe company (pronounced "SAW-con-ee") is headquartered in Pennsylvania. *See also* shoe companies.

Sayre, Ric (b. August 9, 1953). The Oregonian, by way of Ohio, won the 1986 Los Angeles Marathon (in 2:12:59) and the national marathon title in 1987 (2:13:54). *See also* Los Angeles Marathon; national marathon champions, U.S.

Scaff, Dr. Jack (birthdate unavailable). In the 1970s this medical doctor originated the now-popular concept of marathon-training clinics. His Honolulu clinic helped launch that city's marathon into one of the world's largest. He is also famous for being one of the pioneers in helping heart patients recover by training in a marathon lifestyle. *See also* Honolulu Marathon.

scenic races. Some runners will tell you they never notice the scenery when they are racing. But they certainly notice it before and after, and many choose races based on the setting. Among the most beautiful marathons in the United States are Adirondack (www.adirondackmarathon.com), Avenue of the Giants (www.humboldt1.com/~avenue), Big Sur (www.bsim.org), Catalina Island (www.pacificsportsllc.com), Crater Lake, Humboldt Redwoods (www.northcoast.com), Kilauea Volcano (www.bishopmuseum.org/vac/home.html), Napa Valley (www.napa-marathon.com), Lake Tahoe (www.laketahoemarathon.com), Maui (www.mauimarathon.com), Royal Victoria (www.islandnet.com/~rvm), and Twin Cities (www.twincitiesmarathon.org). *See also* Avenue of the Giants Marathon; Big Sur Marathon; Catalina Island Marathon; Humboldt Redwoods Marathon; Kilauea Volcano Marathon; Mackinac Island Run; Napa Valley Marathon; Rim Rock Run; Royal Victoria Marathon; and Twin Cities Marathon.

Schiro, Cathy. *See* O'Brien, Cathy Schiro.

Schul, Bob (b. September 28, 1937). He didn't run road races in his prime years—and you can't get any more prime than the 1964 Olympic gold medal at 5,000 meters—but he later ran the roads as a master and coached many runners for those events. *See also* Hall of Fame, RRCA; Hall of Fame, USATF.

Scott, Steve (b. May 5, 1956). Known mainly as a miler—he has held the American record continuously since the mid-1980s—he twice set world and American 5K records (1986 and 1988, both at Carlsbad) in rare forays onto the roads. Scott now can be seen and heard frequently as a commentator at televised road races. He coaches college runners in southern California. *See also* record progressions, American; record progressions, world.

Scudamore, Dave (b. February 15, 1970). He was cut from the same mold as Bob Kempainen—coached by Vin Lananna and trained as a medical doctor, he took time out from his schooling to win the 1997 national marathon title and place 13th (and 1st American) at the Worlds that year. *See also* national marathon champions, U.S.; World Championships, U.S.

Second Skin. This innovative product protects and prevents blisters by adhering to skin as a gel-like sheath to cushion and protect. Invented by Dr. Wayman Spence, Second Skin was one of the anchor products of his company, Spenco, which he later sold to Johnson & Johnson.

See How She Runs. *See* movies.

Segal, Erich (birthdate unavailable). The classic scholar who became famous as the author of *Love Story*; Segal ran Boston and other races in about three hours during the 1960s and early 1970s. He did a stint as Olympic Marathon commentator at the 1972 Games and is remembered for shouting about an imposter leading Frank Shorter into the stadium. He was also the screenwriter of *Yellow Submarine* and *The Games*, a 1970 film following four long-distance runners from four corners of the globe as they train for the Olympic Marathon. *See also* movies.

Seko, Toshihiko (b. July 15, 1956). Seko, one of the greatest of Japan's long line of intense and dedicated road racers, was also an early example of the debilitating effect American culture can have on the Japanese. Today reports abound from Tokyo of modern youngsters being ruined by embracing American "culture." Toshihiko Seko was at the vanguard. As a youngster, Seko admits he was naturally lazy. Nonetheless (again, as with modern youngsters), he wanted to be famous for something. At first he hoped to be a baseball star. But he became a runner instead, and as both a junior and senior at Kuwana High School, he became the national champion at both the 800 meters and the 1,500. It came easy.

Unfortunately, his studies didn't. And in the supercompetitive atmosphere of Japan in the 1970s, when its Toyotas and electronic equipment were conquering American, Seko failed his entrance exam to Waseda University. Seko's parents decided to send him to the University of Southern California in Los Angeles in hopes he would train harder and become inspired to improve his studies. "I went with two other Japanese runners," Seko revealed in a 1982 interview, "and we played around too much. We spent all our time stuffing ourselves with hamburgers and junk food. I came back to Japan 20 pounds overweight."

When he returned, though, he fell under the influence of controversial coach Kiyoshi Nakamura. Nakamura grew up poor and took every opportunity offered him; he set the Japanese national record at 1,500 meters (3:56.8) that stood for 16 years, became a successful businessman in the wake of World War II, and retired to study world religions. As a hobby he coached at Waseda University for a nominal $150 per year.

As soon as Nakamura saw Seko's flowing running style, he was inspired to have him move up in distance, something that shocked and appalled Seko and his parents—especially in view of his early success

© Mark Shearman, Athletics—Images.

Japan's Toshihiko Seko shows victorious form in the wake of the 1986 London Marathon, sharing the platform with Grete Waitz. Seko was a dominating figure in road racing from the late 1970s through the 1980s. Our favorite quote from Toshihiko came in response to a question about what it takes to win major marathons: "You must run on the edge of death."

at the 800 and 1,500 meters. Nakamura demanded that his devotees give themselves entirely over to him, to the point that some young runners were taken in to live with him at his home. It was more like a martial-arts school than a coaching situation. For years Nakamura was criticized for using corporal punishment on his runners. "I gave up hitting my runners when I discovered that words were more effective," Nakamura admitted.

After some bitter early disagreements, Seko and Nakamura clicked. Seko went on to set the Japanese 10K record of 27:43.5, displaying the speed that accounts for his devastating kick in the final miles of a marathon. He won the prestigious unofficial world marathon championship at Fukuoka three times in a row (1978, 1979, and 1980). Seko finished a strong second to Bill Rodgers at Boston in 1979, as Rodgers set an American record. Seko returned to Boston in 1981 to challenge Rodgers and in the process broke Rodgers's course record by one second. Seko once said that to be successful in the marathon you must be prepared to "run on the edge of death."

The stage was set for the Los Angeles Olympics, where it was believed that a classic duel between Rodgers's heir apparent, Alberto Salazar, and Japan's Toshihiko Seko would be the highlight of the marathon. Having won the Tokyo Men's Marathon with a 2:08:38, Seko ran Japan's Olympic trials at the famed Fukuoka Marathon in 1983 and turned in an extremely credible 2:08:52, while equaling Frank Shorter's record for four Fukuoka wins. Salazar took fifth in 2:09:21. Marathon historian Dave Martin observes that during the year leading to the 1984 Olympic Marathon, "The United States was similar to Japan in that it had so many top marathon runners that the country could have fielded two quality Olympic teams."

Los Angeles was a disaster for the veteran marathoners, however. It was warm (72 degrees) and the course was totally exposed to the sun, which even at the 5:00 P.M. start was intense. Portugal's Carlos Lopes, 37, who had completed only one marathon (Rotterdam, April 1983, 2:08:39), won. Seko and Salazar didn't even make the top 10. Seko did, however, continue to compete. He won the Chicago and London marathons in 1986 and raced in the Olympics again in Seoul in 1988, placing ninth in 2:13:41. Nakamura's and Seko's inspirational influence over younger Japanese road racers cannot be overstated, and some of the results, especially among young female marathoners, are apparent today. *See also* Boston Marathon; Chicago Marathon; Fukuoka Marathon; London Marathon; Tokyo Marathons.

Semple, John "Jock" (b. October 26, 1903, d. March 8, 1988). If there is one person in all road-racing history who fit the description of *crusty*, it would have to be Jock Semple. As far as he was concerned, the Boston Marathon was his race, his personal race, and everyone who ran in it ran at his pleasure. He ruled it not in a dictatorial way, although he frequently acted dictatorial, but in a protective way—protective of the race and the runners. Semple loved the runners, perhaps more than anyone who's ever been associated with Boston or who ever will be. He couldn't abide anything, from tomfoolery to outrageous antics, that would detract from his race or embarrass his runners. At one point in the history of the Boston Marathon, Jock's massage room in the Boston Arena was literally the headquarters of both the marathon and the "sponsoring" Boston Athletic Association. The association and its marathon, in total, were contained in several cardboard boxes piled in a corner.

Jock, who preferred the nickname Johnny, also loved the runners because he was very much one of them. He was born in Glasgow, Scotland, in a second-story apartment near the Dixon's Blazes steel mill, so called because of the hellish light it threw day and night. He was raised to work hard and to get an education, but he preferred having a nickel in his pocket to having a million dollars' worth of education in his head. He left school at 14. He went to work at the Singer Sewing Machine Company in Clydebank, where he took part in a sports day by winning the 100-yard dash.

Johnny moved through several jobs until one night at supper his father asked him if he'd like to go to America. Johnny jumped at the chance and landed in Philadelphia. He got a job putting together the floors of the Japanese exhibition at the city's sesquicentennial. A marathon was part of the celebration. Johnny trained 90 miles a week and took 11th in the race. In 1930, when he was 27, he entered the Boston Marathon and took 7th place after hitchhiking from Philadelphia to

John "Jock" Semple was the man who kept the Boston Athletic Association (and hence, the Boston Marathon) afloat through its meager years in the 1950s and 1960s. He was an accomplished road racer in his youth.

Boston in 26 hours. He ran Boston again in 1932 and placed 10th. The same year he won the Pawtucket Marathon, in the process breaking the course record held by the great Clarence DeMar.

He continued to fall into and out of work during the Depression, and when World War II came he enlisted in the navy. Back from the war in 1945, Jock went to school to become a physical therapist. He got a job with Walter Brown, who'd started the Celtics basketball club. Brown also housed the BAA in the Arena and later in the Garden. He put Jock in charge of the BAA's running club. In 1948 Jock saw John J. Kelley race, went after him as a BAA prospect, and eventually got him signed up. Jock wanted very badly to have a BAA member win the club's marathon as homage to Walter Brown's efforts to keep the BAA and the race alive. He found that member in young Johnny Kelley, who won the race in 1957.

Jock Semple could be incredibly intimidating and insensitive. He dispatched cheaters, fakes, and phonies who tried to sully the Boston Marathon. His verbal invective was similar to a bolt from the blue or the bite of an enraged shark. He is probably best remembered as the official who tried to extricate Kathrine Switzer physically from the race when she managed to get a race number in 1967. On the other hand, his treatment of the authentic, serious runners was like that of a mother taking her child to her breast. Everyone who ever met him has a Jock Semple story to tell. And every story involves his crusty exterior and his heart of gold. *See also* Boston Marathon; Hall of Fame, RRCA; Kelley, John J.; Switzer, Kathrine.

Sensburg, Ingo (birthdate unavailable). The German was a three-time winner of early Berlin Marathons, in 1976, 1979, and 1980. *See also* Berlin Marathon.

Serious Runner's Handbook. *See* Osler, Tom.

Sevene, Bob (b. 1943). The gravel-voiced New Englander coached Joan Benoit Samuelson in her best years while both were affiliated with Nike's Athletics West. He continues to coach in the Boston area. Our favorite quote from Bob was his reference to Joan Benoit as "a bowling ball with legs." *See also* Benoit Samuelson, Joan; coaches.

Shahanga, Gidamis (b. September 4, 1957). The Tanzanian won the 1978 Commonwealth Games Marathon (2:15:40) and 1984 Rotterdam (2:11:12). *See also* Commonwealth Games; Rotterdam Marathon.

Shea, Julie (b. May 3, 1959) and **Shea, Mary** (b. November 26, 1960). Julie held world and American 10K records and was the first to break 35:00. Sister Mary held the world and American 5K marks. Olympic marathoner Jack Bacheler coached the sisters at North Carolina State University. *See also* Bacheler, Jack; record progressions, American; record progressions, world.

Sheehan, Dr. George (b. November 5, 1918; d. November 1, 1993). For all of his renown as a writer and speaker, George was above all a racer. He raced cross country and track as a youth in his native Brooklyn and at Manhattan College, took a hiatus of more than 20 years while fathering a very large family and establishing his medical career on the Jersey Shore, then returned to the sport he was built for at age 44. Running for fitness didn't satisfy him. He had to race. When no other events were available, he often joined the high school races that his sons were running. After he discovered road racing he competed nearly every weekend, and twice when opportunities allowed, for nearly 30 years. He probably raced more than a thousand times in his adult career, though he never bothered to keep a log on any of his running.

George didn't just run through these events as a midpacker. He truly and honestly raced, aiming every time to take home an age-group prize. At age 50 he ran a mile in 4:47, at the time a world record for someone who'd lived a half century or more. His training was better suited to five-mile and 10K racing than to the marathon, yet he ran Boston 21 years in a row starting in 1964. One of his proudest accomplishments was setting a PR of 3:01 at the Marine Corps Marathon when he was just shy of his 61st birthday.

From all this racing George drew lessons that made him the sport's best-loved writer and speaker. He began writing two columns—one philosophical, one medical—for *Runner's World* in 1970, left in the 1980s to do similar work at *The Runner*, then returned to *RW* to finish his career when the two magazines merged in 1987. By then George had written several books, starting with *Dr. Sheehan on Running* (World Publications, 1975) and then his best-seller, *Running & Being* (Simon & Schuster, 1978), which made the national lists at the same time as Jim Fixx's *Complete Book of Running* (Random House, 1977). From the late 1970s through the early 1990s he was in such demand as a speaker that he appeared onstage as many as a hundred times a year.

In 1986 George was diagnosed with advanced prostate cancer. He lived with the disease for another seven years, continuing to run and race (including making the 800-meter final of the 1989 World Veterans Championships) until his final year, speaking until his final months, and writing until his final days when he completed his last book, *Going the Distance* (Villard, 1996). He died at home, in the company of his wife, Mary Jane, and their 12 children, four days short of his 75th birthday. Most of his books remain in print, and a sampling of his columns is available on the family Web site, www.georgesheehan.com. *See also* "Tears for a Winner" on next page; books; Hall of Fame, RRCA; *Runner's World*.

Sheehan on Running, Dr. Dr. Sheehan's first full-length book (World Publications, 1975) is a compilation of many of his *Runner's World* columns. Some consider it his finest book. *See also* books; Sheehan, Dr. George.

Sherring, William (b. September 19, 1878; d. 1964). The Canadian claimed marathon gold at the "extra Olympics" of 1906, held for the only time at a two-year interval. He remains his country's only winner at this Olympic distance. *See also* Olympic medalists.

Billy Sherring of Canada was the winner of the marathon at the 1906 Athens Intercalated Games—the games held on the 10th anniversary of the first modern Olympics.

From the collection of Dr. Edward H. Kozloff—Motor City Striders

Tears for a Winner

From Joe Henderson's *Runner's World* column, March 2000.

My columns and talks are like my runs. No matter how well planned they seem, I never quite know where they'll lead. All take surprising turns on the way to their finish lines.

When I stood up last fall to speak at the Royal Victoria Marathon, I didn't expect to sit down wiping away tears. They were good tears for a great friend. They show he's still much missed but also well remembered.

The theme at the prerace dinner in Victoria was masters running, which has less to do with winning races and setting records after age 40 than with slowing and aging gracefully. The talk started lightly enough and was meant to stay that way. Fidgety runners don't need a heavy message on race eve, only a few laughs and a little inspiration.

I told of a Canadian runner in his 80s, Whitey Sheridan, who'd run for almost 70 of those years. He advised me on my 40th running anniversary, "Hang in there, kid. You're just getting started." This led to talk of winning by surviving. A survivor is the best that most of us can be. If we can't outrun people, we can at least outlast them. I've outlasted Olympic champions and world record-holders while adding up the years of modest efforts.

So far the Victoria talk had stayed on safe emotional ground. But I was about to step into territory where tears lurk. I told of looking up the most to runners who have lasted the longest. The greatest of those heroes is George Sheehan, whose definitions of winning survive him.

Smiling through tears, I wrote a biography of George called *Did I Win?* The title came from one of the last talks he ever gave to runners. Someone from the audience, knowing George's condition, asked, "At this stage of your life what is your biggest concern?"

George was stumped for a moment. Then he put his hands together, looked up in mock prayer, and answered, "Did I win? Have I done enough? Have I been a good enough runner, writer, speaker, and doctor? More importantly, have I been a good enough father and friend?"

He didn't think so. That's why he hadn't retired to "[watch] the waves roll in and out" from his home on the Jersey Shore. That's why he ran for as long as he legs would allow, then walked, then swam. That's why he kept writing columns and worked to finish one more book. That's why he surrounded himself with family and friends right to the end.

One of the last races George ran was the Crim 10-Mile in Michigan. He ran along in last place with another man, a younger one who was injured. That runner turned to George and complained, "You know, Doc, we used to be good."

George came right back with, "We're as good as we ever were. We're doing the best we can with what we have. You have an injury, and I have an illness. But we're still out here, giving our all. No one can do more or should do less."

George Sheehan redefined winning for us. One definition was to "do the best you can with what you are given."

I liked another one even better. The summer after he died, a race was renamed the "George Sheehan Classic" and moved from the neighborhood where he'd lived to the hospital where he'd worked. This was his noontime running course in Red Bank, New Jersey.

As I exited the finish chute, a medal was draped around my neck. One side bore George's likeness. Seeing that, I recalled in the recent talk, I almost broke down. Then I turned the medal over, read one of his lines, and totally lost control. Just then I looked at the Victoria crowd and saw a woman who had dealt with a serious illness of her own this year. She had lowered her head and was mopping her eyes with a dinner napkin.

Tears are contagious, and hers set off mine as I sputtered out the Sheehan line from the medal: "Winning is never having to say I quit." I caught my breath, wiped my cheeks, and added, "He never did, and neither should we."

Shigematsu, Morio (b. June 21, 1940). The Japanese runner broke the world record set by the mythical Abebe Bikila, running 2:12:00 in 1965. *See also* rankings, *Track & Field News*; record progressions, world.

shinsplints. This common road runners' injury term is an umbrella term that can include stress fractures, tibial tendinitis, muscle tears, and inflammation of the bone sheath in the shin area. Shinsplints, whatever the cause, are usually felt as an aching or throbbing along the inside of the shin bone. Overpronation and running on hard surfaces such as concrete sidewalks can aggravate the pain. *See also* injuries.

shoe companies. They were prime movers in the first running boom, allowing runners to take to the roads in greater numbers than ever before, with fewer injuries and other footwear-related problems. New Balance, Tiger (now Asics), Tiger's American spin-off Nike, and adidas led the revolution in materials, design, and models customized to various applications. *See also* "Shoe Business" on next page; adidas; Asics; New Balance; Nike.

Shoe Goo. In response to the soaring price of shoes and higher mileage that wore away the soles faster, runners of the 1970s began patching their shoes with electric glue guns. This practice gave rise to Shoe Goo, a product sold in a tube and formulated for this purpose.

Shorter, Frank. *See* page 329.

Silva, German (b. January 9, 1968). The Mexican is a two-time winner at the New York City Marathon, in 1994 and 1995. The first was memorable because a lead vehicle led Silva and another runner off-course late in the race. *See also* Bloomsday 12K; New York City Marathon.

Simon, Lidia (b. September 4, 1973). The bronze medalist for Romania at the 1997 and 1999 World Championships Marathon, Simon has a knack for cutting her big-time race finishes close. At the 2000 Olympics, she missed gold by just eight seconds. Then she reversed that result at the 2001 World Championships, winning by five seconds (over Reiko Tosa of Japan) in 2:26:01. Winner of the Osaka Ladies' Marathon in 1998 (2:28:31), 1999 (2:23:24), and 2000 (2:22:54), Simon lives and trains, like so many other marathoners, in Boulder, Colorado. *See also* Bolder Boulder 10K; Olympic medalists; Osaka Ladies' Marathon; World Championships medalists.

Sinclair, Jon (b. September 4, 1957). The RRCA Hall of Famer excelled in the middle distances, those longer than 10K and shorter than the marathon. The half-marathon was the perfect length for him, and he won the 1991 national half. *See also* Bloomsday 12K; Hall of Fame, RRCA; national half-marathon champions, U.S.; Peachtree10K.

Sixteen Days of Glory. *See* movies.

Shoe Business

From Joe Henderson's *Running Commentary,* May 1999.

The running-shoe business in the United States is a big business. An estimated 30 million Americans do some running, and several million of them enter races.

These runners each buy two or three pairs of shoes a year. And because running shoes feel so good to wear, they sell well to people who never run a step. (A national sporting-goods association claims that only 40 percent of running shoes sold are ever used for that purpose.)

Many companies, domestic and international, compete vigorously for runner dollars. The largest of the U.S.-based firms are Nike, New Balance, Saucony, and Brooks. Importers include Asics, adidas, Reebok, and, increasingly, Mizuno and Fila. These manufacturers cater to American tastes in shoes. These lean toward the sturdily built models that emphasize support and cushioning over lightness and flexibility.

While vast numbers of runners in this country enter races, very few of them ever purchase lightweight racing shoes. They prefer instead to wear the same pair for training runs and races. This fact makes the "racers" rather difficult to find, even in stores that carry a large selection of "trainers."

Most runners say they prefer to buy shoes from a local shop that specializes in running. Here they find not only the shoes but also well-informed advice on all matters related to the sport. These stores are relatively few in number and small in size. They have difficulty competing with the larger outlets in terms of price.

Runners without such a specialty store nearby, or those intent on bargain shopping, turn in one of two directions. They either shop at the larger multisport stores, many of them national franchises such as Footlocker and Big 5, or they order shoes from catalogs.

Several companies aim to attract the mail-order business. Chief among these are Road Runner Sports and East Bay, which send out millions of catalogs each year. While shoe price and selection are attractive, the major drawback to ordering this way is finding the right fit in an unseen shoe. Some runners select their first pair of a particular model in a store, then have later pairs sent by mail.

The quality of running shoes in this country generally improves from year to year. Change is rapid, and sometimes this appears to happen simply for the sake of style. A common complaint among U.S. runners is, "As soon as I find a shoe I really like, it goes off the market." We runners really become attached to our shoes, and giving them up is like parting with an old friend.

Skah, Khalid (b. January 29, 1967). The 1992 Olympic 10,000-meter champion from Morocco won the 1994 World Half-Marathon title. *See also* World Half-Marathon Championships.

Slaney, Mary Decker Tabb (b. August 4, 1958). She did her best work on the track and was at her very best while winning the 1,500 and 3,000 at the 1983 World Championships. But she had road credentials as well—winner of the first national 10K in 1978, American 10K record-setter twice, and the first American woman to break 32:00 with 31:52 in 1983. *See also* Hall of Fame, RRCA; national 10K champions, U.S.; Peachtree 10K; record progressions, American.

Shorter, Frank (b. October 31, 1947). Frank is often cited as the match that ignited the Running Revolution with his win in the Olympic Marathon in Munich on September 10, 1972. The revolution, however, was already underway. Entries at Boston had increased steadily, and Americans had begun responding to the running prescription in Dr. Kenneth Cooper's *Aerobics*, a bestseller in 1968. But it is impossible to overlook Frank Shorter's contribution to running. Munich, the scene of his dramatic victory (his 2:12:20 was more than two minutes ahead of second-place finisher Karel Lismont of Belgium), was also the place of his birth. His father was an army surgeon stationed in Germany after World War II.

Although a decent college runner, Shorter came into his own after moving to Gainesville, Florida, after college, where he moved up to longer distances and hooked up with a number of other long-distance runners, chief among them Jack Bacheler, who would be a teammate at the 1972 Games. In 1971 on a trip to the West Coast to compete in track meets, he entered the AAU Marathon Championships in Eugene, Oregon, where he placed second behind Kenny Moore; both won spots on the U.S. team for the Pan-American Games later that year. Frank won the Pan-Am Marathon in hot conditions, weather that did not deter Shorter as it often did others. That December he went to Fukuoka to run in the then-unofficial World Marathon Championships, where he won in 2:12:51. (He would ulti-

mately win Fukuoka four years in a row.)

Back in Eugene the following July, he won the U.S. Olympic Trials Marathon and from there went on to win the Munich Olympic Marathon. Shorter was far from finished. He went back to Fukuoka in December 1972 and won with an American-best time of 2:10:30 and followed that with a win in March at Otsu. He had won six world-class marathons in a row.

In 1976 he again won the U.S. Olympic Trials Marathon in Eugene (2:11:51)

Two of America's greatest marathoners battle it out on the track at the AAU 10,000-meter championships in 1969. Frank Shorter (Yale shirt) leads Kenny Moore. At the 1972 Olympic Games, Shorter won the marathon, while Moore (who was also on the 1968 U.S. Olympic Marathon team) took fourth.

and went into the Montreal Olympics the favorite. There he lost to East German Waldemar Cierpinski, whose outstanding performances on the world stage have since become suspect because of strong evidence of the use of performance-enhancing drugs administered by the East German sports federation. Following his silver-medal performance in Montreal, Frank continued to perform at a very high level, entering numerous road races but also dealing with persistent injury problems. In one summer weekend in 1977 he won the 20K Chicago Distance Classic on Saturday, then flew to Atlanta and won the 10K Peachtree road race on Sunday.

He eventually settled in Boulder, Colorado, and an army of distance runners followed his lead. He continues to train regularly but has for several years been gradually recovering from back surgery for a condition that has plagued him for more than a decade. He is involved in a revived Frank Shorter running clothing company, heads the U.S. Anti-Doping Agency, which is attempting to get rid of drugs in sports, and serves as the godfather of American long-distance running. He is a frequent commentator on road racing for several television entities, and he speaks frequently to business and professional organizations and at racing events. *See also* Bloomsday 12K; Bolder Boulder 10K; Fukuoka Marathon; Hall of Fame, National Distance Running; Hall of Fame, RRCA; Hall of Fame, USATF; Olympians, U.S.; Olympic medalists; Olympic Trials Marathon, U.S.; Pan-American Games; Peachtree 10K; rankings, *Track & Field News;* record progressions, American.

Geoff Smith is shown in the Newton Hills on his way to winning the 1984 Boston Marathon.

© Jeff Johnson

Smead, Chuck (b. August 4, 1951). Smead was a prodigy who ran a 2:23 marathon in high school. A few years later he claimed the silver medal for the United States in the 1975 Pan-American Games Marathon at high-altitude Mexico City.

Smith, Bernard "Joe" (birthdate unavailable). His greatest day came during the war-year 1942 Boston Marathon, when he not only won but also set an American record of 2:26:52. A year earlier he'd claimed the national marathon title. *See also* national marathon champions, U.S.; record progressions, American.

Smith, Francie Larrieu. *See* Larrieu Smith, Francie.

Smith, Geoff (b. October 24, 1953). The British-born Smith came to the United States as a college student and stayed on, eventually becoming a citizen. He won the Boston Marathon twice, in the down years of the race in 1984 and 1985, and finished a close second in the dramatic duel with Rod Dixon at New York City in 1983. *See also* Boston Marathon.

Smith, Joyce (b. October 26, 1937). Her major marathon victories all came after ago 40—Avon 1979, Tokyo 1979 and 1980, London 1981 and 1982. Smith was 46 when she ran for Britain in the first Olympic Marathon for women. *See also* Avon Racing Circuits; London Marathon; Tokyo Marathons.

Smith, Les (b. May 10, 1940). An attorney by trade, Smith coordinates the extremely well-organized Portland (Oregon) Marathon weekend, which includes everything from a half-dozen races-within-a-race to a race directors' workshop. *See also* Portland Marathon.

Smith, Linda. *See* Somers, Linda Smith.

Smithee, Larry (b. August 27, 1963). Running on an outrageously downhill 8K course in Utah, he set the "American best" for that distance. Smithee's 21:03 also stands as the world's fastest. *See also* records, American; records, world.

Sohn Kee Chung (b. August 29, 1914). Japan occupied Korea and made Koreans run under the Japanese flag with Japanese names at the 1936 Berlin Olympics. Sohn (a.k.a. Kitei Son) won gold after setting a world marathon record of 2:26:42 in 1935. Fellow Korean Nam Sung Yong, forced to run as Shoryu Nam, placed third in Berlin. *See also* Olympic medalists; record progressions, world.

Somers, Linda Smith (b. May 7, 1961). The U.S. Olympian placed 31st at the 1996 Atlanta Games. She'd done much better at the World Championships the previous year, finishing 7th. Somers's career record also includes victories at Chicago in 1992 (2:37:43) and national titles in 1993 (2:34:11) and 1994 (2:33:42). *See also* Chicago Marathon; national marathon champions, U.S.; Olympians, U.S.; Olympic Trials Marathon, U.S.; World Championships, U.S.

Son, Kitei. *See* Sohn Kee Chung.

Sorbothane (www.sorbothane.com). Resembling rubber but infinitely more absorbent, it is used to absorb impact shock in running-shoe insoles and heel pads. It was originally marketed by having a scientist drop a raw egg onto a sheet of Sorbothane. The egg, of course, would not break because the Sorbothane absorbed the shock of the impact.

Soh, Shigeru (b. January 9, 1953) and **Soh, Takeshi** (b. January 9, 1953) (also spelled So). Contemporaries of Toshihiko Seko, the Japanese twins were world-class competitors for several years in the late 1970s. Shigeru won the 1985 Tokyo Marathon. *See also* Tokyo Marathons.

Spangler, Jenny (b. July 20, 1963). Child prodigies seldom blossom into open-division stars, but Spangler was an exception. At 19 she set an American junior marathon best. Then 13 years later, after a career much interrupted by injuries, she registered a stunning upset victory at the 1996 U.S. Olympic

Trials, breaking 2:30. Alas, the injury bug bit again. She dropped out of the Atlanta Olympic Marathon and has been unable to reclaim her previous form. *See also* national marathon champions, U.S.; Olympians, U.S.; Olympic Trials Marathon, U.S.; records, American age-group.

Spangler, Paul (b. March 18, 1899; d. 1994). The physician didn't begin running until his late 60s but then set a host of age-group records, including the current 90-plus American mark for 10K. He hoped to be the first to finish the New York City Marathon at 100 years of age, thereby claiming a $100,000 prize, but he died while running at 95. *See also* records, American age-group.

Spedding, Charlie (b. May 19, 1952). The Brit did much of his training in the United States during his greatest year, 1984. After winning the London Marathon, he claimed the bronze medal at Los Angeles in the fastest Olympic Marathon ever run. *See also* London Marathon; Olympic medalists.

speed play. *See* fartlek.

speed training. *See* interval training; tempo runs.

Spence, Steve (b. May 9, 1962). A lone American picked up a medal at the international marathon championships in the 1990s. That was Spence, who ran 3rd in the steamy 1991 World Championships race in Tokyo. The Pennsylvanian's success continued the next year, when he won the Olympic Trials and placed 12th at Barcelona. No U.S. male has finished higher at the Games since then. Spence also holds the current American 12K record of 34:26, set at Bloomsday in 1989. *See also* national half-marathon champions, U.S.; national marathon champions, U.S.; Olympians, U.S.; Olympic Trials Marathon, U.S.; records, American; World Championships medalists; World Championships, U.S.

Spenco (www.spenco.com). The late Wayman Spence's company marketed insole inserts to ease the shock of running, along with such wonderful inventions as Second Skin, an artificial damp, clear, plastic sort of material that could be placed over blisters and other raw spots caused by too much running. *See also* Second Skin.

Spiridon. The popular German running magazine, edited by Manfred Steffny, was named for the original Olympic Marathon winner.

splits. The question that stumped 1980 Boston pseudo-winner Rosie Ruiz (as in "What were your splits?") refers to the elapsed time at which a runner reaches key landmarks on a racecourse. *See also* negative splits; pacing.

SportHill (www.sporthill.com). Jim Hill came home from the 1983 World Championships, where he competed for the United States at 10,000 meters, with ideas that would create the clothing company SportHill.

sports bars. *See* bars, sports; PowerBar.

sports drinks. *See* drinks, running; Electrolyte Replacement with Glucose; Gatorade.

sports gels. *See* foods, runners'; gels.

Spring, Michael (b. December 14, 1879). He was another of those rare Olympians who qualified for the Games twice, in 1904 and 1906, and had the dubious distinction of DNFing both times. Spring won the 1904 Boston Marathon. *See also* Boston Marathon; Olympians, U.S.

Springbank Road Races. A professional-quality road race occurred in London, Ontario, in the 1960s, long before there were openly pro races. The races were the brainchild of Dave Prokop, who served as an editor at *Runner's World* and who edited the magazine's 1975 booklet, *The African Running Revolution*, detailing the first African invasion of world distance running.

Springs, Betty. *See* Geiger, Betty Springs.

Squires, Billy (birthdate unavailable). The former Notre Dame runner coached the famed Greater Boston Track Club during its heyday as spawning grounds of great 42Kers: Bill Rodgers, Alberto Salazar, Greg Meyer, Bob Hodge, Randy Thomas, and others. Squires's greatest success story was perhaps Dick Beardsley, who advanced quickly from journeyman runner to sub-2:09 marathoner under Billy's guidance. He was also the coauthor, with Raymond Krise, of the excellent 1982 book *Fast Tracks: The History of Distance Running* (Stephen Greene Press). *See also* Beardsley, Dick; coaches; Salazar, Alberto.

Sri Chinmoy Marathon Team. Founded in 1977 by students of spiritual teacher and athlete Sri Chinmoy, the team's purpose is to serve the running community and help promote spiritual growth through sports. Over the years the group has become the world's largest supporter of ultradistance running events and a major organizer of marathons, triathlons, long-distance swimming events, and masters track and field meets around the globe. The team's first public race was a 10-miler in Greenwich, Connecticut, on October 2, 1977. In 1979 the group organized a marathon in Flushing Meadow Park, New York, that was open to the public.

The Chinmoyists gradually moved well beyond the standard marathon and put on increasingly long races, often along a flat one-mile or two-kilometer loop, where drinks and runner support were more readily available. In 1985 they organized a 1,000-mile race in Flushing Meadow Park, while also hosting monthly marathon-length events. In the summer of 1996 they put together the longest certified race in the world, at 2,700 miles, which they surpassed the following year with a 3,100-mile run. Where they'll stop, nobody knows. *See also* Chinmoy, Sri.

Stack, Walt (b. September 28, 1907; d. 1995). Stack was Mr. Running in the San Francisco Bay Area from the 1960s to 1990s. The blue-collar hod carrier and union activist coined the motto of his club, the Dolphin-South End Runners, "Start slow and taper off." He once said of his own steady running pace, "If you dropped me out of an airplane, I'd fall at an 8:30 mile."

He was known for running bare-chested across the Golden Gate Bridge each morning (17 miles) and following the run with a swim in the icy bay; he rode his one-speed bicycle to and from his workouts and his work. Walt was a triathlete long before the term was coined. Once triathlons became popular, he trained for and completed the Hawaii Ironman—using his one-speed bicycle. Following the race, he was quoted as saying, "I had to have that damned bicycle seat surgically removed from my ass."

Walt's greatest contribution to running was his insistence that everybody—regardless of sex, age, and ethnic background—could and should run. He regularly recruited women to his club and each year put together a bus trip to lead them to ascend Pikes Peak. Salty in speech and irreverent in his approach to life, he always had a contingent of runners surrounding him when he ran a marathon, each hanging on to a stream of off-color stories and jokes. Known for accepting beers along a marathon course, one of Walt's fans created a beer-can holster for him that held a six-pack. "I get four miles per beer," he said.

At his 75th birthday, celebrated aboard the liberty ship *Jeremiah O'Brien* in San Francisco, a special 10K race was organized. In a city where feminism flourished, a contingent of a dozen professional women whom Walt had lured into running ran the race surrounding him while they wore togas and waved palm fronds to keep him cool.

Stahl, Kjell-Erik (b. February 17, 1946). The Swede raced through dozens of sub-2:20 marathons, the highest total recorded until Doug Kurtis broke this "record" with 73. *See also* Kurtis, Doug.

Steamboat Classic (www.steamboatclassic.org). This fast four-mile run in Peoria, Illinois, is directed by Glenn Latimer each June.

Steinfeld, Allan (b. June 7, 1946). Allan has been the race director of the New York City Marathon since the death of Fred Lebow in 1994. Before that he was technical director. Allan joined the NYRRC in 1963. He also wears the title of club president and CEO, positions he assumed in 1993. An accomplished collegiate runner, Steinfeld won the NYRRC eight-mile Handicap Race in 1966. His personal records on the track include a 22.9 200 meters, a 51.6 400 meters, and a 2:00 half-mile. He has run one marathon (Honolulu in 1979), which he completed in 3:27:43.

Allan is a member of the executive committee of USA Track & Field and the president of Running USA, a trade organization for the road-racing industry. He was a chief referee at the 1984 Los Angeles Olympics for the men's and women's marathons, and he has been a technical adviser for television broadcasts of several Olympic Games. He also serves as an adviser for television broadcasts of many NYRRC events.

Allan earned an MS degree in electrical engineering and radio astronomy from Cornell and worked as a high school physics teacher and track coach. He was born at Flower Fifth Avenue Hospital in Manhattan. The location became part of the New York City Marathon course when the event expanded to the five boroughs in 1976. He is married to Alice Schneider, the vice president of computer services and race scoring for the NYRRC and the New York City Marathon. *See also* Lebow, Fred; New York City Marathon; New York Road Runners Club.

Stenroos, Albin (b. February 24, 1889; date of death unknown). Hannes Kohlemainen won the Olympic Marathon title in 1920, and Stenroos made it two in a row for Finland in 1924. No Finn has won since at that distance. *See also* Olympic medalists.

Stewart, Phil (b. February 10, 1950). Stewart, a sub-2:20 marathoner, worked closely with Ed Ayres in the early days of *Running Times*. Phil later founded the *Road Race Management*

From the collection of Dr. Edward H. Kozloff–Motor City Striders

Albin Stenroos trains on a track in New York in 1925. The next year he would go to Boston where he would beat Clarence DeMar, but lose to Johnny Miles.

newsletter, which he still publishes and edits along with directing the Cherry Blossom 10-mile race in Washington, D.C. *See also* Cherry Blossom 10M; publications; *Road Race Management*.

stopwatches. *See* watches, digital.

Stramilano (www.stramilano.it). One of Europe's largest races sends some 45,000 runners through Milan for a half-marathon. The race has produced many of the fastest unaided half-marathons, including Paul Tergat's current men's world record of 59:17, as well as marks at 15K (42:04), 10 miles (45:12), and 20K (56:18) set along the way. *See also* biggest races; fastest races; records, world.

Showing Up

From Joe Henderson's *Running Commentary,* February 2000.

If John Strumsky was miffed at me for snubbing his friend, it didn't show in his letter. He gently corrected the oversight. "In your book *Better Runs,*" he wrote, "you referred to Mark Covert as America's leading streaker. Without meaning to diminish Mark's great accomplishments, I submit a copy of George Hancock's streaking lists."

In this case, streaking isn't running around without clothes but running for years without missing a day. Hancock places Covert's 31-year streak only second among Americans, more than a year behind that of Bob Ray. The retired postal worker from Maryland has run daily since April 1967, averaging $7\frac{1}{4}$ miles a day.

Hancock names eight U.S. runners with streaks of 25 years or more, and 33 who haven't skipped a day in more than 20 years. John Strumsky himself is a 15-year streaker.

Streaking isn't a practice of mine anymore (my longest ended voluntarily at almost five years) and not one I necessarily encourage. But I understand the spirit behind it and admire runners who can tolerate this everydayness.

These are the Cal Ripkens of running. Ripken didn't miss a single baseball game for more than 15 seasons. Admirable as this feat is, Ripken didn't play year-round or daily during the season. Streaking runners have no off-season, no rainouts, and no travel days (but also no big-league curveballs to hit, no sellout crowds to please, and no seven-figure salary to earn). Theirs is a professional approach to running. They show up for work each day, no matter what.

The truest mark of pros in any specialty isn't how much money, if any, they earn but how well they continue to do the job on their bad days. Anyone can do well in good health and high spirits. But a pro keeps doing well when conditions aren't ideal, which they usually aren't.

Anyone can run on a day when the sky is blue, the temperature mild, and the air still. Anyone can get out after a good night's sleep, feeling no fatigue or pain, a fine course at his or her feet, and no need to hurry back.

Not just anyone gets up and out when all the conditions shout, "Forget it!" When the demands of the day shove the run into the dark hours . . . when the course choice is dictated by convenience, not beauty . . . when the temperature leaves the comfort zone, the sky drops rain or snow, or the wind howls . . . when feeling sleep deprived or hung over . . . when tight or sore legs beg for a break.

My hometown of Eugene, Oregon, might house more runners per capita than any city in the country. It's a run capital but also a *rain* capital. Even here the number of runners I see each morning at seven o'clock drops by more than half when the six-month rainy season begins. The fair-weather folks, the amateurs, go into hibernation.

The streakers, the blue-collar workers, the pros, go to work as always. They go out when they feel like staying home, knowing they're likely to feel better afterward than before, knowing they can do good work even on bad days.

streakers. These aren't people who delight in running naked in public but runners who take pleasure—and pride—in never missing a day of running. The world-champion streaker is former world-class marathoner Ron Hill of Britain, who claims not to have taken a day off since 1964. A variation on streaking is the runner who seldom lets a weekend pass without running a marathon. *See also* "Showing Up" above.

strength training. *See* weight training.

Stretching. *See* Anderson, Bob; books.

stretching exercises. Runners can appear to be pushing down walls, toppling trees, or upending cars without drawing a second glance. They're using these objects as stretching props. The practice is almost universal, despite research that shows improper stretching to be one of the leading causes of running injuries rather than a preventive measure. *See also* cross-training.

strides. All running, of course, involves making strides. But this is a specific type of striding—running short distances, seldom more than 100 meters, at a fast pace. Strides are most commonly run as part of a race warmup or at the end of a slow training run.

Strobino, Gaston (b. August 23, 1891; d. March 30, 1969). The U.S. 1912 Olympian won the bronze medal at Stockholm, the fourth Games in a row in which an American won a medal. *See also* Olympians, U.S.; Olympic medalists.

Sub-4. The clothing company of the 1970s and 1980s was named not for the sub-four-hour marathoners it clothed but for the sub-four-minute milers (Steve Scott, John Walker, and others) who represented the company. *See also* clothing.

From the collection of Dr. Edward H. Kozloff–Motor City Striders

Gaston Strobino of the U.S. took third in the 1912 Olympic Marathon in Stockholm.

Subotnick, Dr. Steve (b. 1942). One of the first well-known sports podiatrists and author of one of the earliest podiatry books for runners, he wrote *The Running Foot Doctor* with Stanley Newell (World Publications, 1977) and *Cures for Common Running Injuries* (Anderson World, 1979). *See also* injuries; podiatry.

Sun Run (www.sunrun.com). Canada's largest race is a 10K in Vancouver with a field of more than 20,000. It's sponsored by the city's daily newspaper, the *Vancouver Sun*.

Sun Yingjie (b. January 19, 1979). From the flurry of unbelievable marks set by young Chinese women in the mid-1990s came a world junior marathon record of 2:25:45 by Sun. The 2000 Boston Marathon press guide describes her this way: "At Boston last year, Sun set a blistering opening pace of 15:58 for 5K. Although unfamiliar with the course, she held nothing back, and the elite women had to respond. Sun led through the halfway mark at world-record pace, but by 25K, Fatuma Roba and Catherine Ndereba caught her. Sun dropped back to finish 11th.

Debuting in 1997 with a 2:32:43 10th place at the Chinese National Games and Marathon Championships in Beijing, Sun ran 2:30:10 at the Dalian International Marathon three weeks later for 3rd. In 1998, she placed 1st at Tianjin in 2:25:45, 1st at Dalian, and 5th at Beijing in 2:34:19. Continuing to hone her skills and gather tactical experience, Sun posted two top times in 1999, with a 2:30:29 7th place at the Tokyo Marathon in February, and a 2:30:12 for 12th place at the Seville Marathon World Championships in August. At Beijing in October, Sun finished 2nd in 2:31:19 to countrywoman and Boston competitor Ai Dongmei's 2:29:20." Sun lives in Liaoning, China. *See also* records, world age-group.

supination. The opposite of *pronation*, suppination refers to the way the foot rolls slightly to the outside as it touches the ground when running. Those few runners who do suppinate (most runners overpronate) can find help by choosing the correct shoe for their foot type. *See also* pronation.

Supplex. This is another of the comfortable fabrics developed by DuPont that helped revolutionize runners' clothing. It boasts the softness and breathability of cotton, but is lighterweight, stronger, and faster drying. *See also* clothing.

surges. Call it picking up the pace, making a break, or accelerating. None of these terms is as concise or power-packed as the single word *surge*. Surges are a tactical weapon for the front-runners, but they can serve the rest of us well by helping us break out of a pacing rut.

Sutton, Marian (b. October 7, 1963). The two-time winner at the Chicago Marathon, in 1996 and 1997, is one of the tallest world-class women at, in her words, "five feet twelve." *See also* Chicago Marathon.

Suzuki, Fushige (birthdate unavailable). The Japanese marathoner set a world record of 2:27:49 in 1935. It lasted just four days, then fell to Yasuo Ikenaga (2:26:44), also from Japan. *See also* record progressions, world.

Switzer, Kathrine (b. January 5, 1947). It is difficult to pick from Kathrine's accomplishments and say that this one or that one defines her. She is probably best known as the first female to break the gender barrier at the Boston Marathon by running in 1967 while wearing an official number she obtained by registering as "K. Switzer." (For trivia buffs, the number was 261.) Kathrine was not the first woman to run the race; Roberta Gibb had done so without a number for several years previous.) Equally as memorable as K. Switzer's number was race official Jock Semple's attempt to leap from the press bus and rip it from her. Kathrine was accompanied by her boyfriend, who threw a body block at Jock and sent him flying.

That well-publicized incident did not begin and end Kathrine's fame in running. Instead it launched what continues today to be one of the longest-running and most impressive careers in the sport. Kathrine went on to win the New York City Marathon (1974) and to record the sixth-best time in the world for a woman in 1975. She claims her accomplishments came from lots of hard work and limited talent.

Perhaps her most important contribution to the sport came in 1977 when she convinced Avon Products to sponsor a women's marathon series with the intention of showcasing the fact that women could run marathons well, that women from dozens of countries did so, and that the event should be contested in the Olympic Games. In 1984 that dream became a reality when Joan Benoit won the first-ever women's Olympic Marathon in Los Angeles. Avon disbanded the program in 1985, having proved its point. But Kathrine was far from put out to pasture. Besides speaking on the

© Jeff Johnson

Kathrine Switzer, the first woman to run Boston with a number, celebrates taking second place at the 1975 race in 2:51:37, one of the best times in the world that year.

sport and on the subject of women's sports participation, she used her journalism skills to write about such topics for publications ranging from *Women Today* to *Parade*, from the *New York Times* to *Runner's World*. She also served regularly as a TV commentator, working everything from the Olympic Games and Goodwill Games to dozens of marathons in major cities.

In 1997 she revived her involvement with Avon by creating the Avon Running Global Women's Circuit, an international program that provides millions of women with the opportunity to compete in run- ning and walking events throughout the world. Married to Dr. Roger Robinson, a professor of English literature in New Zealand and a world-class age-group run- ner, she divides her time among New Zealand, New York City, and Virginia. In 1998 St. Martin's Press published her book, *Running and Walking for Women Over 40*. Like Frank Shorter, Kathrine was born in 1947 in Germany, where her par- ents were involved in the occupation fol- lowing World War II. *See also* Avon Rac- ing Circuits; Boston Marathon; New York City Marathon; Robinson, Roger.

Tabb, Ron (b. August 7, 1954). He deserved better than to be known as Mr. Mary Decker. During his brief marriage to Mary, Ron did his best running. He was at his very best while breaking 2:10 (with 2:09:31) and finishing 2nd at the 1983 Boston Marathon. This race qualified him for the first World Championships, and he finished 18th at Helsinki. He took 3rd place in Boston in 1980. *See also* Slaney, Mary Decker Tabb; World Championships, U.S.

TAC. *See* Athletics Congress, The.

Tabori, Laszlo (b. July 6, 1931). The world's third sub-four-minute miler defected from Hungary with his coach, Mihaly Igloi, and eventually took the coaching torch from his mentor. Tabori's athletes included world marathon record-setters Jacqueline Hansen and Miki Gorman. Tabori remains active as a coach in southern California, using his adaptations of the Igloi-interval system with the wide range of talent that he coaches. *See also* coaches; Gorman, Miki; Hansen, Jacqueline.

T&FN. *See Track & Field News.*

Takahashi, Naoko (b. May 6, 1972). In 1998 Naoko ran what may be the best marathon effort by a male or female to date when, at the Asian Games in sultry Bangkok, she recorded an astonishing 2:21:47—the fastest ever for an all-women's race. The fact that the conditions were atrocious didn't seem to bother the five-foot-four-inch, 99-pound terror. She served notice that at marathons with no pacers where the competition between the women would be tough, she would be the toughest. Since that time, she has merely added to her reputation as the queen of all-women's marathons.

It looked, for a while, as if she would be denied the opportunity to notch any more laurels for herself in women-only races. Considering her gutsy performance in sweltering conditions in Bangkok, she was considered a shoo-in for the World Championships in 1999, which were scheduled for extremely warm Seville, Spain. But Naoko ran into troubles getting ready for that race. First she injured her ankle. No sooner had she gotten past that injury than she injured her left hamstring. Yet she was so close to recovering in time that she didn't officially withdraw from the World Championships until the morning of the race.

Without a good showing at Seville, her chances of going to the Sydney Olympics were in doubt. To make the team, she would have to satisfy the selectors. After a rough autumn in which she suffered a broken wrist in a fall and then went through a bout of stomach troubles, she entered the Nagoya International Women's Marathon in March, the last official qualifier marathon available to her. She was nothing short of marvelous. For the first half, the field was running into a headwind. But at 22.5K Naoko took over the race and never faltered. "The wind kind of stood me up in the first half," she reported. She went on to win in an impressive 2:22:19.

That race put her on the Japanese Olympic women's marathon team, of course. At Sydney she never paused or faltered on her way to a dominating win in an Olympic record time of 2:23:14. Once she made the break, the race was virtually over. As staggering as her domination of women-only marathons has been, her coach, Yoshio Koide, feels Naoko has not yet reached her potential. "Her upper body is still like a baby's," Koide stated after her Nagoya win. "When she gets stronger, she can run ever faster times." And faster times she has run. In 2001 she became the first woman to break the 2:20 barrier, running a 2:19:46 at Berlin. She held the record for a week, until Catherine Ndereba ran 2:18:47 in Chicago. Stay tuned. *See also* Asian Games; Berlin Marathon; Ndereba, Catherine; Olympic medalists; rankings, *Track & Field News*; record progressions, world.

© Mark Shearman, Athletics-Images

Naoko Takahashi of Japan made winning the 2000 Sydney Olympic Marathon look easy. From the moment she threw down her sunglasses and went into the zone, she was untouchable.

Taniguchi, Hiromi (b. April 5, 1960). His crowning moment came in his home country of Japan while winning the 1991 World Championships Marathon in Tokyo (with 2:14:57). His other achievements were many: Tokyo Marathon wins in 1987 (2:10:06) and 1989 (2:09:34), London in 1987 (2:09:50), and Rotterdam in 1990 (2:10:56). *See also* London Marathon; rankings, *Track & Field News*; Rotterdam Marathon; Tokyo Marathons; World Championships medalists.

Tanui, Moses (b. August 20, 1965). In an era when the guard among Kenyan stars changes as often as the new month's running magazines, Tanui has endured much longer than most. He's a two-time Boston Marathon winner (1996 and 1998), World Half-Marathon champion (1995), and the first to break one hour in the half-marathon. A resident of Kenya's hotbed marathoner town, Eldoret, Moses broke Cosmas Ndeti's three-year-long stranglehold on Boston in 1996.

Tanui has ranked among the world's top marathoners since his 1993 debut in New York City. His fastest time was his 2:06:16 second-place finish in Chicago in 1999. In 1991 he won gold in the 10,000 meters at the World Championships, and he twice (1990 and 1991) took silver at the World Cross Country Championships. He also was champion three years in a row (1997, 1998, and 1999) at the Kyoto Half-Marathon in Japan. *See also* Boston Marathon; record progressions, world; World Half-Marathon Championships.

© Mark Shearman

Moses Tanui was one of the dominant figures in road racing in the 1990s. Unlike many of his countrymen, Tanui had staying power. He won Boston in 1996 and 1998 and was the first to do the half-marathon in less than an hour.

tapering. Even in a sport that venerates hard work, there are times when it can be counterproductive, such as immediately before and after an important race. "Tapering" one's training somehow sounds more acceptable than "easing off."

Team Diabetes (www. diabetes.org). *See* charity running.

Team in Training (TNT) (www.teamintraining.net). They're the purple people, so-called for the singlets they wear. TNT has an increasingly visible presence in marathons, where they raise money through donations for leukemia research. TNT is an arm of the Leukemia Society. *See also* "Fund Runs" below; charity running.

Fund Runs

From Joe Henderson's *Running Commentary,* September 1998.

American runners are, as a crowd, financially successful. Most of us here have enough money to spend on equipment, publications, and, most of all, travel to races. We even have cash left over for causes, otherwise unrelated to running, that have linked themselves to our sport. In the United States it is hard to find a race that does not contribute to a charity in some way.

At times the event's whole reason for being is to raise funds for the cause of the day, and runners know exactly where their money goes. But much more often the charity is an incidental, almost hidden, recipient of race proceeds.

Americans are of two minds about helping the less blessed. If the giving is voluntary, we freely open our pocketbooks, as if giving help to a friend. Yet we sometimes complain about being forced to contribute, as if we're grudgingly paying taxes to the government. Both traits extend to runners, who can be either generous in our giving or resistant to it. We might balk when the race's pet charity is one that we don't want to support and when the involuntary contribution adds a "tax" to the entry fee.

The protest must be a quiet one, because speaking out against the cause would be like an attack on motherhood or the flag. A common reaction is simply not to enter that race. Hundreds of fund-raising events appear across America each year, then quickly disappear because too few runners support them.

I won't name any negative examples here, preferring to focus on the successes in charitable racing. These come in two types: races built entirely around a worthy cause, and groups organized to support a single cause wherever they might race. One example of each type stands out as a great success story of the 1990s.

The first is the nationwide Race for the Cure series, which contributes to the fight against breast cancer. (A similar program operates in Canada under the name Run for the Cure.) These races-runs-walks are all five kilometers in length, and most are limited to women—yet several of these events rank among the largest in the United States each year with five-figure fields.

Cure races aside, the recent trend in this country has been away from big fund-raising events and toward groups with the same purpose. By far the most successful is Team in Training. TNT groups throughout the country train together for marathons. The target disease of their significant donations is leukemia.

Six thousand TNT members ran the Rock 'n' Roll Marathon in San Diego, California, this summer. They accounted for nearly one-third of the field in this largest first-time marathon in history. Team in Training raised a total of $15.6 million dollars—$2,600 per runner, on average—for their charity on a single day. This represented Americans at their generous best.

Team USA (www.runningusa.org). Following the lead of the Roads Scholars program of RRCA and Discovery USA of Fila, Team USA gives support to rising U.S. road talent. Team USA is a project of Running USA, which has established several training camps across the country. *See also* Discovery USA; Roads Scholars; Running USA; USA Track & Field.

television. Coverage of road racing in the United States is spotty at best. Rarely is a race shown live, nationwide, on a major network. ESPN, however, airs two series on the sport—*Elite Racing* (formerly known as *Road Race of the Month*) and *Running and Racing. See also Elite Racing*; Liquori, Marty; Reavis, Toni; *Running and Racing.*

tempo runs. *Tempo* means "pace," so in a sense a run at any pace is a tempo run. In modern parlance, however, a tempo run has come to mean a run at race pace but at a shorter distance than that race. Or it could be a briskly paced run at the runner's current fastest aerobic pace, or at the anaerobic or lactate threshold. *See also* anaerobic threshold.

tendon injuries. *See* Achilles tendon; injuries.

10K. Ten kilometers (6.2 miles) is the road version of the track 10,000 meters, which has been run in the Olympics since the start but became popular with U.S. road runners only in the 1970s when the metric system was being forced on them. Previously track races had been contested at six miles, and five miles was a more popular road distance. *See also* distances, metric and English.

Terasawa, Toru (b. January 4, 1935). The Japanese runner broke a legend's record, taking a single second off the marathon mark of Abebe Bikila with 2:15:16 in 1963. This time was broken in turn, four months later, by American Buddy Edelen. Terasawa also won the 1962 and 1964 Fukuoka Marathons at a time when that race was second in prestige only to the Olympics. *See also* Fukuoka Marathon; record progressions, world.

Tergat, Paul (b. June 17, 1969). The Kenyan is versatile and focused. Before debuting in the marathon at London in 2001 (with 2:08:15), he had multiple World Cross Country Championships under the elastic of his running shorts and he seems to have set up a private preserve at the half-marathon distance. He holds the world record for the unaided half of 59:17 and the aided record of 59:05. His half-marathon record was so fast that he sucked up en route world records in the 15K, 10-mile, and 20K. It is no surprise, then, that he won the World Half-Marathon Championships in 1999 and 2000.

In the final days leading to one of his international races, Paul leaves his hilltop home and checks himself into the drab, primitive Armed Forces Training Camp in the Ngong Hills of Kenya so that he can concentrate on the fine points of preparation to win. *See also* record progressions, world; records, world; World Half-Marathon Championships.

Teske, Charlotte (b. November 23, 1949). West Germans were fast starters in women's marathoning, winning several major events and setting world records in the 1970s and 1980s. One of their stars from that era was Teske, 1982 Boston (2:29:33) and 1986 Berlin (2:32:10) winner. *See also* Berlin Marathon; Boston Marathon.

Tewanima, Lewis (b. 1888; d. January 18, 1969). Although fellow American Indian Jim Thorpe was the toast of the 1912 Olympics, Tewanima ran 16th in the Stockholm Games marathon (with 2:52:42). That was his second Olympics—he'd finished 9th in 1908 (with 3:09:15). *See also* Olympians, U.S.

Theato, Michel (b. March 22, 1878; date of death unknown). The French delivery boy, familiar with shortcuts through the city, beat favored American Arthur Newton at the Paris Games in 1900. Theato was born in Luxembourg, outside France, as were the two other "French" winners of Olympic Marathons, Boughera El Ouafi (1928) and Alain Mimoun (1956), who were both Algerian born. *See also* Olympic medalists.

Thompson, Ian (b. November 16, 1949). One of the first sub-2:10 marathoners, Thompson won the 1974 Commonwealth Games Marathon (in 2:09:12) and that year's European Championships race (in 2:13:19) for England. He claimed the top world ranking for 1974. *See also* Commonwealth Games; European Championships; rankings, *Track & Field News*.

three-hour marathon. "Breaking three," as in 2:59:59 or faster, was the big goal of the average marathoner in Running Boom I. Breaking that barrier guaranteed that men would appear in the *Runner's World* year-end listings, and it was the mark of world-class running for women in their early years of competing officially. *See also* four-hour marathon.

Few people know of Gert Thys of South Africa, yet he is one of the greats in the world of marathoning.

© Mark Shearman, Athletics–Images

threshold runs. *See* anaerobic threshold.

Thugwane, Josia See page 348.

Thys, Gert (b. November 12, 1971). At the time he ran 2:06:33 to win the 1999 Tokyo Marathon, the South African was the second fastest in history. His top five marathons average 2:08:02! *See* page 334. *See also* "World Leader" on next page; Tokyo Marathons.

World Leader

From Joe Henderson's *Running Commentary,* August 1999.

I stood in the presence of greatness, close enough to reach out and shake the great man's hand. I looked a world leader in the eye and listened to him speak of what he planned to do the rest of the summer.

His name is Gert Thys. I'd seen it printed but until now hadn't heard it spoken correctly. The name looks as if it would be pronounced "Girt Thighs." But it's "Hairt Tays," said his Peoria-based agent, Glenn Latimer, by way of introduction.

We met in the unlikely spot of Cedar Rapids, Iowa—the other side of the world from Thys's South African home. He was here on the U.S. Independence weekend to run the Fifth Season Race at less than one-fifth his best distance. The race paid just $2,000 to win, which he didn't; he finished a close second. Thys ran here as a favor to Latimer, as part of a wider visit to this country.

Thys knows something about national independence. Dark-skinned South Africans have earned it within his own recent memory.

Despite his Afrikaner name, Thys is mixed race. Like Mark Plaatjes (who emigrated to the United States, with help from Glenn Latimer, and won the 1993 World Championship Marathon), Thys suffered doubly—in his country for being "coloured" and internationally for being South African. That all changed in this decade when Nelson Mandela came to power and South Africa rejoined the world. Gert Thys can now run anywhere he wants—as far from home as Cedar Rapids.

He has done more fast running in 1998–99 than any marathoner in history—three sub-2:08s within 10 months. The fastest of those, 2:06:33, is the second-best ever and leads the world this year. With those times he could name his price at any big-money race of the spring or fall. But he said, "I choose not to do that for the rest of this year or next. I prefer to concentrate on the World Championships and the Olympic Games."

Runners with that focus are increasingly rare, especially for the Worlds. That meet could be the off-year "Olympics," but it never has acquired the luster of the Games for marathoners. And no wonder. It's an out-of-season race almost always run in miserably hot places like Athens, Tokyo, or Rome—and often in the heat of the day. The Worlds promise a harder-than-normal effort for a slower-than-normal time and a smaller-than-normal payday.

Conditions don't improve this summer. The meet goes to Seville, Spain, where the locals take vacations to cooler places in August or take siestas in midday when the marathon is to be run. Most of the top marathoners in the world will bypass the race in favor of bigger checks (often guaranteed by appearance fees) and better times later in the year. But not Thys.

I hope he wins in Seville, not just because I've stood closer to him than to any other world leader, but because the best current runner chose the race that should matter the most this year.

[Thys didn't have a good day in overheated Seville, finishing 15th. South Africa's selectors didn't pick him to run in the Sydney Olympics, despite his being the fourth fastest marathoner in history.]

Thugwane, Josia (also spelled Josiah) (b. April 15, 1971). This talented, slight (under 100 pounds, five feet two inches) runner from South Africa is one of the hard-luck but winning-through-adversity stories of the 1990s. Several months before he competed at the Atlanta Olympic Games in 1996, he was carjacked. In the process he suffered a back injury and was shot in the face. The setback didn't stop him from going for his goal. Less than six months later he was standing on the winner's platform at Atlanta, the first South African Olympic marathon medalist since 1912, and the first black South African ever to win an Olympic gold. His win (2:12:36) was one of the closest finishes in Olympic history. He won over South Korea's Lee Bong Ju by three seconds and was eight seconds in front of third-place Eric Wainaina of Kenya.

His priority at home involved education. An uneducated man himself, he wanted to have his children well schooled, and he wanted to learn English so that he would be more conversant on the world stage.

Josia did not come into Atlanta with a great deal of international marathon experience beyond winning the 1995 Honolulu Marathon, but his talent was evident. In 1995 he had run a 1:02:06 half-marathon in South Africa. His instant fame from Atlanta did not serve him well in his native South Africa. He had no sooner returned than he was attacked and robbed. Again, nothing deterred him. In 1997 he took third at London in 2:08:06 and later in the year won Fukuoka with a 2:07:27.

In 1999 he ran a 1:02:47 half-marathon at the Great Scottish Half-Marathon but dropped out of the New York City Marathon after stepping into a pothole. In 2000 he ran 1:04:32 (10th place) in the Great Scottish Half-Marathon, 2:10:29 (8th place) at London, and

2:16:59 (20th place) at the Sydney Olympics. *See also* Fukuoka Marathon; Honolulu Marathon; Olympic medalists.

© Mark Shearman. Athletics–Images

South African Josia Thugwane was carjacked and shot before the 1996 Olympic Games. He won the marathon and returned home, where he was attacked and robbed.

Tiger (now Asics). The Japanese shoe company started a revolution by making the "Marathon" model shoe the first to feature a nylon upper. A previous model had been canvas and had sold for less than $10 in the United States. The company that became Asics is perhaps even more important for what became of Tiger's early distributors in the United States. In the early 1970s they set up their own manufacturing company and named it Nike. *See also* Asics; Blue Ribbon Sports; Bowerman, Bill; Johnson, Jeff; Knight, Phil; shoe companies.

time off. *See* rest.

time running. Runners typically keep score by adding up their daily and weekly miles or kilometers. A much simpler system—another favorite of legendary New Zealand coach Arthur Lydiard—is to run by time instead of distance. This frees a runner from measuring courses and sticking to prescribed routes. Minutes and hours add up the same way anywhere. *See* Lydiard, Arthur; watches, digital.

timing. *See* watches, digital.

Tinari, Nancy Rooks (b. May 13, 1959). The top-class Canadian runner, winner of the 1987 Bolder Boulder 10K, has one of the greatest last names in the sport. Spelled backwards, it becomes "I ran it." *See also* Bolder Boulder 10K.

TNT. *See* Team in Training.

Toivonen, Armas (b. January 20, 1899; date of death unknown). The long line of Finnish stars between World Wars I and II included this bronze medalist in the 1932 Olympic Marathon. In 1934 Toivonen won the first European Marathon title ever awarded. *See also* European Championships; Olympic medalists.

Tokyo. It's one of the few cities ever to host both an Olympics (1964) and a World Championships (1991) centered on the same stadium. *See also* historic sites; Olympic Marathon, 1900 to 2000; World Championships medalists.

Tokyo Marathons. Japan's tradition in high-level marathons is to separate the sexes and conduct invitation-only events. The men run in Tokyo each spring, and the women in fall.

Tokyo Olympiad. *See* movies.

Tolstikov, Yakov (b. May 20, 1959). The Russian gathered two big prizes for one effort in 1991 when the London Marathon doubled as the World Cup. Tolstikov won both. *See also* London Marathon; World Cup Marathon.

Tokyo Ladies' Marathon Winners

Winners of the Japanese race, run in November, follow. Note that Eri Yamaguchi's 1999 time was the fastest ever in an all-women's marathon on an unaided course. * = race record.

Year	Athlete	Time
1979	Joyce Smith (Britain)	2:37:48
1980	Joyce Smith (Britain)	2:30:27
1981	Linda Staudt (Canada)	2:34:28
1982	Zoya Ivanova (USSR)	2:34:26
1983	Nanae Sasaki (Japan)	2:37:09
1984	Katrin Dorre (East Germany)	2:33:23
1985	Katrin Dorre (East Germany)	2:34:21
1986	Rosa Mota (Portugal)	2:27:15
1987	Katrin Dorre (East Germany)	2:25:24
1988	Aurora Cunha (Portugal)	2:31:26
1989	Lyubov Klochko (USSR)	2:31:33
1990	Xie Lihua (China)	2:33:04
1991	Mari Tanigawa (Japan)	2:31:27
1992	Liz McColgan (Britain)	2:27:38
1993	Valentina Yegorova (Russia)	2:26:40
1994	Valentina Yegorova (Russia)	2:30:09
1995	Junko Asari (Japan)	2:28:46
1996	Nobuki Fujimura (Japan)	2:28:58
1997	Makiko Ito (Japan)	2:27:45
1998	Junko Asari (Japan)	2:28:29
1999	Eri Yamaguchi (Japan)	2:22:12*
2000	Joyce Chepchumba (Kenya)	2:24:02

Tokyo Men's Marathon Winners

Winners of the men-only race, originally known as Tokyo Yomiuri International Marathon, follow. It is usually run in March. * = race record.

Year	Athlete	Time
1980	Hideki Kita (Japan)	2:12:04
1981	Rodolfo Gomez (Mexico)	2:11:00
1982	Vadim Sidorov (USSR)	2:10:33
1983	Toshihiko Seko (Japan)	2:08:38
1984	Juma Ikangaa (Tanzania)	2:10:49
1985	Shigeru Soh (Japan)	2:10:32
1986	Juma Ikangaa (Tanzania)	2:08:10
1987	Hiromi Taniguchi (Japan)	2:10:06
1988	Abebe Mekonnen (Ethiopia)	2:08:33
1989	Hiromi Taniguchi (Japan)	2:09:34
1990	Takeyuki Nakayama (Japan)	2:10:57
1991	Abebe Mekonnen (Ethiopia)	2:10:26
1992	Koichi Morishita (Japan)	2:10:19
1993	Abebe Mekonnen (Ethiopia)	2:12:00
1994	Steve Moneghetti (Australia)	2:08:55
1995	Eric Wainaina (Kenya)	2:10:31
1996	Vanderlei Lima (Brazil)	2:08:38
1997	Koji Shimizu (Japan)	2:10:09
1998	Alberto Juzdado (Spain)	2:08:01
1999	Gert Thys (South Africa)	2:06:33*
2000	Japhet Kosgei (Kenya)	2:07:15
2001	Kenichi Takahashi (Japan)	2:10:51

Track & Field News (www.trackandfieldnews.com). Founded in 1948 by brothers Bert and Cordner Nelson, *T&FN* is the oldest—and arguably the most respected—of U.S. running publications. The magazine emphasizes the stadium events but also covers road racing and ranks the world's marathoners each year. The company has long published and distributed books on running. *See also* Nelson, Bert and Nelson, Cordner; publications; rankings, *Track & Field News.*

Track & Field News marathon rankings. *See* rankings, *Track & Field News.*

track racing. Although track falls outside the realm of this book, nothing prevents the best track racers from racing on the roads, and vice versa. Olympic 10,000-meter champion and record-holder Haile Gebrselassie, for instance, has marathon ambitions. Paul Tergat was an Olympic track medalist after setting world marks on the road, and he moved up to the marathon in 2000. Emil Zatopek jumped into the 1952 Olympic Marathon and won after taking the 5,000 and 10,000 golds on the track. Grete Waitz and Alberto Salazar both contended for years that they were not road racers, just track racers doing an occasional road race, but obviously they did very well while slumming.

training heart rate. *See* heart-rate monitor.

training log. *See* logbooks.

Trason, Ann (b. August 30, 1960). The woman who owns the Western States 100-mile race (as 11-time winner) can also show her speed during rare ventures onto the roads. She's a 2:39 marathoner. *See also* Hall of Fame, RRCA; ultramarathons.

Trent, Marcie (b. December 22, 1917; d. 1995). The masters running pioneer and record-setter was killed by a grizzly bear while running with family members in Alaska. She holds the current over-70 records for the half-marathon and marathon. *See also* records, American age-group.

triathlon and duathlon. These multisport competitions have a brief history, dating only from the late 1970s, but have experienced spectacular growth. Triathlon (swimming, cycling, and running) became an Olympic sport in 2000, ending with a 10K run. Although we don't cover the sport in this book, we acknowledge its close ties to road racing, especially in its formative years. Run-bike duathlons are sometimes referred to as biathlons, but technically the biathlon is cross-country skiing and target shooting in winter and running and target shooting in summer.

Trujillo, Maria (now DeRios) (b. October 19, 1959). In 1984 she competed in the Olympic Marathon for her native Mexico. Then she gained U.S. citizenship and ran internationally for her new country, winning the 1995 Pan-American Games Marathon gold medal (in 2:43:56), taking a national marathon title (2:35:39 in 1991), and competing twice in the World Championships (14th in 2:39:28 in 1991 and 35th in 2:46:36 in 1999). *See also* national marathon champions, U.S.; Pan-American Games; rankings, *Runner's World*; World Championships, U.S.

Tsuburaya, Kokichi (b. May 13, 1940). He was the bronze medalist in the 1964 Olympic Marathon, in his home nation of Japan. Tsuburaya later committed suicide from depression caused by a chronic injury that ended his running career. *See also* Olympic medalists.

Tulu, Derartu (b. March 21, 1972). Ethiopia's two-time Olympic gold medalist in the 10,000 won the 2001 London Marathon in 2:23:56. She also was the 2000 Bolder Boulder 10K champion while training for the 2000 Games. *See also* Bolder Boulder 10K; London Marathon.

Turbull, Derek (b. December 5, 1926). A New Zealand sheepherder, Derek is one of the handful of runners who in the 1970s redefined how masters runners should be regarded—as tough and fast. Training by instinct and for a break from the daily routine of raising 3,000 sheep, Derek's accomplishments are astounding. In 1987 at age 60 he ran a 2:38:46 marathon in Adelaide, Australia; it was the first time a 60-year-old had dipped under 2:40. Not satisfied, at age 65 in 1992 he ran the London Marathon in 2:42. A half-hour documentary titled *The Fastest Old Man in the World* was constructed around his feats. His talents aren't confined to long-distance running, though. At age 70 he could still uncork a sub-2:30 800 meters on the track. Once he reached 70, he expanded his interest to include triathlons.

Tuttle, Gary (b. October 12, 1947). Although to this day he claims to be anything but a marathoner, the southern Californian won the 1975 and 1976 national marathon championships. He also placed second at Boston in 1985 during one of Boston's down years. *See also* Bay to Breakers 12K; national marathon champions, U.S.

Tuttle, John (b. October 16, 1958). The 1984 Olympian DNFed at Los Angeles but continued to race well through the years—until he became a leading masters runner and RRCA Hall of Famer. *See also* Hall of Fame, RRCA; Olympians, U.S.; Olympic Trials Marathon, U.S.; rankings, *Runner's World*; records, American age-group.

12K. This odd distance became semistandard with the popularity of Bay to Breakers. It is also the length of Bloomsday, and Falmouth and Bix are a slightly shorter seven miles. Twelve kilometers also is one of the distances the men run in the World Cross Country Championships. *See also* distances, metric and English.

Twin Cities Marathon (www.twincitiesmarathon.org). One of the country's biggest, fastest, and most attractive races, it starts each fall in Minneapolis and finishes in St. Paul, passing many lakes and crossing the Mississippi. *See also* oldest races; scenic races.

Twomey, Cathie (now Bellamy) (b. October 14, 1956). Her long career spanned track, cross country, and roads. In 1979 she won Bloomsday, and in 1987 she ran in (but didn't finish) the World Championships Marathon. She now coaches in Eugene, Oregon. *See also* Bloomsday 12K; World Championships, U.S.

Tymn, Mike (b. April 2, 1937). Once a 2:28 masters marathoner, he's now the sport's longest-running columnist. His work has appeared in *National Masters News* for more than 250 consecutive months. He has written for *Running Times* and *Runner's World* as well as the *Honolulu Advertiser* newspaper.

Ullyot, Dr. Joan (b. July 1, 1940). One of the early female pioneers in both medicine and long-distance running, Joan attended Wellesley College and the Free University of Berlin, then went on to become one of the early female graduates of the Harvard Medical School (1966). "I was your typical woman of 30, the ultimate creampuff," she said. "I always say that if I could become an athlete, anyone could do it."

At 30 she took up running, and it literally changed her life. She started by running a mile. A few years later she was a world-class marathoner during the formative years of women's distance running. She ran her first marathon in 1973. By the following year, she was competing in the U.S. women's marathon championships and then in the informal world championships. She finished sixth in the latter race, and fourth in the 1975 U.S. championships. She has a marathon PR of 2:47, which she ran at age 48.

Her involvement in running caused her to change her medical concentration from pathology to exercise physiology. She was also one of the pioneers in spreading the word about women's running. Her 1976 book of that title was a runaway best-seller for World Publications. Four years later she wrote *Running Free* for Putnam. She was Bloomsday's first-ever women's winner (1977), and during the late 1970s and onward she frequently tried her hand at ultrarunning. *See also* Bloomsday 12K.

Ultimate Guide to Marathons, The. Dennis Craythorn and Rich Hanna of Sacramento published a slick 300-plus-page guide to American marathons in 1997, rating each race. They followed with an international edition and a second edition (1999–2000) of the American version. In spite of the wide popularity of the book, we have not seen a 2001–2002 edition as we go to press. Rich Hanna was twice a U.S. 100K champion, finished second in the 2001 World 100K Championships, and has a 2:17 marathon PR. *See also* books.

Ultimate Runner. A short-lived competition in Jackson, Michigan, combined a road 10K, a track 400 meters, a 100 meters, a mile, and a marathon—all on the same day! The event was scored decathlon style, with a points table for weighing the quality of times at each distance. A scaled-down version of this race, sans the marathon but using the same Ultimate Runner name, is now run annually in Winston-Salem, North Carolina. *See also* oddest races.

ultramarathons. These races, which typically begin with the 50K, are outside the realm of this book, but ultrarunners cross over successfully to standard road races, and some of them even use the marathon as a training run. One of the finest is Ann Trason, 11-time winner of the Western States 100-mile ultramarathon, a winner of the Comrades Ultramarathon in South Africa, and a sub-2:40 marathoner. *See also* Trason, Ann.

ultras. *See* ultramarathons.

USA Road Circuit (www.usaldr.org). One of the many activities overseen by the USATF long-distance office in Santa Barbara is the annual ranking of runners from selected races on this road circuit.

USA Track & Field (USATF) (www.usatf.org). The sport's current governing body in the United States was formerly known as The Athletics Congress (TAC), which grew out of the old Amateur Athletic Union (AAU). USATF's primary duties in road racing are fielding international teams, keeping records, and managing the course-certification program. *See also* Amateur Athletic Union; Athletics Congress, The; Masback, Craig.

USA Track & Field Hall of Fame. *See* Hall of Fame, USATF.

USA Track & Field Road Running Information Center. *See* Road Running Information Center.

U.S. champions. *See national champions for 5K, 10K, half-marathon, and marathon.*

U.S. Olympic Committee (USOC). This group holds the franchise for sending U.S. teams to the Olympics but has little real power in selecting teams. That is the job of USATF.

U.S. Olympic Trials Marathon. *See* Olympic Trials, U.S.

Utes, Warren (b. June 25, 1920). He was to the shorter road races what John Keston was to the longer ones when both men were in their 70s—phenomenal. Utes, father of national-class female runner Cindy James, holds current American records for the 5K (65–69 18:21, 70–74 18:01, and 75–79 19:24), the 10K (75–79 40:12), and the half-marathon (75–79 1:30:19). He also has a pending 5K mark of 22:14 for 80-plus. *See also* Keston, John; records, American age-group.

V

Vahlensieck, Christa (b. May 27, 1949). The West German was the first female marathoner to break 2:35; her 2:34:48 in 1977 was her second world mark (the first was her 2:40:16 in 1975). Her greatest competitive successes came at Košice, where she was a five-time winner. *Track & Field News* ranked her number one in the world for 1976 and 1977. *See also* Košice Peace Marathon; rankings; *Track & Field News*; record progressions, world; Waldniel, Germany.

Van Aaken, Dr. Ernst (b. May 16, 1910). The father of women's marathon running in Europe was a medical doctor and coach, before and after a traffic accident that resulted in amputation of both legs. During the 1970s he hosted an international marathon for women in his hometown of Waldniel, West Germany. His book, *The Van Aaken Method* (World Publications, 1976), was translated into English by George Beinhorn. *See also* coaches; Waldniel, Germany.

Van Alphen, Piet (b. August 16, 1930; d. 1987). Van Alphen of the Netherlands was an extraordinary age-group road racer. In 1982 at the Rotterdam Marathon he ran 2:22:14—at age 53! He was described by masters racer and author Roger Robinson, who raced against him in 1984 in Belgium, as "a stocky, silver-haired man with an over-50 number and a brisk, economical stride." He died at age 57.

Van Blunk, Elaine (b. September 11, 1964). In 1993 Van Blunk won the U.S. national half-marathon title. She qualified for the 1995 World Championships Marathon, where she DNFed. *See also* national half-marathon champions, U.S.; World Championships, U.S.

Vandendriessche, Aurele (b. July 4, 1932). The Belgian won the Boston Marathon twice (1963 and 1964) and wins the all-time prize for the winner with the longest last name. Headline writers in

When Belgian Aurele Vandendriessche came to Boston in 1963 he didn't let the presence of Ethiopians Abebe Bikila and Mamo Wolde stand in the way of a victory.

From the collection of Dr. Edward H. Kozloff—Motor City Striders

Boston naturally shortened it to "Vandy." *See also* Boston Marathon.

Van Zant, Jesse (birthdate unavailable). The 1951 national marathon champion later went on a tear at Bay to Breakers, winning four times in five years (1953, 1954, 1955, and 1957). *See also* Bay to Breakers 12K; national marathon champions, U.S.

Varsha, Bob (b. April 21, 1951). The former top marathoner (sixth in the 1976 U.S. Olympic Trials) was reincarnated as a broadcaster of human running, cycling, and auto racing. *See also* television.

Vaseline. The time-tested lubrication minimizes chafing problems during running.

Vasquez, Sal (b. December 15, 1939). The Mexican-born runner and reformed soccer player had few peers in his 40s and 50s. He still holds the American 50-plus record for 5K with 15:38. *See also* records, American age-group.

© Mark Shearman. Athletics–Images.

Lasse Viren is one of the all-time greats in distance running. Not known as a road racer, he won the 5,000 and the 10,000 at the 1976 Olympics and then finished fifth in the marathon.

Vera, Rolando (b. April 27, 1965). The Ecuadorian runner won the Bolder Boulder 10K in 1988 and the Los Angeles Marathon in 1995. *See also* Bolder Boulder 10K; Los Angeles Marathon.

Vigueras, Alfredo (b. January 12, 1963). Born in Mexico, he won the 1996 national half-marathon and 1999 marathon championships after gaining U.S. citizenship. *See also* national half-marathon champions, U.S.; national marathon champions, U.S.

Viren, Lasse (b. July 22, 1949). The Finn came within four places of pulling a Zatopek. After winning the 5,000 and 10,000 at the Montreal Olympics, Viren placed fifth in the marathon—his debut at this distance. The 5-10 double at the 1976 Games was his second straight.

Virgin, Craig (b. August 2, 1955). It would be difficult to find a male American runner as wide-ranging in endurance talent as Craig. His road credentials ranged from a 28-minute 10K to a 2:10:26 marathon. He set world and American 10K bests three times. His cross country and track work were even better, as he won two World Cross Country titles and made three Olympic 10,000-meter teams.

Craig grew up in Lebanon, Illinois, about 30 miles east of St. Louis. Living in a basketball-mad area, Craig learned early that it wasn't his sport, so he tried cross country. His coach was Hank Feldt, who said of Craig, "From day number one his attitude was his biggest asset. He takes the ability he has and excels with it. I don't mean to slight Craig, but I think I've had other kids with better talent. The difference is that he just sets goals and goes for them. He understands the rules of the game—that you don't get anything without paying for it." By the end of his senior year at Lebanon Community High School he ran 8:41 for two miles, breaking Steve Prefontaine's national high school record.

His focus on setting goals and then attaining them pretty much summarizes his 1979 season. He wanted to break 2:15 in his debut marathon (he ran 2:14:40 at Mission Bay, an American debut record), he wanted to break 27:40 at 10,000 meters on the track (he ran 27:39.4 at the national championships, an American record), he wanted to win a major road race (he won the Trevira 10-Mile Twosome in 46:33, beating Bill Rodgers by more than a minute), and he wanted to win some famous summer road races (he won both Peachtree and Falmouth, setting course records at both). "I don't like people setting any limits on me," he told Amby Burfoot for a *Runner's World* story in 1980. Point noted. *See also* Bay to Breakers 12K; Hall of Fame, National Distance Running; Hall of Fame, RRCA; Peachtree 10K.

Visions of Eight. *See* movies.

V̇O₂max. Also known as *maximal oxygen uptake*, this is a reading of the body's ability to get oxygen from the lungs to the blood and therefore to the working muscles (and also to remove carbon dioxide and lactate) during maximal exertion. An athlete's V̇O₂max and the percentage of V̇O₂max that he or she can maintain for a prolonged period are key measuring sticks of endurance potential. V̇O₂max is generally expressed relative to a person's body weight, in milliliters of oxygen per kilogram or body weight per minute. Perhaps the best way to optimize a runner's V̇O₂max is by interval training—alternating race pace running with short rests. *See also* maximum oxygen uptake.

Vogel, Ted (b. July 17, 1925). The 1948 U.S. Olympic marathoner placed 14th at London. A year earlier Vogel won a national marathon title at age 22. *See also* national marathon champions, U.S.; Olympians, U.S.

volunteers. They stand along the course, and at the start and finish, so that others may run. Without them, there's no such thing as road racing; they make the sport possible. Most events are long on runners and short on volunteer help. To correct this imbalance, and to help runners appreciate what goes on

Giving Back

From Joe Henderson's *Running Commentary,* May 1999.

One of the great strengths of American running is also one of its subtle weaknesses. We rarely suffer a shortage of runners willing to run any distance, anywhere there is a race that weekend. We often suffer from a shortage of workers willing to help conduct the races.

In this sport we are a nation of doers, not viewers. We would rather run in a race ourselves than watch others run it, no matter how fast they are and how slow we are.

Few events here are in danger of disappearing for lack of entrants. Many must limit their fields by setting a maximum number (New York City Marathon) or by imposing qualifying times (Boston Marathon).

The demand for space at starting lines is high and growing higher. The demand for volunteer workers grows too, and the supply remains short. Race directors—who usually are volunteers themselves—forever beg for help. They never seem to have quite enough of it on race day.

The volunteers give up a weekend day to stand shivering in the cold or baking in the sun, delivering the aid that runners demand. For this the workers usually receive no more than a free T-shirt.

I often go to races as a guest of the directors. This lets me follow them through their race day, which usually begins after a sleepless night for them. They and their support troops arrive before the first runner and stay long after the last one goes home.

Watching the start area come together, seeing the course from the standpoint of the workers, then observing the finish-line cleanup is something every runner should experience at least once. It tells several truths about this sport:

- Running the race may be one of the easiest tasks that day. At least it takes much less time than the scene-setting work that makes the running possible.

- Runners are abundant, and each has only one job to perform—running his or her own race. Workers are scarce, and each often does multiple jobs.

- Runners as a group are quick to complain and slow to compliment these workers. Volunteers hear little or nothing from the 99 percent of runners who go home happy but hear much from the 1 percent who are not pleased.

The least we can do as runners is to say more thank-yous. Let the volunteers, those too-often-invisible heroes of the sport, know that we appreciate them. The best we can do is to give back to the sport by serving as volunteers ourselves. Set aside an occasional race to stand and deliver assistance to the runners.

Christian churches promote the concept of the tithe, which means giving 10 percent of one's earnings to the church. Runners of all religions, or none, would do well to practice a form of tithing. For every 10 races we run, we might agree to work at one. Hand out the race packets, work at an aid station, direct the traffic, read the splits, award the winners, assist the injured, distribute the food.

Doing this would help a sport that is always long on runners and short on volunteers. It would also help us to be slower with complaints and quicker with compliments when next we run a race.

in the background, everyone who runs should volunteer occasionally. It would make every corner of the sport much more harmonious. *See also* "Giving Back" on page 360; directors, race.

Von Hasse, Jutta (birthdate unavailable). The women's winner of the first Berlin Marathon in 1974 had additional victories there in 1976 and 1979. *See also* Berlin Marathon.

W

waffle sole. The first great marketing advance for fledgling Nike shoes was created when Bill Bowerman melted rubber using his wife's waffle iron; Bill introduced the waffle sole at the 1972 U.S. Olympic Trials. It is supposed that Bill's later neurological problems were the result of performing his waffle-sole experiments in an unventilated garage. *See also* Bowerman, Bill; Nike; shoe companies.

Wainaina, Eric (b. December 19, 1973). Some people are just plain incredible at peaking at the perfect time. After victory at the 1995 Tokyo Marathon, Kenyan Wainaina managed to be picked for the Olympic Marathon team going to Atlanta. There were some frowns and questions over the choice, but he came through in Atlanta with a bronze medal. With no world-beating accomplishments between Atlanta and Sydney, it seemed a questionable choice to put him on the 2000 team.

But again in Sydney he came through with a strong silver-medal performance (2:10:31) after dueling with two Ethiopians (Gezahegne Abera and Tesaye Tola) when the three broke the field open at 31K. Tola and Wainaina worked against the headwind, while Abera laid back waiting. At 38K Wainaina was leading, but Abera was hanging on his shoulder, looking for a place to make his move. Wainaina was coming off a 2:10:17 marathon at Nagano, a PR; Abera was coming off a stirring second-place 2:09:50 finish at Boston, where he was outkicked at the end by Elijah Lagat. When Abera made his move at Sydney, the best Wainaina could do was hold on. He lost by 20 seconds, but no other Kenyans finished in the top 10. *See also* Olympic medalists; Tokyo Marathons.

Waitz, Grete (b. October 1, 1953). While a vocal group of both male and female runners were raging in public and lobbying in private for a women's Olympic Marathon, Grete Waitz was doing no such thing. Purely a track and cross country runner, Waitz occasionally trained on the roads and more often on the trails in her native Norway. With Olympic events for women restricted to the 800 and 1,500 meters, Grete's chances to shine seemed limited. Her talents lay in endurance—the longer the race, the greater her success.

As a 19-year-old physical education student, she went to the Munich Games and ran a personal best at 1,500 meters (4:16)—but she was out of the running against Eastern Bloc women, who it is apparent in hindsight ran with the aid of performance-enhancing drugs. She did set world records in the 3,000 meters in both 1975 and 1976. Building toward the Montreal Olympics, she trained extremely hard (125 miles per week with intense afternoon workouts), but she was mentally defeated because in spite of her hard work, she could not approach the performances of the Soviet women. In the semifinal in Montreal, Grete allowed herself to be boxed in and finished sixth (in 4:04.6).

Fortunately, the 3,000 meters had just been added to international competition. At the World Cup in Dusseldorf in September 1977, she went out strong in the 3,000 and burned the other runners down, winning in 8:43.5. In March 1978 she won the World Cross Country Championships in Glasgow, Scotland. But the summer was brutal. She went to the European Championships in Prague expecting to win the 3,000, but Svetlana Ulmasova of the USSR outpowered her and Waitz finished third.

Grete's countryman Knut Kvalheim was also stunned. In spite of being the Norwegian record-holder for the mile, 3,000 meters, and 5,000 meters, and the fact that he ran a Norwegian record that afternoon in the 10,000 (27:41.3), he placed ninth. Grete's hus-

Grete Waitz never claimed to be a road racer, but when she set a world record at the New York City Marathon in 1978, she started on a spree that spanned a decade.

© Jeff Johnson

band and coach, Jack, felt that the Eastern Europeans were winning through drug use. The whole racing scene was disheartening. As they strolled through Prague, Knut half-convinced Grete that she should focus on something more fun—running the New York City Marathon in the fall. When he ran the race in 1976, he had gone out with the leaders but dropped out at 10 miles; he hoped to go back and try it again.

Grete was strong but did not train beyond 20K (12 miles). Jack began to read up on the female competitors at the marathon; Grete began to feel that a free plane ticket to New York for her and Jack would provide a much-needed vacation. Fred Lebow, New York's race director, recalled that Bill Rodgers had set an American record in the marathon in 1975 coming off a third-place finish in the World Cross Country Championships. He took a chance on Grete Waitz, feeling that as a track runner she'd probably go out too fast and pull some of the other more experienced women along to faster times, perhaps even to a world record. And indeed there was a world record that day. Grete had found her groove as she ran 2:32:30.

Yet Grete claimed that it was not a world record, because there are no world records on the roads, only on precisely measured tracks. *Runner's World* brought Grete and several members of her family to northern California over the Christmas holidays for the magazine's National Running Week, where she continued to maintain that she was not a road racer. She proceeded to set a world record of 25:28 for five miles running through the streets of Los Altos, California, in the *Runner's World* Midnight Run on New Year's Eve—streets that featured many turns of more than 90 degrees. "I do not run races on the road," she said. "I am a track runner."

Over the next two years Grete became a legend. She traveled to the United States frequently to race on the roads. She ran the L'eggs Mini-Marathon in Central Park and won. She again ran the New York City Marathon and lowered her own world record by 4:57 to 2:27:33. She won the Falmouth seven-mile road race on Cape Cod. She again won the *Runner's World* Midnight Run. She won the World Cross Country Championships again; no runner finished within 30 seconds of her. All the while, her quiet charm enchanted people. And the quiet and efficient way in which she approached winning marathons (she lowered the record to 2:25:42 at her third New York City Marathon) went a long way toward weighing in favor of an Olympic Marathon for women. The men and women attempting to get the women's marathon in the Games had in Grete Waitz an understated yet effective champion of their cause.

With all the successes in women's road racing today, it is difficult to appreciate Grete Waitz's role as a pioneer of women's running. She took second place to Joan Benoit at the inaugural women's Olympic Marathon in Los Angeles in 1984, and that defeat somewhat shades her tremendous accomplishments. Grete won the Peachtree 10K four times in six years. Of the 15 marathons she completed, she won 13, including 9 New York City Marathons. She continues to work for women's running on the international scene. And she has come a long way on other levels. Now she admits to being a road racer occasionally. *See also* Bay to Breakers 12K; Hall of Fame, National Distance Running; London Marathon; New York City Marathon; Peachtree 10K; Olympic medalists; rankings, *Runner's World*; rankings, *Track & Field News*; record progressions, world; World Championships medalists.

Trained in Japan, Kenyan Douglas Wakiihuri has won more major championship marathons than any other Kenyan.

© Mark Shearman. Athletics-Images.

Wakiihuri, Douglas (b. September 26, 1963). The Japanese-trained Kenyan (coached by legendary Kiyoshi Nakamura) remains the most successful of his countrymen to date in championship marathons: 1987 World Championships winner, 1988 Olympic silver medalist, 1990 Commonwealth Games winner, 1995 World Cup winner. He also won at London (1989) and New York City (1990). *See also* Commonwealth Games; London Marathon; New York City Marathon; Olympic medalists; World Championships medalists; World Cup Marathon.

Waldniel, Germany. This small town in the former West Germany was home to a first attempt at conducting a worldwide marathon for women in 1975, organized by Ernst Van Aaken. He accomplished what he'd set out to do by inspiring others to promote international marathons for women. Avon stepped in next. *See also* Avon Racing Circuits; Van Aaken, Dr. Ernst.

Waldniel World Championships Winners

German doctor-coach Ernst Van Aaken was an early provider of encouragement and opportunities for women in long-distance running. Twice in the 1970s he promoted international marathons, bringing women from around the world to his hometown of Waldniel, West Germany. The winners were both German.

Year	Athlete	Time
1974	Liane Winter (West Germany)	2:50:32
1976	Christa Vahlensieck (West Germany)	2:45:25

walk breaks. A trick of using planned walks, early and often, was adopted from ultrarunners for extending runs and easing pains. Tom Osler brought the idea to the attention of marathoners in his *Serious Runner's Handbook*, published in 1978 (World Publications). Jeff Galloway popularized the practice in the 1990s with his writing, his speaking, and his teaching of marathon-training groups. *See also* Galloway, Jeff; Osler, Tom.

Walker, Caroline (b. 1953). The then-sixteen-year-old Oregonian set a world and American record of 3:02:53 in her only marathon, the Trail's End in 1970. She later ran in the World Cross Country Championships. *See also* record progressions, American; record progressions, world.

Walkman. Sony's product, released in the 1980s, helped runners who can't stand silence or the sound of their own heart beating by setting their workouts to music.

wall, the. The infamous stopping or slowing point for many a road racer doesn't have a fixed location, as at 20 miles of a marathon, but is related to a runner's inadequate preparation or unwise pacing. It is physiologically tied to the point at which a runner runs out of stored glycogen in the muscles. It's also being referred to these days as "bonking," a term borrowed from bicycle racers. *See also* bonk.

Walters, Lloyd (birthdate unavailable). At his age it was amazing enough that he ran at all. Walters set the current 90–94 American record for 5K in 1992 with 40:32. *See also* records, American age-group.

Wang Junxia (b. January 9, 1973). The year of Chinese women was 1993. En masse they broke world records by huge margins, but their times are now generally discredited—particularly after China pulled most of its distance team out of the 2000 Olympics for failed drug tests at home. Most successful of these women was Wang Junxia, who set world track 3,000- and 10,000-meter records, then won the World Cup Marathon in 1993. She collected gold (at 5,000) and silver (at 10,000) medals at the 1996 Olympics. *See also* World Cup Marathon.

Wanjiru, Esther (b. March 27, 1977). The Kenyan ran a pending world best for 20K in late 2000. Her 1:04:01 bettered Colleen de Reuck's mark by 70 seconds. *See also* records, world.

warm-up. It becomes less important the longer the runner's distance and the slower the pace. Speedsters warm up longer for a 5K than the race lasts, including some running *(strides)* at race pace. But a four-hour-plus marathoner simply warms up in the early miles of the race itself. *See also* strides.

Warner, Debbie (b. March 17, 1952). The American grabbed the marathon silver medal at the 1987 Pan-American Games behind Maricarmen Cardenas of Mexico.

Washington's Birthday Marathon (www.dcroadrunners.org). Founded in 1962, the Beltsville, Maryland, race ranks among the 10 oldest marathons in the United States. It is run on or near George Washington's birthday in February. *See also* oldest races.

watches, digital. One of the greatest advances in running technology, these little gems first marketed in the late 1970s put instant results on the wrist of every runner. *See also* Casio; MircoSel.

water running. Flotation belts or vests allow runners to take near-normal workouts to the pool. Runners "run" through the water in an upright position while recovering from injury or when they need a break from land-based training. Water running has proved to be one of the most effective forms of substitute or supplementary training because it is low impact but mimics the movements of running. *See also* AquaJogger; cross-training; Wet Vest.

WAVA (World Association of Veterans Athletics). *See* World Masters Association.

Web sites. *See entries for specific events, organizations, and companies.*

weekly mileage. Ever since Arthur Lydiard's New Zealanders credited their base-building 100-mile weeks for their success in the early 1960s, weekly mileage has been the gold standard for measuring running effort. But Lydiard himself later tried to take the emphasis away from counting miles, preferring that most long runs be done by time instead of distance. In a predominately metric world the term *mileage* means little anyway, and kilometer counting isn't as common, though the totals sound more impressive because 100 miles equals 160K. *See also* Lydiard, Arthur; time running.

Weidenbach, Lisa Larsen (now Rainsberger) (b. December 13, 1961). She's forever remembered as the hard-luck runner who ran in three straight U.S. Olympic Marathon Trials (1984, 1988, and 1992) and missed the team by a single place each time. Better to remember her, though, as someone only three Americans could beat on those days . . . and as a winner of Boston (2:34:06 in 1985) and Chicago (2:29:17 in 1988 and 2:28:15 in 1989) . . . and as the current claimant of world and American aided bests for 30K (1:43:27 in 1985) . . . and as the standing American record-holder for 15K (48:28 in 1989). *See also* Bloomsday 12K; Boston Marathon; Chicago Marathon; Olympic Trials Marathon, U.S.; rankings, *Runner's World*; records, American; records, world.

weight divisions. *See* Clydesdale division.

weight training. The practice has gone in and out of favor among runners and their coaches. Percy Cerutty, the great Australian coach of the midcentury, swore by weights, lifted often himself, and oversaw the strength workouts of undefeated miler Herb Elliott. Another influential coach of that era, however, took the opposite view. Arthur Lydiard of New Zealand said, "Deer are some of nature's greatest runners, yet you never see them lifting any weight other than their own." Today's runners, if they lift at all, tend to treat it as a balancing act. They do it more for the muscles that running ignores (mostly in the upper body) than for direct improvement in their main sport. *See also* cross-training.

Weintraub, Abe (b. February 3, 1910). By running 7:25:12 at the 2000 New York City Marathon, he broke world and American records for ages 90 and older held by G-men Josef Galia of Germany and Sam Gadless of the United States. *See also* records, American age-group; records, world age-group.

Welch, Priscilla. *See* next page.

Wells, Jeff (b. May 25, 1954). He never received proper credit at the time, but Wells was an American record-holder on an unaided marathon course. He tied with Tony Sandoval at the 1979 Nike–Oregon Track Club race with 2:10:20. Two years earlier Jeff had won the Honolulu Marathon. *See also* Honolulu Marathon; record progressions, American.

Welzel, Jane (b. April 24, 1955). She recovered from a near-fatal auto accident to win the 1990 national marathon title in 2:33:25 and compete in

One of the most dramatic marathon finishes of all time came at the 1978 Boston Marathon, when Jeff Wells (#14) mounted a late-race charge on Bill Rodgers's lead. Sidestepping a motorcycle police officer and a protester, Wells missed first place by two seconds.

© Jeff Johnson

Welch, Priscilla (b. November 22, 1944). At one point in road-racing history, the awesome 12-year reign of Derek Clayton's marathon record of 2:08:34 seemed astonishing. But every passing day, another marathon mark threatens to live through eternity. The numbers are these: 2:26:51 and 1987. On an April day in London, Priscilla Welch took second place (behind Ingrid Kristiansen) in the London Marathon. Priscilla was then 42 years old. No female masters runner has come close to her time since. And as though to prove that the incredible accomplishment was not a fluke, in the fall of that same year Priscilla won outright the women's side of the New York City Marathon with a 2:30:17.

More astonishing still is the fact that nine years before, she wasn't even a runner. She smoked cigarettes and spent evenings in bars while serving in the British military stationed in Oslo, Norway. She took up running at age 35, coming under the influence of Dave Welch, then a sergeant in the British army.

Born and raised near the town of Bedfordshire in England, "Priscilla had a typical English childhood," her brother commented in a chapter in Mike Sandrock's book *Running With the Legends* (Human Kinetics 1996). He added, "She was no different than any of the other children in the area, though she was always full of energy as a child. When our Mom would ask where Cilla was, she'd always be off on a bicycle somewhere."

She left school at 15 and took courses to become a typist. At age 16 she left home and over the next several years lived with two different aunts while taking additional secretarial courses. She enlisted in the British Royal Naval Service at age 17. She was assigned to British NATO forces in Oslo, where she met Dave, who changed her life by challenging her to begin racing after

© Jeff Johnson

Priscilla Welch has been the world record-holder in the women's masters marathon since 1987 (2:26:51) when she took second place (at age 42) to Ingrid Kristiansen at London.

she took up casual running with an American friend. She entered a Norwegian Independence Day 10K and came in second, surprising both herself and Dave with her innate abilities, for there were several top runners and international cross-country skiers entered.

In 1978 Dave (who has a marathon PR of 2:46) entered the Stockholm Marathon. Although Priscilla was running only four miles per day, she decided to enter the marathon and ran 3:26. In the wake of the race, Priscilla estimated that she'd be capable of taking an hour off her time. Dave was incredulous because a 2:26 would be a world record. Still in Oslo, Priscilla raced frequently at every distance offered, usually running against women in lower age groups because there was no competition in her own.

Then in July 1981 Dave was transferred to the Shetland Islands for the next two years. A bleaker station would be hard to find. There wasn't much else to do but train seriously, in really lousy weather. In that same year a little knot of their running fraternity went to run the first London Marathon; Priscilla broke three hours (2:59:29). The next year she ran the Glasgow Marathon in Scotland and did 2:46:41. Then Dave introduced her to speedwork. Back at the London Marathon in 1983, she ran 2:39. In July she won the Enschede Marathon in Holland in 2:36. She wanted to do more work to see what she could accomplish, but Dave wisely served as a governor to her ambitions, holding her back so she didn't overdo it.

In November 1983 they went to the New York City Marathon, where Priscilla ran 2:32:32. In February 1984 she placed sixth at Osaka, Japan, in 2:36, in spite of huge blisters. But it wasn't a good enough effort for the British Olympic selection committee to pick her for the marathon team scheduled to go to Los Angeles for the first-ever women's Olympic marathon. So she returned to the London Marathon

in April and took second place under horrendous conditions in 2:30:06. She now had a sponsor, Nike, which had given her a choice of training in either Eugene or Boulder. Dave and Priscilla chose Boulder strictly for the altitude, and it apparently worked. At Los Angeles, in spite of 68-degree heat, she placed sixth with a British women's record performance of 2:28:54.

The Welches liked America and decided to stay. Through the decade of the 1980s Priscilla was a formidable force in road racing. The fact that she turned 40 in the fall of 1984 didn't seem to matter. "I don't think '40,' and I certainly don't feel 40," she is quoted as saying. But she began to overrace, an easy thing to do in the United States, where there were more than a handful of road races each weekend. She and Dave decided to scale back the program during 1986. It worked. She came back full tilt in 1987, setting the masters world record of 2:26:51 in London in May, winning every masters title available over the summer, then going to New York in the fall to win outright.

In 1990 she won the masters division in 9 of the 10 major road races she entered. But by the fall, she began to burn out, to feel lethargic. She made a few attempts at a comeback, but each time she'd get tired. She discovered a strange lump under her breast and on November 19, 1992, a surgical team operated on her for 8½ hours to remove her breast and attempt to reconstruct it using skin from her abdomen. Today she runs for pleasure and occasionally enters a race for fun, but she tries to hold herself in check when the competitive juices flow. "I'm getting pretty fast again," she said in early 2000. "But I don't ever want to go back to the intensity I put myself through for more than a decade back then." *See also* "Running Well" on next page; New York City Marathon; rankings, *Runner's World*; records, world age-group.

Running Well

From Joe Henderson's *Running Commentary,* March 2000.

Ask Priscilla Welch how she's doing these days, and she'll say, "Quite well indeed, thank you very much." Much has happened to and for her since her biggest year of running. That was 1987. First she set the world masters marathon record of 2:26:51 that no one has come close to breaking. Later that same year she beat all women at the New York City Marathon.

British-born Priscilla started late as a runner and knew, as younger stars sometimes don't realize, that her top years weren't unlimited. She called this star-treatment time "a pleasant interlude between what I did before and what might come next."

One of her next steps was to coauthor a book, *Masters Running and Racing* (Rodale, 1991), with Bill Rodgers. I got to know them better while working as their editor. Soon after we finished that writing, Priscilla was diagnosed with and treated for breast cancer.

I'd seen or heard little from her until we got together in California this weekend for the Napa Valley Marathon. Seven years past chemotherapy, she looks great, says she feels fine, and has moved happily into her next phase. "We're U.S. citizens now—and both of us are coaches," she said of herself and husband Dave Welch, who had been her coach. They've settled in the Colorado mountain town of Tabernash.

Priscilla has no comeback-racing plans of her own, though she still runs regularly at 55. Her work in the sport just took a new turn. "We have just started coaching the high school distance runners in our town," she said. "At this time of year their workouts and ours include shoveling snow off the track." She added, "We have no children of our own, so already we are thinking of these runners as our kids."

the 1993 Worlds, placing 19th there in 2:46:08. Welzel remains competitive as a master at a wide range of road distances. *See also* national marathon champions, U.S.; rankings, *Runner's World;* World Championships, U.S.

Western Hemisphere Marathon. The oldest U.S. marathon west of Boston has run continuously in Culver City, California, since 1948. In its glory days the event played host to an Olympic Trials (1964) and several national championships. Culver City was the scene of world women's records for Merry Lepper (1963), Cheryl Bridges (1971), Miki Gorman (1973), and Jacqueline Hansen (1974). The race is run in December. *See also* "Old Western" on next page; oldest races.

Wet Vest (www.wetvest.com). Water running made its first splash in the 1980s with the introduction of this flotation product from Bioenergetics. *See also* AquaJogger; water running.

Wharf to Wharf. This six-mile midsummer romp along the California coastline between Santa Cruz and Capitola draws about 15,000 runners. *See also* biggest races.

Old Western

From Joe Henderson's *Running Commentary,* December 1997.

It's no Boston, but what is? Another long-running U.S. marathon isn't in the same league as the leader—in age, size, wealth, or fame. So the 50th running of the Western Hemisphere Marathon needs no qualifying times to limit entries. No one is throwing a party to honor past winners. No one is paying anyone to appear or to win. No one is writing a book to mark the occasion.

Boston didn't need me to write a birthday greeting when it turned 100. Everyone already knew. But Western Hemisphere does need to be remembered at 50. Technically, it's the third-oldest marathon in the country. Yonkers began in 1935 but has had several interruptions, whereas the race in Culver City, California, has continued without pause since 1948 and has the second-longest unbroken streak behind Boston's.

A few hundred runners will compete in Culver City this December, running through the movie lots as jets from LAX land and take off overhead. About the same number ran here in 1967, the first of my three Westerns.

The race was already 20 years old, the longest-lasting marathon in the West. It had already hosted an Olympic Trials, in 1964. Billy Mills ran his first race longer than nine miles in that Trials. "I had no idea how to run a marathon," he says now, "so I asked experienced marathoner Hal Higdon what I should do. He said, 'You damn sprinters! Stay with me and I'll tell you when to quit.' Later I passed him at around 20 miles," and Mills made the team for the Games where he became better known for his 10,000-meter running.

Men ran as fast as 2:15:21 on this course (Bill Scobey, 1971). Women set three world records in four years (Cheryl Bridges, 2:49:40 in 1971; Miki Gorman, 2:46:36 in 1973; and Jacqueline Hansen, 2:43:55 in 1974). "The Western Hemisphere Marathon was ahead of its time," says Hansen. It welcomed women in the early 1960s, a decade before full racing privileges were granted across the country. Fittingly the first Olympic Marathon for women touched parts of the Culver City course in 1984.

Western Hemisphere no longer attracts runners capable of breaking course records, let alone American or world marks. It can't compete for entrants with the other big regional marathons of the season, in Sacramento, San Diego, and Las Vegas.

Western Hemisphere hasn't kept up with the trends of growth and wealth in the sport. But it has kept going. Its strength is its endurance. "It's really a people's marathon," says Syd Kronenthal, a founder of the race. "We never got into the hype. When everyone else was turning toward marathons as exhibitions, we stayed focused on the marathon as a day for running."

At its core marathon running isn't about big crowds, wide media coverage, record times, or hefty prize purses. Marathoning is about enduring and surviving. No race stands as a better symbol of this sport than the Western Hemisphere Marathon. It endured for 25 years before anyone talked about a running boom, when there wasn't another big marathon on the West Coast. And it has continued another 25 years in the face of increasing competition in the area. No other marathon in the United States has gone through its first 50 years without interruption. Not even Boston.

White, Martha (b. October 31, 1959). In 1978 she became the first woman to break 34 minutes for the 10K, dropping the world and American mark to 33:30. *See also* record progressions, American; record progressions, world.

Whitely, Greg (b. January 6, 1967). He held the world and American 5K best for aided courses and the American 5K record, unaided. The latter mark was 13:26, set in 1993. *See also* record progressions, American.

Whitlock, Ed (b. 1931). The British-born Canadian ran 2:52:47 at the 2000 Columbus Marathon. The significance of that mark is that it made him the oldest runner (at 69 years, 237 days) ever to break three hours. After turning 70 in 2001, Whitlock ran a 3:00:24 marathon for the world record in his new age group. *See* records, world age-group.

Williams, Gar (b. January 30, 1933). The RRCA Hall of Famer served as the organization's president. As a runner, he won the 1965 national marathon in 2:33:51. *See also* Hall of Fame, RRCA; national marathon champions, U.S.

Williams, Lynn (b. June 11, 1960). The Canadian Olympic medalist—a bronze in the 3,000 at the 1984 Los Angeles Games—once held the world 5K road record. She was first to break 15:30, going 10 seconds under on the famously fast Carlsbad course. *See also* Bloomsday 12K; record progressions, world.

Williams, Todd (b. March 7, 1969). The two-time track Olympian in the 10,000 has come closer than any other American to breaking one hour for a half-marathon. He holds the current national best, aided, of 1:00:10. Williams also owns the American 15K record (42:22 in 1995) and has won national titles at 10K and half-marathon. He debuted in the marathon with a highly promising 2:11 but has yet to go faster. *See also* national half-marathon champions, U.S.; national 10K champions, U.S.; record progressions, American; records, American.

Wilt, Fred (b. December 14, 1920; d. 1994). This Olympian and FBI agent invented the modern running book with *How They Train* (*Track & Field News*, 1959) and was the founding editor of *Track Technique* magazine, later re-named *Track Coach*. He also coached Buddy Edelen (by mail between himself in Indiana and Edelen in England) to his world marathon record. After retiring from the FBI, Wilt coached the women's team at Purdue University. *See also* books; Edelen, Leonard "Buddy"; Hall of Fame, RRCA; Hall of Fame, USATF.

Wilton, Maureen (birthdate unavailable). The Canadian teenager set a world marathon record of 3:15:22 in 1967. She was coached by Sy Mah, who later became something of a record-setter himself by running more than 500 life-time marathons. *See also* Mah, Sy; record progressions, world.

Winfrey, Oprah (b. January 29, 1954). Her efforts were something of a joke among running purists. But the talk-show diva's 4½-hour marathon at Marine Corps undoubtedly inspired many formerly inactive women—and a few men—to get out from in front of the TV and start running. Oprah prided herself on running every step of her Marine Corps effort. *See also* Connectors; Gomes, Tawni.

Winter, Liane (b. June 24, 1942). The German set the world women's marathon record of 2:42:24 in 1975 while winning at Boston. *See also* Boston Marathon; record progressions, world; Waldniel, Germany.

WMA. *See* World Masters Association.

Wolde, Mamo (b. June 12, 1932). The teammate of Abebe Bikila never received the acclaim of his Ethiopian countryman. Despite Wolde's Olympic gold in 1968 (with 2:20:27 at high altitude) and bronze in 1972 (with 2:15:09 at age 40!), he was treated dismally at home, being jailed for taking the wrong side in a political dispute. *See also* African Games; Ethiopian runners; Olympic medalists.

© Mark Shearman, Athletics-Images.

When Ethiopian Abebe Bikila couldn't manage a threepeat of his 1960s Olympic victories (he won in 1960 and 1964), countryman Mamo Wolde (pictured here on the left) stepped forward in 1968 and won; he was subsequently jailed in Ethiopia for his political convictions.

Following Women

From Joe Henderson's *Running Commentary,* July 1999.

Some of my favorite runners are women. There are more of them to like now than ever before, but I've been around long enough to remember when there were none. This long memory allowed me to emcee a program at the Napa Valley Marathon devoted to women in running. Panelists included three runners who'd lived much of the history of the event: Ruth Anderson, a pioneer among female masters; Gayle Barron, 1978 Boston Marathon Winner; and Lorraine Moller, who rose from 800-meter runner to Olympic Marathon medalist.

They and the audience allowed me some introductory reminiscences. I told them that men go back more than a century in the marathon, and I'm a little younger than that, so much of the learning about them has been long after the fact. But I've lived the women's history race by race, year by year, almost from day one. I ran with the earliest female marathoners, supported them in print, cheered their first successes, and watched them grow into equality.

I saw my first female marathoner in 1963, at the old Ocean to Bay race across the mountains of the San Francisco Peninsula. Lyn Carman finished that day; I didn't. My first full marathon was Boston 1967. You know what happened there—as Jock Semple struck an unintended blow for women's marathoning. I never saw Kathrine Switzer that day (or Bobbi Gibb, who ran an hour faster than Kathrine), but all female runners have her to thank for marketing the event then and in the years since.

I even welcomed losing to a woman for the first time (not counting DNFing against Lyn Carman). Tens of thousands of women have outrun me since 1971, but it happened first in an eight-mile race at Napa. I couldn't have picked a better person to lose to—Francie Larrieu. She was just a teenager then and made the Olympic team the next year when the 1,500 was the longest distance for women. Twenty years later, at 39, she ran in the Games as a marathoner.

I played a minor role in winning Olympic recognition for the marathon by serving with a group grandiosely calling itself the International Runners Committee. We specialized in making pests of ourselves with officials until they finally relented and gave women the race they deserved.

U.S. women qualified for the Los Angeles Games at the Trials in Olympia, Washington. Joan Benoit won there, 17 days after knee surgery. I joined the shouts of joy for how far women had come and how far they now could go.

Little more than a decade before, an official—female, no less—had dismissed women's marathoning as a lark indulged in mainly by bored housewives. It became an Olympic event, and then a phenomenon.

I remember when no woman ran this far, then one, then two, followed by a few. Little more than 30 years later they are closing in on their rightful 50 percent of the marathoning population. Women staged a peaceful revolution in this event and won. Men who fought for them, not against, now cheer this as a victory for all of us.

women's running. The most important movement in the last third of the 20th century was the arrival of women in the sport. They were a trickle in the 1960s, but by the 1980s had won a marathon on the Olympic program, and by the late 1990s made up their rightful half of many race fields. *See also* "Following Women" above.

Women's Running. *See* Ullyot, Dr. Joan.

World Association of Veteran Athletes (WAVA). *See* World Masters Association.

World Masters Association (www.nationalmastersnews.com). Formerly known as the World Association of Veteran Athletes, this governing body for masters track and field and road racing has sponsored regular world championships since 1975 that include a marathon. WMA also oversees an age-graded running-performance system that covers all track events and many road distances.

World Championships medalists. Inaugurated in 1983 at Helsinki, the World Championships began as an every-four-years meet, then switched to a two-year cycle in 1993. Grete Waitz and Rob de Castella won its first marathon. *See also* de Castella, Rob; Waitz, Grete.

World Championships Marathon Medalists

This meet of Olympic quality started as an every-fourth-year supplement to those Games. In 1993 the Worlds went to every other year. In 1997 it incorporated the World Cup by expanding to five runners per country with team competition. * = event record.

WOMEN

Year	Place	Athlete	Time
1983	Helsinki	1. Grete Waitz (Norway)	2:28:09
		2. Marianne Dickerson (U.S.)	2:31:09
		3. Raisa Smekhnova (USSR)	2:31:13
1987	Rome	1. Rosa Mota (Portugal)	2:25:17*
		2. Zoya Ivanova (USSR)	2:32:38
		3. Jocelyn Villeton (France)	2:32:53
1991	Tokyo	1. Wanda Panfil (Poland)	2:29:53
		2. Sachiko Yamashita (Japan)	2:29:57
		3. Katrin Dorre (Germany)	2:30:10
1993	Stuttgart	1. Junko Asari (Japan)	2:30:03
		2. Manuela Machado (Portugal)	2:30:54
		3. Tomoe Abe (Japan)	2:31:01
1995	Göteborg	1. Manuela Machado (Portugal)	2:25:39
		2. Anuta Catuna (Romania)	2:26:25
		3. Ornella Ferrara (Italy)	2:30:11
1997	Athens	1. Hiromi Suzuki (Japan)	2:29:48
		2. Manuela Machado (Portugal)	2:31:12
		3. Lidia Simon (Romania)	2:31:55
1999	Seville	1. Jong Song Ok (North Korea)	2:26:59
		2. Ari Ichihashi (Japan)	2:27:02
		3. Lidia Simon (Romania)	2:27:41
2001	Edmonton	1. Lidia Simon (Romania)	2:26:01
		2. Reiko Tosa (Japan)	2:26:06
		3. Svetlana Zakharova (Russia)	2:26:18

(continued)

World Championships Marathon Medalists, *continued*

MEN

Year	Place	Athlete	Time
1983	Helsinki	1. Rob de Castella (Australia)	2:10:03*
		2. Kebede Balcha (Ethiopia)	2:10:27
		3. Waldemar Cierpinski (East Germany)	2:10:37
1987	Rome	1. Douglas Wakiihuri (Kenya)	2:11:48
		2. Ahmed Salah (Djibouti)	2:12:30
		3. Gelindo Bordin (Italy)	2:12:40
1991	Tokyo	1. Hiromi Taniguchi (Japan)	2:14:57
		2. Ahmed Salah (Djibouti)	2:15:26
		3. Steve Spence (U.S.)	2:15:36
1993	Stuttgart	1. Mark Plaatjes (U.S.)	2:13:57
		2. Lucketz Swartbooi (Namibia)	2:14:11
		3. Bert van Vlaanderen (Holland)	2:15:12
1995	Göteborg	1. Martin Fiz (Spain)	2:11:41
		2. Dionicio Ceron (Mexico)	2:12:13
		3. Luiz Dos Santos (Brazil)	2:12:49
1997	Athens	1. Abel Anton (Spain)	2:13:16
		2. Martin Fiz (Spain)	2:13:21
		3. Steve Moneghetti (Australia)	2:14:16
1999	Seville	1. Abel Anton (Spain)	2:13:26
		2. Vincenzo Modica (Italy)	2:14:03
		3. Nobuyuki Sato (Japan)	2:14:07
2001	Edmonton	1. Gezahegne Abera (Ethiopia)	2:12:42
		2. Simon Biwott (Kenya)	2:12:43
		3. Stefano Baldini (Italy)	2:13:18

World Championships, U.S. American men have run considerably better marathons at this meet than in the Olympics from the 1980s onward. Steve Spence took a bronze medal in 1991, and Mark Plaatjes won the race in 1993. Marianne Dickerson was a silver medalist for the U.S. in the first World Championships Marathon. *See also* Dickerson, Marianne; Plaatjes, Mark; Spence, Steve.

World Cup Marathon. The first attempt at a worldwide race outside the Olympics was launched in 1985 and run at two-year intervals. In 1997, this event became part of the World Championships Marathon, which expanded to accommodate five-member teams.

World Half-Marathon Championships. Begun in 1992, this is the only annual international championship road race.

World Marathon Relay. The relay grew out of Japan's popular ekidens, with three runners going 5K, two running 10K, and the anchor running the odd 7.2K. The World Marathon Relay, begun in 1992, ran every other year until it was discontinued in 1998.

U.S. World Championships Marathoners

The Worlds are like the Olympics—only in some ways more so. The Championships have been contested every other year since 1993, and countries have up to five runners apiece since 1997. Here are all the Americans who have competed. Note that Marianne Dickerson's medal-winning performance in 1983 is still the fastest time for a U.S. woman in this meet.

WOMEN

Year	Place	Athlete	Time
1983	Helsinki	2. Marianne Dickerson	2:31:09
		12. Debbie Eide	2:36:17
		Julie Brown	DNF
1987	Rome	7. Nancy Ditz	2:34:54
		Kim Jones	DNF
		Cathie Twomey	DNF
1991	Tokyo	13. Joy Smith	2:39:16
		14. Maria Trujillo	2:39:28
		Gordon Bakoulis	DNF
1993	Stuttgart	8. Kim Jones	2:36:33
		19. Jane Welzel	2:46:08
		no third runner entered	
1995	Göteborg	7. Linda Somers	2:32:12
		16. Kim Jones	2:37:06
		Elaine Van Blunk	DNF
1997	Athens	25. Cheryl Collins	2:43:42
		36. Julia Kirtland	2:49:43
		40. Julie Peterson	2:51:59
		Mary Alico	DNF
		Patty Valadka	DNF
1999	Seville	32. Marie Boyd	2:44:16
		35. Maria Trujillo	2:46:36
		36. Mary Lynn Currier	2:48:05
		37. Mimi Corcoran	2:49:21
		38. Cindy Keeler	2:53:04
2001	Edmonton	32. Jill Gaitenby	2:39:20
		41. Michelle Simonaitis	2:46:40
		42. Rosa Guitierrez	2:49:08
		45. Rachel Cook	2:53:21
		Jennifer Tonkin	DNF

MEN

Year	Place	Athlete	Time
1983	Helsinki	18. Ron Tabb	2:13:38
		39. Benji Durden	2:20:38
		Ed Mendoza	DNF
1987	Rome	21. Don Janicki	2:20:46
		Dave Gordon	DNF
		Dan Grimes	DNF

(continued)

World Championships Marathoners, *continued*

1991	Tokyo	3. Steve Spence	2:15:36
		26. Steve Taylor	2:29:09
		Brad Hudson	DNF
1993	Stuttgart	1. Mark Plaatjes	2:13:57
		33. Chad Bennion	2:29:37
		Brad Hudson	DNF
1995	Göteborg	10. Steve Plasencia	2:16:56
		21. Ed Eyestone	2:20:17
		Paul Pilkington	DNF
1997	Athens	13. Dave Scudamore	2:19:06
		56. Dan Held	2:20:08
		62. Marco Ochoa	2:23:50
		63. Jon Warren	2:30:04
		Don Janicki	DNF
1999	Seville	24. Rod DeHaven	2:19:06
		26. Eddy Hellebuyck	2:20:08
		34. Jonathan Hume	2:23:50
		47. Steve Swift	2:30:04
		Keith Brantly	DNF
2001	Edmonton	35. Josh Cox	2:26:52
		38. Eddy Hellebuyck	2:28:01
		48. Mike Dudley	2:30:45
		Khalid Khannouchi	DNF
		David Morris	DNF

World Cup Marathon Winners

In the 1980s the number of international title opportunities for marathoners suddenly jumped from one to three with the addition of the World Championships and then the World Cup. The last two often competed with each other in the same year until they combined into one race, the Championships, in 1997. * = event record.

WOMEN

Year	Place	Athlete	Time
1985	Hiroshima	Katrin Dorre (East Germany)	2:33:30
1987	Seoul	Zoya Ivanova (USSR)	2:30:39
1989	Milan	Sue Marchiano (U.S.)	2:30:48
1991	London	Rosa Mota (Portugal)	2:26:14*
1993	San Sebastian	Wang Junxia (China)	2:28:16
1995	Athens	Anuta Catuna (Romania)	2:31:10

MEN

Year	Place	Athlete	Time
1985	Hiroshima	Ahmed Salah (Djibouti)	2:08:09*
1987	Seoul	Ahmed Salah (Djibouti)	2:10:55
1989	Milan	Zekele Meteferia (Ethiopia)	2:10:28
1991	London	Yakov Tolstikov (USSR)	2:09:17
1993	San Sebastian	Richard Nerurkar (Britain)	2:10:03
1995	Athens	Douglas Wakiihuri (Kenya)	2:12:01

World Half-Marathon Winners

This is the only annual international championship event in road racing. Note Tegla Loroupe's three straight victories starting in 1997. * = event record.

WOMEN

Year	Place	Athlete	Time
1992	Tyneside	Liz McColgan (Britain)	1:08:53
1993	Brussels	Conceicao Ferreira (Portugal)	1:10:07
1994	Oslo	Elana Meyer (South Africa)	1:08:36
1995	Montbeliard	Valentina Yegorova (Russia)	1:09:58
1996	Palma	Ren Xiujuan (China)	1:10:39
1997	Košice	Tegla Loroupe (Kenya)	1:08:14
1998	Uster	Tegla Loroupe (Kenya)	1:08:29
1999	Palermo	Tegla Loroupe (Kenya)	1:08:48
2000	Vera Cruz	Paula Radcliffe (Britain)	1:09:07
2001	Bristol	Paula Radcliffe (Britain)	1:06:47*

MEN

Year	Place	Athlete	Time
1992	Tyneside	Benson Masya (Kenya)	1:00:24
1993	Brussels	Vincent Rousseau (Belgium)	1:01:16
1994	Oslo	Khalid Skah (Morocco)	1:00:27
1995	Montbeliard	Moses Tanui (Kenya)	1:01:45
1996	Palma	Stefano Baldini (Italy)	1:01:17
1997	Košice	Shem Kororia (Kenya)	59:56*
1998	Uster	Paul Koech (Kenya)	1:00:01
1999	Palermo	Paul Tergat (Kenya)	1:01:50
2000	Vera Cruz	Paul Tergat (Kenya)	1:03:47
2001	Bristol	Haile Gebrselassie (Kenya)	1:00:03

World Publications. The book-publishing arm of *Runner's World*, later known as Anderson World, was the most active publisher of running books from the mid-1970s through the early 1980s. See also *Runner's World*.

world rankings. *See* rankings, *Track & Field News*.

world records. *See* record progressions, world; records, world; records, world age-group.

World's Largest Run (www.ymca.net). Launched in 2001, this is a series of 5Ks, run simultaneously at hundreds of YMCAs around the world. All events start at the same time, which could be noon in one time zone and midnight in another.

Worley, Rick (b. 1947). The Texan ran 200 marathons in 159 consecutive weekends between January 1997 and January 2000. He also ran all U.S. states and Canadian provinces in calendar year 1998. *See also* streakers.

World Marathon Relay Winners

The format for this event, which ended with its 1998 running, was five-member teams with two running 5K, two running 10K, and one adding the odd 12.2K. Note that while the Kenyan men won three of the four relays, Kenya's women were shut out. * = event record.

WOMEN'S TEAMS

Year	Place	Team	Time
1992	Madeira	Portugal	2:30:14
1994	Lijokhoban	Russia	2:17:19
1996	Copenhagen	Ethiopia	2:16:04*
1998	Manaus	Ethiopia	2:21:15

MEN'S TEAMS

Year	Place	Team	Time
1992	Madeira	Kenya	2:00:02
1994	Lijokhoban	Morocco	1:57:56*
1996	Copenhagen	Kenya	2:00:40
1998	Manaus	Kenya	2:01:13

Wysocki, Ruth (b. March 8, 1957). The track Olympian in 1984 is the current American age-40-plus record-holder for both the 5K (16:06) and 10K (33:22). *See also* records, American age-group.

Xie Lihua (b. July 19, 1965). Our lone X-named entrant won the 1990 Tokyo Ladies' Marathon in 2:33:04. *See also* Tokyo Marathons.

Y

Yamada, Keizo (b. November 20, 1927). After spending his teenage years in tumultuous wartime Japan, he won the 1953 Boston Marathon and 1956 Fukuoka. *See also* Boston Marathon; Fukuoka Marathon.

Yamaguchi, Eri (b. January 13, 1973). The Japanese woman has run with near world-record times, including the Asian mark on an unaided course and the fastest unaided time in an all-women's race, 2:22:12 at Tokyo in 1999. *See also* Tokyo Marathons.

Yegorova, Valentina (b. February 16, 1964). Through the end of 1999 Yegorova had completed 23 marathons, running at least one per year since she entered the marathoning world on June 26, 1988, with a sixth-place finish at Tallinn (2:37:05). Although she has not been overwhelmingly consistent in winning (she won 5 of her 23 completed marathons), she has peaked well for international competition, winning the Barcelona Olympic Marathon in 1992 and taking second in the Atlanta Olympics in 1996. Her 1992 win was by a mere eight seconds (2:32:41) over Japan's Yuko Arimori; in 1996 Yegorova was two minutes behind Fatuma Roba. Although she did not compete in the 1988 Olympic Games, Yegorova raced her second marathon a month later at Ufa and won in 2:30:59, a seven-minute improvement on her debut marathon.

Yegorova was born in Cheboksary, east of Moscow. She was a decent track runner on a national level, and her leg speed carried over to the marathon and took her to the international level rather quickly. By her fourth marathon (Osaka in January 1990) she had broken under 2:30 (2:29:47) in taking 3rd place. She ran only one marathon in 1989, taking 15th place at the World Cup in Milan in 2:40. She ran three more marathons in 1990, rare for a world-class runner—taking 21st at London in April (2:35), 2nd at Split in August (2:31), and 4th at Tokyo in December (2:36). She had better luck at the World Cup in London in April 1991, taking 3rd in 2:28:18.

Her Barcelona gold medal was only her second marathon win in 14 marathons to that point. After the Olympic win, however, she made a point of accepting invitations to the Tokyo Marathon on a consistent basis and she did very well there: fourth in 1992 (2:31), first in 1993 (2:26:40), first again in 1994 (2:30:09), second in 1995 (2:28), and third in 1999 (2:28). In the wake of the Atlanta Olympics, she moved (with her husband-coach and then 10-year-old son) to Gainesville, Florida. *See also* Olympic medalists; rankings, *Track & Field News;* Tokyo Marathons; World Half-Marathon Championships.

yoga. *See* stretching exercises.

Yonkers Marathon. America's second-oldest marathon, after Boston, was first run in 1907 and serves as the longtime site of the U.S. marathon championships. John J. Kelley won this tough race eight times in a row in the late 1950s and early 1960s. *See also* national marathon champions, U.S.; oldest races.

The Yonkers Marathon, held a month after Boston, was for many years the U.S. national championships. At the 1949 race Victor Dyrgall (right), John A. Kelley (center), and Thomas Brogan (left) were at the top of their form.

From the collection of Dr. Edward H. Kozloff–Motor City Striders.

Young, Craig (b. July 16, 1956). The toy maker from Colorado holds the American 40-plus best time for an aided 10K (29:27 in 1997) and has a pending half-marathon national record (1:05:01 in 1999) for that age group. *See also* rankings, *Runner's World*; records, American age-group.

Young, George (b. July 24, 1937). The four-time Olympian's road career consisted of only two marathons, but they netted him a national title and a slot on the 1968 Olympic team. He placed 16th at Mexico City after winning a medal in the steeplechase. *See also* Hall of Fame, RRCA; Hall of Fame, USATF; national marathon champions, U.S.; Olympians, U.S.; Olympic Trials Marathon, U.S.

Young, Ken (b. November 9, 1941). As a runner he achieved such oddities as a record time for a marathon on an indoor track. He's better known, though, for bringing order to road record-keeping by founding and operating with his ex-wife Jennifer the National Running Data Center, which is now operated by others within the USATF organization as the Road Running Information Center.

Ken lives in a remote area in Humboldt County, California, near the underground archives of Scientology, from where he continues to run long distances. More interestingly he publishes a statistical newsletter called *The Analytical Distance Runner* (www.mattoleriver.com), which is a number cruncher's delight. In the newsletter he handicaps upcoming road races by statistically analyzing recent performances of entrants. He has also developed a penchant for tattoos. *See also* Hall of Fame, RRCA; Road Running Information Center.

Yun Bok Suh (b. January 9, 1923). In the brief interval between World War II and the Korean conflict, he gave his countrymen an emotional boost by winning the 1947 Boston Marathon; his 2:25:39 there was a world record that held for more than five years. The Korean was *Track & Field News*'s first number-one-ranked marathoner. *See also* Boston Marathon; rankings, *Track & Field News*; record progressions, world.

Z

Zabala, Juan Carlos (b. September 21, 1911). The Argentinean was the first Latin American to win an Olympic Marathon title, in 1932 at Los Angeles. His curious career record comprises two victories (the other at Košice) and three DNFs, including the 1936 Games. *See also* Košice Peace Marathon; Olympic medalists.

Zatopek, Emil (b. September 19, 1922; d. November 22, 2000). Arguably the greatest distance runner of all time, Emil did very little of his racing on the roads. He was first and foremost a track runner and in his time set numerous world records, many for distances seldom raced today—20K and the hour run, for instance. Emil was born in Koprinivince, a poor village in Moravia. His father was a carpenter. Emil himself began his working life early, in a shoe factory.

His running career began with a race through the streets for young boys; his name was mentioned in the local paper, and for years he carried the clipping with him. He was not a runner of enormous talent, but he was intelligent and he was willing to work—hard. He took the training methods of Paavo Nurmi and built upon them. When Emil entered the military, he did workouts while on guard duty, running back and forth endlessly at his post while wearing heavy military boots.

It is difficult in modern days to place Emil Zatopek in perspective because some of his running achievements seem too extraordinary to be true, even though many of them were accomplished on dirt tracks that were nothing like the modern all-weather tracks that are designed specifically to accommodate records. He was the first runner to break 28 minutes for six miles; he was the first to break 29 minutes for 10,000 meters; he was the world record-holder in the 10,000, 10 miles, 20,000, and one-hour run simultaneously; and he won 69 straight races at 5,000 and 10,000 meters.

At the 1952 Helsinki Olympic Games, he won the 5,000 meters and the 10,000 meters, and then entered the marathon (an event he had never previously run) and won it in Olympic record time (2:23:04). This distance-running gold-medal triple play has never been equaled, although Finland's Lasse Viren came close in the 1976 Olympic Games in Montreal when he won the 5,000, the 10,000, and then took fifth in the marathon.

Emil Zatopek's only other marathon produced a sixth-place finish at the 1956 Melbourne Olympic Games. He was not in terribly good condition, having undergone a hernia operation some weeks before. The condition was brought on by his strength-training technique of carrying his wife Dana on his shoulders when he ran—

The great Emil Zatopek. No more need be said.

From the collection of Dr. Edward H. Kozloff–Motor City Striders

servers, however, pointed out that it was what was happening below the waist that mattered. Below the waist, Emil was a strong, efficient machine capable of unexpected bursts of speed and power when he needed them to take the win.

Many nicknames were attached to the ever-popular Emil. His pained running style and his fighting spirit won him the nickname "The Beast of Prague." He was also referred to as "The Czech Locomotive." One *New York Times* writer referred to him as "The Colossus of the Roads," in spite of his seldom racing on roads.

When the Soviets invaded Czechoslovakia in 1968, Colonel Zatopek defied the invading tanks.

a trick he hoped would compensate for his advancing age. (Dana had won a gold medal of her own in the javelin throw for Czechoslovakia in the 1952 Games; the two were born on the same day, September 19, 1922.)

Zatopek spoke a half-dozen languages and was one of the most well-liked and well-respected competitors of all time. Besides his incredible string of accomplishments in running and his good humor, he is most remembered for his unique running style and a slew of nicknames. His style was painful to watch, as his face contorted in grimaces of pain while his arms flailed wildly. One journalist described Emil's style as being that of a man "stabbed through the chest." Canny ob-

For his efforts he was sent to live in a trailer in the woods where he was put to work doing manual labor in a uranium mine. He undertook that task in his usual no-holds-barred style, although the many years of forced labor may have contributed to his ill health later in life.

In 1991 he traveled to Stanford University in search of relief from growing arthritis problems, but no solution was found. In the years before his death, he was closely associated with the Prague International Marathon, while he remained an indefatigable ambassador for the sport of running. *See also* "Hero of the Half-Century" on next page; Olympic Marathon, 1900 to 2000; Olympic medalists; rankings, *Track & Field News.*

Hero of the Half-Century

From Joe Henderson's *Runner's World* column, January 2000.

No one now running can remember the turn of the last century. Many of us, though, are old enough and long enough connected to the sport to have memories reaching back a half century. I'm happy to make that claim.

The first foreign name to pierce my consciousness in family talk about track was Emil Zatopek. He had won the 10,000 at the first post-World War II Olympics, then broke records repeatedly during the next few years. He peaked at the 1952 Games when he won the 5,000, 10,000, and marathon—a triple never accomplished before and not since.

To me, Zatopek is the finest runner of the past 50 years. I remember him that way for how he once raced but more so for how he continued to live and give.

I never expected to meet the great man from a then-remote land. But by chance we came together briefly while waiting to board separate flights out of Munich after the 1972 Olympics. He blew kisses to friends outside the boarding area and spoke his last words of thanks to them in German. Working up courage, I approached him. "Uh, excuse me, are you Emil Zatopek?" I asked, already knowing he was but not knowing if he understood English.

"Why yes, Zatopek," he answered without missing a beat. "And what is your name, please?" It meant nothing to him, but he still took time to talk for 20 minutes. Word quickly spread through the *Runner's World* tour group that we were in the presence of track royalty. Passengers dropped out of line to shake his hand and ask for his autograph.

Now 50 years old, he had come to Munich as a guest of the Olympic Committee to celebrate the 20th anniversary of his triple. "It is odd," he said, "to have all this . . . how do you say it? . . . acclaim. In my country I am just a common man . . . a nobody."

Zatopek didn't talk politics, but he was officially a nobody in Czechoslovakia. When a revolt against the Soviets broke out in 1968, he took the wrong side in the struggle and lost his rank as an army colonel. The national hero was reduced to working as a garbage collector and then as a street-sweeper, jobs normally reserved in his country for the mentally retarded. When Czechs in his hometown learned of this, they rushed out to help him carry the cans and push the broom.

He said, "I am now a simple worker. I drill for mineral water."

Zatopek excused himself and walked toward the plane that would take him to Prague, back to his simple life as a nobody whose name will forever live in Olympic history. I've never seen him again but have followed him from afar through news stories.

He outlasted the vindictive government in his country (now the Czech Republic). The current rulers realize what a treasure he is and allow him to accept acclaim freely. By all accounts he handles it well.

One of his finest moves was a quiet one. Ron Clarke, a frequent setter of world records but never an Olympic medalist, came to visit the man who had won so many. As they parted, Zatopek handed the Australian a small package and told him to open it later. Clarke's worries that he was smuggling something out of the country vanished when he found a gold medal with a note saying, "You earned this."

[Emil Zatopek died in November 2000 after suffering a stroke.]

Zuna, Frank (b. January 2, 1893). He contrasted sharply with his friend and contemporary, Clarence DeMar, who called the extremely laid-back Zuna "bohemian." Yet Frank ran well enough to win Boston in 1921, to run in the 1924 Olympics, and to become the first American marathoner to break 2:40 (with 2:38:28 in 1925). *See also* Boston Marathon; Olympians, U.S.; record progressions, American.

Frank Zuna, described by his friend and complete opposite Clarence DeMar as "bohemian," was a force to be reckoned with. He took second to DeMar's win at Boston in 1923; both were on the U.S. Olympic team in 1924.

From the collection of Dr. Edward H. Kozloff—Motor City Striders

Supplemental Index

We don't include a traditional index because the encyclopedia itself is an alphabetized index of sorts. This index includes not only a list of the entries covered in the book, but also names of people that do not receive their own alphabetical listing in the body of the book. These supplemental names appear only within other entries (and their sidebar essays or statistical lists) as noted in the parentheses that follow their listing here. Those entries not followed by a parenthetical note appear within the book on their own.

A

Birch Bay Marathon

Biwott, Simon (*See* Berlin Marathon; World Championships medalists)

Bix 7

Bizaw, Hiywot (*See* African Games)

Bjorkund, Garry

Blake Arthur

Blaschke, Ursula (*See* Berlin Marathon)

Blewett, Bill (*See* Peachtree 10K)

blisters

blood doping

blood lactate (*See* anaerobic threshold)

Bloom, Marc

Bloomsday 12K

Blue Ribbon Sports (*See* Asics; Nike)

Blum, Steve (*See* records, American age-group)

Bochroder, Christin (*See* Berlin Marathon)

Bochroder, Ralf (*See* Berlin Marathon)

body composition

body temperature

Bogacheva, Irina

Bohannon, Dr. Richard (*See* American Running Association)

Boileau, Art

Boitano, Mary Etta

Bolder Boulder 10K

Bone Fone

bonk

Bonner, Beth

books

Bor, Simon (*See* Los Angeles Marathon)

Bordin, Gelindo

Borg, Gunnar (*See* perceived exertion)

Borschel, Tom (*See* Rim Rock Run; "Monumental Event")

Bortz, Dr. Walter (*See* Fifty-Plus Fitness Association)

Boston Marathon

Boston Marathon, The (*See* books; Derderian, Tom)

Boulder, Colorado

Bowerman, Bill

Bowers, Jim (*See* records, American age-group)

Boychuk, Andy (*See* Drayton, Jerome; Pan-American Games)

Boyd, Marie (*See* World Championships, U.S.)

Boyle, Kathy (*See* national 10K champions, U.S.)

Brace, Steve (*See* Berlin Marathon)

Brahm, Terry (*See* national 5K champions, U.S.)

Brandt, Angelika (*See* Berlin Marathon)

Brantly, Keith

Brasher, Chris

Brawley, Henry (*See* Olympians, U.S.)

Breal, Michel (*See* Olympic Marathon, 1896)

Breathe Right

Breckinridge, Alex (*See* Olympians, U.S.)

Brenner, Eric (*See* Bay to Breakers 12K)

Breslin, Jimmy (*See* Hirsch, George)

Brewer, Diane Bussa (*See* national half-marathon champions, U.S.)

Bridges, Cheryl

Bright, Bob

Bright, Norman (*See* Bay to Breakers 12K)

Brignolia, Lawrence (*See* Boston Marathon)

Brokaw, Tom (*See* Lebow, Fred)

Broloppet Half

Brooks

Brown, Barry

Brown, Dick (*See* AquaJogger; Lauck, Anne Marie Letko)

Brown, Doris (*See* Heritage, Doris Severtson Brown)

Brown, Ellison "Tarzan"

Brown, Julie

Brown, Walter (*See* Semple, John "Jock")

Browne, Dan

Buerkle, Dick

Buffone, Gary (*See* Sachs, M.L. and Sacks, M.H.)

Bukovjan, Vlastimil (*See* Košice Peace Marathon)

Buniak, Peter (*See* Drayton, Jerome)

Burfoot, Amby

Burangulova, Ramila (*See* Honolulu Marathon)

Burley, Gillian (*See* Košice Peace Marathon)

Bush, George W.

Byelayeva, Lucia (*See* Košice Peace Marathon)

C

Cabrera, Delfo

Caffery, John

Calcaterra, Giorgio (*See* Kurtis, Doug)

Cameron, Fred (*See* Boston Marathon)

Campbell, Bob (*See* Hall of Fame, RRCA)

Campbell, John

camps, running

Capitol 10K

carbohydrate loading

Cardenas, Maricarmen (*See* Pan-American Games; Warner, Debbi)

Carlip, Freddi

Carlsbad 5K

Carlton, Fritz (*See* Boston Marathon)

Carman, Lyn (*See* women's running; "Following Women")

Carmichael, Heather (*See* Peachtree 10K)

Carr, Edward (*See* Olympians, U.S.)

Carrefour International 9K

Carroll, Billy (*See* Around the Bay 30K; "Bay Watch")

Keim, George (*See* rankings, *Runner's World*)
Keino, Kip (*See* Hussein, Ibrahim; Kenyan runners)
Kelley, Don (*See* Bay to Breakers 12K)
Kelley, John A.
Kelley, John J.
Kellner, Gyula
Kempainen, Bob
Kenah, Cheri Goddard (*See* national 5K champions, U.S.)
Kennedy, Thomas (*See* Olympians, U.S.)
Kennedy, William (*See* Boston Marathon)
Kenyan runners
Kesey, Ken (See *Running* magazine)
Keston, John
Khannouchi, Khalid
Khannouchi, Sandra (*See* Khannouchi, Khalid)
Kiddy, Sandra (*See* records, American age-group)
kids' running
Kigen, Simeon (*See* rankings, *Runner's World*)
Kilauea Volcano Marathon
Kilby, Brian
kilometer distances (*See* distances, metric and English)
Kim Won Tak (*See* Asian Games)
Kim Yang Kon (*See* Asian Games)
Kimaiyo, Eric
Kimaiyo, Hellen
Kimani, Joseph
Kimihara, Kenji
Kimondiu, Ben (*See* Chicago Marathon)
King, Wilford (*See* Bay to Breakers 12K)
Kipketer, Sammy
Kiplagat, Lornah
Kiprono, Josephat
Kipyego, Ernest (*See* Košice Peace Marathon)
Kiraly, Pal (*See* Košice Peace Marathon)
Kirtland, Julia
Kirui, Dominic (*See* Bloomsday 12K)
Kirui, Ismail
Kita, Hideki (*See* Tokyo Marathons)
Klecker, Barney (*See* Klecker, Janis)
Klecker, Janis
Kleinerman, Joe
Klein, Helen (*See* records, American age group)
Kleyweg, Joke (*See* Rotterdam Marathon)
Kline, Fred (*See* Bay to Breakers 12K)
Klochko, Lyubov
knee injuries (*See* injuries)
Kneeland, David (*See* Olympians, U.S.)
Knight, Phil
Knox, Merle (*See* Bay to Breakers 12K)
Koech, Paul (*See* records, world; World Half-Marathon Championships)

Koech, Peter (*See* rankings, Runner's World)
Koga, Sinzo (*See* Fukuoka Marathon)
Kogo, Steve (*See* rankings, *Runner's World*))
Koide, Yoshio (*See* Takahashi, Naoko)
Kokamo, Yumi (*See* Osaka Ladies' Marathon)
Kokesh, Jerry (*See* Hall of Fame, RRCA)
Kokowska, Renata
Kolehmainen, Hannes
Kolesnikov, Nikolay (*See* Košice Peace Marathon)
Komonen, Dave (*See* Boston Marathon)
Konstantinos, Crown Prince (*See* Louis, Spiridon; Olympic Marathon, 1896)
Korir, John (*See* Peachtree 10K; rankings, *Runner's World*)
Kororia, Shem (*See* World Half-Marathon Championships)
Kortelainen, Jouni (*See* Košice Peace Marathon)
Kosgei, Japhet
Košice Peace Marathon
Koskei, James (*See* Bay to Breakers 12K; Bolder Boulder 10K)
Koski, Karl (*See* national marathon champions, U.S.)
Kostrubala, Thaddeus
Kotila, Paavo (*See* Boston Marathon)
Kowalchik, Claire (See *Complete Book of Running for Women, The*)
Koyanagi, Shunji (*See* Fukuoka Marathon)
Kristiansen, Ingrid
Krise, Raymond (*See* Squires, Billy)
Kronenthal, Syd (*See* Western Hemisphere Marathon; "Old Western")
Kryza, Violetta (*See* Košice Peace Marathon)
Krzyacin, Andzej (*See* Košice Peace Marathon)
Kuehls, Dave
Kurtis, Doug
Kuscsik, Nina
Kvalheim, Knut (*See* Waitz, Grete)
Kyriakides, Stylianos (*See* Boston Marathon)

L

lactate threshold (*See* anaerobic threshold)
Lafferty, John (*See* national marathon champions, U.S.)
Lagat, Elijah
Lakeman, Dirk (*See* national 10K champions, U.S.)
Lake Tahoe Marathon
Lamppa, Ryan
Lananna, Vin (*See* Johnson, Jeff; Kempainen, Bob; Scudamore, Dave)
Langlace, Chantal
largest races (*See* biggest races)
Laris, Tom (*See* Bay to Breakers 12K)

Mini-Marathon, New York City
Mintz, Ida
Miranda, Oscar
Mirkin, Dr. Gabe
Mizuno
Modica, Vincenzo (*See* World Championships medalists)
Moiseyev, Leonid
Molina, Jose Luis (*See* Los Angeles Marathon)
Moller, Lorraine
Mondragon, Martin (*See* Los Angeles Marathon; rankings, *Runner's World*)
Moneghetti, Steve
monitor, heart-rate (*See* heart-rate monitor; Polar)
Monti, David
Moore, Kenny
Moqhabi, Thabiso (*See* Commonwealth Games)
Morgan, Bill (*See* Bay to Breakers 12K)
Morgunova, Lyubov (*See* Honolulu Marathon)
Morishita, Koichi
Morita, Shuichi (*See* Fukuoka Marathon)
Moroccan runners
Morolong, Simon (*See* Peachtree 10K)
Morris, David
Morris, Debbie K. (*See* national marathon champions, U.S.)
Morrisey, Thomas
Morse, Guy
Moseyev, Vladimir (*See* Košice Peace Marathon)
Moss Brown (*See* Gore-Tex)
Mota, Rosa
Motmillers, Arturs (*See* Košice Peace Marathon)
Motshwarateu, Matthews (*See* record progressions, world)
Moumou, El Hadi (*See* Kurtis, Doug)
Mount Evans Race
Mount Washington Race
movies
Moving Comfort
Mtolo, Willie (*See* New York City Marathon)
Muhrcke, Gary
Muindi, Jimmy
Muinonen, Vaino (*See* European Championships)
Munday, Susan (*See* national marathon champions, U.S.)
Murgoci, Elena (*See* Rotterdam Marathon)
Murphy, Colette (*See* national 10K champions, U.S.)
Murphy, Frank
Murphy, John and Murphy, Suzanne
Murphy, Suzanne (*See* Murphy, John and Murphy, Suzanne)

Musyoki, Michael
Mutisya, Gideon (*See* Charleston Distance Run, "Doing the Charleston")
Mutwol, William (*See* record progressions, world)

N

Naali, Simon Robert (*See* Honolulu Marathon)
NAIA (*See* National Association of Intercollegiate Athletics)
Nagata, Masayuka (*See* Asian Games)
Nakamura, Kiyoshi (*See* Kenyan runners; Seko, Toshihiko; Wakiihuri, Douglas)
Nakayama, Takeyuki
Nam, Shoryu. (*See* Sohn Kee Chung)
Nam Sung Yong (*See* Sohn Kee Chung)
Napa Valley Marathon
nasal strips (*See* Breathe Right)
Nason, Jerry
National Association of Intercollegiate Athletics (NAIA)
National Distance Running Hall of Fame (*See* Hall of Fame, National Distance Running)
national 5K champions, U.S.
national half-marathon champions, U.S.
national marathon champions, U.S.
National Masters News
national records (*See* record progressions, American; records, American; records, American age-group)
National Running Center (*See* mail-order companies)
national 10K champions, U.S.
Ndayisenga, J.P. (*See* Peachtree 10K)
Ndereba, Catherine
Ndeti, Cosmas
Ndungu, Stephen (*See* Los Angeles Marathon)
Nederlof, Erwin (*See* Košice Peace Marathon)
negative splits
Negere, Tena
Negrete, Fidel (*See* Pan-American Games)
Nehi, John (*See* Bay to Breakers 12K)
Nelson, Bert and Nelson, Cordner
Nenow, Mark
Neppel Darrah, Peg
Nerurkar, Richard (*See* World Cup Marathon)
Nesbit, Joan (*See* Peachtree 10K)
New Balance
Newton, Arthur (*See* long slow distance)
Newton, Arthur (runner)
New York City Marathon
New York City Road Runners Club
Ngolepus, Joseph (See Berlin Marathon)
Ngotho, Jane (*See* Bay to Breakers 12K)

Run to the Top

Rusman, Wilma (*See* Rotterdam Marathon)

RW (*See* Runner's World)

Ryan, Kevin (*See* Honolulu Marathon)

Ryan, Mike (b. January 1, 1889)

Ryan, Mike (b. December 26, 1941)

Ryun, Jim (*See* Anderson, Bob; Kenyan runners)

S

Sachs, M.L. and Sacks, M.H.

Sacks, M.H. (*See* Sachs, M.L.)

Sadanaga, Nobuyoshi (*See* Fukuoka Marathon)

Sadreydinova, Raisa (*See* Košice Peace Marathon)

St. George Marathon

St. Hilaire, Judi

St. Louis

Sakamoto, Mineteru (*See* Asian Games)

Salah, Ahmed

Salazar, Alberto

Salmini Films

Salumae, Jane (*See* Los Angeles Marathon)

Sampson, Millie (*See* record progressions, world)

Samuelson, Joan Benoit (*See* Benoit Samuelson, Joan)

San Blas Half-Marathon

Sander, Norbert (*See* New York City Marathon)

Sanders, Gordon (*See* national 10K champions, U.S.)

Sanders, Odis

San Diego Marathon

Sandoval, Tony

Sandrock, Mike

São Sylvestre

Sasaki, Nanae (*See* Tokyo Marathons)

Sasaki, Seiichiro (*See* Clayton, Derek)

Sato, Nobuyuki (*See* World Championships medalists)

Saucony

Sayre, Ric

Scaff, Dr. Jack

Scandurra, Aldo (*See* Hall of Fame, RRCA)

Scannell, Karen (*See* rankings, *Runner's World*)

scenic races

Schiro, Cathy (*See* O'Brien, Cathy Schiro)

Schilly, Katy (*See* national marathon champions, U.S.)

Schlau, Bob (*See* rankings *Runner's World*; records, American age-group)

Schelegle, Ed (*See* national marathon champions, U.S.)

Schmenk, Doug (*See* national marathon champions, U.S.)

Schneider, Alice (*See* Steinfeld, Allan)

Schrivener, Leslie (*See* Fox, Terry)

Schul, Bob

Schuster, Richard (*See* podiatry)

Schwaber, David (*See* ethylene vinyl acetate)

Schwarzenegger, Arnold (*See* movies; "Moving Pictures")

Scobey, Bill (*See* Western Hemisphere Marathon; "Old Western")

Scott, Steve

Scrutton, Mark (*See* Bolder Boulder 10K)

Scudamore, Dave

Sears, Ray (*See* Hall of Fame, RRCA)

Second Skin

See How She Runs (*See* movies; "Moving Pictures")

Seeley, Jan (See *Marathon & Beyond)*

Segal, Erich

Seko, Toshihiko

Selassie, Haile (*See* Bikila, Abebe; Ethiopian runners)

Semer, Whayong (*See* records, American age-group)

Semple, John "Jock"

Senorski, Midde Hamrin (*See* Chicago Marathon)

Sensburg, Ingo

Serious Runner's Handbook (*See* Osler, Tom)

Sevene, Bob

Shahanga, Alfredo (*See* Berlin Marathon)

Shahanga, Gidamis

Shapiro, Judy (*See* Ikenberry, Judy; "Living History")

Shea, Julie and Shea, Mary

Shea, Mary (*See* Shea, Julie and Shea, Mary)

Sheahen, Al (See *National Masters News*)

Sheehan, Dr. George

Sheehan, George III (*See* Beardsley, Dick; "Where's Dick?")

Sheehan on Running, Dr.

Shepherd, Jack (*See* Glover, Bob)

Sheridan, Whitey (*See* Sheehan, Dr. George; "Tears for a Winner")

Sherring, William

Shettler, Jim (*See* Bay to Breakers 12K)

Shibui, Yoko (*See* Osaka Ladies' Marathon)

Shibutani, Toshihiro (*See* Fukuoka Marathon)

Shigematsu, Morio

Shimizu, Koji (*See* Tokyo Marathons)

shinsplints

Shintaku, Masanari (*See* Fukuoka Marathon)

shoe companies

Shoe Goo

Shorter, Frank

Sidorov, Vadim (*See* Tokyo Marathons)

Sigei, William (*See* record progressions, world)

Sun Run

Sun Yingjie

Suomelainen, Olavi (*See* Boston Marathon)

supination

Supplex

surges

Sutton, Marian

Sutton, Percy (*See* New York City Marathon)

Suzuki, Fushige

Suzuki, Hiromi (*See* rankings, Track & Field News; World Championships medalists)

Svanberg, Johan (*See* Olympic medalists)

Swannack, Skip (*See* Bay to Breakers 12K)

Swartbooi, Luketz (*See* World Championships medalists)

Swift, Steve (*See* World Championships, U.S.)

Switzer, Kathrine

T

Tabb, Ron

Tabori, Laszlo

TAC (*See* Athletics Congress, The)

T&FN (See *Track & Field News*)

Takahashi, Kenichi (*See* Tokyo Marathons)

Takahashi, Naoko

Talley, James (*See* records, American age-group)

Tanaka, Shigeki (*See* Boston Marathon)

Tanigawa, Mari (*See* Tokyo Marathons)

Taniguchi, Hiromi

Tanui, Moses

tapering

Taylor, Steve (*See* World Championships, U.S.)

Tazetdinova, Guliya (*See* Košice Peace Marathon)

Team Diabetes

Team in Training (TNT)

Team USA

television

Temane, Matthews (*See* record progressions, world)

tempo runs

Temu, Naftali (*See* Kenyan runners)

tendon injuries (*See* Achilles tendon; injuries)

10K

Terasawa, Toru

Tergat, Paul

Teske, Charlotte

Tewanima, Lewis

Thackwray, Dean (*See* Olympians, U.S.)

Theato, Michel

Thomas, Randy (*See* Squires, Billy)

Thompson, Hunter S. (*See Running* Magazine)

Thompson, Ian

Thorpe, Jim (*See* Tewanima, Lewis)

three-hour marathon

threshold runs (*See* anaerobic threshold)

Thugwane, Josia (also spelled Josiah)

Thys, Gert

Tibaduiza, Domingo (*See* Berlin Marathon; Leydig, Jack)

Tiger (now Asics)

Tikkanen, Paivi (*See* Berlin Marathon)

time off (*See* rest)

time running

timing (*See* watches, digital)

Tinari, Nancy Rooks

Tinsley, Harold (*See* Hall of Fame, RRCA)

TNT (*See* Team in Training)

Toivonen, Armas

Tokyo

Tokyo Marathons

Tokyo Olympiad (*See* movies; "Moving Pictures")

Tola, Tesaye (*See* Olympic medalists)

Tolstikov, Yakov

Tonkin, Jennifer (*See* World Championships, U.S.)

Tosa, Reiko (*See* Simon, Lidia; World Championships medalists)

Toth, Gyula (*See* Košice Peace Marathon)

Towne, Robert (*See* Moore, Kenny)

Track & Field News

Track & Field News marathon rankings (*See* rankings, *Track & Field News*)

track racing

Tracy, Dick (*See* products for runners)

training heart rate (*See* heart-rate monitor)

training log (*See* logbooks)

Trason, Ann

Trautmann, John (*See* national 10K champions, U.S.)

Treacy, John (*See* Barrios, Arturo; Los Angeles Marathon; Olympic medalists)

Trent, Marcie

triathlon and duathlon

Trickett, Pat (*See* records, world age-group)

Trivoulides, Peter (*See* Boston Marathon)

Truex, Max (*See* Hall of Fame, RRCA; Igloi, Mihaly; "Igloi's Boys")

Trujillo, Maria (now DeRios)

Truppel, Hans-Joachim (*See* Košice Peace Marathon)

Tsebe, David (*See* Berlin Marathon)

Tsuburaya, Kokichi

Tulu, Derartu

Turbull, Derek

Turland, Heather (*See* Commonwealth Games)

Tuttle, Gary

Tuttle, John

12K

About the Authors

© Ken Lee

Richard Benyo (b. March 10, 1936) ran as a child—usually as a means of avoiding being pummeled by older kids hoping to dispel their boredom. He grew up in central eastern Pennsylvania, where he and his brother ran over, under, around, and through the mountains and abandoned coal mines. The practice served him well in college, where he ran cross country at Bloomsburg State.

After graduation in 1968, he worked at a daily newspaper in eastern Pennsylvania, where he and fellow editor Ed Gildea organized the Switchback Scamper race in 1971 in an attempt to save the right-of-way of the oldest gravity railroad in America; the race continues today under the direction of Rich's younger brother Drew. In 1972 Rich moved to Virginia to edit *Stock Car Racing* magazine, where he ran little, traveled much, and wrote his first book, *Superspeedway* (Mason Charter, 1976).

In 1977 Rich moved to California to work as managing editor of *Runner's World* magazine, where editor Joe Henderson had decided to move over to the book division. Rich was promoted to executive editor and vice president–editorial. He wrote several books while at *Runner's World*, including *Return to Running* (World Publications, 1978) and *Masters of the Marathon* (Atheneum, 1983). He also became more serious about his running, completing eight marathons and several ultras in 1978. In 1980 he broke three hours in the marathon for the first time.

Rich left *Runner's World* in late 1984 and became the running columnist for the *San Francisco Chronicle* until 1990. He also wrote five books with Jack LaLanne's wife, Elaine, and three with his own wife, Rhonda. In 1989 he and running partner Tom Crawford became the first runners to run from Badwater in Death Valley (the hottest spot on earth and lowest point in the Western Hemisphere) to the top of Mount Whitney (at 14,494 feet the highest point in the continental United States) and back to Badwater, a distance of roughly 300 miles. In 1992 Rich became the first person to do the out-and-back a second time.

He has continued to write books, among them *Making the Marathon Your Event* (Random House, 1992) and *Running Past 50* (Human Kinetics, 1998). He also wrote an account of his adventures on the Death Valley course, titled *The Death Valley 300* (Specific Publications, 1991). In 1997, in conjunction with Human Kinetics, he launched *Marathon & Beyond* magazine, a bimonthly journal devoted to marathoning and ultrarunning (www.marathonandbeyond.com). Two years later he and managing editor Jan Seeley took over the magazine, forming their own company, 42K. Rich lives with his wife, Rhonda (the only female in the world to have done the Death Valley to Mount Whitney out-and-back course), in northern California. Besides running and hiking, they have been learning to sail on the San Francisco Bay.

Joe Henderson (b. June 3, 1943) began his magazine career began in 1967 with *Track & Field News*. He was editor of *Runner's World* from 1970 to 1977 and has been a columnist for the magazine most of the years since. He is also editor of *Running Commentary* newsletter (www.joehenderson.com) and had written 22 books before cowriting this encyclopedia.

Although he grew up in Iowa and attended Drake University there, he believed that California would be a prominent center of distance running. Joe accepted a job at Kansan Bob Anderson's *Distance Running News*, then talked Anderson into moving to northern California in 1970 and changing the magazine's name to *The Runner's World* (*"The"* was later dropped).

Joe was an early proponent of what came to be known as LSD (long slow distance) and his first book, published in 1969, was titled *LSD: The Humane Way to Train* (Tafnews). Perhaps his most influential book in the 1970s was *The Long Run Solution* (World Publications, 1976), a mix of philosophy and practical advice.

One of Joe's first acts as *Runner's World's* editor was to talk Dr. George Sheehan, a New Jersey cardiologist he'd met on a trip to the 1968 Mexico City Olympic Games, to write a column in the magazine. Dr. Sheehan quickly became *RW*'s most-read writer, and Joe would eventually write a biography about his good friend, titled *Did I Win?* (WRS, 1995)

In 1977 Joe left the *RW* editorship to devote more time to his writing. Eventually he landed in running mecca Eugene, Oregon, where for several years he worked on the Nike magazine, *Running.* After that publication folded, he gravitated back to *Runner's World,* where since 1983 he has served as the West Coast editor and has been a columnist.

Since 1982 Joe has published the newsletter *Running Commentary* (originally a printed monthly, now an e-mail weekly). Besides writing an occasional book, he speaks to running groups on a regular basis and teaches classes in both writing and running at the University of Oregon. He is a two-time winner (1978 and 1996) of the RRCA Jerry Little Memorial Journalism Excellence Award, is a recipient of the Emil Zatopek Award from the 50-Plus Fitness Association, and is an adviser to the RRCA.

Joe is a second-generation journalist, and one of his greatest joys is that his daughter Sarah is following in his journalistic footsteps. He is also married to a writer, Barbara Shaw, and they live in Eugene.

*You'll find
other outstanding
running resources at*

www.humankinetics.com

In the U.S. call

1-800-747-4457

Australia 08 8277 1555
Canada 1-800-465-7301
Europe .... +44 (0) 113 278 1708
New Zealand 09-523-3462

HUMAN KINETICS
The Premier Publisher in Sports and Fitness
P.O. Box 5076 • Champaign, IL 61825-5076 USA